A PRACTICAL GUIDE TO DATA ANALYSIS USING R

Using diverse real-world examples, this text examines what models used for data analysis mean in a specific research context. What assumptions underlie analyses, and how can you check them?

Building on the successful *Data Analysis and Graphics Using R*, third edition (Cambridge, 2010), it expands upon topics including cluster analysis, exponential time series, matching, seasonality, and resampling approaches. An extended look at p-values leads to an exploration of replicability issues and of contexts where numerous p-values exist, including gene expression.

Developing practical intuition, this book assists scientists in the analysis of their own data, and familiarizes students in statistical theory with practical data analysis. The worked examples and accompanying commentary teach readers to recognize when a method works and, more importantly, when it doesn't. Each chapter contains copious exercises. Selected solutions, notes, slides, and R code are available online, with extensive references pointing to detailed guides to R.

JOHN H. MAINDONALD is Contract Associate at Statistics Research Associates and was previously Visiting Fellow at the Australian National University. He has had wide experience both as a university lecturer and as a quantitative problem solver, working with researchers in diverse areas. He is the author of *Statistical Computation* (1984), and the senior author of *Data Analysis and Graphics Using R* (third edition, 2010).

W. JOHN BRAUN is Professor at the University of British Columbia, where he is Director of the UBCO campus of the Banff International Research Station for Mathematical Innovation and Discovery. In 2020, he received the Statistical Society of Canada Award for Impact of Applied and Collaborative Work.

JEFFREY L. ANDREWS is Associate Professor at the University of British Columbia. He currently serves as Principal Co-director of the Master of Data Science program and President-elect of The Classification Society (TCS). He is the 2013 Distinguished Dissertation Award winner from TCS and a recipient of the 2017 Chikio Hayashi Award for Young Researchers from the International Federation of Classification Societies.

A PRACTICAL GUIDE TO DATA ANALYSIS USING R

An Example-Based Approach

JOHN H. MAINDONALD
Statistics Research Associates, Wellington, New Zealand

W. JOHN BRAUN
University of British Columbia, Okanagan

JEFFREY L. ANDREWS
University of British Columbia, Okanagan

CAMBRIDGE
UNIVERSITY PRESS

CAMBRIDGE
UNIVERSITY PRESS

Shaftesbury Road, Cambridge CB2 8EA, United Kingdom

One Liberty Plaza, 20th Floor, New York, NY 10006, USA

477 Williamstown Road, Port Melbourne, VIC 3207, Australia

314–321, 3rd Floor, Plot 3, Splendor Forum, Jasola District Centre, New Delhi – 110025, India

103 Penang Road, #05–06/07, Visioncrest Commercial, Singapore 238467

Cambridge University Press is part of Cambridge University Press & Assessment, a department of the University of Cambridge

We share the University's mission to contribute to society through the pursuit of education, learning and research at the highest international levels of excellence.

www.cambridge.org
Information on this title: www.cambridge.org/9781009282277

DOI: 10.1017/9781009282284

First published 2024

Printed in the United Kingdom by CPI Group Ltd, Croydon CR0 4YY

A catalogue record for this publication is available from the British Library

A Cataloging-in-Publication data record for this book is available from the Library of Congress

ISBN 978-1-009-28227-7 Hardback

For my grandchildren Luke, Amelia, and Ted

For my children, Matthew, Phillip, and Reese

For my family (Irene, Charlie, and Mia) and my parents (Dave and Marleen)

Contents

	List of Figures		*page* xi
	Preface		xvii
1	**Learning from Data, and Tools for the Task**		1
	1.1	Questions, and Data That May Point to Answers	2
	1.2	Graphical Tools for Data Exploration	12
	1.3	Data Summary	22
	1.4	Distributions: Quantifying Uncertainty	30
	1.5	Simple Forms of Regression Model	42
	1.6	Data-Based Judgments – Frequentist, in a Bayesian World	48
	1.7	Information Statistics and Bayesian Methods with Bayes Factors	58
	1.8	Resampling Methods for SEs, Tests, and Confidence Intervals	66
	1.9	Organizing and Managing Work, and Tools That Can Assist	70
	1.10	The Changing Environment for Data Analysis	72
	1.11	Further, or Supplementary, Reading	79
	1.12	Exercises	80
2	**Generalizing from Models**		88
	2.1	Model Assumptions	88
	2.2	t-Statistics, Binomial Proportions, and Correlations	91
	2.3	Extra-Binomial and Extra-Poisson Variation	95
	2.4	Contingency Tables	100
	2.5	Issues for Regression with a Single Explanatory Variable	104
	2.6	Empirical Assessment of Predictive Accuracy	116
	2.7	One- and Two-Way Comparisons	121
	2.8	Data with a Nested Variation Structure	130
	2.9	Bayesian Estimation – Further Commentary and Approaches	131
	2.10	Recap	136
	2.11	Further Reading	137
	2.12	Exercises	137
3	**Multiple Linear Regression**		144
	3.1	Basic Ideas: the `allbacks` Book Weight Data	144
	3.2	The Interpretation of Model Coefficients	148

3.3	Choosing the Model, and Checking It Out	161
3.4	Robust Regression, Outliers, and Influence	171
3.5	Assessment and Comparison of Regression Models	176
3.6	Problems with Many Explanatory Variables	183
3.7	Errors in x	191
3.8	Multiple Regression Models – Additional Points	195
3.9	Recap	201
3.10	Further Reading	202
3.11	Exercises	203
4	**Exploiting the Linear Model Framework**	208
4.1	Levels of a Factor – Using Indicator Variables	209
4.2	Block Designs and Balanced Incomplete Block Designs	213
4.3	Fitting Multiple Lines	216
4.4	Methods for Fitting Smooth Curves	219
4.5	* Quantile Regression	238
4.6	Further Reading and Remarks	240
4.7	Exercises	240
5	**Generalized Linear Models, and Survival Analysis**	245
5.1	Generalized Linear Models	245
5.2	Logistic Multiple Regression	250
5.3	Logistic Models for Categorical Data – an Example	260
5.4	Models for Counts – Poisson, Quasipoisson, and Negative Binomial	261
5.5	Fitting Smooths	274
5.6	Additional Notes on Generalized Linear Models	276
5.7	Models with an Ordered Categorical or Categorical Response	278
5.8	Survival Analysis	281
5.9	Transformations for Proportions and Counts	288
5.10	Further Reading	289
5.11	Exercises	290
6	**Time Series Models**	292
6.1	Time Series – Some Basic Ideas	293
6.2	Regression Modeling with ARIMA Errors	304
6.3	* Nonlinear Time Series	313
6.4	Further Reading	314
6.5	Exercises	315
7	**Multilevel Models, and Repeated Measures**	318
7.1	Corn Yield Data – Analysis Using `aov()`	320
7.2	Analysis Using `lme4::lmer()`	325
7.3	Survey Data, with Clustering	329
7.4	A Multilevel Experimental Design	335
7.5	Within- and Between-Subject Effects	344
7.6	A Mixed Model with a Betabinomial Error	349

7.7 Observation-Level Random Effects – the `moths` Dataset 356
7.8 Repeated Measures in Time 357
7.9 Further Notes on Multilevel Models 367
7.10 Recap 371
7.11 Further Reading 371
7.12 Exercises 371

8 Tree-Based Classification and Regression 373
8.1 Tree-Based Methods – Uses and Basic Notions 374
8.2 Splitting Criteria, with Illustrative Examples 378
8.3 The Practicalities of Tree Construction – Two Examples 384
8.4 From One Tree to a Forest – a More Global Optimality 390
8.5 Additional Notes – One Tree, or Many Trees? 393
8.6 Further Reading and Extensions 395
8.7 Exercises 396

9 Multivariate Data Exploration and Discrimination 400
9.1 Multivariate Exploratory Data Analysis 401
9.2 Principal Component Scores in Regression 408
9.3 Cluster Analysis 412
9.4 Discriminant Analysis 422
9.5* High-Dimensional Data – RNA-Seq Gene Expression 429
9.6 High-Dimensional Data from Expression Arrays 433
9.7 Balance and Matching – Causal Inference from Observational Data 443
9.8 Multiple Imputation 457
9.9 Further Reading 462
9.10 Exercises 463

Epilogue 467

Appendix A **The R System: a Brief Overview 469**
A.1 Getting Started with R 469
A.2 R Data Structures 473
A.3 Functions and Operators 483
A.4 Calculations with Matrices, Arrays, Lists, and Data Frames 487
A.5 Brief Notes on R Graphics Packages and Functions 490
A.6 Plotting Characters, Symbols, Line Types, and Colors 493

References 495
References to R Packages 508
Index of R Functions 514
Index of Terms 519

Figures

1.1	(A) Dotplot and (B) boxplot displays of cuckoo egg lengths	4
1.2	(A) Boxplot with annotation, compared with (B) histogram with overlaid density plot	12
1.3	Total lengths of possums, by `sex` and geographical location	13
1.4	Mortality from measles, London: (A) 1629–1939; (B) 1841–1881	14
1.5	Brain vs. body weight: (A) untransformed; (B) log transformed scales	15
1.6	Distance traveled up a 20° ramp, vs. starting point	16
1.7	Quarterly labor force numbers, by Canadian region, 1995–1996: (A) same log scale; (B) sliced log scale	18
1.8	Alternative logarithmic scale labeling choices, labor force numbers	19
1.9	Outcomes for two different surgery types – Simpson's paradox example	20
1.10	Boxplot showing `weights` (inverse sampling fractions), in the dataset `DAAG::nassCDS`	23
1.11	Individual plot-level yields of kiwifruit, by season and by block	25
1.12	Different y vs. x relationships, and Pearson vs. Spearman correlation	29
1.13	Normal density plot, with associated statistical measures	34
1.14	Plots for five samples of 50 from a normal distribution	35
1.15	Quantile–quantile plots – data vs. simulated normal values	36
1.16	Simulations of the sampling distribution of the mean	38
1.17	Normal densities with t_8 and t_3 overlaid	40
1.18	A fitted line, as against a fitted lowess curve	44
1.19	Quantile–quantile plots – regression residuals vs. normal samples	46
1.20	Boxplots for 200 simulated p-values – one-sided one-sample t-test	52
1.21	Post-study probability (PPV) vs. pre-study odds, given power	55
1.22	Sampling distribution of difference in AIC statistics	60
1.23	Alternative Cauchy priors, and posteriors, for the sleep data	62
1.24	Change in Bayes Factor with sample size, for different p-values	64
1.25	Permutation distribution density curves	67
2.1	Female vs. male admission rates – Simpson's paradox example	89
2.2	Second vs. first member of paired data – two examples	92
2.3	Quantile–quantile and *worm* plots for binomial and betabinomial fits	97
2.4	Worm plots for Poisson and negative binomial type I fits	98
2.5	Chemical vs. magnetic measure – line vs. loess smooth	105
2.6	Weight vs. volume, for eight softback books, with regression line	107
2.7	Diagnostic plots for Figure 2.6	108

2.8 Pointwise bounds for line, and for new predicted values 110
2.9 Confidence bounds – pairwise differences vs. difference of means 111
2.10 Regression lines – y on x and x on y 112
2.11 Graphs that illustrate the use of power transformations 113
2.12 Heart weight vs. body weight, for 30 Cape fur seals 115
2.13 Graphical summary of three-fold cross-validation – house sale data 117
2.14 Plots that relate to bootstrap distributions of prediction errors 120
2.15 LSD and HSD comparisons of means for three treatments 122
2.16 Test for linear trend vs. anova test – p-value comparison 125
2.17 False-color image of two channel microarray gene expression values 126
2.18 Rice shoot dry mass data – plots that show interactions 129
2.19 Diagnostic plots – `MCMCregress()` Bayesian analysis 135
3.1 Weight vs. volume, for seven hardback and eight softback books 145
3.2 Diagnostic plots – `lm(weight ~ 0+volume+area)` 147
3.3 Scatterplot matrices for Northern Ireland hill race data 149
3.4 Variation in distance per unit time with distance 151
3.5 Diagnostic plots – `lm(mph ~ log(dist)+log(gradient)` 152
3.6 Diagnostic plots – `lm(logtime ~ logdist + logclimb)` 153
3.7 Scatterplot matrices – log transformed `oddbooks` data 154
3.8 Scatterplot matrix for the `DAAG::litters` data 157
3.9 Termplots for regression with `oddbooks` data 164
3.10 Confidence intervals, compared with prediction intervals 167
3.11 Scatterplot matrix with power transformations – hurricane deaths data 169
3.12 Diagnostic plots – model for hurricane death data 170
3.13 Scatterplot matrix for `hills2000` data, logarithmic scales 172
3.14 Residuals vs. fitted – least squares compared with resistant fit 173
3.15 (A) A 2D plot that shows leverages; (b) a 3D dynamic graphic plot 175
3.16 Standardized changes in regression coefficients 175
3.17 Increase in penalty term difference for unit increase in the number of parameters p, for AIC, BIC, and AICc 177
3.18 Diagnostic plot, compared with simulated diagnostic plots 182
3.19 p-Values vs. number of variables available for selection 186
3.20 Scatterplot matrix for `Coxite` data 187
3.21 Observed porosities, and fitted values with 95 percent confidence bounds 188
3.22 Change in regression line as error in x changes 192
3.23 Apparent differences between groups, resulting from errors in x 194
3.24 Does preoperative baclofen reduce pain – Simpson's paradox example? 196
3.25 Added variable plots (a termplot variant) 198
3.26 Residuals vs. fitted values, for each of the three regressions 199
4.1 Weights of extracted sugar – wild-type plant vs. other types 209
4.2 Apple taste scores – `panelist` and `product` effects 215
4.3 Plots relate to alternative models fitted to the `leaftemp` data 219
4.4 Diagnostic plots for the parallel line model – `leaftemp` data 219
4.5 Number of grains per head vs. barley seeding rate 221
4.6 Line vs. quadratic curve, and residual plots, for barley seeding rate data 223
4.7 Resistance vs. apparent juice content for kiwifruit slabs 226
4.8 Thin plate spline basis curves, and contributions to fitted curve 228

4.9 Use of `gam.check()` with model for `fruitohms` data 229
4.10 Plots that relate to a monotonic decreasing spline fit 231
4.11 Gas consumption vs. external temperature – before and after insulation 232
4.12 Minimum and maximum temperature effects on dewpoint 234
4.13 Residuals vs. maximum temperature, for three minimum temperature ranges 235
4.14 Hurricane deaths – plots for fitted terms, and for residuals 236
4.15 Hurricane deaths – logarithmic vs. untransformed base damage measure 236
4.16 Plots show quantile curves (A) the 50 percent curve with two SE bounds; (B) 10 percent and 90 percent curves, unweighted and weighted by population 239
5.1 Plot illustrating the logit link function 246
5.2 Proportion moving vs. alveolar concentration – `anesthetic` data 249
5.3 Empirical log(odds) vs. concentration – `anesthetic` data 250
5.4 Location of sites for `DAAG::frogs` data 251
5.5 Scatterplot matrices that relate to `frogs` data 252
5.6 Scatterplot matrix, with suggested transformations – `frogs` data 254
5.7 Color density scale shows predicted probability of finding a frog 256
5.8 Explanatory variable contributions to fit, linear predictor scale 256
5.9 Contributions of model terms to fit, relative to means from other terms 258
5.10 Number of simple aberrant crypt foci, plotted against time 262
5.11 Dotplot summaries of numbers of two moth species, by habitat type 264
5.12 Dispersion estimates vs. mean, for `moths` data 267
5.13 Diagnostic plots – model for numbers of species A moths 269
5.14 Diagnostic plots – hurricane death model with `quasipoisson` error 271
5.15 Fitted values for NBI model, and quantile–quantile plot of residuals 273
5.16 Proportion of lefthanders, as smooth function of year of birth 275
5.17 Leverage vs. fitted proportion, for three common link functions 278
5.18 Graphical representation of survival data collection process 282
5.19 Survival curves – female vs. male AIDS contaminated blood infections 284
5.20 Survival curve for males who contracted AIDS from sexual contact 285
5.21 Time-dependent coefficients – Cox proportional hazards model 287
5.22 Time-dependent coefficients – Cox proportional hazards, cricketers 289
6.1 Trace plot of annual Lake Huron depth measurements 294
6.2 (A) First four lag plots of Lake Huron depth data; (B) autocorrelations for AR(1) and AR(2) fits vs. data; (C) partial autocorrelations 295
6.3 Autocorrelations and partial autocorrelations for an MA process 298
6.4 Predictions with pointwise CIs – ARIMA(1,1,2) vs. ETS 301
6.5 Two simulation runs each for alternative MA3 processes 302
6.6 Original and seasonally adjusted series, and plot of seasonal component 303
6.7 `mdbrtRain` and `mdbAVt`, and `SOI` and `IOD` yearly values 304
6.8 Termplots for model `gam(mdbrtRain ~ s(CO2)+s(SOI)+s(IOD)` 305
6.9 Termplots for model `gam(mdbAVt ~ s(CO2)+s(SOI)` 307
6.10 (A) Rainfall; (B) temperature vs. year, with fitted values 307
6.11 Scatterplot matrix for air quality data 310
6.12 Predicted values of `IA400/Lab` ratio – ARIMA vs. ETS model 312
7.1 Stripplots – corn yields for four parcels on each of eight sites 319

7.2 Profile likelihoods – model fitted to Antiguan corn data 328
7.3 Boxplots for average class scores (`like`) – public vs. private schools 329
7.4 Plots of parameter estimates for fit to `DAAG::science` data 333
7.5 Field layout for the kiwifruit shading trial 336
7.6 Variation at the different levels, for the kiwifruit shading data 340
7.7 Plots of residuals, of plot effects, and of simulated plot effects 343
7.8 Effects of car window tinting on visual performance, plots of data 345
7.9 Cold-storage fruitfly mortality, fitted curves and 95 percent bounds 351
7.10 Fruitfly mortality model – intra-class correlations for different links 352
7.11 Diagnostics for model fitted to insect cool-storage time–mortality data: (A) quantile–quantile plot of quantile residuals; (B) boxplots comparing treatment groups; (C) data-based quartiles vs. model-based; (D) quartiles as a function of number of insects 354
7.12 LT99 95 percent CIs – complementary log–log link and logit link 355
7.13 Oxygen intake vs. power output, for five athletes in the Daedalus project 360
7.14 Distance between two positions on the skull vs. age, for 27 children 363
7.15 Slopes of profiles, vs. means of distance and log(distance) 364
8.1 Boxplots for six selected variables, from 500 rows in the SPAM database 375
8.2 Tree diagram, from use of `rpart()` with email spam data 376
8.3 Illustrative tree from `rpart()` output 378
8.4 `Mileage` (mpg) vs. `Weight`, for 60 cars, with *loess* curve 381
8.5 Tree-based model for `Mileage` given `Weight`, for 60 cars 381
8.6 CV error eventual increase vs. error decrease, with later splits 384
8.7 CV error vs. `cp`, for female heart attack data 386
8.8 Tree from use of one standard error rule for email spam data 388
8.9 Error rates – random forest OOB vs. test set and `rpart()` test set 394
9.1 Brushtail possum morphometric measurements: (A) scatterplot matrix; (B) cloud plot 402
9.2 Second vs. first principal component, columns 6–14 of `possum` data 404
9.3 This repeats Figure 9.2, now for bootstrap data 406
9.4 Two-dimensional, obtained from nine-dimensional Euclidean, by two different scaling methods 407
9.5 Pairs plot of first three principal components 410
9.6 Plot of `BDI` against scores on first principal component 411
9.7 Four "blobs" of bivariate normal data, with different layouts of means 412
9.8 Single linkage hierarchical clustering plot, and plot that checks results 413
9.9 Cluster dendrograms for Panel B of Figure 9.7 414
9.10 Dendrograms shown are from moving clusters closer together 415
9.11 Four-group k-means makes implicit equal-sized assumption, example 417
9.12 Different two-component mixtures of univariate Gaussians 418
9.13 BIC values (BIC as used elsewhere), plotted against number of groups 420
9.14 Density contours of the fitted mixture model 421
9.15 Leaf length vs. leaf width – untransformed vs. logarithmic scales 423
9.16 Scatterplot matrix for the first three LDA canonical variates 428
9.17 (A) Mean–variance relationship for mRNA gene expression data; (B) use MDS to locate samples in 2D space 431
9.18 (A) LDA analysis for `Golub` data; (B) repeat for random normal data 436

9.19 (A) Mean–variance relationship for cancer gene expression data; (B) use MDS to locate samples in 2D space 437
9.20 Different accuracy measures, in the development of a discriminant rule 440
9.21 How effective is linear discriminant in distinguishing known groups? 442
9.22 Overlaid density plots – treatment groups and experimental controls 447
9.23 Are observations for which `re74` is available detectably different? 448
9.24 Random forest propensity scores – treated vs. controls? 451
9.25 Propensity scores for treatment and control groups after matching 454
9.26 (A) "Love plot"; (B) treatment/control differences for matched items 454
9.27 Love plots for different numbers (5,6) of cutpoints 456
9.28 Term plots for checking GAM model with straight line terms 459
9.29 Means of overimputations (solid points), with confidence bounds 461
A.1 Worldwide annual totals of CO_2 emissions – 1900, 1920, . . . , 2020 471
A.2 Fonts, symbols, and line types 493

Preface

This text is designed as an aid, for learning and for reference, in the navigation of a world in which unprecedented new data sources, and tools for data analysis, are pervasive. It aims to teach, using real-world examples, a style of analysis and critique that, given meaningful data, can generate defensible analysis results. Its focus is on ideas and concepts, with extensive use of graphical presentation. It may be used to give students who have taken courses in statistical theory exposure to practical data analysis. It is designed, also, as a resource for scientists who wish to do statistical analyses on their own data, preferably with reference as necessary to professional statistical advice. It emphasizes the role of statistical design and analysis as part of the wider scientific process.

As far as possible, our account of statistical methodology comes from the coal-face, where the quirks of real data must be faced and addressed. Experience in consulting with researchers in many different areas of application, in supervising research students, and in lectures to researchers, have been strong influences in the text's style and content. We comment extensively on analysis results, noting inferences that seem well founded, and noting limitations on inferences that can be drawn. We emphasize the use of graphs for gaining insight into data – in advance of any formal analysis, for understanding the analysis, and for presenting analysis results. The project has been a tremendous learning experience for all three of us. As is usual, the more we learn, the more we appreciate how much more we have to learn.

The text is suitable for a style of learning where readers work through the text with a computer at their side, running the R code as and when this seems helpful. It complements more mathematically oriented accounts of statistical methodology. The appendix provides a brief account of R, primarily as a starting point for learning. We encourage readers with limited R experience to avail themselves of the wealth of instructional material on the web as well as the hardcopy resources listed in Section 1.11.

While no prior knowledge of specific statistical methods or theory is assumed, readers will need to bring with them, or quickly acquire, a modest level of statistical sophistication. Prior experience with real data, prior exposure to statistical methodology, and some prior familiarity with regression methods, will all be helpful.

Important technical terms will include *random sample*, *independence*, *dependence*, *standard deviation*, and *normal distribution*, with limited attention to formal definition. Our primary concern is with the role and meaning of this language in practical data analysis. While there will be references to theoretical results, it is not our purpose to provide a systematic account of statistical theory.[1] We make only limited use of mathematical symbolism.

Statistical analysis relies heavily on mathematical models. An understanding of the mathematics underlying a model is important only to the extent that it helps in understanding, and where possible in checking, what the model means in the context from which the data came. Is it reasonable to assume that observations are independent? What are the influences, perhaps the time sequence in which the data were collected, that might place this assumption in question? This is just one of the issues, but a very important one, that data analysts need to consider. Comments made by John W. Tukey emphasize the importance, in statistical training and practice, of wrestling with what the models used mean in the context of data that has been presented for analysis:

> ... Statistics is a science ... and it is no more a branch of mathematics than are physics, chemistry and economics; for if its methods fail the test of experience – not the test of logic – they are discarded.
> [Tukey (1953), quoted by Brillinger (2002)]

The methods that we cover have wide application. The datasets, many of which have featured in published papers, are drawn from many different fields. They reflect a journey in learning and understanding, alike for the authors and for those with whom they have worked, that has ranged widely over many different research areas. We hope that our text will stimulate the cross-fertilization that occurs when ideas and applications that have proved effective in one area find use elsewhere, perhaps even leading to new lines of investigation.

To summarize: The strengths of this book include the directness of its encounter with research data, its advice on practical data analysis issues, careful critiques of analysis results, the use of modern data analysis tools and approaches, the use of simulation and other computer-intensive methods where these provide insight or give results that are not otherwise available, attention to graphical and other presentation issues, the use of examples drawn from across the range of statistical applications, the links that it makes into the debate over reproducibility in science, and the inclusion of code that reproduces analyses.

A substantial part of the first edition of *Data Analysis and Graphics Using R* (Maindonald and Braun, 2003) was derived, initially, from the lecture notes of courses for researchers that the first author presented, at the University of Newcastle (Australia) over 1996–1997 and at Australian National University from 1998, through until formal retirement and beyond. It was a privilege to have contacts, arising from consulting work and lectures, across the University. Those contacts were extended as a result of short courses on R-based analysis that were offered,

[1] For an overview of the theory of statistical inference, see, for example, Cox (2006).

across a wide variety of Australian government and academic institutions, between 2003 and 2014.

Influences on the Modern Practice of Statistics

Statistics is a young discipline. Only in the 1920s and 1930s did the modern framework of statistical theory, including ideas of hypothesis testing and estimation, begin to take shape. As documented in Gigerenzer et al. (1989, *The Empire of Chance*), differences in historical development have led to some differences in practice between research areas.

Statistical methods have found wide use, but they have also been widely misused. There has been a widespread reliance on "black box" approaches, used without due consideration of the reasonableness of assumptions made, or attention to diagnostic checks, or attention to the processes that generated the data. In experimental work, the use of p-values and other statistics has too often become a substitute for the checks that independent replication provides on the total experimental process. There has been a renewed attention, both in the wider scientific community and in the statistical community, to the interplay between scientific methodology and statistical design and analysis. Critical reexamination of current scientific processes, and of the role of statistical analysis within those processes, can help ensure that the demands of scientific rationality do in due course win out over accidents of historical development and all-too-human failures to maintain critical standards.

New Data Analysis Tools

The methodology has developed in a synergy with the relevant supporting mathematical theory and, more recently, with computing. This has led to major advances on the methodologies of the precomputer era. "Data Science," or perhaps "Statistical Science," is a good name for the mix of tools and skills required for effective data analysis. Data analysts now have at their disposal vastly new powerful tools than were available even 20 years ago, for exploratory analysis of regression data, for choosing between alternative models, for diagnostic checks, for handling nonlinearity, for assessing the predictive power of models, and for graphical presentation. New computing tools make it straightforward to move data between different systems, to keep a record of calculations, to retrace or adapt earlier calculations, and to edit output and graphics into a form that can be incorporated into published documents. Machine learning and related methodologies emphasize new types of data, new data analysis demands, new data analysis tools, and datasets that may be of unprecedented size. Textual data and image data offer interesting new challenges.

The traditional concerns of professional data analysts remain as important as ever. Irrespective of the size of dataset, questions of data quality, of relevance to the issues that are under investigation, and of the way that the data have been sampled, remain as important as ever. Implicit or explicit claims that results generalize to a relevant wider target population must be justified.

Students in first or second year university courses, in such areas as geography or biology or politics or psychology or business studies, are increasingly likely to encounter R. It is finding its way into the upper levels of secondary schools. While this is to be encouraged, students do need to understand that such courses are at the start of an adventure in statistical understanding. There is no good substitute for professional training in modern tools for data analysis, and experience in using those tools with a wide range of datasets. No one should be embarrassed that they have difficulty with analyses that involve ideas that professional statisticians may take seven or eight years of training and experience to master.

The questions that data analysis is designed to answer can often be stated simply. This may encourage the layperson, or even scientists doing their own analyses, to believe that the answers are similarly simple. Commonly, they are not. Be prepared for unexpected subtleties. Comments made by Stephen Senn are apt:

> I've been studying statistics for over 40 years and still don't understand it. The ease with which non-statisticians master it is staggering.

No amount of statistical or computing technology can be a substitute for good design of data collection, for understanding the context in which data are to be interpreted, or for skill in using available analysis tools. The best any analysis can do is to highlight the information in the data.

The R System

Work on R started in the early 1990s, as a project of Ross Ihaka and Robert Gentleman, when both were at the University of Auckland (New Zealand). The R system implements a dialect of the S language, developed at AT&T by John Chambers and colleagues. Section 1.4 in Chambers (2008) describes the history. Versions of R are available, at no charge, for Microsoft Windows, for Linux and other Unix systems, and for Macintosh systems. It is available through the Comprehensive R Archive Network (CRAN). Go to http://cran.r-project.org/, and find the nearest mirror site. A huge range of packages, contributed by specialists in many different areas, supplement base R. The development model has proved effective in marshaling high levels of computing expertise for continuing improvement, for identifying and fixing bugs, and for responding quickly to the evolving needs and interests of the statistical community. The R Task Views web page[2] lists packages that handle some of the more common R applications. It has become an increasing challenge to keep pace with the new and/or improved abilities that R packages, new and old, continue to develop. Those who rely heavily on R for their day-to-day work will do well to keep attuned to major changes and developments.

The R system has brought into a common framework a huge range of abilities that extend beyond the data analysis and associated data manipulation and graphics abilities that are the focus of this text. Examples include drawing and coloring maps, reading and handling shapefiles, map projections, plotting data collected by balloon-borne weather instruments, creating color palettes, manipulating bitmap images, solving sudoku puzzles, creating magic squares, solving ordinary differential equations, and processing various types of genomic data. Help files and

[2] https://cran.r-project.org/web/views/.

vignettes that are included with packages are a large reservoir of information on the methodologies that they implement.

There are several graphical user interfaces (GUIs) that can be highly helpful in accessing a restricted range of R abilities – examples are *BlueSky*, *Rcmdr*, *R-Instat*, *jamovi*, and *rattle*. Access to the fill range of abilities that R and R packages make available will require use of the command line.

RStudio is a widely used R interactive development environment (IDE) for tasks that include viewing history, debugging, managing the workspace, package management, and data input and output. It has features that greatly assist project management and package development.

Among systems that have the potential to challenge R's dominance for data analysis, Julia (`julialang.org/`) seems particularly interesting. Relative to R, it has high computational efficiency. It has the potential to develop or adapt a range of packages that together match what R packages offer.

Changes and Additions from Data Analysis and Graphics Using R

Chapters 1–5 of *Data Analysis and Graphics Using R*, third edition (Maindonald and Braun, 2010) have been amalgamated and condensed somewhat into Chapters 1–3 of the present book. Here, the focus has moved, from including extensive R tutorial content in the text, to pointing users to the extensive R help resources now available both on the web and in printed form. Supplementary content available online includes R Markdown scripts, one for each chapter, that can be processed to reproduce all computer output, including tables and graphs. This content is available at `https://jhmaindonald.github.io/PGRcode`.

Concerns about reproducibility (or, in the terminology we prefer, "replicability"), especially in wet laboratory biology and in psychology, have attracted extensive attention in the pages of *Nature*, *Science*, *The Economist*, psychology journals, and elsewhere. The uses and limitations of p-values have been an important part of the discussion. Chapter 1 now has a much extended discussion of their use and role, leading on to the wider discussion of replicability issues. Information statistics (AIC, AICc, and BIC) get more detailed attention.

The treatment of p-values extends to noting the new possibilities that arise when there are, potentially, hundreds, or thousands, or more, p-values. The false discovery rate estimates that are then available are more informative, and relate more directly to the questions that are commonly of experimental interest, than p-values. The new Section 9.5 takes up these ideas as they apply to the analysis of RNA-Seq gene expression data.

Other topics that get new or increased attention include: the modeling of extra-binomial or extra-Poisson variation; exponential time series, including their use in forecasting; seasonality; spline smooths with time series error terms; fitting monotonic increasing or decreasing response curves; and quantile regression automatic choice of smoothing parameter.

Changes in the lme4 package for fitting mixed-effects models, and the implementation of the Kenward–Roger approach that is now available in the *afex* package, have required substantial rewrites. In Chapter 7, there is a new section on "A Mixed Model with a Betabinomial Error." The treatment of Principal Component Analysis and of multi-dimensional scaling is now followed by a new section on hierarchical and other forms of clustering.

The treatment of causal inference from observational data has been greatly extended to discuss the role of matching. There is some limited attention to the use of multiple imputation to fill in missing values in data where some observations are incomplete.

Source Files That Combine Text and R Code

Drafts of this text were created from *Sweave* source files that combine marked up code and text into one document, in a form that could then be processed using Yihui Xie's *knitr* package to give the LaTeX files and associated R output and figures from which this text was generated. Rerunning and checking of code is a built-in part of the process, making the revising and updating of text and code easier and less error prone. The R Markdown plain text format, designed to be easier for novices to learn and master, can can be processed using *knitr* abilities in a very similar way. R Markdown is widely used for creating online content, for papers and books, and for the vignettes that many R packages use to supplement help pages. See `https://rmarkdown.rstudio.com/`.

Acknowledgements

The prefaces to the three editions of *Data Analysis and Graphics Using R* give names of those who provided helpful comment. For this new text, James Cone has provided useful comments. Trish Scott has helped with copyediting. Discussions on the R-help and R-devel email lists have contributed greatly to insight and understanding. The failings that remain are, naturally, our responsibility.

This text has drawn on data from many different sources. Following the references is a list of data sources (individuals and/or organizations) that we wish to thank and acknowledge. Thanks are due also to the many researchers whose discussions with us have helped stimulate thinking and understanding, and who in many instances have given us access to their data. We apologize to anyone that we may have inadvertently failed to acknowledge.

Too often, data that have become the basis for a published paper are not made available in any form of public record. The data may not find their way into any permanent record, and cease to be available for checking the analysis, for work that builds on what can be learned when data from multiple sources are brought together, to try a new form of analysis, or for use in teaching. In areas where data are as a matter of course kept available for future researchers to use, this has been a major contributor to advances in scientific understanding. Those benefits can and should extend more widely. Thanks are due to Beverley Lawrence for her efforts as copy-editor, and to Cambridge University Press staff who assisted us through the copy-editing and publication process – Roger Astley, Natalie Tomlinson, Anna Scriven, and Clare Dennison.

Notes for Readers

For many readers, a largely "learn as one goes" approach to mastering what they need to know of R will work well. For this, they can look for the mix of sources of tutorial content that works best for them – online tutorial content such as is noted in Section 1.11, books and other printed material, results from web searches, and such guidance as is provided in Appendix A. We encourage readers who are new to R to skim over the content of Appendix A before or as they work through the first chapter.

A complete set of R code, together with other supplementary material, is available from `https://jhmaindonald.github.io/PGRcode`.

Graphs and Graphics Packages

In Chapter 1, simplified code is given for figures that do not involve relatively complicated code. In later chapters, code is given only for those figures that are specifically targeted at the methodology under discussion.

The main graphics packages that will be used are the base *graphics* package, *lattice* and *latticeExtra*, and *ggplot2*. The `plot()` and related functions in base graphics directly generate a plot. With *lattice* and *ggplot2* functions, an alternative to directly creating a plot is to save the output as a graphics object that can be further updated and/or modified before use to create a plot.

Accessing Data and Functions from Packages

A number of packages are automatically loaded, with their functions and datasets then available, at the start of a new R session. For functions and datasets in packages that are not already available, there is a choice between using `library()` or an equivalent to make all datasets and functions from the package available, or using code such as `lattice::xyplot()` (execute the lattice function from the *lattice* package) or `DAAG::cuckoos` (the `cuckoos` dataset from the *DAAG* package) whenever such a function or dataset is required.

Conventions

Starred headings identify more technical discussions that can be skipped at a first reading. Item numbers for more technical and/or challenging exercises are likewise starred.

Comments, prefaced by `#` or for extra emphasis by `##`, will often be included in code chunks. Where code is included in comments, it will be surrounded by back quotes, as in `` `species ~ length` `` in the final line of code that now follows:

```
## Code for a stripped down version of Figure 1.1A
library(latticeExtra)  # The 'lattice' package will be loaded & attached also
cuckoos <- DAAG::cuckoos
## Panel A: Dotplot without species means added
dotplot(species ~ length, data=cuckoos)  ## `species ~ length` is a 'formula'
```

1

Learning from Data, and Tools for the Task

Chapter Summary

We begin by illustrating the interplay between questions driven by scientific curiosity and the use of data in seeking the answers to such questions. Graphs provide a useful window through which meaning can be extracted from data. Numeric summary statistics and probability distributions provide a form of quantitative scaffolding for models of random as well as nonrandom variation. Simple regression models foreshadow the issues that arise in the more complex models considered later in the book. Frequentist and Bayesian approaches to statistical inference are touched upon, the latter primarily using the Bayes Factor as a summary statistic which moves beyond the limited perspective that p-values offer. Resampling methods, where the one available dataset is used to provide an empirical substitute for a theoretical distribution, are also introduced. Remaining topics are of a more general nature. Section 1.9 will discuss the use of RStudio and other such tools for organizing and managing work. Section 1.10 will include a discussion on the important perspective that replication studies provide, for experimental studies, on the interplay between statistical analysis and scientific practice. The checks provided by independent replication at another time and place are an indispensable complement to statistical analysis. Chapter 2 will extend the discussion of this chapter to consider a wider class of models, methods, and model diagnostics.

A Note on Terminology – Variables, Factors and More!

Much of data analysis is concerned with the statistical modeling of relationships or associations that can be gleaned from data, with a mathematical formula used to specify the model. There is an example at the beginning of Section 1.1.6.

The word *variable* will be used when data values are numeric. These include counts, as for example in `count` from the `DAAG::ACF1` data frame which has numbers of aberrant lesions in the lining of a rat's colon. The term *factor* will be used when values are on a categorical scale. Thus, in the data frame `DAAG::kiwishade`, `yield` is a variable with values such as 101.11, and `block` is a factor with levels `east`, `north`, and `west`. A factor may also represent values on an ordinal scale. Thus the factor `tint` in the data frame `DAAG::tinting` has ordered levels `no`, `lo`, and `hi`.

Continuous measurements can be further classified as having either an *interval* scale or a *ratio* scale. Variables defined on an interval scale can take positive or negative values, and differences in the data values are meaningful. Variables defined on a ratio scale are usually positive only, so quotients are more meaningful.

1.1 Questions, and Data That May Point to Answers

Accounts of observed phenomena become part of established science once we know the circumstances under which they will recur. This process is relatively straightforward when applied to the study of regular events, such as a solar eclipse or the ocean tide levels in the Bay of Fundy in eastern Canada. Mathematical models that are based on sound physical principles can provide very accurate predictions for such events. Not everything is so readily predictable. How effective is a particular vaccine in preventing COVID-19-associated hospitalizations? How fast will a wildfire spread through a region with known topography and vegetation under given wind, temperature, and moisture conditions? Data from a suitable experiment or series of experiments may be able to go at least part of the way towards providing an answer. Thus, results from prescribed burns in designated forest stands where all relevant variables have been measured can provide a starting point for assessing the rate of spread of surface fires.

Or it may be necessary to rely on whatever data are already available. How effective are airbags in reducing the risk of death in car accidents? Data on car accidents in the United States over the period 1997–2002 are available. While careful and critical analyses of these data can help answer the question, caveats apply when the interest is in effectiveness at a later time and in another country. There have been important advances in the subsequent two decades in airbag design, manufacture, and systems that control deployment.

In Canada, there is a tendency for car passengers to use seatbelts at a higher rate than in the United States, so that efficacy assessments based on the American data have to be tempered when applied to the Canadian experience. The decision on which of the available datasets is best designed to provide an answer, and the choice of model, have called for careful and critical assessment. The help pages `?DAAG::nassCDS` and `?gamclass::FARS` provide further commentary. There is a strong interplay between the questions that can reasonably be asked, and the data that are available or can be collected. Keep in mind, also, that different questions, asked of the same data, may demand different analyses.

1.1.1 A Sample Is a Window into the Wider Population

The population comprises all the data that might have been. The sample is the data that we have. Subjects for a sample to be surveyed should be selected randomly. In a clinical trial, it is important to allocate subjects randomly to different treatment groups.

Suppose, for example, that names on an electoral roll are numbered from 1 to 9384. The following uses the function `sample()` to obtain a random sample of 12 individuals:

```
## For the sequence below, precede with set.seed(3676)
sample(1:9384, 12, replace=FALSE)  # NB: `replace=FALSE` is the default
```

```
 [1] 2263 9264 4490 8441 1868 3073 5430   19 1305 2908 5947  915
```

The numbers are the numerical labels for the 12 individuals who are included in the sample. The task is then to find them! The option `replace=FALSE` gives a *without replacement* sample, that is, it ensures that no one is included more than once.

A more realistic example might be the selection of 1200 individuals, perhaps for purposes of conducting an opinion poll, from names numbered 1 to 19,384, on an electoral roll. Suitable code is:

```
chosen1200 <- sample(1:19384, 1200, replace=FALSE)
```

The following randomly assigns 10 plants (labeled from 1 to 10, inclusive) to one of two equal-sized groups, control and treatment:

```
## For the sequence below, precede with set.seed(366)
split(sample(seq(1:10)), rep(c("Control","Treatment"), 5))
```

```
$Control
[1]  5  7  1 10  4

$Treatment
[1] 8 6 3 2 9
```

```
# sample(1:10) gives a random re-arrangement (permutation) of 1, 2, ..., 10
```

This assigns plants 3, 5, 10, 2, and 7 to the control group. This mechanism avoids any unwitting preference for placing healthier-looking plants in the treatment group.

The simple independent random sampling scheme can be modified or extended in ways that take account of structure in the data, with random sampling remaining a part of the data-selection process.

Cluster Sampling

Cluster sampling is one of many probability-based variants on simple random sampling. See Barnett (2002). The function `sample()` can be used as before, but now the numbers from which a selection is made correspond to clusters. For example, households or localities may be selected, with multiple individuals from each. Standard inferential methods then require adaptation to account for the fact that it is the clusters that are independent, not the individuals within the clusters. Donner and Klar (2000) describe methods that are designed for use in health research.

**A Note on With-Replacement Samples*

For data that can be treated as a random sample from the population, one way to get an idea of the extent to which it may be affected by random variation is to take with-replacement random samples from the one available sample, and to do this

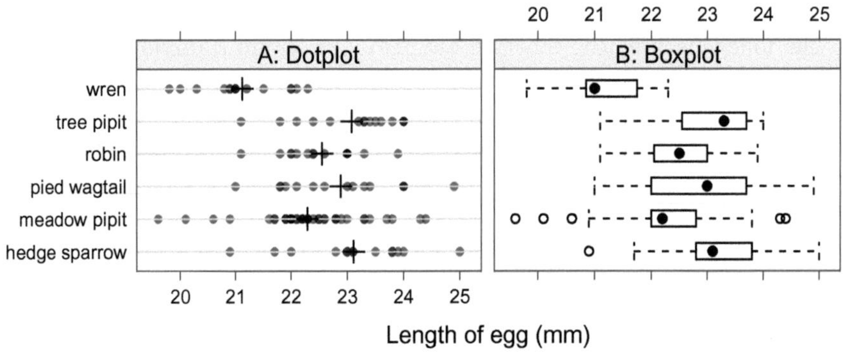

Figure 1.1 Dotplot (Panel A) and boxplot (Panel B) displays of cuckoo egg lengths. In Panel A, points that overlap have a more intense color. Means are shown as +. The boxes in Panel B take in the central 50 percent of the data, from 25 percent of the way through the data to 75 percent of the way through. The dot marks the median. Data are from Latter (1902).

repeatedly. The distribution that results can be an empirical substitute for the use of a theoretical distribution as a basis for inference.

We can randomly sample from the set $\{1, 2, \ldots, 10\}$, allowing repeats, thus:

```
sample(1:10, replace=TRUE)
```

```
[1]  1  3  7  5  5 10  3  3  2  9
```

```
## sample(1:10, replace=FALSE) returns a random permutation of 1,2,...10
```

With-replacement sampling is the basis of *bootstrap* sampling. The effect is that of repeating each value an infinite number of times, and then taking a without-replacement sample. Subsections 1.8.3 and 1.8.4 will demonstrate the methodology.

1.1.2 Formulating the Scientific Question

Questions should be structured with a view both to the intended use of results, and to the limits of what the available data allow. Predictions of numbers in hospital from COVID-19 two weeks into the future do not demand the same level of scientific understanding or detailed data as needed to judge who among those infected are most likely to require hospitalization.

Example: A Question About Cuckoo Eggs

Cuculus canorus is one of several species of cuckoos that lay eggs in the nests of other birds. The eggs are then unwittingly adopted and hatched by the hosts. Latter (1902) collected the data in `DAAG::cuckoos` as shown in Figure 1.1 in order to investigate claims in Newton and Gadow (1896, p. 123) that the cuckoo eggs tend to match the eggs of the host bird in size, shape, and color. Panel A is a dotplot

Table 1.1 *Mean lengths of cuckoo eggs, compared with mean lengths of eggs laid by the host bird species. The table combines information from the two* DAAG *data frames* **cuckoos** *and* **cuckoohosts**.

Host species	Meadow pipit	Hedge sparrow	Robin	Wagtails	Tree pipit	Wren	Yellow hammer
Length (cuckoo)	22.3 (45)	23.1 (14)	22.5 (16)	22.6 (26)	23.1 (15)	21.1 (15)	22.6 (9)
Length (host)	19.7 (74)	20.0 (26)	20.2 (57)	19.9 (16)	20 (27)	17.7 (-)	21.6 (32)

(Numbers in parentheses are numbers of eggs)

display of the raw data. Panel B is the more summary boxplot form of display (to be discussed further in Section 1.1.5) that is designed to give a rough indication of how variation between groups compares with variation within groups.[1]

Table 1.1 adds information that suggests a relationship between the size of the host bird's eggs and the size of the cuckoo eggs that were laid in that nest. Observe that apart from several outlying egg lengths in the meadow pipit nests, the length variability within each host species' nest is fairly uniform.

In the paper (Latter, 1902) that supplied the cuckoo egg data of Figure 1.1 and Table 1.1, the interest was in whether cuckoos do in fact match the eggs that they lay to the host eggs, and if so, in assessing which features match and to what extent.

Uniquely among the birds listed, the architecture of wren nests makes it impossible for the host birds to see the cuckoo's eggs, and the cuckoo's eggs do not match the wren's eggs in color. For the other species the color does mostly match. Latter concluded that the claim in Newton and Gadow (1896) is correct, that the eggs that cuckoos lay tend to match the eggs of the host bird in ways that will make it difficult for hosts to distinguish their own eggs from the cuckoo eggs.

Issues with the data in Table 1.1 and Figure 1.1 are as follows.

- The cuckoo eggs and the host eggs are from different nests, collected over the course of several investigations. Data on the host eggs are from various sources.
- The host egg lengths for the wren are indicative lengths, from Gordon (1894).

There is thus a risk of biases, different for the different sources of data, that limit the inferences that can be drawn. How large, then, relative to statistical variation, is the difference between wrens and other species? Would it require an implausibly large bias to explain the difference? A more formal comparison between lengths for the different species based on an appropriate statistical model will be a useful aid to informed judgment.

Stripped down code for Figure 1.1 is:

```
library(latticeExtra)  # Lattice package will be loaded and attached also
cuckoos <- DAAG::cuckoos
## Panel A: Dotplot without species means added
dotplot(species ~ length, data=cuckoos)  ## `species ~ length` is a 'formula'
## Panel B: Box and whisker plot
bwplot(species ~ length, data=cuckoos)
## The following shows Panel A, including species means & other tweaks
av <- with(cuckoos, aggregate(length, list(species=species), FUN=mean))
```

[1] Subsection A.5.1 has the code that combines the two panels, for display as one graph.

```
dotplot(species ~ length, data=cuckoos, alpha=0.4, xlab="Length of egg (mm)") +
  as.layer(dotplot(species ~ x, pch=3, cex=1.4, col="black", data=av))
  # Use `+` to indicate that more (another 'layer') is to be added.
  # With `alpha=0.4`, 40% is the point color with 60% background color
  # `pch=3`: Plot character 3 is '+'; `cex=1.4`: Default char size X 1.4
```

1.1.3 Planning for a Statistical Analysis

First steps in any coordinated scientific endeavor must include clear identification of the question of interest, followed by careful planning. Consultation with subject-matter specialists, as well as with specialists in statistical aspects of study design, will help avoid obvious mistakes in any of the steps: designing the study, collecting and/or collating data, carrying out analyses, and interpreting results.

If new data are to be acquired, one must decide if a designed experiment is feasible. In human or animal experimentation, such as in clinical trials to test a new drug therapy, ethics are an immediate concern. Data from experiments appear throughout this text – examples are the data on the tinting of car windows that is used for Figure 7.8 in Section 7.5, and the kiwifruit shading data that is discussed in Subsection 1.3.2. Such data can, if the experiment has been well designed with a view to answering the questions of interest, give reliable results. Always, the question must be asked: "How widely do the results generalize?". For example, we might be interested in knowing to what extent the results for the kiwifruit shading conditions can be generalized to other locations with different soil types and weather conditions.

Understand the Data

Most standard elementary statistical methods assume that sample values were all chosen independently and with equal probability from the relevant population. If the data were from an observational study, such as in the cuckoo eggs example of Subsection 1.1.2, special care is required to consider what biases may have been induced by the method of data collection, and to ensure that they do not not lead to incorrect conclusions.

Temporal and spatial dependence are common forms of departure from independence, often leading to more complicated analyses. Data points originating from points that are close together in time and/or space are often more similar. Tests and graphical checks for dependence are necessarily designed to detect specific forms of dependence. Their effectiveness relies on recognizing forms of dependence that can be expected in the specific context.

If the data were acquired earlier and for a different purpose, details of the circumstances that surrounded the data collection are especially important. Were they from a designed experiment? If so, how was the randomization carried out? What factors were controlled? Was there a hierarchical structure to the data, such as would occur in a survey of students, randomly selected from classes, which are themselves randomly selected from schools, and so on? If the data were collected as part of an observational study, such as in the cuckoos example of Subsection

1.1.2, special care is required to ensure that hidden biases induced by the method of data collection do not lead to incorrect conclusions. Biases are likely when data are obtained from "convenience" samples that have the appearance of surveys but which are really poorly designed observational studies. Online voluntary surveys are of this type. Similar biases can arise in experimental studies if care is not taken. For example, an agricultural experimenter may pick one plant from each of several parts of a plot. If the choice is not made according to an appropriate randomization mechanism, a preference bias can easily be introduced.

Nonresponse, so that responses are missing for some respondents, is endemic in most types of sample survey data. Or responses may be incomplete, with answers not provided to some questions. Dietary studies based on the self-reports of participants are prone to measurement error biases. With experimental data on crop or fruit yields, results may be missing for some plots because of natural disturbances caused by animals or harsh weather. One ignores the issue at a certain risk, but treating the problem is nontrivial, and the analyst is advised to determine as well as possible the nature of the missingness. It can be tempting simply to replace a missing height value for a male adult in a dataset by the average of the other male heights. Such a *single imputation* strategy will readily create unwanted biases. Males that are of smaller than average weight and chest measurement are likely to be of smaller than average height. *Multiple imputation* is a generic name for methodologies that, by matching incomplete observations as closely as possible to other observations on the variables for which values are available, aim to fill in the gaps.

Causal Inference

With data from carefully designed experiments, it is often possible to infer causal relationships. Perhaps the most serious danger is that the results will be generalized beyond the limits imposed by the experimental conditions.

Observational data, or data from experiments where there have been failures in design or execution, is another matter. Correlations do not directly indicate causation. A and B may be correlated because A drives B, or because B drives A, or because A and B change together, in concert with a third variable. For inferring causation, other sources of evidence and understanding must come into play.

What Was Measured? Is It the Relevant Measure?

The `DAAG::science` and `DAAG::socsupport` data frames are both from surveys. The former concerns student attitudes towards science in Australian private and public school systems. The latter concerns social and emotional support resources as they might relate to psychological depression in a sample of individuals.

In either case it is necessary to ask: "What was measured?" This question is itself amenable to experimental investigation. For the dataset `science`, what did students understand by "science"? Was science, for them, a way to gain and test knowledge of the world? Or was it a body of knowledge? Or, more likely, was it a label for their experience of science laboratory classes (interesting sights, smells and sounds perhaps) and field trips? Answers to other questions included in the survey shed some limited light.

In the `socsupport` dataset, an important variable is the Beck Depression Inventory or `BDI`, which is based on a 21-question multiple-choice self-report. It is the outcome of a rigorous process of development and testing. Since its first publication in 1961, it has been extensively used, critiqued, and modified. Its results have been well validated, at least for populations on which it has been tested. It has become a standard psychological measure of depression (see, e.g., Streiner et al., 2014).

For therapies that are designed to prolong life, what is the relevant measure? Is it survival time from diagnosis? Or is a measure that takes account of quality of life over that time more appropriate? Two such measures are "Disability Adjusted Life Years" (DALYs) and "Quality Adjusted Life Years" (QALYs). Quality of life may differ greatly between the therapies that are compared.

Use Relevant Prior Information in the Planning Stages

Information from the analysis of earlier data may be invaluable both for the design of data collection for the new study and for planning data analysis. When prior data are not available, a pilot study involving several experimental runs can sometimes provide such information.

Graphical and other checks are needed to identify obvious mistakes and/or quirks in the data. Graphs that draw attention to inadequacies may be suggestive of remedies. For example, they may indicate a need to numerically transform the data, such as by taking a logarithm or square root, in order to more accurately meet the assumptions underlying a more formal analysis. At the same time, one should keep in mind the risk that use of the data to influence the analysis may bias results.

Subject Area Knowledge and Judgments

Data analysis results must be interpreted against a background of subject area knowledge and judgment. Some use of qualitative judgment is inevitable, relating to such matters as the weight that can be placed on claimed subject area knowledge, the measurements that are taken, the details of study design, the analysis choices, and the interpretation of analysis results. These, while they should be as informed as possible, involve elements of qualitative judgment. A well-designed study will often lead to results that challenge the insights and understandings that underpinned the planning.

The Importance of Clear Communication

When there are effective lines of communication, the complementary skills of a data analyst and a subject matter expert can result in effective and insightful analyses. When unclear about the question of interest, or about some feature of the data, analysts should be careful not to appear to know more than is really the case. The subject-matter specialist may be so immersed in the details of their problem that, without clear signals to the contrary, they may assume similar knowledge on the part of the analyst.

Data-Based Selection of Comparisons

In carefully designed studies where subjects have been assigned to different groups, with each group receiving a different treatment, comparisons of outcomes between the various groups, and of subgroups within those groups (e.g., female/male, old/young) will be of interest. Among what may be many possible comparisons, the comparisons that will be considered should be specified in advance. Prior data, if available, can provide guidance. Any investigation of other comparisons may be undertaken as an exploratory investigation, a preliminary to the next study.

Data-based selection of one or two comparisons from a much larger number is not appropriate, since large biases may be introduced. Alternatively, there must be allowance for such selection in the assessment of model accuracy. The issues here are nontrivial, and we defer further discussion until later.

Models Must Be Fit for Their Intended Use

Statistical models must, along with the data upon which they rely, be applied according to their intended use. Architects and engineers have in the past relied heavily on scale models for giving a sense of important features of a planned building. For checking routes through the building, for the plumbing as well as for humans, such models can be very useful. They will not give much insight on how buildings in earthquake-prone regions are likely to respond to a major earthquake – a lively concern in Wellington, New Zealand, where the first author now lives. For that purpose, engineers use mathematical equations that are designed to reflect the relevant physical processes. The credibility of predictions will strongly depend on the accuracy with which the models can be shown to represent those processes.

1.1.4 Results That Withstand Thorough and Informed Challenge

Statistical models aim to give real-world descriptions that are adequate for the purposes for which the model will be used. What checks will give confidence that a model will do the task asked of it? As argued in Tukey (1997), there must be exposure to diverse challenges that can build (or destroy!) confidence in model-based inferences. We should trust those results that have withstood thorough and informed challenge.

A large part of our task in this text is to suggest effective forms of challenge. Specific types of challenge may include the following.

- For experiments, carefully check and critique the design.
- Look into what is known of the processes that generated the data, and consider critically how this may affect its use and the reliance placed on it. Are there possible or likely biases?
- Look for inadequacies in laboratory procedure.
- Use all relevant graphical or other summary checks to critique the model that underpins the analysis.
- Where possible, check the performance of the model on test data that reflects

the manner of use of results. (If, for example, predictions are made that will be applied a year into the future, check how predictions made a year ahead panned out for historical data.)

- For experimental data, have the work replicated independently by another research group, from generation of data through to analysis.

In areas where the nature of the work requires cooperation between scientists with a wide range of skills, and where data are shared, researchers provide checks on each other. For important aspects of the work, the most effective critiques are likely to come from fellow researchers rather than from referees who are inevitably more remote from the details of what has been done. Failures of scientific processes are a greater risk where scientists work as individuals or in small groups with limited outside checks.

There are commonalities with the issues of legal and medical decision making that receive extensive attention in Kahneman et al. (2021, p. 372), on the benefits of "averaging," that is, using the perspectives of multiple judges as a basis for decision making when sentencing; the authors comment:

> The advantage of averaging is further enhanced when judges have diverse skills and complementary judgment patterns.

Also needed is a high level of shared understanding.

For observational data, the challenges that are appropriate will depend strongly on the nature of the claims made as a result of any analysis. Dangers of over-interpretation and/or misinterpretation of results gleaned from observational data will be exemplified later in the text.

1.1.5 Using Graphs to Make Sense of Data

Ideas of *Exploratory Data Analysis* (EDA), as formalized by John W. Tukey, have been a strong influence in the development of many of the forms of graphical display that are now in wide use. See Hoaglin (2003). A key concern is that the data should as far as possible speak for itself, prior to or as part of a formal analysis.

A use of graphics that is broadly in an EDA tradition continues to develop and evolve. The best modern statistical software makes a strong connection between data analysis and graphics, combining the computer's ability to crunch numbers and present graphs with that of a trained human eye to detect pattern. Statistical theory has an important role in suggesting forms of display that may be helpful and interpretable.

Graphical Comparisons

Figure 1.1 was a graphical comparison between the lengths of cuckoo eggs that had been laid in the nests of different host species. The boxes that give boxplots their name focus attention on quartiles of the data, that is, the three points on the axis that split the data into four equal parts. The lower end of the box marks the first quartile, the dot marks the median, and the upper end of the box marks the third quartile. Points that lie out beyond the "whiskers" are plotted individually, and are candidates to be considered outliers. The widths of the boxes will of course vary randomly, leading in some cases to the flagging of points that should not be treated as extreme. The narrow box may largely account for the five values that are flagged for meadow pipit.

Figure 1.1 strongly suggested that eggs planted in wrens' nests were substantially smaller than eggs planted in other birds' nests. The upper quartile (75 percent point) for eggs in wrens' nests lies below all the lower quartiles for other eggs.

1.1.6 Formal Model-Based Comparison

For comparing lengths between species in the cuckoo eggs data, we use the model:

$$\text{Egg length} = \text{Mean for species} + \text{Random variation.}$$

The means in the dataset `cuckoos` are:

```
av <- with(cuckoos, aggregate(length, list(species=species), FUN=mean))
setNames(round(av[["x"]],2), abbreviate(av[["species"]],10))
```

```
hedgsparrw meadowpipt piedwagtal      robin tree pipit       wren
     23.11      22.29      22.89      22.56      23.08      21.12
```

The model postulates that the length of a cuckoo egg found in a given nest depends in some way on the host species. There are likely to be additional factors that have not been observed but which also influence the egg length. The variation due to these unobserved factors is aggregated into one term which is referred to as statistical error or random variation. Where none of these observed factors predominates and their effects add, a normal distribution will often be effective as a model for the random variation.

The species means are estimated from the data and are called *fitted values.* The differences between the data values and those means are called *residuals.* For example, suppose ℓ_i is the length of the ith egg in the nest of a wren, and $\bar{\ell}$ is the average of all eggs in the wrens' nests. Then the ith residual for this group is

$$e_i = \ell_i - \bar{\ell}.$$

The `scale()` function provides a convenient way to calculate such residuals; its usage below *centers* the data by subtracting the average from each data point. Thus, the residuals for the wren length model are:

```
with(cuckoos, scale(length[species=="wren"], scale=FALSE))[,1]
```

```
 [1] -1.32  0.98 0.38 -0.22 0.88 -0.12 1.18 -0.12 -0.82 -0.22 0.88
[12] -1.12 -0.32 0.08 -0.12
```

Is the variability different for different species? The boxes in Figure 1.1, with endpoints set for each species to contain the central 50 percent of the data, hint that variation may be greater for the pied wagtail than for other species. (The box widths equal the inter-quartile range, or IQR. See further, Subsection 1.3.4.)

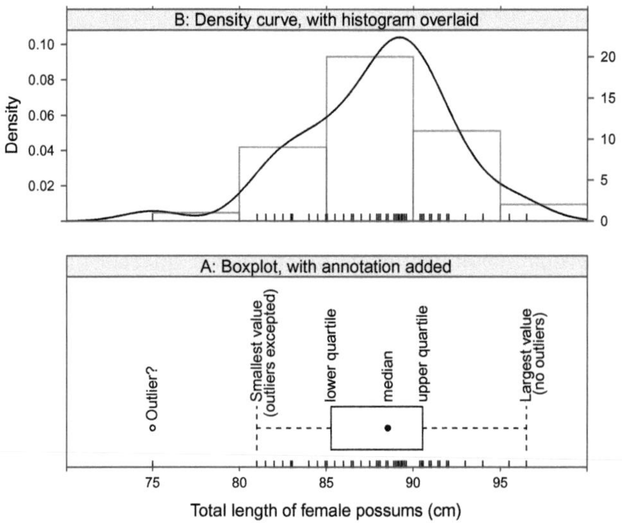

Figure 1.2 Panel A shows a boxplot, with annotation that explains boxplot features. Panel B shows a density plot, with a histogram overlaid. Histogram frequencies are shown on the right axis of Panel B. In both panels, the individual data points appear as a "rug" along the lower side of the bounding box. Where necessary, they have been moved slightly apart to avoid overlap.

1.2 Graphical Tools for Data Exploration

In this section, we illustrate basic approaches to the graphical exploration of data. Three R static graphics systems enjoy wide use. These are: *base* (or "traditional") graphics using `plot()` and associated commands, *lattice* which offers more stylized types of graphs, and *ggplot2* whose rich array of features comes at the cost of extra graphics language complexity.

Later chapters will make extensive use both of *base* graphics and of *lattice* graphics, resorting to *ggplot2* on those occasions when features are needed that are not readily available in the other packages. Some lattice graphs will be printed in a style (use a *theme*) akin to the default ggplot2 style. Section A.5 has further details.

1.2.1 Displays of a Single Variable

A basic form of display for a single numeric variable is the dotplot, which plots the individual data points along a number line or single axis. The boxplot provides a coarser summary of *univariate* data. The histogram and density curve offer more fine-grained alternatives.

Figure 1.2A shows a boxplot of total lengths of females in the `possum` dataset, with annotation added that explains the interpretation of boxplot features. Figure 1.2B shows a density curve, with a histogram overlaid, for the same data. Both panels contain rug plots which are essentially dotplots consisting of vertical bars added along the lower edge.

One data point lies outside the boxplot "whiskers" to the left, and is flagged as a possible outlier. An outlier is a point that is determined to be far from the main body of the data. Under the default criterion, about 1 percent of normally distributed data would be judged as outlying.

A histogram is a crude form of density estimate. A smooth density estimate is, often, a better alternative. The height of the density curve at any point is an estimate of the proportion of sample values per unit interval, locally at that point. Both histograms and density curves involve an element of subjective choice. Histograms require the choice of breakpoints, while density estimates require the choice of a bandwidth parameter that controls the amount of smoothing. In both cases, the software has default choices that should be used with care.

Code for a slightly simplified version of Figure 1.2B is:

```
fossum <- subset(DAAG::possum, sex=="f")
densityplot(~totlngth, plot.points=TRUE, pch="|", data=fossum) +
  layer_(panel.histogram(x, type="density", breaks=c(75,80,85,90,95,100)))
```

Comparing Univariate Displays Across Factor Levels

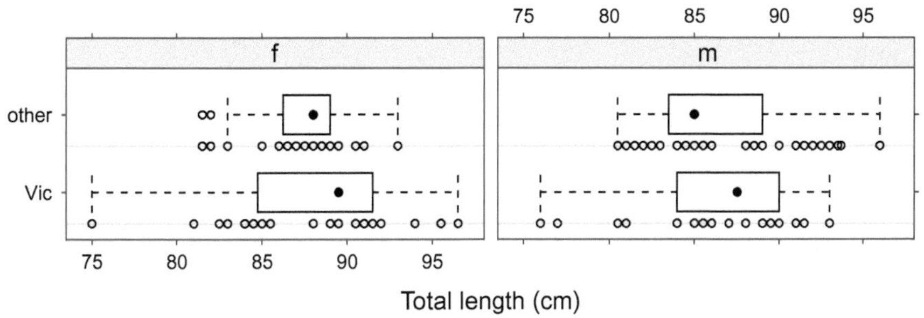

Figure 1.3 Total lengths of possums, by **sex** and (within panels) by geographical location (Victorian or other).

Univariate summaries can be broken down by one or more factors between and/or within panels. Figure 1.3 overlays dotplots on boxplots of the distributions of Australian possum lengths, broken down by sex and (within panels) by geographical region (Victoria or other).

```
## Create boxplot graph object --- Simplified code
gph <- bwplot(Pop~totlngth | sex, data=possum)
## plot graph, with dotplot distribution of points below boxplots
gph + latticeExtra::layer(panel.dotplot(x, unclass(y)-0.4))
```

The normal distribution is not necessarily the appropriate reference. Points may be identified as outliers because the distribution is skew (usually, with a tail to the right). Any needed action will depend on the context, requiring the user to exercise good judgement. Subsection 1.2.8 will comment in more detail.

1.2.2 Patterns in Univariate Time Series

Figure 1.4 shows time plots of historical deaths from measles in London. (Here, "measles" includes both what is nowadays called measles and the closely related rubella or German measles.)

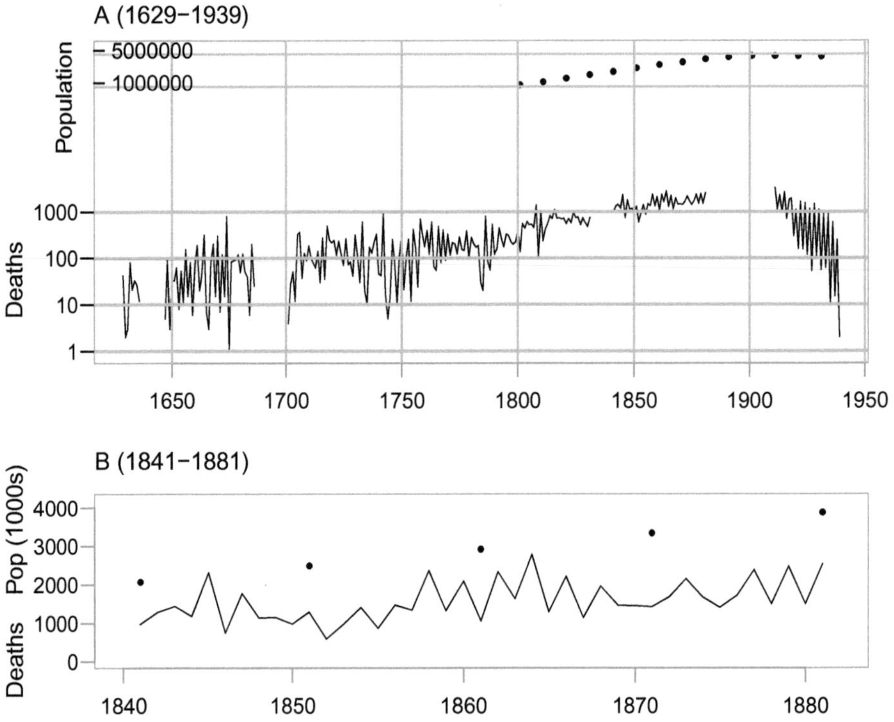

Figure 1.4 The two panels provide different insights into data on mortality from measles, in London over 1629–1939. Panel A uses a logarithmic scale to show the numbers of deaths from measles in London for the period from 1629 through 1939 (black curve). The black dots show, for the period 1800 to 1939 the London population in thousands. Panel B shows, on the linear scale (black curve), the subset of the measles data for the period 1840 through 1882 together with the London population (in thousands, black dots).

Panel A uses a logarithmic vertical scale while Panel B uses a linear scale and takes advantage of the fact that annual deaths from measles were of the order of one in 500 of the population. Thus, deaths in thousands and population in half millions can be shown on the same scale.

Panel A shows broad trends over time, but is of no use for identifying changes on the time-scale of a year or two. In Panel B, the lines that show such changes are, mostly, at an angle that is in the approximate range of 20° to 70° from the horizontal. A sawtooth pattern is evident, indicating that years in which there were many deaths were often followed by years in which there were fewer deaths. To obtain this level of detail for the whole period from 1629 until 1939, multiple panels would be necessary.

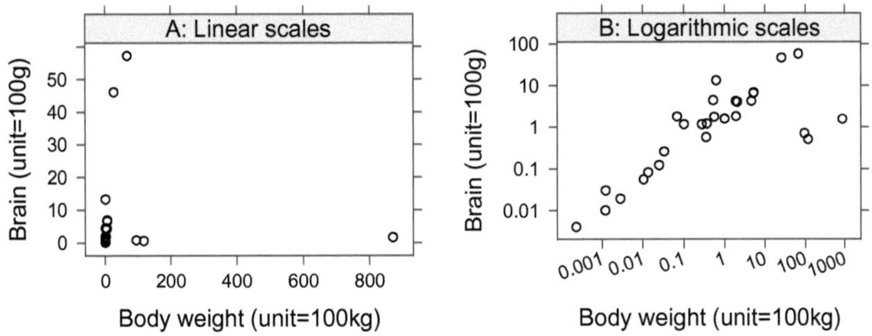

Figure 1.5 Brain weight versus body weight, for 28 animals that vary greatly in size. Panel A has untransformed scales, while Panel B has logarithmic scales, on both axes.

Simplified code is:

```
measles <- DAAG::measles
## Panel A
plot(log10(measles), xlab="", ylim=log10 (c(1,5000*540)),
    ylab=" Deaths; Population", yaxt="n")
ytiks1 <- c(1, 10, 100, 1000); ytiks2 <- c(1000000, 5000000)
## London population in thousands
londonpop <-ts(c(1088,1258,1504,1778,2073,2491,2921,3336,3881,
  4266,4563,4541,4498,4408), start=1801, end=1931, deltat=10)
points(log10(londonpop*600), pch=16, cex=.5)
abline(h=log10(ytiks1), lty = 2, col = "gray", lwd = 2)
abline(h=log10(ytiks2*0.5), lty = 2, col = "gray", lwd = 2)
axis(2, at=log10(ytiks1), labels=paste(ytiks1), lwd=0, lwd.ticks=1)
axis(2, at=log10(ytiks2*0.5), labels=paste(ytiks2), tcl=0.3,
    hadj=0, lwd=0, lwd.ticks=1)
## Panel B
plot(window(measles, start=1840, end=1882), ylim=c (0, 4600), yaxt="n")
points(londonpop, pch=16, cex=0.5)
axis(2, at=(0:4)* 1000, labels=paste(0:4), las=2)
```

For details of the data, and commentary, see Guy (1882), Stocks (1942), and Senn (2003) where interest was in the comparison with smallpox mortality. The population estimates (`londonpop`) are from Mitchell (1988).

1.2.3 Visualizing Relationships Between Pairs of Variables

Patterns and relationships linking multiple variables are a primary focus of data analysis. The following example is concerned with the relationship between two variables and illustrates an important question that often arises: What is the appropriate scale?

Figures 1.5A and B plot brain weight (g) against body weight (kg), for 28 animals. Panel A indicates that the distributions of data values are highly positively skew, on both axes, but is otherwise unhelpful. Panel B's logarithmic scales spread points out more evenly, and the graph tells a clearer story. Note that, on both axes, tick

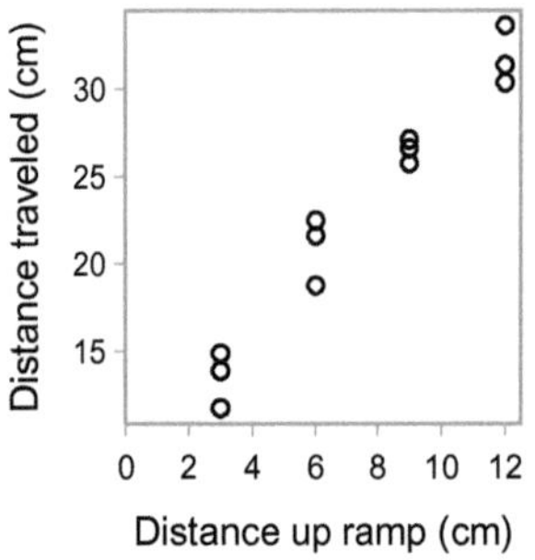

Starting point	Distance traveled		
3	31.38	30.38	33.63
6	26.63	25.75	27.13
9	18.75	22.50	21.63
12	13.88	11.75	14.88

Figure 1.6 Distance traveled (*distance.traveled*) by model car, as a function of starting point (*starting.point*), up a 20° ramp.

marks are separated by an amount that, when translated back from log(weight) to weight, differ by a factor of 100. The argument `aspect="iso"` has ensured that these correspond to the same physical distance on both axes of the graph. Code is:

```
## Untransformed vs log transformed scales
Animals <- MASS::Animals
asp <- with(Animals, sapply(list(log(brain/100), log(body/100)),
                  function(x)diff(range(x)))) |> (\(d)d[1]/d[2])()
xlab <- "Body weight (unit=100kg)"; ylab <- "Brain (unit=100g)"
gphA <- xyplot(I(brain/100) ~ I(body/100), data=Animals, aspect=asp,
        xlab=xlab, ylab=ylab)
gphB <- xyplot(log(brain/100) ~ log(body/100), data=MASS::Animals,  # Panel B
        aspect='iso', xlab=xlab, ylab=ylab)
labx <- 10^c((-3):3); laby <- 10^c((-2):2)
gphB <- update(gphB, scales=list(x=list(at=log(labx), labels=labx, rot=20),
                  y=list(at=log(laby), labels=laby)))
```

A logarithmic scale is appropriate for quantities that change multiplicatively. Thus, if cells in a growing organism divide and produce new cells at a constant rate, then the total number of cells changes multiplicatively, resulting in what is termed exponential growth. Large organisms may similarly increase in a given time interval by the same approximate fraction as smaller organisms. Growth rate on a natural logarithmic scale ($\log_e$) equals the relative growth rate.

Anyone who works with real data – biologists, economists, physical scientists – will do well to make themselves comfortable with the use and interpretation of logarithmic scales. See Subsection 2.5.6 for a brief discussion of other commonly used transformations.

1.2.4 Response Lines (and/or Curves)

The data shown on the right-hand side of Figure 1.6, and plotted in the figure, were generated by releasing a model car three times at each of four different distances (`starting.point`) up a 20° ramp. The experimenter recorded distances traveled from the bottom of the ramp across a concrete floor. Response curve analysis, using regression, is appropriate. It would be a mistake to treat the four starting points as factor levels in a one-way analysis. Data are available in DAAG::modelcars.

For these data, the physics suggests the likely form of response. Where no such help is available, careful examination of the graph, followed by systematic examination of plausible forms of response, may suggest a suitable form of response curve.

1.2.5* Multiple Variables and Times

Overlaying plots of several time series (sequences of measurements taken at regular intervals) might seem appropriate for making direct comparisons. However, this approach will only work if the scales are comparable for the different series.

Figures 1.7A and B show alternative views of labor force numbers (thousands), for various regions of Canada, at quarterly intervals over the 24-month period from January 1995 to December 1996. Over this time, Canada was emerging from a deep economic recession. The ranges of values, for each of the six regions, are:

```
## Apply function range to columns of data frame jobs (DAAG)
sapply(DAAG::jobs, range) ## NB: `BC` = British Columbia
```

```
       BC Alberta Prairies Ontario Quebec Atlantic  Date
[1,] 1737    1366      973    5212   3167      941 95.00
[2,] 1840    1436      999    5360   3257      968 96.92
```

With a logarithmic scale, as in Figure 1.7A, similar changes on the scale correspond to similar proportional changes. The regions have been taken in order of the number of workers in December 1996 (or, in fact, at any other time). This ensures that the order of the labels in the key matches the positioning of the points for the different regions. Code that has been used to create and update the graphics object `basicGphA`, then updating it to obtain the labeling on the x- and y-axes is:

```
## Panel A: Basic plot; all series in a single panel; use log y-scale
formRegions <- Ontario+Quebec+BC+Alberta+Prairies+Atlantic ~ Date
basicGphA <-
  xyplot(formRegions, outer=FALSE, data=DAAG::jobs, type="l", xlab="",
         ylab="Number of workers", scales=list(y=list(log="e")),
         auto.key=list(space="right", lines=TRUE, points=FALSE))
  ## `outer=FALSE`: plot all columns in one panel
## Create improved x- and y-axis tick labels; will update to use
datelabpos <- seq(from=95, by=0.5, length=5)
datelabs <- format(seq(from=as.Date("1Jan1995", format="%d%b%Y"),
                   by="6 month", length=5), "%b%y")
## Now create $y$-labels that have numbers, with log values underneath
ylabposA <- exp(pretty(log(unlist(DAAG::jobs[,-7])), 5))
gphA <- update(basicGphA, scales=list(x=list(at=datelabpos, labels=datelabs),
               y=list(at=ylabposA, labels=ylabelsA)))
```

Because the labor forces in the various regions do not have similar sizes, it is impossible to discern any differences among the regions from this plot. Plotting on the logarithmic scale was not enough on its own. Figure 1.7B, where the six different panels use different *slices* of the same logarithmic scale, is an informative alternative. Simplified code is:

```
## Panel B: Separate panels (`outer=TRUE`); sliced log scale
basicGphB <-
```

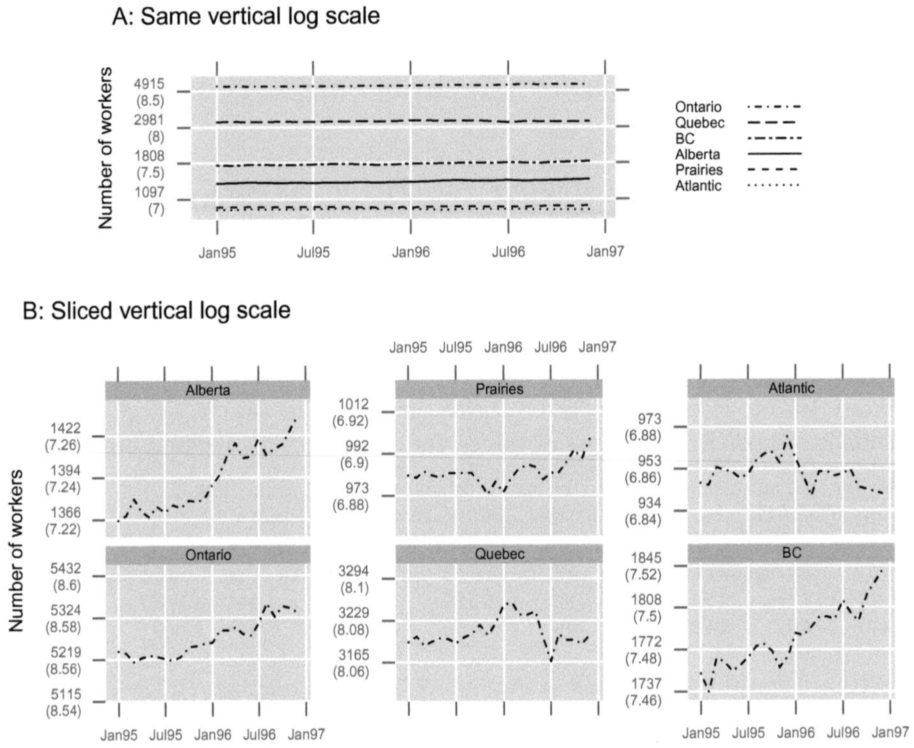

Figure 1.7 Data are labor force numbers (thousands) for various regions of Canada, at quarterly intervals over 1995–1996. Panel A uses the same logarithmic y-scale for all regions. Panel B shows the same data, but now with separate ("sliced") logarithmic y-scales on which the same percentage increase, for example, by 1 percent, corresponds to the same distance on the scale, for all plots. Distances between ticks are 0.02 on the $\log_e$ scale, that is, a change of close to 2 percent.

```
xyplot(formRegions, data=DAAG::jobs, outer=TRUE, type="l", layout=c(3,2),
       xlab="", ylab="Number of workers",
       scales=list(y=list(relation="sliced", log=TRUE)))
```

Use of `outer=TRUE`, causes separate columns (regions) to be plotted on separate panels. As before, equal distances on the scale correspond to equal relative changes. It is now clear that Alberta and BC experienced the fastest job growth and that there was little or no job growth in Quebec and the Atlantic region.

The following are the changes in numbers employed, in each of Alberta and BC, from January 1995 to December 1996. The changes are shown in actual numbers, and on scales of $\log_2$, $\log_e$ and $\log_{10}$. Figure 1.8 shows this graphically.

		Increase		
	Rel. change	$\log_2$	$\log_e$	$\log_{10}$
Alberta (1366 to 1466; increase=70)	1.051	0.072	0.050	0.022
BC (1752 to 1840; increase=88)	1.050	0.070	0.049	0.021

From the beginning of 1995 and the end of 1996, the increase of 70 in Alberta from 1366 to 1436 is by a factor of $1436/1366 \simeq 1.051$). For BC, an increase by 88

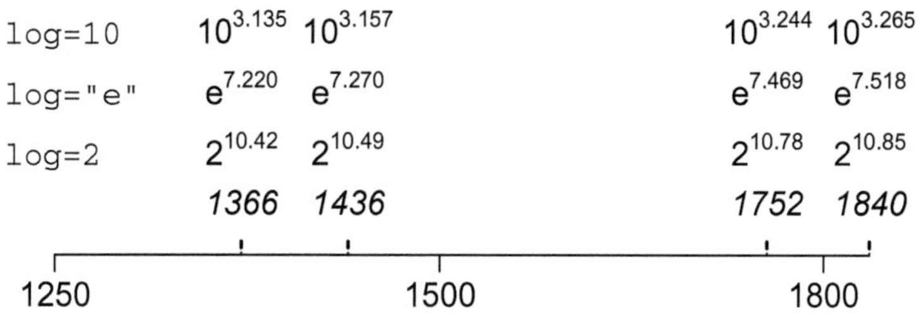

Figure 1.8 Labeling of the values for Alberta (1366, 1436) and BC (1752, 1840), with alternative logarithmic scale choices.

from 1752 to 1840 is by a factor of 1.050. The proper comparison is not between the absolute increases, but between very nearly identical multipliers of 1.051 and 1.050.

Even better than using a logarithmic y-scale, particularly if ready comprehension is important, would be to standardize the labor force numbers by dividing, for example, by the respective number of persons aged 15 years and over at that time. Scales would then be directly comparable. (The `plot` method for time series could then suitably be used to plot the data as a multivariate time series. See `?plot.ts`.)

1.2.6 Labeling Technicalities*

For lattice functions, the arguments `log=2` or `log="e"` or `log=10` are available. The latter two scales are referred to as natural and common log scales, respectively. These use the relevant logarithmic axis labeling, as in Figure 1.8, for axis labels. In base graphics, with one of the arguments `log="x"` or `log="y"` or `log="xy"`, the default is to label the specified axis or axes in the original units.

An alternative, both for traditional and lattice graphics, is to enter the log-transformed values, using whatever base is preferred (`2` or `"e"` or `10`), into the graphics formula. Unless other tick labels are manually entered, ticks will be automatically transformed to the correct scale.

Note again the reason for placing y-axis tick marks a distance 0.02 apart on the $\log_e$ linear scale used in Figure 1.7. On the $\log_e$ scale a change of 0.02 is very nearly a 2 percent change.

1.2.7 Graphical Displays for Categorical Data

Figure 1.9 illustrates the possible hazards of adding values in a multiway table over one of its margins. Data are from a study (Charig, 1986) that compared the use of open surgery for kidney stones with a method that made a small incision and used ultrasound to destroy the stone. Stones were classified by diameter: either at least 2 cm or less than 2 cm. For each subject, the outcome was assessed as successful ("yes") or unsuccessful ("no").

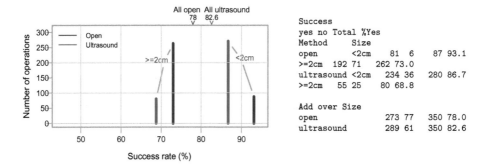

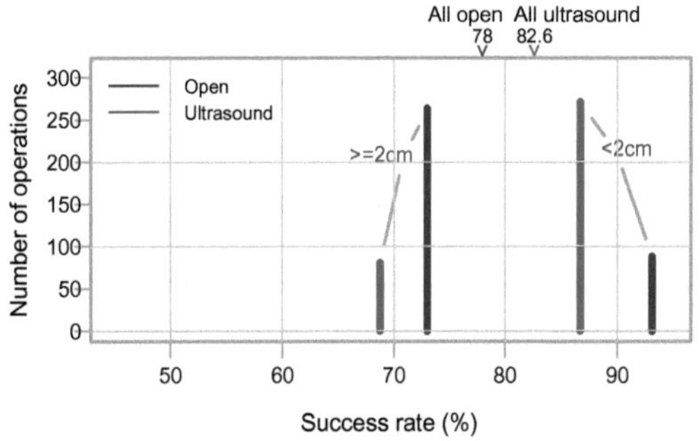


```
Success
yes no Total %Yes
Method       Size
open         <2cm     81  6    87 93.1
>=2cm  192 71   262 73.0
ultrasound <2cm    234 36   280 86.7
>=2cm   55 25    80 68.8

Add over Size
open                 273 77   350 78.0
ultrasound           289 61   350 82.6
```

Figure 1.9 Outcomes are for two different types of surgery for kidney stones. The overall (apparent) success rates (78 percent for open surgery as against 83 percent for ultrasound) favor ultrasound. The success rate for each size of stone separately favors, in each case, open surgery.

If we consider small stones and large stones separately, it appears that surgery is more successful than ultrasound. The blue vertical bar Figure 1.9 is in each case to the right of the corresponding red vertical bar. The overall counts, which favor ultrasound, are thus misleading. For open surgery, the larger number of operations for large stones (263 large, 87 small) weights the overall success rate towards the low overall success rate for large stones. For ultrasound surgery (red bars), the weighting (80 large, 280 small) is towards the high success rate for small stones. This is an example of the phenomenon called the Simpson or Yule–Simpson paradox. (See also Subsection 2.1.2.)

Note that without additional information, the results are not interpretable from a medical standpoint. Different surgeons will have preferred different surgery types, and the prior condition of patients will have affected the choice of surgery type. The consequences of unsuccessful surgery may have been less serious for ultrasound than for open surgery.

The table `stones`, shown to the right of Figure 1.9, has three `margins` – `Success`, `Method`, and `Size`. The table `margin12` that results from adding over `Size` retains the first two of these. Code used is:

```
stones <- array(c(81,6,234,36,192,71,55,25), dim=c(2,2,2),
            dimnames=list(Success=c("yes","no"),
            Method=c("open","ultrasound"), Size=c("<2cm", "≥2cm")))
margin12 <- margin.table(stones, margin=1:2)
```

Mosaic plots are an alternative type of display that can be obtained using either `mosaicplot()` from base graphics or `vcd::mosaic()`. Figure 1.9 makes the point of interest for the kidney stone surgery data more simply and directly.

1.2.8 What to Look for in Plots

We now note points to keep in mind when examining data.

Outliers

Outliers are points that appear, or are judged, isolated from the main body of the data. Such points, whether errors or genuine values, can indicate departure from model assumptions, and may distort any model that is fitted.

Boxplots, and the normal quantile–quantile plot that will be discussed in Subsection 1.4.3, are useful for highlighting outliers in one dimension. Scatterplots may highlight outliers in two dimensions. Some outliers will, however, be apparent only in three or more dimensions.

Asymmetry of the Distribution

Positive skewness (a tail to the right) is a common form of departure from normality. The largest values are widely dispersed, and values near the minimum are likely to be bunched up together. Provided that all values are greater than zero, a logarithmic transformation typically makes such a distribution more symmetric. Negative skewness (a tail to the left) is less common. Severe skewness is typically a more serious problem for the validity of analysis results than other types of nonnormality.

If values of a variable that takes positive values range by a factor of more than 10:1 then, depending on the application area context, positive skewness is to be expected. A logarithmic transformation should be considered.

Changes in Variability

Boxplots and histograms readily convey an impression of the extent of variability or scatter in the data. Side-by-side boxplots, such as in Figure 1.1B, or dotplots such as in Figure 1.1A, allow rough comparisons of the variability across different samples or treatment groups. They provide a visual check on the assumption, common in many statistical models, that variability is constant across treatment groups.

It is easy to over-interpret such plots. Statistical theory offers useful and necessary warnings about the potential for such over-interpretation. (The variability in a sample, typically measured by the variance, is itself highly variable under repeated sampling. Measures of variability will be discussed in Subsection 1.3.3.)

When variability increases as data values increase, the logarithmic transformation will often help. Constant relative variability on the original scale becomes constant absolute variability on a logarithmic scale.

Clustering

Clusters in scatterplots may suggest features of the data that may or may not have been expected. Upon proceeding to a formal analysis, any clustering must be taken into account. Do the clusters correspond to different values of some relevant variable? Outliers are a special form of clustering.

Nonlinearity

Where it seems clear that one or more relationships are nonlinear, a transformation may make it possible to model the relevant effects as linear. Where none of the common standard transformations meets requirements, methodology is available that will fit quite general nonlinear curves. See Subsection 4.4.2.

If there is a theory that suggests the form of model, then this is a good starting point. Available theory may, however, incorporate various approximations, and the data may tell a story that does not altogether match the available theory. The data, unless they are flawed, have the final say!

Time Trends in the Data

It is common to find time trends that are associated with order of data collection. It can be enlightening to plot residuals, or other quantities, against time. Patterns of increase or decrease are common and are readily recognized, but one should also be alert to the possibility of seasonality or periodic behavior.

1.3 Data Summary

Data summaries may: (1) be of interest in themselves; (2) give insight into aspects of data structure that may affect further analysis; (3) be used as data for further analysis. In case (3), it is necessary to ensure that important information, relevant to the analysis, is not lost. Before adding counts across the margins of multiway tables, or otherwise pooling data across different groups, it is important to check the potential for distortions that are artifacts of the way that the data have been summarized. Examples will be given.

If there is no loss of information, use of summary data can allow a helpful simplicity of analysis and interpretation, Do not, however, proceed without careful consideration!

1.3.1 Counts

The data frame `DAAG::nswpsid1` is from a study (Lalonde, 1986) that compared two groups of individuals with a history of unemployment problems – one an "untreated" control group and the other a "treatment" group whose members were exposed to a labor training program. The data include measures that can be used for checks on whether the two groups were, aside from exposure (or not) to the training program, otherwise plausibly similar. The following compares the relative numbers between who had completed high school (`nodeg = 0`) and those who had not (`nodeg = 1`).

```
## Table of counts example: data frame nswpsid1 (DAAG)
## Specify `useNA="ifany"` to ensure that any NAs are tabulated
tab <- with(DAAG::nswpsid1, table(trt, nodeg, useNA="ifany"))
dimnames(tab) <- list(trt=c("none", "training"), educ = c("completed", "dropout"))
tab
```

```
             educ
trt            completed dropout
  none              1730     760
  training            80     217
```

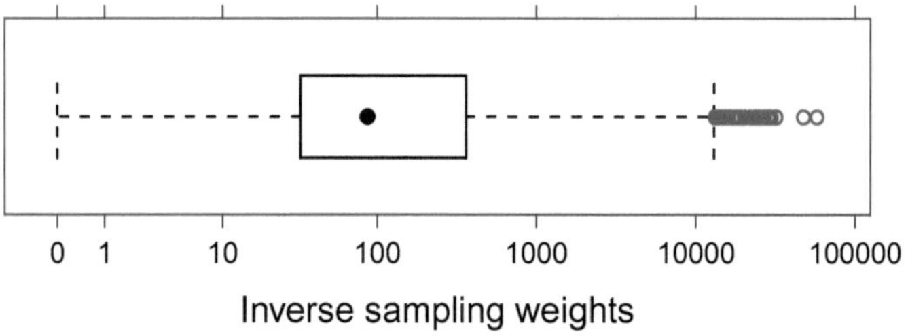

Figure 1.10 Boxplot showing **weights** (inverse sampling fractions), in the dataset **DAAG::nassCDS**. A **log(weight+1)** scale): has been used.

The training group has a much higher proportion of dropouts. Similar comparisons are required for other factors, variables, and combinations of two factors or variables. The data will be investigated further in Section 9.7.1.

Tabulation That Accounts for Frequencies or Weights – the xtabs() Function

Each year the National Highway Traffic Safety Administration in the United States uses a stratified random sampling method to collect data from all police-reported collisions in which there is an injury to people or property and where at least one vehicle is towed. Sampling fractions differ according to class of accident. The subset in DAAG::nassCDS is restricted to front-seat occupants.[2]

Factors whose effect warrant investigation include: **airbag** (was an airbag fitted?), **seatbelt** (was a seatbelt used?), and **dvcat** (a force of impact measure). The column *weight* (*national inflation factor*) holds the inverses of the sampling fraction estimates. The less accurate estimates that come where the sampling fraction is small have to be given an accordingly greater weight in the calculation of overall estimates, in order to fairly represent the population. Very large weights, for some classes of accident, will exaggerate the effect, both of any mistakes in data collection, and of deviations from the prescribed (and relatively complex) sampling scheme. The following contrasts numbers in the sample with estimated total numbers of collisions, obtained by applying the sampling weights:

```
sampNum <- table(nassCDS$dead)
popNum <- as.vector(xtabs(weight ~ dead, data=nassCDS))
rbind(Sample=sampNum, "Total number"=round(popNum,1))
```

```
                alive  dead
Sample          25037  1180
Total number 12067937 65595
```

Use of **xtabs()** to classify the estimated population numbers (in thousands) by airbag use, and adding the marginal death rates per 1000 to the table, gives:

```
nassCDS <- DAAG::nassCDS
```

[2] It holds a subset of the columns from a corrected version of the data analyzed in Meyer and Finney (2005). See also Farmer (2005) and Meyer (2006). More complete data are available from one of the web pages noted on the help page for **nassCDS**.

```
Atab <- xtabs(weight ~ airbag + dead, data=nassCDS)/1000
## Define a function that calculates Deaths per 1000
DeadPer1000 <- function(x)1000*x[2]/sum(x)
Atabm <- ftable(addmargins(Atab, margin=2, FUN=DeadPer1000))
print(Atabm, digits=2, method="compact", big.mark=",")
```

```
airbag | dead    alive    dead DeadPer1000
none           5,445.2    39.7         7.2
airbag         6,622.7    25.9         3.9
```

This might suggest that the fitting of an airbag substantially reduces the risk of mortality. Consider, however:

```
SAtab <- xtabs(weight ~ seatbelt + airbag + dead, data=nassCDS)
## SAtab <- addmargins(SAtab, margin=3, FUN=list(Total=sum))  ## Gdet Totals
SAtabf <- ftable(addmargins(SAtab, margin=3, FUN=DeadPer1000), col.vars=3)
print(SAtabf, digits=2, method="compact", big.mark=",")
```

```
seatbelt airbag | dead          alive         dead DeadPer1000
none     none            1,342,021.9     24,066.7         17.6
         airbag            871,875.4     13,759.9         15.5
belted   none            4,103,224.0     15,609.4          3.8
         airbag          5,750,815.6     12,159.2          2.1
```

The `Total` column gives the weights that are, effectively, applied to the values in the `DeadPer1000` column when the raw numbers are added over the *seatbelt* margin. In the earlier table (*Atab*), the results for *airbag=none* were mildly skewed (4119:1366) to those for *belted*. Results with airbags were strongly skewed (5763:886) to those for *seatbelt=none*. Hence, adding over the *seatbelt* margin gave a spuriously large advantage to the presence of an airbag.

The reader may wish to try an analysis that accounts, additionally, for estimated force of impact (*dvcat*):

```
FSAtab <- xtabs(weight ~ dvcat + seatbelt + airbag + dead, data=nassCDS)
FSAtabf <- ftable(addmargins(FSAtab, margin=4, FUN=DeadPer1000), col.vars=3:4)
print(FSAtabf, digits=1)
```

There is no consistent pattern in the difference between *"none"* and *"airbag"*.

Further terms, including the age of vehicle and the age of driver, demand consideration. The estimated effect of *airbag*, or of any factor other than `seatbelt`, varies depending on what further terms are included in the model. Seatbelts have such a large effect that their contribution stands out irrespective of what other terms appear in the model. These data, tabulated as above, have too many uncertainties and potential sources of bias to give reliable answers.

A better starting point for investigation are the data from the Fatality Analysis Recording System (FARS). The `gamclass::FARS` dataset has data for the years 1998 to 2010. This has, in principle at least, a complete set of records for the more limited class of accidents where there was at least one fatality.

Farmer (2005) used the FARS data for an analysis, limited to cars without passenger airbags, that used front-seat passenger mortality as a standard against which to compare driver mortality. In the absence of any effect from airbags, the ratio of driver mortality to passenger mortality should be the same, irrespective of whether

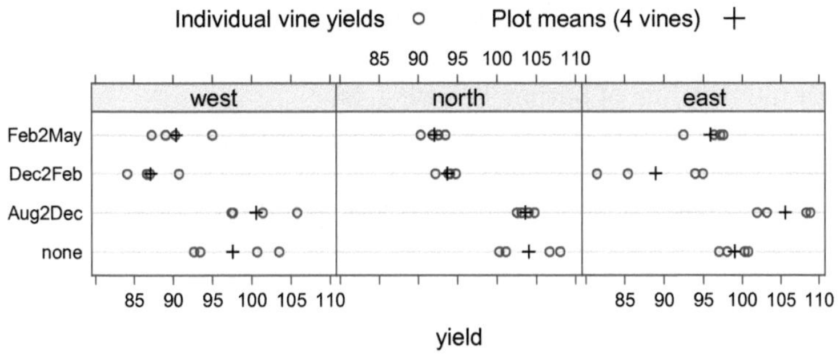

Figure 1.11 Individual yields and plot-level mean yields of kiwifruit (in kg) for each of four treatments (season) and blocks (exposure).

there was a driver airbag. Farmer found a ratio of driver fatalities to passenger fatalities that was 11 percent lower in the cars with driver airbags. Factors that have a large effect on the absolute risk can be expected to have a much smaller effect on the relative risk.

In addition to the functions discussed, note the function `gmodels::CrossTable()`, which offers a choice of SPSS-like and SAS-like output formats.

1.3.2 Summaries of Information from Data Frames

The data frame `DAAG::kiwishade` has yield measurements from 48 kiwifruit vines. Plots, made up of four vines each, were the experimental units. Figure 1.11 plots both the aggregated means and the individual vine results.

The 12 plots were divided into three blocks of four plots each. One block of four was north-facing, a second block west-facing, and a third block east-facing. (Because the trial was conducted in the Southern hemisphere, there is no south-facing block.) Shading treatments were applied to whole plots, that is, to groups of four vines, with each treatment occurring once per block. The shading treatments were applied either from August to December, December to February, February to May, or not at all. For more details of the experiment, look ahead to Figure 7.5.

As treatments were applied to whole plots, a focus on the individual vines exaggerates the extent of information that is available, in each block, for comparing treatments. To gain an accurate impression of the strength of the evidence, focus on the means, represented by +. The code is given as a footnote.[3] The code includes

[3]
```
## Individual vine yields, with means by block and treatment overlaid
kiwishade <- DAAG::kiwishade
kiwishade$block <- factor(kiwishade$block, levels=c("west","north","east"))
keyset <- list(space="top", columns=2,
text=list(c("Individual vine yields", "Plot means (4 vines)")),
points=list(pch=c(1,3), cex=c(1,1.35), col=c("gray40","black")))
panelfun <- function(x,y,...){panel.dotplot(x,y, pch=1, ...)
av <- sapply(split(x,y),mean); ypos <- unique(y)
lpoints(ypos~av, pch=3, col="black")}
dotplot(shade~yield | block, data=kiwishade, col="gray40", aspect=0.65,
        panel=panelfun, key=keyset, layout=c(3,1))
## Note that parameter settings were given both in the calls
## to the panel functions and in the list supplied to key.
```

a user-defined panel function to take means, for each combination of block and shading treatment, "on the fly." Code that creates the means separately from the graph, with the first line of output following, is:

```
## mean yield by block by shade: data frame kiwishade (DAAG)
kiwimeans <- with(DAAG::kiwishade,
                  aggregate(yield, by=list(block, shade), mean))
names(kiwimeans) <- c("block","shade","meanyield")
head(kiwimeans, 4)  # First 4 rows
```

```
  block   shade meanyield
1  east    none     99.03
2 north    none    104.03
3  west    none     97.56
4  east Aug2Dec    105.56
```

The `aggregate()` function splits the data frame according to the specified combinations of factor levels, and then applies a specified function to each of the resulting subgroups.

Should the analysis then use the aggregated data? The form of analysis of variance that will be applied to these data in Subsection 7.4.1 will give, for treatment comparison purposes, the same results as an analysis based directly on the plot means, tacitly assuming that the mean is the appropriate form of summary. If there were occasional highly aberrant values, use of medians might be preferable. Use of aggregated data gives the analyst more control over which summary statistic to use.

The Benefits of Data Summary – Dengue Status Example

Hales et al. (2002) examined the implications of climate change projections for the worldwide distribution of dengue, a mosquito-borne disease that is a risk in hot and humid regions. Dengue status, that is, information on whether dengue had been reported during 1965–1973, was available for 2000 administrative regions. Climate information was available on a much finer grid of about 80,000 pixels at 0.5° latitude and longitude resolution. Should the analysis work with summary data for 2000 administrative regions, or with the much larger dataset that has one row for each of the 80,000 pixels?[4] The following are reasons that might suggest working with the summary data.

- Use of the values at the pixel level to calculate summary climate statistics prior to the analysis, by administrative region, gives the user control over the choice of statistical summary statistic. If, for example, values for some pixels are extreme relative to other pixels in the administrative region, medians may be more appropriate than means. The mean will give the same weight to sparsely populated cold mountainous locations as to highly populated hot and humid locations on nearby plains.

[4] Working with spatio-temporal data aggregated over different subregions can require highly complex analysis procedures. Lee et al. (2017) describes a Canadian bladder cancer study where data from postal code regions was merged in a nontrivial manner with data from census regions.

- Correlation between nearby observations, though still substantial, will be less of an issue for the dataset in which each row is an administrative region. Points that repeat essentially identical information are a problem for the interpretation of plots and can be a problem for the analysis. Regions that are close together tend to have similar climates and the same dengue status.
- Analysis and data screening are simpler with the reduced dataset. Scatterplots are less likely to degenerate into a dense mass of black ink.

The mean and the median are the most commonly used measures of central value, among several alternatives. (In fact, the paper used the disaggregated data.)

1.3.3 Measures of Variation

The *standard deviation* (often represented by the symbol σ) is a standard form of summary of variability (or *spread*) of sample or population values. Given a random sample $x_1, x_2, \ldots, x_n$, σ can be estimated by the sample standard deviation:

$$s = \sqrt{\frac{\sum_{i=1}^{n}(x_i - \bar{x})^2}{n-1}}.$$

For s to be an accurate estimator for σ, the sample must be large. In R, `sd()` can be used to calculate s.

The square of the standard deviation, termed the *variance*, is widely used in formal inference. The standard deviation lends itself to easier interpretation because it is in the same units as the original measurements.

Cuckoo Eggs Example

Consider the cuckoo eggs data from Subsection 1.1.2. The standard deviations for each group, with numbers of eggs shown in parentheses, are as follows.

```
hedgsparrow meadowpipit piedwagtail       robin  tree pipit        wren
  1.05 (14)   0.92 (45)   1.07 (15)   0.68 (16)   0.88 (15)   0.75 (15)
```

The variability in egg length is smallest when the robin is the host. Note, however, that the numbers are all, except for meadow pipit, 14 or 15 or 16. The standard deviations are subject to large statistical uncertainty.

The footnote has code for the calculations used to create the table.[5]

Degrees of Freedom

The denominator $n-1$ in the formula used to calculate s is the number of degrees of freedom remaining after estimating the mean. With one data point, the sum of squares about the mean is zero, the degrees of freedom are zero, and no estimate of variability is possible.

In later chapters, standard deviation calculations will be based on the variation that remains after fitting a model (most simply, a line), to the data. Degrees of freedom are reduced by 1 for each model parameter that is estimated.

[5]
```
## SD of length, by species: data frame cuckoos (DAAG)
z <- with(cuckoos, sapply(split(length,species), function(x)c(sd(x),length(x))))
print(setNames(paste0(round(z[1,],2)," (",z[2,],")"),
```

1.3.4 Inter-quartile Range and Median Absolute Deviation

In a boxplot, as in Figure 1.2 in Section 1.1.5, the box spans the range between the lower and upper quartiles. The inter-quartile range is the width of the box. For data that are close to normally distributed $s \approx 0.75H$.

The median absolute deviation (MAD) is the median of the absolute deviations from the median. When multiplied by the value 1.4286, this statistic provides an approximately unbiased estimator for the standard deviation of a normally distributed population. The calculation is carried out by the function `mad()`. The value of the multiplier is set by the parameter `constant`. The MAD is a more robust estimate of the standard deviation than that based on the inter-quartile range, meaning that if a normally distributed sample were to be contaminated by a few outlying erroneous observations, the MAD is least affected. See the Exercises for a simple demonstration of this.

1.3.5 A Pooled Standard Deviation Estimate

Suppose independent random samples have been taken from each of two populations that have the same standard deviation σ. If the respective sample sizes are n_1 and n_2, then the number of degrees of freedom for estimating the (common) variance is $n_1 + n_2 - 2$, after estimation of the possibly different population means. The pooled standard deviation estimator for σ is:

$$s_p = \sqrt{\frac{\sum(x - \bar{x})^2 + \sum(y - \bar{y})^2}{n_1 + n_2 - 2}}.$$

Diagnostic checks that the common variance assumption is plausible, and/or transformations that will assist in making variances more homogeneous, can be crucial. A logarithmic transformation will often be effective in making variances more homogeneous.

Elastic Bands Example

A set of 21 elastic bands was randomly divided into two groups of 10 and 11. The amount of stretch under a weight of 1.35 kg was immediately measured for bands in the first group. The other bands were immersed in hot water at 65 °C for four minutes, then left at air temperature for 10 minutes, with their stretch then measured under a weight of 1.35 kg. The means and standard deviations for the two groups were:

```
sapply(DAAG::two65, function(x) c(Mean=mean(x), sd=sd(x))) |> round(2)
```

```
     heated ambient
Mean 253.50  244.09
sd     9.92   11.73
```

The pooled standard deviation estimate is $s = 10.91$, with 19 $(= 10 + 11 - 2)$ degrees of freedom. Since the separate standard deviations ($s_1 = 9.92$; $s_2 = 11.73$) are similar, the pooled standard deviation estimate is an acceptable summary of the variation in the data.

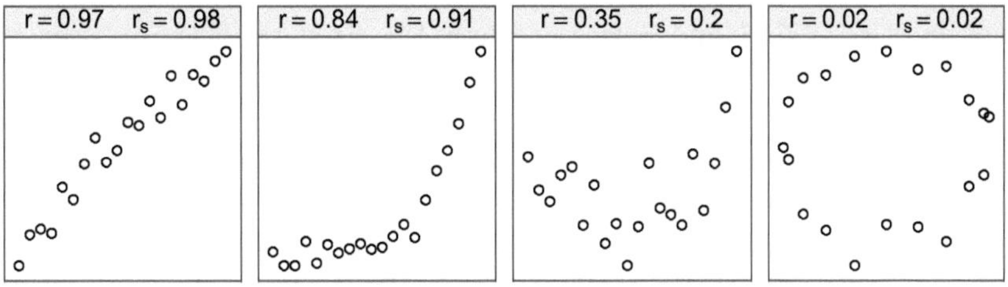

Figure 1.12 Different relationships between y and x. The Pearson (linear) correlation is r, while the Spearman rank correlation is r_h.

1.3.6 *Effect Size*

Effect sizes and effect size estimates offer a standardized measure of a difference that is of interest, relative to variation in the population or in the data. The *effect size* that will be discussed here is that known as Cohen's d, obtained by dividing the effect of interest by its standard deviation. For the elastic bands data listed above, the estimated effect size is:

```
setNames(diff(c(ambient=244.1, heated=253.5))/c(sd=10.91), "Effect size")
```

```
Effect size
     0.8616
```

If a drug (e.g., one designed to reduce blood pressure) makes on average a very small difference relative to variation in a relevant defined population, its effect will be hard to demonstrate in clinical trials. Its usefulness for individual patients will be too much a matter of chance to justify its use in medical practice.

For more on effect measures that may be defined for use in a range of contexts, including with correlations, see the vignette in the *effectsize* package that can be displayed by typing:

```
vignette('effectsize', package='effectsize')
```

1.3.7 *Correlation*

The Pearson or product–moment correlation is a summary measure of linear relationship. Calculation of a correlation should always be accompanied by a check that the relevant scatterplot shows a linear relationship. It can be helpful to add a smooth trend line. Separate distributions of the two variables should be roughly normal, or at least not highly skew. If the relationship between the variables appears to be nonlinear or the separate distributions are asymmetric, a Spearman rank correlation may be more appropriate.

The four panels in Figure 1.12 show four different types of relationship. In the first panel, the Pearson correlation is close is to 1.0, and the evident nonlinearity is not of much consequence. The magnitude of the correlation r, or of the squared correlation r^2, does not of itself indicate whether the underlying fit is adequate.

For the second panel, the Pearson correlation is $r = 0.84$, while the Spearman correlation is $r_h = 0.91$ and better captures the strength of the relationship. A linear fit is clearly inadequate.

The `cor()` function provides both measures. In addition, or as an alternative to the function `cor()`, note `cor.test()`. This returns a confidence interval and a test for no association. Subsection 2.2.4 describes the underlying assumptions.

A further possibility is to specify `method="kendall"` when `cor.test()` is called, giving the Kendall correlation. This is applicable, for example, where the same individuals are assessed by two different judges, and is related to the probability that the two judges will assign the same ranking to an individual.

The following are ways in which correlations may mislead.

- There may be a subgroup structure in the data. If, for example, random samples are taken from each of a number of villages and the data are pooled, then any overall correlation at the level of individuals may reflect a correlation between village averages or a correlation between individuals within villages, or some of each. The two correlations may not be the same, or may even go in different directions. See Cox and Wermuth (1996).
- Any correlation between a constituent and a total amount is likely to be, in part at least, a mathematical artifact. In a study of an anti-hypertensive drug that hopes to determine whether the change $y - x$ is larger for those with higher initial blood pressure x. If x and y have similar variances then $y - x$ will have a negative correlation with x, whatever the influence of x.

While a correlation coefficient provides a single number summary of the relationship between x and y, regression methods offer a richer framework for the examination of such relationships.

1.4 Distributions: Quantifying Uncertainty

The models that will be used in later chapters will typically have both deterministic (or *signal*) and random (or *noise*) components. The simplest type of model takes the form

$$y = \mu + \varepsilon,$$

where μ is a constant, and ε is the random component. In the models that will be discussed in this section, μ will be the population mean, alternatively termed the *expected value*. More generally, and this will be a major focus in later chapters, μ can be replaced by a function of one or more variables and/or factors.

The random component is sometimes referred to as *error*. Both *noise* and *error* are technical terms. Use of the word *error* does not imply that there have been mistakes in the collection of the data, though mistakes can of course contribute to the variability.

The R *stats* package has many functions that return theoretical values of statistics for specific distributions. See `?Distributions` for details. The CRAN *Distributions* task view gives details of contributed R packages that extend the range of possibilities.

For each distribution, there are four functions, with names whose first letter is, respectively, `d` (**d**ensity), `p` (cumulative **p**robability), `q` (**q**uantile), and `r` (generate a **r**andom sample).

1.4.1 Discrete Distributions

The usual starting points for discussing discrete distributions are the binomial and the Poisson. Examples for both now follow.

Binomial Functions are `dbinom()`, `pbinom()`, and `qbinom()`, `rbinom()`
Values are 0, 1, 2, ..., n, where the argument `size` specifies n, and the argument `prob` specifies the probability π. The name Bernoulli is used for the special case when `size` $n = 1$. A Bernoulli random variable takes the value 1, with probability π and 0, with probability $1 - \pi$. For example, if a fair six-sided die is tossed once, the number of times a "2" appears is Bernoulli with $\pi = 1/6$.

A binomial random variable with `size` $n > 1$ is the sum of n independent Bernoulli variables. For an example, suppose a sample of 10 items is taken from an assembly line that produces 15 percent defective items, on average. The probabilities of 0, 1, 2, ..., 10 defectives are (rounded to three decimal places):

```
## dbinom(0:10, size=10, prob=0.15)
```

```
    0     1     2     3     4     5     6     7     8     9    10
0.197 0.347 0.276 0.130 0.040 0.008 0.001 0.000 0.000 0.000 0.000
```

The probability of observing four or fewer defectives in a sample of size 10 is:

```
pbinom(q=4, size=10, prob=0.15)
```

```
[1] 0.9901
```

The function `qbinom()` goes in the other direction, from cumulative probabilities to numbers of events. It generates *quantiles*, a generalization of the more familiar term *percentiles.* To calculate a seventieth percentile of the distribution of the number of defectives in a sample of 10, with Pr[defective=0.15], type:

```
qbinom(p = 0.70, size = 10, prob = 0.15)
```

```
[1] 2
```

```
## Check that this lies between the two cumulative probabilities:
## pbinom(q = 1:2, size=10, prob=0.15)
```

The following generates a random sample of 15 values from a binomial distribution with `p`=0.5 and `size`=4.

```
rbinom(15, size=4, p=0.5)
```

```
 [1] 0 2 3 3 3 2 2 3 1 2 2 1 3 1 2
```

The Poisson distribution `dpois()`, `ppois()`, `qpois()`, `rpois()`
Values are 0, 1, 2, ..., where the argument `lambda` specifies the theoretical mean.

The Poisson distribution is often used to model the number of events that occur in a certain time interval, or the numbers of defects observed in, for example, manufactured products. The distribution has a single parameter λ (the Greek letter "lambda") which coincides with the mean or expected value.

As an example, consider a population of raisin buns for which there are an average of three raisins per bun, that is, $\lambda = 3$. The possible numbers of raisins are 0, 1, 2, ... Under the Poisson model, which assumes that raisins appear independently in different buns, probabilities for numbers of raisins in a bun are:

```
## dpois(x = 0:8, lambda = 3)
```

```
     0      1      2      3      4      5      6      7      8
0.0498 0.1494 0.2240 0.2240 0.1680 0.1008 0.0504 0.0216 0.0081
```

The functions `ppois()`, `qpois()`, and `rpois()` can be used in exactly the same way as binomial family functions. Thus, in the raisin buns example, the probability of more than eight raisins (equals 0.0038) can be calculated in any of the following ways:

```
1 - ppois(q = 8, lambda = 3)
ppois(q=8, lambda=3, lower.tail=FALSE)  ## Alternative
1-sum(dpois(x = 0:8, lambda = 3))        ## Another alternative
```

The following simulates numbers of raisins in 20 raisin buns, where the expected number of raisins per bun is three:

```
raisins <- rpois(20, 3)
raisins
```

```
 [1] 4 2 3 3 1 4 3 0 6 3 3 2 4 2 5 4 3 1 2 2
```

Note that the average of these values is 57/20 which is, not accidentally, near the expected value 3.

In the practical situation, raisins may tend to stick together, or the mixing may not be even through the baking mixture. Something more sophisticated than a simple Poisson model may be required.

Initializing the Random Number Generator

In a number of our earlier examples, we have seen calls to the function `set.seed()`. The seed for the random number generator is stored in the workspace, in a hidden variable (`.Random.seed`) that changes whenever there has been a call to the random number generator. Where it is required to repeat the same sequence on successive occasions, the function `set.seed()` can be used to set an initial seed and thus ensure the same sequence. The following uses `set.seed()` to make the call to `rbinom(10, size=1, p=0.5)` thus reproducible:

```
set.seed(23286) # Use to reproduce the sample below
rbinom(15, size=1, p=0.5)
```

```
 [1] 0 0 0 0 1 0 1 0 1 1 1 1 1 0 0
```

When the workspace is saved, `.Random.seed` is stored in the workspace. When the workspace is loaded again, the value stored in the workspace will be restored. Any new simulations will then be independent of those prior to saving the workspace.

Means and Variances

Binomial In a sample of 10 manufactured items from a population where 15 percent are defective, we expect to see 1.5 defectives on average. More generally, the *expected value* or *mean* of a binomial random variable with `size` $= n$ and probability `prob` $= \pi$ is $n\pi$. The variance of a binomial random variable is $n\pi(1-\pi)$.

For the number of defectives in our sample of 10 items with $\pi = 0.15$, the variance is $10 \times 0.15 \times 0.85 \simeq 1.275$.

In practice, the probability of a defective may change from one sample item to the next, perhaps because of unevenness in the quality of the raw material. Thus, there may be a tendency for defects to cluster together. This can lead to a distribution that has a larger variance relative to the mean than predicted by the binomial distribution.

Poisson The variance of a Poisson random variable is equal to its mean, often denoted λ. Thus if the number of raisins in a bun is Poisson with mean $\lambda = 3$, the variance is also 3.

1.4.2 Continuous Distributions

Models for measurement data usually take the form of a *continuous* distribution. The probability that a measurement takes a particular value is then 0. Instead, the distribution of a continuous random variable is modeled by its density function. The area under the density curve between $x = a$ and $x = b$ gives the probability that the random variable lies between those limits. The total area under the density curve is 1.

The normal distribution The *normal*, or Gaussian, distribution, which has the bell-shaped density curve pictured in Figure 1.13, is widely used to model continuous measurement data. A transformation may be required, as in Figure 1.5 in Subsection 1.2.3, for the normal model to be useful. The density (height) of the curve is given as a function of the distance from the mean.

The density curve shown in Figure 1.13 is for a *standard* normal distribution that has mean 0 and standard deviation 1. Replacing each value z in a population of standard normal variates by $\mu + \sigma z$ changes the mean to μ and the variance to σ.

Code to plot the normal density function is:

```
## Plot the normal density, in the range -3 to 3
z <- pretty(c(-3,3), 30)  # Find ~30 equally spaced points
ht <- dnorm(z)            # Equivalent to dnorm(z, mean=0, sd=1)
plot(z, ht, type="l", xlab="Normal variate", ylab="Density", yaxs="i")
# yaxs="i" locates the axes at the limits of the data
```

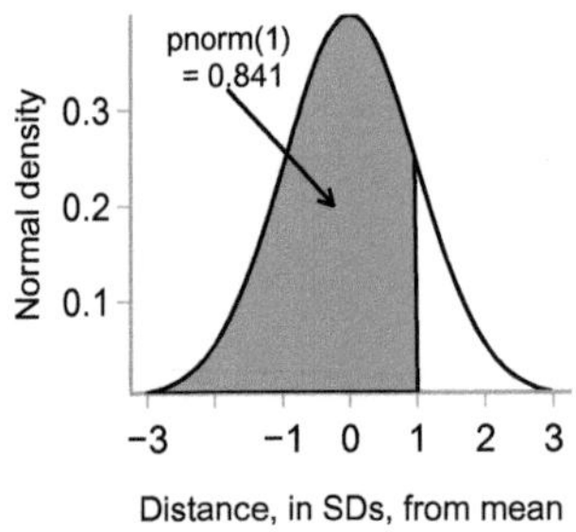

Calculations using `pnorm()`

	Prob
pnorm(0)	0.500
pnorm(1)	0.841
pnorm(-1.96)	0.025
pnorm(1.96)	0.975
pnorm(1.96, mean=2)	0.484
pnorm(1.96, sd=2)	0.836

Figure 1.13 A plot of the normal density. The horizontal axis is labeled in standard deviations (SDs) distance from the mean. The area of the shaded region is the probability that a normal random variable has a value less than one standard deviation above the mean.

Functions for calculations relating to the normal distributions are `dnorm()` (used for plotting the density curve in Figure 1.13), `pnorm()`, `qnorm()`, and `rnorm()`. The function `pnorm()` calculates the cumulative probability, that is, the area under the curve up to the specified ordinate or x-value. Thus, the probability that a normal variate with mean 0 and standard deviation 1 is less than 1.0 is `pnorm(1)` $= 0.841$. This corresponds to the area of the shaded region in Figure 1.13. To obtain the probability in the upper tail, supply the argument `lower.tail=FALSE`.

The function `qnorm()` computes normal quantiles. Thus, the 90th percentile is:

```
qnorm(.9)          # 90th percentile; mean=0 and SD=1
```

```
[1] 1.282
```

The footnote has additional examples.[6]

Other continuous distributions A simple model is the *uniform distribution*, for which an observation is equally likely to take any value in a given interval. The probability density is constant over that interval.

The *exponential distribution* gives high probability density to positive values lying near 0, with the density decaying exponentially as the values increase. It is the simplest of a class of distributions that have been used to model times between arrivals of customers to a queue. The exponential is a special case of the chi-squared distribution which arises, for example, when checking for dependence between row and column numbers in contingency tables.

Different Ways to Represent Distributions

As noted in Section 1.1.5, the boxplot defaults are set so that 1 percent of values that are drawn at random from a normal distribution will on average be flagged as possible outliers. If the distribution is not symmetric, more than 1 percent of

[6]
```
## Additional examples:
setNames(qnorm(c(.5,.841,.975)), nm=c(.5,.841,.975))
qnorm(c(.1,.2,.3))   # -1.282 -0.842 -0.524  (10th, 20th and 30th percentiles)
qnorm(.1, mean=100, sd=10)  # 87.2 (10th percentile, mean=100, SD=10)
```

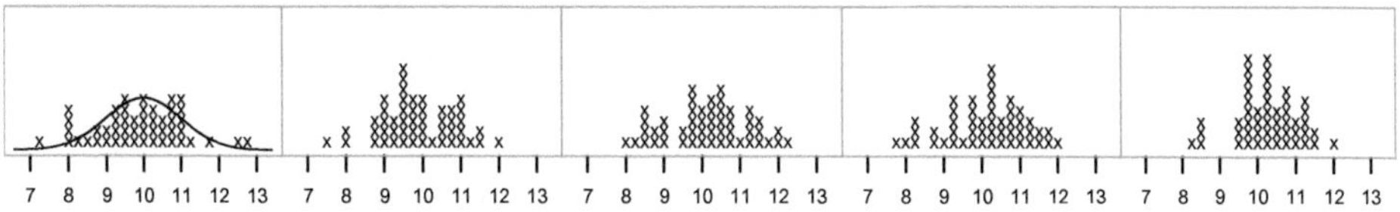

Figure 1.14 Each panel shows a simulated distribution of 50 values from a normal distribution with mean = 10 and sd = 1. The underlying theoretical normal curve is overlaid on the far left panel.

points are likely to lie outside the whiskers, at the lower end if the distribution is left-skewed or at the upper end if the distribution is right-skewed. If the distribution is symmetric, but "heavy-tailed," then we would expect more than 1 percent of the values to plot beyond the boxplot whiskers with no preference for either end.

Generating Simulated Samples from the Normal and Other Distributions

The function `rnorm()` generates random samples of values from the normal distribution. To generate 10 random values from a standard normal distribution, we type:

```
options(digits=2)  # Suggest number of digits to display
rnorm(10)          # 10 random values from the normal distribution
```

```
[1]  0.42  1.15 -1.40  0.18  0.21 -1.13 -0.69  0.29  0.23 -0.21
```

Figure 1.14 demonstrates the use of simulation to indicate the extent of sample-to-sample variation in histogram summaries of the data, when five independent random samples of 50 values are taken from a normal distribution.[7]

Calculations for other distributions, for example `runif()` to generate uniform random numbers, or `rexp()` to generate exponential random numbers, follow the same pattern.

```
runif(n = 20, min=0, max=1) # 20 numbers, uniform distn on (0, 1)
rexp(n=10, rate=3)          # 10 numbers, exponential, mean 1/3.
```

Exercises at the end of this chapter explore further possibilities.

Histograms are not a good basis for deciding whether sample values are consistent with a normal distribution. A more effective tool is the normal quantile–quantile plot.

1.4.3 Graphical Checks for Normality

In a normal quantile–quantile plot the sorted data values are plotted against the expected ordered values for a normal distribution. Thus for data from a normal distribution, the points should scatter about a straight line.

The `DAAG::pair65` dataset has data from an experiment that tested the effect of heat on the stretchiness of elastic bands. Following an initial check for

[7]
```
## The following gives conventional histogram representations:
set.seed (21)          # Use to reproduce the data in the figure
df <- data.frame(x=rnorm(250), gp=rep(1:5, rep(50,5)))
lattice::histogram(~x|gp, data=df, layout=c(5,1))
```

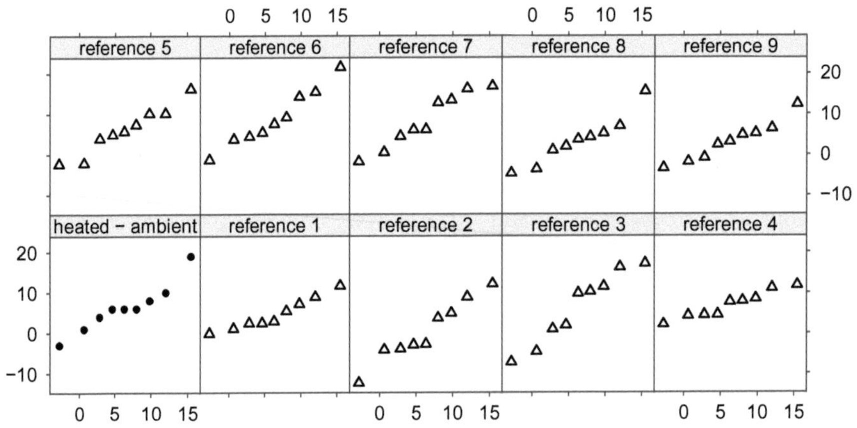

Figure 1.15 The lower left panel is the normal quantile–quantile plot for heated–ambient differences. Remaining panels show normal quantile–quantile plots for samples of nine numbers from a normal distribution.

"stretchiness," the bands were arranged into nine pairs, such that the two members of a pair appeared similarly "stretchy." One member of each pair, chosen at random, was placed in hot water (60–65 °C) for four minutes, while the other was left at ambient temperature. After a wait of about 10 minutes, the amounts of stretch, under a 1.35 kg weight, were recorded. The following were the amounts of stretch, and the differences, for each pair:

	1	2	3	4	5	6	7	8	9
heated	244	255	253	254	251	269	248	252	292
ambient	225	247	249	253	245	259	242	255	286
heated-ambient	19	8	4	1	6	10	6	-3	6

The normal quantile–quantile plot for these differences is in the lower left panel of Figure 1.15. The other seven plots are for samples (all of size nine) of simulated random normal values. As judged against these plots, the distribution of the sample differences appears consistent with normality. The code is:

```
## Normal quantile-quantile plot for heated-ambient differences,
## compared with plots for random normal samples of the same size
plt <- with(DAAG::pair65, DAAG::qreference(heated−ambient, nrep=10, nrows=2))
update(plt, scales=list(tck=0.4), xlab="")
```

Displays in the style of Figure 1.15 help to calibrate the eye, giving a sense of the nature and extent of departures from linearity that can be expected in random normal samples of the specified size, here nine. The process should be repeated several times. With a sample size of just nine, large departures from a linear pattern will be needed to provide convincing evidence of nonnormality.

The base graphics function `qqnorm()` may be used to obtain such plots one at a time. Specify, for example, `qqnorm(rnorm(9))`.

The methodology extends to allow a comparison of ordered sample values with expected ordered values for any distribution that is of interest. See `?qqplot`.

In practice exact normality is unlikely, and is for most inferential purpose not required. Concern arises when there are gross departures from normality, such as skewed or heavy-tailed data. In small samples (e.g., of the order of 10 or less), large departures from normality, of an extent that affect the validity of results, will frequently go undetected. It is typically necessary to rely on sources of evidence that are external to the data, including where possible previous experience with similar data.

1.4.4 Population Parameters and Sample Statistics

Parameters, such as the mean (μ) or standard deviation (σ), numerically summarize various aspects of a population. Such parameters are usually unknown and are estimated using *statistics* that are calculated for a sample (which should be a random sample) from the population. Thus the sample mean is used to estimate the population mean, and the sample standard deviation estimates the population standard deviation.

Other commonly used statistics are the proportion, variance, median, the quartiles, the extremes, the slope of a regression line, and the correlation coefficient. Each may be used as an estimate of the corresponding population parameter.

To what extent is it possible to use the one sample that we have as the basis for some wider generalization? If another sample were taken, would it very likely give a similar result? The sampling distribution plays a central role in assessing the extent to which results can be generalized beyond the one available sample.

The sampling distribution of the mean, and extensions to the sampling distributions of regression coefficients, underpin a large part of the methodology described in this text. They allow the extension of results that apply to random samples from normal populations, for use with populations that show various types of deviations from normality. Is it then important to assess, in any particular case, the extent to which the normal distribution result can be trusted? Recourse to simulation allows a value of the statistic of interest to be calculated from each of a multiple repeated random samples from the relevant distribution. The collection of simulated sample statistics can be summarized by a distribution called the *sampling distribution* of the statistic.

The information on the sampling distributions of the statistics of interest offers an *empirical*, that is, sampling-based, alternative to the direct use of statistical theory. It can be used when theoretical results are not available or are of uncertain relevance. Here, it will be used to investigate what the relevant theoretical result – the Central Limit Theorem – may mean in practice.

In practice, even if the main part of the population distribution appears symmetric, there will often be occasional aberrant values. Such aberrant values do, perhaps fortunately, work in a conservative direction – they reduce the chances that genuine differences will be detected. A take-home message is that, especially in small samples, the probabilities and quantiles can be quite imprecise. They are rough guides, intended to assist in making a judgment.

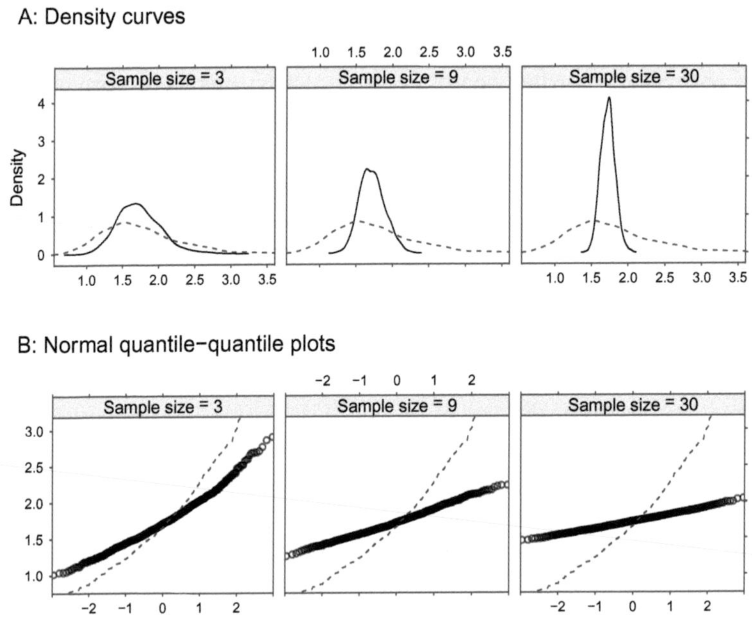

Figure 1.16 Data values are from simulations of the sampling distribution of the mean, for a mildly skew distribution. Panel A shows density curves, while Panel B shows normal quantile–quantile plots. The plot for the population, repeated in each panel, is shown as a dashed curve. Simulated sampling distributions, each from 1000 simulations, are shown as solid curves. The three panels show the plots for samples of respective sizes 3, 9, and 30.

The Sampling Distribution of the Mean

The standard deviation of the sampling distribution of the mean is termed the *standard error of the mean* (SEM). If the population mean is μ and the standard deviation is σ, then given independent random samples

$$\text{SEM} = \frac{\sigma}{\sqrt{n}}.$$

A consequence of the Central Limit Theorem is that for a statistic such as a mean or a regression slope, an averaged value may have a sampling distribution that is close to normal, even if the underlying population distribution is clearly not normal.[8]

In practice, if the sampled population has a distribution that is approximately normal, the average of samples of size $n = 3$ or $n = 4$ can usually, for most practical purposes, be treated as coming from a normal distribution. Skewed or heavy-tailed distributions will require larger (perhaps much larger) samples than distributions that have lighter tails than the normal.

[8] More precisely, the distribution of the sample mean approximates the normal distribution with increasing accuracy, as the sample size increases, assuming values are independent, and the population standard deviation is finite. There are similar results for many other sample statistics.

Figure 1.16 shows density curves and normal quantile–quantile plots for simulated sampling distributions of the mean (sample sizes 3, 9, and 30), for sample values from a mildly skewed distribution. As the sample size increases from $n = 3$ to $n = 9$ to $n = 30$, the density curves become more nearly symmetric with a decreasing standard deviation, while the normal quantile–quantile plots become more nearly linear, with a reduced slope. The reductions in slope in Panel B reflect the reduced SEMs, from $\frac{\sigma}{\sqrt{3}}$ to $\frac{\sigma}{\sqrt{9}}$ to $\frac{\sigma}{\sqrt{30}}$. Even for a sample size of 3, much of the skewness has gone.

Code for the plots in Figure 1.16A is:

```
library(lattice)
## Generate n sample values; skew population
sampfun = function(n) exp(rnorm(n, mean = 0.5, sd = 0.3))
gph <- DAAG::sampdist(sampsize = c(3, 9, 30), seed = 23, nsamp = 1000,
  FUN = mean, sampvals=sampfun, plot.type = "density")
```

For Figure 1.16B, replace `plot.type="density"` in the call to `DAAG::sampdist()` with `plot.type="qq"`. The skewness of the population can be increased by increasing `sd` in the call to `sampfun()`. For example, try `sd = 0.8`.

** The Sampling Distribution of s*

It is usually simplest to work with the sampling distribution of

$$\frac{(n-1)s^2}{\sigma^2}.$$

Under the independently and identically distributed (iid) normal assumption, this quantity has a chi-squared distribution with $n-1$ degrees of freedom, independently of $\bar{x}$. Its distribution is close to normal for very large n. Exercise 2.20 in Subsection 2.12 investigates transformations that improve the approximation to normality.

For nonnormal data, the distribution of $\frac{(n-1)s^2}{\sigma^2}$ will differ from the chi-squared. Simulation can be a useful mechanism for investigating the extent of the difference that can be expected for specific patterns of departure from normality.

** The Standard Error of the Median*

For data from a normal distribution, the standard error of the median can be calculated using

$$\text{SE}_{\text{median}} = \sqrt{\frac{\pi}{2}}\frac{s}{\sqrt{n}} \approx 1.25\frac{s}{\sqrt{n}}.$$

This quantity is about 25 percent greater than the standard error of the mean. For the `cuckoos` data, median length of eggs in nests of wrens is 21.0 mm, with standard error of the median equal to 0.244.

The median is often employed when the distribution is positively skewed. The median is then less than the mean, and the standard error formula given above is not applicable.

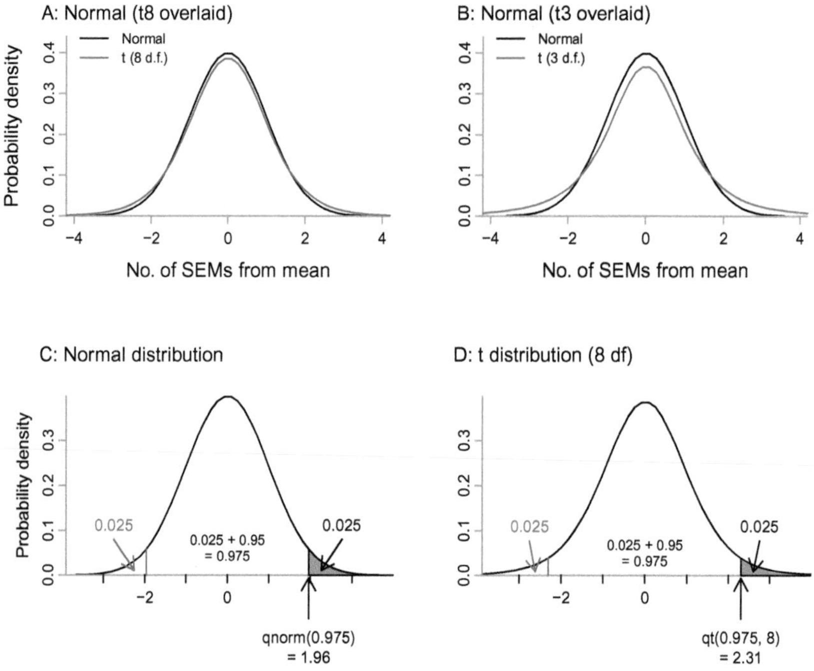

Figure 1.17 Panels A and B overlay the density for a normal distribution with the density for a t-distribution, in Panel A t with eight degrees of freedom, and in Panel B t with three degrees of freedom. Panels C and D show the endpoints of symmetrically placed regions that enclose 95 percent of the probability, in Panel C for a normal distribution, and in Panel D for t with eight degrees of freedom. In each panel, the upper 2.5 percent of the area under the curve is shaded in gray.

Simulation in Learning and Research

In statistical theory and in practice, simulation is widely used, when analytical results are not available. It can be a useful tool in teaching and learning. The R package *animation* (Xie and Cheng, 2008) has a variety of simulations that are intended for use in teaching or self-instruction.

1.4.5 The t-Distribution

We have previously noted that, under Central Limit Theorem conditions, the sampling distribution of the mean could be approximated by normal distributions with standard deviations given thus.

One-sample case: The standard deviation of $\bar{x}$ is termed *standard error of the mean* (SEM), and equals $\frac{\sigma}{\sqrt{n}}$.

Two-sample case: The standard deviation of $\bar{x_1} - \bar{x_2}$ is termed the *standard error of difference* (SED). Assuming a common variance, it equals $\sigma\left(\frac{1}{n_1} + \frac{1}{n_2}\right)$.

Table 1.2 *Comparison of normal distribution endpoints (multipliers for the SEM) with the corresponding t-distribution endpoints on eight degrees of freedom.*

Probability enclosed between limits	Cumulative probability	Number of SEMs: Normal distribution	Number of SEMs: t-Distribution (8 df)
68.3%	84.1%	1.0	1.07
95%	97.5%	1.96	2.31
99%	99.5%	2.58	3.36
99.9%	99.95%	3.29	5.04

In the usual case where σ has to be replaced by an estimate s, the relevant standardized differences are as follows.

$$\text{One-sample:} \quad t = \frac{(\bar{x} - \mu)}{SEM}, \text{ where } SEM = \frac{s}{\sqrt{n}}. \tag{1.1}$$

$$\text{Two-sample:} \quad t = \frac{\bar{x_1} - \bar{x_2} - \mu}{SED}, \text{ where } SED = s\sqrt{\frac{1}{n_1} + \frac{1}{n_2}}. \tag{1.2}$$

The statistic t expresses the difference of interest in standard error units. In the one-sample case the sampling distribution is t with $n-1$ degrees of freedom. In the two-sample case, assuming a common variance, degrees of freedom are $n_1 + n_2 - 2$. Figures 1.17 A and B show the density curve for a normal distribution overlaid with those for t-distributions with eight and three degrees of freedom respectively. Replacing σ by s introduces a source of uncertainty additional to that in $\bar{x}$, an uncertainty that is larger as the degrees of freedom for s are smaller.

Figures 1.17 C and D compare area under the curve calculations for a t-distribution with those for a normal distribution. The difference is most obvious in the tails. In the terminology of Subsection 1.4.2, the t-distribution is heavy-tailed – heavier for smaller than for larger degrees of freedom. The "limiting" distribution as degrees of freedom increase is the standard normal.

Changing from a normal distribution to a t-distribution with eight degrees of freedom leads to a small change, from 1.0 to 1.07, in the t-distribution quantile for enclosing the central 68.3 percent of the area. There is a substantial difference, an increase from 1.96 to 2.31, for enclosing 95 percent of the area. The t-distribution underpins a wide range of statistical analysis approaches, both in frequentist and in Bayesian methodology. It will feature extensively in Chapter 2.

Table 1.2 compares the multipliers for a normal distribution with those for an eight degrees of freedom t-distribution, for several different choices of area under the curve. Examples of the calculations required are:

```
qnorm(c(0.975,0.995), mean=0)   # normal distribution
```

```
[1] 2.0 2.6
```

```
qt(c(0.975, 0.995), df=8)       # t-distribution with 8 d.f.
```

```
[1] 2.3 3.4
```

The sampling distribution of the t statistic will be the starting point for the confidence interval and hypothesis testing approaches of Section 1.6.

1.4.6 The Likelihood, and Maximum Likelihood Estimation

Consider the model

$$y_i = \mu + \epsilon_i, i = 1, 2, \ldots, n,$$

where μ is an unknown constant, and where the errors ϵ are assumed to be independent and normally distributed with mean 0 and variance σ^2. More generally, and this will be the main focus of interest in the later text, the elements μ_i of μ may themselves be functions of explanatory variables and/or factors.

The probability density for the ith y-value is normal with mean μ and variance σ^2. Because of the independence assumption, the probability density of the entire sample of ys is simply the product of these normal densities. This product, when viewed as a function of μ and σ, has the name *likelihood.* The *maximum likelihood estimates* are the values of μ and σ which maximize this function. A calculus argument can be used to show that the estimates are $\bar{y}$ and $s\sqrt{(n-1)/n}$. Thus, the usual estimator of the standard deviation differs slightly from the maximum likelihood estimator. The denominator in the usual variance estimate is the number of degrees of freedom ($n - 1$ in this case), while it is n for the maximum likelihood estimate. This difference is negligible in large samples.

In practice, it is usually most convenient to work with the log-likelihood, rather than with the likelihood. Instead of multiplying densities to obtain the likelihood, the logarithms of the densities are added to obtain the log-likelihood. Maximizing on the log scale leads to exactly the same estimates as on the original scale.

Where a model m_1 with maximum likelihood L_1 is obtained from a model m_0 with maximum likelihood L_0 by fitting an additional term or terms, the log-likelihood ratio $\log(\lambda_{lr}) = \log\left(\frac{L_1}{L_0}\right)$ may be used to compare them. As L_1 has more parameters to estimate, $L_1 \geq L_0$.

Exact expressions for the distribution of the log-likelihood ratio λ_{lr} are not in general available. Where the sample size n is large enough, use can be made of the result that in the large sample limit, $2\log(\lambda_{lr}) = 2(\log(L1) - \log(L_0))$ is distributed as chi-squared with degrees of freedom equal to the number of additional parameters estimated in the more complex model.

1.5 Simple Forms of Regression Model

In this introductory account, the primary focus of attention will be models for data that can be displayed as a scatterplot. By convention, the x-variable, plotted on the horizontal axis, has the role of explanatory or predictor variable. The y-variable, by convention plotted on the vertical axis, has the role of response or outcome variable. Many of the issues that arise for these simple regression models are fundamental to all regression methods. Size and shape data, discussed in Section 2.5.8, are one of a number of applications that raise their own specific issues.

Scrutiny of the scatterplot should precede regression calculations. It can be useful to compare the fitted line with a fitted smooth curve such as will be a major focus in Chapter 4, as a help in judging whether a straight line is appropriate.

1.5.1 Line or Curve?

The data shown in Figure 1.18 is from an experiment where different weights of roller were rolled over different parts of a lawn and the depression noted (data are from Stewart et al., 1988). The data are:

```
roller <- DAAG::roller
t(cbind(roller, "depression/weight ratio"=round(roller[,2]/roller[,1],2)))
```

	1	2	3	4	5	6	7	8	9	10
weight	1.9	3.10	3.3	4.8	5.3	6.1	6.4	7.6	9.8	12
depression	2.0	1.00	5.0	5.0	20.0	20.0	23.0	10.0	30.0	25
depression/weight ratio	1.1	0.32	1.5	1.0	3.8	3.3	3.6	1.3	3.1	2

Write (x_i, y_i) $(i = 1, 2, \ldots 10)$ for the 10 (`weight`, `depression`) pairs. Three possible models, all modeling the dependent value as the sum of a deterministic or *signal* component and a *noise* component ε_i for each (x_i, y_i) pair, are:

1. $\frac{y_i}{x_i} = \mu + \varepsilon_i$ (the signal is a ratio that is constant across observations);
2. $y_i = \beta x_i + \varepsilon_i$ (the "line through the origin" model);
3. $y_i = \alpha + \beta x_i + \varepsilon_i$ (allows an arbitrary line).

Model 3, which fitted a line using the linear modeling function `lm()`, gave the fitted line in Figure 1.18A. This used a least squares approach to calculate the intercept and slope, that is, minimize

$$\sum_{i=1}^{10} \varepsilon_i^2.$$

The strict requirement for calculation of standard error and p-value information is the *iid normal* assumption that the ε_i are independently and identically distributed as normal variables with mean 0 and variance σ^2. Equivalently, it is assumed that, given x_i, the responses y_i are sampled independently from a normal distribution with mean $\alpha + \beta x_i$. The output from `lm()` includes an estimate of the variance σ^2.

Independence implies that the size and sign (negative or positive) of one element give no information on the likely size and sign of any other element. It implies that elements are uncorrelated. With different assumptions (e.g., a sequential correlation between successive data points), the standard errors will be different.

Using Models to Predict

Interest may be in the rate of increase of depression with increasing roller weight. For models 2 and 3 above, the slope of the line (β) is then the focus of interest. Alternatively, or additionally, the aim may be the prediction of values for new data. Different models may serve different purposes.

A data-based assessment of how results may generalize to other lawns would require data from multiple lawns, then using a modeling approach that (such as will be discussed in Chapter 7) that accounts for between-lawn variation as well as for the within-lawn variation on which the present data gives limited information. The mechanical properties of the soil would usefully feature in such a model.

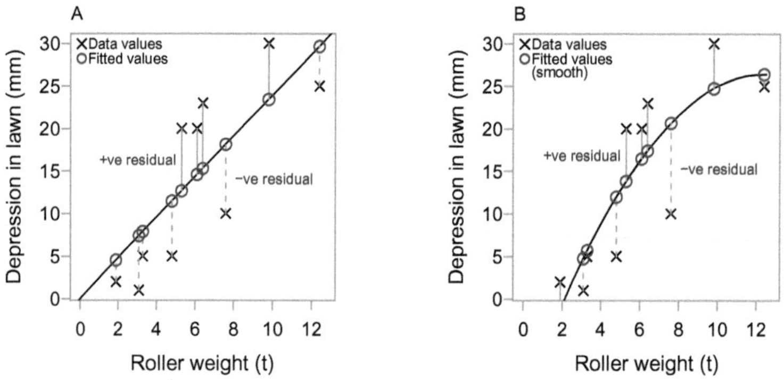

Figure 1.18 In Panel A, a line has been fitted, while Panel B has used the function `lowess()` to fit a smooth curve. Residuals (the "rough") appear as vertical lines. Positive residuals are solid lines, while negative residuals are dashed. For code used to create the figures, see the web page for the book.

Which Model is Best – Line or Curve?

The fitting of a curve, as in Figure 1.18B, can help in judging whether a line, as in Figure 1.18A, really is appropriate. Here there is just one point that seems to be causing the line, and the fitted curve, to bend down. As might be expected, a formal statistical analysis suggests that the curve in Figure 1.18B is an "over-fit." See further Exercise 4.2 in Chapter 4.

1.5.2 Fitting Models – the Model Formula

The same model formula `depression ~ weight` can be used both with the function `lm()` to specify the fitting of a line to the data of Figure 1.18, and with the function `plot()` to specify the y- and x-variables for a plot:

```
## Fit line - by default, this fits intercept & slope.
roller.lm <- lm(depression ~ weight, data=DAAG::roller)
## Compare with the code used to plot the data
plot(depression ~ weight, data=DAAG::roller)
## Add the fitted line to the plot
abline(roller.lm)
```

In the formula, `weight` is the *predictor* or *explanatory* variable, while `depression` is the *response*.[9]

Model Objects

The model object, saved above as `roller.lm`, is a list. The element names give clues on what the elements contain:

```
roller.lm <- lm(depression ~ weight, data=DAAG::roller)
names(roller.lm)    # Get names of list elements
```

9
```
## For a model that omits the intercept term, specify
lm(depression ~ 0 + weight, data=roller)  # Or, if preferred, replace `0` by `-1`
```

```
 [1] "coefficients"  "residuals"     "effects"       "rank"
 [5] "fitted.values" "assign"        "qr"            "df.residual"
 [9] "xlevels"       "call"          "terms"         "model"
```

Most information that is commonly required from model objects can be obtained by the use of an *extractor* function. Note in particular:

```
coef(roller.lm)          # Extract coefficients
summary(roller.lm)       # Extract model summary information
coef(summary(roller.lm)) # Extract coefficients and SEs
fitted(roller.lm)        # Extract fitted values
predict(roller.lm)       # Predictions for existing or new data, with SE
                         # or confidence interval information if required.
resid(roller.lm)         # Extract residuals
```

Information in the list object `roller.lm` can be accessed directly, thus:

```
roller.lm$coef           # An alternative is roller.lm[["coef"]]
```

Use of an extractor function, when available, is preferable.

The default summary information for the `roller.lm` model object is:

```
print(summary(roller.lm), digits=3)
```

```
Call:
lm(formula = depression ~ weight, data = DAAG::roller)

Residuals:
   Min     1Q Median     3Q    Max
 -8.18  -5.58  -1.35   5.92   8.02

Coefficients:
            Estimate Std. Error t value Pr(>|t|)
(Intercept)    -2.09       4.75   -0.44   0.6723
weight          2.67       0.70    3.81   0.0052

Residual standard error: 6.7 on 8 degrees of freedom
Multiple R^2:  0.644,    Adjusted R^2:    0.6
F-statistic: 14.5 on 1 and 8 DF,  p-value: 0.00518
```

The intercept of the fitted line is $a = -2.09$ (SE $= 4.75$), while the estimated slope is $b = 2.67$ (SE $= 0.70$). The p-value for the slope (testing the null hypothesis that β = true slope $= 0$) is small, consistent with the evident linear trend. The p-value for the intercept (testing $\alpha = 0$) is 0.67, that is, the difference from zero may well be random sampling error. Thus, consistently with the intuition that depression should be proportional to weight, the intercept term should be dropped. We leave this as an exercise.

The standard deviation of the noise term, here identified as the residual standard error, is 6.735. We defer comment on R^2 and the F-statistic until Subsection 2.5.2.

Residual Plots

The residuals allow limited checks on model assumptions. (Here, the dataset is not large enough to allow detection of any except extreme departures.) The function

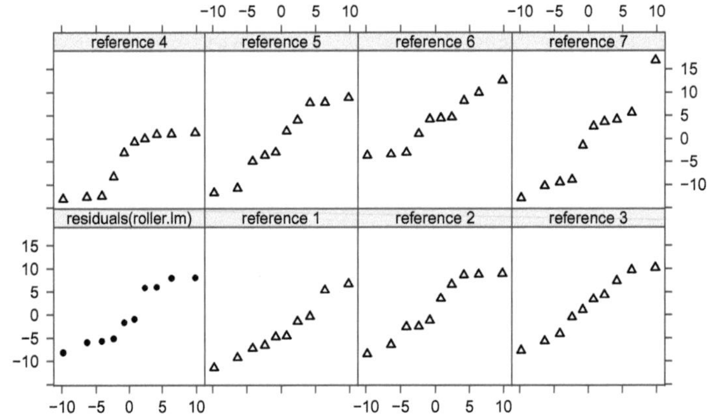

Figure 1.19 The normal quantile–quantile plot for the regression of Figure 1.18A is shown in the lower left panel. Other panels show normal quantile–quantile plots for computer-generated normal data.

`plot()`, used with an `lm` object as argument, has as its default the display of four standard diagnostic plots. Its use will be demonstrated in Subsection 2.5.3. See also Exercise 1.11b.

The third of the default plots is the normal quantile–quantile plot. As an aid to judging whether this differs from a straight line by more than can be expected as a result of random generation, this is suitably compared with plots for computer-generated random normal data. Figure 1.19 uses the function `DAAG::qreference()` to display 7 such plots alongside the normal quantile–quantile plot for the residuals from the model. Such plots provide the eye with a reference standard.

```
## Normal quantile-quantile plot, plus 7 reference plots
DAAG::qreference(residuals(roller.lm), nrep=8, nrows=2, xlab="")
```

Simulation of Regression Data

It is often useful to repeatedly simulate data from a fitted model, then refit to each new set of simulated data. This provides a check on variation under such repeated simulation. The function `simulate()` can be used for this purpose.

Thus, to obtain 10 sets of simulated outcome values for the model that was fitted to the `roller` data, do:

```
roller.lm <- lm(depression ~ weight, data=DAAG::roller)
roller.sim <- simulate(roller.lm, nsim=20)  # 20 simulations
```

The object `roller.sim` is a data frame with one column for each of the 20 sets of simulated values of `depression`. These are obtained from the column of fitted values by adding normal random deviates with mean 0 and residual standard deviation as given by `sigma(roller.lm)`. To visualize this output, try:

```
with(DAAG::roller, matplot(weight, roller.sim, pch=1, ylim=range(depression)))
points(DAAG::roller, pch=16)
```

Table 1.3 *Details are for the first three rows of the model matrix, for calculations of fitted values and residuals, in the straight line fit to the lawn roller data.*

Model matrix					
Multiply by −2.09	Multiply by 2.67	Add multiplied values to give fitted value $\widehat{y}$		Observed y	Residual = $y - \widehat{y}$
1	1.9	$-2.09 + 2.67 \times 1.9 =$	2.98	2	$2 - 2.98$
1	3.1	$-2.09 + 2.67 \times 3.1 =$	6.18	1	$1 - 6.18$
1	3.3	$-2.09 + 2.67 \times 3.3 =$	6.71	5	$5 - 6.71$
...	...	...		...	...

1.5.3 The Model Matrix in Regression

For the use of `lm()` and related functions, the model matrix has a crucial role.

In straight line regression, the model or X matrix has two columns – a column of 1s and a column that holds values of the explanatory variable x. The fitted straight line model is

$$\begin{aligned}\widehat{y} &= a + bx \\ &= 1 \times a + x \times b.\end{aligned}$$

The first two columns of Table 1.3 show (first three rows only) the model matrix used in fitting a straight line model to the lawn roller data. To extract the model matrix from the model object, use the extractor function `model.matrix()`, thus:

```
model.matrix(roller.lm)
## Specify coef(roller.lm) to obtain the column multipliers.
```

For each row, fitted values are multiple of the value 1 in the first column (here, to two decimal places, −2.09), another multiple (here 2.67) of the value in the second column, and adding them.

For the simpler (no intercept) model $\widehat{y} = bx$. The model matrix then has only a single column, holding the values of x.

From Straight Line Regression to Multiple Regression

Above, we considered a model that had a `weight`^{2} explanatory term as well as a `weight` term. In principle, there is no limit to the terms that can be added. Much of the content of following chapters will be an exploration of the possibilities afforded by adding explanatory terms that add further columns to the model matrix.

The `DAAG::litters` data frame has observations on brain weight, body weight, and litter size of 20 mice. A model that will be considered in Subsection 3.2.5 is:

```
mouse.lm <- lm(brainwt ~ lsize+bodywt, data=DAAG::litters)
coef(summary(mouse.lm))
```

Are both the explanatory variables `lsize` and `bodywt` contributing to the predictive power of the equation?

1.6 Data-Based Judgments – Frequentist, in a Bayesian World

Here, the attention will be on approaches that depend on distributional assumptions. Section 1.8 will be concerned with approaches that are more empirically based.

1.6.1 Inference with Known Prior Probabilities

In daily life we continually update the information on which we rely as better or more complete information has become available. It may be that the old completely supplants the new. Or it may be that the old provides a wider context in which to understand the new information. Bayesian approaches use what is already known or surmised as a context for the analysis and interpretation of new data.

In a medical context, consider a rare disease that occurs in 2 in 1000 in a target population. Suppose that in a person with the disease (a true positive) the disease will be detected with a probability of 0.8 (this is termed the *sensitivity*), while a person who does not have the disease (a true negative) will be detected as negative with a probability of 0.95 (this is termed the *specificity*). Then, in a population of 10,000 where 20 have the disease and 9800 do not (a prevalence of 0.002), the results will on average divide up thus:

	Test $+ve$	Test $-ve$	TOTAL	
True $+ve$	16	4	20	*Sensitivity* $= 16/20 = 80\%$
True $-ve$	499	9481	9980	*Specificity* $= 9481/9900 = 95\%$

Thus, among those who test positive, a fraction of only $16/(16{+}499) \simeq 0.03$ will be true positives.

Prior knowledge of the prevalence of the disease in the target population is crucial for judging the risk indicated by the test result. Additionally, accurate estimation of sensitivity and specificity requires large trials, with results that apply to individuals who would meet the entry criteria for the study.

Bayes' theorem gives this result in a manner that does not depend on a specific numerical example, and makes it easy to change the assumptions:

$$\begin{aligned}\Pr[\mathrm{D}\mid\text{test } {+}\text{ve}] &= \frac{\Pr[\text{test } {+}\text{ve} \mid \mathrm{D}] \times \Pr[\mathrm{D}]}{\Pr[\textit{test} + \textit{ve}]} \\ &= \frac{\Pr[\textit{test} + \textit{ve} \mid \mathrm{D}] \times \Pr[\mathrm{D}]}{\Pr[\textit{test} + \textit{ve} \mid \mathrm{D}] \times \Pr[\mathrm{D}] + \Pr[\textit{test} + \textit{ve} \mid \neg\mathrm{D}] \times \Pr[\neg\mathrm{D}]}.\end{aligned}$$

The following function can be used to calculate the probability that a patient who tests positive has the disease:

```
## `before` is the `prevalence` or `prior`.
after <- function(prevalence, sens, spec){
  prPos <- sens*prevalence + (1-spec)*(1-prevalence)
  sens*prevalence/prPos}
## Compare posterior for a prior of 0.002 with those for 0.02 and 0.2
setNames(round(after(prevalence=c(0.002, 0.02, 0.2), sens=.8, spec=.95), 3),
       c("Prevalence=0.002", "Prevalence=0.02", "Prevalence=0.2"))
```

```
Prevalence=0.002  Prevalence=0.02    Prevalence=0.2
           0.031             0.246              0.800
```

With a prevalence of 0.002 in a population of 10,000, 99.98 percent of those tested will not have the disease, but will contribute 499 out of the 515 of those who test positive. With a prevalence that equals 0.02, the probability of a positive is much less strongly weighted toward the figure for those who do not have the disease. The finding of a positive has then to be placed in the context of an assessment of the prevalence in the relevant wider population, if necessary using a ballpark estimate. This is especially necessary if the prevalence is very small.

One can think of the probability $\Pr[\mathit{test}+ve \mid \neg \mathrm{D}]$, here equal to 0.05 as a p-value for testing the null hypothesis that a patient who does not have a disease will test positive. In this context it is very clear that in order to get a reasonable sense of what $p = 0.05$ might mean, there has to be attention to the best available estimate of, or guess at, the prior probability.

Relating "Incriminating" Evidence to the Probability of Guilt

Consider the case where there is a police search of a DNA database of 5000 individuals, with the incriminating DNA type found in 1 individual in 1000. The following summarizes the expected result of the police search for a DNA match, optimistically assuming that the person whose DNA was found at the crime scene will be among those netted.

Not from crime scene	From crime scene
4 (false) positives	1 true positive

Odds are then 1:4 or worse that the DNA belongs to the defendant. The DNA match falls well short, on its own, of identifying the defendant as the person whose DNA was found at the crime scene. Writing Pr[I] for Pr[innocence] and Pr[E] for the Pr[evidence], $\Pr[\mathrm{I} \mid \mathrm{E}]$ is very different from $\Pr[\mathrm{E} \mid \mathrm{I}]$. In order to establish a link there has to be other evidence that explains why this particular individual was identified as the suspect, rather than others with the same DNA match. Quoting the 0.001 figure as the probability that the DNA is not from the defendant is a version of what is termed the *prosecutor's fallacy.*

1.6.2 Treatment Differences That Are on a Continuous Scale

We will start by demonstrating, and critiquing, a frequentist hypothesis testing approach. Consider now `sleep` data from a 1905 study that has change in hours of sleep for 10 individuals, for each of two soporific drugs.

```
## Use pipe syntax, introduced in R 4.1.0
pairedDiffs <- with(datasets::sleep, extra[group==2] - extra[group==1])
pairedDiffs |> (function(x)c(mean = mean(x), SD = sd(x), n=length(x)))() |>
   (function(x)c(x, SEM=x['SD']/sqrt(x['n'])))() |>
   setNames(c("mean","SD","n","SEM")) -> stats
   print(stats, digits=3)
```

```
 mean     SD      n     SEM
1.580  1.230 10.000  0.389
```

For assessing the difference between the drugs, a relevant statistic is then

$$t = \frac{\bar{d}}{s/\sqrt{n}} = \frac{6.33}{2.03} = 3.11.$$

The mean is $t = 3.11$ times the SEM. The symbol t is used because the relevant reference for a formal statistical hypothesis test is, under normal distribution assumptions, a t-distribution, here with eight degrees of freedom. We may report: "The mean difference is 1.58 [SEM = 0.389], based on $n = 10$ differences."

Formal hypothesis testing requires the setting out of *null* and *alternative* hypotheses. Taking the population mean to be μ, a common choice of (*point*) null hypothesis is

$$\mathrm{H}_0 : \mu = 0 \qquad \text{with alternative hypothesis } \mu \neq 0.$$

The (two-sided) p-value is twice the probability that the t-statistic is greater than

$$\text{mean/SEM} = 1.580/0.389 = 4.062.$$

```
## Sum of tail probabilities
2*pt(1.580/0.389, 9, lower.tail=FALSE)
```

```
[1] 0.0028
```

A standard form of summary statement is: "Based on the sample mean of 1.58, the population mean is greater than zero ($p = 0.0028$)."

A confidence interval offers a different perspective on the result, one that focuses on the estimate and on its accuracy. Assuming that data are from a normal distribution with mean μ, values of t_9 will with probability 0.95 lie between −2.262 and 2.262, that is, in 95 percent of such samples $\bar{d}$ will lie within a distance 2.262 SEMs of μ. These are the endpoints of what is known as the 95 percent "confidence" interval for μ:

$$(1.58 - 2.262 \times 0.389, 1.58 + 2.262 \times 0.389) = (0.7, 2.46).$$

For a 99 percent confidence interval, replace the multiplier 2.26 by 3.25. This leads to the wider interval $(0.316, 2.84)$.

Code that short-circuits the above calculations, for a 95 percent confidence interval, is:

```
## 95% CI for mean of heated-ambient: data frame DAAG::pair65
t.test(sleep, conf.level=0.95)
```

An Hypothesis Test

If the 95 percent confidence interval for the population mean does not contain zero then, using the language of hypothesis testing, the null hypothesis that the population mean is zero will be rejected at a "significance level" of $\alpha = 1 - 0.95 = 0.05$. The value of p that is on the borderline between rejection and nonrejection is termed the critical value, commonly denoted α.

Note that $p = 0.00283$ is at the upper end of a range of values, extending from 0 to 0.00283, that under the distributional assumptions made, would all be equally likely if the true mean is zero. With $t = 4.06$, the p-value is a $|t| \geq 4.06$ ("as large or larger") probability, not a $|t| = 4.06$ probability, and has to be understood accordingly.

If the only interest was in whether the first drug gave a greater increase than the second drug, the relevant probability is that in the upper tail:

```
pt(4.06, 9, lower.tail=F)
```

```
[1] 0.0014
```

The p-Value Probability Relates to a Decision Process

The direct interpretation of a p-value as a probability is to a decision process that lumps together all p-values that are smaller than a set threshold α. Common practice has been to set $\alpha = 0.05$, or to 0.01 or less if greater assurance is required.

When planning an experiment or sampling scheme, in a case where the interest is in a possible difference between two groups, the $p \leq \alpha$ perspective makes a certain sense, with commonly used values are 0.05, or 0.01, or 0.005. Once the results are available, it makes sense to look at the specific p-value, and ask what that means. In this text, the Bayes Factors that will be treated in Subsection 1.7.2 will be used as a source of insight.

1.6.3 Use of Simulation with p-Values

All a p-value offers is an assessment of implications that flow from accepting the null hypothesis. It is important to ask: "How much more likely does the test statistic become under the alternative?" In the extreme case where data are random noise, no given p-value is any more likely under the alternative than under the null!

In order to assess the probability under the alternative, assumptions must be made regarding a prior distribution. For any given prior, the probability under the alternative depends, in the one- or two-sample case, on a standardized difference, known as the *effect size*, as noted in Subsection 1.3.6.

Observe the following.

- The substantial reduction in variation in the p-values returned as effect sizes increase is most noticeable at an effect size of 1.2 for `n=10`, and at 0.8 and 1.2 for `n=40`.
- With an effect size of 0.2, the proportion of p-values that are greater than 0.05 changes from 172 percent at `n=10` to 130 percent at `n=40`. It remains more likely than not that the p-value will be greater than 0.05.
- Again with `eff=0.2`, the lower and upper quartiles shift down from 0.105 and 0.532 at `n=10` to 0.024 and 0.283 at `n=40`. The difference, or *inter-quartile range*, reduces from 0.43 to 0.26. The use of a $p^{0.25}$ scale gives a misleading visual impression of the relative widths of the two boxes.

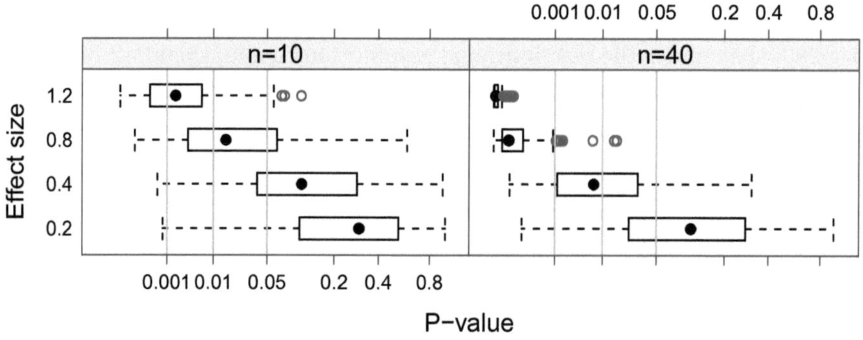

Figure 1.20 Boxplots are for 200 simulated p-values for a one-sided one-sample t-test, for the specified effect sizes `eff` and sample sizes `n`. The $p^{0.25}$ scale on the x-axis is used to reduce the extreme asymmetry in the distributions of values that are returned. See Exercise 1.24a for further comment.

The following function was used for the simulations:

```
eff2stat <- function(eff=c(.2,.4,.8,1.2), n=c(10,40), numreps=200,
                     FUN=function(x,N)pt(sqrt(N)*mean(x)/sd(x), df=N-1,
                                         lower.tail=FALSE)){
  simStat <- function(eff=c(.2,.4,.8,1.2), N=10, nrep=200, FUN){
    num <- N*nrep*length(eff)
    array(rnorm(num, mean=eff), dim=c(length(eff),nrep,N)) |>
      apply(2:1, FUN, N=N)
  }
  mat <- matrix(nrow=numreps*length(eff),ncol=length(n))
  for(j in 1:length(n)) mat[,j] <-
    as.vector(simStat(eff, N=n[j], numreps, FUN=FUN))  ## length(eff)*numep
  data.frame(effsize=rep(rep(eff, each=numreps), length(n)),
           N=rep(n, each=numreps*length(eff)), stat=as.vector(mat))
}
```

Code for Figure 1.20 is then:

```
set.seed(31)
df200 <- eff2stat(eff=c(.2,.4,.8,1.2), n=c(10, 40), numreps=200)
labx <- c(0.001,0.01,0.05,0.2,0.4,0.8)
gph <- bwplot(factor(effsize) ~ I(stat^0.25) | factor(N), data=df200,
              layout=c(2,1), xlab="P-value", ylab="Effect size",
              scales=list(x=list(at=labx^0.25, labels =labx)))
update(gph+latticeExtra::layer(panel.abline(v=labx[1:3]^0.25, col='lightgray')),
       strip=strip.custom(factor.levels=paste0("n=",c(10,40))),
       par.settings=DAAG::DAAGtheme(color=F, col.points="gray50"))
```

The code can readily be adapted to show the equivalent plots for sample effect sizes, for t-statistics, and in principle for the Bayes Factors that will be introduced in the next section. See Exercise 1.24a at the end of the chapter.

1.6.4 Power – Minimizing the Chance of False Positives

The p-value focuses on what can be expected under the null. When designing a new experiment or sampling scheme, it is important to assess the probability of detecting a "positive" (i.e., ultimately concluding that the null is false) when the alternative is true. For this purpose it is necessary to specify the size of difference that is of interest. In the one-sample and two-sample t-tests, this is the Cohen's d measure, defined as the mean difference (one-sample case) or difference in means (two-sample case), divided by the standard deviation.[10]

Given that a decision has been made in advance to regard as *significant* any p-value that is less than α, the *power* P_w is the probability of detecting an effect of the specified size. (Note that $\beta = 1 - P_w$ has the name "Type II error".)

Suppose for example that the power is $P_w = 0.8$, relative to the $\alpha = 0.05$ cutoff. This is high relative to the standards of much published work. Consider three scenarios, where 300 tests for a drug are divided between true positives and true negatives in one of the ratios 0.2:1, 1:1, 5:1. Results will then, on average, divide up as follows:

```
       True positives False positives
R=0.2  0.05x250=12.5  0.8 x50=40
R=1    0.05x150=7.5   0.8x150=120
R=5    0.05 x50=2.5   0.8x250=160
```

As the prior odds increase from 0, the probability that $p \leq 0.05$ will indicate a real effect will, unless $P_w = 0$, increase from zero. In the extreme case where $P_w = 0$, the probability of a real effect will be be the same (equal to the prior probability) irrespective of the p-value.

Power calculations, as implemented in the base R function `power.t.test()` and in the *pwr* package, allow experimenters to determine the size of experiment that can on average be expected to detect, at a specified significance level α, a specified Cohen's `d` effect size.

The effect size for which it is reasonable to plan depends on the context. In medicine, the effect size should be large enough to be distinguishable from natural variation in the population. It is useful to check previous trials in related areas of research, being mindful that the refereeing processes involved in publication will in many areas generate substantial positive biases.

Power Calculations – Examples

Examples of power calculations, for two-sided tests with effect size `d=0.5`, are:

```
power.t.test(d=0.5, sig.level=0.05, type="one.sample", power=0.8)
```

```

     One-sample t test power calculation

              n = 33
          delta = 0.5
             sd = 1
      sig.level = 0.05
          power = 0.8
    alternative = two.sided
```

[10] We are assuming a common standard deviation in the case of two samples.

```
pwr1 <- power.t.test(d=0.5, sig.level=0.005, type="one.sample", power=0.8)
pwr2 <- power.t.test(d=0.5, sig.level=0.005, type="two.sample", power=0.8)
## d=0.5, sig.level=0.005, One- and two-sample numbers
c("One sample"=pwr1$n, "Two sample"=pwr2$n)
```

```
One sample Two sample
        57        108
```

Figure 1.20 in Subsection 1.3.6 provided strong indications of the range of p-values that could be expected, given a specified effect size and specified sample size. Those who are planning an experiment would do well to plot the equivalent graph that relates the effect size of interest and the planned sample size.

The simulations are, effectively, experiments. The following shows, based on the simulation results for the combinations shown of effect size (ES) and sample sizes (number of pairs or paired differences), the proportion of simulations where the p-value for the null hypothesis of no effect fell under the specified significance level.

α=0.05

	n=10	n=20	n=40
ES=0.05	0.035	0.04	0.049
ES=0.2	0.082	0.134	0.234
ES=0.4	0.204	0.397	0.694
ES=0.8	0.6162	0.9239	0.9985
ES=1.2	0.9203	0.9991	~1.0000

α=0.005

	n=10	n=20	n=40
ES=0.05	0.004	0.005	0.006
ES=0.2	0.011	0.023	0.054
ES=0.4	0.037	0.116	0.343
ES=0.8	0.2119	0.655	0.9768
ES=1.2	0.5666	0.9762	~1.0000

Thus, for n = 10 and an effect size of 0.2, close to 8 percent of "positives" (where $p \leq 0.05$ is used as the criterion) will be detected as such, as against 5 percent under the null. Subsection 1.10.2 will discuss estimated effect sizes from replications of published social psychology studies, where a high proportion were in the vicinity of 0.05. For sample sizes of 40 or less, the power is under 0.05, so that more than 19 out of 20 true positives will be missed under an $\alpha = 0.05$ cutoff. The experimental results mainly add noise.

Code for the calculations, for the two different choices of significance level, is:

```
effsize <- c(.05,.2,.4,.8,1.2); npairs <- c(10,20,40)
pwr0.05 <- matrix(nrow=length(effsize), ncol=length(npairs),
              dimnames=list(paste0('ES=',effsize), paste0('n=',npairs)))
pwr0.005 <- matrix(nrow=length(effsize), ncol=length(npairs),
              dimnames=list(paste0(effsize), paste0('n=',npairs)))
for(i in 1:length(effsize)) for(j in 1:length(npairs)){
   pwr0.05[i,j] <- power.t.test(n=npairs[j],d=effsize[i],sig.level=0.05,
                             type='one.sample')$power
   pwr0.005[i,j] <- power.t.test(n=npairs[j],d=effsize[i],sig.level=0.005,
                             type='one.sample')$power}
tab <- cbind(round(pwr0.05,4), round(pwr0.005,4))
```

**Positive Predictive Values*

In the example at the start of this subsection, the prior odds R was an actual but unknown ratio of number of drugs with a potentially detectable effect to the number with no effect, giving a prior probability of $R/(R+1)$. The reasoning carries

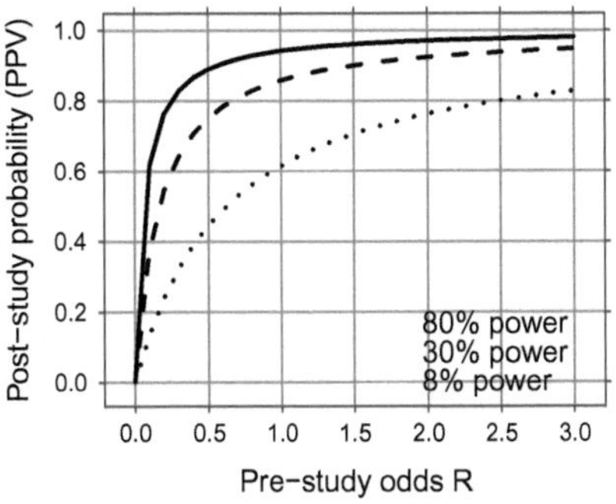

Example: With R = 1:15 (e.g., 100 true +ves to 1500 true -ves), $\alpha = 0.05$, and $P_w = 0.3$, the posterior odds are:

$$\frac{RP_w}{\alpha} = \frac{0.3}{15 \times 0.05} = 0.4,$$

$$\text{PPV} = \frac{0.4}{1 + 0.4} \simeq 0.29.$$

Figure 1.21 Post-study probability (PPV)), as a function of the pre-study odds, for different levels of statistical power.

through in the same way if R is a guess at a prior odds ratio, perhaps based on earlier studies.

The effect size (ES) for identifying a detectable effect may be chosen as the smallest change that is of interest. For instance, in an experiment to compare drugs that induce sleep (as in the dataset `datasets::sleep`), a minimum effect size of ES = 30 min might be reasonable.

The (posterior) probability of a genuine effect of the given size is known as the *positive predictive value* or PPV. Examples that will be given shortly should make the idea clear. The *false discovery rate* or FDR is related to the PPV thus:

$$\text{FDR} = 1 - \text{PPV}.$$

With $\alpha = 0.05$, 5 percent of tests are expected, under the null hypothesis, to show $p \leq \alpha$. Thus, given that the ratio of positives to negatives is $R : 1$, the odds that an apparent positive will be a true positive is

$$\frac{RP_w}{\alpha} = R\frac{P_w}{\alpha}, \tag{1.3}$$

that is, multiply the prior odds R by $\frac{P_w}{\alpha}$ to get an odds ratio that accounts for the new evidence. Ioannidis (2005) has a modification of Equation (1.3) that allows for bias.

The positive predictive value (PPV), or posterior probability, is then

$$PPV = \frac{RP_w}{RP_w + \alpha}. \tag{1.4}$$

Figure 1.21 illustrates what the formula means in practice.

Based on eight journal articles published between 2006 and 2009, Button et al. (2013) reported an astonishing median power of 0.08 across 461 individual studies of brain volume abnormalities. Results were better, but still not encouraging, in neuroscience more generally. Based on meta-analysis reports published in 2011, Button et al. (2013) found a median power of 0.21 for 730 individual primary studies.

Prinz et al. (2011) reported a success rate of around 30 percent in their efforts to reproduce the main result in 67 published studies. Two scenarios that, in the absence of other faults, would on average reproduce this approximate success rate are:

- $R = 1{:}15$, $\alpha = 0.05$, $P_w = 0.3$,
- $R = 1{:}4$, $\alpha = 0.05$, $P_w = 0.08$.

Calculations for the first of these are shown to the right of Figure 1.21. These scenarios ignore the likely contributions of design, data, execution, and presentation faults. Such faults will increase the risk of finding a spurious effect, the risk of failing to detect a genuine effect, and the risk of biases that distort the result.

Small studies with low power compromise the use of p-values for any purpose – whether as a screening device, or to confirm an earlier result. Button et al. (2013) note that the magnitude of a true effect, when found, is on average exaggerated. Additionally, small studies may not be conducted with the same care as larger studies that require more careful organization, and the smaller datasets that result are more susceptible to minor changes in the analysis process.

The issues to which Equation (1.4) and Figure 1.21 relate are of central importance for large areas of laboratory science. See, in particular, Ioannidis (2005). In practical use, for estimating the PPV, such formulae provide only broad guidelines. The estimate of the power P_w, and an assessment of what is a reasonable effect size, is often based on pilot-study information from a convenience sample and not a random sample, and is susceptible to selection bias. Estimates that are accurate enough to be a good basis for design may be available when a trial is the latest in a series of comparable trials. Gelman and Carlin (2014) argue for the use of information external to the specific study as a basis for choosing the effect size. A literature review will often provide useful leads.

The results given in this subsection rely on setting a threshold α and not distinguishing between p-values that lie within a range from 0 to α. That makes sense when designing an experiment, but preferably setting α somewhat less than 0.05. Once results are in, it becomes important to take note of the specific p-value, and ask what it means.

1.6.5 The Future for p-Values

The critical test for laboratory science is replicability – are other scientists able to replicate the results? p-Values and other relevant statistics should be seen as a complement to, and not as a substitute for, independent replication. Two quotes from Ronald Fisher, who introduced the use of p-values, emphasize the importance of replication:

> Personally, the writer prefers to set a low standard of significance at the 5 per cent point, and ignore entirely all results which fail to reach this level. A scientific fact should be regarded as experimentally established only if a properly designed experiment *rarely* fails to give this level of significance.
> [Fisher (1926)]

Fisher commented, also, that a level of 0.02 or 0.01 might be used if 0.05 did not seem low enough:

> ... no isolated experiment, however significant in itself, can suffice for the experimental demonstration of any natural phenomenon ...
>
> ... we may say that a phenomenon is experimentally demonstrable when we know how to conduct an experiment which will rarely fail to give us a statistically significant result. [Fisher (1935, pp 13–14)]

Independent replication at another time and place is the crucial check, irrespective of the statistical summary measures used. It provides checks on the experimental processes, on mistakes in statistical analysis, and on factors that may be local to the place and time of the original experiment. It checks that the published article and supplementary materials are sufficiently accurate and detailed that others can repeat the experiment. Where mistakes have been made, it is unlikely that another research group will repeat the same mistakes.

If both the original study and the replication have been carried out with impeccable care and give clearly different results, identification of the different factor that has been at play may yield new and important insight. The low power of much of what is reported in the literature makes it difficult to be sure that results are "clearly different."

How Small a p-Value Is Needed?

p-Values are designed to decrease as the weight of evidence shifts to favor the alternative. They are not absolute measures of the weight of evidence. In a context where positive results are thought to be as likely as not, $p \leq 0.05$ has to be regarded as providing only weak evidence for an effect.

The Bayes Factors that will be discussed in Section 1.7 will be used alongside p-values and can help in assessing what a given p-value may mean for the relative probabilities of the null and the alternative.

1.6.6 Reporting Results

It is important to report effect sizes. As the sample size increases, the p-value for a given estimated effect size will decrease. For large enough sample sizes, a small p-value (using whatever value is taken as "small") will correspond to an effect size that is so small as to be of no consequence. Rather than testing for a point null, it commonly makes much better sense to set a minimum difference μ_0 that is of interest, and test $\mu > \mu_0$ against the null $\mu = \mu_0$.

The quoting of multiple p-value or equivalent test results raises awkward questions about what to make of the combined results. In general, significance tests should be closely tied to key points in the paper. Where possible, make a rough assessment of the prior probabilities, at least to the extent of distinguishing between studies with "low prior odds" and those with prior odds that may be of the order of 1:1 or higher. Once it seems clear that an effect is real, the focus of interest should shift to its pattern and magnitude, and to its scientific significance.

It is a poor use of the data to perform tests for each comparison between treatments when the real interest is (or should be) in the overall pattern of response. Where the response depends on a continuous variable, it may be pertinent to ask whether, for example, the response keeps on rising (falling), or whether it rises (falls) to a maximum (minimum) and then falls (rises).

Is There an Alternative That Is More Likely?

Finding $p \leq \alpha$ (commonly with $\alpha = 0.05$) is all very well. The important question is whether there is an alternative that is substantially more likely. Comments in Berkson (1942) highlight the point that p-values relate only to what can be expected under the null.

> If an event has occurred, the definitive question is not, "Is this an event which would be rare if the null hypothesis is true?" but "Is there an alternative hypothesis under which the event would be relatively frequent?"

The approaches to be described in the next section address this point very directly.

1.7 Information Statistics and Bayesian Methods with Bayes Factors

Information statistics and Bayes Factors both offer ways to establish a preference for one model over another. Information statistics rely on large sample results, though for the Akaike Information Criterion (AIC) that is in common use, a correction is available that is designed to improve the small sample properties. Bayes Factors rely on the choice of a specific prior. Although a large sample approximation is not involved, the prior is both more important and harder to choose with confidence when sample sizes are small. Unlike the AIC, Bayes Factors have not to date found common use in the statistical mainstream.

1.7.1 Information Statistics – Using Likelihoods for Model Choice

For using likelihoods to express a preference for one model over another rather than as a basis for a significance test, the likelihood must be adjusted for the number of parameters estimated. Setting p equal to the number of parameters estimated (here, this includes any scale parameters), the AIC is one of two widely used criteria that take the form:

$$kp - 2\log(\hat{L}), \quad \text{where, for AIC, } k = 2.$$

For the Bayesian Information Criterion (BIC), $k = \log(n)$, where n is the number of observations. In either case, the model that gives the smallest value is preferred. The descriptor "Bayesian" appears in the name because the choice of k can be motivated by arguments that have a Bayesian connection, albeit in a large sample limit.

The AIC penalty term is designed so that, in the large sample limit with n much larger than p, the statistic will select the model with the lowest prediction error. Where p is an overly large fraction of n the criterion is inclined to select overly complex models. For models for which it is available, there is then a strong case for increasing the amount of the correction, as for the AICc statistic that will be discussed below.

The BIC sets $k = \log(n)$, thus for $n > 7$ penalizing complex models (many parameters) more strongly. It is designed, in the large sample limit, to select the correct model. As for the AIC, it is important that the number of observations n is much larger than the number p of parameters that are estimated.[11]

For normal theory models the AIC statistic is, in the usual case where the variance has to be estimated:

$$\text{AIC} \; = n \log\left(\frac{\text{RSS}}{n}\right) + 2p + \text{const}, \quad \text{where} \quad \text{const} = n(1 + log(2\pi)). \qquad (1.5)$$

Note again the reason for placing y-axis tick marks a distance 0.02 apart on the $\log_e$ linear scale used in Figure 1.7. On the $\log_e$ scale a change of 0.02 is very nearly a 2 percent change. where RSS is the residual sum of squares and the constant term arises from the assumption of an iid normal distribution for the errors.

Corrections are available, different for different error families that improve the small sample properties of the AIC statistic. For normal theory models, the AICc statistic replaces the AIC penalty term $2p$ by:

$$2\frac{n}{n-p-1}p, \quad \text{that is, an increase of } 2p\frac{p+1}{n-p-1}.$$

The penalty is then larger for smaller values of `n`, with the consequence that the difference in AICc statistics for a `d` degree of freedom increase is smaller for smaller values of `n`. For the comparison between a model with `p` parameters and one with `p+d` parameters, the change in the AICc statistic is less than the change in the AICc statistic by an amount:

$$2(p+d)\frac{n}{n-(p+d)-1} - 2p\frac{n}{n-p-1} - 2d.$$

The function `AICcmodavg::AICc()` implements this, as well as corrections for a number of other error families. A vignette that gives an overview of the package has extensive advice on model comparison.[12]

The following checks on the formula just given for the AICc statistic:

```
## Calculations using mouse brain weight data
mouse.lm <- lm(brainwt ~ lsize+bodywt, data=DAAG::litters)
n <- nrow(DAAG::litters)
RSSlogLik <- with(mouse.lm, n*(log(sum(residuals^2)/n)+1+log(2*pi)))
p <- length(coef(mouse.lm))+1 # NB: p=4 (3 coefficients + 1 scale parameter)
k <- 2*n/(n-p-1)
c("AICc" = AICcmodavg::AICc(mouse.lm), fromlogL=k*p-2*logLik(mouse.lm)[1],
  fromFit=k*p + RSSlogLik) |> print(digits=4)
```

```
   AICc fromlogL  fromFit
 -112.9   -112.9   -112.9
```

11 In more technical language the AIC statistic is designed to be *asymptotically efficient*, where the BIC statistic is designed to be *asymptotically consistent*.

12 Type `vignette("AICcmodavg", package="AICcmodavg")` to see the vignette.

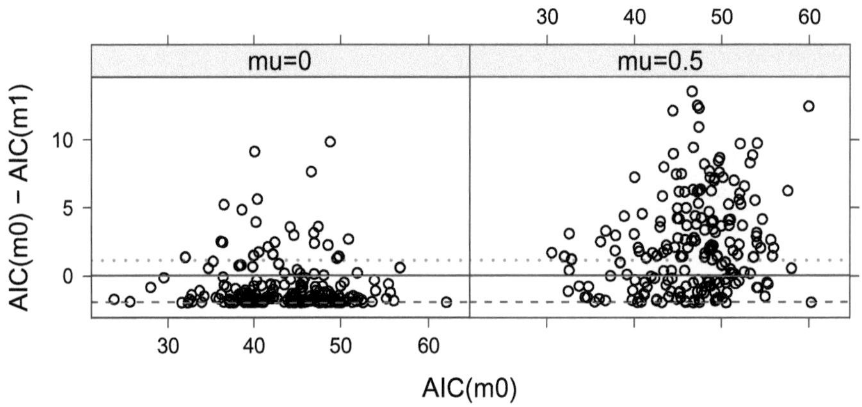

Figure 1.22 Points are from simulations of the sampling properties of the difference in AIC statistics between a model that fits a zero mean and a model that fits a nonzero mean.

Look ahead to Figure 3.17 in Subsection 3.5.1 for a graph that compares the change in penalty terms between the three statistics, for $5 \leq n \leq 35$ from a unit increase in the number of parameters estimated. For the AICc statistic, the cases shown are for an increase from p=1 to p=2, or from p=3 to p=4.

The Sampling Properties of the Difference in AIC Statistics

Figure 1.22 shows results from simulation of the sampling properties of the difference in AIC statistics between a model that fits a zero mean and one that fits a nonzero mean. Panel A is for the case where 15 observations are from a normal distribution with mean 0, while for Panel B the mean was set to 0.5σ. The red solid line is for $y = 0$, while the dashed line is for $y = -2$. Notice that in Panel A, points are relatively dense close to the line $y = -2$, with many more points shifted above this limiting line in Panel B. If the graph is repeated for the AICc statistic, the effect is to shift the solid red horizontal zero line upwards to the fainter dotted red line. Code for Figure 1.22 is:

```
sim0vs1 <- function(mu=0, n=15, ntimes=200){
a0 <- a1 <- numeric(ntimes)
for(i in 1:ntimes){
  y <- rnorm(n, mean=mu, sd=1)
  m0 <- lm(y ~ 0); m1 <- lm(y ~ 1)
  a0[i] <- AIC(m0); a1[i] <- AIC(m1)
}
data.frame(a0=a0, a1=a1, diff01=a0-a1, mu=rep(paste0("mu=",mu)))
}
sim0 <- sim0vs1(mu=0)
sim0.5 <- sim0vs1(mu=0.5)
simboth <- rbind(sim0, sim0.5)
cdiff <- with(list(n=15, p=2), 2*(p+1)*p/(n-(p+1)-1))
xyplot(diff01 ~ a0 | mu, data=simboth, xlab="AIC(m0)", ylab="AIC(m0) - AIC(m1)") +
  latticeExtra::layer({panel.abline(h=0, col='red');
        panel.abline(h=cdiff, lwd=1.5, lty=3, col='red', alpha=0.5);
        panel.abline(h=-2, lty=2, col='red')})
```

The following are the proportions of samples for which the statistic for "m1" is smaller than that for "m0," so that "m1" is preferred:

```
                          True model is m0 True model is m1
AIC: Proportion choosing m1           0.18             0.66
AICc: Proportion choosing m1          0.32             0.80
```

Kass and Raftery (1993) give reasons why AIC is likely to choose overly complex models in the large sample context. When samples are small, even AICc should be used with caution. Checks on distributional assumptions become increasingly less helpful as sample sizes decrease relative to the number of parameters estimated.

1.7.2 Bayesian Methods with Bayes Factors

In this text, Bayesian methods are primarily used to complement the use of *p*-values, and to help clarify what they do and do not imply. *p*-Values, Bayes Factors, and other forms of Bayesian summary, offer different and complementary perspectives on inferences from data.

In a Bayesian approach, the density for the prior is used to weight the density that is fitted to the data, yielding a posterior distribution. There is, in most contexts, an inevitable arbitrariness in the choice of prior. A Bayes Factor is the ratio of the (marginal) likelihood under the alternative to the likelihood under the null. To obtain the odds for the alternative over against the null multiply the Bayes Factor by the prior odds, which in many contexts has likewise to be guessed. Uncertainties in what a *p*-value can be taken to imply are replaced by uncertainties associated with the assumptions made in calculating the Bayes Factor.

Once decisions have been made on the choice of priors, Bayes Factors allow, as *p*-values do not, a probability to be assigned to the null relative to the alternative. The null can in principle be an interval rather than a point.

Here, use will be made of functions in the *BayesFactor* package. The class of priors used places a Cauchy prior (i.e., a *t*-distribution with one degree of freedom) on a difference that is of interest. The default scale parameter is $1/\sqrt{2}$, where a value of 1 corresponds to half the inter-quartile range. The difference made by a different choice of scale parameter is relatively small:

```
     pcauchy(1, scale=1)    pcauchy(1, scale=1/sqrt(2))
                    0.75                           0.80
```

The family of priors used, commonly referred to as the JZS (Jeffreys–Zellner–Siow) family, has been extensively researched. It has the benefit of allowing, for a wide range of models, a numerical approximation to the required integral. See Rouder et al. (2009). It may reasonably be the default in contexts where priors are required that do not overly reflect the judgment of an individual experimenter. It is not at all intuitively obvious how priors should be chosen.

Various upper limits are available in the literature that apply across a wide class of priors that are centered at the null, for distributions that include the Cauchy and the normal. See Subsection 2.9.2. Subsection 2.9.3 will demonstrate computations that can be adapted for use with other families of priors.

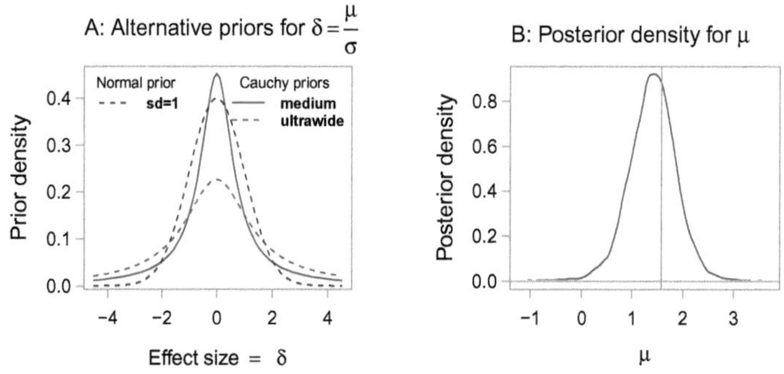

Figure 1.23 Panel A compares alternative Cauchy priors for the standardized effect size δ (or μ) with a normal distribution. Panel B shows the posterior for the sleep data, obtained using the default prior. A vertical line shows the mean increase in hours of sleep in the sample.

Bayes Factors are compared with two other Bayesian approaches for comparing a null with an alternative in Linde et al. (2021). The R package *bayesplay* has several vignettes that provide a step-by-step introduction to Bayes Factors as implemented in the *BayesFactor* package. Kass and Raftery (1993) give a useful overview that discusses also the AIC and BIC statistics. See also the text "An introduction to Bayesian thinking" (Clyde et al., 2022), which is available from `https://statswithr.github.io/book/`.

The Cauchy Prior with Different Choices of Scale Parameter

Figure 1.23A compares alternative priors that might be used for the `sleep` data of Subsection 1.6.2. Panel B shows a posterior density for δ was obtained assuming the default `rscale`$=\sqrt{2}/2$ *BayesFactor* prior.

Note that the default is to use a scale parameter that is data dependent, where ideally the user would supply a scale that was based on previous experience with comparable data. The default use of a data-dependent scale introduces an uncertainty that becomes an increasing issue for small samples.

```
## Calculate and plot density for default prior - Selected lines of code
x <- seq(from=-4.5, to=4.5, by=0.1)
densMed <- dcauchy(x, scale=sqrt(2)/2)
plot(x, densMed, type='l')
## Panel B
pairedDiffs <- with(datasets::sleep, extra[group==2] - extra[group==1])
ttBF0 <- BayesFactor::ttestBF(pairedDiffs)
## Sample from posterior, and show density plot for mu
simpost <- BayesFactor::posterior(ttBF0, iterations=10000)
plot(density(simpost[,'mu']))
```

A Thought Experiment

Consider as a thought experiment three alternatives, in a study that tests 300 drugs:

1. 50 have an effect that is in principle detectable, while 250 are inactive. The (usually unknown) prior odds $R:1$ are, in this thought experiment, 50:250 = 1:5 or 0.2:1, so that R=0.2, strongly favoring the null hypothesis of no effect.

Table 1.4 *Posterior odds, as returned by* **BayesFactor::ttest.tstat()**, *when the Bayes factor is multiplied by the respective the prior odds R.*

p-value (t_{19})	Bayes Factor	Posterior odds R = 0.2	R = 1	R = 5
0.05 (2.1)	1.39	0.28	1.39	6.9
0.01 (2.9)	5.12	1.02	5.12	25.6
0.005 (3.2)	9.17	1.83	9.17	45.9

2. 150 have an effect, and 150 are inactive, so that R=1.
3. 250 have an effect, and 50 are inactive, so that R=5.

Now consider three sets of 20 paired differences, the first resulting in a two-sided p-value equal to 0.05, the second 0.01, and the third 0.005. Code that calculates the Bayes Factors that will be used here is:

```
tval <- setNames(qt(1-c(.05,.01,.005)/2, df=19), paste(c(.05,.01,.005)))
bf01 <- setNames(numeric(3), paste(c(.05,.01,.005)))
for(i in 1:3)bf01[i] <- BayesFactor::ttest.tstat(tval[i],n1=20, simple=T)
```

The final three columns of Table 1.4 show the posterior odds from multiplying the relevant Bayes Factors by prior odds of 0.2, 1.0, and 5.0 respectively.

As with p-values, it may make more sense to specify the minimum effect size that is of interest, rather than to work with a point null. This is, at the same time, a less important issue for Bayes Factors than for p-values. Look ahead to Figure 1.24.

Now compare calculations for the `sleep` data that use the *BayesFactor* package for the three suggested choices of scale factor:

```
pairedDiffs <- with(datasets::sleep, extra[group==2] - extra[group==1])
ttBF0 <- BayesFactor::ttestBF(pairedDiffs)
ttBFwide <- BayesFactor::ttestBF(pairedDiffs, rscale=1)
ttBFultra <- BayesFactor::ttestBF(pairedDiffs, rscale=sqrt(2))
rscales <- c("medium"=sqrt(2)/2, "wide"=1, ultrawide=sqrt(2))
BF3 <- c(as.data.frame(ttBF0)[['bf']], as.data.frame(ttBFwide)[['bf']],
        as.data.frame(ttBFultra)[['bf']])
setNames(round(BF3,2), c("medium", "wide", "ultrawide"))
```

```
medium       wide ultrawide
    17         18        18
```

Note for comparison the Sellke et al. (2001) upper limit, which applies for a wide range of priors, centered at the null, with densities that tail off in much the same manner as for the normal. With the p-value equal to 0, this is:

```
pval <- t.test(pairedDiffs)[['p.value']]
1/(-exp(1)*pval*log(pval))
```

```
[1] 22
```

For degrees of freedom around 10, the value returned by **ttestBF** is not greatly below this lower bound. See Subsection 2.9.2 for further comment.

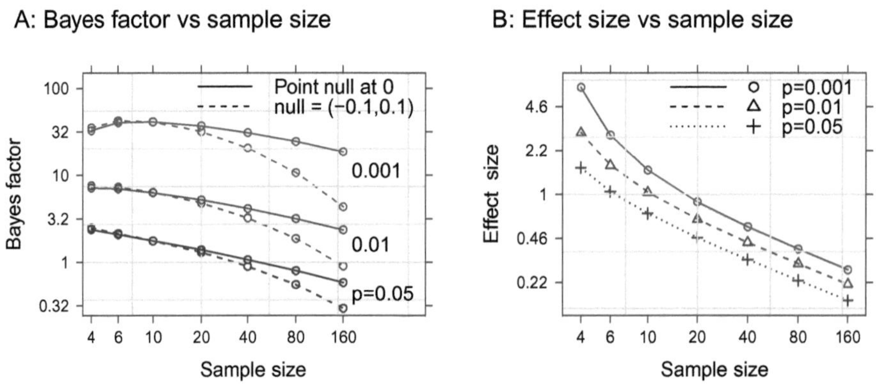

Figure 1.24 Bayes factors are shown that correspond to a given two-sided p-value, for a range of sample sizes, calculated using the function `BayesFactor::ttest.tstat()`. Note that calculations for the null (−0.1,0.1) interval case require *BayesFactor* version 0.9.12-4.5 or later. Earlier versions used, for $t>5$, an approximation that failed and gave, for $p = 0.01$ with $n \leq 4$ and for $p = 0.001$ with $n \leq 9$, grossly inflated values.

A Null Interval May Make Better Sense

A simple change in the code for the one-sample case gives, instead of a comparison with a point null, a comparison between a null interval and its complement. Thus, for the `sleep` data, consider a null interval that extends 45 minutes (0.75 hr) either side of 0. The SD is $s = 1.23$, so that 0.75 hr gives a standardized difference of $d = 0.75/1.23 = 0.61$.

The first line of the following output compares the interval $-0.61 < d < 0.61$ with 0, while the second line compares the region outside that interval with 0.

```
min45 <- round(0.75/sd(pairedDiffs),2)  ## Use standardized units
ttBFint <- BayesFactor::ttestBF(pairedDiffs, nullInterval=c(-min45,min45))
round(as.data.frame(ttBFint)['bf'],3)
```

```
                                bf
Alt., r=0.707 -0.61<d<0.61       5
Alt., r=0.707 !(-0.61<d<0.61)   27
```

```
bf01 <- as.data.frame(ttBFint)[['bf']]
```

The ratio $27.39/5.03 = 5.45$ is the Bayes factor that compares an absolute difference $|d| \geq 0.61$ with $|d| < 0.61$.

The Effect of Changing Sample Size

Figure 1.24 shows, for three choices of p-value and for a range of sample sizes, Bayes Factor estimates as returned by `BayesFactor::ttest.tstat()`. Panel B shows the effect sizes – these are as estimated from a sample that yields the specified p-value.

For all three choices of p-value, the Bayes Factor soon starts to decrease with increasing degrees of freedom. For p=0.05 sooner than for smaller p-values, a point is in due course reached where the sample effect size is too small to be of consequence. The Bayes Factor reflects this, giving a perspective on the information in the data that is different from that offered by p-values.

The somewhat larger Bayes Factors at smaller sample sizes, relative to a given p-value, come with a caution. Even more than for p-values, sampling variation is a greater concern when samples are small.

Exercise 1.31 looks at the effect of replacing `rscale="medium"` with `rscale="wide"`. Exercise 1.32 shows results with the JUI family of priors for which the function `statsr:bayes_inference` has provision.[13] In the example considered, the Bayes Factor is smaller.

Different Statistics Give Different Perspectives

A difference between $p = 0.00001$ and $p = 0.000001$, in a one-sample and one-sided t-test with n=40, will not ordinarily attract much attention. The corresponding Bayes Factors, calculated using `BayesFactor::ttest.tstat()` and rounded to whole numbers, are 1012 and 8328. While the difference looks impressive, it is readily explainable by statistical variation and/or small departures from assumptions.

```
bf1 <- BayesFactor::ttest.tstat(qt(0.00001, df=40), n1=40, simple=T)
bf2 <- BayesFactor::ttest.tstat(qt(0.000001, df=40), n1=40, simple=T)
rbind("Bayes Factors"=setNames(c(bf1,bf2), c("p=0.00001","p=0.000001")),
  "t-statistics"=c(qt(0.00001, df=40), qt(0.000001, df=40)))
```

```
              p=0.00001 p=0.000001
Bayes Factors    1012.0     8327.8
t-statistics       -4.8       -5.6
```

Various authors (see, e.g., Kass and Raftery, 1995) suggest a scale of evidence akin to the following for Bayes Factors:

1 – 3	3 – 20	20 – 150	>150
A bare mention	Positive	Strong	Very strong

Small Bayes Factors (much less than 1.0) can be interpreted as evidence against the alternative and in favour of the null.

* *Technical Details of the Family of Priors Used in* BayesFactor

The Cauchy distribution is a t-distribution with a single degree of freedom, used as a relatively uninformative prior. It results from assuming a normal distribution for the difference δ, with the variance of δ distributed as inverse chi-square. The median is its location parameter, while its scale parameter is half the inter-quartile range. The mean and variance are not defined. The Jeffreys distribution has a similar role for the variance of the normal distributions that are assumed both under the null and under the alternative. See `?dcauchy` and `?BAS::Jeffreys`.

[13] Differently from the unit information prior used in Subsection 2.9.2 to motivate the BIC statistic, it is here centered on the null.

1.8 Resampling Methods for SEs, Tests, and Confidence Intervals

Resampling methods rely on the selection of repeated samples from a "population" that is constructed from the sample data. They can be an effective recourse when departures from normality are an issue.

As there are in general too many possible distinct samples to take them all, reliance is on repeated random samples. In this section, we demonstrate permutation and bootstrap methods. We start by demonstrating the use of permutation tests for the equivalent of one-sample and two-sample t-tests.

1.8.1 The One-Sample Permutation Test

Consider the paired elastic band data from the data frame `DAAG::pair65`:

```
                  1   2   3   4   5   6   7   8   9
heated          244 255 253 254 251 269 248 252 292
ambient         225 247 249 253 245 259 242 255 286
heated-ambient   19   8   4   1   6  10   6  -3   6
```

If the treatment has made no difference, then an outcome of 244 for the heated band and 225 for the ambient band might equally well have been 225 for the heated band and 244 for the ambient band. A difference of 19 becomes a difference of -19. The assumption is that each of the $2^9 = 512$ permutations, and thus its associated mean difference, is equally likely. This *exchangeability* assumption is weaker than independence. It may be seen as a weak form of independence.

We then locate the mean difference for the data that we observed within this permutation distribution. The p-value is the proportion of values that are as large in absolute value as, or larger than, the mean for the data.

The first row of the following table shows absolute values of the nine differences:

Difference	19	8	4	1	6	10	6	3	6
	19	8	4	−1	6	10	6	3	6
	19	8	4	1	6	10	6	−3	6

In the permutation distribution, these each have an equal probability of taking a positive or a negative sign. There are 2^9 possibilities, and hence $2^9 = 512$ different values for $\bar{d}$. Rows 1 to 3 of the table show the possibilities that give a mean difference that is as large as or larger than in the actual sample. There are another three possibilities that give a mean difference that is of the same absolute value, but negative. (These three possibilities are obtained by reversing the signs of all elements in rows 1 to 3 of the table.) Hence, $p = 6/512 = 0.0117$.

In general, when the number of pairs is large, the computational demands of an enumeration approach such as has been demonstrated become severe. A suitable recourse is to take repeated random samples from the permutation distribution. The function `DAAG::onetPermutation()` may be used for this.

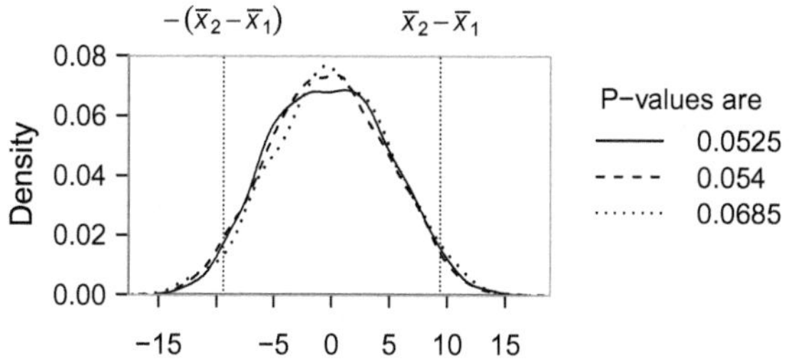

Figure 1.25 Density curves for two samples of 2000 each from the permutation distribution of the difference in means, for the two-sample elastic band data.

1.8.2 The Two-Sample Permutation Test

Suppose we have n_1 values in one group and n_2 in a second, with $n = n_1 + n_2$. The permutation distribution results from taking all possible samples of n_2 values from the total of n values. For each such sample, we calculate

mean of the n_2 values that are selected – mean of remaining n_1 values.

The permutation distribution is the distribution of all such differences of means. We locate the differences of means for the actual samples within this permutation distribution. Thus, consider the data from the dataset `DAAG::two65`. In order to keep computational demands within reasonable bounds, we will take samples of 2000 or more from the permutation distribution.

Ambient: 254 252 239 240 250 256 267 249 259 269 (Mean = 253.5).
Heated: 233 252 237 246 255 244 248 242 217 257 254 (Mean = 244.1).

The proportion of samples (here out of 2000) where the absolute value of the difference of the two resampled means was greater than or equal to that for the observed means can be used as a p-value. A much larger sample size than 2000 is not warranted, given the sampling uncertainty inherent in the initial sample sizes of 10 for the ambient bands and 11 for the heated bands.

Figure 1.25 overlays three estimates of the permutation distribution that were obtained by taking, in each instance, 2000 random samples from the permutation distribution. The point where the difference in means falls with respect to the sampled values ($253.5 - 244.1 = 9.4$) has been marked, as has minus this difference. The code used for the first of the density curves was in essence that for the function `DAAG::twotPermutation`, preceded by `set.seed(47)`.

1.8.3* Estimating the Standard Error of the Median: Bootstrapping

The bootstrap idea is to treat the one sample that we have, for purposes of estimating the sampling distribution of a sample statistic, as an approximation to the entire population. We take repeated resamples with replacement from the given sample, compute the median for each of the resamples and calculate the standard deviation of all of these medians. Even though the resamples are not genuine new samples, this estimate for the standard error of the median has good statistical properties. A similar approach works well for estimating the standard error of such statistics as the median, lower and upper quartiles, and correlation. The bootstrap approach contrasts with simulation, sometimes termed the *parametric bootstrap*, where sampling is from a theoretical distribution.

The formula given in Subsection 1.4.4 for the SEM has the same form, irrespective of the distribution, as long as the sample has been chosen randomly. By contrast, the formula for the standard error of the median (Subsection 1.4.4) applies only when data are normally distributed. Use of the bootstrap estimate of the standard error of the median reduces also any need to look for an alternative theoretical distribution that may be a better fit to the data.

A comparison between the bootstrap estimate and the normal theory estimate allows an assessment of the seriousness of any bias that may result from non-normality. We proceed to calculate the bootstrap estimate of the standard error for the median length for the eggs that were in wrens' nests. The *boot* package is needed for all bootstrap examples. The result will serve as a check on our earlier computation.

Output from R for the lengths of eggs from the wrens' nests is:

```
## Bootstrap estimate of median of wren length: data frame cuckoos
wren <- subset(DAAG::cuckoos, species=="wren")[, "length"]
library(boot)
## First define median.fun(), with two required arguments:
##          data specifies the data vector,
##          indices selects vector elements for each resample
median.fun <- function(data, indices){median(data[indices])}
## Call boot(), with statistic=median.fun, R = # of resamples
set.seed(23)
(wren.boot <- boot(data = wren, statistic = median.fun, R = 4999))
```

```
ORDINARY NONPARAMETRIC BOOTSTRAP


Call:
boot(data = wren, statistic = median.fun, R = 4999)


Bootstrap Statistics :
    original  bias    std. error
t1*       21   0.054        0.21
```

The original estimate of the median was 21. The bootstrap estimate of the standard error is 0.215, based on 4999 resamples. Compare this with the slightly larger standard error estimate of 0.244 given by the normal theory formula in Section 1.4.4. The bootstrap estimate of the standard error will of course differ somewhat between different runs of the calculation. Also given is an estimate of the bias, that is, of the tendency to under- or over-estimate the median.

1.8.4 Bootstrap Estimates of Confidence Intervals

The usual approach to constructing confidence intervals is based on a statistical theory that relies, in part, on normal distribution assumptions. If the normal assumption is not applicable and an alternative theory is not available, the bootstrap may be helpful. Calculation for the median and for the correlation now follow.

The function `boot.ci()` implements five different methods for using bootstrap estimates of a statistic to calculate confidence intervals. The `perc` (percentile) type is the most the most commonly used. The `bca` type (bias corrected accelerated or BC_a) may give a substantial improvement. A sample size of $n = 15$, as in the wren egg length data that follows, is too small for the difference to be of consequence. Efron and Tibshirani (1993) describes these methods, together with a theoretical justification for the use of the BC_a method.

Bootstrap 95 Percent Confidence Intervals for the Median

We will construct 95 percent confidence intervals for the median of the cuckoo egg lengths in wrens' nests. Results are given for the BC_a method, as well as for the percentile method that may be preferred for symmetric distributions.

The object `wren.boot` from Subsection 1.8.3 can be used as a starting point The endpoints for the 95 percent percentile confidence interval are calculated as the 2.5 and 97.5 percentiles of the bootstrap distribution of medians:

```
## Call the function boot.ci() , with boot.out=wren.boot
boot.ci(boot.out=wren.boot, type=c("perc","bca"))
```

```
BOOTSTRAP CONFIDENCE INTERVAL CALCULATIONS
Based on 4999 bootstrap replicates

CALL :
boot.ci(boot.out = wren.boot, type = c("perc", "bca"))

Intervals :
Level      Percentile            BCa
95%    (21, 22 )    (20, 21 )
Calculations and Intervals on Original Scale
Some BCa intervals may be unstable
```

The Correlation Coefficient

Bootstrap methods do not require bivariate normality. Independence between observations, that is, between (x, y) pairs, is as important as ever. Note, however, that a correlation of, for example, 0.75 for a nonnormal distribution may have quite different implications from a correlation of 0.75 when normality assumptions apply.

We will compute 95 percent confidence intervals for the correlation between `chest` and `belly` for the `possum` data frame. Results are given for BC_a as well as for percentile confidence intervals.

```
## Bootstrap estimate of 95% CI for `cor(chest, belly)`: `DAAG::possum`
corr.fun <- function(data, indices)
  with(data, cor(belly[indices], chest[indices]))
set.seed(29)
```

```
corr.boot <- boot(DAAG::possum, corr.fun, R=9999)
```

```
boot.ci(boot.out = corr.boot, type = c("perc", "bca"))
```

```
BOOTSTRAP CONFIDENCE INTERVAL CALCULATIONS
Based on 9999 bootstrap replicates

CALL :
boot.ci(boot.out = corr.boot, type = c("perc", "bca"))

Intervals :
Level      Percentile            BCa
95%    ( 0.48,  0.71 )   ( 0.47,  0.71 )
Calculations and Intervals on Original Scale
```

The Bootstrap – Parting Comments

Bootstrap methods are not a panacea. They must respect the structure of the data. Any form of dependence in the data must be taken into account. There are contexts where the bootstrap is invalid and will mislead. The bootstrap is unlikely to be satisfactory for statistics, including maximum, minimum, and range, that are functions of sample extremes. The bootstrap is usually appropriate for statistics from regression analysis – means, variances, coefficient estimates, and correlation coefficients. It also works reasonably well for medians and quartiles, and other such statistics. See the references in `boot::boot`.

1.9 Organizing and Managing Work, and Tools That Can Assist

Each R session starts in a specific *working directory*, which can be changed using the command `setwd()`, or the equivalent menu item. It can be a challenge to keep track of the resources – R packages, other software, other internet resources, relevant publications, other data – that bear on the task. Work will typically break down into several separate subtasks, with occasional need to move between them. Analyses need to be documented, with a description that may become part of a report or paper.

Full advantage should then be taken of tools that can help remove complexity from the analyst's mind or notebook and place it in the external world. The tools now noted can be classified, broadly, as either *integrated development environments* (IDEs), or *graphical user interfaces* (GUIs). R binaries come with a very basic GUI.

As an alternative to the R GUI that is supplied with R binaries, there are several GUIs that provide, also, graphical and analysis abilities. The web page `https://r4stats.com/` lists and compares a number of the possibilities. Look under Articles | Software Reviews | r-gui-comparison.

Especially for novices or infrequent users of R, a GUI interface can be helpful for handling data input, for creating simple graphs, for simple tabulation and summarization, and for fitting standard models. The balance of preference is likely to change in favor of the command line as familiarity with R increases.

Menu and command line modes of use can be mixed. for inspection and/or modification and/or for audit trail purposes. The user can examine the help page for the relevant function(s), modify the code as required, and reexecute it. For ease of presentation, our discussion will usually assume use of the command line, either directly, or from an editor window in a GUI or IDE.

The RStudio Integrated Development Environment

Once an R user moves from simple exercises in typing code at the command line to serious work with R, workspace management can be a challenge. For managing work with R, we recommend the highly rated RStudio IDE (go to `www.rstudio.com`). RStudio is designed to organize work by *projects*. Notwithstanding its name, the abilities available in RStudio now extend to working with languages other than R.

The RStudio IDE has extensive features that assist with the following.

- The organization of work into projects. Moving to a new project will at the same time change the working directory to that for the new project.
- A GUI for handling a wide range of tasks that it is often most convenient to initiate from the menu.
- Maintaining a record of files that have been accessed from RStudio, of help pages accessed, and of plots. The record of files is maintained from one session of a project to the next.
- The editing, maintenance, and display of code files.
- Abilities that assist reproducible reporting, using the *knitr* package for processing file formats that include code and code markup that specifies how the code is to be used and processed. Currently, most of the attention is on R Markdown and Sweave. Subsection 1.9.1 has further details.
- The development and maintenance of R packages.

Click on View | Show Tutorial to be taken to extensive interactive R-related tutorial material, powered by the *learnr* package.

RStudio has very extensive web-based documentation. Within the R main menu panel, click on Help | RStudio Docs to go to links to a wide range of online resources. The RStudio website has, additionally, extensive help on getting started with R.

Among alternatives to RStudio, note the ESS interface to Emacs (`http://ess.r-project.org/`), aimed at advanced users who are comfortable working with the Emacs editor. The R interface is one of several interfaces to different language or statistical package environments.

1.9.1 Reproducible Reporting – the knitr Package

The R package *knitr* has extensive abilities that allow the mixing of text and R code for automatic report generation. There has been heavy reliance on its abilities in the preparation of this text.

The R code chunks are embedded within markup that includes options to control the display of code and of any computer output. When suitably processed, a document is generated that contains the text, and the specified combination of R code and computer output. The functionality of *knitr* is automatically available, via a GUI interface, to RStudio users.

There are several different types of document where markup code can be used to control how text and other document features will appear after processing for printing. Sweave, used for the present text, is LaTeX with R markup added. R Markdown, which is Markdown with a similar style of markup added, is much simpler to learn and use. It is widely used for preparation of R-related documents and texts. Output alternatives are PDF, or HTML, or Word.

A short R Markdown document that introductory help details can be created from the File menu on the main RStudio panel. Click on New File | R Markdown. This will display a skeleton R Markdown document that can be edited as required, or processed as it stands. Clicking on the **Knit** button will generate a document that includes text as well as output from any embedded R code chunks. Note also the reference material available by clicking on Markdown Quick Reference under Help on the R main menu panel.

1.10 The Changing Environment for Data Analysis

This is a time when new and rich sources of data abound, with new ways to extract meaning from the available data. The use of open databases has been crucial to progress in such areas as earthquake science, the study of viruses and vaccines, modeling of epidemics, and climate science. In molecular biology, freely accessible databases have played a pivotal role in the technology that allowed a much more effective response to the COVID-19 pandemic than would have been possible two decades earlier. This sharing of data and skills, and use of modern technology, also helps in the critique of what has been published earlier.

There remain too many areas that, because potential gains are less obvious, have not put in place measures that ensure open access to the original data on which reported results are based. Data should, unless there are strong countervailing confidentiality reasons, be available both for other researchers to check and for uses that extend beyond the individual paper. A published result attracts greater confidence if it has been checked out over multiple datasets where a comparable pattern of response would be expected. Multiple datasets may together allow investigation of questions that individual datasets cannot on their own address. Meta-analyses, or systematic reviews that aim to bring together results of a range of studies that bear on the same issue, can be really effective only if carried out with access to the original data.

1.10.1 Models and Machine Learning

The models described in this chapter have had, to a varying extent, a theoretical motivation. The tree-based models that are the subject of Chapter 8 have, by contrast, a largely algorithmic motivation. Their use, and checks to examine whether they are serving their intended purpose, do, however, involve a modeling of the processes involved. The limited assumptions made are important. Tree-based models have been widely used in "machine learning".

The Limits of Current Machine Learning Systems

In an era when new and rich data sources abound, there is more need than ever for tools and approaches that will assist in critical evaluation both of the data and of consequent analyses. Automation of numerical computations makes obvious sense; it frees the analyst to focus on those parts of the exercise that really do require conscious attention. Can machines extend their role beyond this? Can they acquire the skills needed to do the job of a skilled data analyst, as the term *machine learning* (or, more recently, *deep learning*) might seem to suggest?

Machine learning approaches have been very successful in, for example, the creation of automated guidance systems, and in robotics. These are, in key respects, highly automated statistical processing machines. They take large amounts of often noisy data from their sensors, then using that data as a basis for action. Extreme care is needed to avoid or reduce the risk of faults in the data inputs or in the data processing that have an immediate and obvious result. Automated aircraft guidance systems have been, for the most part, extraordinarily successful. Two Boeing 737 Max 8 crashes in 2019, with a total of 346 deaths, tell a story of human failure to take meticulous care in moving such a system to a new context.[14]

When machine learning algorithms extend their reach into social, business, and government decision making, very different types of feedback issues come into play. In contrast to automated guidance systems, there may be little or no direct feedback that can be used to check on data or analysis inadequacies. Consider, in this connection, systems that make judgments on job applicants, on rehiring and promotion, on the risk that prisoners will reoffend, on loan applications, on hedge fund investments, and on much more besides.

Issues of this type, for systems currently in place, are documented at length in O'Neil (2016, *Weapons of Math Destruction*). O'Neil cites the example of a teacher who was fired because of a low score from an automated rating system. The reason was, apparently, that under her tutelage the reading scores of her incoming fifth graders had not progressed from the inflated levels that they had been given, at a feeder school, at the previous year's end. Automated systems must, to be effective, allow room for the human ability to step back and reflect, to learn from failures, and to correct mistakes. As O'Neil (2016) comments:

> ... it's not enough to just know how to run a black box algorithm. You actually need to know how and why it works, so that when it doesn't work, you can adjust.

"Interpretable machine learning" is designed to address such challenges. See, for example, Rudin et al. (2022).

Traps in Big Data Analysis

Primary interest may be in accurate prediction. Or interest may be in the drivers of model predictions. In a study of the effectiveness of seatbelts and airbags reducing

[14] `https://en.wikipedia.org/wiki/Boeing_737_MAX#cite_note-Leap-228`, (2023-2-7).

fatalities in vehicle accidents, the interest is in the factors – seatbelt use, airbag deployment, and other factors that may influence survival. In the various approaches that have been used to predict flu trends, a primary aim has been accurate prediction. The story of Google Flu Trends highlights the importance of attention to the drivers, even where the chief interest is in prediction.

Google Flu Trends was launched in 2008 and updated in 2009, with the aim of using Google search queries to make accurate and timely prediction of flu outbreaks. The account that now follows is based on the Lazer et al. (2014) article "The parable of Google Flu: Traps in big data analysis."

In early 2010 the algorithm predicted an outbreak in the mid-Atlantic region of the United States two weeks in advance of official sources. Thereafter, until the publication of estimates ceased in 2013, the system consistently overestimated flu prevalence. In February 2013, the system made headlines by over-predicting doctor visits for influenza-like illness by a factor of more than two. The methodology had large ad hoc elements, and was not taking advantage of time series structure in the data, resulting in a performance that was inferior to that of forward projection methods that used Center for Disease Control data. Google shut down the prediction function in 2015. Lazer et al. (2014) use this history as a warning they term "Big data hubris":

> Big data hubris is the often implicit assumption that big data are a substitute for, rather than a supplement to, traditional data collection and analysis. ... quantity of data does not mean that one can ignore foundational issues of measurement, construct validity and reliability, and dependencies among data.

The insights that informed more conventional approaches can be incorporated into algorithms in the style of Google Flu Trends, as argued in Guo et al. (2021).

Of Mice and Machine Learning – Missing Data Values

Missing data, noted earlier in Subsection 1.1.3, are a persistent nuisance to the data analyst. A version of *Multiple Imputation* is the strategy that is usually preferred when some observations are incomplete. The `Amelia` and `mice` packages both contain a number of functions for this purpose. See further Section 9.8.

A number of machine learning algorithms have been proposed recently to tackle missing data problems as well. Wang et al. (2021) carried out an extensive and carefully conducted simulation comparison of several popular and promising deep learning algorithms with two of the `mice` functions, one based on classification and regression trees, and the other based on random forests. The simulation study was based on repeated removal of swaths of a large survey. The findings of the study indicate that the deep learning algorithms are much faster than the functions in `mice`. Also, for the goal of predicting a particular missing value, the deep learning algorithms possess some advantage. However, the accuracy of repeated-sampling properties of the estimates (i.e., bias and variance) based on `mice` turn out to be vastly superior to those of the deep learning algorithms. Code and data for this study can be found at `https://github.com/zhenhua-wang/MissingData_DL`.

On R resources for multiple imputation, and helpful references, see Sections 9.7 and 9.8. Sangari and Ray (2021) give an overview of studies that compare imputation methods, do a comparison of their own, and provide helpful brief summary details of the methods that are compared.

Humans Are Not Good Intuitive Statisticians

While the human mind has remarkable intuitive abilities (consider the ability, without apparent effort, to recognize a familiar face), it is not a good intuitive statistician. Kahneman's ground-breaking book (Kahneman, 2013) on human judgment and decision making argues the case at length. Hence the need for training, and especially for training in forms of critical scrutiny that will help analysts to recognize and learn from their mistakes.

The Yule–Simpson "paradox," discussed in Subsection 1.2.7, is one of a number of traps for overly simplistic use of data that highlight the limits of untrained human intuition. Smith (2014) gives a number of examples from the public sphere. The traps that such paradoxes set for data analysis results can readily get built into black box automated systems, where there may be no ready way either to discover how the black box reached apparently faulty conclusions, or to get attention to problems that have been identified.

Disturbingly often, the careful examination of published analyses reveals serious flaws. Over the course of the COVID-19 pandemic, a number of papers have been published which have a focus on matters of strong public interest. They attracted critical expert scrutiny and were quickly withdrawn, though not before they had fed viral online media activity, exacerbating a COVID-19 misinformation crisis. An example is a June 2021 paper in *Vaccines*, titled "The safety of COVID-19 vaccinations – We should rethink the policy." Among other issues, it treated reports of death from any cause following vaccination as attributable to COVID-19, and took data on benefits from a study of a different population that examined deaths over a six-week period only, with no adjustment for the different age distributions.[15]

Researchers who wish to focus on the subject-specific aspects of their work may find close attention to the statistical methodology an annoying diversion. There is no good way to escape those challenges. Difficulties arise when, as often, research institutions have not made effective provision for access to high-quality statistical advice. Our hope is that this text will be a help along the way.

1.10.2 Replicability Is the Definitive Check

Where a total study is independently repeated, we will use the terms *replicate* and *replicability*. These are used in preference to the terms *reproduce* and *reproducibility* that in some literature relates to the reproducing of the statistical analysis.

Statistical methodology, and scientific processes more generally, have to be justified by their effectiveness in answering questions of interest. Their effectiveness

[15] See `www.bmj.com/content/374/bmj.n1726` (2022-02-24) for commentary.

can and should be open to empirical investigation. The critical test for laboratory science is replicability – are other scientists able to reproduce the results?

To What Extent Is Published Work Replicable? What Is the Evidence?

In important areas of laboratory science, worrying evidence has emerged that suggests that a majority of published results are not replicable. In one widely quoted case (Begley and Ellis, 2012), scientists from the bio-pharmaceutical company Amgen who attempted to reproduce 53 "landmark" cancer studies were successful in six cases only. The main issues appear to have been with faults in laboratory procedure and in statistical analysis (Begley, 2013). Among other such reports from attempts by industry scientists to reproduce published work see, for example, Prinz et al. (2011), where results were marginally more encouraging.

How has this happened? Journal editors, and the scientific community at large, have fallen for the seductive notion that the statistical analysis of data, generated at one time and in one laboratory and leading to a suitably small p-value, is an effective replacement for the more stringent requirement that other scientists should reproduce the reported results.

Some Major Replication Studies

Concerns raised by the Begley and Ellis paper, and by other reports that point in the same direction, have been the impetus for several systematic attempts to replicate published results. Such studies are important for the light they shed on the interplay between statistical analysis issues (and especially on the role of p-values) and issues that relate to the funding, planning, executing, and reporting of experimental studies.

Other replication studies, looking at studies more generally, have shown a much higher failure rate. The "Reproducibility: Psychology" project replicated 97 studies, published in 2008 in one of three journals. Using a simplistic $p \leq 0.05$, around 40 percent of the studies were successfully reproduced. See Open Science Collaboration (2015). Data and R code are available from `https://osf.io/fgjvw/`.

The median Cohen's `d` effect size for the 43 cognitive psychology papers dropped from 1.16 in the original to 0.52 in the replicate. For social psychology (54 papers), the drop was from 0.64 to 0.15. For the 47 studies with an original effect size of 0.5 or less, the median was 0.044, with a mean of 0.072. Unless features of an individual study can be identified that set it apart, an individual researcher who tries to replicate such a study might expect, on average, a difference of similar magnitude from that in the original study. Exercise 3.17f in Chapter 3 pursues further the analysis of data where the original effect sizes were 0.5 or less.

In an article that is primarily about the replicability of laboratory experiments in economics, Camerer et al. (2016) report on two studies on the replicability of macroeconomic studies, from 1986 and 2006. Only 13 percent and 23 percent, respectively, of original results were replicable, even when the original data and code were available.

Replicability in Preclinical Cancer Research

A $1.3 million grant from the Laura and John Arnold Foundation funded an exercise, reported in Rodgers and Collings (2021), that aimed to replicate the 53 "most impactful" preclinical cancer biology studies published over 2010–2012. In the end, 50 experiments from 23 papers were repeated.[16] In 92 percent of the completed experiments, replication effect sizes were smaller than the original, with the median effect size 85 percent smaller than reported for the original experiment. Barriers to repeating experiments included shortcomings in documentation of the original methodology; failures of transparency in original findings and protocols; failures to share original data, reagents, and other materials; and methodological challenges encountered during the execution of the replication experiments. These challenges meant that only 50 of the planned 193 replication experiments were able to proceed. The challenge to established practices has generated controversy in the research community, and highlighted questions on just what constitutes replication.[17]

Studies Where There May Be Strong Social Influences

Especially where there may be strong social influences at play, it can be important to check the extent to which results generalize to different countries and cultures. The Klein et al. (2014) study was specifically designed to check the extent to which results from 13 widely quoted "classic and contemporary psychology studies could be reproduced across different samples and settings internationally." Results were obtained, for each of the 13 studies, from 36 independent samples, 25 from the United States and 13 from elsewhere, with a total of 6344 subjects participating. Plots showed a relatively similar pattern of between study variation for all 13 studies. Replications were successful for 10 of the 13 studies, weakly successful in one case, and unsuccessful in two cases. The data are available online (at `https://osf.io/wx7ck/?view_only=`). See also Yong (2012).

The Scientific Study of Scientific Processes

Results from replication studies are important in establishing the extent to which publications (even in very reputable journals) can be relied upon. They provide important evidence, in the areas covered, on the extent of problems with current scientific processes.

Replicability demands can and should go hand in hand with the fostering of informed imaginative exploration and insight. Imaginative exploration provides necessary leads into new areas of work and investigation, but requires checks against allowing an unrestrained imagination to take research down blind alleys.

The issues that these studies raise bear directly on the aims that we have set for this text. Failures in experimental design and in laboratory procedure all too frequently compromise the trustworthiness of the data used for analysis. While

[16] See the web link Errington (2021), and the papers Errington et al. (2021), and Rodgers and Collings (2021).

[17] Nosek and Errington (2020).

experimental design and more general data collection issues are not a particular focus of this text, we do want to emphasize their importance.

The package *ReplicationSuccess* has functionality that is designed to assist in planning and analysing replication studies.[18]

A key component of replicability is the reproducibility of the analysis, whether with the data used for the published paper, or with new data. The technology that is now available leaves little excuse for failure to attend both to the maintenance of data records through time, and to reproducible reporting.

Would Lowering the p-Value Threshold Help

There have in some quarters been calls to lower the p-value significance threshold to $\alpha = 0.005$ (Benjamin et al., 2018). Ioannidis (2018) argues that such a move should be considered only as a temporary recourse, put in place until such time as more durable solutions emerge. A different threshold, perhaps as low as 10^{-6}, is suggested for observational studies. Especially for large studies, it is important to report estimated effect sizes. An estimated effect size of 0.1 gives, for a one-sample t-test with n=800, a p-value that is a little under 0.005.

Other types of summary statistic, such as Bayes Factors, should be used where appropriate. For Bayes Factors, details of the prior that was assumed would be an essential accompaniment. Given the large element of individual judgment involved in the choice of a prior, it is hard to see how Bayes Factors or other such statistics could readily be a complete replacement for p-values. Irrespective of changes that may be made to reporting protocols, there is a clear need for greater attention to statistical literacy as part of research training.

Peer Review at the Study Planning Stage

Starting in 2013, the Center for Open Science (see `http://cos.io/rr`) has facilitated the submission of registered reports (RRs) for review prior to observing study outcomes, with more than 300 journals now offering this route to publication. As noted on the COS website (`http://cos.io/rr`):

> Manuscripts that survive pre-study peer review receive an in-principle acceptance that will not be revoked based on the outcomes, but only on failings of quality assurance, following through on the registered protocol, or unresolvable problems in reporting clarity or style.

Results that appear in published work provide later researchers with starting points on which to build. They may also have an important role in drawing attention to lines of inquiry that have been pursued earlier and have lead nowhere.

Scheel et al. (2021) describe a comparison between 71 papers that had used the RR mechanism as of November 2018 with a random sample of 152 hypothesis-testing studies from the standard literature in psychology. The authors found 96 percent (146/152) of "positive" results in the standard literature, as opposed to 44 percent (31/71) for RRs. This suggests strong selection effects in what appears in the published literature.

[18] Enter `vignette('ReplicationSuccess', package='ReplicationSuccess')` to see the extensive commentary in the package vignette.

1.11 Further, or Supplementary, Reading

Extensive R-related tutorial material is available online. The Learn R web page on the website `www.r-bloggers.com/` has extensive tutorial content, and includes links to content that is available elsewhere (Galili, 2015). See also **`https://r4ds.had.co.nz/`**.

Reference was made earlier to the extensive interactive R-related tutorial material, powered by the *learnr* package, which can be accessed by clicking on View | Show Tutorial on the main RStudio menu panel.

Introductions to R include Dalgaard (2008). Braun and Murdoch (2021) is an elementary introduction to the R programming language. More technical and detailed accounts of the R language include: Aphalo (2020), Chambers (2008), Matloff (2011), Wickham (2015), and Wickham (2016).

Kahneman (2013) gives important insight into human propensities for misinterpreting statistical data. O'Neil (2016) has insightful commentary on the nature and limitations of mathematical models, and on the limitations of machine learning technology in current use as a replacement for human judgement. They become, if trained on data that has inherent biases, "weapons of math destruction"! Thaler (2015) is an extended commentary on the mismatch between the decision making processes of the idealized agents of the models of classical economics (he calls these "Econs") and human agents, with serious implications for economic and social policy.

On planning experimental trials, see Robinson (2000). The detailed discussion, with detailed practical examples, has much to say that is relevant to studies more generally. See also Cox (1958).

Papers that comment on statistical presentation issues, and on deficiencies in the published literature, include Andersen (1990), Maindonald (1992), Wilkinson and Task Force on Statistical Inference (1999), and Allison et al. (2016). On errors in the interpretation of p-values, see Greenland et al. (2016), and the extensive list of references given in that paper. Wilkinson and Task Force on Statistical Inference (1999) makes helpful comments on the planning of data analysis, on the role of exploratory data analysis, and more.

On formal hypothesis testing, see Gigerenzer (1998) and Wilkinson and Task Force on Statistical Inference (1999). The misuse of p-values has been a strong focus in the debate over reproducibility. Greenland et al. (2016) make the point that p-values test the total context in which work has been undertaken. The role of failures in experimental design and execution has not received the same level of attention in the scientific literature as issues that relate to the use and meaning of p-values.

Ioannidis (2005) has been a key reference in the debate on reproducibility. Changes are needed in the conduct of major areas of science – in publication, in management, and in reward systems. Nosek et al. (2015) and Mogil and Macleod (2017) make detailed proposals. Allison et al. (2016) note common errors. They discuss roadblocks to getting corrections or retractions published. Button et al. (2013) discuss in detail the issues posed by the use of small under-powered studies. They note the huge transformation in the reliability of gene association studies that has resulted from the collaboration of groups of researchers to increase the sample size and minimize the labor and resource input of any one contributor.

Gigerenzer et al. (1989) discuss the history that has led to differences in styles and approaches to inference in different area of statistical application. Wonnacott and Wonnacott (1990) have an elementary account of Bayesian Methodology. See also Gelman et al. (2003). Gigerenzer (2002) demonstrates the use of Bayesian arguments in several important practical contexts, including AIDS testing and screening for breast cancer. Chapters 3 and later of Ellenberg (2015) are largely occupied with statistical issues, using real-world examples as points of departure. Note, in particular, Part II, titled "Inference," moving finally to Bayesian inference. Kass and Raftery (1993) remains an informative source of comment on the history of Bayes Factors, and on their use and interpretation.

Books and papers that set out principles of good graphics include Robbins (2012). See also the imaginative uses of R's graphical abilities that are demonstrated in Murrell (2011). Chang (2013) is a helpful resource for *ggplot2*. Bowman et al. (2019) discuss aspects of graphical presentation that are too easily ignored.

1.12 Exercises

1.1. The data frame `DAAG::orings` has details of damage that had occurred in US space shuttle launches prior to the disastrous *Challenger* launch of January 28, 1986. Observations in rows 1, 2, 4, 11, 13, and 18 were shown in the prelaunch charts used in deciding whether to proceed with the launch, with remaining rows omitted.

Compare plots of `Total` incidents against `Temperature`: (i) including only the observations shown in the prelaunch charts; and (ii) using all rows of data. What did the full set of data strongly suggest that was less clear from the plot that showed only the selected rows?

1.2. For the purposes of the exercises that follow, type `?sample` at the R command line, and take a careful look at the help page that appears. Note in particular the arguments `size` and `replace`.

   a. Write out and execute the code required to select a random sample of 25 numbers, *with replacement*, from the numbers from 100 through 200.
   b. Write and execute code that randomly assigns 30 patient labels in such a way that 20 patients are assigned to a treatment group, and 10 patients are to a control group.
   c. Suppose 30 patients are to be assigned randomly to treatment, control and placebo groups. Write and execute code that randomly assigns 10 patient labels to each of the three groups.

1.3. For the data frame `DAAG::possum`

   a. Use the function `str()` to get information on each of the columns.
   b. Using the function `complete.cases()`, determine the rows in which one or more values is missing. Print those rows. In which columns do the missing values appear?

1.4. The following plots four different transformations for the columns `brain` and `body` in the `Animals` dataset. What different aspects of the data do these different graphs emphasize? Consider the effect on low values of the variables, as contrasted with the effect on high values.

```
Animals <- MASS::Animals
manyMals <- rbind(Animals, sqrt(Animals), Animals^0.1, log(Animals))
manyMals$transgp <- rep(c("Untransformed", "Square root transform",
  "Power transform, lambda=0.1", "log transform"),
rep(nrow(Animals),4))
manyMals$transgp <- with(manyMals, factor(transgp, levels=unique(transgp)))
lattice::xyplot(brain~body|transgp, data=manyMals,
  scales=list(relation='free'), layout=c(2,2))
```

1.5. Calculate the following correlations:

```
with(Animals, c(cor(brain,body), cor(brain,body, method="spearman")))
with(Animals, c(cor(log(brain),log(body)),
  cor(log(brain),log(body), method="spearman")))
```

Comment on the different results. Which is the most appropriate measure?

1.6. Use the function `abbreviate()` to obtain six-character abbreviations for the row names in the data frame `DAAG::cottonworkers`. Plot `survey1889` against `census1886`, and plot `avwage*survey1889` against `avwage*census1886`, in each case using the six-letter abbreviations to label the points. What indications, different from those of the 1886 survey data, do the 1886 census data give of the contributions of the different classes of worker to the overall wage bill?

1.7. Plot a histogram of the `earconch` measurements for the `DAAG::possum` data. The distribution should appear *bimodal* (two peaks). This is a simple indication of clustering, possibly due to sex differences. Obtain side-by-side boxplots of the male and female `earconch` measurements. How do these measurement distributions differ? Can you predict what the corresponding histograms would look like? Plot them to check your answer.

1.8. For the data frame `DAAG::ais`, draw graphs that show how the values of the hematological measures (red cell count, hemoglobin concentration, hematocrit, white cell count, and plasma ferritin concentration) vary with the sport and sex of the athlete.

1.9. In the data frame `DAAG::cuckoohosts`, column names with first letter `c` refer to cuckoos, while names starting with `h` refer to hosts. Plot `clength` against `cbreadth`, and `hlength` against `hbreadth`, all on the same graph and using different colors to distinguish points for the cuckoo eggs from points for the host eggs. Join the two points that relate to the same host species with a line. What does a line that is long, relative to other lines, imply? Code that you may wish to use or adapt is:

```
usableDF <- DAAG::cuckoohosts[c(1:6,8),]
nr <- nrow(usableDF)
with(usableDF, {
  plot(c(clength, hlength), c(cbreadth, hbreadth), col=rep(1:2,c(nr,nr)))
  for(i in 1:nr)lines(c(clength[i], hlength[i]), c(cbreadth[i], hbreadth[i]))
  text(hlength, hbreadth, abbreviate(rownames(usableDF),8), pos=c(2,4,2,1,2,4,2))
})
```

1.10. The following uses a graph to illustrate least squares estimation of the mean:

```
## Take a random sample of 100 values from the normal distribution
x <- rnorm(100, mean=3, sd=5)
(xbar <- mean(x))
## Plot, against `xbar`, the sum of squared deviations from `xbar`
lsfun <- function(xbar) apply(outer(x, xbar, "-")^2, 2, sum)
curve(lsfun, from=xbar-0.01, to=xbar+0.01)
```

Write code that repeats the calculations 500 times, storing the sample means in a vector `avs` and the sample medians in a vector `meds`. Create the plot:

```
boxplot(avs, meds, horizontal=T)
```

Interpret what you see in light of what Subsection 1.4.4 had to say about the sampling distribution of the median.

1.11. In the data frame `DAAG::nswdemo`, plot `re78` (1978 income) against `re75` (1975 income). What features of the plot call for attention, if the interest is in finding a relationship?

a. Restricting attention to observations for which both `re78` and `re75` are nonzero, plot `log(re78)` against `log(re75)`, and fit a trend curve. Additionally, fit a regression line to the plot. Does the regression line accurately describe the relationship? In what respects is it deficient?
b. Now examine the diagnostic plot that is obtained by using `plot()` with the regression object as parameter. What further light does this shed on the regression line model?

1.12. The `MASS::galaxies` data frame gives speeds of 82 galaxies (see the help file and the references listed there for more information). Construct a density plot for these data. Is the distribution strongly skewed? Is there evidence of clustering?

1.13. Figure 1.5B plotted brain weight (units of 100 g) versus body weight (units of 100 kg), for 28 animals, using logarithmic scales. Copy the plot and use a ruler or other straight edge to draw a line through the main body of points. Use the ratio of vertical to horizontal distance, between the points where the line intersects the left and right boundaries of the plotting region, to estimate the slope of the line. The slope can be interpreted as the ratio between the relative rate of increase of brain weight, and that for body weight. For a body weight increase of 5 percent (this counts for this purpose as a small increase), what increase might be expected in brain weight? Compare the line that you have drawn with the regression line for `log(brain)` on `log(body)`.

1.14. An experimenter intends to arrange experimental plots in four blocks. In each block there are seven plots, one for each of seven treatments. Use the function `sample()` to find four random permutations (i.e., orderings or arrangements) of the numbers 1 to 7 that will be used, one set in each block, to make the assignments of treatments to plots.

1.15. The following are total numbers of aberrant crypt foci (abnormal growths in the colon) observed in seven rats that had been administered a single dose of the carcinogen azoxymethane and sacrificed after six weeks (thanks to Ranjana Bird, Faculty of Human Ecology, University of Manitoba for use of these data):

```
87 53 72 90 78 85 83
```

Calculate the sample mean and variance. Is the Poisson model appropriate? To investigate how the sample variance and sample mean differ under the Poisson assumption, repeat the following simulation experiment several times:

```
x <- rpois(7, 78.3)
mean(x); var(x)
```

1.16. The following simulates 100 normal random variates from each of (i) a normal distribution and t-distributions with (ii) four degrees of freedom and (iii) two degrees of freedom. Run the code several times, on each occasion counting the number of points that appear out beyond the whiskers in each of the two boxplots.

```
nvals100 <- rnorm(100)
heavytail <- rt(100, df = 4)
veryheavytail <- rt(100, df = 2)
boxplot(nvals100, heavytail, veryheavytail, horizontal=TRUE)
```

Comment on the differences between the three distributions in the number of points that are tagged as potential outliers.

1.17. Use `t.test()` to test the null hypothesis that the mean is 0 for random samples of 10 values from a normal distribution:

a. with mean 0 and standard deviation 2;
b. with mean 1.5 and standard deviation 2.

Finally, write a function that generates a random sample of n numbers from a normal distribution with mean μ and standard deviation 1, and returns the p-value for the test that the mean is 0.

1.18. Use the function that was created in Exercise 1.17 to generate 50 independent p-values, all with a sample size $n = 10$ and with mean $\mu = 0$. Use `qqplot()`, with the argument setting `x = qunif(ppoints(50))`, to compare the distribution of the p-values with that of a uniform random variable, on the interval [0, 1]. Comment on the plot.

1.19. The following function draws, when called with `n=1000`, 10 boxplots of random samples of 1000 from a normal distribution, and ten boxplots of random samples of 1000 from a t-distribution with seven degrees of freedom:

```
boxdists <- function(n=1000, times=10){
  df <- data.frame(normal=rnorm(n*times), t=rt(n*times, 7),
  sampnum <- rep(1:times, rep(n,times)))
  lattice::bwplot(sampnum ~ normal+t, data=df, outer=TRUE, xlab="",
                  horizontal=T)
}
```

Run the function, first with `n=1000`, and then with `n=200`. Refer back to the Subsection 1.4.2 note on heavy-tailed distributions, and comment on the different numbers of points that are flagged as possible outliers.

1.20. Run the following code:

```
a <- 1
form <- ~rchisq(1000,1)^a+rchisq(1000,25)^a+rchisq(1000,500)^a
lattice::qqmath(form, scales=list(relation="free"), outer=TRUE)
```

Repeat, first with `a = 0.5`, and then with `a = 0.33`. Which choice of `a` appears to give the best approximation to a normal distribution?

1.21. The following code generates random normal numbers with a sequential dependence structure:

```
y <- rnorm(51)
ydep <- y1[-1] + y1[-51]
acf(y)     # acf plots `autocorrelation function'(see Chapter 6)
acf(ydep)
```

Repeat this several times. There should be no consistent pattern in the acf plot for different random samples `y`, and a fairly consistent pattern in the acf plot for `ycor` that reflects the correlation that is introduced by adding to each value of `y` the next value in the sequence.

1.22. Assuming that the variability in egg length in the cuckoo eggs data is the same for all host birds, obtain an estimate of the pooled standard deviation as a way of summarizing this variability. [Hint: Remember to divide the appropriate sums of squares by the number of degrees of freedom remaining after estimating the six different means.]

1.23. Write a function that simulates simple linear regression data from the model

$$y = 2 + 3x + \varepsilon,$$

where the noise terms are independent normal random variables with mean 0 and variance 1.

Using the function, simulate two samples of size 10. Consider two designs: First, assume that the x-values are independent uniform variates on the interval $[-1, 1]$; second, assume that half of the x-values are -1s, and the remainder are 1s. In each case, compute slope estimates, standard error estimates and estimates of the noise standard deviation. What are the advantages and disadvantages of each type of design?

1.24. * The following code can be used to obtain and plot, for a specific choice of `eff` and `N`, a set of simulated p-values as in Figure 1.20 in Subsection 1.3.6:

```
ptFun <- function(x,N)pt(sqrt(N)*mean(x)/sd(x), df=N-1, lower.tail=FALSE)
simStat <- function(eff=.4, N=10, nrep=200, FUN)
   array(rnorm(n=N*nrep*length(eff), mean=eff), dim=c(length(eff),nrep,N)) |>
     apply(2:1, FUN, N=N)
pval <- simStat(eff=.4, N=10, nrep=200, FUN=ptFun)
# Suggest a power transform that makes the distribution more symmetric
car::powerTransform(pval)  # See Subsection 2.5.6
labx <- c(0.0001, 0.001, 0.005, 0.01, 0.05, 0.1, 0.25)
bwplot(~I(pval^0.2), scales=list(x=list(at=labx^0.2, labels=paste(labx))),
       xlab=expression("P-value (scale is "*p^{0.2}*")") )
```

a. Use the following to compare the distribution from direct use of `simStat()` with that from the data frame `df200` that was created in Subsection 1.3.6:

```
pvalDF <- subset(df200, effsize==0.4 & N==10)$stat
plot(sort(pval^0.2), sort(pvalDF^0.2))
abline(0,1)
```

Compare with the plot of sort(pval) against sort(pvalDF). Which plot is more useful, and why?

b. Repeat the calculations using eff2stat() with the argument 'FUN' set to calculate two-sided p-values. (In the argument FUN, replace mean(x) by abs(mean(x))) and double the value returned by pt().)

c. Repeat with 'FUN' set to simulate sample effect sizes, thus:

```
## Estimated effect sizes: Set `FUN=effFun` in the call to `eff2stat()`
effFun <- function(x,N)mean(x)/sd(x)
  # Try: `labx <- ((-1):6)/2`; `at = log(labx)`; `v = log(labx)
## NB also, Bayes Factors: Set `FUN=BFfun` in the call to `eff2stat()`
BFfun <- function(x,N)BayesFactor::ttest.tstat(sqrt(N)*mean(x)/sd(x), n1=N,
                                               simple=T)
  # A few very large Bayes Factors are likely to dominate the plots
```

d. Create an equivalent of effFun() that returns t-statistics. For one combination of eff and N, plot the 100 simulated values.

1.25. Using the data frame cars (*datasets*), plot dist (i.e., stopping distance) versus speed. Fit and plot the a line. Then try fitting and plotting a quadratic curve. Does the quadratic curve give a useful improvement to the fit? [Readers who have studied the relevant physics might develop a model for the change in stopping distance with speed, and check the data against this model.]

1.26. The distance that a body, starting at rest, falls under gravity in t seconds is well approximated as $d = \frac{1}{2}gt^2$, where $g \simeq 9.8\,\text{m.s}^{-2}$. The equation can be modified to take account of the effects of air resistance, which will vary with barometric pressure and other atmospheric conditions. How useful will a time–distance relationship for a human dummy that falls from a height of some thousands of meters be for predicting the time–distance relationship for another dummy, or for a human, falling at another time from a similar height? How is the challenge similar to, and how different from, the use of the lawn roller data of Subsection 1.5.1 for such indications as it can provide that are relevant to another time and place? (Humans have very occasionally survived falls from such heights. See www.greenharbor.com/fffolder/ffresearch.html.)

1.27. The dataset MPV::radon gives percentages of radon released when radon-enriched water was used in showers with differently sized orifices. The temperatures were:

```
(degC <- setNames(c(21,30,38,46),paste('rep',1:4)) )
```

```
rep 1 rep 2 rep 3 rep 4
   21    30    38    46
```

a. Use the following code to manipulate the data into the form required and plot the observations against temperature for each orifice diameter:

```
radonC <- tidyr::pivot_longer(MPV::radon, names_to='key',
                     cols=names(degC), values_to='percent')
radonC$temp <- degC[radonC$key]
lattice::xyplot(percent ~ temp|factor(diameter), data = radonC)
```

(On *tidyr* and other *tidyverse* packages, see Subsection A.2.5.)

b. What common pattern do you observe in each of the six time plots? What does this tell you about the measurements?

c. A clearer pattern can be obtained by plotting the residuals or scaled residuals. The latter are obtained by subtracting the treatment means and then dividing by the treatment standard deviations, as in

```
matplot(scale(t(MPV::radon[,-1])), type="l", ylab="scaled residuals")
```

Execute this code and then modify it to obtain the time plots of the raw residuals.

d. The raw residuals can be calculated by applying `aggregate()` to the case-by-variable form of the data obtained in part (a):

```
radon.res <- aggregate(percent ~ diameter, data = radonC, FUN = scale,
   scale = FALSE)
```

The technique of part (a) involving the `pivot_longer()` function yields the residual time plots. Modify the code above appropriately to obtain the scaled residual time plots.

1.28. * In the unusual case where the variance is known, the function `AIC()` defines the AIC statistic for normal theory regression models as:

$$\text{AIC} = \frac{\text{RSS}}{\sigma^2} + 2p + \text{const}, \quad \text{where} \quad \text{const} = n(1 + \log(2\pi)).$$

Show that, if σ^2 is replaced by the maximum likelihood estimate $\frac{\text{RSS}}{n}$, this reduces to Equation (1.5).

1.29. Conduct the following simulation experiment to verify the robustness property of the mean absolute deviation relative to the sample standard deviation and the inter-quartile range.

a. Generate 100 independent standard normal random variates using the `rnorm()` function assigning them to an object called `x`.

b. Estimate σ using `sd()`, `IQR()`, and `mad()`, using the results in Subsection 1.3.4. Observe how close each estimate is to the true value ($\sigma = 1$).

c. Now replace the first 20 observations in `x` with independent normal variates having mean 0 and standard deviation 10. Reestimate σ for this contaminated dataset using each of the three estimators. Which estimate is closest to the value 1?

d. Repeat the preceding experiment using different numbers of contaminated data points and different standard deviations.

1.30. Compare the two plots:

```
diamonds <- ggplot2::diamonds
with(diamonds, plot(carat, price, pch=16, cex=0.25))
with(diamonds, smoothScatter(carat, price))
```

Why does the first plot give the impression that the price values are truncated at the upper end, while the second plot suggests that this may not be real? Check the help page `?adjustcolor`, and repeat the first plot with the argument `col=adjustcolor('blue', alpha=0.1)`. What does this tell you that was not obvious from the first two plots?

1.31. The following function can be used to obtain the data for Figure 1.24:

```
t2BF <- function(t, n=10, rscale="medium", mu=0){
if(!(length(mu)%in%(1:2)))stop("mu must be of length 1 or 2")
if(length(mu)==1){
   BayesFactor::ttest.tstat(t=t, n1=n, rscale=rscale, simple=TRUE)} else {
    null0 <- BayesFactor::ttest.tstat(t=t, n1=n, nullInterval=mu,
                                  rscale=rscale,simple=TRUE)
alt0 <- BayesFactor::ttest.tstat(t=t, n1=n, nullInterval=mu, rscale=rscale,
                              complement=TRUE, simple=TRUE)
alt0/null0}
}
```

The following is a cut-down version of the needed calculations:

```
bfDF <- expand.grid(p=c(0.05,0.01,0.002),n=c(10,40,160))
bfDF[,'t'] <- apply(bfDF,1,function(x){qt(x['p']/2, df=x['n']-1, lower.tail=FALSE)})
bfDF[,'bf'] <- apply(bfDF,1,function(x)t2BF(t=x['t'], n=x['n'], mu=0,
                  rscale="medium"))
bfDF[,'bfw'] <- apply(bfDF,1,function(x)t2BF(t=x['t'], n=x['n'], mu=0,
                  rscale="wide"))
## Now specify a null interval
bfDF[,'bfInterval'] <- apply(bfDF,1,function(x)t2BF(t=x['t'], n=x['n'],
                  mu=c(-0.1,0.1),rscale="medium"))
bfDF[,'bfIntervalw'] <- apply(bfDF,1,function(x)t2BF(t=x['t'], n=x['n'],
                  mu=c(-0.1,0.1),rscale="wide"))
```

Comment (i) on the effect of changing from `rscale="medium"` to `rscale="wide"`, and (ii) on the effect of the change from a point null to the specific null interval that was chosen.

1.32. *The function `bayes_inference` in the *statsr* package implements, in addition to the JZS priors that are implemented in the *BayesFactor* package, the JUI (Jeffreys unit information) prior that replaces the Cauchy distribution for the mean with a normal distribution. Also, it returns Bayesian credible intervals which (unlike frequentist confidence intervals) can be interpreted as a probability that the statistic of interest lies within the interval. Try the following calculations:

```
df <- data.frame(d = with(datasets::sleep, extra[group==2] - extra[group==1]))
library(statsr)
BayesFactor::ttestBF(df$d, rscale=1/sqrt(2))  # Make default setting explicit
bayes_inference(d, type='ht', data=df, statistic='mean', method='t', null=0,
             rscale=1/sqrt(2), alternative='twosided', prior_family = "JZS")
  # Set `rscale=1/sqrt(2)` (`bayes_inference()` default is 1.0)
  # `prior_family = "JZS"` is the default
# Compare with `prior_family = "JUI"`, with default settings
bayes_inference(d, type='ht', data=df, statistic='mean', method='t',
             alternative='twosided', null=0, prior_family = "JUI")
```

a. Compare the 95 percent Bayesian credible interval that is obtained with the corresponding frequentist confidence interval. What difference has it made, to the Bayes Factor and to the Bayesian credible interval, to replace the JZS family by the JUI family?
b. Repeat the comparisons for the comparison between `horsebean` and `linseed` feeds in the `statsr:chickwts` dataset. (See the example in the help page `?statsr:chickwts`.)

2

Generalizing from Models

Statistical analysis has as a major aim the assessment of the extent to which available data support conclusions that extend beyond the circumstances that generated the data. This chapter will discuss a range of approaches and perspectives, as they apply to binary comparisons, to one-way comparisons, to contingency tables, and to linear regression. The ideas and issues considered will be important through the remainder of the text.

2.1 Model Assumptions

A common model requirement is that *error* terms are independently and identically normally distributed. This *iid* assumption involves the separate assumptions of independence, homogeneity of variance (i.e., the standard deviations of all values are the same), and normality. As was explained in Subsection 1.4.3, strict normality is, depending on the use that will be made of model results, usually unnecessary. Much of the art of statistical analysis lies in recognizing those assumptions that are important and need careful checking. Models are said to be *robust* against those assumptions that are of minor consequence.

2.1.1 Inferences Are Never Assumption Free

Subsections 1.8.1 and 1.8.2 discussed permutation test alternatives to *t*-tests, for use in situations where normality assumptions are in doubt. Rank tests are another such possibility. Contrary to what is sometimes claimed, such tests are not assumption free. Independence assumptions will be no less important than for methods that rely on normality assumptions. Consider carefully what assumptions are made, and how this may affect or limit results.

There is a tradeoff between the strength of model assumptions and the ability to find effects. Simple nonparametric approaches may assume less than can reasonably be assumed to be true. If structure in data is ignored, one risks missing insights that parametric methods might provide. Thus, with size and shape (*morphometric*) data from biological organisms, such as the animal `body` and `brain` weight data in Figure 1.5 in Subsection 1.2.3, it makes sense to check for an allometric relationship (linear on logarithmic scales) such as is common with such data.

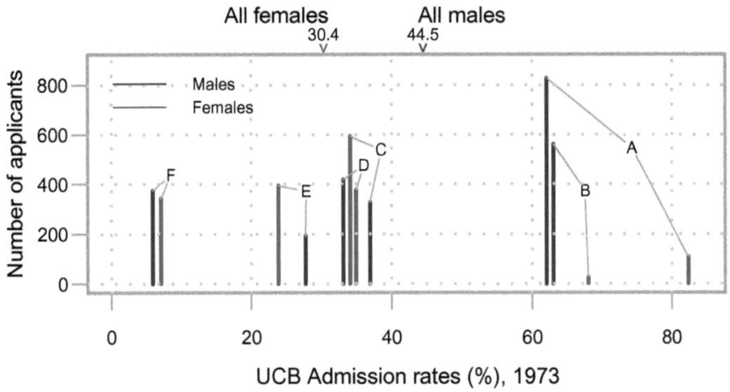

Figure 2.1 The high numbers of males (blue vertical lines) who applied to departments A and B have weighted overall male admission rates towards the high admission rates for those departments (all rates over 60 percent, both for both males and for the small numbers of female applicants). The overall female admission rate has been strongly weighted towards the low admission rates (under 40 percent, both for males and females) in departments C, D, E, and F.

2.1.2 Has Account Been Taken of All Relevant Effects?

Subsection 1.2.7 made the point that failure to account for relevant factors may seriously distort estimated effect(s) for term(s) that remain. There are implications for the conclusions that may be drawn from such standard forms of data summary as multiway tables or means. The multiway table `UCBAdmissions` (*datasets* package) provides an example. Figure 2.1 is a graphical summary.

Admission percentages, by sex, totaled across the six largest departments at the University of California at Berkeley in 1973 were (Bickel et al., 1975):

```
## Tabulate by Admit and Gender
byGender <- 100*prop.table(margin.table(UCBAdmissions, margin=1:2), margin=2)
round(byGender,1)
```

```
            Gender
Admit        Male Female
  Admitted 44.5   30.4
  Rejected 55.5   69.6
```

For individual departments, the numbers are:

```
## Admission rates, by department
pcAdmit <- 100*prop.table(UCBAdmissions, margin=2:3)["Admitted", , ]
round(pcAdmit,1)
```

```
        Dept
Gender      A    B    C    D    E    F
  Male   62.1 63.0 36.9 33.1 27.7  5.9
  Female 82.4 68.0 34.1 34.9 23.9  7.0
```

As a fraction of those who applied, females were strongly favored in department A, and males somewhat favored in departments C and E. To understand why the overall proportions favor males, it is necessary to look at the relative numbers applying in the various departments. The numbers were:

```
## Calculate totals, by department, of males & females applying
margin.table(UCBAdmissions, margin=2:3)
```

```
        Dept
Gender     A   B   C   D   E   F
  Male   825 560 325 417 191 373
  Female 108  25 593 375 393 341
```

The overall bias was due to males favoring departments where admission rates were highest. Figure 2.1, which plots admission rates against numbers of applicants, separately for males and females, uses a graph to make this point.

What question is in mind? Is the aim to compare the chances of admission for a randomly chosen female with the chances for a randomly chosen male? The relevant figure is then the overall admission rate of 30.35 percent for females, as against 44.52 percent for males. Or, is the interest in the chances of a particular student who has decided on a department? A female had a much better chance than a male in department A, while a male had a slightly better chance in departments C and E.

Here, information was available on the classifying factor on which it was necessary to condition. This will not always be the case. In any tabulation where there is large imbalance in the numbers, the possibility remains open that conditioning on another variable, possibly unobserved, would reverse or modify an observed association. See Aldrich (1995) and Simpson (1951).

In any overall analysis, the classifying (or *conditioning*) factor `Department` must be explicitly incorporated in the model. Section 5.3 demonstrates one suitable approach. See also Exercise 2.2 at the end of the chapter. The help page that can be accessed by typing `?mantelhaen.test` has further comments and examples.

2.1.3 The Limitations of Models

Comments in Tukey (1997) are apt:

- Do not assume "that we always know what in fact we never know – the exact probability structure ..."
- "No dataset is large enough to provide complete information about how it should be analyzed."

Subject area knowledge can only to a limited extent make up the deficiency.

Models require critical evaluation to determine the extent to which they give, for their intended use, valid and reliable results. We should trust only those results that have survived informed critical evaluation.

2.1.4 Use the Methodology That Best Suits the Task in Hand?

In the frequentist approach parameter values are assumed to be unknown constants, and estimates are in most contexts chosen to maximize the "likelihood." Frequentist approaches further divide into those that place a strong focus on the use of p-values and on significance testing, and those that focus on comparing likelihoods. Bayesian values treat parameter values as random variables, to be updated as new data becomes available. An approach that relies on repeated resampling from the one available sample will be the subject of Subsections 1.8.3 and 1.8.4, here treated within a frequentist framework.

The different approaches provide different sources of insight. Likelihood and Bayesian perspectives are important both in their own right, and because they can in principle provide answers to questions that p-values are often wrongly thought to answer.

2.2 t-Statistics, Binomial Proportions, and Correlations

This section will note further practical issues for one- and two-sample comparisons. An issue for two-sample comparisons is that the variances may not be equal. One-sample comparisons are commonly appropriate when the interest is in differences of paired values for each of a number n of experimental or observational units.

More generally, the interest may be in correlations between the members of the pair, as a measure of the strength of relationship, in a case where the measures are different quantities such as perhaps hours of sleep and calories consumed.

2.2.1 *One- and Two-Sample t-Tests*

The one-sample t-test was introduced in Subsection 1.6.2. The discussion that follows will now be extended to two-sample tests, noting also issues that arise for both types of test.

2.2.2 *A Two-Sample Comparison*

The dataset `DAAG::two65` has amounts of stretch for each of 21 elastic bands, 10 of which were placed in warm water (60–65 °C) for four minutes, while the other 11 were left at ambient temperature. After a wait of about 10 minutes, the amounts of stretch, under a 1.35 kg weight, were recorded. Means, standard deviations, and standard errors, for the stretch of the two sets of bands are:

```
stats2 <- sapply(DAAG::two65,
                 function(x) c(av=mean(x), sd=sd(x), n=length(x)))
pooledsd <- sqrt( sum(stats2['n',]*stats2['sd',]^2)/sum(stats2['n',]-1) )
stats2 <- setNames(c(as.vector(stats2), pooledsd),
                   c('av1','sd1','n1','av2','sd2','n2','pooledsd'))
print(stats2, digits=4)
```

```
      av1       sd1        n1       av2       sd2        n2 pooledsd
  253.500     9.925    10.000   244.091    11.734    11.000   11.470
```

The heated versus ambient difference is $\bar{x}_1 - \bar{x}_2 = 9.41$. The pooled standard deviation estimate, calculated as described in Subsection 1.3.3, is $s = 11.47$. The standard error of difference (SED) is thus:

$$\text{SED} = 10.91\sqrt{\frac{1}{10} + \frac{1}{11}} = 5.01.$$

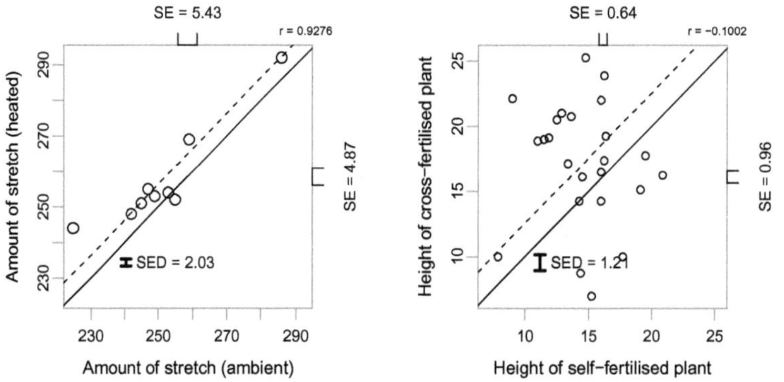

Figure 2.2 Second versus first member, for each pair. The first panel is for the ambient/heated elastic band data (**DAAG::pair65**) from Subsection 1.4.5, while the second is for Darwin's plants (**DAAG::mignonette**).

Use of the function `t.test()` gives:

```
with(DAAG::two65, t.test(heated, ambient, var.equal=TRUE))
```

```
        Two Sample t-test

data:  heated and ambient
t = 2, df = 19, p-value = 0.06
alternative hypothesis: true difference in means is not equal to 0
95 percent confidence interval:
 -0.5723 19.3905
sample estimates:
mean of x mean of y
    253.5     244.1
```

For a one-sided test, $p = 0.03$, that is, half of that just given.

This gives, on its own, weak evidence for a difference. The two-sided p-value is at the upper end of a class of results for which $p \leq 0.06$. (It makes as much sense to attach the probability 0.06 to this specific result as it does to argue that, because it is at the lower end of a class of results for which $p \geq 0.06$, it should be regarded as occurring with probability 0.94!)

When Is Pairing Helpful?

Figure 2.2 shows, for two different sets of paired data, a plot of the second member of the pair against the first. The left panel is for the paired elastic band data of Subsection 1.4.5, while the right panel (for the dataset **DAAG::mignonette**) is from Charles Darwin's experiments that compared the heights of crossed wild mignonette plants with the heights of self-fertilized plants. Plants were paired within the pots in which they were grown, with one plant on one side and one on the other.

For the paired elastic band data there is a clear correlation, and the standard error of the difference is much less than the root mean square of the two separate standard errors. For Darwin's data there is little evidence of correlation. The standard error of differences of pairs is about equal to the root mean square of the two separate standard errors. For the elastic band data, the pairing was helpful; it led to a low SED. The pairing was not helpful for Darwin's data (note that Darwin gives other datasets where the pairing was helpful, in the sense of allowing a more accurate comparison.)

If the data are paired, then the two-sample t-test corresponds to the wrong model! The one-sample approach is valid, whether or not there is evidence of correlation between members of the same pair.

What if the Standard Deviations Are Unequal?

If variances are heterogeneous (unequal variances or standard deviations), the t-statistic based on the pooled variance estimate is inappropriate. The Welch procedure gives, unless degrees of freedom are very small, an adequate approximation. The Welch statistic is the difference in means divided by a standard error of difference that allows for unequal variances, that is,

$$t = \frac{\bar{x}_1 - \bar{x}_2}{\text{SED}}, \quad \text{where SED} = \sqrt{\frac{s_1^2}{n_1} + \frac{s_2^2}{n_2}}.$$

If the two variances are unequal this does not have a t-distribution. However, critical values are quite well approximated by the critical values of a t-distribution with degrees of freedom given by a function of variances and sample sizes that is due to Welch (1949). The test has the name *Welch test.* For details, see Miller (1986). The function `t.test()` has the Welch test as its default; unequal variances are assumed unless the argument `var.equal=TRUE` is given.

If $n_1 = n_2$ then the statistic is the same as for the t-test that is based on the pooled estimate of variance, but with reduced degrees of freedom.

2.2.3 The Normal Approximation to the Binomial

We assume that individuals are drawn independently and at random from a binomial population where individuals are in one of two categories – male as opposed to female, a favorable treatment outcome as opposed to an unfavorable outcome, survival as opposed to nonsurvival, defective as opposed to nondefective, Democrat as opposed to Republican, etc. Let π be the population proportion. In a sample of size n, the proportion in the category of interest is denoted by p. Then,

$$\text{SE}[p] = \sqrt{\pi(1-\pi)/n}.$$

An approximate 95 percent confidence bound for the proportion π is:

$$p \pm 1.96\sqrt{\frac{p(1-p)}{n}}.$$

An upper bound for SE$[p]$ is $1/(2\sqrt{n})$. If π is between about 0.35 and 0.65, the inaccuracy in taking SE$[p]$ as $1/(2\sqrt{n})$ is small. This approximation leads to the confidence intervals shown in Table 2.1. See `?binom.test` for calculation of confidence intervals for binomial proportions more generally.

Table 2.1 *Approximate 95 percent confidence interval, assuming* $0.35 \leq \pi \leq 0.65$.

Sample size n	25	100	400	1000
Approximate 95% confidence interval	$p \pm 20\%$	$p \pm 10\%$	$p \pm 5\%$	$p \pm 3.1\%$

2.2.4 The Pearson or Product–Moment Correlation

The Pearson correlation measures linear association. It equals:

$$\frac{\sum(x-\bar{x})(y-\bar{y})}{\sqrt{\sum(x-\bar{x})^2\sum(y-\bar{y})^2}},$$

where the sums are taken over all observations.

The usual interpretation of the magnitude of the Pearson correlation assumes that sample pairs (x, y) have been taken at random from a bivariate normal distribution. Observations must be independent, and the marginal distributions of x and y both approximately normal. If the marginal distributions are highly asymmetric, the correlation is likely to be smaller, with increased statistical variability.

The following is an extreme example that makes a comparison with the Spearman rank correlation. For calculating the Spearman correlation variable values for each of x and y are in each case ranked by order of magnitude (1,2, ...), with the Pearson correlation then calculated between the ranked values.[1]

```
## Pearson correlation between `body` and `brain`: Animals
Animals <- MASS::Animals
rho <- with(Animals, cor(body, brain))
## Pearson correlation, after log transformation
rhoLogged <- with(log(Animals), cor(body, brain))
## Spearman rank correlation
rhoSpearman <- with(Animals, cor(body, brain, method="spearman"))
c(Pearson=round(rho,2), " Pearson:log values"=round(rhoLogged,2),
  Spearman=round(rhoSpearman,2))
```

```
             Pearson  Pearson:log values              Spearman
               -0.01                0.78                  0.72
```

The standard error of the correlation coefficient is, for most inferential purposes, not a useful statistic. The distribution of the sample correlation, under the usual assumptions (e.g., bivariate normality), is too skew. Where it is reasonable to assume that the joint distribution of (x, y) pairs from which it has been calculated is bivariate normal, Fisher's z-transformation can be used to transform the Pearson statistic to a distribution that is close to normal and can be used for inference. (In practice, assuming independence between different (x, y) pairs, it may be enough to check that both x and y have normal distributions. The test that the population correlation ρ is zero requires only that, for given x, the distribution of y is normal, independently for different values of x.)

Fisher's z-statistic is:

$$z = 0.5 \log\left(\frac{1+r}{1-r}\right).$$

[1] Values that are equal in magnitude are commonly given the average of the relevant ranks.

The standard deviation, again to a close approximation, is $1/\sqrt{n-3}$, where n is the number of observations.

The function `cor.test()` may be used for the calculations, for the Kendall correlation that was mentioned in Subsection 1.3.7 as well as for the Pearson and Spearman correlations. For `method="pearson"` (the default), with at least four pairs of (x, y) values, `cor.test()` outputs a confidence interval for the correlation.

Methods for comparing Pearson correlations are implemented in the *cocor* package. An accompanying vignette that reproduces the Diedenhofen and Musch (2015) paper has extensive methodological and historical details.

2.3 Extra-Binomial and Extra-Poisson Variation

Both for the binomial and for the Poisson, one parameter determines both the mean and the variance. This limits the data for which they can provide useful models. The most commonly implemented alternative to the binomial is the betabinomial. There are a number of alternatives to the Poisson that have been widely implemented, with the negative binomial the best known. Attention has mainly been on distributions for *overdispersed* data where the variance is greater than for the binomial or Poisson, with more limited attention on the more unusual *underdispersion.*

Event processes lead to the Poisson distribution and its generalization. Or it may be seen as a limiting case of the binomial as the size n goes to infinity and probability π goes to zero, with the binomial mean constant at $n\pi = \lambda$.

For an event process (e.g., radioactive decay events), the number of counts in any time interval will be Poisson if:

- events occur independently – the occurrence of one event does not change the probability of a further event, and
- the rate λ at which events occur is constant.

Thus, in radioactive decay, atoms appear to decay independently (and emit ionizing radiation), at a rate that is the same for all atoms. The mean is λ, which is also the variance. If the sample mean and the sample variance differ only by statistical error, data are to this extent consistent with a Poisson distribution.

2.3.1 Checks for Extra-Binomial and Extra-Poisson Variation

The probabilities returned by `pbinom()` and `ppois()`, and by other functions that return "quantiles" for discrete distributions, change in discrete jumps. As an example where the jumps are large, the probabilities of number of heads in two coin tosses change from 0.25 (no heads) to 0.5 (1 head or less) to 1.0 (2 heads or less). This complicates providing an equivalent of the normal quantile–quantile plot that has the same visual effectiveness. Randomized quantile residuals are obtained by replacing the quantiles of the fitted distribution by the equivalent normal quantile. A randomization process is then used to obtain "residuals" that, aside from sampling variability, have a normal distribution if distributional assumptions are correct. The discussion in Subsection 7.6.2 has further details.

Now consider two datasets, one of which shows systematic clear departures from a binomial fit, while the second shows clear departures from a Poisson fit.

Extra-Binomial Variation in the Male/Female Balance in Large Families

The dataset qra::malesINfirst12, from hospital records in Saxony in the nineteenth century, gives the number of males among the first 12 children of family size 13 in 6115 families. The probability that a child will be male varies, within and/or between families. (The thirteenth child is ignored to counter the effect of families nonrandomly stopping when a desired gender is reached.) Data, with fitted binomial values, residuals, and standard deviations of fitted binomial values, are:

```
maleDF <- data.frame(number=0:12, freq=unname(qra::malesINfirst12[["freq"]]))
N <- sum(maleDF$freq)
pihat <- with(maleDF, weighted.mean(number, freq))/12
probBin <- dbinom(0:12, size=12, prob=pihat)
rbind(Frequency=setNames(maleDF$freq, nm=0:12),
      binomialFit=setNames(probBin*N, nm=0:12),
      rawResiduals = maleDF$freq-probBin*N,
      SDbinomial=sqrt(probBin*(1-probBin)*N)) |>
  formatC(digits=2, format="fg") |> print(digits=2, quote=F, right=T)
```

```
                0   1   2   3   4    5    6    7   8   9  10  11  12
Frequency       3  24 104 286 670 1033 1343 1112 829 478 181  45   7
binomialFit  0.93  12  72 258 628 1085 1367 1266 854 410 133  26 2.3
rawResiduals  2.1  12  32  28  42  -52  -24 -154 -25  68  48  19 4.7
SDbinomial   0.97 3.5 8.4  16  24   30   33   32  27  20  11 5.1 1.5
```

Notice the systematic manner in which the residuals go from positive to negative to positive. This happens because the standard deviation of the binomial number of successes is much smaller in the tails.

We now proceed to examine plots that check, first on the binomial fit to the Saxony data, and then a fit that uses, as an alternative, the betabinomial distribution. The betabinomial distribution has a scale parameter that allows the variance to increase beyond that for a binomial distribution. The function `gamlss::gamlss` is used to fit the model, in preference to implementations in other packages, because of its convenience for use with associated functions that provide plots of residuals.

Figure 2.3 compares, for each model, the quantile–quantile (Q–Q) plot of randomized quantile residuals with the corresponding worm plot. The worm plots show departures from a line with slope 1.0, with the same horizontal scale as for the Q-Q plot. Worm plots can show substantial variation from one plot to the next, so that can be important to repeat the plot several times.

The steady change from negative to positive differences from the line with unit slope in Panel A is very obvious in Panel B. The absence of this clear pattern, apparent in Panel D and very obvious in Panels E and F, suggest a well-fitting model. The curved boundary lines in Panels B and D are pointwise 95 percent bounds, assuming the fitted distribution.

Code for fitting the models is:

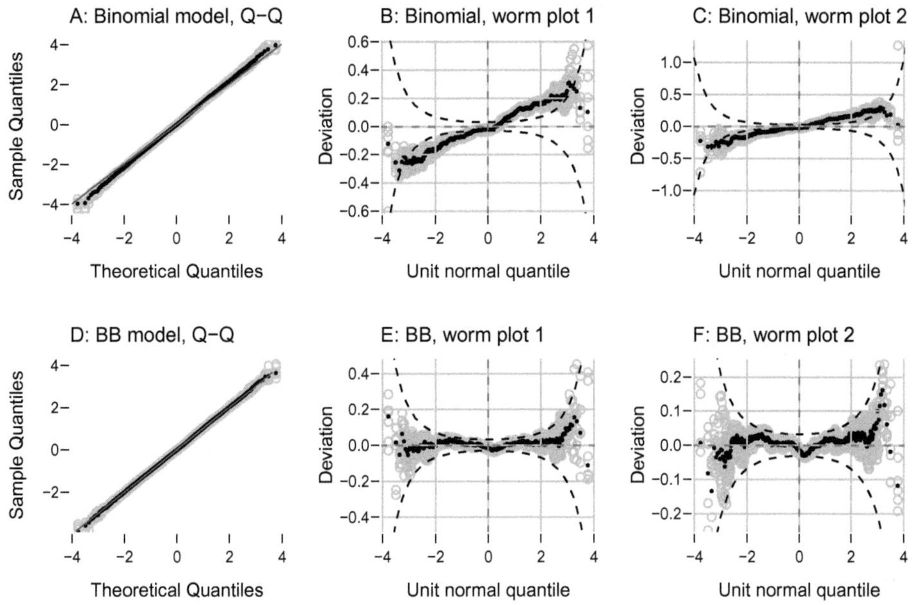

Figure 2.3 Panel A is a Q-Q plot and Panels B and C are worm plots, that show medians from six sets of randomized quantile residuals, for the fit to a binomial distribution. Panels D, E, and F show the corresponding plots for the fit to a betabinomial distribution.

```
## Fit binomial and betabinomial distributions.
suppressPackageStartupMessages(library(gamlss))
doBI <- gamlss(cbind(number, 12−number)~1, weights=freq,
               family=BI, data=maleDF, trace=FALSE)
doBB <- gamlss(cbind(number, 12−number)~1, weights=freq,
                     family=BB, data=maleDF, trace=FALSE)
```

Code for Panels A and B is:

```
rqres.plot(doBI, plot.type='all', type="QQ", main=""); box(col='white')
rqres.plot(doBI, plot.type='all', type="wp", main=""); box(col='white')
## Plots C, D, E, F: Set object name; set`type="wp" (C, E, F), or`"QQ"` (D)
```

The AIC statistic that was described in Subsection 1.7.1, calculated using the relevant methods for *gamlss* models, shows a substantially smaller value and thus a clear preference for the betabinomial:

```
aicStat <- AIC(doBI, doBB)
rownames(aicStat) <-
  c(doBI="Binomial", doBB="Betabinomial")[rownames(aicStat)]
aicStat$dAIC <- with(aicStat, round(AIC−AIC[1],1))
aicStat
```

```
             df   AIC dAIC
Betabinomial  2 24990  0.0
Binomial      1 25070 80.6
```

Data with Strong Extra-Poisson Variation

Consider now counts of numbers of accidents among 414 machinists from a three-months study conducted around the end of World War I (Greenwood and Woods, 1919). In data such as these, it is entirely to be expected that there will be substantial variation – some are much more prone to accidents than others:

```
## Numbers of accidents in three months, with Poisson fit
machinists <- data.frame(number=0:8, freq=c(296, 74, 26, 8, 4, 4, 1, 0, 1))
N <- sum(machinists[['freq']])
lambda <- with(machinists, weighted.mean(number, freq))
fitPoisson <- dpois(0:8, lambda)*sum(machinists[['freq']])
rbind(Frequency=with(machinists, setNames(freq, number)),
      poissonFit=fitPoisson) |>
  formatC(digits=2, format="fg") |> print(quote=F, digits=2, right=T)
```

```
             0   1  2   3    4     5      6       7        8
Frequency  296  74 26   8    4     4      1       0        1
poissonFit 255 123 30 4.8 0.58 0.056 0.0045 0.00031 0.000019
```

The very poor fit for 0 or 1 accidents is obvious, with no need to check residuals.

The negative binomial is the most frequently used generalization of the Poisson that is designed for count data where the variance is greater than the mean. Figure 2.4 shows the worm plots for each of the two models.

Code that fits the models is:

```
doPO <- gamlss(number~1, weights=freq,
               family=PO, data=machinists, trace=FALSE)
doNBI <- gamlss(number~1, weights=freq,
                family=NBI, data=machinists, trace=FALSE)
```

Code for Panels A and B (or C) is:

```
rqres.plot(doPO, plot.type='all', type="QQ", main=""); box(col='white')
## Repeat, changing the argument, for remaining plots
```

There are two variants, labeled in the *gamlss* package as NBI and NBII. Here, with counts for one distributional mean, NBI and NBII provide different ways

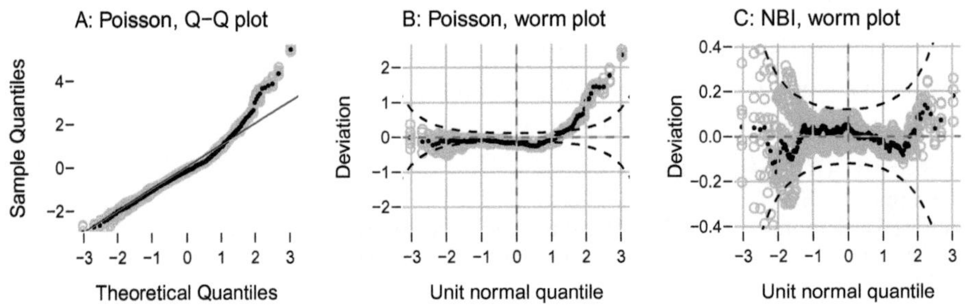

Figure 2.4 Panel A is a worm plot, showing medians from six sets of randomized quantile residuals, for the fit to a Poisson distribution. Panels B and C show corresponding plots for the fit to a negative binomial type I distribution.

to parameterize the distribution. In Subsection 5.4.3, where the interest is in the effect of habitat on the densities of two species of moths, NBI and NBII will lead to different fitted values.

2.3.2 Technical Details – Extra-Binomial or Extra-Poisson Variation*

The `stats::glm()` function provides for `quasibinomial` (and `quasipoisson` families. These are not formally defined distributions. Instead, they fit just as for the "binomial" or "Poisson," but estimate a "dispersion" Φ from the fitted model that is a multiplier for the variance, allowing it to be larger (or, much less commonly, smaller) than the respective binomial or Poisson variance. With Φ thus defined, the variance for the binomial-like number x of "successes" out of n is $n\pi(1-\pi)\Phi$. The variance for the Poisson-like count x with mean λ is $\lambda\Phi$.

The *gamlss* implementation of the betabinomial has a probability parameter `mu` and "dispersion" (or "scale") parameter `sigma`. The parameter σ has its own link function, by default log(). The dispersion index Φ that is the direct analogue of the dispersion as defined for `glm()` models, is $(1+n\sigma)/(1+\sigma)$. The betabinomial distribution is derived by assuming that the probability of "success," rather than being fixed, varies randomly according to a beta distribution. As well as the betabinomial, the *gamlss* package has also the double binomial. As for the betabinomial, the binomial ($\Phi = 1$) is a limiting case.

Section 7.6 will demonstrate the use of the betabinomial in the *glmmTMB* package. This provides a "dispersion" parameter ϕ which is the inverse of the parameter σ in *gamlss*, that is, $\phi = \sigma^{-1}$. As for other distributional families, the way that the variance relates to the particular "dispersion" (or "scale") parameter can be different between implementations in different R packages.

There are, in addition, zero-inflated versions of the distributions noted, and zero-adjusted versions of all except the double binomial. These have a further parameter, named "nu" in the *gamlss* implementation, that is described as a *shape* parameter.

An insightful way to relate the different parameterizations of the betabinomial is to express the dispersion parameter as a function of the intra-class correlation ρ. A positive correlation leads to more homogeneous responses within replicates, with greater between replicate differences, leading to a dispersion index Φ that is greater than one. Then:

$$\rho = \frac{\sigma}{\sigma+1} \quad (\sigma \text{ is the dispersion parameter in gamlss}).$$

The dispersion index Φ (multiplier for $n\pi(\pi-1)$) is then

$$\Phi = 1 + (n-1)\rho \tag{2.1}$$

$$= \frac{1+n\sigma}{1+\sigma}. \tag{2.2}$$

The following calculates the "dispersion index" for the betabinomial fit to the Saxony family male/female split data, equivalent to the "dispersion" as defined for glm() models with quasibinomial errors:

```
sigma <- exp(coef(doBB, "sigma"))
cat("Phi =", (1+12*sigma)/(1+sigma))
```

```
Phi = 1.165
```

The increase relative to the binomial is small, but because of the large numbers in the dataset, stands out clearly.

For more details on the betabinomial see, for example, Morgan (1992). Morgan and Ridout (2008) is interesting because it compares use of a binomial distribution, a betabinomial, and a mixture of the two distributions.

As parameterized in the *gamlss* package, the negative binomial type I (NBI) distribution has variance, with multiplier Φ:

$$\text{Variance} == \mu(1+\mu\sigma), \quad \text{so that } \Phi = (1+\mu\sigma).$$

For the machinist accidents data, this equals:

```
mu <- exp(coef(doNBI, "mu"))
sigma <- exp(coef(doNBI, "sigma"))
cat("Phi =", (1+sigma*mu))
```

```
Phi = 2.019
```

For the negative binomial type II (NBII) distribution, the variance is $\mu(1+\sigma)$, so that $\Phi = 1+\sigma$.

Where μ varies as a function of factors or other terms in a model, the difference between the negative binomial types NBI and NBII models is of consequence. For NBI the variance changes by a factor $\Phi = (1+\mu\sigma)$ as μ changes, while for NBII the variance is a constant multiple $1+\sigma$ of μ.

The packages *gamlss* and *VGAM*, and a number of others, implement a number of other distributions that are designed to model extra-Poisson variation. There is a much wider choice than for distributions that model extra-binomial variation.

2.4 Contingency Tables

The `psid3` and `nswdemo` datasets (*DAAG*) relate to US studies that evaluated labor training programs. For details, see `?DAAG::nswdemo`. The following two-way table gives number of observations, classified according to high school graduates versus number of dropouts, and according to nonparticipation in a labor training program (PSID3 group) or participation (NSW group).

```
## 'Untreated' rows (no training) from psid3, 'treated' rows from nswdemo
nswpsid3 <- rbind(DAAG::psid3, subset(DAAG::nswdemo, trt==1))
degTAB <- with(nswpsid3, table(trt,nodeg))
# Code 'Yes' if completed high school; 'No' if dropout
dimnames(degTAB) <- list(trt=c("PSID3_males","NSW_male_trainees"),
                         deg =c("Yes","No"))
degTAB
```

Table 2.2 *Calculated expected values for a contingency table.*

	High School Graduate			
	Yes	No	Total	Row proportion
PSID3	63 (43.07)	65 (84.93)	128	128/425 = 0.3012
NSW74 trainees	80 (99.93)	217 (197.07)	297	297/425 = 0.6988
Total	143	282	425	
Column proportion	143/425 = 0.3365	282/425 = 0.6635		

```
                     deg
trt                   Yes  No
  PSID3_males          63  65
  NSW_male_trainees    80 217
```

Table 2.2 is designed to accompany an explanation, given in the following subsection, of details of the calculations for a chi-squared test for no association. The datasets, and other related datasets, will be further discussed in Subsection 9.7.1.

The table shows a much higher proportion of high school dropouts in the NSW group than in the PSID3 group. The chi-squared test for no association, described in the next subsection, can be used for a formal test of significance:

```
# To agree with hand calculation below, specify correct=FALSE
chisq.test(degTAB, correct=FALSE)
```

```

        Pearson's Chi-squared test

data:  degTAB
X-squared = 20, df = 1, p-value = 0.000008
```

Statistical variability is an unlikely explanation for the much stronger representation of high school dropouts in the NSW data.

The Mechanics of the Chi-Squared Test

The null hypothesis is that the proportion of the total in each cell is, to within random error, the result of multiplying a row proportion by a column proportion. The independence assumption, that is, the assumption of independent allocation to the cells of the table, is crucial. Where it is possible to form replicate tables, the assumption should be checked.

Given I rows and J columns, the expected value in cell (i, j) is calculated as

$$E_{ij} = \text{(proportion for row } i) \times \text{(proportion for column } j) \times \text{total}. \quad (2.3)$$

It follows that the expected values can be found by multiplying the column totals by the row proportions. (Alternatively, the row totals can be multiplied by the column proportions.) Thus, $128 \times 0.3365 = 43.07$, $128 \times 0.3365 = 84.93$, etc.

A chi-squared residual for each cell of the table can be calculated as

$$\frac{O_{ij} - E_{ij}}{\sqrt{E_{ij}}}, \text{ where } O_{ij} \text{ is the observed value in cell } (i,j).$$

Table 2.3 *Dreamer and object movements, compiled from Hobson (1988, Table 12.1, p. 248).*

	Object moves	
Dreamer moves	Yes	No
Yes	5	17
No	3	85

Squaring these values, and summing over all cells of the table gives a value for the chi-squared statistic that is the same as that returned by the R function `chisq.test()` when the default `correct=TRUE` is changed to `correct=FALSE`. See `?chisq.test` for details.

Under the null hypothesis the chi-squared statistic has an approximate chi-squared distribution with $(I-1)(J-1)$ degrees of freedom. In Table 2.2, the values in parentheses are the expected values E_{ij}.

An Example Where a Chi-Squared Test May Not Be Valid

Table 2.3 summarizes information that Hobson (1988) derived from drawings of dreams, made by an unknown person whom he names "The Engine Man." For each of 110 drawings Hobson notes whether the dreamer moves, whether an object moves, and other details also. Dreamer movement may occur if an object moves, but is relatively rare if there is no object movement. (Note that the Table 2.3 form of summary is ours, based on the summaries that Hobson provides.)

It may seem natural to do a chi-squared test for no association.[2] This gives $X^2 = 7.1$ (1 d.f.), $p = 0.008$. Note, however, that there is a time sequence to the dreams. There might well be runs of dreams of the same type. If the sequence in which Hobson records details represents the sequence in time, this will allow a check of the strength of any evidence for runs.

A further point concerns the adequacy of the chi-squared approximation, under the assumption that counts enter independently into the cells of the table. The commonly used rule that all expected values should be at least 2 (Miller, 1986) is satisfied for the data of Table 2.3. A check is to do a Fisher "exact" test. In this instance the Fisher exact test[3] gives, surprisingly, the same result as the chi-squared test, i.e., $p = 0.008$.

Rare and Endangered Plant Species

The calculations for a test for no association in a two-way table can sometimes give useful insight, even where a formal test of statistical significance would be invalid. The example that now follows illustrates this point. Data are from species lists for various regions of Australia. Species were classified `CC`, `CR`, `RC`, and `RR`, with `C` denoting common and `R` denoting rare. The first code letter relates to South

[2]
```
## Engine man data
engineman <- matrix(c(5,3,17,85), 2,2)
chisq.test(engineman)
```
[3]
```
fisher.test(engineman)
```

Australia and Victoria, and the second to Tasmania. They were further classified by habitat according to the Victorian register, where `D` = dry only, `W` = wet only, and `WD` = wet or dry.

Data can be entered thus:

```
## Enter the data thus:
rareplants <- matrix(c(37,190,94,23, 59,23,10,141, 28,15,58,16), ncol=3,
  byrow=TRUE, dimnames=list(c("CC","CR","RC","RR"), c("D","W","WD")))
```

We use a chi-squared calculation to check whether the classification into the different habitats is similar for the different rows. Details of the calculations are:

```
(x2 <- chisq.test(rareplants))
```

```
        Pearson's Chi-squared test

data:  rareplants
X-squared = 35, df = 6, p-value = 0.000004
```

This low p-value should attract a level of skepticism. We do not have a random sample from some meaningful larger population. Some species may be commonly found together, for reasons unconnected with habitat type. As a simplistic thought experiment suppose that species come in closely linked pairs, with both members of the pair always falling into the same cell of the table. This would inflate the chi-squared statistic by a factor of 2 (the net effect of inflating the numerator by 2^2, and the denominator by 2). Available information does not allow estimation of the extent of any such clustering.

Examination of Departures from a Consistent Overall Row Pattern

The following shows the observed values, together with expected values and residuals, that are generated as part of the `chisq.test()` calculations:

```
## Observed
## values
rareplants
```

```
    D   W WD
CC 37 190 94
CR 23  59 23
RC 10 141 28
RR 15  58 16
```

```
## Expected
## values
x2$expected
```

```
      D     W   WD
CC 39.3 207.2 74.5
CR 12.9  67.8 24.4
RC 21.9 115.6 41.5
RR 10.9  57.5 20.6
```

```
## Standardized
## residuals
residuals(x2)
```

```
         D      W
WD
CC -0.37 -1.196
2.26
CR
2.83 -1.067 -0.28
RC -2.55
2.368 -2.10
RR  1.24
0.072 -1.02
```

Under the null hypothesis, the expected relative numbers in different columns are the same in every row. The chi-squared residuals are measures of departures from this pattern.

The null hypothesis assumption is that allocation to cells is independent, with probabilities (row probabiliy) × (column probability) and expected values as given by Equation (2.3). If numbers are large enough, residuals will then for all practical purposes behave like random normal deviates with mean zero and variance one.

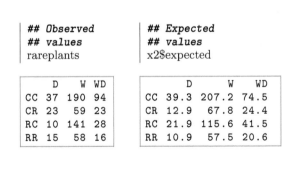

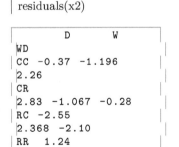

If numbers are large enough the residuals will, assuming that allocation to cells is independent with probabilities (row probabiliy) × (column probability), behave like random normal deviates with mean zero and variance one, so that the expected values are as given by Equation (2.3).

The `CC` species are, relative to the overall average, over-represented in the `WD` classification; the `CR` species are over-represented in the `D` classification; the `RC` species are under-represented in `D` and `WD`, and over-represented in `W`.

Interpretation Issues

Having found an association in a contingency table, what does it mean? The interpretation will differ depending on the context. The incidence of gastric cancer is relatively high in Japan and China. Do screening programs help? Here are two ways in which the problem has been studied.

- In a long term follow-up study, patients who had surgery for gastric cancer may be classified into two groups – a "screened" group whose cancer was detected by mass screening, and an "unscreened" group who presented at a clinic or hospital with gastric cancer. The five-year mortality may be around 58 percent in the unscreened group, compared with 72 percent in the screened group, out of approximately 300 patients in each group.
- In a prospective cohort study, two populations – a screened population and an unscreened population – may be compared. The death rates in the two populations over a ten-year period may then be compared. For example, the annual death rate may be of the order of 60 per 100,000 for the unscreened group, compared with 30 per 100,000 for the screened group, in populations of several thousand individuals.

In the long-term follow-up study, the process that led to the detection of cancer was different between the screened and unscreened groups. The screening may lead to surgery for some cancers that would otherwise lie dormant long enough that they would never attract clinical attention. It is necessary, as in the prospective cohort study, to compare all patients in a screened group with all patients in an unscreened group. As patients were not divided randomly between the two groups, results are even so not conclusive.

2.5 Issues for Regression with a Single Explanatory Variable

2.5.1 Iron Slag Example – Check Residuals with Care!

In the example now considered, there is an evident pattern in residuals from a straight line regression. The data compare two methods for measuring the iron content in slag – a magnetic method and a chemical method (data are from Hand et al. (1993)). The chemical method required greater effort and was presumably more expensive, while the magnetic method was quicker and easier.

The plot of residuals against fitted values in Figure 2.5A gives a strong hint of pattern in the residuals. In Panel B, the argument `span` to the function that plots the smooth has been increased from the default, from 2/3 to 0.8, in order to prevent the large positive residual on the left from obscuring the pattern.

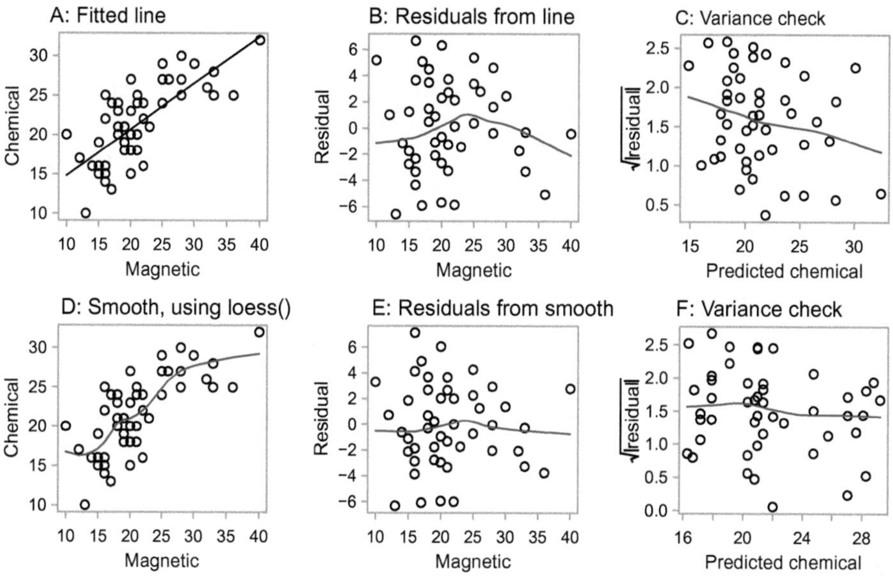

Figure 2.5 Panels A, B, and C (top row) are from adding a line to the plot of `chemical` against `magnetic`. Panels D, E, and F (bottom row) are from adding a loess smooth. In C, the downward slope might appear to suggest lower variance for larger fitted values. Panel F is the equivalent plot from fitting a loess curve. Any suggestion that variance changes with fitted value has gone.

Panel C gives a visual check on whether the error variance is constant. (Taking the square root of absolute values of the residuals symmetrizes their distribution, giving a more meaningful smooth and a plot that makes better visual sense.) Panel C gives a strong, but misleading, suggestion that the variance decreases with increasing value of `magnetic`. The smooth in Panel C, because it relates to the straight line model that Figures 2.5A and B indicate is inappropriate, is misleading.

Now, use the function `loess()` to fit a smooth curve to the data in Figure 2.5A. Figure 2.5D shows the scatterplot, with a smooth curve fitted. Panel E shows the plot of residuals versus `magnetic` that then results, with a smooth curve fitted that is designed to help in checking whether there is any remaining trend. Panel F plots the square root of absolute values of residuals against predicted chemical. There is now no suggestion of variance heterogeneity.

The code used to fit the line and extract the fitted values and residuals was:

```
ord <- order(DAAG::ironslag[["magnetic"]])
ironslag <- DAAG::ironslag[ord,]
slagAlpha.lm <- lm(chemical~magnetic, data=ironslag)
resval <- residuals(slagAlpha.lm)
fitchem <- fitted(slagAlpha.lm)
```

The code used to fit the loess curve and extract the fitted values and residuals was:

```
slag.loess <- loess(chemical~magnetic, data=ironslag, span=0.8)
```

```
resval2 <- slag.loess[["residuals"]]
fitchem2 <- slag.loess[["fitted"]]
```

Panels B, C, E, and F were plotted using the function `scatter.smooth()`.

Where there is genuine heterogeneity of variance, and an accurate estimate of the variance at each data point is available, data points should be weighted proportionately to the reciprocal of the variance. Getting an estimate to within some constant of proportionality is enough. It may be possible to guess at a suitable functional form for the change in variance with x or (equivalently, since $y = a + bx$) with y. For example, the variance may be proportional to y.

2.5.2 The Analysis of Variance Table

The analysis of variance table breaks the sum of squares for a linear model into two parts: a part accounted for by the deterministic component, which is in this case the line, and a part attributed to the noise component or residual. For the lawn roller linear model, the analysis of variance table is:

```
roller.lm <- lm(depression ~ weight, data=DAAG::roller)
anova(roller.lm)
```

```
Analysis of Variance Table

Response: depression
          Df Sum Sq Mean Sq F value Pr(>F)
weight     1    658     658    14.5 0.0052
Residuals  8    363      45
```

The total sum of squares (about the mean) for the 10 observations is 1020.9 (= 658.0 + 362.9; we round to one decimal place). Including weight reduced this by 658.0, giving a residual sum of squares (RSS) equal to 362.9. The column headed `Mean Sq` (*mean square*) gives a fair comparison. The mean square for `weight` is 658.0; this compares with a mean square of 45.4 for the residual.

The degrees of freedom can be understood thus: with just two observations determining a line both residuals would be zero, yielding no information about the noise. Every additional observation beyond two yields one additional degree of freedom for estimating the noise variance. Thus with 10 points, $10 - 2$ (= 8) degrees of freedom are available (in the residuals) for estimating the noise variance. (Where a line is constrained to pass through the origin, one point is enough to determine the line, and with 10 points the variance would be estimated with nine degrees of freedom.)

This table has the information needed for calculating R^2 (also known as the "coefficient of determination") and adjusted R^2. The R^2 statistic is the square of the correlation coefficient, and is the sum of squares due to weight divided by the total sum of squares:

$$R^2 = \frac{658.0}{1020.9} = 0.64.$$

Compare this with

$$\text{adjusted } R^2 = 1 - \frac{362.9/8}{1020.9/9} = 0.60.$$

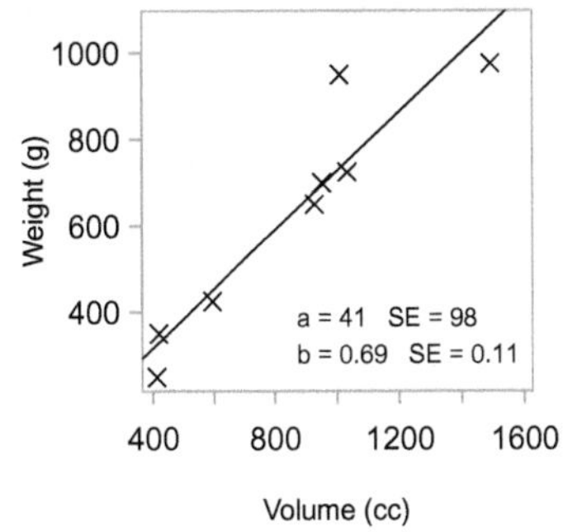

volume	weight
412	250
953	700
929	650
1492	975
419	350
1010	950
595	425
1034	725

Figure 2.6 Weights (g) versus volume ($\leq$m^3) for eight softback books, with the fitted regression line added.

Adjusted R^2 takes into account the number of degrees of freedom, and is in general preferable to R^2. A small adjusted R^2 indicates large variability about the fitted line, relative to the variability explained by the line. It is useful as a measure of the extent to which the total scatter of outcome values is explained by the model. Neither R^2 nor adjusted R^2 is appropriate for comparisons between different studies, where the range of values of the outcome variable may be different. Both are likely to be largest in those studies where the range of values of the outcome variable is greatest. AIC and BIC, introduced in Section 1.7, are in general much preferable for model comparison purposes. See also Section 2.6.

2.5.3 Outliers, Influence, and Robust Regression

The data displayed in Figure 2.6, with data shown on the right, are for a collection of eight softback books. Additionally, the figure shows the fitted regression line. Output from the regression calculations is:

```
softbacks.lm <- lm(weight ~ volume, data=DAAG::softbacks)
print(coef(summary(softbacks.lm)), digits=3)
```

```
            Estimate Std. Error t value Pr(>|t|)
(Intercept)   41.372     97.559   0.424 0.686293
volume         0.686      0.106   6.475 0.000644
```

Figure 2.7 shows regression diagnostics. Code that gives the plots is:

```
plot(softbacks.lm, fg="gray")
```

For regression with one explanatory variable, Plot A is equivalent to a plot of residuals against the explanatory variable. Plot C is designed for examining the constancy of the variance. Plot D plots residuals against leverage. Leverage, which depends only on explanatory variable values, is a measure of the potential for an observation to have a large influence in determining the regression line. Observations that are well away from the mean (or where there are multiple explanatory variables, the *centroid*) can exert a greater pull than those closer to the mean (or centroid). See Subsection 3.4.2 for further details.

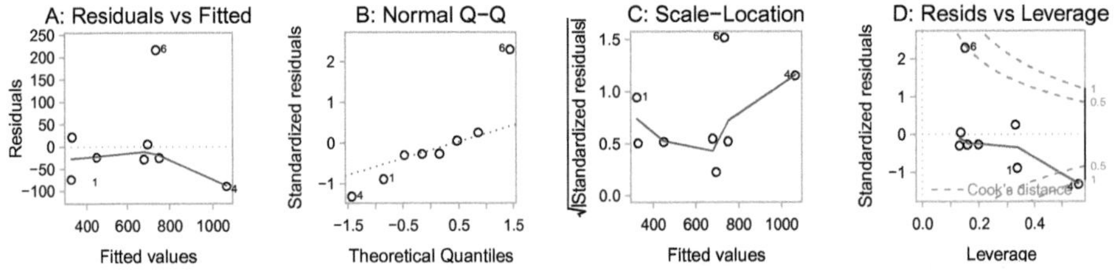

Figure 2.7 Diagnostic plots for Figure 2.6.

Contours of Cook's distances of 0.1 and 1 are shown in red. Cook's distance is a measure of *influence*; it measures the extent to which the line would change if the point were omitted. Observation 4's position at the extreme end of the range of x-values gives it a high *leverage*. Since its y-value is lower than would be predicted by the line, it pulls the line downward. This large leverage, combined with a residual that is the second largest, gives it the largest Cook's distance. Observation 6, which has the largest residual, has a much smaller leverage and, accordingly, a smaller Cook's distance.

Diagnostic plots, such as Figure 2.7, are not definitive. Rather, they draw attention to points that require further investigation. Here, with only eight points, it would not make sense to omit any of them, especially as points 4 and 6 are both, for different reasons, candidates for omission.

It may turn out, upon subsequent checking, that an outlier has arisen from a recording or similar error. Where an outlier seems a genuine data value, it is good practice to do the analysis both with and without the outlier. If retention of an apparent outlier makes little difference to the practical use and interpretation of the results, it is usually best to retain it in the main analysis. If an outlier that seems a genuine data value is omitted from the main analysis, it should be reported along with the main analysis, and included in graphs.

Robust Regression

Robust regression offers a halfway house between including outliers and omitting them entirely. Rather than omitting outliers, it downweights them, reducing their influence on the fitted regression line. This has the additional advantage of making outliers stand out more strongly against the line. Available functions include `MASS::rlm()`, `MASS::lqs()`, and **`robustbase::lmrob()`**. Resistant methods, such as `MASS::lqs()` implements, are a subclass of robust methods that focus directly on ensuring that outliers do not contribute to the regression fit. For all methods, it can be important that residuals have an approximately symmetric distribution. See, further, Section 3.4 and Exercise 3.16 in Section 3.11.

2.5.4 Standard Errors and Confidence Intervals

Recall that since two parameters (the slope and intercept) have been estimated, the error mean square is calculated with $n-2$ degrees of freedom. As a consequence,

Table 2.4 *Observed and fitted values of* `depression` *at the given* `weight` *value. SE (*standard error*) is the standard error for a new predicted value. SE.OBS is the standard error for a new observation.*

	Predictor `weight`	Observed `depression`	Fitted	SE	SE.OBS	
1	1.9	2	3.0	3.61	7.6	$\sqrt{3.61^2+6.74^2}$
2	3.1	1	6.2	2.98	7.4	$\sqrt{2.98^2+6.74^2}$
3	3.3	5	6.7	2.88	7.3	
. . . . 10	12.4	25	31.0	4.92	8.3	

the standard errors for the slope and for predicted values are calculated with $n-2$ degrees of freedom. Both involve the use of the square root of the error mean square.

Confidence Intervals and Test for the Slope

A 95 percent confidence interval for the regression slope is

$$b \pm t_{0.975}\mathrm{SE}_b,$$

where $t_{0.975}$ is the 97.5 percent point of the t-distribution with $n-2$ degrees of freedom, and SE_b is the standard error of b.

For the `roller.lm` model, a 95 percent confidence interval may be calculated thus:

```
SEb <- coef(summary(roller.lm))[2, 2]
coef(roller.lm)[2] + qt(c(0.025,.975), 8)*SEb
```

```
[1] 1.1 4.3
```

SEs and Confidence Intervals for Predicted Values

There are two types of predictions: prediction of points on the line, and prediction of a new data value. The SE estimates of predictions for new data values account for uncertainty in variation of individual points about the line. It is thus larger, perhaps much larger, than the SE for prediction of points on the line.

Table 2.4 shows expected values of the depression, with values of SE (for points on the line) and of SE.OBS (for new observations), for a range of roller weights. These may be calculated thus:

```
## Code to obtain fitted values and standard errors (SE, then SE.OBS)
fit.with.se <- predict(roller.lm, se.fit=TRUE)
fit.with.se$se.fit                                    # SE
sqrt(fit.with.se[["se.fit"]]^2+fit.with.se$residual.scale^2)  # SE.OBS
```

The SE.OBS estimate accounts both for the standard error for the fitted value (estimated at 3.6 in row 1), and for the noise standard error (estimated at 6.74) for a new observation.

To calculate confidence intervals for predicted values, specify, for example:

```
predict(roller.lm, interval="confidence", level=0.95)
```

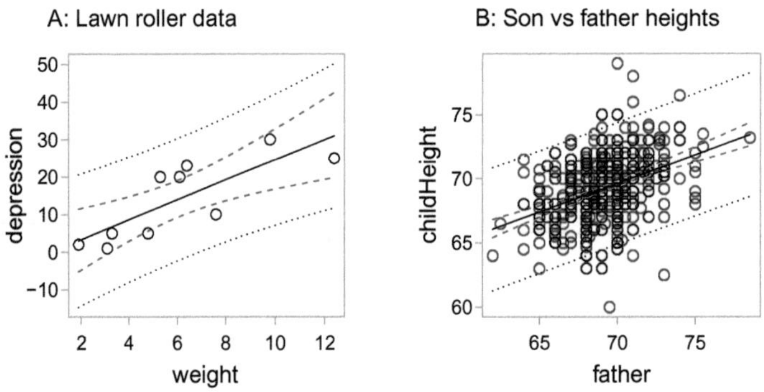

Figure 2.8 Panel A relates to the lawn roller data. Panel B relates to Galton's data that compares son's height with father's height. The two panels both show points, fitted line, 95 percent pointwise bounds for line (dashed, in red), and 95 percent pointwise bounds for predicted values.

To obtain confidence bounds for new predictions, replace `interval="confidence"` by `interval="prediction"`. If these are required for new x-values, use the argument `newdata` to supply the name of a data frame that has the new values for `weight`.

Figure 2.8A shows 95 percent pointwise confidence bounds, both for the fitted line, and for predictions of new data values. Figure 2.8B shows shows the equivalent points, and confidence bounds, for Galton's data that compares son's heights with father's heights. Both panels use the function `investr::plotFit()` to create the graphs simply and directly. Code for Figure 2.8B is:

```
galtonMales <- subset(HistData::GaltonFamilies, gender=="male")
galton.lm <- lm(childHeight~father, data=galtonMales)
investr::plotFit(galton.lm, interval="both", col.conf="red", hide=FALSE,
            col=adjustcolor('black',alpha=0.5), fg="gray")
```

For the plot shown in Panel B, summary information on the coefficients is:

```
             Estimate Std. Error t value
(Intercept)     38.36       3.31    11.6
father           0.45       0.05     9.3
```

A t-statistic that equals 9.34 and may seem large contrasts with a small adjusted R^2 statistic that equals 0.15. The fitted line explains only just over 0.15 of the variance of the heights of sons.

It bears emphasizing that the validity of these calculations depends crucially on model assumptions. Confidence bounds for the fitted line rely on normality for the sampling distribution of the slopes, while prediction bounds for future observations assume normally distributed heights.

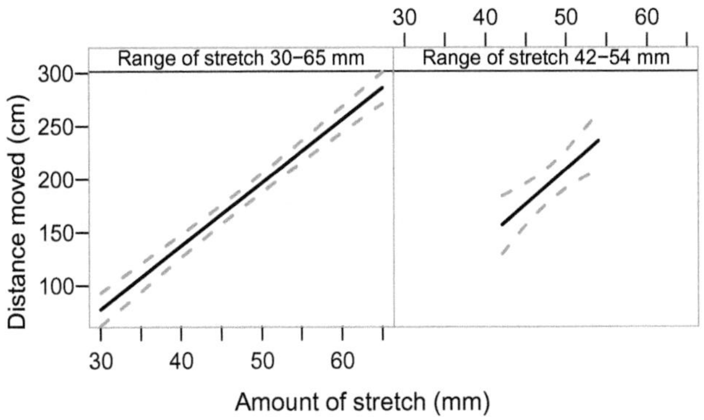

Figure 2.9 Data for the left panel (`elastic1`, seven points) spanned a much wider range of values than that for the right panel (`elastic2`, nine points). Even with the slightly larger number of points (nine as against seven), the right panel has much wider confidence bounds.

* *Implications for Design*

An emphasis of this subsection is that the choice of location of the x-values, which is a design issue, is closely connected with sample size considerations. Increasing the sample size is not the only, or necessarily the best, way to improve precision.

The estimated variance of the slope estimate is

$$\mathrm{SE}_b{}^2 = \frac{s^2}{ns_x^2}, \quad \text{where we define } s_x^2 = \frac{\sum_i (x_i - \bar{x})^2}{n}.$$

Here s^2 is the error mean square, that is, s is the estimated SD for the population from which the residuals are taken. The expected value of $\mathrm{SE}_b{}^2$ is

$$\mathrm{E}[\mathrm{SE}_b^2] = \frac{\sigma^2}{ns_x^2}.$$

Now consider two alternative ways to reduce SE_b by a factor of 2.

- By fixing the configuration of x-values, but multiplying by 4 the number of values at each discrete x-value, s_x is unchanged. As n increases by a factor of 4, the expected value of SE_b^2 reduces by a factor of 4, and SE_b by a factor of 2.
- Alternatively, increasing the average separation between x-values by a factor of 2 will reduce SE_b by a factor of 2. Checking for linearity over the extended range of x-values is, however, important.

Reducing SE_b reduces, at the same time, the standard error of the fitted values. Figure 2.9 shows the effect of increasing the range of x-values (the code for both panels is a ready adaptation of the code for Figure 2.8). Both experiments used the same rubber band. The first experiment used a much wider range of values of x (= amount by which the rubber band was stretched). For the left panel of Figure 2.9, $s_x = 10.8$, while for the right panel $s_x = 4.3$.

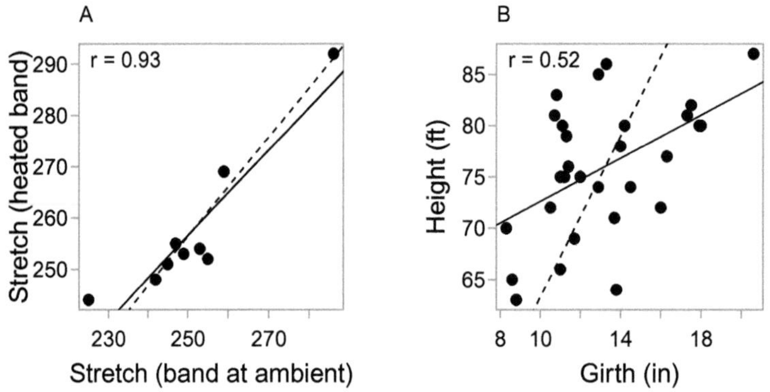

Figure 2.10 Each plot shows both regression lines, for y on x (solid line) and x on y (dotted line). In Panel A, for the `DAAG::pair65` dataset, the lines are quite similar. (Note, however, that the most extreme point is driving the relatively high correlation.) In Panel B, for two of the columns from the `trees` dataset, the correlation is smaller, with the result that the lines are more different.

2.5.5 There Are Two Regression Lines!

At this point, we note that there are two regression lines – a regression line for y on x, and a regression line for x on y. It makes a difference which is the explanatory variable, and which the dependent variable. Writing $b_{y|x}$ for the slope of the regression line of y on x, and $b_{x|y}$ for that for x on y, it follows that:

$$b_{y|x} b_{x|y} = r^2, \text{ where } r \text{ is the Pearson correlation.}$$

When $r = 1$, so that the two lines coincide, $b_{x|y} = b_{y|x}^{-1}$. The two lines are quite different if the correlation is small.

Figure 2.10 illustrates the point for two different datasets. The correlation for the data on Panel A reduces sharply, to 0.78, if the point in the top right of the panel is left out.

An Alternative to a Regression Line

There are yet other possibilities. A perspective that makes good sense for the seal organ growth data that will feature in Subsection 2.5.8 is that there is an underlying linear functional relationship. The analysis assumes that observed values of log(organ weight) and log(body weight) differ from the values for this underlying functional relationship by independent random amounts. The line that is obtained will lie between the regression line for y on x and the line for x on y. See Sprent (1966). Exercise 2.14 demonstrates a method for finding such a line.

2.5.6 Logarithmic and Power Transformations*

The discussion accompanying Figure 1.5 drew attention to the use of a logarithmic transformation to transform data with a strong right skew to give a more nearly

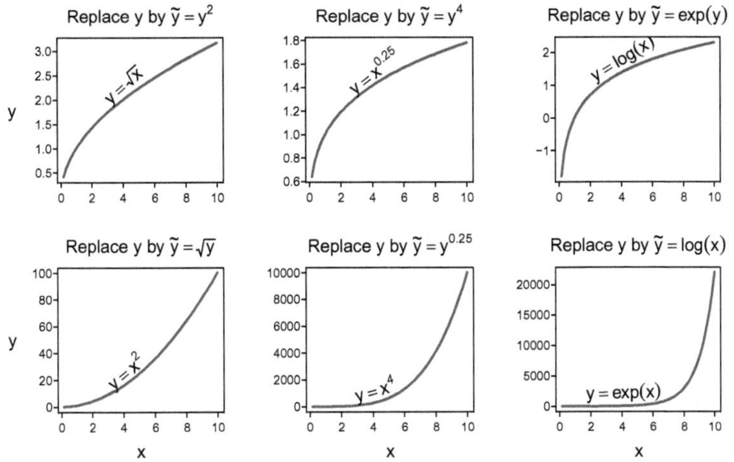

Figure 2.11 This figure shows some alternative response curves. The formula for $\tilde{y}$ gives the power family transformation of y that will make $\tilde{y}$ a linear function of x. Thus, if $y = \log(x)$, then taking $\tilde{y} = \exp(y)$ will make $\tilde{y}$ a linear function of x. Negative powers are also possible, for example, $\tilde{y} = y^{-1}$.

symmetric distribution. A logarithmic transformation is often appropriate for size measurements (linear, surface, volume, or weight) of biological organisms. If the ratio of largest to smallest data value is greater than 10, and especially if it is more than 100, then the logarithmic transformation should be tried as a matter of course. Check this advice against the response curves shown in Figure 2.11.

The logarithmic transformation belongs to the wider class of power transformations that includes square root and cube root transformations. The square root transformation is sometimes used for counts of rare events, and the cube root for rainfall data. The connection to the logarithmic transformation will be explained shortly. Figure 2.11 shows a number of response curves, and describes the particular transformation that would make the relationship linear.

We have so far mentioned only transformation of y. We might alternatively transform x, or transform both x and y.

* *General Power Transformations – Box–Cox and Yeo–Johnson*

For $\lambda \neq 0$, the power transformation replaces a value y by y^λ. The logarithmic transformation corresponds to $\lambda = 0$. In order to make this connection, the Box–Cox transformation (Box and Cox, 1964), makes a location and scale correction, so that the transformation is:

$$
\begin{aligned}
y(\lambda) &= \frac{y^\lambda - 1}{\lambda}, \quad \text{if } \lambda \neq 0, \\
y(\lambda) &= \log(y), \quad \text{if } \lambda = 0.
\end{aligned}
$$

- If the small values of a variable need to be spread, make λ smaller.
- If the large values of a variable need to be spread, make λ larger.

Use `summary()` with the object returned by `car::powerTransform()` to get a range of plausible values for λ. An alternative to `powerTransform()`, with fewer options, is `MASS::boxcox()`. Both `powerTransform()` and `boxcox()` accept as argument a regression formula or regression object where y is the outcome variable. An estimate is then given for λ that makes the distribution of residuals as close as possible (as measured by the likelihood function) to iid (independently and identically distributed) normal with mean 0.

The Yeo–Johnson family of transformations modifies and generalizes the Box–Cox family to handle data where the smallest value of y may be zero or negative. For nonnegative values of y, it finds the Box–Cox transformation of $y + 1$. For negative values of y, it is the Box–Cox transformation of $|y| + 1$ with parameter $2 - \lambda$. Use the function `powerTransform()`, specifying `family = "yjPower"`, to obtain an optimal Yeo–Johnson transformation.

As an alternative to a model formula or `lm` regression object, a data frame or matrix can be supplied as argument. For use of a model formula as argument, the left-hand side can be a matrix rather than a variable. Residuals from the regressions for all columns are then transformed, each column with its own transformation, so that the joint distribution is as close as possible to multivariate normal.

The use of `boxcox()` and `powerTransform()` is pursued in exercises at the end of the chapter. Subsection 3.3.3 has further details on the use of the function `powerTransform()`, with an example.

2.5.7 General Forms of Nonlinear Response

Low-order polynomial fits – quadratics or cubics – are often effective. Checks for quadratic as opposed to linear, and/or for cubic as opposed to quadratic, can be useful as part of a process of checking for variation for which the model has not accounted. Higher-order polynomial fits are in general unsatisfactory. The tradeoff for accurate approximation of observed data values becomes increasingly, as the order of polynomial increases, an erratic pattern of variation at intermediate data points. Spline approximations, used to fit a general form of curve with a slope that is constrained to change slowly in each local part of the curve, are in general a better choice. Section 4.4 will provide details.

2.5.8 Size and Shape Data – Allometric Growth

The logarithmic transformation is commonly important for morphometric data, i.e., for data on the size and shape of organisms. Figure 2.12 uses logarithmic scales to plot heart weight against body weight, for 30 seals that had been snared in trawl nets as an unintended consequence of commercial fishing (Stewardson et al., 1999).

For each animal, the data provide information at just one point in time, when they died. The data thus have limited usefulness for the study of growth profiles through time. At best, if conditions have not changed too much over the lifetimes of the animals in the sample, the data may provide an indication of the average of the population growth profiles. If, for example, sample ages range from 1 to 10 years, it is pertinent to ask how food availability may have changed over the past

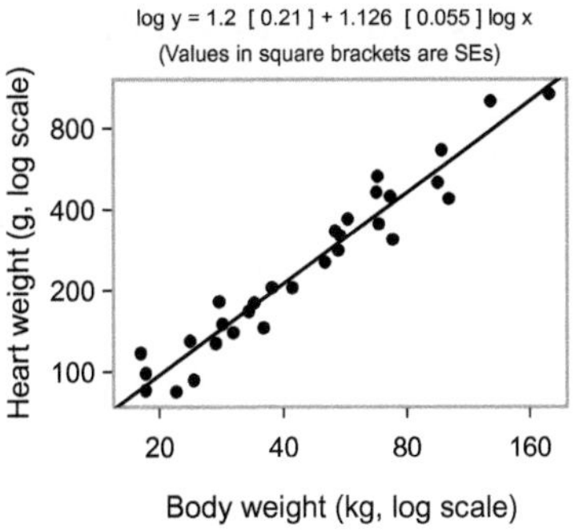

Figure 2.12 Heart weight versus body weight, for 30 Cape fur seals.

10 years, and whether this may have had differential effects on the different ages of animal in the sample.

The Allometric Growth Equation

The allometric growth equation is

$$y = ax^b$$

where x may, for example, be body weight and y heart weight. It may alternatively be written

$$\log y = \log a + b \log x,$$

that is,

$$Y = A + bX, \quad \text{where} \quad Y = \log y, \quad A = \log a, \quad \text{and } X = \log x.$$

Summary information on the coefficients of the regression line in Figure 2.12 is:

```
cfseal.lm <- lm(log(heart) ~ log(weight), data=DAAG::cfseal)
print(coef(summary(cfseal.lm)), digits=4)
```

```
            Estimate Std. Error t value  Pr(>|t|)
(Intercept)    1.204    0.21131   5.699 4.121e-06
log(weight)    1.126    0.05467  20.597 1.872e-18
```

The estimate of the exponent b (= 1.126) differs from 1.0 by 2.3 (= 0.126/0.05467) times its standard error. The relative rate of increase appears, then, slightly greater for heart weight than for body weight. (The t-statistic and p-value in the regression output relate to the comparison between b and zero, which is not of interest. Authors sometimes present p-values that focus on the comparison with zero, even though their interest is in the comparison with 1.0. See Table 10 and other similar tables in Gihr and Pilleri (1969, p. 43).) For an elementary discussion of allometric growth, see Schmidt-Nielsen (1984).

2.6 Empirical Assessment of Predictive Accuracy

The *training data* estimate of predictive accuracy, derived by direct application of model predictions to the data from which the regression relationship was derived, gives in general an optimistic assessment. There is a mutual dependence between the model prediction and the data used to derive that prediction. It is because of this dependence that degrees of freedom for the variance are adjusted to take account of the number of parameters estimated.

The issue becomes a more serious concern in contexts such as the classification models that will be discussed in Chapter 8 and Section 9.4, where no satisfactory theoretical adjustment for the dependence is available. The simple models discussed in the present chapter will be used as a context in which to demonstrate general approaches that address this issue.

2.6.1 The Training/Test Approach, and Cross-Validation

An ideal is to assess the performance of the model on a new dataset. With a large dataset, it is good practice to split the data into two sets: The *training* set is for developing the model, and the *test* set is for testing predictions. The assumption is, then, that the test data can be treated as a random sample from the population to which results will be applied, or otherwise sampled in the same way. If there are too few data to make it reasonable to divide data into training and test sets then the method of cross-validation can be used.

Cross-Validation – a Tutorial Example

In cross-validation, the data are divided into k subsets, where k is typically in the range 3 to 10. Each split between one of the k subsets and remaining data sets up a *fold* in which the subset is used as “test” data, with remaining data (from the other $k-1$ subsets) used to fit (‘train’) the model. The predictive accuracy assessments from the k folds are combined to give a measure of the predictive performance of the model. This may be done for more than one measure of predictive performance. In what follows, the interest will be in sums of squared differences between y-values and the line to which they relate.

For simplicity, we will use three-fold validation only, with a smallish dataset where a standard form of regression estimate might be preferred. Figure 2.13 relates to data on floor area and sale price for 15 houses in a suburb of Canberra (Australia), in 1999.

```
set.seed(29)        # Generate results shown
rand <- sample(rep(1:3, length=15))
## sample() randomly permutes the vector of values 1:3
for(i in 1:3) cat(paste0(i,":"), (1:15)[rand == i],"\n")
```

```
1:  3 4 8 9 11
2:  1 5 10 12 15
3:  2 6 7 13 14
```

The dataset was randomly divided into three groups of five observations, so that there were three folds, that is, test/training splits. In each fold, the sum of squares

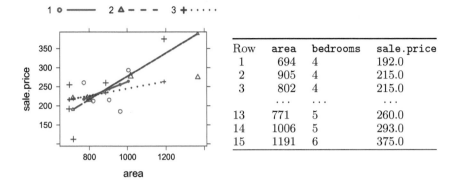

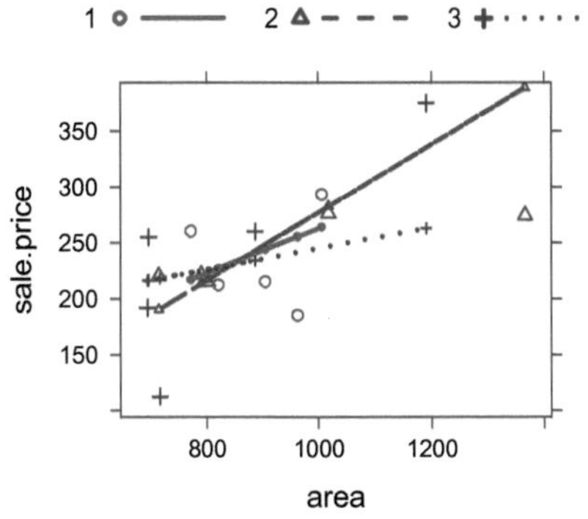

Row	area	bedrooms	sale.price
1	694	4	192.0
2	905	4	215.0
3	802	4	215.0
...	...	...	...
13	771	5	260.0
14	1006	5	293.0
15	1191	6	375.0

Figure 2.13 Graphical summary of three-fold cross-validation for the house sale data in the dataset **houseprices**. Points were assigned a plot character (and color) according to the *fold* at which they made up the "test" subset, with remaining points comprising the "training data." Line color identifies the line fitted to the corresponding training data.

of the differences of test data y-values from the fitted line gave a contribution to a total the residual sum of squares, with degrees of freedom here equal to 15; y-values are in each case independent of the fitted value that has been subtracted. Figure 2.13 is a visual summary, obtained by using the function `DAAG::CVlm()` with the default setting `plotit=TRUE`.

The following summary of the cross-validation results includes, for each fold, estimates of the mean square error.

```
fold 1
Observations in test set: 5
                 2     6     7    13     14
area         905.0 963.0 821.0 771.0 1006.0
cvpred       243.6 255.2 226.9 216.9  263.8
sale.price   215.0 185.0 212.0 260.0  293.0
CV residual  -28.6 -70.2 -14.9  43.1   29.2

Sum of squares = 8684    Mean square = 1737    n = 5

fold 2
Observations in test set: 5
                  3    4   8      9     11
area         802.00 1366 714 1018.0 790.00
cvpred       216.81  388 190  282.5 213.16
sale.price   215.00  274 220  276.0 221.50
CV residual   -1.81 -114  30   -6.5   8.34

Sum of squares = 14083    Mean square = 2817    n = 5

fold 3
Observations in test set: 5
                 1   5    10    12   15
area         694.0 716 887.0 696.0 1191
```

```
cvpred        216.3   218 234.5 216.5   263
sale.price    192.0   113 260.0 255.0   375
CV residual  -24.3  -106   25.5  38.5   112

Sum of squares = 26421    Mean square = 5284    n = 5

Overall (Sum over all 5 folds)
  ms
3279
```

The DAAG function `CVlm()` can be used to give either or both of the above graphs as well as the printed summary. To obtain the estimate of the error mean square, the total of the sums of squares is divided by 15.

This gives

$$s^2 = (24,351 + 20,416 + 14,241)/15 = 3934.$$

Actually, what we have is an estimate of the error mean square when we use only 2/3 of the data. Thus, we expect the cross-validated error to be on average larger than the error if all the data could be used. We can reduce the error by doing 10-fold rather than three-fold cross-validation. Or we can do leave-one-out cross-validation, which for these data is 15-fold cross-validation. Contrast $s^2 = 3934$ with the estimate $s^2 = 2323$ from the model-based estimate in the regression output for the total data.[4]

The methodology can be used in a variety of contexts where the standard least squares theory no longer applies. Thus, in multiple regression, this may happen because there is use of a variable selection process. Valid estimates of the error mean square can be obtained by repeating the variable selection process at each cross-validation fold. Independence assumptions are as important as in standard forms of regression modeling.

2.6.2* Bootstrapping in Regression

We first indicate how resampling methods can be used to estimate the standard error of slope of a regression line. Recalling that the standard error of the slope is the standard deviation of the sampling distribution of the slope, we need a way to approximate this sampling distribution. One approach is to resample the observations or cases directly. For example, suppose five observations have been taken on a predictor x and response y:

$$(x_1,y_1),(x_2,y_2),(x_3,y_3),(x_4,y_4),(x_5,y_5).$$

Generate five random numbers with replacement from the set $\{1,2,3,4,5\}$: 3, 5, 5, 1, 2, say. The corresponding resample is then

$$(x_3,y_3),(x_5,y_5),(x_5,y_5),(x_1,y_1),(x_2,y_2).$$

[4]
```
## Estimate of sigma^2 from regression output
summary(lm(sale.price ~ area, DAAG::houseprices))[["sigma"]]^2
```

Note we are demonstrating only the so-called case-resampling approach. Another approach involves fitting a model and resampling the residuals. Details for both methods are in Davison and Hinkley (1997, chapter 6). A regression line can be fit to the resampled observations, yielding a slope estimate. Repeatedly taking such resamples, we obtain a distribution of slope estimates, the bootstrap distribution.

As an example, consider the regression relating `sale.price` to `area` in the `houseprices` data. We will compute a bootstrap estimate of the standard error of the slope. For comparison purposes, note first the estimate given by `lm()`: .0664.

```
houseprices <- DAAG::houseprices
houseprices.lm <- lm(sale.price ~ area, houseprices)
print(coef(summary(houseprices.lm)),digits=2)
```

```
            Estimate Std. Error t value Pr(>|t|)
(Intercept)    70.75     60.348     1.2    0.262
area            0.19      0.066     2.8    0.014
```

In order to use the `boot()` function, we need a function that will evaluate the slope for each of the bootstrap resamples:

```
houseprices.fn <-
  function (houseprices, index,
            statfun=function(obj)coef(obj)[2]){
            house.resample <- houseprices[index, ]
            house.lm <- lm(sale.price ~ area, data=house.resample)
            statfun(house.lm)   # slope estimate for resampled data
            }
```

We then use the function `boot::boot()` to make repeated calls to `houseprices.fn()`, with different randomly generated resamples from the data frame `houseprices`.

```
set.seed(1028)     # use to replicate the exact results below
library(boot)      # ensure that the boot package is loaded
## requires the data frame houseprices (DAAG)
(houseprices.boot <- boot(houseprices, R=999, statistic=houseprices.fn))
```

```
ORDINARY NONPARAMETRIC BOOTSTRAP


Call:
boot(data = houseprices, statistic = houseprices.fn, R = 999)


Bootstrap Statistics :
    original  bias     std. error
t1*    0.188 0.00972       0.085
```

The output shows the original slope estimate, a bootstrap estimate of the bias of this estimate, and the standard error estimate. The standard error was computed from the standard deviation of the 1000 (data + 999 resamples) slope estimates.

By changing the statistic argument in the `boot()` function appropriately, we can compute standard errors and confidence intervals for fitted values. The change of

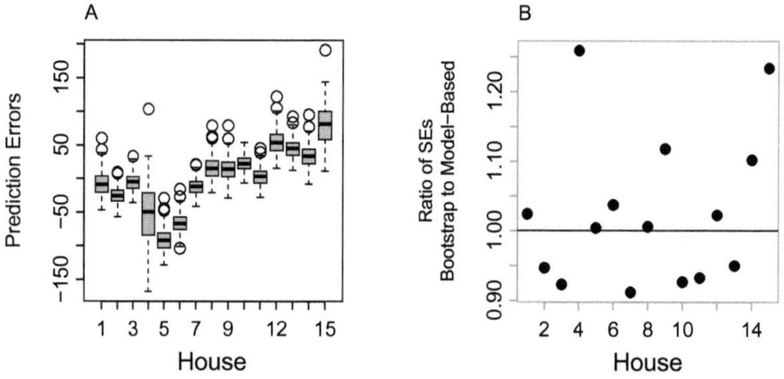

Figure 2.14 (A) Plot of bootstrap distributions of prediction errors for regression relating **sale.price** to **area**, each based on 200 bootstrap estimates of the prediction error. (B) Ratios of bootstrap prediction standard errors to model-based prediction standard errors.

argument can be passed (using the ... mechanism) as an argument with that name to `boot()`. Thus, the following returns bootstrap predictions for house with an area of 1200 square feet, with the function `boot.ci()` then used to obtain a 95 percent confidence interval:

```
statfun1200 <- function(obj)predict(obj, newdata=data.frame(area=1200))
price1200.boot <- boot(houseprices, R=999, statistic=houseprices.fn,
statfun=statfun1200)
boot.ci(price1200.boot, type="perc") # "basic" is an alternative to "perc"
```

```
BOOTSTRAP CONFIDENCE INTERVAL CALCULATIONS
Based on 999 bootstrap replicates

CALL :
boot.ci(boot.out = price1200.boot, type = "perc")

Intervals :
Level     Percentile
95%   (247, 368 )
Calculations and Intervals on Original Scale
```

Regression estimates for each resample can be used to compute predicted values at the original values of the predictor, and compared with model-based predictions. Repeating this procedure a number of times (here $R = 199$) gives a distribution of the prediction errors at each observation. Figure 2.14A displays a prediction error plot for the **houseprices** data.[5] Note the large variability in the prediction error

[5]
```
## Bootstrap estimates of prediction errors of house prices
houseprices2.fn <- function (houseprices, index){
house.resample <- houseprices[index, ]
house.lm <- lm(sale.price ~ area, data=house.resample)
houseprices$sale.price - predict(house.lm, houseprices)
  ## prediction errors from resamples
}
n <- length(houseprices$area);  R <- 199
houseprices2.boot <- boot(houseprices, R=R, statistic=houseprices2.fn)
house.fac <- factor(rep(1:n, rep(R, n)))
```

associated with observation 4. Figure 2.14B shows ratios of the bootstrap standard errors to the model-based standard errors.[6] The standard errors that are calculated from the bootstrap output are generally larger than those given by the `lm` regression model, and should perhaps be used in preference.

We can also compute an estimate of the aggregate prediction error, as an alternative to the cross-validation estimate obtained in the previous subsection. There are a number of ways to do this, and some care should be taken. We refer the interested reader to Davison and Hinkley (1997, section 6.4).

Commentary

The cross-validation and bootstrap estimates of mean square error require the assumption that the variance is homogeneous. The estimate of predictive error applies only to data that have been sampled in the same way as the data that are used as the basis for the calculations. It assumes that the `target` population will be highly comparable to the `source` population that generated the data.

Here, the estimate of predictive accuracy applies only to 1999 house prices in the same city suburb. Such standard errors may have little relevance to the prediction of house prices in another suburb, even if thought to be comparable, or to prediction for more than a very short time into the future. This point has relevance to the use of regression methods in business "data mining" applications. A prediction that a change will make cost savings of $500,000 in the current year may have little relevance to subsequent years. The point has special force if changes will take years rather than months to implement.

A realistic, though still not very adequate, assessment of accuracy may be derived by testing a model that is based on data from previous years on a test set that is formed from the current year's data. Predictions based on the current year's data may, if other features of the business environment do not change, have a roughly comparable accuracy for prediction a year into the future. If the data series is long enough, we might, starting at a point part-way through the series, compare predictions one year into the future with data for that year. The estimated predictive accuracy would be the average accuracy for all such predictions. A more sophisticated approach might involve incorporation of temporal components into the model, that is, use of a time series model. See Maindonald (2003) for more extended commentary on such issues.

2.7 One- and Two-Way Comparisons

This section introduces examples where one or more factors, that is, categorical effects, have the role of explanatory variables.

[6]
```
## Ratios of bootstrap to model-based standard errors
bootse <- apply(houseprices2.boot$t, 2, sd)
usualse <- predict.lm(houseprices.lm, se.fit=TRUE)$se.fit
plot(bootse/usualse, xlab="House",
ylab="Ratio of SEs\nBootstrap to Model-Based", pch=16)
```

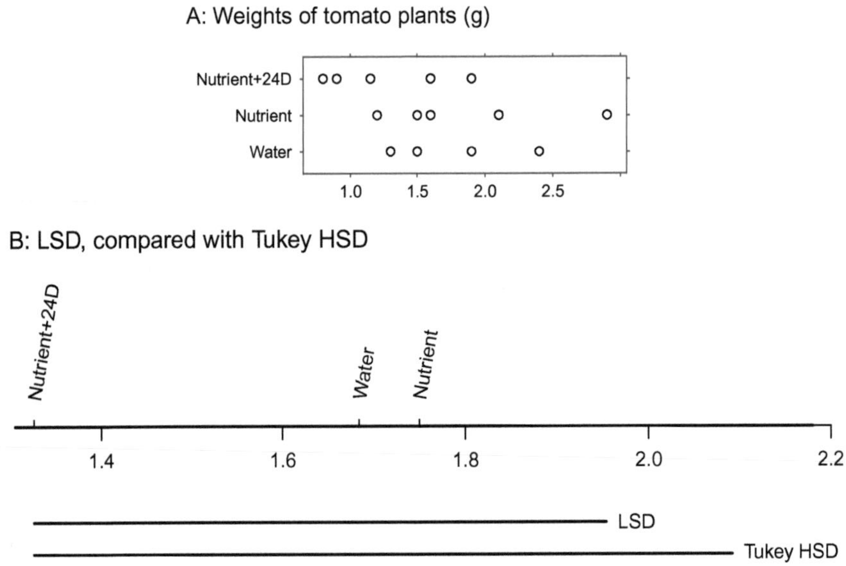

Figure 2.15 Panel A compares weights of tomato plants, after two months of the three treatments. In Panel B means that differ by more than the LSD (least significant difference) are different, at the 5 percent level, in a *t*-test that compares the two means. Tukey's honest significant difference (HSD) takes into account the number of means that are compared. See the text for details.

2.7.1 One-Way Comparisons

Figure 2.15A displays data from a one-way unstructured comparison between three treatments. The weights of the plants were measured after two months on the respective treatments: water, concentrated nutrient, and concentrated nutrient plus the selective herbicide 2,4-D.

```
tomato <- data.frame(Weight = c(1.5, 1.9, 1.3, 1.5, 2.4, 1.5,  # Water
                          1.5, 1.2, 1.2, 2.1, 2.9, 1.6,  # Nutrient
                          1.9, 1.6, 0.8, 1.15, 0.9, 1.6), # Nutrient+24D
  trt = factor(rep(c("Water", "Nutrient", "Nutrient+24D"), c(6, 6, 6))))
## Make `Water` the first level of trt.  In aov or lm calculations, it is
## then taken as the baseline or reference level.
tomato$trt <- relevel(tomato$trt, ref="Water")
```

The code has three treatments only from the four that are in the data frame `DAAG::tomato`.

The strip plots display "within group" variability, as well as giving an indication of differences among the group means. Variances seem similar for the three treatments.

Summary code is:

```
## A: Weights of tomato plants (g)
library(lattice, quietly=TRUE)
gph <- stripplot(trt~Weight, aspect=0.35, scale=list(tck=0.6), data=tomato)
```

```
## B: Summarize comparison between LSD and Tukey's HSD graphically
tomato.aov <- aov(Weight ~ trt, data=tomato)
```

```
DAAG::onewayPlot(obj=tomato.aov)
```

Figure 2.15 compares two different statistics that, for data where there is more than one comparison, are commonly used as measures of the difference in treatment means that is "significant" at the 5 percent level.

- For the 5 percent least significant difference (LSD), the 5 percent is the proportion of all comparisons between treatment means in which the difference can be expected to exceed the LSD.
- For the 5 percent honest significant difference (HSD), the 5 percent is the proportion of experiments in which the maximum difference between treatments can be expected to exceed the HSD. Ignoring changes in degrees of freedom and possible associated changes in the standard error, the HSD will increase as the number of treatment groups that are to be compared increases.

The LSD is overly lax, while the HSD may be overly conservative. Note the assumption that the standard error of difference is the same for all treatment comparisons. As all three treatments have the same number of observations, it is enough for the variance to be the same for all treatments.

The function `BHH2::anovaPlot()` offers alternative graphical perspectives:

```
BHH2::anovaPlot(tomato.aov)
```

Two dot plots are presented, one for the residuals and one for the treatment means, suitably rescaled so that they are comparable to the residuals. Such plots, advocated by Box et al. (2005), provide a clear visualization of the strength and direction of the statistical evidence, while also highlighting possible problems, such as outliers, in the data. Braun (2012) describes some graphical alternatives.

The Analysis of Variance Table

The analysis of variance table is given by the `anova()` function, thus:

```
## Do analysis of variance calculations
anova(tomato.aov)
```

```
Analysis of Variance Table

Response: Weight
          Df Sum Sq Mean Sq F value Pr(>F)
trt        2   0.63   0.314     1.2   0.33
Residuals 15   3.91   0.261
```

The residual mean squared error is 0.261. The mean square for the the differences of the three group means from the overall mean accounts for two degrees of freedom. Each treatment contributes $6 - 1 = 5$ degrees of freedom to the pooled or residual sum of squares, giving $3 \times 5 = 15$ d.f. in all. Note that 2 (for trt) plus 15 (for residuals) equals 17, which is one less than the number of observations. Estimation of the overall mean accounts for the remaining degree of freedom.

The `Mean Sq` ("mean square") column has estimates of between sample (`trt`) and within sample variability (`Residuals`). The between sample variance can be calculated by applying the function `var()` to the vector of treatment means, then multiplying by the common sample size, in this case 6. The within sample variability estimate is, effectively, a pooled variance estimate for the three treatments. Each mean square is the result from dividing the `Sum Sq` ("sum of squares") column by the appropriate degrees of freedom.

In the absence of systematic differences between the sample means, the two mean squares have the same expected value, with a ratio (the F-statistic) near 1. Systematic differences between the sample means will add extra variation into the treatment mean square, with no effect on the residual mean square, giving an expected F-statistic that is larger than 1. Where the evidence for differences is convincing, interest will then turn to teasing out the nature of those differences. A strategy that is sometimes adopted is to use a preliminary F-test to decide whether to apply the LSD criterion.

In the output above, the F-statistic is 1.2, on three and eight degrees of freedom, with $p = 0.33$. There is no convincing indication that there are indeed differences among the means. With four treatments, as in the complete `DAAG::tomato` dataset, there are six comparisons. The case for accounting for the number of of comparisons made is then very strong, whether or not starting with an overall analysis of variance F-test.

Other Multiple Comparison Sets

Tukey's HSD is one of a number of criteria that may be used for comparisons when more than two group means are compared. See `?p.adjust`, and tests available in the package *agricolae*, for other possibilities.

The discussion will now move on from examples where the number of comparisons that are of interest is relatively small to cases where the number of comparisons is large – hundreds, or thousands, or tens of thousands. The proliferation of p-values then allows the calculation of a false discovery rate. Subsection 2.7.2 that follows will be a brief diversion, before returning to consider the new possibilities that severe multiplicity can offer.

Multiple range tests should not be used when there is an ordering in the explanatory variable that allows the response to be modeled as a line or as a curve. The simulations in Subsection 2.7.2 that now follows illustrate the loss of power that can result.

There is a large literature on multiple range tests and simultaneous inference. See Hothorn et al. (2008), and references given on the help page `?p.adjust`. See also the CRAN *SocialSciences* task view.

2.7.2 Regression versus Qualitative Comparisons – Issues of Power

Figure 2.16 plots results from 200 simulations from a straight line model with slope 0.8, SD = 2, and four replications at each of the levels 1, 2, . . . 5. Both axes use a scale of $\log(p/(1-p))$. The vertical axis shows the p-values for a test for linear trend, while the horizontal axis shows p-values for an analysis of variance test for qualitative differences. Most points (for the simulation shown, 89 percent) lie below

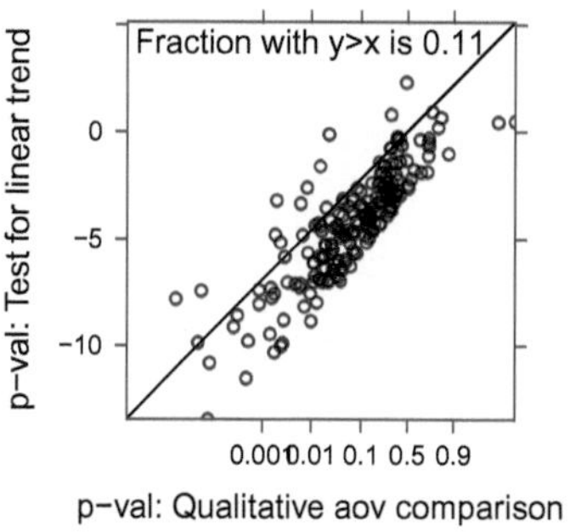

Figure 2.16 The plot compares p-values for a test for linear trend with p-values from an analysis of variance test for qualitative differences, in each of 200 sets of simulated data. The line $y = x$ is superimposed.

the line $y = x$, showing the greater power of a test for linear trend. (Note that the test for linear trend is equivalent to using `aov()` to test for a linear contrast when the explanatory term is an ordered factor.)

The function `DAAG::simulateLinear()` automates such simulations. Write the p-values for a test for linear trend as p_l, and the p-values for the analysis of variance test for qualitative differences as p_a. Specifying `type="density"` gives overlaid plots of the densities for the two sets of p-values, both on a scale of $\log(p/(1-p))$, together with a plot of the density of $\log(p_l/(1-p_l)) - \log(p_a/(1-p_a))$. As the data are paired, this last plot is the preferred form of comparison.

Fitting a line (or a curve) allows interpolation between successive levels of the explanatory variable. It may be reasonable to hazard prediction a small distance beyond the range of the data. The pattern of response may give scientific insight.

2.7.3* Severe Multiplicity – the False Discovery Rate

The dataset `DAAG::coralPval` that is the subject of the following discussion was generated using a microarray gene expression technology. Microarrays are now increasingly being replaced by the more direct measurements of gene activity in the cell that the RNA-Seq technology provides. In either case, a single experiment may yield information on thousands, or tens of thousands, of genes. The present data are from experimental work that was designed to compare gene expression, for the 3042 genes investigated, between two life-stages of coral – the presettlement free-swimming stage, and postsettlement. Each of the full complement of six panels (two only are shown in Figure 2.17) had 3072 spots; this included 30 blanks. Where there was an increase, the spot should be fairly consistently red, or reddish, over all six panels. Where there was a decrease, the spot should be fairly consistently green, or greenish. Results from the six sets of comparisons were used to generate 3042 p-values, one for each of 3042 sets of spots.

The methodology that will be described has wide application, to any form of comparison that generates large numbers of p-values – hundreds, or thousands, or more. The multiplicity of p-values allows inferences that an individual p-value does not provide. It allows the estimation of a false discovery rate (FDR).

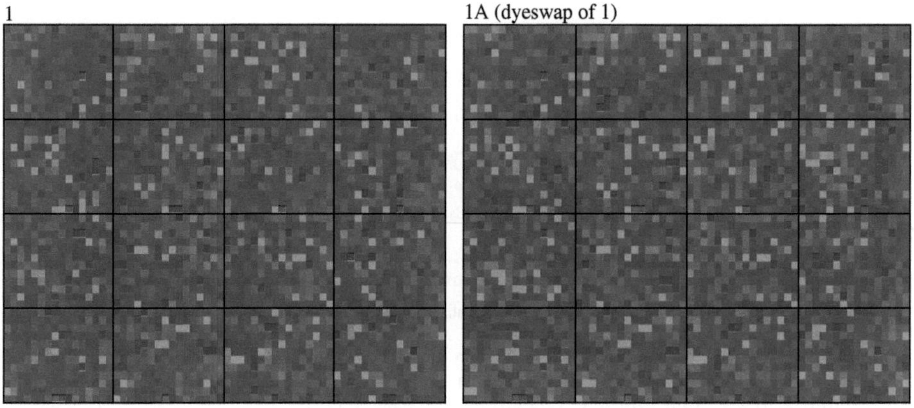

Figure 2.17 This false color image shows the intensity of the post-signal (red), relative to the pre-signal (green), for the first two of six half-slides ("panels") in a two-channel microarray gene expression experiment. Use of one dye-swap pair per slide was designed to allow adjustment for any systematic red–green bias.

**Microarrays and Alternatives – Technical Note*

In the experimental procedure and subsequent processing that led to the plots shown in Figure 2.17, the slides are first printed with probes, with one probe per spot, each designed to check for the expression of one gene. The two samples carry labeling with separate fluorescent dyes so that when later a spot "lights up" under a scanner, the relative intensities of the two dye frequencies will provide a measure of differences in the signal intensity.

After labeling the separate samples, mixing them, and wiping the mixture over the slide or half-slide, and various laboratory processing steps, a scanner was used to determine, for each spot, the intensities generated from the two samples. Various corrections are then necessary, leading finally to the calculation of logarithms of intensity ratios. Essentially, it is logarithms of intensity ratios that are shown in Figure 2.17.

For further information on the statistical analysis of microarray data, see Smyth (2004). With suitable preprocessing of the data, the methods carry over to the analysis of RNA-Seq data. See Law et al. (2014). For background on the coral data, see Grasso et al. (2008).

The False Discovery Rate (FDR)

The object `DAAG::coralPval` has 3072 p-values from the gene expression data represented in Figure 2.17. The following calculates, for several different thresholds `pcrit` $= p_{crit}$, the total number of genes detected as differentially expressed with threshold as the threshold:

```
coralPval <- DAAG::coralPval
pcrit <- c(0.05, 0.02, 0.01, 0.001)
under <- sapply(pcrit, function(x)sum(coralPval<=x))
```

The numbers expected under the null hypothesis, in each case, are:

```
expected <- pcrit*length(coralPval)
```

These numbers can be set out in a table that allows a comparison of the implications of choosing one threshold rather than another.

```
fdrtab <- data.frame(Threshold=pcrit, Expected=expected,
Discoveries=under, FDR=round(expected/under, 4))
print(xtable::xtable(fdrtab), include.rownames=FALSE, hline.after=FALSE)
```

Threshold	Expected	Discoveries	FDR
0.05	153.60	1310	0.12
0.02	61.44	1068	0.06
0.01	30.72	900	0.03
0.00	3.07	491	0.01

The column headed FDR is just the number of detections ("discoveries") expected under the null hypothesis, divided by the actual number detected. Although often described as an adjusted p-value, the result of the adjustment is not a p-value, but an estimate of the false discovery rate. For the false discovery rate to equal 0.05, the unadjusted p-value threshold should be set somewhere between 0.01 and 0.02.

The Benjamini–Hochberg method for adjusting p-values relies, in essence, on the argument just given. Rather than finding an unadjusted p-value threshold, it is, however, more straightforward to work directly with adjusted values, calculated as will now be described. After sorting the p-values from smallest to largest, the calculation is:

$$p_{adj[i]} = \frac{m}{i} p_i\,; \quad i = 1,2,\ldots,m.$$

A further tweak is to set each $p_{adj[i]}$ to the smallest value, if any, that appears later in the sequence. This ensures that $p_{adj[i]}$ is a monotonic function of p_i. (Also, any value that is greater than 1.0 is set to 1.) The function `p.adjust()` (*stats* package in base R), can be used (specify `method="BH"`) to do the adjustments, thus:

```
fdr <- p.adjust(coralPval, method="BH")
```

Here are numbers that fall under thresholds 0.05, 0.04, 0.02, and 0.01:

```
fdrcrit <- c(0.05, 0.04, 0.02, 0.01)
under <- sapply(fdrcrit, function(x)sum(coralPval<=x))
setNames(under, paste(fdrcrit))
```

```
0.05 0.04 0.02 0.01
1310 1234 1068  900
```

The FDR for a cutoff of 0.05 is a composite value, with some genes that fall under this threshold having an FDR much greater than 0.05, and many more having an FDR that is much less. The discussion that now follows shows how this composite FDR can be broken apart. Take p_{45} as the false discovery rate for genes in the range $0.04 <$ fdrcrit ≤ 0.05. Then the 1310 genes with fdrcrit ≤ 0.05 are comprised thus:

- $1310 - 1234 = 76$ genes with an average FDR of p_{45}
- 1234 genes with an average FDR of 0.04.

Then

$$p_{45} \times 76 + 0.04 \times 1234 = 0.05 \times 1310.$$

Solving for p_{45} yields, rounded to two decimal places,

$$p_{45} = 0.21.$$

As with use of the $p \leq 0.05$ criterion for a single p-value, it is tempting to place greater weight than is warranted on an FDR statistic that falls just under 0.05.

The average estimated false discovery rate for genes with $0.01 < \text{fdrcrit} \leq 0.02$, is:

$$\frac{0.02 \times 1068 - 0.01 \times 900}{1068 - 900} = 0.07.$$

This line of argument can be combined with the assumption of a smooth change in the FDR to provide a local FDR estimate. These bear the same relationship to the FDR that a density, for the relevant distribution, bears to the corresponding p-value, that is, to an area in the tail or tails of the distribution. The function `locfdr::locfdr()` is designed to provide, as well as estimates of local FDRs, an estimate of the proportion of p-values that correspond to cases where the null hypothesis is true. Estimates of the proportion of nulls may vary widely, depending on the method used.

As noted, the FDR estimates are not p-values in the conventional sense. They give a frequency based probability that a detected difference is a real difference – information that p-values do not provide. Why insist on working with p-values when there is a better alternative? When m is large, the estimate provided has high statistical accuracy.

The `p.adjust()` FDR estimate remains valid in a wide range of contexts where p-values are positively correlated. Also available is `method="BY"`, designed for contexts where there may be quite general dependence structures. This gives a very conservative adjustment. Other available adjustment methods (see `?p.adjust`) are more in the style of p-values.

The number 3072 of p-values is small relative to much other expression array data. The experimental data that will be considered in Section 9.5, from an experiment with RNA-Seq data, yielded 18658 p-values for each comparison of interest.

2.7.4 Data with a Two-Way Structure (Two Factors)

Consider now data from an experiment that compared wild type (`wt`) and genetically modified rice plants (`ANU843`), each with three different chemical treatments. A first factor relates to whether `F10` or `NH4Cl` or `NH4NO3` is applied. A second factor relates to whether the plant is wild type (`wt`) or `ANU843`.

There are 72 sets of results, that is, two types (`variety`) × three chemical treatments (`fert`) × 6 replicates, with the setup repeated across each of two blocks (`Block`). Figures 2.18A and B show alternative perspectives on these data.

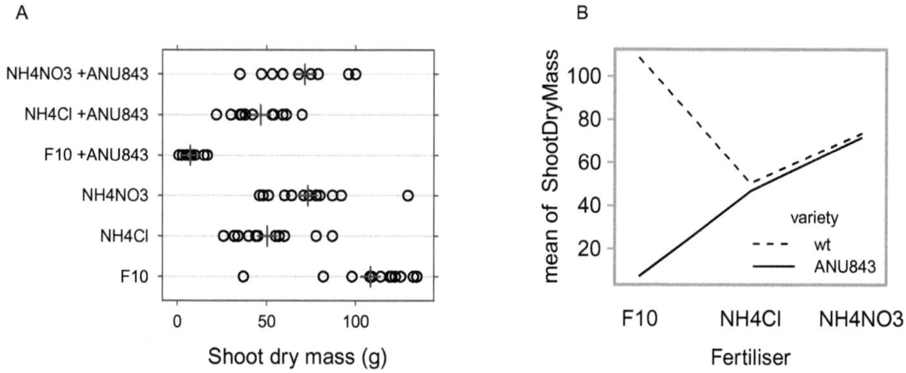

Figure 2.18 Both panels are for rice shoot dry mass data. Panel A shows a one-way strip plot, with different strips for different treatment regimes. Treatment means are shown with a large `+`. The interaction plot in Panel B shows how the effect of fertilizer (the first factor) changes with variety (the second factor). Data relate to Perrine et al. (2001).

Figure 2.18B shows a large difference between `ANU843` and wild type (`wt`) for the `F10` treatment. For the other treatments, there is no detectable difference. A two-way analysis will show a large interaction.[7]

Note, finally, that the treatments were arranged in two blocks. In general, this has implications for the analysis. This example will be discussed again in Chapter 4, where block effects will be taken into account.

2.7.5 Presentation Issues

The discussion so far has treated all comparisons as of equal interest. Often they are not. There are several possibilities.

- Interest may be in comparing treatments with a control, with comparisons between treatments of lesser interest.
- Interest may be in comparing treatments with one another, with any controls used as a check that the order of magnitude of the treatment effect is pretty much what was expected.
- There may be several groups of treatments, with the chief interest in comparisons between the different groups.

Any of these situations should lead to specifying in advance the specific treatment comparisons that are of interest.

Often, however, scientists prefer to regard all treatments as of equal interest. Results may be presented in a graph that displays, for each factor level, the mean and its associated standard error. Alternatives to displaying bars that show the standard error may be to show a 95 percent confidence interval for the mean, or to show the standard deviation. Displaying or quoting the standard deviation may be appropriate when the interest is, not in comparing level means, but in obtaining an idea of the extent to which the different levels are clearly separated. In any case, the following hold.

[7]
```
## Simplified version of code, Panel B only
with(DAAG::rice, interaction.plot(fert, variety, ShootDryMass, xlab="Fertiliser"))
```

Table 2.5 *Each tester made two firmness tests on each of five fruit.*

Fruit	Tester	Firmness	Mean
1	1	6.8, 7.3	*7.05*
2	1	7.2, 7.3	*7.25*
3	1	7.4, 7.3	*7.35*
4	1	6.8, 7.6	*7.2*
5	1	7.2, 6.5	*6.85*
6	2	7.7, 7.7	*7.7*
7	2	7.4, 7.0	*7.2*
8	2	7.2, 7.6	*7.4*
9	2	6.7, 6.7	*6.7*
10	2	7.2, 6.8	*7.0*

- For graphical presentation, use a layout that reflects the data structure, that is, a one-way layout for a one-way data structure, and a two-way layout for a two-way data structure.
- Explain clearly how error bars should be interpreted: ± SE limits, ± 95 percent confidence interval, ± SED limits, or whatever. Or if the intention is to indicate the variation in observed values, the SD (standard deviation) may be appropriate.
- Where there is more than one source of variation, explain what source(s) of "error" is/are represented. It is pointless and potentially misleading to present information on a source of error that is of little or no interest, for example, on analytical error when the relevant error for the treatment comparisons that are of interest arises from fruit to fruit or tree to tree variation.

2.8 Data with a Nested Variation Structure

Ten apples are taken from a box. A randomization procedure assigns five to one tester, and the other five to another tester. Each tester makes two firmness tests on each of their five fruit. Firmness is measured by the pressure needed to push the flat end of a piece of rod through the surface of the fruit. Table 2.5 gives the results, in N/m^2.

For comparing the testers, we have five experimental units for each tester, not 10. One way to do a *t*-test is to take means for each fruit. We then have five values (means, italicized) for one treatment, that we can compare with the five values for the other treatment.

If the data structure is ignored, and ten values for one tester are compared with 10 values for the other tester (the pretense is that we have ten experimental units for each tester), the analysis will suggest that the treatment means are more accurate than is really the case. It is likely to underestimate the standard error of the treatment difference.

2.8.1 Degrees of Freedom Considerations

For comparison of two means when the sample sizes n_1 and n_2 are small, it is important to have as many degrees of freedom as possible for the denominator of the t-test. A small bias in a calculated SED may be a reasonable tradeoff for extra degrees of freedom.

The same considerations arise in the one-way analysis of variance, and we pursue the issue in that context. It is illuminating to plot out, side by side, say 10 SEDs based on randomly generated normal variates, first for a comparison based on 2 d.f., then 10 SEDs for a comparison based on 4 d.f., etc.

A formal statistical test is thus unlikely, unless the sample is large, to detect differences in variance that may have a large effect on the result of the test. It is therefore necessary to rely on judgment. Both past experience with similar data and subject area knowledge may be important. In comparing two treatments that are qualitatively similar, differences in the population variance may be unlikely, unless the difference in means is at least of the same order of magnitude as the individual means. If the means are of similar magnitude, then it is reasonable to expect that the variances will be similar, though this is by no means inevitable,

If the treatments are qualitatively different, then differences in variance may be expected. Thus in weed control experiments there will be few weeds in all plots where there is effective weed control, and thus little variation. In control plots, or for plots given ineffective treatments, there may be huge variation.

If there do seem to be differences in variance, it may be possible to model the variance as a function of the mean. It may be possible to apply a variance-stabilizing transformation. Or the variance may be a smooth function of the mean. Otherwise, if there are just one or two degrees of freedom per mean, use a pooled estimate of variance unless the assumption of equal variance seems clearly unacceptable.

2.8.2 General Multiway Analysis of Variance Designs

Generalization to multiway analysis of variance raises a variety of new issues. If each combination of factor levels has the same number of observations, and if there is no structure in the *error* (or *noise*), the extension is straightforward. The extension is less straightforward when one or both of these conditions are not met. For unbalanced data from designs with a simple error structure, it is necessary to use the `lm()` (linear model) function. The functions `nlme::lme()` and `lme4::lmer()` are both able to handle problems where there is structure in the error term. Data from unbalanced as well as from balanced designs can be handled. Chapter 7 will take up the discussion of models of this type.

2.9 Bayesian Estimation – Further Commentary and Approaches

The account of Bayesian methods given in this text should be enough to give a sense of the broad difference in perspective that they offer, relative to the role that p-values have in frequentist approaches. As well as providing for the calculation of Bayes Factors and/or posterior probability distributions for one- and two-sample t-tests, the *BayesFactor* package has provision for tests that relate to linear models more generally. Further possibilities include tests for proportions (assuming observations are independent with the same probability), contingency tables (under the independence assumption relevant to the sampling design), and for correlations (assuming normality for y given x). Readers are encouraged to work through, as a minimum, the first two of the vignettes that come with the *BayesFactor* package. Calculation of Bayes Factors in other contexts, and the use of other forms of summary statistics, will in general require resort to the Markov Chain Monte Carlo (MCMC) simulation approach that will be demonstrated in Subsection 2.9.3. To get details of the wide range of R packages that implement Bayesian methods, check the CRAN task view for Bayesian inference.[8]

2.9.1 * Bayesian Estimation with Normal Priors and Likelihood

A relatively simple example is that of a normal likelihood (as considered in Subsection 1.4.6) where the unobserved true mean is now also assumed to have a normal distribution, now with mean μ_0 and variance σ_0^2. The posterior density of the mean is then normal with

$$\text{mean} = \frac{n\bar{y} + \mu_0\,\sigma^2/\sigma_0^2}{n + \sigma^2/\sigma_0^2}; \text{ variance} = \frac{\sigma^2}{n + \sigma^2/\sigma_0^2}.$$

This assumes that σ^2 is known; the sample variance can be used as an estimate. An alternative is to put a prior distribution on this parameter as well.

In problems where the model has many parameters, direct evaluation of the relevant posterior distributions for parameters of interest is commonly computationally intractable. Fortunately, a simulation technique called Markov Chain Monte Carlo (or MCMC) will usually give effective approximations to these posterior distributions. Calculations must run for long enough that the posterior distribution reaches a steady state that is independent of the starting values of parameters.

Exercise 2.16a at the end of the chapter demonstrates the simulation of a finite state Markov chain. Subsection 2.9.3 will use Bayesian MCMC for straight line regression.

2.9.2 Further Comments on Bayes Factors

The Sellke et al. (2001) upper limit

For $p < e^{-1}$, Sellke et al. (2001) give an upper bound, applying to a wide class of priors, on the Bayes Factor that corresponds to a given p-value. The posterior odds in favor of the alternative are no greater than:

$$\frac{R}{-ep\log(p)}. \tag{2.4}$$

For $p = 0.05$, this upper bound is $2.46R$, while for $p = 0.01$ it is $7.99R$.

The result applies to a class of frequently used priors for the effect size that includes among others the normal distribution, with the mean centered at the (point) null hypothesis. The requirement is that for any fixed tail probability p_0,

[8] `https://cloud.r-project.org/web/views/Bayesian.html`

the distribution of $p/p_0|p < p_0$ is nonincreasing as the test statistic increases in absolute value.

Held and Ott (2018) discuss other bounds that are available, including bounds that account for sample size. In their account, the bound given is a lower bound in favor of the null, which better reflects what priors that are centered at the null are designed to do.

*A Note on the Bayesian Information Criterion

For models where the number of observations is large relative to the number of parameters estimated, an argument can be made for using the the Bayesian Information Criterion function `BIC()` statistic that was introduced in Subsection 1.7.1 as a starting point for calculating a Bayes Factor. Given BIC statistics `BIC1` and `BIC2`, the factor favoring the second model over the first is taken to be:

$$\exp\left(\frac{\text{BIC2} - \text{BIC1}}{2}\right).$$

This is the Bayes Factor obtained when the difference between the BIC2 and the BIC1 model is assumed to have a "unit information" prior. In the case of one- and two-sample comparisons, the prior is a normal distribution that is centered on the mean of the data, with variance for the difference δ that estimated for a single observation. See, for example, Neath and Cavanaugh (2012). Such a prior is unreasonably favorable to the alternative when the sample size is small. Note that because the mean is centered on the mean of the data, the conditions under which the Sellke et al. (2001) upper limit apply are violated.

The following uses a result from Rouder et al. (2009) that, for two-sided p-values from a one-sample t-test, gives the corresponding BIC based Bayes Factor. The Bayes Factor that is derived using `BayesFactor::ttest.tstat()` as in shown in Figure 1.24 is given for comparison.

```
pval <- c(.05,.01,.001); np <- length(pval)
Nval <- c(4,6,10,20,40,80,160); nlen <- length(Nval)
## Difference in BIC statistics, interpreted as Bayes factor
t2BFbic <- function(p,N){t <- qt(p/2, df=N-1, lower.tail=FALSE)
                    exp((N*log(1+t^2/(N-1))-log(N))/2)}
bicVal <- outer(pval, Nval, t2BFbic)
## Bayes factor, calculated using BayesFactor::ttest.tstat()
t2BF <- function(p, N){t <- qt(p/2, df=N-1, lower.tail=FALSE)
          BayesFactor::ttest.tstat(t=t, n1=N, simple=TRUE, rscale = "medium")}
BFval <- matrix(nrow=np, ncol=nlen)
for(i in 1:np)for(j in 1:nlen) BFval[i,j] <- t2BF(pval[i], Nval[j])
cfVal <- rbind(BFval, bicVal)[c(1,4,2,5,3,6),]
dimnames(cfVal) <- list(
  paste(rep(pval,rep(2,np)), rep(c("- from ttest.tstat", "- from BIC"),np)),
      paste0(c("n=",rep("",nlen-1)),Nval))
round(cfVal,1)
```

```
                          n=4    6   10   20   40   80  160
0.05 - from ttest.tstat   2.4  2.1  1.8  1.4  1.1  0.8  0.6
0.05 - from BIC           9.6  5.1  3.0  1.8  1.2  0.8  0.5
0.01 - from ttest.tstat   7.0  6.9  6.2  5.1  4.1  3.1  2.3
```

```
0.01  - from BIC             76.5   31.4   15.3   8.0   5.0   3.3   2.3
0.001  - from ttest.tstat    32.3   40.0   40.9  36.6  30.5  24.2  18.4
0.001  - from BIC          1606.1  464.0  175.7  77.1  43.7  27.8  18.7
```

For $p = 0.001$ and $n = 4$, the ratio 1606:1 is much larger and makes even less sense than the 999:1 ratio that results from wrongly interpreting the null hypothesis 1 in 1000 value as giving a relative probability. With large samples, the data overwhelms the prior. The estimates are then very similar to those returned by `BayesFactor::ttest.tstat()` with its Cauchy prior that is centered on the point null.

These results reinforce the point that the "Bayes Factor" that is calculated from BIC statistics will overly favor the alternative when sample sizes are small. Bear in mind that the small sample context is the one where other model assumptions are of most consequence.

The article `www.rpubs.com/lindeloev/bayes_factors` describes and compares results from different models used to calculate Bayes factors in several relevant R packages.

2.9.3 Bayesian Regression Estimation using the* MCMCpack *Package*

Subsection 2.9 discussed ideas of Bayesian estimation, drawing attention to the use of the Markov Chain Monte Carlo (MCMC) simulation technique to generates successive parameter estimates. The simulation process must be allowed to *burn in*, that is, run for long enough that the posterior distribution reaches a steady state that is independent of the starting values of parameters. The function `MCMCpack::MCMCregress()`, with a similar syntax to `lm()`, can be used for the calculations. The default is to assume independent uniform priors for the regression coefficients, to allow the simulation to run for 10,000 iterations, and to take the first 1000 iterations as burn-in.

The example that now follows fits a regression model to the `roller` data of Subsection 1.5.2. It is designed for illustrative purposes, for a regression fit where most data analysts would consider this level of sophistication overdone. Code and accompanying output are:

```
suppressPackageStartupMessages(library(MCMCpack))
roller.mcmc <- MCMCregress(depression ~ weight, data=DAAG::roller)
summary(roller.mcmc)
```

```
Iterations = 1001:11000
Thinning interval = 1
Number of chains = 1
Sample size per chain = 10000

1. Empirical mean and standard deviation for each variable,
   plus standard error of the mean:

             Mean     SD Naive SE Time-series SE
(Intercept) -2.00  5.486  0.05486        0.05316
weight       2.65  0.812  0.00812        0.00765
```

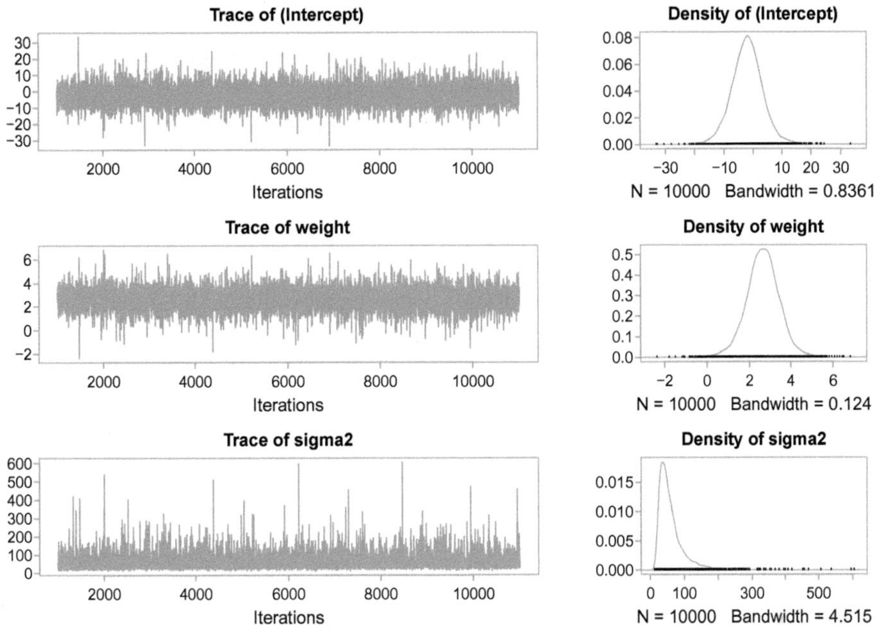

Figure 2.19 Diagnostic plots for the Bayesian analysis that used `MCMCregress()`.

```
sigma2        60.47 40.610  0.40610          0.52264

2. Quantiles for each variable:

               2.5%    25%    50%    75%  97.5%
(Intercept) -12.80  -5.38  -1.99   1.29   9.25
weight        1.01   2.17   2.66   3.16   4.26
sigma2       21.01  35.40  49.39  71.42 166.23
```

Because estimates from the previous iteration are the starting values for the current iteration, the sequence of estimates is Markovian and there is a lag 1 partial autocorrelation. The time series SE in the final column is designed to adjust for this partial autocorrelation. (Specifically, it is assumed that they follow an autoregressive process of order 1.) The standard error is inflated to take account of the partial autocorrelation between successive estimates. Notice that the coefficient estimates are very similar to those obtained in Subsection 1.5.2 using `lm()`, while the SEs (both sets) are slightly larger.

Figure 2.19 uses a plot method, for objects of class `mcmc` that can be used as a check on whether an adequate number of iterations were allowed for burn-in. The layout has been changed somewhat from the default. The code is:

```
mat <- matrix(c(1:6), byrow=TRUE, ncol=2)
# panels are 1, then 2, ... 6. Layout=dim(mat), i.e., 3 by 2
layout(mat, widths=rep(c(2,1),3), heights=rep(1,6))
# NB: widths & heights are relative
plot(roller.mcmc, auto.layout=FALSE, ask=FALSE, col="gray40")
# The method is plot.mcmc()
```

These plots are unremarkable. For this very simple model, burn-in occurs quickly, and none of the plots show any indication of a trend. The posterior distributions of the model coefficients all look plausibly normal.

The *coda* package, on which *MCMCpack* depends, has several other functions that give diagnostic information that may be helpful in interpreting the MCMC results. See `help(package="coda")`.

2.10 Recap

- The aim should be an insightful and coherent account of the data, placing it in the context of what is already known. Ensure that the statistical analysis assists this larger purpose. Ensure that the analysis and graphs reflect any important structure in the data.
- In group comparisons, present means, standard errors, and numbers for each group. Results from formal significance tests have secondary usefulness.
- The use of many significance tests readily leads to data summaries that lack coherence and insight. Look for coherent forms of analysis that are effective in summing up what can be learned from the data.
- Reserve multiple range tests for unstructured comparisons.
- Think about the science behind the data. What analysis (or analyses) will best reflect that science?

Statistical models have both deterministic (*signal*) and random error (*noise*) components. In simpler cases, as in the present chapter, the model takes the form:

$$\text{observation} = \text{signal} + \text{noise}.$$

The hope is that the fitted value will recapture most of the signal, and that the residual will contain mostly noise. Unfortunately, as the relative contribution of the noise increases,

- it becomes harder to distinguish between signal and noise,
- it becomes harder to decide between competing models.

Model assumptions, such as normality, independence, and constancy of the variance, should be checked to the extent possible. Plots of residuals are important diagnostic tools. The function `plot()`, with an `lm` model object as argument, gives a basic set of diagnostic plots, as in Figure 2.7. A separate check is needed, where data have a time or other such sequence that may affect results, for sequential correlation. A course check can be performed by applying the function `acf()` to the vector of residuals. See Subsection 6.1.2.

Model coefficients give the values by which the values in the respective columns of the model matrix must be multiplied. These are then summed over all columns. Later chapters will use the model matrix formulation to fit models where fitted values are the sum of linear combinations of nonlinear terms.

Keep in mind that the usual product–moment correlation measures linear association. Wherever possible, use the richer and more insightful regression framework.

Alternatives to straight line regression with x and y as measured are as follows.

- Transform x and/or y.
- Use polynomial regression.
- Fit a smoothing curve.

Regress y on x, or x on y?

The line for the regression of y on x is different from the line for the regression of x on y. The difference between the two lines is most marked when the correlation is small.

2.11 Further Reading

Finding the right statistical model is an important part of statistical problem solving. Chatfield (2003) has helpful comments. Clarke (1968) has a useful discussion of the use of models in archaeology. See, also, the very different points of view of Breiman and Cox (as discussant) in Breiman (2001). Our stance is much closer to Cox than to Breiman.

Miller (1986) has extensive comment on consequences of failure of assumptions, and on how to handle such failures. Smith (2014) is a wide-ranging compendium of examples of errors in data interpretation. Discussion stays at an elementary, mostly nonmathematical, level. Johnson (1995) comments critically on the limitations of widely used nonparametric methods.

Bayesian methodology is used, in this text, primarily as a commentary on what can be achieved using frequentist approaches. Chapters 4, 6, and 7 of Bolker (2008) give a brief summary of Bayesian methodology, including Bayesian modeling. Spiegelhalter et al. (2000) is a helpful 130-page overview of practical issues for the use of Bayesian methods. See also Doorn et al. (2021).

2.12 Exercises

2.1. In a study that examined the use of acupuncture to treat migraine headaches, consenting patients on a waiting list for treatment for migraine were randomly assigned in a 2:1:1 ratio to acupuncture treatment, a "sham" acupuncture treatment in which needles were inserted at nonacupuncture points, and waiting-list patients whose only treatment was self-administered (Linde et al., 2005). (The "sham" acupuncture treatment was described to trial participants as an acupuncture treatment that did not follow the principles of Chinese medicine.) The two tables that follow summarize results.

a. Numbers of patients who experienced a more than 50 percent reduction in headaches over a four-week period, relative to a prerandomization baseline were as follows.

	Acupuncture	Sham acupuncture	Waiting list
$\geq$ 50% reduction	74	43	11
$<$ 50% reduction	71	38	65

b. Patients who received the acupuncture and sham acupuncture treatments were asked to guess their treatment. Results were as follows.

	Acupuncture	Sham acupuncture
Chinese	82	30
Other	17	26
Don't know	30	16

Analyze the two tables. What, in each case, are the conclusions that should be drawn? Comment on implications for patient treatment and further research.

2.2. The table `UCBAdmissions` was discussed in Section 1.3.1. The following gives a table that adds the 2 × 2 tables of admission data over all departments:

```
## UCBAdmissions is in the datasets package
## For each combination of margins 1 and 2, calculate the sum
UCBtotal <- apply(UCBAdmissions, c(1,2), sum)
```

a. Compare the information in the table `UCBtotal` with the result from applying the function `mantelhaen.test()` (see `?mantelhaen.test`) to the dataset `UCBAdmissions`. Comment on the difference.

b. The Mantel–Haenzel test is valid only if the male-to–female odds ratio for admission is similar across departments. The following code calculates the relevant odds ratios:

```
apply(UCBAdmissions, 3, function(x) (x[1,1]*x[2,2])/(x[1,2]*x[2,1]))
```

Is the odds ratio consistent across departments? Which department(s) stand(s) out as different? What is the nature of the difference?

2.3. The following fictitious data is designed to illustrate issues for combining data across tables.

Table A:

	Engineering			Sociology			Total	
	Male	Female		Male	Female		Male	Female
Admit	30	10	Admit	15	30	Admit	45	40
Deny	30	10	Deny	5	10	Deny	35	20

Table B:

	Engineering			Sociology			Total	
	Male	Female		Male	Female		Male	Female
Admit	30	20	Admit	10	20	Admit	40	40
Deny	30	10	Deny	5	25	Deny	35	35

To enter the data for Table A, type:

```
tabA <- array(c(30,30,10,10,15,5,30,10), dim=c(2,2,2))
```

and similarly for Table B. The third dimension in each table is faculty, as required for using faculty as a stratification variable for the Mantel–Haenzel test. From the help page for `mantelhaen.test()`, extract and enter the code for the function `woolf()`. Apply the function `woolf()`, followed by the function `mantelhaen.test()`, to the data of each of Tables A and B. Explain, in words, the meaning of each of the outputs. Then apply the Mantel–Haenzel test to each of these tables.

2.4. In a sequence of 1000 experiments, let $P = 0.8$ (power) be the probability that an effect of interest will be detected at $p \leq \alpha$, where $\alpha = 0.05$. How many of the 1000 experiments can be expected to show an apparent effect at the $\alpha = 0.05$ cutoff level? Use Equation (1.4) in Subsection 1.6.4 to estimate the PPV, that is, what proportion is expected to be real, where the number of genuine cases is 200, 300, ..., 900, in each case out of 1000.

2.5. *For constructing bootstrap confidence intervals for the correlation coefficient, the Fisher z-transformation of the correlation gives, under bivariate normality assumptions for the (x, y) combinations from which the correlation was calculated, a statistic with an approximately normal sampling distribution. The following lines of R code obtain a bootstrap confidence interval for the z-transformed correlation between `chest` and `belly` in the `possum` data frame. The final step applies the inverse of the z-transformation to the confidence interval to return it to the original scale. Run the code and compare the resulting interval with the one computed without transformation. Is the z-transform necessary here?

```
z.transform <- function(r) .5*log((1+r)/(1-r))
z.inverse <- function(z) (exp(2*z)-1)/(exp(2*z)+1)
  possum.fun <- function(data, indices) {
    chest <- data$chest[indices]
    belly <- data$belly[indices]
    z.transform(cor(belly, chest))}
possum.boot <- boot(possum, possum.fun, R=999)
z.inverse(boot.ci(possum.boot, type="perc")$percent[4:5])
# The 4th and 5th elements of the percent list element
# hold the interval endpoints. See ?boot.ci
```

2.6. Use the function `rexp()` to simulate 100 random observations from an exponential distribution with rate 1. Use the bootstrap (with 99,999 replications) to estimate the standard error of the median. Repeat several times. Compare with the result that would be obtained using the normal approximation, that is, $\sqrt{\pi/(2n)}$.

2.7. Low doses of the insecticide toxaphene may cause weight gain in rats (Chu et al., 1988). A sample of 20 rats are given toxaphene in their diet, while a control group of eight rats are not given toxaphene. Assume further that weight gain among the treated rats is normally distributed with a mean of 60 g and standard deviation 30 g, while weight gain among the control rats is normally distributed with a mean of 10 g and a standard deviation of 50 g. Using simulation, compare confidence intervals for the difference in mean weight gain, using the pooled variance estimate and the Welch approximation. Which type of interval is correct more often?

Repeat the simulation experiment under the assumption that the standard deviations are 40 g for both samples. Is one of the methods now giving systematically larger confidence intervals? Which type of interval do you consider best?

2.8. *Experiment with the `DAAG::pair65` example and plot various views of the likelihood function, either as a surface using the `persp()` function or as one-dimensional profiles using the `curve()` function. Is there a single maximizer? Where does it occur?

2.9. *Suppose the mean reaction time to a particular stimulus has been estimated in several previous studies, and appears to be approximately normally distributed with mean 0.35 s with standard deviation 0.1 s. On the basis of 10 new observations, the mean reaction time is estimated to be 0.45 s with an estimated standard deviation of 0.15 s. Based on the sample information, what is the likelihood estimator for the true mean reaction time? What is the Bayes' estimate of the mean reaction time?

2.10. Use the robust regression function `MASS::rlm()` to fit lines to the data in `elastic1` and `elastic2`. Compare the results with those from use of `lm()`. Compare regression coefficients, standard errors of coefficients, and plots of residuals against fitted values.

2.11. In the dataset `pressure` (*datasets*), examine the dependence of pressure on temperature. Try:

```
with(pressure, MASS::boxcox(pressure ~ I(1/(temperature+273))))
```

What transformation does this suggest?
[Theory suggests that the logarithm of the vapor pressure should be approximately inversely proportional to the absolute temperature. Search on the internet for "Claudius–Clapeyron equation", or look in a suitable reference text.]

2.12. *Use the function `car::powerTransform()` to determine transformations for, for both variables, for use in connection with Exercise 2.11. (Be sure to work with absolute temperature.)

a. Examine diagnostics for the regression fit that results following the suggested transformations. In particular, examine the plot of residuals against temperature. Comment on the plot. What are its implications for further investigation of these data?
b. Use `summary()` with the output from `car::powerTransform()`. Are the results consistent with the Claudius–Clapeyron equation? [Note that Subsection 3.3.3 supplements the discussion of `powerTransform()` in Subsection 2.5.6.]

2.13. Fit the double binomial distribution to the `qra::malesINfirst12` data from Subsection 2.3.1 that gave numbers of male and female children in large families in Saxony in the nineteenth century.

a. Compare the worm plots. Is there any consistent difference in the patterns?
b. Use `AIC` or `GAIC` to compare the fits obtained using `gamlss::gamlss()`. Repeat with the argument `c=TRUE` that is available for the *gamlss* AIC method. Why does this make almost no difference? What is n in this context?

2.14. *The following function returns the coefficient of the estimated linear functional relationship between `x` and `y`:

```
"funRel" <-
function(x=leafshape$logpet, y=leafshape$loglen, scale=c(1,1)){
  ## Find principal components rotation; see Subsection 9.1.2
  ## Here (unlike 9.1.2) the interest is in the final component
  xy.prc <- prcomp(cbind(x,y), scale=scale)
  b <- xy.prc$rotation[,2]/scale
  c(bxy = -b[1]/b[2])    # slope of functional equation line
}
## Try the following:
leafshape <- DAAG::leafshape
funRel(scale=c(1,1))   # Take x and y errors as equally important
## Note that all lines pass through (mean(x), mean(y))
```

a. Write $b_{y.x}$ for the slope of the regression line of y on x and $b_{x.y}$ for the slope of the regression line of x on y. For each of the three settings `scale=c(1,10)`, `scale=c(1,1)`, `scale=c(10,1)`, of the argument `scale`, note where the values of the functional coefficient lie in the range between $b_{y.x}$ and $b_{x.y}^{-1}$.
b. Repeat this for each of the data frames `softbacks`, `elastic2`, and (with the variables `logpet` and `loglen`) `leafshape17`.
c. Explain the effect of changing the settings of the argument `scale`.

2.15. *A Markov chain is a data sequence which has a special kind of dependence. For example, a fair coin is tossed repetitively by a player who begins with \$2. If "heads" appear, the player receives \$1; otherwise, she pays \$1. The game stops when the player has either \$0 or \$5. The amount of money that the player has before any coin flip can be recorded – this is a Markov chain. A possible sequence of plays is as follows:

Player's fortune:	2	1	2	3	4	3	2	3	2	3	2	1	0
Coin toss result:	T	H	H	H	T	T	H	T	H	T	T	T	

Note that all we need to know in order to determine the player's fortune at any time is the fortune at the previous time as well as the coin flip result at the current time. The probability of an increase in the fortune is 0.5 and the probability of a decrease in the fortune is 0.5. The transition probabilities can be summarized in a transition matrix:

```
    0   1   2   3   4   5
0 1.0 0.0 0.0 0.0 0.0 0.0
1 0.5 0.0 0.5 0.0 0.0 0.0
2 0.0 0.5 0.0 0.5 0.0 0.0
3 0.0 0.0 0.5 0.0 0.5 0.0
4 0.0 0.0 0.0 0.5 0.0 0.5
5 0.0 0.0 0.0 0.0 0.0 1.0
```

The $(i+1,j+1)$ entry of this matrix is the probability of making a change from the value i to the value j. Here, the possible values of i and j are $0,1,2,\ldots,5$. According to the matrix, there is a probability of 0 of making a transition from \$2 to \$4 in one play, since the (2,4) element is 0; the probability of moving from \$2 to \$1 in one transition is 0.5, since the (2,1) element is 0.5.

The following function can be used to simulate N values of a Markov chain sequence, with transition matrix P:

```
Markov <- function(N=15, initial.value=1, transition=P, stopval=NULL)
  {X <- numeric(N)
   X[1] <- initial.value + 1 # States 0:(n-1); subscripts 1:n
   n <- nrow(transition)
   for (i in 2:N){
    X[i] <- sample(1:n, size=1, prob=transition[X[i-1], ])
    if(length(stopval)>0)if(X[i] %in% (stopval+1)){X <- X[1:i]; break}}
  X - 1
}
## Set `stopval=c(0,5)` to stop when  the player's fortune is $0 or $5
```

Simulate 15 values of the coin flip game, starting with an initial value of \$2. Repeat the simulation several times.

2.16. *A Markov chain for the weather in a particular season of the year has the transition matrix, from one day to the next:

```
        Sun Cloud Rain
Sun     0.6   0.2  0.2
Cloud   0.2   0.4  0.4
Rain    0.4   0.3  0.3
```

The (i,j) entry of this matrix is the probability of making a change from the value i to the value j, where `Sun` is 1, `Cloud` is 2, and `Rain` is 3. It can be shown, using linear algebra, that in the long run this Markov chain will visit the states according to the *stationary* distribution:

Sun	Cloud	Rain
0.429	0.286	0.286

A result called the *ergodic* theorem allows us to estimate this distribution by simulating the Markov chain for a long enough time.

a. Simulate 1000 values, and calculate the proportion of times the chain visits each of the states. Compare the proportions given by the simulation with above theoretical proportions.
b. Here is code that uses the function `zoo::rollmean()` to calculate rolling averages of the proportions over a number of simulations and plot the result:

```
plotmarkov <-
  function(n=1000, width=101, start=0, transition=Pb, npanels=5){
    xc2 <- Markov(n, initial.value=start, transition)
    mav0 <- zoo::rollmean(as.integer(xc2==0), k=width)
    mav1 <- zoo::rollmean(as.integer(xc2==1), k=width)
    npanel <- cut(1:length(mav0), breaks=seq(from=1, to=length(mav0),
                  length=npanels+1), include.lowest=TRUE)
    df <- data.frame(av0=mav0, av1=mav1, x=1:length(mav0), gp=npanel)
    print(xyplot(av0+av1 ~ x | gp, data=df, layout=c(1,npanels), type="l",
          par.strip.text=list(cex=0.65), auto.key=list(columns=2),
          scales=list(x=list(relation="free"))))
}
```

Try varying the number of simulations and the width of window. How wide a window is needed to get a good sense of the stationary distribution? This series settles down rather quickly to its stationary distribution (it "burns in" quite quickly). A reasonable width of window is however needed to give an accurate indication of the stationary distribution.

2.17. The Monty Hall problem (Franco-Watkins et al., 2003) arose from a 1970s-era television game show in which a contestant is provided with an opportunity to win an expensive prize. The prize is hidden behind one of three doors, and the contestant is asked to choose one of the doors. Upon making the choice, the game show host chooses one of the other two doors to be opened, according to a rule that ensures that the door hiding the prize is not opened. If neither door hides the prize, then the door to be opened is chosen at random. The contestant is then allowed the option of choosing from among the remaining two unopened doors; in other words, they may switch to a new door or remain with their first choice. The final door chosen is then opened, either revealing the prize or revealing nothing.

a. Prior to starting the game, what should be the contestant's assessment of the probability that the prize is behind door 1?

b. Suppose the contestant first chooses door 1. Calculate the probability that the host will choose to open door 3, under the following hypotheses.

$$H_1: \text{ the prize is hidden behind door 1}$$

$$H_2: \text{ the prize is hidden behind door 2}$$

$$H_3: \text{ the prize is hidden behind door 3}$$

c. Suppose the host opens door 3 (revealing no prize). Which of the three hypotheses, H_1, H_2, and H_3 maximizes the likelihood? In other words, under which of them is the probability that the host chooses door 3 highest?

d. By calculating the ratio of the likelihood under H_2 to the likelihood under H_1, show that the Bayes Factor that door 2 hides the prize is 2.0.

e. Use Bayes' Theorem to show that the probability of H_1, given the host's choice of door 3, is $1/3$, and the probability of H_2, under that same choice is $2/3$. Alternatively, use the Bayes Factor calculated above, together with the prior probabilities to arrive at these posterior probabilities of H_1 and H_2.

3

Multiple Linear Regression

Multiple linear regression generalizes straight line regression to allow multiple explanatory (or predictor) variables. The focus may be on accurate prediction. Or it may, alternatively or additionally, be on the regression coefficients themselves. Be warned that simple-minded interpretations of regression coefficients can be grossly misleading. Later chapters will elaborate on the ideas and methods developed in this chapter, applying them in new contexts.

Graphical and other diagnostics can be important sources of insight, bringing to attention common types of departure from model assumptions. A check of the residuals may identify one or more influential outliers that unduly skew the model fit and render it unsatisfactory for use for predictions with new data. A plot of partial residuals may show a systematic departure from linearity for a term that has been assumed linear.

3.1 Basic Ideas: the `allbacks` Book Weight Data

The data now considered have been put together for primarily didactic purposes. Seven books with hardback covers, together with eight softbacks, were selected in a relatively haphazard fashion from the first author's shelves. Data are plotted in Figure 3.1 with selected rows printed to the right of the figure. Explanatory variables are the volume of the book ignoring the covers, and the total area of the front and back covers. Assuming that the hard covers are all similar in their construction, we might expect that

$$\text{weight of book } = b_0 + b_1 \times \text{volume } + b_2 \times \text{area of covers.}$$

For the moment, we will retain the intercept, b_0. It may not be needed.

Code used, with the output that relates to the regression coefficients, is:

```
allbacks <- DAAG::allbacks # Place the data in the workspace
allbacks.lm <- lm(weight ~ volume+area, data=allbacks)
print(coef(summary(allbacks.lm)), digits=2)
```

```
            Estimate Std. Error t value    Pr(>|t|)
(Intercept)    22.41     58.402    0.38 0.707858178
volume          0.71      0.061   11.60 0.000000071
area            0.47      0.102    4.59 0.000616455
```

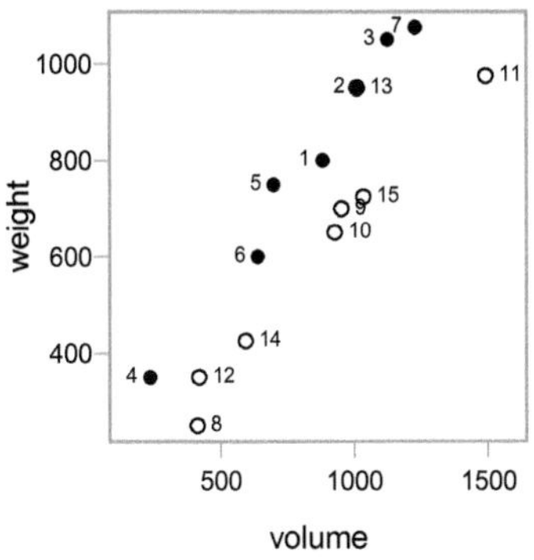

	volume (cm^3)	area (cm^2)	weight (g)	cover
1	885	382	800	hb
....				
7	1228	396	1075	hb
8	412	0	250	pb
....				
15	1034	0	725	pb

Figure 3.1 Weight versus volume, for seven hardback and eight softback books. Filled dots are hardbacks, while open dots are softbacks. Selected data are shown to the right of the graph.

The correlations between parameter estimates are:

```
## Correlations between estimates -- model with intercept
round(summary(allbacks.lm, corr=TRUE)$correlation, 3)
```

```
            (Intercept) volume   area
(Intercept)       1.000 -0.883 -0.318
volume           -0.883  1.000 -0.002
area             -0.318 -0.002  1.000
```

The intercept is given as $b_0 = 22.4$, with a p-value $(=0.7)$ that suggests that it should be omitted. Other coefficient estimates are $b_1 = 0.708$ and $b_2 = 0.468$, with p-values that are so small that the precise value no longer has much meaning. It makes more sense to focus on the t-statistics, here 11.6 for `volume` and 4.6 for `area`, which convert the coefficients to multiples of their standard error.

The correlation between the coefficient for `volume` and that for `area` is -0.002, so the t-statistics are very nearly independent between coefficients. The final three lines of the default summary output are:

```
Residual standard error: 77.7 on 12 degrees of freedom
Multiple R^2:  0.928,    Adjusted R^2:  0.917
F-statistic: 77.9 on 2 and 12 DF,  p-value: 0.000000134
```

The estimate of the noise standard deviation (the "residual standard error") is 77.7. There are $15 - 3 = 12$ degrees of freedom for the residual; starting with 15 observations and 3 parameters were estimated. In addition, there are two versions of R^2. The F-statistic allows an overall test for the null hypothesis that coefficients other than the intercept are 0.

The 5 percent critical value for a t-statistic with 12 degrees of freedom, used for calculating 95 percent confidence intervals for coefficients, is 2.18.[1] Thus, a 95 percent confidence interval for `volume` is $0.708 \pm 2.18 \times 0.0611$, that is, it ranges from 0.575 to 0.841. Here, because of the very small correlation between the coefficient estimates, these confidence intervals are for all practical purposes independent.

[1]
```
## 5% critical value; t-statistic with 12 d.f.
qt(0.975, 12)
```

The default summary output includes coarse information on the distribution of residuals:

```
Residuals:
    Min      1Q Median      3Q     Max
-104.1   -30.0  -15.5    16.8   212.3
```

Note: The output for the data and associated model considered here, where both b_1 and b_2 are clearly required, contrasts with output where there are a number of coefficients, with several whose p-values are around the conventional $p = 0.05$ level that has commonly been used to judge "significance," and with varying amounts of dependence. Omission of one variable will lead to large increases in the t-statistics, and smaller p-values, for variables with which it had a large positive correlation. Additionally, prior probabilities become important when p-values are in the region of 0.05 or somewhat smaller. Here, because of issues in the selection of books, and of available explanatory variables, there is a real question whether the results generalize in any meaningful way to a larger "population" of books that may be of interest.

3.1.1 A Sequential Analysis of Variance Table

The `anova()` function outputs a sequential analysis of variance table that assesses the contribution of each predictor variable to the model in turn, given predictors from earlier rows of the table.

```
anova(allbacks.lm)
```

```
Analysis of Variance Table

Response: weight
          Df Sum Sq Mean Sq F value     Pr(>F)
volume     1 812132  812132   134.7 0.00000007
area       1 127328  127328    21.1    0.00062
Residuals 12  72373    6031
```

The contribution of `volume` after fitting overall mean is given first, then the contribution of `area` after fitting both the overall mean and `volume`. The p-value for area in the anova table must agree with that in the main regression output, since both these p-values test the contribution of `area` after including `volume` in the model. In general, the p-values for any earlier coefficients will differ from those shown in the table of coefficients and associated statistics shown earlier. Here, because the correlation between `volume` and `area` is so small as to be inconsequential, the difference is not apparent in the printed values.

The model matrix that has been used in the least square calculations is:

```
## Show rows 1, 7, 8 and 15 only
model.matrix(allbacks.lm)[c(1,7,8,15), ]
```

```
   (Intercept) volume area
1            1    885  382
7            1   1228  396
8            1    412    0
15           1   1034    0
```

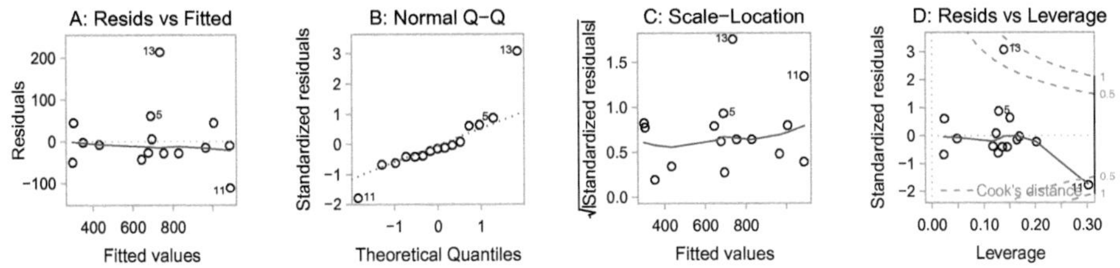

Figure 3.2 Diagnostic plots for the model that fits **weight** as a function of **volume** and **area**, omitting the intercept.

```
## NB, also, code that returns the data frame used
## model.frame(allbacks.lm)
```

Predicted values are given by multiplying the first column by b_0 (=22.4), the second by b_1 (= 0.708), the third by b_2 (= 0.468), and adding.

Omission of the Intercept Term

Now investigate the effect of leaving out the intercept, which had p = 0.7079. Regression output, when the intercept is omitted, is:

```
allbacks.lm0 <- lm(weight ~ -1+volume+area, data=allbacks)
print(coef(summary(allbacks.lm0)), digits=2)
```

```
       Estimate Std. Error t value        Pr(>|t|)
volume     0.73      0.028    26.3 0.0000000000011
area       0.48      0.093     5.1 0.0001879245500
```

The larger standard errors in the model that included the intercept were a consequence of the substantial negative correlations between the estimates for the intercept and those for **volume** and **area**. The reduction in standard error is greater for the coefficient of **volume**, where the correlation was −0.883, than for **area**, where the correlation was −0.318. (See Section 3.6.3.)

Omission of the intercept term results in a substantial increase in the correlation between the coefficients for **volume** and **area**:

```
## Correlations between estimates -- no intercept
print(round(summary(allbacks.lm0, corr=TRUE)$correlation, 3))
```

```
       volume   area
volume  1.000 -0.635
area   -0.635  1.000
```

3.1.2 Diagnostic Plots

The plots shown in Figure 3.2 provide graphical checks on the adequacy of the model fit to the **allbacks** data. Simplified code is: [2]

```
## The following has the default captions
plot(allbacks.lm0)
```

[2]
```
## To show all plots in the one row, precede with
par(mfrow=c(1,4))       # Follow with par(mfrow=c(1,1))
```

Note the large residual in Panel A for observation 13. In Panel D, it lies outside the 0.5 contour of Cook's distance, well out towards the contour for a Cook's distance of 1. Thus, it is a (mildly) influential point. The Cook's distance measure, which was mentioned in Section 2.5.3, will be discussed in Subsection 3.4.2.

Should we omit observation 13? The first task is make such checks of the data as are possible. In this case, the purpose was served by checking back to the book itself, on the author's shelves. The book was a computing book, with a smaller height to width ratio than any of the other books. It had heavier paper, though differences in the paper were not immediately obvious. If the sample of books had been selected in a way that made generalization to some wider population of books meaningful, it might be legitimate to omit it from the main analysis, but noting that this one book (with a much higher weight to volume ratio than other books) had been omitted for purposes of the analysis. The following omits observation 13:

```
allbacks.lm13 <- lm(weight ~ -1+volume+area, data=allbacks[-13, ])
print(coef(summary(allbacks.lm13)), digits=2)
```

```
       Estimate Std. Error t value Pr(>|t|)
volume     0.69      0.016      43  1.8e-14
area       0.55      0.053      11  2.1e-07
```

The residual standard error is substantially smaller (41 instead of 75.1) in the absence of observation 13. Observation 11 now has a Cook's distance that is close to 1, but does not stand out in the plot of residuals. This is about as far as it is reasonable to go in the investigation of diagnostic plots.

With just 15 points, and books selected that were immediately available from one person's shelves, the small p-values should be treated with skepticism. The fitted model is unlikely to do well at predicting weights for a very different set of books on another set of shelves.

3.2 The Interpretation of Model Coefficients

If an aim is a scientific understanding that involves interpretation of model coefficients, then it is important to fit a model whose coefficients are open to the relevant interpretations. Different formulations of the regression model, or different models, may serve different explanatory purposes. Predictive accuracy is in any case a consideration, and may be the main interest.

Three datasets will be considered. The first dataset has record times, distances, and amounts of climb for Northern Irish hill races. The second has data on book dimensions and weight, from a highly biased sample of books. The third has data on mouse brain weight, litter size, and body weight.

3.2.1 Times for Northern Irish Hill Races

The dataset `DAAG::nihills`, from which Table 3.1 has selected observations, gives distances (`dist`), heights climbed (`climb`), male record times (`time`), and female record times (`timef`), for 23 Northern Irish hill races. Initially, the interest will be in an equation that predicts `mph`, that is, miles traversed per hour.

Table 3.1 *Distance (`dist`), height climbed (`climb`), and record times (`time`), for four of the 23 Northern Irish hill races.*

	Name	`dist` (mi)	`climb` (ft)	`time` (h)	`timef` (h)
1	Binevenagh	7.5	1740	0.86	1.06
2	Slieve Gullion	4.2	1110	0.47	0.62
3	Glenariff Mountain	5.9	1210	0.70	0.89
...	...	...	...	...	...
23	BARF Turkey Trot	5.7	1430	0.71	0.94

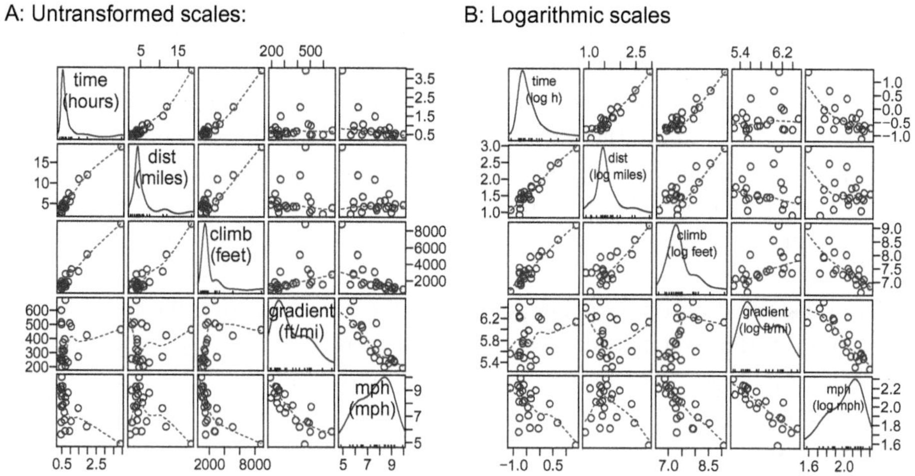

Figure 3.3 Scatterplot matrices for the **`nihills`** data (Table 3.1), drawn using the function `car::spm()`. Panel A uses untransformed scales, while Panel B uses logarithmic scales. The density plots in the diagonal panels give indications of the extent of distributional asymmetry. Smooth curves have been added to the individual plots. For instructions of how a measure of spread can be added around the smooths, see **Details** for `spread` under `?car::spm`.

Figure 3.3 shows scatterplot matrices, in Panel A for untransformed data, and in Panel B for log-transformed data. The diagonal panels give the x-variable names for plots in the column (above or below), and the y-variable names for plots in the same row (left or right). Observe that the vertical axis labels alternate between the axis on the left and the axis on the right, and similarly for the horizontal axis labels. This avoids a proliferation of axis labels on the left and lower axes.

A simplified version of Panels A and B can be obtained by typing

```
nihr <- within(DAAG::nihills, {mph <- dist/time; gradient <- climb/dist})
nihr <- nihr[, c("time","dist", "climb", "gradient", "mph")]
sm <- list(spread=0, col.smooth='red')
car::spm(nihr, regLine=FALSE, col='blue', smooth=sm)
car::spm(log(nihr), regLine=FALSE, col='blue', smooth=sm,
      var.labels=paste("ln", names(nihr)))
```

The logarithmic transformation does make the distributions of `time`, `dist`, and `climb` more symmetric, and that for `gradient` mildly so. The transformation for `mph` pushes its mode somewhat more to the right. It is thus best left untransformed, if the alternative is a logarithmic transformation.

What is Special about Logarithmic Transformations?

The effect of a logarithmic transformation is that values that differ by the same factor on the untransformed scale (e.g., 4/2, 8/4) are then the same absolute distance apart on the log-transformed scale.

The following are ways in which a logarithmic transformation may help.

- Where there is a long tail to the right, the transformation can be expected to give a more symmetric distribution, with a much reduced tail to the right.
- In a regression that uses the untransformed variables, point(s) in the extreme right tail will, where the distribution has a long tail to the right, have a larger *leverage* in determining the regression coefficient than those closer to the mean – a point on which Subsection 3.4.2 will comment further. Even after taking logarithms (in Figure 3.3B), where values have been log transformed, the leverage of the points with largest values of `time`, `dist`, and `climb` remain large, but are less dominating.
- The transformation often makes good scientific sense. Because the physiological demands on the human athlete increase with `time`, it can be expected that `time` will increase more than linearly with `dist`, and similarly for `climb`. Working with logarithmically transformed variables allows for this possibility, though in a specific way.
- Where the variance increases with increasing values of the dependent variable, use of a logarithmic scale may help stabilize the variance.
- Such relationship as is evident between the explanatory variables may be more nearly linear on the logarithmic scale. Linear relationships make diagnostic plots more readily interpretable.
- The ratio of maximum to minimum value varies from 7.6 for distance to 12 for male times and 14.6 for female times. Values of `dist` vary by a factor of 7.56, and those of `climb` by a factor of 11.7. As a general guide, a logarithmic transformation should be considered if the ratio of maximum to minimum value is more than 5.

3.2.2 An Equation That Predicts dist/time

We fit two equations with `log(dist)` as the first of two explanatory variables. In the first of these `log(climb)` is used as a further explanatory variable, while in the second `log(gradient)` = `log(climb/dist)` is used as the second explanatory variable. Code that fits the models, with the two equations obtained, is:

```
## Hold climb constant at mean on logarithmic scale
mphClimb.lm <- lm(mph ~ log(dist)+log(climb), data = nihr)
## Hold `gradient=climb/dist` constant at mean on logarithmic scale
mphGradient.lm <- lm(mph ~ log(dist)+log(gradient), data = nihr)
avRate <- mean(nihr$mph)
```

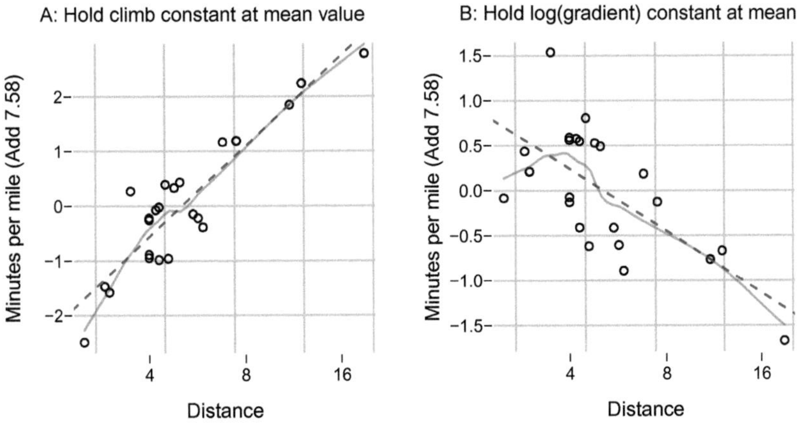

Figure 3.4 Variation in distance per unit time (in miles per hour) with distance. Panel A shows the pattern of change when **log(climb)** is held constant at its mean value, while Panel B shows the pattern of change when **log(climb/dist)** is held constant at its mean value. On the y-axis, tick labels show variation about a mean that equals 7.58. These are termed "component plus residual" plots.

```
bClimb <- coef(mphClimb.lm)
```

```
(Intercept)    log(dist)   log(climb)
     28.947        2.397       -3.390
```

```
  (Intercept)        log(dist) log(gradient)
      28.9475          -0.9937       -3.3903
```

The explanatory terms in two models differ only in the parameterization used, and give the same fitted values. The `plot` method for `lm` models gives the same diagnostic plots in the two cases.

Figure 3.4 uses the function `car::crPlots()` to show in a visually striking way the importance of the choice of the second variable for the interpretation of the coefficient of `log(dist)`. The plots that are produced, termed "component plus residual" plots, are a variation on termplots, as described in Subsection 3.3.2. They have been used here in preference to termplots because they allow the replacement of default x-axis that are centered values of `log(dist)` values by values of `dist`. For each term specified in the `terms` argument, a plot is generated that shows how outcome values change as a function of values of that term when other explanatory variables are held constant.

Code that shows a simplified version of the plot in Figure 3.4A is:

```
car::crPlots(climb.lm, terms = . ~ log(dist), xaxt='n', xlab="Distance")
## `terms = . ~ log(dist)` picks out the part of the model formula for which
## the component+residual plot is required.  The `.` on the left of the `~`
## operator is shorthand for the response on the left of the model formula.
axis(1, at=log(2^(2:5)), labels=paste(2^(2:5)))
```

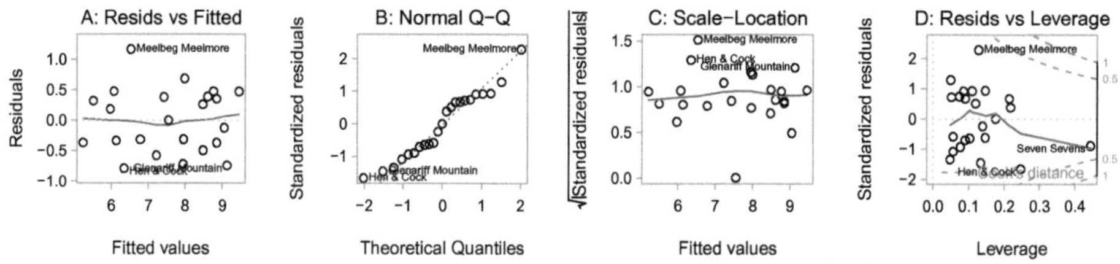

Figure 3.5 Diagnostic plots for the model **mphGradient.lm** that regressed **mph** on **logdist** and **loggradient**. The diagnostics are the same as for the model **mphClimb.lm**.

The smooth suggests that the relationship is not quite linear. The difference made by using a model that allows for curvature is minor, as the reader may care to check. See, further, Subsection 3.3.1.

This equation implies that for a given height of climb, the average rate (mph) at which the route is traversed increases with increasing distance. To understand what is happening, think carefully about the implications of holding climb constant. For a given value of climb, short races will be steep while for long races the gradient will be relatively gentle. Thus, the increase in average rate is not altogether surprising.

Correlations between the coefficients for the two models are:

```
summary(mphClimb.lm, corr=T)$correlation["log(dist)", "log(climb)"]
```

```
[1] -0.7801
```

```
summary(mphGradient.lm, corr=T)$correlation["log(dist)", "log(gradient)"]
```

```
[1] 0.06529
```

Thus, a side benefit of working with mphGradient.lm is that the two coefficients have negligible correlation.

Diagnostic plots are given in Figure 3.5:

```
## Show the plots, with default captions
plot(mphClimb.lm, fg='gray')
```

The importance of contextual information for the interpretation of regression results will be a common theme in later examples.

3.2.3 Equations That Predict log(time)

Models will be fitted with the same two respective choices of explanatory variables as before, but now with log(time) as the dependent variable. This would make good sense if the interest is in predicting the likely best time for a race that is run over a new route. The first equation to be fitted is:

$$\log(\texttt{time}) = a + b_1 \log(\texttt{dist}) + b_2 \log(\texttt{climb}),$$

```
lognihr <- setNames(log(nihr), paste0("log", names(nihr)))
timeClimb.lm <- lm(logtime ~ logdist + logclimb, data = lognihr)
```

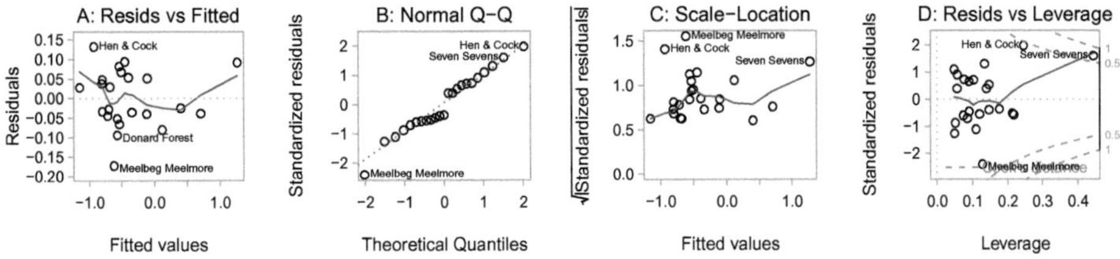

Figure 3.6 Diagnostic plots for the regression of `logtime` on `logdist` and `logclimb`.

Figure 3.6 shows the diagnostic plots:

```
## Show the plots, with default captions
plot(timeClimb.lm, fg='gray')
```

The diagnostic plots do not indicate any major issue. The Meelbeg Meelmore race has a moderately large residual. There is a hint of saucer-shaped curvature in the plot of residuals against fitted values. We will look at this in more detail shortly.

The estimates of the coefficients (a,b_1, and b_2) are:

```
print(coef(summary(timeClimb.lm)), digits=2)
```

	Estimate	Std. Error	t value	Pr(>|t|)
(Intercept)	-4.96	0.274	-18	7.1e-14
logdist	0.68	0.055	12	8.2e-11
logclimb	0.47	0.045	10	2.0e-09

The fitted equation is

$$\begin{array}{llll} \log(\texttt{time}) = & -4.96 & +0.68 \quad \times \log(\texttt{dist}) + & 0.47 \quad \times \log(\texttt{climb}). \\ & [\text{SE}=0.27] & [\text{SE}=0.055] & [\text{SE}=0.045] \end{array}$$

Exponentiating both sides of this equation, and noting that $\exp(-4.96) = 0.0070$, gives

$$\texttt{time} = 0.0070 \times \texttt{dist}^{0.68} \times \texttt{climb}^{0.0.47}.$$

This equation implies that for a given height of climb, the time taken to traverse a given distance is less for longer races. The relative rate of increase in time is 68 percent of the relative rate of increase in distance. As before, the issue is that short races will be steep while for long races the gradient will be relatively gentle.

Now regress on `logdist` and `log(climb/dist)`:

```
timeGradient.lm <- lm(logtime ~ logdist + loggradient, data=lognihr)
print(coef(summary(timeGradient.lm)), digits=3)
```

	Estimate	Std. Error	t value	Pr(>|t|)
(Intercept)	-4.961	0.2739	-18.1	7.09e-14
logdist	1.147	0.0346	33.2	5.90e-19
loggradient	0.466	0.0453	10.3	1.98e-09

The coefficient of `logdist` is now, reassuringly, greater than 1. A related benefit is that the correlation between `logdist` and `logradient` is −0.065, which is negligible relative to the correlation of 0.78 between `logdist` and `logclimb`.[3] Because the correlation between `logdist` and `loggradient` is so small, the coefficient of `logdist` (=1.124) in the regression on `logdist` alone is almost identical to the coefficient of `logdist` (=1.147) in the regression on `logdist` and `logGradient`.

The standard error of the coefficient of `logdist` is smaller, 0.035 as against 0.055, when the second explanatory variable is `logGradient` rather than `logclimb`. Note that the predicted values do not change. The models `timeClimb.lm` and `timeGradient.lm` are different parameterizations of the same underlying model.

3.2.4 Book Dimensions – the `oddbooks` *Dataset*

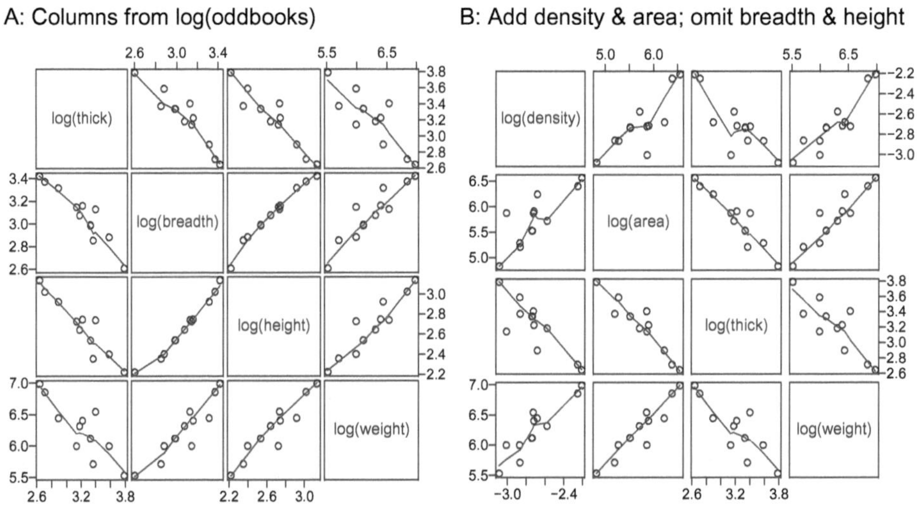

Figure 3.7 Panel A shows the scatterplot matrix for the logarithms of the variables in the `oddbooks` data frame. Panel B has the derived variables `log(density)` and `log(area)`, plus original variables `log(thick)` and `log(weight)`. These plots used the function `pairs()` from the base R *graphics* package.

The way that data are sampled can lead to large biases in the estimated coefficients. Figure 3.7A shows a scatterplot matrix for logged measurements, from the data frame `oddbooks`, on 12 soft-cover books.[4] The books were taken from one particular section of one particular bookshelf.

[3]
```
## Correlations of logGrad and logclimb with logdist
with(lognihr, cor(cbind(loggradient, logclimb), logdist))
```

[4]
```
## Code for Panel A, omitting the title; use 'pairs()'
oddbooks <- DAAG::oddbooks
pairs(log(oddbooks), lower.panel=panel.smooth, upper.panel=panel.smooth,
```

Figure 3.7B repeats two of the variables from Panel A, adding two derived variables:[5] Books were selected in such a way that weight increased with decreasing thickness, reflected in the strong negative correlation between log(`weight`) and log(`thick`).

The interest will be in what the regression could tell us if the dimensions (`thick`, `breadth`, `height`) were all the information available that might explain the weight, and this was a context where these did not multiply to give a volume to which the weight could be directly related.

We will start by fitting all three explanatory variables:

```
lob3.lm <- lm(log(weight) ~ log(thick)+log(breadth)+log(height),
              data=oddbooks)
# coef(summary(lob3.lm))
```

We leave readers to examine the table of coefficients and standard errors, with p-values that, rounded to 2 decimal places, range from 0.12 for `log(breadth)` to 0.91 for `log(height)`. The AIC statistics for single term deletions are:

```
setNames(drop1(lob3.lm)$AIC, rownames(drop1(lob3.lm)))
```

```
      <none>   log(thick) log(breadth)  log(height)
      -40.68       -41.07       -38.77       -42.66
```

There is a clear case for dropping `log(height)`. The resulting equation is:

```
lob2.lm <- lm(log(weight) ~ log(thick)+log(breadth), data=oddbooks)
coef(summary(lob2.lm))
```

```
             Estimate Std. Error t value Pr(>|t|)
(Intercept)   -0.5028     2.5202 -0.1995 0.846285
log(thick)     0.4507     0.3950  1.1411 0.283297
log(breadth)   1.9904     0.4845  4.1084 0.002643
```

Output from `add1()` with the model that has only the constant term will be used to choose between the three models with a single explanatory variable. We will then fit the model that appears preferred:

```
lob0.lm <- lm(log(weight) ~ 1, data=oddbooks)
add1(lob0.lm, scope=~log(breadth) + log(thick) + log(height))
```

```
Single term additions

Model:
log(weight) ~ 1
             Df Sum of Sq   RSS   AIC
<none>                    2.033 -19.3
log(breadth)  1      1.79 0.238 -43.0
log(thick)    1      1.43 0.598 -32.0
log(height)   1      1.73 0.302 -40.2
```

```
lob1.lm <- update(lob0.lm, formula=. ~ .+log(breadth))
```

[5]
```
## Panel B, omitting the title
oddothers <- with(oddbooks,
  data.frame(density = weight/(breadth*height*thick),
  area = breadth*height, thick=thick, weight=weight))
pairs(log(oddothers), lower.panel=panel.smooth, upper.panel=panel.smooth, gap=0.5)
```

Coefficients in the fitted equations, with SEs in square brackets underneath, are:

$$\begin{aligned}
\log(\text{weight}) &= \underset{[3.2]}{-0.72} + \underset{[0.43]}{0.46}\log(\text{thick}) + \underset{[1.07]}{1.88}\log(\text{breadth}) + \underset{[1.27]}{0.15}\log(\text{height}),\\
\log(\text{weight}) &= \underset{[2.52]}{-0.5} + \underset{[0.49]}{0.35}\log(\text{thick}) + \underset{[0.48]}{1.99}\log(\text{breadth}),\\
\log(\text{weight}) &= \underset{[SE=0.45]}{2.33} + \underset{[0.17]}{1.47}\log(\text{breadth}).
\end{aligned}$$

The predicted values for the three very different models are very similar:

```
round(rbind("lob1.lm"=predict(lob1.lm), "lob2.lm"=predict(lob2.lm),
       "lob3.lm"=predict(lob3.lm)),2)
```

	1	2	3	4	5	6	7	8	9	10	11	12
lob1.lm	6.94	6.77	6.62	6.33	6.21	6.36	6.06	6.06	5.79	6.35	5.86	5.59
lob2.lm	6.93	6.73	6.61	6.33	6.18	6.40	6.04	6.04	5.70	6.47	5.89	5.62
lob3.lm	6.92	6.73	6.61	6.33	6.18	6.41	6.04	6.04	5.70	6.47	5.89	5.61

Figure 3.7A made it clear that `weight` increases with increasing values of `density`. In essence, it is the omission of `log(density)` from the regression equations that has skewed the regression coefficient estimates. The plot of `log(weight)` against `log(density)` in Panel B shows the strong relationship. The regression equation is:

```
oddbooks <- within(oddbooks, density <- weight/(thick*breadth*height))
lm(log(weight) ~ log(density), data=oddbooks) |> summary() |> coef() |>
  round(3)
```

	Estimate	Std. Error	t value	Pr(>|t|)
(Intercept)	10.284	0.586	17.555	0
log(density)	1.492	0.215	6.924	0

As a check, the following code generates a message to say that the equation gives what is essentially a perfect fit:

```
## Not run. It is left to the reader to run this code.
lm(log(weight) ~ log(thick)+log(breadth)+log(height)+log(density),
   data=oddbooks) |> summary() |> coef() |> round(3)
```

The `oddbooks` dataset was contrived to give a skewed picture of the way that book weight varies with dimensions. Correlations between `area` and `thick`, and between both `area` and `thick` and `density`, make it impossible to separate the effects of these three variables. Solid results require use of equations that capture the relevant physical relationships. Where the best that can be done is to guess, it is hazardous to try to attach a causal interpretation to regression coefficients.

For the `oddbooks` data, we know how the relevant variables (`thick`, `breadth`, `height`, `density`) drive and in that sense "cause" "weight," and could verify that leaving `log(density)` out of the equation gives coefficients that are uninterpretable. With observational data, there will in general be no way to know for sure how results may be affected by variables that have been left out or incorrectly modeled. For the `oddbooks` data, it was important that effects were additive on a logarithmic scale.

Observational data is very susceptible to such bias. For example, solar radiation, windspeed, temperature, and rainfall may change systematically with distance up

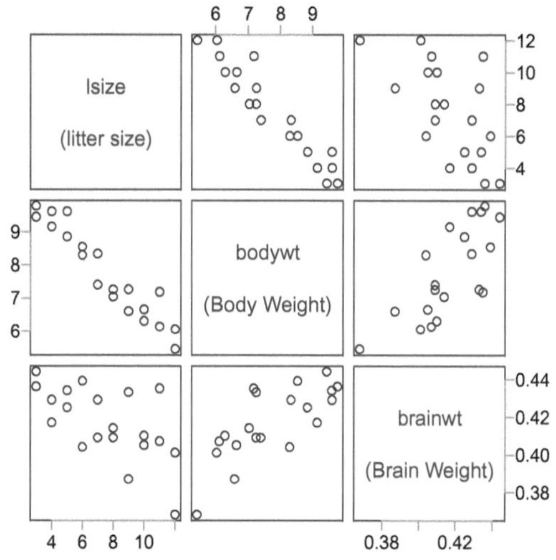

Figure 3.8 Scatterplot matrix for the litters dataset. Data relate to Wainright et al. (1989).

a hillside, making it impossible to distinguish the effects of the different factors on plant growth or on the ecology. There may be effects, crucial for making sense of the data, that are not obvious from the data themselves.

3.2.5 Mouse Brain Weight Example

The `DAAG::litters` data frame has values of brain weight, body weight, and litter size for each of 20 mice. As Figure 3.8 makes clear, the explanatory variables `lsize` and `bodywt` are strongly correlated. Stripped-down code for Figure 3.8 is:

```
litters <- DAAG::litters
pairs(litters)
```

Observe now that, in a regression with `brainwt` as the response variable, the coefficient for `lsize` has a different sign (−ve versus +ve) depending on whether `bodywt` also appears as an explanatory variable. Here are the calculations:

```
## Regression of brainwt on lsize
summary(lm(brainwt ~ lsize, data = litters), digits=3)$coef
```

```
              Estimate Std. Error t value  Pr(>|t|)
(Intercept)   0.447000   0.009625  46.443 3.391e-20
lsize        -0.004033   0.001198  -3.366 3.445e-03
```

```
## Regression of brainwt on lsize and bodywt
summary(lm(brainwt ~ lsize + bodywt, data = litters), digits=3)$coef
```

```
            Estimate Std. Error t value Pr(>|t|)
(Intercept)  0.17825   0.075323   2.366 0.030097
lsize        0.00669   0.003132   2.136 0.047513
bodywt       0.02431   0.006779   3.586 0.002278
```

The coefficients have different interpretations in the two cases.

- In the first regression, variation in `brainwt` depends on `lsize`, regardless of `bodywt`. No adjustment has been made for the increase in `bodywt` as `lsize` decreases. Individuals from small litters (small `lsize`) have, on average, large large `bodywt` and large `brainwt`. Individuals from large litters have, on average, low `bodywt` and low `brainwt`.
- In the multiple regression, the coefficient for `lsize` is a measure of the change in `brainwt` with `lsize`, when `bodywt` is held constant. For any particular value of `bodywt`, `brainwt` increases with `lsize`. This was a noteworthy finding for the purposes of the study.

The results are consistent with the biological concept of brain sparing, whereby the nutritional deprivation that results from large litter sizes has a proportionately smaller effect on brain weight than on body weight.

3.2.6 Issues for causal interpretation

The literature on conditions and checks that are needed in contexts where the hope is to give a regression coefficient a causal interpretation is large and growing. In an introduction titled "Towards less casual causal inferences," Hernán and Robins (2020) comment on the need to bring together evidence from multiple sources (in what is termed "triangulation") and consider multiple methodological approaches. They go on to comment:

> No book can possibly provide a comprehensive description of methodologies for causal inference across the sciences.

Note also the influential Bradford Hill criteria, discussed at length in Höfler (2005), with extensive accompanying commentary. With the limited attention given in this present text to issues of causation, the best that can be done is to highlight some of the important themes.

There may be variables whose effects are not of primary interest, but which nonetheless have important explanatory power. These are termed *covariates*. Where they affect the both the outcome and the variable of interest, they are known as *confounders*. As the number of variates and covariates increases, it becomes an increasing challenge to find a model that effectively accounts for observed outcomes, and to convincingly justify causal interpretations.

The following are contexts where coefficients may, with reasonable confidence, be interpretable.

- The coefficient of interest is not much affected by the choice of covariates, once all clearly relevant covariates are included. This will happen if the variable of interest is independent of such covariates.
- The effect is so large relative to other influences (as, e.g., in the effect from smoking in many health studies) that its contribution is not in doubt.
- The regression model reflects well-understood scientific laws.

- Accidents of nature or society have created conditions that, it can be argued, closely mirror the requirements for a randomized experiment. For example, in a large-scale study of a chemical pollutant, it may be possible to identify cases where one of a pair of identical twins has been exposed to the pollutant, while the other has not.
- Different sources of evidence, with different biases, all point to the same conclusion. Thus, it was a confluence of evidence, including the development of an understanding of the mechanisms involved, that settled debate on the link between smoking and lung cancer.
  - Subgroups can in some instances be analyzed separately in a manner that provides what are effectively independent sources of evidence. There may be grounds for arguing that any biases are likely to go in different directions.

Where the groups that are compared may differ on more than one or two covariates, any use of regression methods that claims to identify a causative effect has to meet stringent requirements.

- All relevant covariates have been taken into account.
- There must have been checks that allow for the possibility of nonlinear effects and/or interactions.
- It has to be established that causation goes from from the variable or factor to the dependent variable, conditional on other covariates being held constant.

These are difficult to demonstrate convincingly, unless the groups are already closely matched on everything except the variable or factor whose effect it is hoped to demonstrate. A plot akin to Figure 9.24 should be provided as a matter of course. Propensity scores, described in Subsection 9.7.2, provide a more limited one-dimensional comparison. Matching approaches, described in Section 9.7, can be an effective complement to regression methods. There remain issues of how close the matches need to be.

Where there is complexity in the causal pathways, graphs in the style of "directed acyclic graphs" (DAGs) can be helpful in making clear what is known and what is assumed. Cunningham (2021, pp. 96–118) is a helpful overview of basic concepts and terminology. Vignettes that accompany the *ggdag* package provide a brief introduction to some of the important ideas.

Effects of Lifestyle on Health

Does cutting down on sugar reduce risk to health, in particular from Type 2 diabetes? Is it important whether sugar comes from fruit, or from cooked or processed foods that contain large amounts of refined sugar? Are fats a major problem? If so, which fats? Are ketogenic diets – low carbohydrate and high fat – effective as claimed? Lichtenstein et al. (2021) is an assessment of the evidence on effects of diet on cardiovascular health. How important is regular exercise? What is the effect of environmental pollution? What is the effect of moderate alcohol consumption.[6]

[6] See the fact sheet at `www.cdc.gov/alcohol/fact-sheets/moderate-drinking.htm`.

It is relatively easy to demonstrate that a given factor is associated with good health but difficult to know the extent the health effects are caused by the factor rather than just an indicator of a generally healthy diet and lifestyle.

Mokdad et al. (2018) used results from multiple studies to bring together and balance carefully critiqued evidence from a wide range of studies on human health effects, for the population of the United States between 1990 and 2016. Their assessments (notably their figure 2) suggested that, depending on the measure used, dietary effects on risk of death were around six times those from low physical activity, and similar to those of tobacco use. Air pollution appeared a somewhat greater risk than low physical activity.

Contrast the assessments in Mokdad et al. (2018) with those in Paluch et al. (2021). Paluch et al. report on the relationship between steps per day and all-cause mortality for 5115 adults, aged 18 to 35 when recruited in 1985 and 1986 for a prospective study. Participants were from four locations in the United States, with the sample balanced to reflect the wider population in race (black/white), sex, and age distribution. They wore an accelerometer over 2005 to 2006, and were then followed for a mean of 10.8 years, with deaths recorded through to 2018. Adjustments were made for age, sex, race, accelerometer wear time, education, center, BMI,[7] smoking, and alcohol (with or without diet variable).

Three categories were compared: under 7000 steps per day (used as baseline), 7000 to <10,000, and ≥10,000. The hazard rate, measuring risk of death given survival up to a point in time, were reported as reduced, for the two higher step rate groups relative relative to baseline, as:

7000 to <10,000 steps per day: 0.22 (95% CI 0.11 – 0.43)
≥10,000 steps per day: 0.29 (0.15 – 0.54)

These estimates and confidence intervals (see Paluch et al.'s table 6) were reported as exactly the same irrespective of whether a "healthy eating index" (a diet variable) was included in the model.[8]

The results are not readily reconciled with those of Mokdad et al. (2018). Was number of steps per day serving as a measure of general fitness rather than measuring a direct effect on the risk of death?

The Studies Mostly Agree. But What Do They Say?

A number of studies have found that, as one might expect, mortality in the first year after birth was higher for babies of mothers who smoked during pregnancy than for nonsmokers. On the other hand, if attention is limited to low-birthweight babies, here defined as weighing less than 2.5 kg at birth, the risk was lower when the mother was a smoker. The likely explanation is that a baby may have a low birthweight for reasons other than having a mother who smokes. The other factors, whatever they are, bring a risk of death that is greater than that of smoking as the primary cause of low birthweight. See Hernández-Díaz et al. (2006), and the

[7] Body Mass Index, used as a measure of obesity
[8] This seems unlikely. Was this a mistake? Presumably they were not much different.

commentary in Wilcox (2006). The authors state that, for babies with a birthweight of less than 2 kg, the mortality for nonsmoking mothers relative to smokers is 0.79. This appears to contradict a graph where the ratio is never less than around 0.96. Just possibly, the 0.79 figure is an artifact of very different distributions of numbers within the under 2 kg category. In any case, the 0.96 figure is the more pertinent.

Adjusting for Confounders

Hernández-Díaz et al. (2006) comment

> It is the mantra of observational studies that we can never rule out unobserved confounding. Perhaps we need a second mantra: Never adjust for covariates just because they are handy.

The birthweight paradox provides a further example of the need to think carefully about the causal pathways involved when interpreting regression coefficients. For the `nihills` data, it was necessary to recognize the very different consequences that would flow from holding `climb`, as opposed to `gradient`, constant. Especially where a number of covariates are involved, the physical processes that determine the causal pathways may, as with the birthweight data, be difficult or impossible to identify. The key requirement is that, as noted in Imbens (2015) "the comparison of units with different treatments but identical pretreatment variables can be given a causal interpretation." All confounders must be identified, and their role correctly modeled. Effects may not be linear, and interactions must be accounted for. Glass et al. (2013) discuss the issues involved in detail. Because the causal pathways are usually not well understood, regression coefficients will often be suggestive rather than definitive.

Where there are two groups to be compared, a propensity score may sometimes be effective. The score, measuring the "propensity" of observations to belong to one group rather than the other, is used to replace the explanatory terms in the model that would otherwise be needed to account for group differences other than the factor (e.g., a treatment effect) of interest. While it will sometimes be possible to show that a propensity score is not doing the task required of it, it is in general not possible to verify empirically that a propensity score has been effective in accounting for all "nuisance" differences. See further Subsection 9.7.2.

3.3 Choosing the Model, and Checking It Out

As a preliminary to setting out a general strategy for fitting multiple regression models, we describe the assumptions that underpin multiple regression modeling. Can the equation be trusted to give reliable predictions for a suitably defined population from which the data have been taken? The meaning that can be attached to individual coefficients are not, for purposes of the checks that will be described here, an immediate concern.

We have explanatory variables $x_1, x_2, \ldots, x_p$. Or, more generally, the x_i may be columns of the model matrix.

- The expectation E[y] is some linear combination of $x_1, x_2, \ldots, x_p$:

$$\mathrm{E}[y] = \alpha + \beta_1 x_1 + \beta_2 x_2 + \cdots + \beta_p x_p. \tag{3.1}$$

- The distribution of y is normal with mean E[y] and constant variance, independently between observations.

Independence and constant variance are crucial. The role of normality can be overstated. For inference regarding model coefficients, it is enough that the sampling distributions of the coefficients are close to normal.[9]

The assumption that E[y] is a linear combination of the explanatory variables is a common starting point for investigation. Diagnostic plots, and other checks, are important, both in detecting common types of failure of assumptions and in indicating the nature of the failure. Assumptions may be hard to fault if the noise component of the variation in y is a substantial fraction of the variation for which the model is able to account. It becomes, for example, harder to detect any nonlinearity in the effects of explanatory variables.

3.3.1 Criteria for Model Choice

Criteria that may influence the choice of model include the following.

1. The model should do an effective job in accounting for the bulk of the data. Models where a few very large points (or, just possibly, a few very small points) determine the form of the fitted model are unsatisfactory.
2. Equation (3.1) implies that, if other variables in the model are held constant, the relationship between y and x_i will be a straight line, with independent and normally distributed errors. That is, the relationship between y and x_i is linear, conditional on $x_1, \ldots, x_{i-1}, x_i, \ldots, x_p$. If transformations can be found such that most of the p pairwise scatterplots of y against x_i appear linear, that will be a good starting point for identifying an appropriate linear model. It is then likely, though not guaranteed, that the unconditional relationships will be linear or close to linear,
3. Models should, where relevant, be scientifically meaningful.

In Subsection 3.2.1 (Figure 3.3), a comparison of the scatterplot matrix for the untransformed data with that for the log-transformed data was used to justify the use of log transformed variables. Figure 3.3B is preferable to Figure 3.3A on both of the criteria 1 and 2. A more general approach, in which logarithmic transformations are viewed as a special case of power transformations, will be discussed in Subsection 3.3.3.

Linear relations between y and individual x_i imply, also, that there will be linear relations between the x_i. One possibility is to look for transformations, for each variable separately, that give a distribution that is close to symmetric. For power

[9] Strictly, the requirement is that the joint distribution is close to multinormal. Normality of the individual distributions will in most practical contexts ensure this.

transformations, the function `car::powerTransform()` can be used to check for transformations for all variables at the same time. See Subsection 3.3.3.

When considering possible fine tuning of an initially chosen model that makes reasonable scientific and statistical sense, care is needed that such fine tuning does bring with it selection effects that may in fact reduce predictive power.

3.3.2 Plots That Show the Contribution of Individual Terms

Termplots, implemented using R's function `termplot()`) or as *component plus residual plots* by the function `car::crPlots()`, take advantage of a point noted in connection with Equation (3.1) – conditional on all variables except x_i, the plot of y against x_i should exhibit random normal scatter about a straight line.

For simplicity, assume a model with three explanatory variables: x_1, x_2, and x_3, as in the `oddbooks` data. The interest is in examining the contribution of each in turn to the model. The fitting of a regression model makes it possible to write:

$$y = b_0 + b_1 x_1 + b_2 x_2 + b_3 x_3 + e \tag{3.2}$$

$$= \widehat{y} + e, \text{ where } \widehat{y} = b_0 + b_1 x_1 + b_2 x_2. \tag{3.3}$$

Another way to write the model that is to be fitted is:

$$y - b_0 = b_1(x_1 - \bar{x}_1) + b_2(x_2 - \bar{x}_2) + b_3(x_3 - \bar{x}_3) + e.$$

It is a fairly straightforward algebraic exercise to show that $b_0 = \bar{y}$. Thus, we have

$$y - \bar{y} = t_1 + t_2 + t_3 + e,$$

where $t_1 = b_1(x_1 - \bar{x}_1)$, $t_2 = b_2(x_2 - \bar{x}_2)$, $t_3 = b_3(x_3 - \bar{x}_3)$.

Termplots are an exercise in leaving out each of t_1, t_2, and t_3 in turn. Omission of t_1 from $t_1 + t_2 + t_3 + e$ leaves $t_2 + t_3 + e$ to be explained by $t_1 = b_1(x_1 - \bar{x}_1)$. The quantity $r_1 = t_2 + t_3 + e$ is the partial residual for x_1. Then each of the following plots should show random variation about a line:

1. $r_1 = t_2 + t_3 + e$ against x_1,
2. r_2 against x_2, which leaves t_2 out,
3. r_3 against x_3, which leaves t_3 out.

If one or more of the plots shows clear nonlinearity in the scatter of points, this is an indication that a more complex model is needed.

In the terminology of *component plus residual plots*, the quantities r_i have the form *component* + *residual*. Thus, for $r_1 = t_2 + t_3 + e$, $t_2 + t_3$ is the component, while e is the residual; the sum r_1 is plotted against x_1. The argument generalizes in the obvious way when there are more than three terms.

The `predict()` function has an option (`type="terms"`) that gives the t_i, here for the model fitted to the `oddbooks` data.

```
oddbooks.lm <- lm((weight) ~ log(thick)+log(height)+log(breadth),
data=DAAG::oddbooks)
yterms <- predict(oddbooks.lm, type="terms")
```

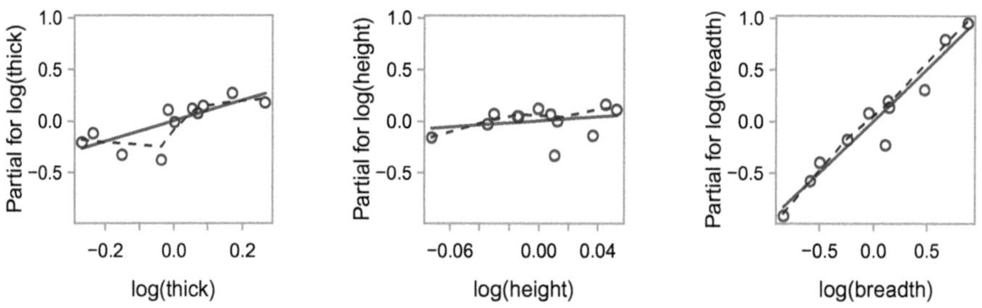

Figure 3.9 The solid lines in the termplots show the respective contribution of the model term, in the regression of `log(weight)` on `log(thick)`, `log(height)`, and `log(breadth)`. Partial residuals (specify `partial.resid=TRUE`), and an associated smooth curve (specify `smooth=panel.smooth`) have been added. With `transform.x=TRUE` the fitted responses appear as straight lines.

The first column of `yterms` has values of t_1, the second has values of t_2, and so on. This information is used to construct the *component plus residual* plots that are given by R's function `termplot()`. (The function does not return anything sensible for terms where interactions are involved, e.g., `x1 + x1:fac` where `fac` is a factor.)

Figure 3.9 shows the contributions of the individual terms to the model. The solid line in the left panel plots $b_1(x_1 - \bar{x}_1)$ against x_1, while the solid line in right panel plots $b_2(x_2 - \bar{x}_2)$ against x_2. Here is code that may be used to create the plots:

```
## To show points, specify partial.resid=TRUE
## For a smooth curve, specify smooth=panel.smooth
termplot(oddbooks.lm, partial.resid=TRUE, smooth=panel.smooth,
col.res="gray30", transform.x=TRUE)
```

If new log-transformed variables are created and used in the model formula, that is, `logthick = log(thick)`, etc., argument `transform.x = TRUE` is unnecessary.

3.3.3 A More Formal Approach to the Choice of Transformation*

Subsection 2.5.6 drew attention to the power family of transformations, defined for this purpose by:

$$\tilde{y} = \frac{y^\lambda - 1}{\lambda}. \tag{3.4}$$

This formulation, used in place of the simpler $\tilde{y} = y^\lambda$, has the advantage that the logarithmic transformation then corresponds to $\lambda = 0$; it is the limiting transformation as λ goes to zero. Values of λ between 0 and 1 give transformations that lie, in a mathematically meaningful sense, between the logarithmic and no transformation. If evident right skewness remains after taking logarithms, something "stronger" than a log transformation is required. A negative λ may be effective.

The function `car::powerTransform()` is designed, when applied to values of a single variable, to guide the choice of a power transformation that brings the distribution as close as possible to normal. Optimizing for closeness to normality can be expected to yield, where the data allow it, an approximately symmetric and unimodal distribution.[10] The following are possible alternative modes of use.

- If applied to a matrix or data frame, a transformation will be found for each of the columns, designed to bring the joint distribution as close as possible to multivariate normality. The indicated transformations for the explanatory variables may be different, depending on whether the outcome variable is included.
- If applied to a regression model object, it finds a transformation of the outcome variable such that the distribution of residuals is as close as possible to normality.

Application of the function to the columns `mph`, `dist` and `gradient` of the data frame `nihr` with which we worked in Subsection 3.2.1 yields:

```
## Use car::powerTransform
nihr <- within(DAAG::nihills, {mph <- dist/time; gradient <- climb/dist})
summary(car::powerTransform(nihr[, c("dist", "gradient")]), digits=3)
```

```
bcPower Transformations to Multinormality
         Est Power Rounded Pwr Wald Lwr Bnd Wald Upr Bnd
dist       -0.9709          -1       -1.782      -0.1594
gradient   -0.4833           0       -1.830       0.8631

Likelihood ratio test that transformation parameters are equal to 0
 (all log transformations)
                           LRT df  pval
LR test, lambda = (0 0) 6.533  2 0.038

Likelihood ratio test that no transformations are needed
                           LRT df       pval
LR test, lambda = (1 1) 30.78  2 0.00000021
```

For `dist` and `gradient`, the intervals with endpoints defined by the Wald lower and upper 95 percent confidence interval bounds contains 0, suggesting that a log transformation is a reasonable choice, while `mph` might be left untransformed.

If we allow `powerTransform()` to choose the transformation that does best in providing normally distributed residuals, we find:

```
form <- mph ~ log(dist) + log(gradient)
summary(car::powerTransform(form, data=nihr))
```

```
bcPower Transformation to Normality
   Est Power Rounded Pwr Wald Lwr Bnd Wald Upr Bnd
Y1     1.009           1      -0.4183        2.437

Likelihood ratio test that transformation parameter is equal to 0
 (log transformation)
                         LRT df pval
LR test, lambda = (0) 1.985  1 0.16

Likelihood ratio test that no transformation is needed
                            LRT df pval
LR test, lambda = (1) 0.000157  1 0.99
```

[10] In fact, `powerTransform()` implements two families of power transformations – the Box–Cox family as defined in Equation (3.4), and the more general Yeo–Johnson family of transformations that will be used in Subsection 3.3.5.

GAM models, discussed in Subsection 4.4.2, provide a more general context in which to examine whether a parametric model adequately captures the contributions of the several terms. GAM models are able, in principle, to capture arbitrary curvilinear contributions to the model fit.

The Use of Transformations – Further Comments

Often there are scientific reasons for transformations. Thus, suppose we have weights w of individual apples, but the effects under study are more likely to be related to surface area. It then makes sense to consider using $x = w^{\frac{2}{3}}$ as the explanatory variable. If the interest is in studying relative, rather than absolute, changes, consider working with the logarithms of measurements.

A logarithmic transformation may both remove an interaction and give more nearly normal data. It can, on the other hand, introduce an interaction where there was none before. Or a transformation can reduce skewness while increasing heterogeneity. The availability of direct methods for fitting special classes of model with nonnormal errors, for example the generalized linear models that we will discuss in Chapter 5, has reduced the need for transformation prior to analysis.

3.3.4 Accuracy Estimates, for Fitted Values and for New Observations

The interest may be in accuracy assessments for one or more fitted values. Or it may be in the accuracy with which the fitted value predicts the value for a new observation. The following table gives both 95 percent coverage (confidence) intervals and 5 percent prediction intervals for `time`, for the first four observations in the data frame `DAAG::nihills`. For predicting future observations, scatter about the fitted values needs to be taken into account, resulting in much wider intervals. Note the change from the default `interval="confidence"` to `interval="prediction"` in the call to `predict()`.

```
lognihr <- log(DAAG::nihills)
names(lognihr) <- paste0("log", names(lognihr))
timeClimb.lm <- lm(logtime ~ logdist + logclimb, data = lognihr)
## Coverage intervals; use exp() to undo the log transformation
citimes <- exp(predict(timeClimb.lm, interval="confidence"))
## Prediction intervals, i.e., for new observations
pitimes <- exp(predict(timeClimb.lm, newdata=lognihr, interval="prediction"))
## fit ci:lwr ci:pwr pi:lwr pi:upr
ci_then_pi <- cbind(citimes, pitimes[,2:3])
colnames(ci_then_pi) <- paste0(c("", rep(c("ci-","pi-"), c(2,2))),
                        colnames(ci_then_pi))
## First 4 rows
print(ci_then_pi[1:4,], digits=2)
```

```
                     fit ci-lwr ci-upr pi-lwr pi-upr
Binevenagh          0.89   0.85   0.94   0.75   1.06
Slieve Gullion      0.49   0.47   0.51   0.41   0.58
Glenariff Mountain  0.64   0.60   0.68   0.54   0.76
Donard & Commedagh  1.13   1.07   1.19   0.95   1.33
```

Figure 3.10A shows these confidence and prediction intervals graphically. The narrower 95 percent confidence bands are in red, while the wider 95 percent

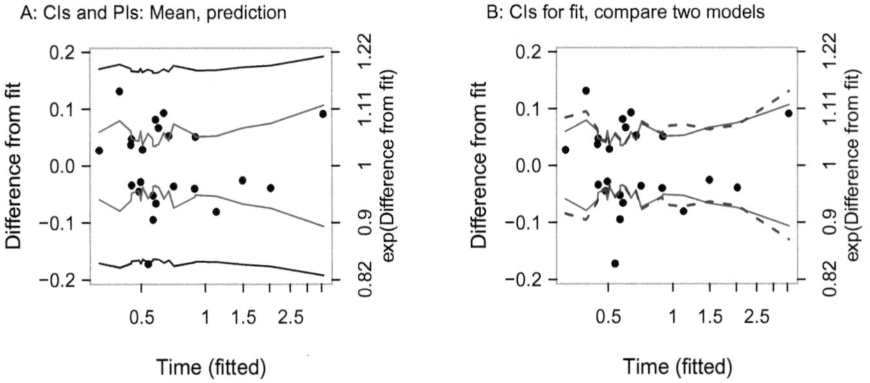

Figure 3.10 Both panels show differences of observed values (black dots) and differences of predicted confidence intervals (in red), from fitted values, with fitted values on the x-axis. As these differences are on a logarithmic scale, the back transformed values (take exponents) are Observed/Fit, where "Fit" is on the back transformed scale. In both panels, pointwise 95 percent confidence intervals for fitted values are in red, with the fitted values subtracted off. Panel A has, in addition, the wider 95 percent prediction intervals, shown in black. Panel B adds confidence intervals for the model that has a quadratic term in `log(dist)` (blue dashes).

prediction bands are shown in black. The prediction bands are relevant for calculating bounds for new races, possibly as here on the same courses. Note the following.

- Because the combinations of distance and time vary from race to race, the bounds are not smooth functions of the predicted times.
- The model that replaces `log(climb)` with `log(gradient)` gives the same predicted values and the same intervals.

Figure 3.10B repeats the confidence bound information from Figure 3.10A (but omits the prediction bound information), now adding confidence bound information for a model that has a quadratic term in `log(dist)`:

```
timeClimb2.lm <- update(timeClimb.lm, formula = . ~ . + I(logdist^2))
```

(The dots (`"."`) on the left and right of the argument `new` repeat, respectively, the left and right parts of the model formula used on `timeClimb.lm`.)

Note that we had to write `I(logdist^2)`. The wrapper function `I()` ensures that its argument is handled as an arithmetic expression rather than as a model formula. (Within a model formula, `log(dist)^2` is interpreted as `log(dist)`. More helpfully, `(a+b+c)^2` is shorthand for `a+b+c+a:b+b:c+c:a`. Terms such as `a:b` are, technically, interactions.)

Observe that the bounds for the model `timeClimb2.lm` (dashed lines) are similar to those for `timeClimb.lm` (solid lines) within the main body of the data, but fan out at either extreme. The extra degree of freedom for the quadratic term leads to bounds that may better reflect the uncertainty in the predictions for large times.

There is a tradeoff between bias for `timeClimb.lm`, and increased variance for `timeClimb2.lm`.

These confidence and prediction bound estimates have important limitations.

1. Failure of assumptions of independence of the data points and homogeneity of variance, perhaps because of clustering or other forms of dependence, will bias or invalidate both types of interval.
2. The normality assumption is crucial for prediction intervals. Normality plays a less directly important role in the accuracy of the confidence bands.
3. Both types of bands apply only to the population from which the data have been sampled. It might be hazardous to use the above model to predict winning times for hill races in England or Mexico or Tasmania.

Point 3 can be addressed by testing the model against data from these other locations. Subsection 3.5 will compare results from the Scottish `hills2000` data with results from the Northern Irish `nihills` data. The results are broadly comparable.

3.3.5 Choosing the Model – Deaths from Atlantic Hurricanes

The dataset `DAAG::hurricNamed` has data on fatalities caused in the United States by the 94 Atlantic hurricanes that made landfall over 1950–2012 inclusive. Explanatory variables that will be used here are `BaseDam2014` (damage converted to 2014 dollars) and `LF.PressureMB` (barometric pressure at the time of landfall in the United States; if more than one landfall, then the minimum was taken), with `deaths` as the dependent variable.[11]

The analysis now given will treat `deaths` as a continuous variable. It will be desirable to check, to the extent possible, that this does not have any effect of consequence on the model choice and model fit. Figure 3.11 shows power-transformed values of `deaths`, `LF.PressureMB`, and `BaseDam2014`, as suggested by output from the code:

```
hurric <- DAAG::hurricNamed[,c("LF.PressureMB", "BaseDam2014", "deaths")]
thurric <- car::powerTransform(hurric, family="yjPower")
transY <- car::yjPower(hurric, coef(thurric, round=TRUE))
smoothPars <- list(col.smooth='red', lty.smooth=2, lwd.smooth=1, spread=0)
car::spm(transY, lwd=0.5, regLine=FALSE, oma=rep(2.5,4), gap=0.5,
        col="blue", smooth=smoothPars, cex.labels=1)
```

As `deaths` has some zero values, the Yeo–Johnson family of transformations, described in Subsection 2.5.6, has been specified. The range of values of `LF.PressureMB` (909 – 1003) and of `BaseDam2014` (1.04 – 98195.4) is in each case so large that adding 1 to their values makes little difference to the suggested transformation.

[11] The controversial *PNAS* article (Jung et al., 2014) used the estimate of the dollar damage for a comparable hurricane in 2013, that is, the 2013 equivalent of `NDAM2014`, rather than the more relevant inflation adjusted damage at the time measure. It claimed that hurricanes with female sounding names were, because treated less seriously, more dangerous than those with male names.

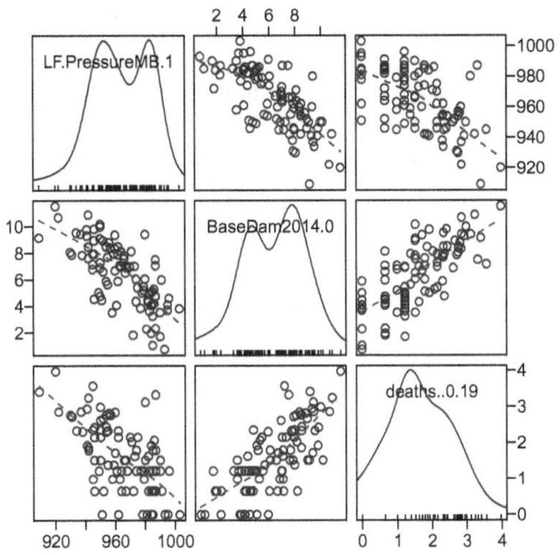

Figure 3.11 Scatterplot matrix, with automatically chosen power transformations, for hurricane death data.

Notice that `LF.PressureMB`, which has been left untransformed, has a bimodal distribution. Its relationship with the transformed values of `BaseDam2014` is nonlinear. The choice $\lambda = 0$ for `BaseDam2014` implies a logarithmic transformation. We then work with `log(BaseDam2014` and with `LF.PressureMB`.

The primary concern is for the distribution of the outcome variable to be as close to normal after accounting for the explanatory terms. A further use of the function `powerTransform()`, directly with the relevant model formula to suggest a transformation, then gives:

```
modelform <- deaths ~ log(BaseDam2014) + LF.PressureMB
powerT <- car::powerTransform(modelform, data=as.data.frame(hurric),
                              family="yjPower")
summary(powerT, digits=3)
```

```
yjPower Transformation to Normality
   Est Power Rounded Pwr Wald Lwr Bnd Wald Upr Bnd
Y1    -0.2033        -0.2       -0.3111      -0.0955

 Likelihood ratio test that transformation parameter is equal to 0
                             LRT df      pval
LR test, lambda = (0) 15.41  1 0.000087
```

This suggests use of a power transformation with $\lambda = -0.20$. This is not much different from that used in Figure 3.11, for the unconditioned values of `deaths+1`. Now fit a line, using the function `car::yjPower()` to create the transformed values of the outcome variable:

```
deathP <- with(hurric, car::yjPower(deaths, lambda=-0.2))
power.lm <- MASS::rlm(deathP ~ log(BaseDam2014) + LF.PressureMB, data=hurric)
print(coef(summary(power.lm)),digits=2)
```

```
## Use (deaths+1)^(-0.2) as outcome variable
plot(power.lm, cex.caption=0.85, fg="gray",
  caption=list('A: Resids vs Fitted', 'B: Normal Q-Q', 'C: Scale-Location', '',
            'D: Resids vs Leverage'))
```

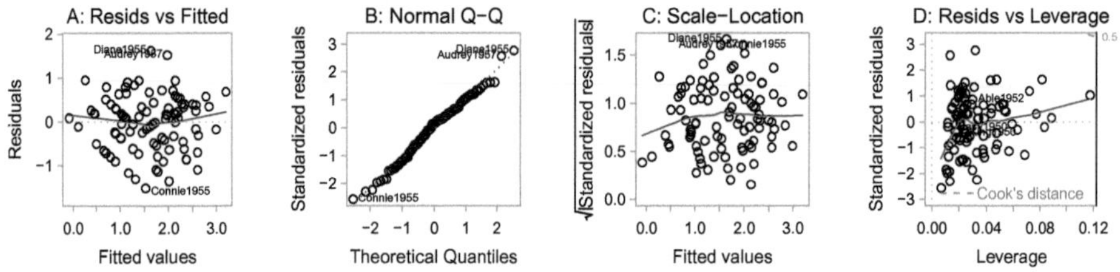

Figure 3.12 Diagnostic plots for a model that used power transformed values of **deaths** ($\lambda = -0.20$) for the outcome variable.

```
                     Value  Std. Error  t value
(Intercept)         9.6289       4.978      1.9
log(BaseDam2014)    0.2247       0.040      5.6
LF.PressureMB      -0.0098       0.005     -2.0
```

Figure 3.12 shows the diagnostic plots: Notice the slight curvature in the plot of residuals versus fitted values. Diane and Audrey stand out in several of the plots, but not to an extent that identifies them as outliers. The points with low leverage, where the smooth dips down in Panel D, are likely to be for data where there were no deaths. This is not a particular concern, as interest is primarily in points for cases where deaths occurred. Otherwise, these plots appear unexceptional. This dataset will be examined further in Subsection 5.4.4.

3.3.6 Strategies for Fitting Models – Suggested Steps

- Examine the distribution of each of the explanatory variables, and of the response variable. Look for any instances where distributions are highly skew, or where there are outlying values. Check whether any outlying values may be mistakes.
- Where a variable has a skewed distribution, consider whether a transformation may give a more symmetric distribution. Surprisingly often, logarithmic transformation of one or more explanatory variables gives a more symmetric distribution, leads to a regression relationship on the transformed scale(s) that are more nearly linear, and makes it easier to identify a regression equation that has good predictive power.
- Examine the scatterplot matrix involving all the explanatory variables. (Including the response is, at this point, optional.)
  - Look for values that appear as outliers in any of the pairwise scatterplots.
  - Look for evidence of nonlinearity in the plots of explanatory variables against each other. Such nonlinearity is often a result of skewness in one of the distributions, or of differences in the extent of skewness. In such cases consider transformation of one or both variables.

- Note the ranges of each of the explanatory variables. Do they vary sufficiently to affect values of the response variable?
- How accurately are each of the explanatory variables measured? At worst, the inaccuracy may be so serious that coefficients of other explanatory variables will be seriously in error and/or that any effect is unlikely to be detected. On implications for estimating coefficients of other variables, see Section 3.7.
- Look for pairs of explanatory variables that are so highly correlated that they appear to give the same information. Do scientific considerations help judge whether both variables should be retained? For example, the two members of the pair may measure what is essentially the same quantity. Note, however, that the difference, although small, can be important. Section 5.2 has an example, where the replacing of variables x_1 and x_2 by new variables $x_1 + x_2$ and $x_1 - x_2$ gave a better and more usable summary of the information in the data.

Note that if relationships between explanatory variables are nonlinear, diagnostic plots may be misleading. See Cook and Weisberg (1999).

Diagnostic Checks

Checks should include the following.

- Plot residuals against fitted values. For initial checks, consider the use of residuals from a resistant regression model. Check for patterns in the residuals, and for the fanning out (or in) of residuals as the fitted values change. (Do not plot residuals against observed values. This is potentially deceptive; there is an inevitable positive correlation.)
- Examine the Cook's distance statistics.
- If it seems helpful, examine standardized versions of the drop-1 coefficients that are available using the function `dfbetas()`. See Subsection 3.4.2. It may be necessary to delete influential data points and refit the model.
- For each explanatory variable, construct a component plus residual plot, to check whether any of the explanatory variables require transformation.
- If observations follow a time sequence, use the function `acf()` to check for sequential correlation in the residuals. (See Section 9.2.)

The *dr* package implements and demonstrates a suite of tools that use ideas of "structural dimension" to guide the choice of a suitable form of nonlinear equation. This methodology is beyond the scope of this text.

3.4 Robust Regression, Outliers, and Influence

This section gives additional detail on diagnostic graphs and statistics that may be useful in critiquing and/or interpreting regression models. There will be an especial focus on tools that can be effective in drawing attention to outliers and in assessing their effect, if included on the model.

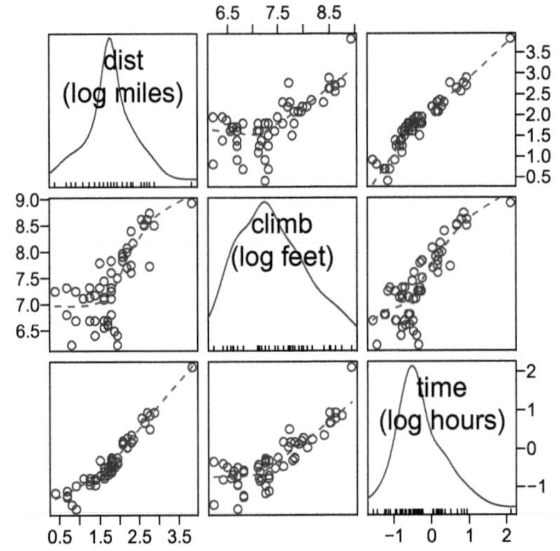

Figure 3.13 Scatterplot matrix for the `hills2000` data, with logarithmic scales.

3.4.1 Making Outliers Obvious – Robust Regression

Outliers can be hard to detect. Two (or more) outliers that are influential may mask each other. If this seems a possible issue, a useful recourse is to work with residuals from a resistant fit. A resistant fit is a type of robust fit that aims to ignore completely the effect of outliers, to give a fitted model against which outliers stand out.

The Scottish hillrace dataset `hills2000` is directly comparable with the Northern Irish dataset `nihills`. Again, we will use logarithmic scales and limit attention to the male results. Figure 3.13 shows the scatterplot matrix. Apart from a possible outlier, the relationship between `dist` and `climb` seems approximately linear on the log scale. Code is a ready adaptation of the code for Figure 3.3B.

The help page for `races2000` (`hills2000` is a subset of `races2000`) suggests uncertainty about the distance for the Caerketton race in row 42. We will include Caerketton during our initial analysis and check whether it appears to be an outlier.

Figure 3.14 shows residuals (A) from a least squares (`lm`) fit and (B) from a resistant `lqs` fit, in both cases plotted against fitted values. By default, even if almost half the observations are outliers, a resistant fit should ensure that the effect on the fitted model will be small. See the help page for `lqs` for details. The code for the regression fits is:

```
## Panel A
lhills2k.lm <- lm(log(time) ~ log(climb) + log(dist), data = hills2000)
## Panel B
lhills2k.lqs <- MASS::lqs(log(time) ~ log(climb) + log(dist), data = hills2000)
reres <- residuals(lhills2k.lqs)
```

Caerketton shows up clearly as an outlier, in both panels. Its residual in panel 1 is -0.356 (visual inspection might suggest -0.35). The predicted `logtime` for this

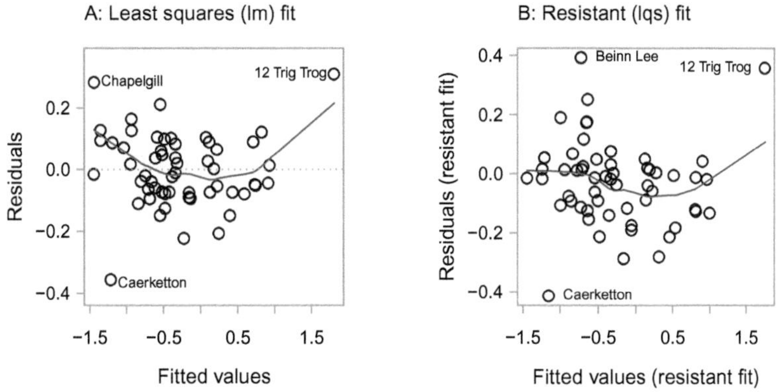

Figure 3.14 Plots of residuals against fitted values from the regression of `logtime` on `logclimb` and `logdist`. Panel A is from the least squares (`lm`) fit, while Panel B is for a resistant fit that uses `MASS::lqs()`. Note that the resistant fit relies on repeated sampling of the data, and will differ slightly from one run to the next.

race is conveniently written as $\log(\widehat{\text{time}})$. Then

$$\log(\text{time}) - \log(\widehat{\text{time}}) = -0.356.$$

Thus

$$\log(\frac{\text{time}}{\widehat{\text{time}}}) = -0.356, \text{ that is, } \frac{\text{time}}{\widehat{\text{time}}} \simeq \exp -0.356 = 0.7.$$

The time given for this race is 70 percent of that predicted by the regression equation. The standardized difference is −3; this can be seen by use of

```
plot(lhills2k.lm, which=2)
```

The resistant fit in Panel B suggests that Beinn Lee and 12 Trig Trog are also outliers. These outliers may be a result of nonlinearity.

Dynamic graphic exploration can be helpful. See, further, Figure 3.15A in the subsection that follows.

Outliers, Influential or Not, Should Be Taken Seriously

Outliers, influential or not, should never be disregarded. Careful scrutiny of the original data may reveal an error in data entry. Alternatively, use of an inappropriate model may result in one or more outliers. If apparently genuine outliers remain excluded from the final fitted model, they should be noted in the eventual report or paper. They should be included, separately identified, in graphs.

3.4.2 Leverage, Influence, and Cook's Distance

This extends earlier discussions of diagnostics in Subsections 2.5.3 and 3.1.2.

What difference does replacing y_i by $y_i + \Delta_i$, while leaving other y-values unchanged, make to the fitted surface? There is a straightforward answer; the fitted value changes from $\widehat{y}_i$ to $\widehat{y}_i + h_{ii}\Delta_i$, where h_{ii} is the *leverage* for that point.

* *Leverage and the Hat Matrix – Technical Details*

In a regression with outcome variable y and model matrix X, the *hat* matrix is

$$\mathrm{H} = \mathrm{X}(\mathrm{X}^T\mathrm{X})^{-1}\mathrm{X}^T.$$

The leverage values h_{ii} are the diagonal elements of the hat matrix H that can be derived from the model matrix. They sum to give the number p of columns of the model matrix. (The vector $\widehat{\mathrm{y}}$ of fitted or *hat* values is given by the matrix calculation $\widehat{\mathrm{y}} = \mathrm{Hy}$. The hat matrix puts the hat on y.) A large h_{ii} gives the ith observation high leverage. Use the function `hatvalues()` to obtain the leverages, thus:

```
round(unname(hatvalues(timeClimb.lm)),2)
```

```
 [1] 0.12 0.07 0.13 0.11 0.09 0.15 0.05 0.15 0.25 0.22 0.09 0.06 0.06
[14] 0.13 0.05 0.10 0.18 0.21 0.44 0.09 0.14 0.05 0.08
```

The largest leverage, for observation 19, is 0.44. As this is more than three times the average value of 0.13, it may call for attention. (The model matrix has $p = 3$ columns. With $n = 23$ observations, the average is $p/n = 0.13$.)

Influential Points and Cook's Distance

The Cook's distance statistic is a commonly used measure of "influence," that is, of the combined effect of the size of the residual and its leverage in determining fitted values. Recall the guideline given in Section 2.5.3, that any Cook's distance that is 1.0 or more, or that is substantially larger than other Cook's distances, warrants careful examination.

Any serious distortion of the fitted response may lead to residuals that are hard to interpret or even misleading. It is wise to check the effect of removing any highly influential data points before proceeding far with the analysis.

Dynamic Graphics

The left panel of Figure 3.15 is a plot of residuals against leverage values, with the Cook's distances are shown as contours. The right panel is a snapshot, created using the abilities of the *rgl* package, of a three-dimensional dynamic graphic plot that shows the regression plane in the regression of `log(time)` on `log(dist)` and `log(climb)`. The two points that in the perspective shown appear most extreme have been labeled. The left panel can be obtained thus:

```
## Residuals versus leverages
plot(timeClimb.lm, which=5, add.smooth=FALSE)
## The points can alternatively be plotted using
## plot(hatvalues(model.matrix(timeClimb.lm)), residuals(timeClimb.lm))
```

The right panel can be obtained thus:

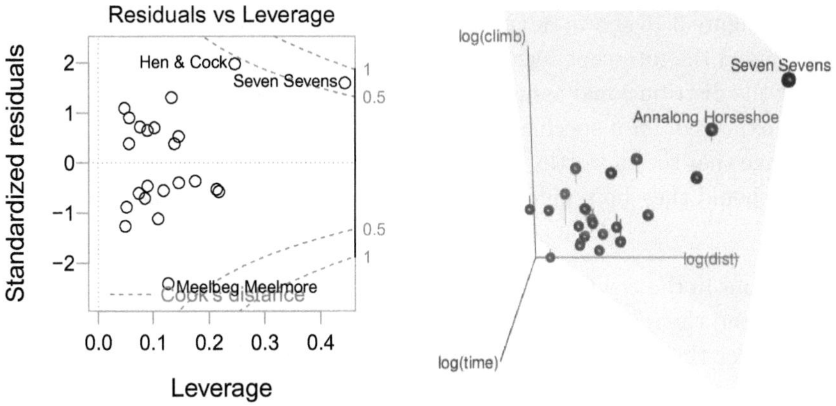

Figure 3.15 In the left panel, standardized residuals are plotted against leverages. Contours are shown for Cook's distances of 0.5 and 1.0. The right panel is a snapshot of a three-dimensional dynamic graphic plot.

```
with(nihills, scatter3d(x=log(dist), y=log(climb), z=log(time), grid=FALSE,
                        point.col="black", surface.col="gray60",
                        surface.alpha=0.2, axis.scales=FALSE))
with(nihills, Identify3d(x=log(dist), y=log(climb), z=log(time),
                labels=row.names(DAAG::nihills), minlength=8), offset=0.05)
## To rotate display, hold down the left mouse button and move the mouse.
## To put labels on points, right-click and drag a box around them, perhaps
## repeatedly.  Create an empty box to exit from point identification mode.
```

Dynamic graphic three-dimensional (3D) plots can be useful in calling attention to any clustering in the points, or points that lie away from the main body of points.

The abilities of the *rgl* package can be conveniently accessed from the 3D graph submenu of the R Commander GUI's graphics pull-down menu.

Influence on the Regression Coefficients

In addition to diagnostic plots, it is useful to investigate the effect of each observation on the estimated regression coefficients. The function `dfbetas()` calculates the differences in the coefficient estimates obtained with and without each observation, then dividing by the respective standard error estimate to give a standardized

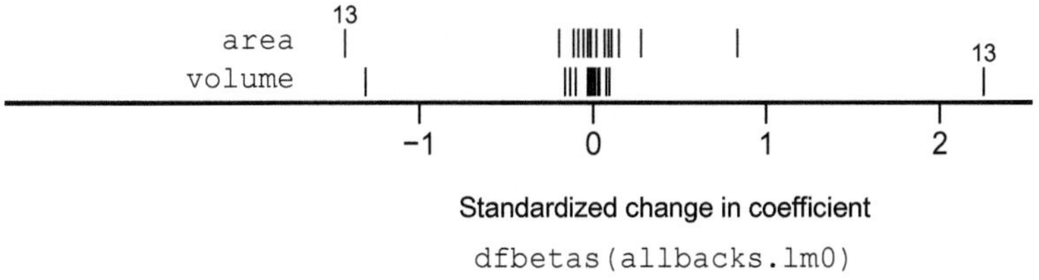

Figure 3.16 Standardized changes in regression coefficients, for the model fitted to the `allbacks` dataset. The points for the one row (row 13) where the change for one of the coefficients was greater than 2 in absolute value are labeled with the row number.

estimate. Figure 3.16 shows values for the regression model fit to the `allbacks` data that excluded the intercept term.

Under the distributional assumptions, standardized changes that are larger than 2 can be expected, for a specified coefficient, in about 1 observation in 20. Here, the only change that seems worthy of note is for `volume` in observation 13. For absolute changes, should they be required, use the function `lm.influence()`.

**Additional Diagnostic Plots*

The functions in the *car* package, designed to accompany Fox and Weisberg (2018), greatly extend the range of diagnostic plots. See the examples and references in the help pages for this package. As an indication of what is available, try

```
car::influencePlot(allbacks.lm)
```

3.5 Assessment and Comparison of Regression Models

The R^2 and adjusted R^2 statistics (discussed in Subsection 2.5.2) are included in the default output from `summary.lm()`. Note also the F-statistic that compares the *mean square* explained by the model with the *residual mean square* that is used as a variance estimate. Other statistics that may be used appear in output from functions that will be discussed shortly – `add1()`, `drop1()`, and `anova()`. The use of such statistical measures should be accompanied by careful scrutiny of diagnostic plots, term plots, and other relevant graphical checks. Finally, we will look briefly at the use of Bayes Factors to compare regression models.

While adjusted R^2 is in general a more meaningful statistic, it is not a good basis for model comparison. The AIC (or AICc) and BIC *information* statistics that were introduced in Subsection 1.7.1 are preferred for this purpose. These are among measures that are designed to choose, from among a small number of alternatives, the model with the best predictive power. While predictive accuracy is not necessarily the only or the most important consideration, it is always an important consideration.

3.5.1 AIC, AICc, BIC, and Bayes Factors for Normal Theory Regression Models*

Consider now the use of a regression model that relates `brainwt` (brain weight), in the dataset `DAAG::litters`, to `lsize` (litter size) and `bodywt` (body weight). How strong is the case for including `lsize` as an explanatory factor? The following fits models that do and do not include `lsize`:

```
## Calculations using mouse brain weight data
mouse.lm <- lm(brainwt ~ lsize+bodywt, data=DAAG::litters)
mouse0.lm <- update(mouse.lm, formula = . ~ . - lsize)
```

Now look at alternative ways to compare the two models:

```
aicc <- sapply(list(mouse0.lm, mouse.lm), AICcmodavg::AICc)
infstats <- cbind(AIC(mouse0.lm, mouse.lm), AICc=aicc,
                  BIC=BIC(mouse0.lm, mouse.lm)[,-1])
print(rbind(infstats, "Difference"=apply(infstats,2,diff)), digits=3)
```

```
              df      AIC     AICc      BIC
mouse0.lm      3  -112.81  -111.31  -109.82
mouse.lm       4  -115.57  -112.90  -111.58
Difference     1    -2.76    -1.59    -1.76
```

More generally, how do the statistics compare when the number of parameters estimated is a modest proportion, perhaps 5 percent or more, of the number of observations? Figure 3.17 looks, for a range of values of n (number of observations), at how the AIC, AICc, and BIC statistics compare. The lines all show the increase in the penalty term difference for an increase of one in the number of parameters estimated. The change (negative if the statistic decreases) in the relevant statistic in moving from a model with log likelihood L_1 to a log likelihood L_2 that results from adding one more degree of freedom is:

$$-2L_2 + 2L_1 + \text{ penalty increase,}$$

where the penalty difference is that shown in Figure 3.17.

```
df <- data.frame(n=5:35, AIC=rep(2,31), BIC=log(5:35))
cfAICc <- function(n,p,d) 2*(p+d)*n/(n-(p+d)-1) - 2*p*n/(n-p-1)
df <- cbind(df, AICc12=cfAICc(5:35,1,1), AICc34=cfAICc(5:35,3,1))
labs <- sort(c(2^(0:6),2^(0:6)*1.5))
xyplot(AICc12+AICc34+AIC+BIC ~ n, data=df, type='l', auto.key=list(columns=4),
       scales=list(y=list(log=T, at=labs, labels=paste(labs))),
 par.settings=simpleTheme(lty=c(1,1:3), lwd=2, col=rep(c('gray','black'), c(1,3))))
```

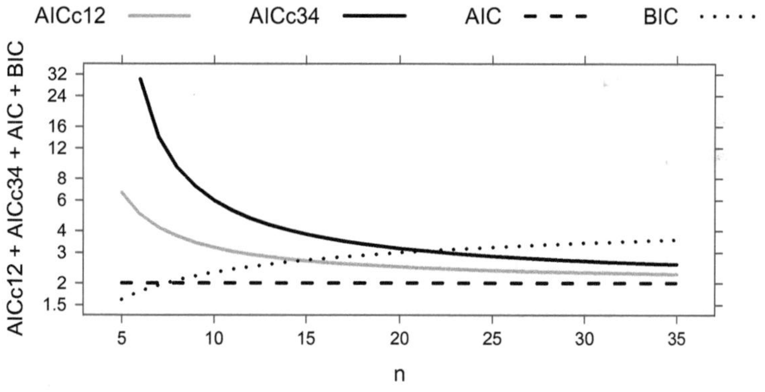

Figure 3.17 The increase in the penalty term difference is shown for an increase of one in the number of parameters p. For the AIC statistic, this equals the constant 2. For the BIC statistic, this depends only on n. For the AICc statistic, the number of parameters p makes a huge difference when n is small, as shown by the difference between the black (4 vs. 3) and gray (2 vs. 1) solid lines

There is a strong case for consistently using AICc in place of AIC. Once n/p is small enough that the BIC difference is smaller than the AICc difference, this may reasonably be taken as evidence that the asymptotic results no longer apply, whether for BIC as well as for AIC. Note that the sampling variation is large for all three statistics when n/p is small.

The Functions `drop1()` *and* `add1()`

Readers may care to check that the AIC and BIC information can be obtained by using `drop1()` with `mouse.lm` as argument, or `add1()` with the *scope* extended to include `lsize`. The default is to show AIC statistics. Setting `k=log(n)`, where `n=nrow(DAAG::litters)`, gives the BIC statistics.

```
n <- nrow(DAAG::litters)
drop1(mouse.lm, scope=~lsize)              # AIC, with/without `lsize`
drop1(mouse.lm, scope=~lsize, k=log(n))  # BIC, w/wo `lsize`
add1(mouse0.lm, scope=~bodywt+lsize)      # AIC, w/wo `lsize`, alternative
```

In this context where the number of observations to maximum number of parameters ratio is $20/4 = 5$, neither of these statistics makes much sense.

The Use of `BayesFactor::lmBF` *to Compare the Two Models*

A further possibility is to use a *BayesFactor* package style Bayes Factor to compare the two models. Separate factors `bf1` and `bf2` are first calculated that are for comparisons with the model that has only the constant term. The ratio `bf2/bf1` is then used to compare the two models.

```
suppressPackageStartupMessages(library(BayesFactor))
bf1 <- lmBF(brainwt ~ bodywt, data=DAAG::litters)
bf2 <- lmBF(brainwt ~ bodywt+lsize, data=DAAG::litters)
bf2/bf1
```

```
Bayes factor analysis
--------------
[1] bodywt + lsize : 1.512 \pm0%

Against denominator:
  brainwt ~ bodywt
---
Bayes factor type: BFlinearModel, JZS
```

The `bf1/bf0` ratio of 1.51 can be compared with a Bayes Factor-type relative preference statistic that is calculated from the BIC, thus:

```
## Relative support statistics
setNames(exp(-apply(infstats[,-1],2,diff)/2), c("AIC","AICc","BIC"))
```

```
  AIC  AICc   BIC
3.965 2.213 2.410
```

Note also the C_p statistic. The `anova` method for models fitted using `lm()` sets the C_p statistic to be:[12]

$$C_p = \text{RSS} + 2p\sigma^2.$$

In the linear regression context, with the smallest value preferred, this will choose the same model as the AIC statistic.

[12] The function `olsrr:ols_mallows_cp()` implements, instead, the more usual: $C_p = \frac{\text{RSS}}{\sigma^2} + 2p - n$.

3.5.2 *Using* anova() *to Compare Models – the* nihills *Data*

The function anova(), used in Subsection 2.5.2 and Section 3.1 to give a sum of squares breakdown for a regression model, can be used to compare models. The sum of squares breakdown, and the use of an F-statistic to compare models, makes sense only if the models are *nested*, that is, the more complex model can be formed by adding a term or terms to a simpler model.

If as usually happens the variance has to be estimated, σ^2 is replaced by the estimated variance s^2 for the "largest" model considered. An alternative to the default test="F" is test="Cp", which (as with AIC, AICc, and BIC), does not require nested models.[13]

Figure 3.6 suggested some curvature in the contribution of the term logdist that was fitted to the nihills data. The following investigates adding a squared term, giving the model nihills2.lm.

```
lognihr <- log(DAAG::nihills)
lognihr <- setNames(log(nihr), paste0("log", names(nihr)))
timeClimb.lm <- lm(logtime ~ logdist + logclimb, data = lognihr)
timeClimb2.lm <- update(timeClimb.lm, formula = . ~ . + I(logdist^2))
print(anova(timeClimb.lm, timeClimb2.lm, test="F"), digits=4)
```

```
Analysis of Variance Table

Model 1: logtime ~ logdist + logclimb
Model 2: logtime ~ logdist + logclimb + I(logdist^2)
  Res.Df    RSS Df Sum of Sq     F Pr(>F)
1     20 0.1173
2     19 0.0999  1   0.01744 3.318 0.0843
```

The result from the alternative argument test="Cp" is:

```
print(anova(timeClimb.lm, timeClimb2.lm, test="Cp"), digits=3)
```

```
Analysis of Variance Table

Model 1: logtime ~ logdist + logclimb
Model 2: logtime ~ logdist + logclimb + I(logdist^2)
  Res.Df    RSS Df Sum of Sq   Cp
1     20 0.1173                0.15
2     19 0.0999  1    0.0174 0.14
```

```
## Compare with the AICc difference
sapply(list(timeClimb.lm, timeClimb2.lm), AICcmodavg::AICc)
```

```
[1] -45.9 -46.3
```

Both suggests a slight preference for the model with the squared term.

Now investigate adding, in turn, each of I(logdist^2) and logdist:logclimb. The interaction term logdist:logclimb may equivalently (as these are continuous variables) be written I(logdist*logclimb):

[13] For comparing nested models in a context where the argument scale is used to specify a known residual variance, specify test="Chisq". This is not relevant here.

```
form1 <- update(formula(timeClimb.lm), ~ . + I(logdist^2) + logdist:logclimb)
addcheck <- add1(timeClimb.lm, scope=form1, test="F")
print(addcheck, digits=4)
```

```
Single term additions

Model:
logtime ~ logdist + logclimb
                 Df Sum of Sq     RSS    AIC F value Pr(>F)
<none>                        0.1173 -115.4
I(logdist^2)      1   0.01744 0.0999 -117.1   3.318 0.0843
logdist:logclimb  1   0.01172 0.1056 -115.8   2.108 0.1628
```

The model formula `form1` includes, in addition to the terms already in the model, the terms `I(logdist^2)` and `logdist:logclimb`. The function `add1()` checks the effect of adding each of these additional terms, one at a time, to the model.

3.5.3 Training/Test Approaches, and Cross-Validation

The surest check is to use the chosen model to make predictions for "test" data that is separate from the "training" data used to fit the model, and that reflects the conditions under which predictions will be used. For testing the accuracy of predictions when the model is applied one year into the future, a useful check is to compare past predictions made one year into the future with what eventuated. (In times of relative stability, what this gives is a best case scenario, with no accounting for what a pandemic, or a war, or a freak of nature, may throw up.)

As noted earlier, the *DAAG* package has two hill race datasets – **nihills** for Northern Ireland, and **hills2000** for Scotland. The square of the "residual standard error" from **timeClimb.lm** is a mean squared error (MSE) estimate, with **nihills** in the role of training data. We will use the dataset **hills2000** as test data, but omitting the seemingly erroneous Caerketton observation. The mean square prediction error (MSPE) estimate for **hills2000** as test data is the mean squared difference between predictions for that data from the model **timeClimb.lm**, and observed values for the Scottish hill race data.

If the two datasets can be treated as different random samples from the combined dataset, the expected values of the MSE and the MSPE will be the same. Degrees of freedom are number of rows (23) minus 3 for the MSE, and number of of rows (55, after omitting Caerketton) for the MSPE estimate. As the **hills2000** data are independent of the data used to fit the model **timeClimb.lm**, there is no adjustment for number of parameters estimated.

```
## Check how well timeClimb.lm model predicts for hills2000 data
timeClimb.lm <- lm(logtime ~ logdist + logclimb, data = lognihr)
logscot <- log(subset(DAAG::hills2000,
              !row.names(DAAG::hills2000)=="Caerketton"))
names(logscot) <- paste0("log", names(hills2000))
scotpred <- predict(timeClimb.lm, newdata=logscot, se=TRUE)
trainVar <- summary(timeClimb.lm)[["sigma"]]^2
trainDF <- summary(timeClimb.lm)[["df"]][2]
mspe <- mean((logscot[,'logtime']-scotpred[['fit']])^2)
```

```
mspeDF <- nrow(logscot)
```

The two estimates are as follows, to four significant figures.

- Training data (`nihr`): 0.0059 on 20 degrees of freedom. Note that degrees of freedom are number of rows (23), less number of parameters estimated.
- Test data (`hills2000`): 0.0173 on 55 degrees of freedom. Degrees of freedom are number of rows (55) of test data.

The two mean square error estimates are independent, and can be compared using an F-test:

```
pf(mspe/trainVar, mspeDF, trainDF, lower.tail=FALSE)
```

```
[1] 0.004789
```

The increase in the mean square error arises, in part, because the squared "residual standard error" when the model is fitted to the `hills2000` data is larger than for the `timeClimb.lm` fitted model. There is more inherent variability in the `hills2000` data.

```
scot.lm <- lm(logtime ~ logdist+logclimb, data=logscot)
signif(summary(scot.lm)[['sigma']]^2, 4)
```

```
[1] 0.01228
```

3.5.4 Further Points and Issues

Patterns in the Diagnostic PLots – Are They More Than Hints?

The smooths added to the plots of residuals against fitted values in Figures 3.6 and 3.12 had saucer-like shapes. Were these likely to be a result of statistical noise? As a guide to judgment, we can use the function `DAAG::plotSimDiags()` to simulate from the fitted model and examine the diagnostic plots. If plots from simulated data give comparable curvature with modest frequency, the hints can be ignored.

Thus, consider again the model for which Figure 3.6 gives the diagnostic plots. Code that generates eight simulated sets of y-values, then showing the eight sets of plots of residuals against fitted values, is:

```
set.seed(91)     # Reproduce plots as shown here
plotSimDiags(timeClimb.lm, layout=c(4,2), which=1, caption=list(""))
```

Figure 3.18 shows the resulting plots. Panels 1 and 5 show saucer-shaped curvature that is comparable to that in the first of the plots in Figure 3.6. A hint that the model is not quite capturing the trend in the response should probably be ignored.

What Is the Scatter About the Fitted Response?

When there are extensive data, it can happen that the scatter about the fitted model is so large that the relatively small amount of the total variation explained by the model makes it of limited practical use. See Soyer and Hogarth (2012) for

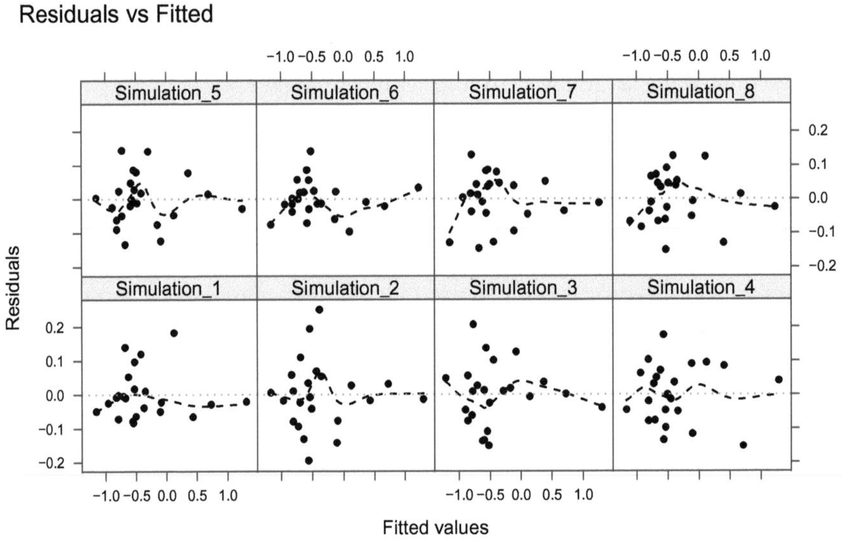

Figure 3.18 Eight sets of simulated time values were generated by adding random normal noise, with standard deviation equal to the fitted model error root mean square, to the fitted `log(time)` (`ltime`) values for the model. Panels show diagnostic plots of residuals against fitted values.

extended commentary. Termplots are a good way to check how this feeds into the contribution of individual variables when other variables are held constant.

In the component plus residual plots in Figure 3.4, the scatter was small relative to the explanatory power of the terms individually. Figure 2.8B related to data (the dataset `HistData::GaltonFamilies`) where, notwithstanding a t-statistic of 9.3 for the gradient of the fitted line, the line explained only 15 percent of the variation.

Model Selection and Tuning Risks

Selection bias is a concern whenever a model performance measure is used to choose from a number of alternative models. Criteria that suggest transformations for explanatory variables, if this is done independently of the effect on the model fit, do not introduce this bias. They become an increasing concern as, using a model with linear terms as a starting point, ever more modifications or alternatives are considered. These may include the addition of one or more or other quadratic terms, or the transformation of one or more variables. Excessive fine tuning is both a waste of time and counterproductive.

As discussed in Subsection 3.5.3, a safe way to proceed is to fit the model to data that are separate from the data used to develop the model. In principle, cross-validation can be used to address the issue, but that requires the model development steps to be repeated for each cross-validation fold.

Generalization to New Contexts Requires a Random Sample of Contexts

Chapter 7 discusses models that in principle allow generalization to new contexts, accounting for variation between contexts (perhaps countries) as well as variation within countries. Development of such a model for hillraces would require data from more than two countries, preferably at least 5 or 6.

What Happens If We Do Not Transform the Hillrace Data?

If we avoid transformation and do not allow for increasing variability for the longer races (see, further, Exercise 3.8 at the end of the chapter), several observations appear to be outliers, with the race that has the longest time highly influential.

Venables and Ripley (2002, p. 154) point out (in connection with the Scottish hillrace data) that it is reasonable to expect that variances will be larger for longer races. Using `dist` as a surrogate for time, they give observations weights of `1/dist^2`. This is roughly equivalent, in its effect on the variance, to our use of `logtime` as the response variable.

Are "Errors in x" an Issue?

As explained in Subsection 3.7, random errors in the measured values of the explanatory variables can bias the model coefficients, and/or lead to spurious indications that one or more other variable is having an important effect. In the dataset `nihills`, most distances are given to the nearest half mile, and may in any case not be known at all accurately. The error is, however, likely to be small relative to the range of values of distances, so that the attenuation effects that will be discussed in Subsection 3.7 are likely to be small and of minor consequence.

3.6 Problems with Many Explanatory Variables

Variable selection is an issue when the aim is to obtain the best prediction possible. If instead the interest is in which variables have useful explanatory power, then the choice of variables will, in general, depend on which variables are to be held constant when the effects of other variables are estimated. In unusually favorable circumstances, it may turn out that one or perhaps two variables stand out as having a dominant effect, with coefficients not much affected by what other variables are included in the regression equation. There should in any case be an initial exploratory investigation of explanatory variables, as described in Subsection 3.3.6, leading perhaps to transformation of one or more of the variables.

One suggested rule is that there should be at least 10 times as many observations as variables, before any use of variable selection takes place. For any qualitative factor, subtract one from the number of levels, and count this as the number of variables contributed by that factor. While this may be a reasonable working rule when working with relatively noisy data where none of the variables has a dominant effect, there are important contexts where it is clearly inapplicable.

The following strategies, individually or in combination, can help keep to a minimum the number of different models that are to be compared.

1. Start with an informed guess on what variables/factors are likely to be important. Where there are many explanatory variables, consider classifying them into groups according to an assessment of scientific "importance." Fit the most important variables first, then add the next set as a group, checking whether this improves the fit.
2. Use an omnibus check to compare a model that has, for example, all first-order interaction terms (i.e., model formulae terms of the form `x1:x2`), against a main effects model, rather than checking for interaction effects one at a time.
3. Principal components analysis is one of several methods that may be able to identify a few components, that is, combinations of the explanatory variables, that together account for most of the variation in the explanatory variables. In favorable circumstances, one or more of the first few principal components will prove to be useful explanatory variables, or may suggest useful simple forms of summary of the original variables. In unfavorable circumstances, the components will prove irrelevant! See Section 9.2 and Harrell (2015, sections 4.7 and 8.6) for further commentary and examples. See Section 9.7 for examples.
4. Discriminant analysis can sometimes be used to identify a summary variable. There is an example in Section 9.7.

3.6.1 Variable Selection Issues

We caution against giving much credence to p-values that appear in output from conventional automatic variable selection techniques – various forms of stepwise regression, and best subsets regression. The resulting regression equation may have poorer genuine predictive power than the regression that includes all explanatory variables. The standard errors and t-statistics typically ignore the effects of the selection process; estimates of standard errors, p-values, and F-statistics will be optimistic. Estimates of regression coefficients are biased upwards in absolute value – positive coefficients will be larger than they should be, and negative coefficients will be smaller than they should be. See Harrell (2015) for further discussion.

Selection effects of various types arise in an increasing variety of contexts. In part this is a consequence of new automated technologies for data collection, and of the ease with which large data collections can be exposed to automated scrutiny.

Variable Selection – a Simulation with Random Data

Repeated simulation of a regression problem where the data consist entirely of noise will demonstrate the extent of the problem. In each regression there are 41 vectors of 100 numbers that have been generated independently and at random from a normal distribution. In these data:[14]

1. the first vector is the response variable y,
2. the remaining 40 vectors are the variables x_1, x_2, ..., x_{40}.

[14]
```
## Generate a 100 by 40 matrix of random normal data
y <- rnorm(100)
xx <- matrix(rnorm(4000), ncol = 40)
dimnames(xx)<- list(NULL, paste("X",1:40, sep=""))
```

If we find any regression relationships in these data, this will indicate faults with our methodology. (In computer simulation, we should not, however, totally discount the possibility that a quirk of the random number generator will affect results. This is unlikely to be an issue for the present simulation!)

The footnote has code that performs a best subsets regression that looks for the three x-variables that best explain y.[15] The function `DAAG::bestsetNoise()` automates the calculation:

```
## DAAG::bestsetNoise(m=100, n=40)
```

```
Loading required namespace: leaps
```

```
Coefficients:
            Estimate Std. Error t value Pr(>|t|)
(Intercept)   0.1438     0.0957    1.50   0.1363
xV4          -0.1918     0.0992   -1.93   0.0561
xV10         -0.3075     0.0948   -3.24   0.0016
xV14          0.2643     0.0961    2.75   0.0071
```

When repeated 10 times, the outcomes were as follows. Categories are exclusive.

	Instances
All three variables selected had $p < 0.01$	1
All three variables had $p < 0.05$	3
Two out of three variables had $p < 0.05$	3
One variable with $p < 0.05$	3
Total	10

In the modeling process there are two steps.

1. Select variables.
2. Do a regression and determine SEs and p-values, etc.

The p-value calculations have taken no account of step 1. Such finding of "significance" in datasets that consist only of noise is evidence of a large bias.

The Extent of Selection Effects – a Detailed Simulation

As previously, datasets of random normal data were created, always with 100 observations and with the number of variables varying between three and 50. For three variables, there was no selection, while in other cases an exhaustive search selected the "best" three variables. Figure 3.19 plots the p-values for the three variables that were selected against the total number of variables. The fitted line estimates the median p-value.

When all three variables are taken, the p-values are expected to average 0.5. Notice that, for selection of the best three variables out of 10, the median p-value has reduced to about 0.1. Code for Figure 3.19 is:

[15]
```
## Find the best fitting model. (The 'leaps' package must be installed.)
xx.subsets <- leaps::regsubsets(xx, y, method = "exhaustive", nvmax = 3, nbest = 1)
subvar <- summary(xx.subsets)$which[3,-1]
best3.lm <- lm(y ~ -1+xx[, subvar])
print(summary(best3.lm, corr = FALSE))
```

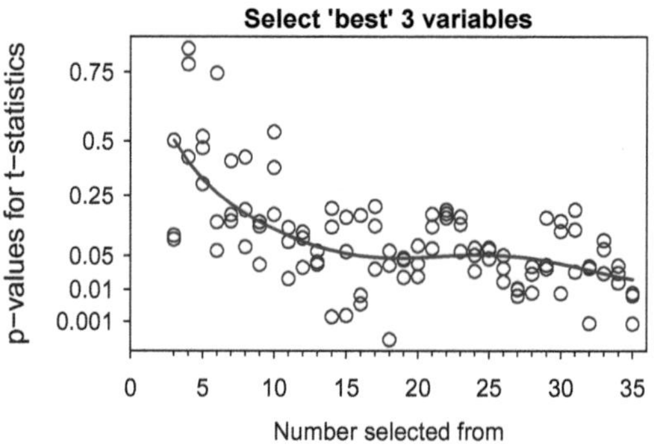

Figure 3.19 p-Values, versus number of variables available for selection, when an exhaustive search selected the "best" three variables. The fitted line estimates the median p-value. The function `bsnVaryNvar()` makes repeated calls to `bestsetNoise()`. Results will vary somewhat from one run to another.

```
library(splines)
DAAG::bsnVaryNvar(nvmax=3, nvar = 3:35, xlab="Number selected from")
```

Cross-Validation That Accounts for the Variable Selection Process

Subsection 2.6.1 introduced the use of cross-validation. In the variable selection context it is important, at each fold, to repeat both the variable selection step and the calculation of the sum of squares of the outcome values for the test data for that fold about the fitted values for a model fit that used the training data for that fold. The sums of squares for the separate folds are added and divided by the total number of observations to give an overall variance estimate.

**Regularization Approaches*

Regularization approaches are available that add to the sum of squares a penalty term that is a multiple λ of a penalty that is a function of the model coefficients. See Breheny and Huang (2011) and Breheny (2019) and the vignette that accompanies the *ncvreg* package. A number of different types of penalty have been proposed, with lasso perhaps the best known (Efron et al., 2003). Methods of this type are a resort when there are too many possible subsets to allow a best-subsets approach. Cross-validation can be used to choose the value of λ that gives the lowest error mean square, or when there are more variables than observations.

3.6.2 Multicollinearity

Some explanatory variables may be linearly related to combinations of one or more of the other explanatory variables. Technically, this is known as multicollinearity. For each multicollinear relationship, there is one redundant variable.

The approaches that we have advocated – careful thinking about the background science, careful initial scrutiny of the data, and removal of variables whose effect is

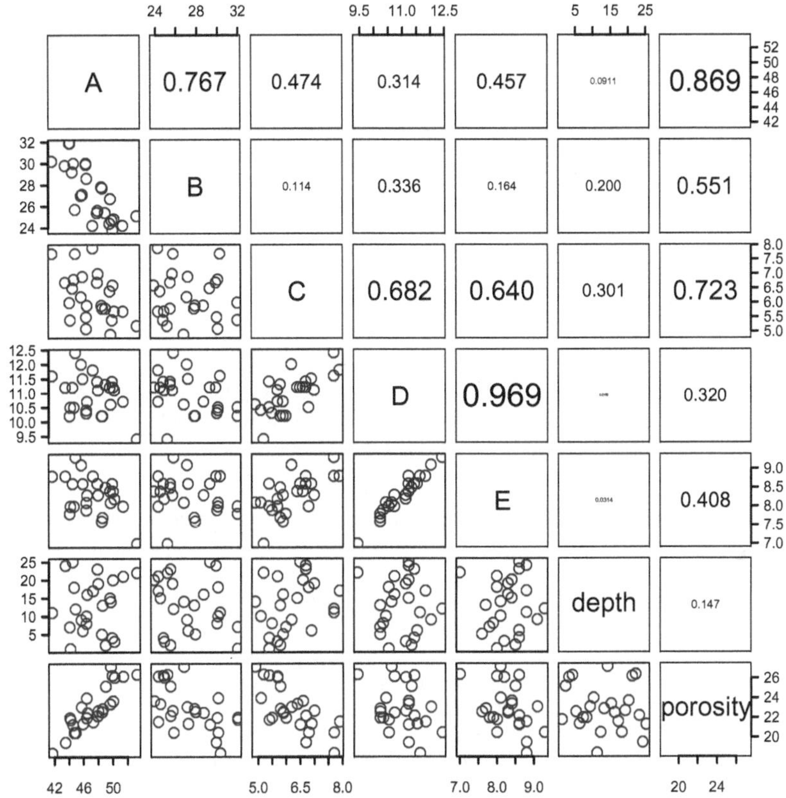

Figure 3.20 Scatterplot matrix for the variables in the `Coxite` data, with absolute values of pairwise correlations shown in the upper panel.

already accounted for by other variables – will generally avoid the more extreme effects of multicollinearity that we will illustrate. Milder consequences are pervasive, especially for observational data.

An Example – Compositional Data

The matrix `compositions::Coxite` has the mineral compositions of 25 coxite type rock specimens. Each composition consists of the percentage by weight of each of five minerals (`A` = albite, `B` = blandite, `C` = cornite, `D` = daubite, and `E` = endite), the depth of location, and porosity. The analysis that follows is a relatively crude use of these data. For an analysis that uses a method that is designed for compositional data, see Aitchison (2003).

Figure 3.20 shows the scatterplot matrix.[16] The relationship between `D` and `E` appears close to linear.

[16]
```
## Simplified plot
data(Coxite, package="compositions")  # Places Coxite in the workspace
  # NB: Proceed thus because `Coxite` is not exported from `compositions`
coxite <- as.data.frame(Coxite)
pairs(coxite)
```

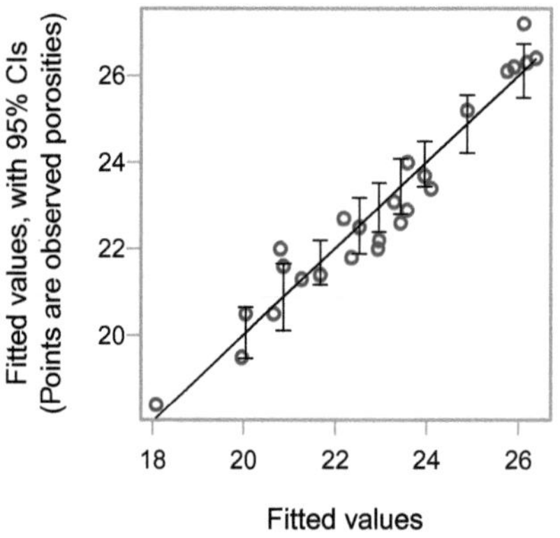

Figure 3.21 Line $y = x$, with 95 percent pointwise confidence bounds for fitted values shown at several locations along the range of fitted values. The points show the observed porosities at each of the fitted values.

We will look for a model that explains `porosity` as a function of mineral composition. Inclusion of all six explanatory variables in the model formula gives:

```
coxiteAll.lm <- lm(porosity ~ A+B+C+D+E+depth, data=coxite)
print(coef(summary(coxiteAll.lm)), digits=2)
```

	Estimate	Std. Error	t value	Pr(>|t|)
(Intercept)	-217.747	253.444	-0.859	0.40
A	2.649	2.483	1.067	0.30
B	2.191	2.601	0.842	0.41
C	0.211	2.227	0.095	0.93
D	4.949	4.672	1.059	0.30
depth	0.014	0.033	0.435	0.67

The percentages of the five minerals sum, for each observation, to very close to 100. The very slight differences from 100, for some of the rows, are enough that the model fits without complaint. Observe the following.

- The variable `E`, because it is a linear combination of earlier variables, has been "aliased," that is, left out. Effectively, its coefficient has been set to zero.
- None of the individual coefficients comes anywhere near the usual standards of statistical significance.
- For the overall regression fit, $p = 1.18 \times 10^{-10}$.

The overall regression fit has good predictive power, notwithstanding the inability to tease out the contributions of the individual coefficients. Figure 3.21 shows 95 percent pointwise confidence intervals for fitted values at several points within the range.

Pointwise confidence bounds can be obtained thus:

```
hat <- predict(coxiteAll.lm, interval="confidence", level=0.95)
```

The object that is returned is a matrix, with columns `fit` (fitted values), `lwr` (lower confidence limits) and `upr` (upper confidence limits). Data points that distort the fitted response are "influential."

3.6.3 The Variance Inflation Factor (VIF)

The variance inflation factor (VIF) measures the effect of correlation with other variables in increasing the standard error of a regression coefficient. If x_j, with values x_{ij} $(i = 1, \ldots, n)$ is the only variable in a straight line regression model, and b_j is the estimated coefficient, then

$$\text{var}(b_j) = \frac{\sigma^2}{s_{jj}}, \quad \text{where } s_{jj} = \sum_{i=1}^{n}(x_{ij} - \bar{x}_j)^2,$$

and σ^2 is the variance of the error term in the model. When further terms are included in the regression model, this variance is inflated, as a multiple of σ^2, by the VIF. Notice that the VIF depends only on the model matrix. It does not reflect changes in the residual variance.

Because the model `coxiteAll.lm` was singular (one variable was a linear combination of earlier variables), VIFs are not available. To demonstrate the calculation of VIFs, we explicitly omit `E` from the model (omitting one of `A`, `B`, `C`, or `D` would also allow the calculation of VIFs), thus:

```
print(DAAG::vif(lm(porosity ~ A+B+C+D+depth, data=coxite)), digits=2)
```

```
     A      B      C      D  depth
2717.8 2485.0  192.6  566.1    3.4
```

The size of these factors has made it impossible to obtain meaningful estimates of the individual coefficients.

We now investigate the use of the function `leaps::regsubsets()` to choose the "best" subsets with 1, 2, 3, and 4 of the explanatory variables:

```
b <- leaps::regsubsets(porosity ~ ., data=coxite, nvmax=4, method='exhaustive')
## The calculation fails for nvmax=5
inOut <- summary(b)[["which"]]
## Extract and print the coefficents for the four regressions
dimnam <- list(rep("",4),c("Intercept", colnames(coxite)[-7]))
cmat <- matrix(nrow=4, ncol=7, dimnames=dimnam)
for(i in 1:4)cmat[i,inOut[i,]] <- signif(coef(b,id=1:4)[[i]],3)
outMat <- cbind(cmat," "=rep(NA,4),
as.matrix(as.data.frame(summary(b)[c("adjr2", "cp", "bic")])))
print(signif(outMat,3),na.print="")
```

```
 Intercept    A      B     C    D E   depth    adjr2    cp   bic
     -10.6 0.71                                0.745 50.60 -28.7
      52.3      -0.575 -2.19                   0.924  1.40 -56.9
    -184.0 2.33  1.840       4.27              0.925  2.15 -55.3
    -194.0 2.41  1.950       4.51    0.0122    0.923  3.86 -52.4
```

Observe the following.

- `E` does not appear in any of the models.
- Both for the *cp* (or C_p) criterion and the *bic* (or *BIC*) criterion, the model with the smallest value is preferred. (Refer back to Section 3.5.) Both choose the model with the two explanatory variables `B` and `C`.

The preferred model is, noting also the variance inflation factors:

```
BC.lm <- lm(porosity ~ B+C, data=coxite)
print(signif(coef(summary(BC.lm)), digits=3))
```

```
            Estimate Std. Error t value Pr(>|t|)
(Intercept)   52.300     1.7800    29.3 4.01e-19
B             -0.575     0.0508   -11.3 1.19e-10
C             -2.190     0.1560   -14.1 1.81e-12
```

```
car::vif(BC.lm)
```

```
    B     C
1.013 1.013
```

The variance inflation factors are $(1 - r^2)^{-1}$, where $r = 0.114$ is the correlation between the two variables.

Readers may care to check the diagnostic plots.[17]

Numbers That Do Not Quite Add Up

Now round all the percentages to whole numbers, and repeat the analysis that uses all six available explanatory variables.

```
coxiteR <- coxite
coxiteR[, 1:5] <- round(coxiteR[, 1:5])
coxiteR.lm <- lm(porosity ~ ., data=coxiteR)
print(coef(summary(coxiteR.lm)), digits=2)
```

```
            Estimate Std. Error t value Pr(>|t|)
(Intercept)   -1.425     23.404  -0.061  0.95212
A              0.560      0.246   2.278  0.03515
B              0.016      0.240   0.065  0.94865
C             -1.318      0.294  -4.484  0.00029
D              0.975      0.422   2.309  0.03305
E             -0.553      0.524  -1.055  0.30543
depth         -0.015      0.022  -0.667  0.51310
```

```
print(DAAG::vif(lm(porosity ~ .-E, data=coxiteR)), digits=2)
```

```
   A    B    C    D depth
17.0 16.5  3.3  4.7   1.3
```

This result may seem surprising. Adding noise has reduced the correlation, so that `C` now appears significant even when all other explanatory variables are included. Perhaps more surprising is the $p = 0.033$ for `D`.

While this is contrived, we have occasionally seen comparable effects in computer output that researchers have brought for scrutiny.

[17] `plot(BC.lm)`

Remedies for Multicollinearity

As noted at the beginning of the section, careful initial choice of variables, based on scientific knowledge and careful scrutiny of relevant exploratory plots, will often avert the problem. Occasionally, it may be possible to find or collect additional data that will reduce correlations among the explanatory variables.

A variety of "regularization" methods have been proposed for alleviating the effects of multicollinearity, in inflating coefficients and their standard errors. There is an overlap with variable selection issues. A good place to start is Breheny and Huang (2011) and the vignette that accompanies the *ncvreg* package.

3.7 Errors in x

The discussion so far has assumed either that the explanatory variables are measured with negligible error, or that the interest is in the regression relationship given the observed values of explanatory variables. The present section is designed to draw attention to the major effect that errors in the explanatory variables can have on the regression gradients. The implications of the theoretical results, for particular practical circumstances, can be quite different from what might be intuitively expected. Discussion will mainly focus on the "classical" errors in x model.

With a single explanatory variable, the effect under the classical "errors in x" model is to reduce the expected magnitude of the gradient. The attenuated gradient is less likely, relative to use of an x that is measured without error, to be distinguishable from statistical noise.

Measurement of Dietary Intake

The 36-page Diet History Questionnaire is a Food Frequency Questionnaire (FFQ) that was developed and evaluated at the US National Cancer Institute. In large-scale trials that look for dietary effects on cancer and on other diseases, it has been important to have an instrument for measuring food intake that is relatively cheap and convenient. (Some trials have cost US$100,000,000 or more.)

The Schatzkin et al. (2003) study used the FFQ to ask for details of food intake over the previous year for 124 food items. It queried frequency of intake and, for most items, portion sizes. They investigated, also, the supplementary use of an instrument that questioned participants on their dietary intake in the previous 24 hours, then used the 24-hour dietary recall to calibrate the FFQ assessments.

Schatzkin et al. (2003) then compared FFQ measurements with those from Doubly Labeled Water, used as an accurate but expensive biomarker. They concluded that the FFQ was too inaccurate for its intended purpose. The 24-hour dietary recall, although better, was still seriously inaccurate. In some instances, the standard deviation for estimated energy intake was seven times the standard deviation, between different individuals, of the reference. A bias in the relationship between FFQ and reference further reduced the attenuation factor, to 0.04 for women and to 0.08 for men. For the relationship between the 24-hour recalls and the reference, the attenuation factors were 0.1 for women and 0.18 for men, though these could be improved by use of repeated 24-hour recalls.

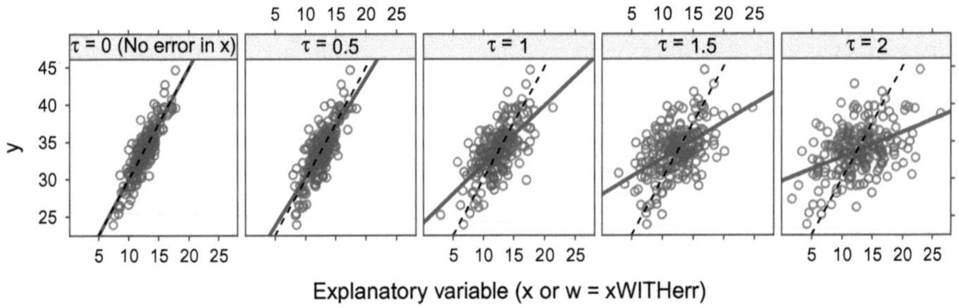

Figure 3.22 The fitted solid lines show how the change in the regression line as the error in x changes. The underlying relationship, shown with the dashed line, is in each instance $y = 15 + 1.5\ x$. For the definition of τ, see the text.

These results raise serious questions about what such studies can achieve, using presently available instruments whose cost and convenience makes them viable for use in large studies. Carroll (2004) gives an accessible summary of the issues. Subsection 7.9.6 has further brief comment on the modeling issues.

Simulations of the Effect of Measurement Error

Suppose that the underlying regression relationship that is of interest is

$$y_i = \alpha + \beta x_i + \epsilon_i, \text{ where } \mathrm{var}(\epsilon_i) = \sigma^2 \ (i = 1, \ldots, n).$$

Let $s_x = \sqrt{\sum_{i=1}^{n}(x_i - \bar{x})^2/(n-1)}$ be the standard deviation of the values that are measured without error. Take the measured values as

$$w_i = x_i + \eta_i, \text{ where } \mathrm{var}(\eta_i) = s_x^2\, \tau^2.$$

The η_i are assumed independent of the ϵ_i.

Figure 3.22 shows results from a number of simulations that use the w_i as the explanatory values. If $\tau = 0.4$ (the added error has a variance that is 40 percent of s_x), the effect on the gradient is modest. If $\tau = 2$, the attenuation is severe. The function `DAAG::errorsINx()` can be used for additional simulations such as in Figure 3.22.

Estimation of the magnitude of the error and consequent attenuation of the slope requires a direct comparison with values that are measured with negligible error. More is required than the w and y values used to create scatterplots such as in Figure 3.22.

An estimate of the attenuation in the gradient is, to a close approximation:

$$\lambda = \frac{1}{1+\tau^2}, \text{ where } \lambda \text{ has the name reliability ratio.}$$

If for example $\tau = 0.4$, then $\lambda \simeq 0.86$. The study context will be important in deciding whether a reduction in the estimated gradient by a factor of 0.86 is of consequence. There may be more important concerns. Very small attenuation factors (large attenuations), for example, less than 0.1 such as were found in the Schatzkin et al. (2003) study, are likely to seriously compromise the use of analysis results. Points to note are as follows.

- From the data used in the panels of Figure 3.22, it is impossible to estimate τ, or to know the underlying x_i values. For this, an investigation is required that compares the w_i with an accurate, that is, for all practical purposes error-free, determination of the x_i.
- A test for $\beta = 0$ can be undertaken in the usual way, but with reduced power to detect an effect that may be of interest.
- The t-statistic for testing $\beta = 0$ is affected in two ways; the numerator reduces by an expected factor of λ, while the standard error that appears in the numerator increases. Thus, if $\lambda = 0.1$, the sample size required to detect a nonzero gradient increases by more than the factor of 100 that is suggested by the effect on the gradient alone.

*Two Explanatory Variables

Consider first the case where one predictor is measured with error, and others without error. The coefficient of the variable that is measured with error is attenuated, as in the single variable case. The coefficients of other variables may be reversed in sign, or show an effect when there is none. See Carroll et al. (2006, pp. 52–55) for summary comment.

Suppose that

$$y = \beta_1 x_1 + \beta_2 x_2 + \epsilon.$$

If w_1 is unbiased for x_1 and the measurement error η is independent of x_1 and x_2, then least squares regression with explanatory variables w_1 and x_2 yields an estimate of $\lambda\beta_1$, where if ρ is the correlation between x_1 and x_2,

$$\lambda = \frac{1-\rho^2}{1-\rho^2+\tau^2}.$$

A new feature is the bias in the least squares estimate of β_2. The naive least squares estimator estimates

$$\beta_2 + \beta_1(1-\lambda)\,\gamma_{12}, \text{ where } \gamma_{12} = \rho\frac{s_1}{s_2}. \tag{3.5}$$

Here γ_{12} is the coefficient of x_2 in the least squares regression of x_1 on x_2, $s_1 = \text{SD}[x_1]$, $s_2 = \text{SD}[x_2]$. The estimate of β_2 may be quite different from zero, even though $\beta_2 = 0$. Where $\beta_2 \neq 0$, the least squares estimate can be reversed in sign from β_2. Some of the effect of x_1 is transferred to the estimate of the effect of x_2.

Two Explanatory Variables, One Measured without Error – a Simulation

The function `DAAG::errorsINx()`, when supplied with a nonzero value for the argument `gpdiff`, simulates the effect when the variable that is measured without error codes for a categorical effect. Figure 3.23 had `gpdiff=1.5`. Two lines appear, suggesting a "treatment" effect where there was none.

The function `errsINseveral()` simulates a model where there are two continuous variables x_1 and x_2. The default choice of arguments has

$$\beta_1 = 1.5,\ \beta_1 = 0,\ \rho = -0.5,\ s_1 = s_2 = 2,\ \tau = 1.5,\ \text{var}[\epsilon] = 0.25.$$

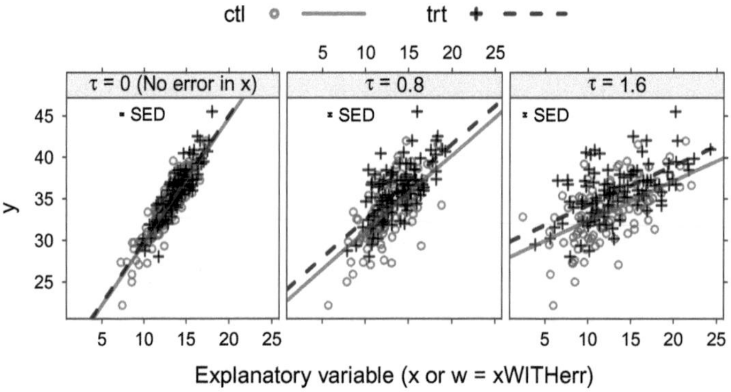

Figure 3.23 Errors in x may readily generate spurious differences between groups. For the simulations whose results are shown, y is a linear function of x. The mean value of x is 12.5 for the first group level (`"ctl"`), and 14.0 for the second (`"trt"`) level. In the left panel, values of x are measured without error. In the middle and right panels, independent errors have been added to x from distributions with SDs that are respectively 0.8 and 1.6 times that of the within-group standard deviation of x. The SEDs are conditional on w = `xWITHerr`.

Measurement error variances are x_1: $s_1^2\tau^2$, x_2: 0. Then $\lambda = 0.25$, $\gamma_{12} = -0.5$, and the expected value for the naive least squares estimator of β_2 is

$$\beta_2 + \beta_1(1 - \lambda) = 0 + 1.5 \times 0.75 \times (-0.5) = -0.5675.$$

An Arbitrary Number of Variables

Where two or more explanatory variables are measured with substantial error, this widens the range of possibilities for transferring some part or parts of effects between variables. The function `DAAG::errorsINseveral()` can be used for simulations with an arbitrary correlation structure for explanatory variables, and with an arbitrary variance–covariance matrix for the added errors.[18]

**The Classical Error Model versus the Berkson Error Model*

In the classical model $\mathrm{E}[w_i|x_i] = x_i$. In the Berkson model $\mathrm{E}[x_i|w_i] = w_i$. The Berkson model may be a realistic model in an experiment where w_i is an instrument setting, but the true value varies randomly about the instrument setting. For example, the temperature in an oven or kiln may be set to w_i, but the resulting (and unknown) actual temperature is x_i. In straight line regression, the coefficient is then unbiased, but the variance of the estimate of the coefficient is increased.

[18] If $\boldsymbol{\beta}$ is the vector of coefficients in the model without errors in the measured values, V corresponds in the obvious way to `V`, and U to `xerrV`, then an estimate for the resulting least squares estimates when for regression on the values that are measured with error is $\boldsymbol{\beta}'V(V+U)^{-1}$. Note that Zeger et al. (2000, p. 421) have an initial T (our U), where V is required.

Zeger et al. (2000) discuss the practical consequences of both types of error, though giving most of their attention to the classical model. In their context, realistic models may have elements of both the classical and Berkson models.

Using Missing Value Approaches to Address Measurement Error

Errors that arise from multiple imputation, to be discussed in Section 9.8, can be treated as a form of measurement error. Blackwell et al. (2017) offer a methodology.

3.8 Multiple Regression Models – Additional Points

The notes that follow should dispel any residual notion that this chapter's account of multiple regression models has covered everything of importance.

3.8.1 Confusion between Explanatory and Response Variables

As an example, we return to the `allbacks` data. We compare the coefficients in the equation that predicts `area` given `volume` and `weight`, with the rearranged coefficients from the equation that predicts `weight` given `volume` and `area`:

```
coef(lm(area ~ volume + weight, data=allbacks))
```

```
(Intercept)      volume      weight
    35.4587     -0.9636      1.3611
```

```
b <- as.vector(coef(lm(weight ~ volume + area, data=allbacks)))
c("_Intercept_"=-b[1]/b[3], volume=-b[2]/b[3], weight=1/b[3])
```

```
_Intercept_      volume      weight
    -47.847      -1.512       2.135
```

Only if the relationship is exact, so that predicted time is the same as observed time, will the equations be the same. Williams (1983) gives examples from the earth sciences literature.

Unintended Correlations

Suppose that x_i ($i = 1, 2, \ldots, n$) are results from a series of controls, while y_i ($i = 1, 2, \ldots, n$) are the results from the corresponding treated group. It is tempting to plot $y - x$ versus x. Unfortunately, there is likely to be a negative correlation between $y - x$ and x, though this is not inevitable. This emphasizes the desirability of maintaining a clear distinction between explanatory and response variables. See the example in Sharp et al. (1996).

3.8.2 Missing Explanatory Variables

Here the issue is use of the wrong model for the expected value. With the right "balance" in the data, the expected values are unbiased or nearly unbiased. Where there is serious imbalance, the bias may be large.

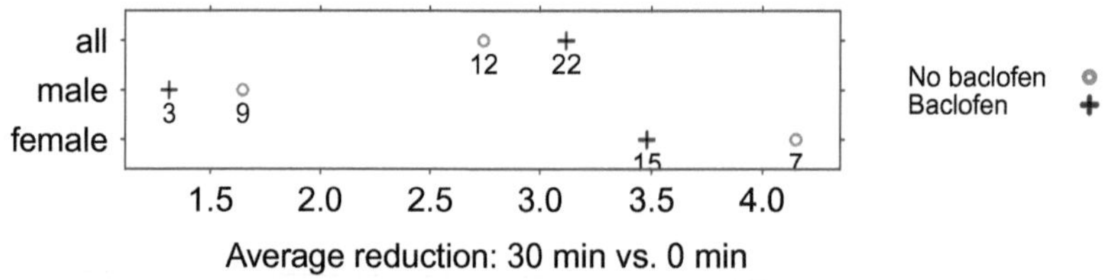

Figure 3.24 Does preoperative baclofen (additional to earlier painkiller), reduce pain? Subgroup numbers, shown below each point, weight the overall averages when sex is ignored.

Figure 3.24 relates to data collected in an experiment on the use of painkillers (Gordon et al., 1995). Pain was measured as a VAS (Visual-Analogue Scale) score. Researchers were investigating differences in the pain score between the two analgesic treatments, without and with baclofen.

Notice that the overall comparison (average for baclofen versus average for no baclofen) goes in a different direction from the comparison for the two sexes separately. As the two treatment groups had very different numbers of men and women, and as there was a strong sex effect, an analysis that does not account for the sex effect gives an incorrect estimate of the treatment effect (Cohen, 1996).

The overall averages in Figure 3.24 reflect the following subgroup weighting effects (f is shorthand for female and m for male).

Baclofen: 15f to 3m, i.e., $\frac{15}{18}$ to $\frac{3}{18}$ (a little less than f average)
No baclofen: 7f to 9m, i.e., $\frac{7}{16}$ to $\frac{9}{16}$ ($\approx$ half-way between m & f)

There is a sequel. More careful investigation revealed that the response to pain has a different pattern over time. For males, the sensation of pain declined more rapidly over time.

Strategies

(i) Simple approach Calculate means for each subgroup separately.
Overall treatment effect is average of subgroup differences.
Effect of baclofen (reduction in pain score from time 0) is as follows.

Females: $3.479 - 4.151 = -0.672$ ($-$ve, therefore an increase)
Males: $1.311 - 1.647 = -0.336$
Average over male and female $= -0.5 \times (0.672 + 0.336) = -0.504$

(ii) Fit a model that accounts for sex and baclofen effects

$$y = \text{overall mean} + \text{sex effect} + \text{baclofen effect} + \text{interaction}$$

(At this point, we are not including an error term.)

When variables or factors are omitted from models, values of the outcome variable are as far as possible accounted for using those that remain. The mouse brain weight example in Subsection 3.2.5 can be understood in this way. Bland and Altman (2005) give several examples of published results where conclusions have been vitiated by effects of this type.

Another example of this same type, albeit in the context of contingency tables, was discussed in Subsection 2.1.2. The analysis of the UCB admissions data in Section 5.3 formulates the analysis of contingency table data as a regression problem.

3.8.3* Added Variable Plots

Added variable plots are a partial alternative to the use of termplots, described in Section 3.3. They can be created using the function `avPlots()` in the *car* package. Such plots are designed to examine the contribution of a variable z, given variables already in the model. Here, variables already in the model will be collectively represented by the symbol x.

As a starting point for understanding added variable plots, observe that a multiple regression calculation can be handled as a sequence of straight line regressions. As an example, consider calculations based on the **nihills** dataset, with y = `ltime` = `log(time)`, x = `lclimb` = `log(climb)` and z = `ldist` = `log(dist)`. As x is here a single variable, comprising a single column of the model matrix, the individual calculation steps can be performed using straight line regression.

The sequence of steps is as follows.

1. Regress y on x, with vector of residuals $e_{y|x}$. For the example data:

```
yONx.lm <- lm(logtime ~ logclimb, data=lognihr)
e_yONx <- resid(yONx.lm)
print(coef(yONx.lm), digits=4)
```

```
(Intercept)     logclimb
    -7.1047       0.9021
```

2. Regress z on x, with vector of residuals $e_{z|x}$.

```
zONx.lm <- lm(logdist ~ logclimb, data=lognihr)
e_zONx <- resid(zONx.lm)
print(coef(yONx.lm), digits=4)
```

```
(Intercept)     logclimb
    -7.1047       0.9021
```

3. Regress $e_{y|x}$ (from 1 above) on $e_{z|x}$ (from 2 above), with vector of residuals $e_{y|xz}$.

```
ey_xONez_x.lm <- lm(e_yONx ~ 0+e_zONx)
e_yONxz <- resid(ey_xONez_x.lm)
print(coef(ey_xONez_x.lm), digits=4)
```

```
e_zONx
0.6814
```

Note that as $e_{y|x}$ and $e_{z|x}$ have mean 0, the constant term in the regression equation is zero. The effect is to reduce the residual sum of squares from $\sum_{i=1}^{n} e_{y|z}(i)^2$ to $\sum_{i=1}^{n} e_{y|xz}(i)^2$. (Use of $e_{z|x}$ as an explanatory variable can only decrease the sum of squares, or perhaps leave it unchanged.)

The coefficients for the regression of y on x and z can be recovered by putting together the results from the regressions in items 1 – 3 above. Details of the algebra that recovers the regression parameters, which are a little intricate, are given below.

For each of the regressions 1, 2, and 3, there is a plot of residuals against fitted values. In the simplest case to consider, all three relationships are linear. Or if one of them is not linear there must, to obtain a multiple linear regression, be a compensating nonlinear trend in one or both of the other two. The following shows the plots of residuals against fitted values, for each of the three regressions.

The plot of $e_{y|x}$ against $e_{z|x}$ has the name *added variable plot*, here for $z =$ `ldist`. Panel A in Figure 3.25 has the added variable plot for `ldist`, while Panel B has the added variable plot for `lclimb`. Both panels use the function `car::avPlots()`, which is designed to leave out one variable (or, more generally, term) only at a time:

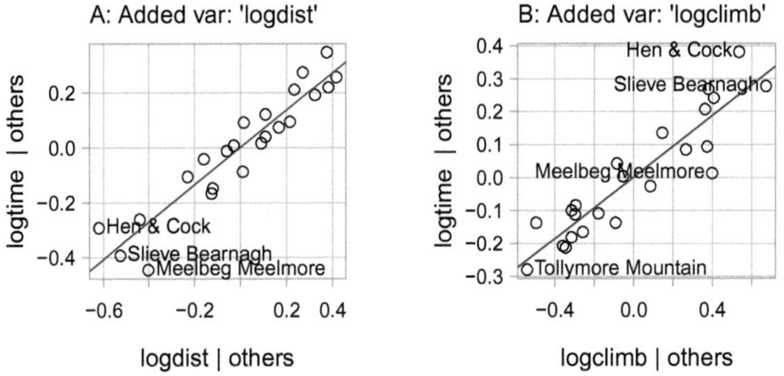

Figure 3.25 Added variable plots: (A) for `ldist` (after fitting `lclimb`), and (B) for `lclimb` (after fitting `ldist`). Panel A provides a check whether, given that $x =$ `lclimb` is included as an explanatory variable, $z =$ `ldist` should be also included. In Panel B, the roles of the two variables are reversed.

```
## Code for added variable plots
logtime.lm <- lm(logtime ~ logclimb+logdist, data=lognihr)
car::avPlots(logtime.lm, lwd=1, terms="logdist", fg="gray")
car::avPlots(logtime.lm, lwd=1, terms="logclimb", fg="gray")
```

The following single call gives both plots:

```
car::avPlots(timeClimb.lm, terms=~.)
```

The first of the plots can alternatively be obtained, based on the straight-line calculations given above, from:

```
plot(e_yONx ~ e_zONx)
```

Figure 3.26 has plots of residuals against fitted values, for each of the three regressions. The final plot is for the residuals and fitted values from the added variable plot for `lclimb`. This is interesting because apparent nonlinearities in the first two plots have, in the final plot, largely canceled out.
Slightly modified code is:

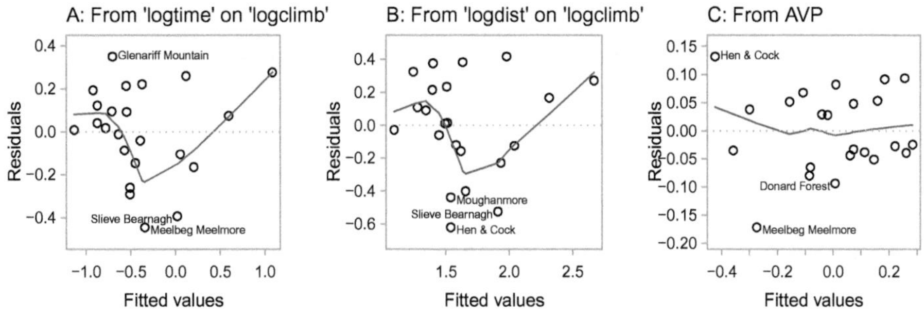

Figure 3.26 The vertical axis shows, respectively, residuals from the regressions: (A) `logtime` on `logclimb`; (B) `logtime` on `logdist`; and (C) residuals from (A) versus residuals from (B) (AVP = added variable plot). These are in each case plotted against fitted values from the corresponding regression.

```
plot(yONx.lm, which=1, caption="A: ... 'logtime' on 'logclimb'")
plot(zONx.lm, which=1, caption="B: ... 'logdist' on 'logclimb'")
plot(ey_xONez_x.lm, which=1, caption="C: From Added Variable plot")
```

Alternatives to Added Variable Plots

The plot of $e_{y|x}$ against z, that is, regress y on x and plot the residuals against z, is not satisfactory for judging whether z should be included in the regression. Observe that residuals from the regression of y on x take the form

$$e_{y|x} = y - a_{y|x} - b_{y|x}\, x.$$

If x and z have a nonzero correlation, this will lead to a nonzero correlation between z and the term $b_{y|x}\, x$) in $e_{y|x}$. Termplots, also known as "component plus residual" plots, avoid this issue because the residuals in the "component plus residual" are residuals from the model with all terms fitted.

Termplots may on the whole be more informative than added variable plots. While systematic departures from linearity in one or more of the added variable plots may indicate the need for transforming one or more variables, the fact that both ordinates represent residuals from a regression calculation can make it difficult to establish a direct connection back to the original variables.

**Algebraic Details*

The algebraic details are given for completeness. While not essential for understanding the account just given, they may help reinforce understanding.

The regression equations can be written as follows.

1. $y = a_{y|x} + b_{y|x}\, x + e_{y|x}$.
   Coefficients are $a_{y|x} = -7.1047$; $b_{y|x} = 0.9021$ [Type `coef(yONx.lm)`]
2. $z = a_{z|x} + b_{z|x}\, x + e_{z|x}$, i.e., $e_{z|x} = z - a_{z|x} - b_{z|x}\, x$.
   Coefficients are $a_{z|x} = -3.146$; $b_{z|x} = 0.6404$ [Type `coef(zONx.lm)`]
3. $e_{y|x} = b_{y|xz}\, e_{z|x} + e_{y|xz}$.

The coefficient is $b_{y|xz} = 0.6814$. There is no intercept term because both sets of residuals have mean equal to 0. [Type `coef(e_yxONe_zx.lm)`]

Thus:

$$\begin{aligned} y &= a_{y|x} + b_{y|x}x + e_{y|x} \quad \text{(from 1)} \\ &= a_{y|x} + b_{y|x}x + b_{y|xz}e_{z|x} + e_{y|xz} \quad \text{(substituting from 3)} \\ &= a_{y|x} + b_{y|x}x + b_{y|xz}\left(z - a_{z|x} - b_{z|x}\, x\right) + e_{y|xz} \quad \text{(substituting from 2)} \\ &= a_{y|x} - b_{y|xz}\, a_{z|x} + \left(b_{y|x} - b_{z|x}\right) x + b_{y|xz}\, z + e_{y|xz}. \end{aligned}$$

Then the terms in the fitted equation $\widehat{y} = a + b_1 x + b_2 z$ are:

$$\begin{aligned} &a = a_{y|x} - b_{y|xz}\, a_{z|x} = -7.1047 - 0.6814 \times (-3.146) = -4.9611, \\ &b_1 = b_{y|x} - b_{y|xz}\, b_{z|x} = 0.9021 - 0.6814 \times 0.6404 = 0.4658, \\ &b_2 = b_{y|xz} = 0.6814. \end{aligned}$$

Compare the above coefficients with:

```
coef(lm(logtime ~ logclimb + logdist, data=lognihr))
```

```
(Intercept)     logclimb      logdist
    -4.9611       0.4658       0.6814
```

As noted above, wherever x appears, any number of explanatory variables can be fitted. The argument is essentially unchanged.

3.8.4* Nonlinear Methods – an Alternative to Transformation?

Aside from the brief discussion that follows, we have not found room for this important topic in the present text. We will investigate the use of the R `nls()` function (*stats* package) to shed light on the loglinear model that Subsection 3.2.1 used for the hillrace data.

The analysis of Subsection 3.2.1 assumed additive errors on the transformed logarithmic scale. This implies, on the untransformed scale, multiplicative errors. We noted that the assumption of homogeneity of errors was in doubt.

One might alternatively assume that the noise term is additive on the untransformed scale, leading to the nonlinear model

$$y = x_1^{\alpha}\, x_2^{\beta} + \varepsilon,$$

where y = `time`, x_1 = `dist`, and x_2 = `climb`. We will use the `nls()` nonlinear least squares function to estimate α and β. The iterative procedure used requires starting values for α and β. Here, the estimates from the earlier loglinear regression will be used for this purpose. Because we could be taking a square or cube of the `climb` term, we prefer to work with the variable `climb.mi` that is obtained by dividing `climb` by 5280, so that numbers are of modest size:

```
nihr$climb.mi <- nihr$climb/5280
nihr.nls0 <- nls(time ~ (dist^alpha)*(climb.mi^beta), start =
                 c(alpha = 0.68, beta = 0.465), data = nihr)
## plot(residuals(nihr.nls0) ~ log(predict(nihr.nls0)))
```

The parameter estimates are:

```
signif(coef(summary(nihr.nls0)),3)
```

```
      Estimate Std. Error t value Pr(>|t|)
alpha    0.315    0.00806    39.1 4.25e-21
beta     0.814    0.02950    27.6 5.46e-18
```

These parameter estimates differ substantially from those obtained under the assumption of multiplicative errors. This is not an unusual occurrence; the nonlinear least squares problem has an error structure that is different from the linearized least squares problem solved earlier. Residuals suggest a nonlinear pattern.

Another possibility, that allows `time` to increase nonlinearly with `climb.mi`, is

$$y = \alpha + \beta x_1 + \gamma x_2^\delta + \varepsilon.$$

We then fit the model, using an arbitrary starting guess:

```
nihr.nls <- nls(time ~ gamma + delta1*dist^alpha + delta2*climb.mi^beta,
start=c(gamma = .045, delta1 = .09, alpha = 1,
delta2=.9, beta = 1.65), data=nihr)
## plot(residuals(nihr.nls) ~ log(predict(nihr.nls)))
```

The starting values were obtained from an initial model in which `alpha` was constrained to equal 1. The result is:

```
signif(coef(summary(nihr.nls)),3)
```

```
       Estimate Std. Error t value     Pr(>|t|)
gamma    0.1520     0.0714    2.13 0.0471000000
delta1   0.0399     0.0284    1.41 0.1770000000
alpha    1.3100     0.2710    4.84 0.0001330000
delta2   0.8660     0.0922    9.39 0.0000000234
beta     1.5100     0.1810    8.32 0.0000001380
```

There are no obvious outliers in the residual plot. In addition, there is no indication of an increase in the variance as the fitted values increase. Thus, a variance-stabilizing transformation or the use of weighted least squares is unnecessary.

3.9 Recap

A coefficient in a multiple regression equation predicts the effect of a variable when other variables are held constant. Coefficients can thus be different, sometimes dramatically, for a different choice of explanatory variables.

Regression equation predictions are for the data used to derive the equation, and reflect any sampling biases that affect that data. Biases that arise because data were not randomly sampled from the population can lead to predictions that, for the population as a whole, are seriously astray.

Plots that can be useful for checking regression assumptions and/or for checking whether individual data points may unduly influence results include: scatterplot matrices of the variables in the regression equation, plots of residuals against fitted values, partial residual plots such as are provided by the `termplot()` function (these are a better guide than plots of residuals against individual explanatory variables), normal quantile–quantile plots of residuals, scale–location plots, and Cook's distance and related plots.

Watch for variables whose measurements may be affected by large inaccuracies. Where the interest is in the regression coefficients, their effects will be attenuated. They have the potential to generate spurious effects from other explanatory variables.

Robust methods downweight points that may be outliers. Methods that are resistant to outliers aim, as far as possible, to completely remove the contribution of outliers to the regression fit.

3.10 Further Reading

Faraway (2014), and the more detailed and wide-ranging account Gelman et al. (2020), are both highly recommended. Both address many important practical issues, with chapters 20 and 21 of the Gelman et al. book a good starting point for considering issues of causal inference.

Cook and Weisberg (1999) rely heavily on graphical explorations to uncover regression relationships. Tu and Gilthorpe (2011) explore in detail a wide range of issues that arise for the interpretation of regression coefficients. Its insightful commentary has wide general relevance. Venables and Ripley (2002) is a basic reference for using R for regression calculations. See also Fox and Weisberg (2018). Harrell (2015) is wide ranging and has extensive practical advice, but does makes strong technical demands on the reader. Hastie et al. (2009) explore beyond the models and modeling approaches that we have described.

Cunningham (2021) weaves a wide-ranging review of the causal inference literature into an engaging story, replete with examples that highlight important issues. Code is provided for R, Stata, and Python. While directed in the first place at economics students, the methodology and examples have wide social science, public health, and other relevance. Hernán and Robins (2020) is a more conventional style of text that is similarly wide ranging and practically oriented, with R, SAS, Stata, and Python code. Rosenbaum (2002) is another good starting point for engaging with the issues that observational studies raise. See, further, Section 9.7 and additional references noted therein. Results from observational studies can rarely be interpreted with the same confidence as for a carefully designed experimental study.

Several of the studies that are discussed in Levitt and Dubner (2005), some with major public policy relevance, relied to a greater or lesser extent on regression methods. References in the notes at the end of their book allow interested readers to pursue technical details of the statistical and other methodology. The conflation of multiple sources of insight and evidence is invariably necessary, if conclusions are to carry conviction. Emphasizing the difficulty of reaching watertight conclusions, Levitt's claim that legalizing abortion reduced the US crime rate has generated extensive controversy in the literature. See Shoesmith (2017) and Donohue and Levitt (2019).

Especially hazardous is the use of analyses where there are multiple potential confounding variables, that is, variables which must be available and whose effects (including possible interaction effects) must be properly modeled if coefficients for other variables are to be genuinely suggestive of a causal link. These issues get further consideration in Section 9.7.3.

On variable selection, which warrants more attention than we have given it, see Bolker (2008), Harrell (2015), Hastie et al. (2009), and Venables (1998). Bolker's account extends (p. 215) to approaches that weight and average models.

On errors in variables, see Carroll et al. (2006). Linear models are a special case of nonlinear models!

Structural equation models allow, in addition to explanatory variables and response variables, intermediate variables that are response with respect to one or more of the explanatory variables, and explanatory with respect to one or more of the response variables. Cox and Wermuth (1996) and Edwards (2000) describe approaches that use regression methods to elucidate the relationships. Cox and Wermuth is useful for the large number of examples and for its illuminating comments on practical issues, while Edwards has a more up-to-date account of the methodology.

Bates et al. (1988) discuss nonlinear models in detail. A more elementary presentation is given in one of the chapters of Myers (1990).

3.11 Exercises

3.1. The dataset `cities` lists the populations (in thousands) of Canada's largest cities over 1992–1996. There is a division between Ontario and the West (the so-called "have" regions) and other regions of the country (the "have-not" regions) that show less-rapid growth. To identify the "have" cities we can specify

```
## Set up factor that identifies the `have' cities
cities <- DAAG::cities
cities$have <- with(cities, factor(REGION %in% c("ON","WEST"),
                                   labels=c("Have-not","Have")))
```

Plot the 1996 population against that for 1992, distinguishing the two categories of city, both using the raw data and using the log-transformed values, thus:

```
lattice::xyplot(POP1996~POP1992, groups=have, data=cities,
                auto.key=list(columns=2))
lattice::xyplot(log(POP1996)~log(POP1992), groups=have, data=cities,
                auto.key=list(columns=2))
```

Which of these plots is preferable? Explain.

Now carry out the regressions

```
cities.lm1 <- lm(POP1996 ~ have+POP1992, data=cities)
cities.lm2 <- lm(log(POP1996) ~ have+log(POP1992), data=cities)
```

Examine diagnostic plots. Which model seems preferable? Interpret the results.

3.2. Calculate volumes (`volume`) and page areas (`area`) for the books on which information is given in the data frame `DAAG::oddbooks`.

   a. Plot `log(weight)` against `log(volume)`, and fit a regression line.
   b. Plot `log(weight)` against `log(area)`, and again fit a regression line.
   c. Which of the lines (a) and (b) gives the better fit?
   d. Repeat (a) and (b), now with `log(density)` in place of `log(weight)` as the dependent variable. Comment on how results from these regressions may help explain the results obtained in (a) and (b).

3.3. The `MASS::cpus` data frame gives information on eight aspects for each of 209 different types of computers. Read the help page for more information.

   a. Construct a scatterplot matrix for these data, as in Figure 3.3 in Subsection 3.2.1. Should any of the variables be transformed before further analysis is conducted?
   b. How well does estimated performance (`estperf`) predict performance (`perf`)? Study this question by constructing a scatterplot of these two variables, after taking logarithms. Do the plotted points scatter about a straight line or is there an indication of nonlinearity? Is variability in performance the same at each level of performance?

3.4. In the dataset `MASS::cement`, examine the dependence of `y` (amount of heat produced) on `x1`, `x2`, `x3`, and `x4` (which are proportions of four constituents). Begin by examining the scatterplot matrix. As the explanatory variables are proportions, do they require transformation, perhaps by taking $\log(x/(100-x))$? What alternative strategies might help identify an equation for predicting heat?

3.5. Use the model fitted to the data in `nihills` to give predicted values for the data in `hills2000`. Plot these against predicted values from the model fitted to `hills2000`, and use differences from observed values of `logtime` to estimate a prediction variance that is relevant when Northern Irish data are used to predict Scottish times. Would you expect this variance to be larger or smaller than the estimated error variance from the `hills2000` model fit? Is this what you see?

3.6. The data frame `DAAG::hills2000` updates the 1984 information in the dataset `DAAG::hills`. Fit regression models, for men and women separately, based on the data in `hills`. Check whether they fit satisfactorily over the whole range of race times. Compare the two equations.

3.7. Section 3.1 used `lm()` to analyze the allbacks data that are presented in Figure 3.1. Repeat the analysis using (1) the function `MASS::rlm()`, and (2) the function `MASS::lqs()`. Compare the two sets of results with the results in Section 3.1.

3.8. The following investigates the consequences of not using a logarithmic transformation for the `nihills` data analysis. The second differs from the first in having a `dist` × `climb` interaction term, additional to linear terms in `dist` and `climb`.

   a. Fit and compare the two models:

```
nihills.lm <- lm(time ~ dist+climb, data=DAAG::nihills)
nihillsX.lm <- lm(time ~ dist+climb+dist:climb, data=DAAG::nihills)
```

```
anova(nihills.lm, nihillsX.lm) # Use `anova()` to make the comparison
coef(summary(nihillsX.lm))     # Check coefficient for interaction term
drop1(nihillsX.lm)
```

b. Using the F-test result, make a tentative choice of model, and proceed to examine diagnostic plots. Are there any problematic observations? What happens if these points are removed? Refit both of the above models, and check the diagnostics again.

3.9. Fit the model `brainwt ~ bodywt + lsize` to the `DAAG::litters` dataset, then checking the variance inflation factors for `bodywt` and for `lsize`. Comment.

3.10. Apply the `lm.ridge()` function to the `litters` data, using the generalized cross-validation (GCV) criterion to choose the tuning parameter. (GCV is an approximation to cross-validation.)

a. In particular, estimate the coefficients of the model relating `brainwt` to `bodywt` and `lsize` and compare with the results obtained using `lm()`.

b. Using both ridge and ordinary regression, estimate the mean brain weight when litter size is 10 and body weight is 7. Use the bootstrap, with case-resampling, to compute approximate 95 percent percentile confidence intervals using each method. Compare with the interval obtained using `predict.lm()`.

3.11. *Compare the ranges of `dist` and `climb` in the data frames `nihills` and `hills2000`. In which case would you expect it to be harder to find a well-fitting model? For each of these data frames, fit the models based on each of the formulae:

```
log(time) ~ log(dist) + log(climb)    ## lm model
time ~ alpha*dist + beta*I(climb^2)   ## nls model
```

Is there one model that gives the best fit in both cases?

3.12. The data frame `MPV::table.b3` has data on gas mileage and 11 other variables for a sample of 32 automobiles.

a. Construct a scatterplot of `y` (mpg) versus `x1` (displacement). Is the relationship between these variables nonlinear?

b. Use the `xyplot()` function, and `x11` (type of transmission) as a `group` variable. Is a linear model reasonable for these data?

c. Fit the model, relating `y` to `x1` and `x11`, which gives two lines having possibly different gradients and intercepts. Check the diagnostics. Are there any influential observations? Are there any influential outliers?

d. Plot the residuals against the variable `x7` (number of transmission speeds), again using `x11` as a `group` variable. Comment on anything unusual about this plot.

3.13. The following code is designed to explore effects that can result from the omission of explanatory variables:

```
x1 <- runif(10)           # predictor which will be missing
x2 <- rbinom(10, 1, 1-x1)
  ## observed predictor, depends on missing predictor
y <- 5*x1 + x2 + rnorm(10,sd=.1) # simulated model; coef of x2 is positive
```

```
y.lm <- lm(y ~ factor(x2)) # model fitted to observed data
coef(y.lm)
```

```
(Intercept) factor(x2)1
      3.971      -0.827
```

```
y.lm2 <- lm(y ~ x1 + factor(x2))  # correct model
coef(y.lm2)
```

```
(Intercept)          x1 factor(x2)1
     0.3744      4.5778      0.8724
```

What happens if x2 is generated according to `x2 <- rbinom(10, 1, x1)`? Repeat with `x2 <- rbinom(10, 1, .5)`.

3.14. Fit the model investigated in Subsection 3.8.4, omitting the parameter α. Investigate and comment on changes in the fitted coefficients, standard errors, and fitted values.

3.15. Figure 3.23 used the function `errorsINx()`, with the argument `gpdiff=1.5`, to simulate data in which the regression relationship $y = 15 + 1.5x$ is the same in each of two groups (called `ctl` and `trt`). The left panel identifies the two fitted lines when the explanatory variable is measured without error. These are, to within statistical error, identical. The right panel shows the fitted regression lines when random error of the same order of magnitude as the within groups variation in x is added to x, giving the column of values $zWITHerr$.

a. Run the function for several different values of `gpdiff` in the interval (0,1.5), and plot the estimate of the treatment effect against `gpdiff`.
b. Run the function for several different values of `timesSDz` in the interval (0,1.5) and plot the estimate of the treatment effect against `gpdiff`.
c. Run the function with `beta = c(-1.5,0)`. How does the estimate of the treatment effect change, as compared with `b = c(1.5,0)`? Explain the change.

3.16. Fit the following two resistant regressions, in each case plotting the residuals against `Year`.

```
bomData <- DAAG::bomregions2021
nraw.lqs <- MASS::lqs(northRain ~ SOI + CO2, data=bomData)
north.lqs <- MASS::lqs(I(northRain^(1/3)) ~ SOI + CO2, data=bomData)
plot(residuals(nraw.lqs) ~ Year, data=bomData)
plot(residuals(north.lqs) ~ Year, data=bomData)
```

Compare, also, normal quantile–quantile plots for the two sets of residuals.

a. Repeat the calculations several times. Comment on the extent of variation, from one run to the next, in the regression coefficients.
b. Based on examination of the residuals, which regression model seems more acceptable: `nraw.lqs` or `north.lqs`?
c. Compare the two sets of regression coefficients. Can you explain why they are so very different?

(More careful modeling will take into account the temporal sequence in the observations. See Section 6.2 for an analysis that does this.)

3.17. Consider the National Football League (NFL) 1976 team performance data in `MPV::table.b1`. The data frame has 28 observations on 10 variables, including `y`, the number of games won.

a. Fit a model relating `y` to the main effects of all other variables, assigning the `lm` object to `full.lm`.
b. Fit a model relating `y` to `x2` and `x8` (opponents' rushing yards) together, assigning the `lm` object to `reduced2.lm`.
c. Fit a model relating `y` to `x2` (passing yards) only, assigning the `lm` object to `reduced1.lm`.
d. Use the `anova()` function with `test="Cp"` to decide which of the three models should be preferred.
e. Compare the AICc statistics. Do they tell a similar story?
f. Use the following code to create a plot that compares estimated effect sizes for the replicate with those for the original, for the social psychology studies in the dataset `DAAG::repPsych`, discussed in Subsection 1.10.2, that relates to the paper Open Science Collaboration (2015).

```
socpsych <- subset(DAAG::repPsych, Discipline=='Social')
with(socpsych, scatter.smooth(T_r.R~T_r.O))
abline(v=.5)
```

Now fit a robust regression to the points for which the original estimated effect size was 0.5 or less:

```
soc.rlm <- MASS::rlm(T_r.R~T_r.O, data=subset(socpsych, T_r.O<=0.5))
## Look at summary plots
termplot(soc.rlm, partial.resid=T, se=T)
```

```
plot(soc.rlm)
```

Which points appear to differ from the fitted line by an amount that is greater than comfortably explained as statistical variation?

4

Exploiting the Linear Model Framework

In Chapter 3, the columns of the model matrix contained the observed values of the explanatory variables, perhaps after transformation. This chapter will explore less direct ways to relate the columns of the model matrix to the explanatory variables and/or factors, thus greatly extending the range of available models.

The function `lm()`, and several other regression modeling functions, call a routine that automatically creates suitable columns of *contrasts* when a factor appears in a model formula. These columns of contrasts serve as the columns of "dummy variables" that some older statistical software systems required users to create for themselves.

For modeling a quadratic form of response, a suitable recourse is to take x as one of the columns and values of x^2 as another, but the use of orthogonal polynomial columns may often be preferable. More generally, the columns can include arbitrary sets of *basis* functions that can be used to fit, in principle, curves and surfaces of arbitrary complexity. The basis functions effectively form a set of building blocks from which the curve or surface can be constructed. The resulting curves and surfaces, while often complex to describe mathematically, allow the calculation of predicted values and associated standard error estimates. For many purposes, this is all that is needed.

Quantile regression is an alternative to least squares regression, still taking advantage of the machinery of model matrices. It opens interesting new possibilities, and can provide useful perspectives on least squares or more general maximum likelihood model fits.

The latter part of this chapter will explore approaches that are available in the generalized additive model (GAM) framework, using the `gam()` function in the *mgcv* package. These allow use of an optimality criterion to control the complexity of the fitted model. The `gam()` and allied functions are able to fit, also, generalized linear models such as will be described in Chapter 5, and more besides.

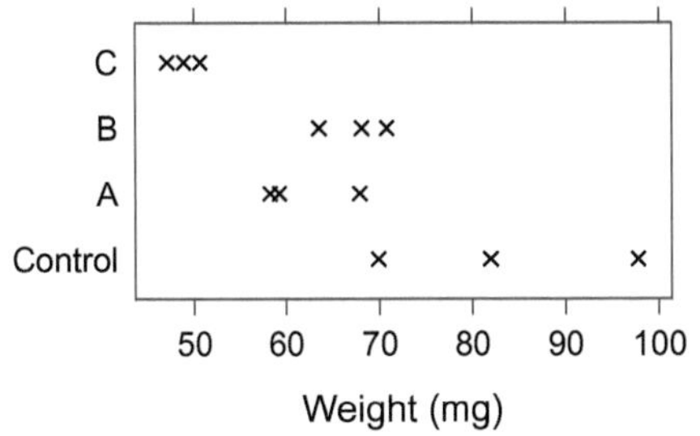

Control (WT[a])	A (GM1)	B (GM2)	C (GM3)
82.0	58.3	68.1	50.7
97.8	67.9	70.8	47.1
69.9	59.3	63.6	48.9
Mean =			
83.2	61.8	67.5	48.9

[a] WT = Wild Type; GM = Genetically Modified

Figure 4.1 Weights (*weight*) of sugar extracted from a control (wild-type) plant, and from three different genetically modified plant types.

4.1 Levels of a Factor – Using Indicator Variables

4.1.1 Example – Sugar Weight

The dataset `DAAG::sugar` is from an experiment that compared weights (mg) of sugar from the breakdown of cellulose, between an unmodified wild-type plant and three different genetically modified (GM) forms. The different plant types are distinguished by the different levels `Control` (Wild), `A` (GM1), `B` (GM2) and `C` (GM3) of the factor `trt`. Figure 4.1 displays the data. The following sets the data up ready for subsequent calculations:

```
sugar <- DAAG::sugar # Copy dataset 'sugar' into the workspace
## Ensure that "Control" is the first level
sugar[["trt"]] <- relevel(sugar[["trt"]], ref="Control")
options()[["contrasts"]]  # Check the default factor contrasts
```

```
        unordered              ordered
"contr.treatment"        "contr.poly"
```

```
## If your output does not agree with the above, then enter
## options(contrasts=c("contr.treatment", "contr.poly"))
```

For any problem that involves factors, there are multiple ways to set up the model matrix. In the out-of-the-box setup, the first of the treatment levels is used as a reference (or baseline), with the effects of other treatment levels then measured from the reference. Here it makes sense to set `Control` (Wild) as the reference.

For present purposes, we will work with the outcome variable `weight`, noting that use of `log(weight)` might be preferred because this reduces the apparent between-treatment difference in within-treatment variability. The analysis that works with `log(weight)` is left as an exercise for the reader.

The model can be fitted using either one of the functions `lm()` or `aov()`. The two functions differ only in their default output. With `Control` as reference, the model matrix is shown in Table 4.1. Values of the response (`sugar$weight`) have been added in the final column.

The following uses `aov()` to fit the model and a combination of `coef` and `summary` to summarize the output:

Table 4.1 *Model matrix for the analysis of variance model for the data in Figure 4.1. The values of the response are in the final column.*

Control (reference)	A	B	C	weight
1	0	0	0	82.0
1	0	0	0	97.8
1	0	0	0	69.9
1	1	0	0	58.3
1	1	0	0	67.9
1	1	0	0	59.3
1	0	1	0	68.1
1	0	1	0	70.8
1	0	1	0	63.6
1	0	0	1	50.7
1	0	0	1	47.1
1	0	0	1	48.9

Table 4.2 *At the head of each column is the multiple, as determined by least squares, that is taken in forming the fitted values.*

Control: 83.2	A: −21.4	B: −15.7	C: −34.3	Fitted value
1	0	0	0	83.2
1	1	0	0	61.8
1	0	1	0	67.5
1	0	0	1	48.9

```
sugar.aov <- aov(weight ~ trt, data=sugar)
## To display the model matrix, enter: model.matrix(sugar.aov)
## Note the use of summary.lm(), not summary() or summary.aov()
round(signif(coef(summary.lm(sugar.aov)), 3), 4)
```

```
            Estimate Std. Error t value Pr(>|t|)
(Intercept)     83.2       4.47   18.60   0.0000
trtA           -21.4       6.33   -3.38   0.0096
trtB           -15.7       6.33   -2.49   0.0377
trtC           -34.3       6.33   -5.43   0.0006
```

Note the use of `signif` to yield results with three significant figures while `round` displays these results with up to four decimal places.

The row labeled `(Intercept)` gives the estimate (= 83.2) for the reference, namely, `Control`. The remaining coefficients (differences from the reference) are:

A: weight differs by −21.4,
B: weight differs by −15.7,
C: weight differs by −34.3.

All three differences from the control are significant at the conventional 5 percent level.

Table 4.2 has one row for each of the four treatment groups. It shows, above each column, the multiplier determined by the least squares calculations. The fitted values in the final column may be calculated either as `fitted(sugar.aov)` or as `predict(sugar.aov)`. Residuals are the difference of the observed weight from the fitted values (shown in the final column) for the relevant treatment group.

In this example, regression calculations have been a complicated way to compute treatment means! The methodology shows its power to better effect in more-complex models, where there is no such simple alternative.

Use of the overall analysis of variance *F*-test, prior to these individual comparisons, is a limited safeguard against over-interpretation of the results of such comparisons. A more stringent alternative is to assess differences against Tukey's experimentwise HSD criterion that was discussed in Subsection 2.7.1.

```
sem <- summary.lm(sugar.aov)$sigma/sqrt(3)  # 3 results/trt
# Alternatively, sem <- 6.33/sqrt(2)
qtukey(p=.95, nmeans=4, df=8) * sem
```

```
[1] 20.26
```

Using this stricter criterion, B cannot be distinguished from the control, and A, B, and C cannot be distinguished from each other.

4.1.2 Different Choices for the Model Matrix When There Are Factors

In the language used in the relevant R help pages, different choices of *contrasts* are available, with each different choice leading to a different model matrix. The different choices give different mathematical descriptions for the same model. The coefficients (parameters) change and must be interpreted differently. The fitted values and the analysis of variance table do not change. The choice of contrasts may call for careful consideration, to obtain the coefficient estimates that best relate to the problem at hand. It can be helpful to have the different perspectives offered by one or more repeats of the analysis with different choices of contrasts.

The default (*treatment*) choice of *contrasts* uses the initial factor level as reference. For `contr.SAS()`, the final level is used as reference. The other common choice is *sum* contrasts, which use the mean of treatment effects as reference. The assignment `contrasts(sugar$trt) <- 'contr.sum'` sets sum contrasts for the factor `sugar$trt`. Enter `options(contrasts=c("contr.sum", "contr.poly"))` to make the setting globally. (The first vector element specifies the choice for factors for which no ordering has been specified, while the second specifies the choice for ordered factors.)

For `contr.sum()`, the mean of the means for the three levels is the reference. The estimate for the final level is, then, minus the sum for the first two levels.

Here is the output from use of the *sum* contrasts:

```
contrasts(sugar$trt) <- 'contr.sum'
sugarSum.aov <- aov(weight ~ trt, data = sugar)
round(signif(coef(summary.lm(sugarSum.aov)), 3),4)
```

```
             Estimate Std. Error t value Pr(>|t|)
(Intercept)     65.40       2.24  29.200   0.0000
trt1            17.90       3.87   4.610   0.0017
trt2            -3.53       3.87  -0.912   0.3880
trt3             2.13       3.87   0.551   0.5970
```

The reference, labeled `(Intercept)` and given as 65.4, is the mean of the treatment means. Remaining coefficients are differences, for `Control` (*trt1*) and two of the three other treatment levels (`A` and `B`), from this mean. The sum of the differences for all three treatments is zero. Thus, the difference for `C` is:

$$-(17.9 - 3.53 + 2.13) = -16.5.$$

The estimates (means) are, rounding to one decimal place:

Control: $65.4 + 17.9 = 83.3$,
A: $65.4 - 3.53 = 61.9$,
B: $65.4 + 2.1 = 67.5$,
C: $65.4 - 16.5 = 48.9$.

All four estimates can be obtained thus:

```
dummy.coef(sugarSum.aov)
```

```
Full coefficients are

(Intercept):       65.37
trt:             Control        A         B          C
                  17.867   -3.533     2.133   -16.467
```

Factor Contrasts – Further Details

Use the function `contrasts()` to set contrasts for an individual factor:

```
contrasts(sugar$trt) <- "contr.sum"
```

The coding for any particular choice of contrasts can be inspected directly, using the relevant function in the style of `contr.treatment()`:

```
fish <- factor(1:3, labels=c("Trout","Cod","Perch"))
```

```
contr.treatment(fish)
```

```
      Cod Perch
Trout   0     0
Cod     1     0
Perch   0     1
```

```
# Base is "Trout"
```

```
contr.SAS(fish)
```

```
      Trout Cod
Trout     1   0
Cod       0   1
Perch     0   0
```

```
# Base is "Perch"
```

```
contr.sum(fish)
```

```
      [,1] [,2]
Trout    1    0
Cod      0    1
Perch   -1   -1
```

```
# Base is mean of levels
```

Also available are *helmert* contrasts, used in some specialized contexts. See `?contr.helmert`.

** Tests for Main Effects in the Presence of Interactions?*

With rare exceptions, tests for main effects in the presence of interactions are a bad idea. The function `anova.lme()` in the *nlme* package allows the argument `type = "m"`. This gives marginal tests of the effect of dropping each term in the model in turn, while retaining other terms. This includes tests on the effect of "dropping" each factor main effect, while retaining all interaction terms. A difficulty is that the choice of contrasts implicitly sets constraints that determine just what is "dropped," with the consequence that the null hypothesis that is tested depends on the choice of contrasts. It is incumbent on anyone who specifies `type = "m"` to show that the contrasts used correspond a null hypothesis that is meaningful for purposes of their particular study. See Venables (1998) for further commentary.

4.2 Block Designs and Balanced Incomplete Block Designs

Data in the data frame `DAAG::rice`, shown in Figure 2.18, are from an experiment where the plants were laid out in blocks, with each treatment combination occurring once in each block. As all combinations of factors occur equally often in each block, the experimental design is a complete block design.

The data in `appletaste` are from a *balanced incomplete block design* (BIBD). In this particular BIBD, one treatment is left out of each block, but in such a way that the number of blocks in which a treatment is left out is the same for all treatments. (More generally, a BIBD is a design in which all treatments occur together equally often in the same block.)

Blocks should be chosen so that conditions are as uniform as possible within each block. In a glasshouse (or greenhouse) experiment all plants in a single block should be in a similar position in the glasshouse, with a similar exposure to light.

4.2.1 Analysis of the Rice Data, Allowing for Block Effects

Data from block designs require the use of a model that adjusts for block differences. Otherwise, if there are substantial differences between blocks, these are likely to mask treatment effects. The usual model assumption (which should, where possible, be checked) is that any differences will have an equal effect on all plants in any one block. The interest is, then, in knowing the extent to which treatment differences are consistent across blocks.

The analysis of variance table is a useful initial summary:

```
rice <- DAAG::rice
ricebl.aov <- aov(ShootDryMass ~ Block + variety * fert, data=rice)
print(summary(ricebl.aov), digits=3)
```

```
              Df Sum Sq Mean Sq F value  Pr(>F)
Block          1   3528    3528    10.9  0.0016
variety        1  22685   22685    70.1 6.4e-12
fert           2   7019    3509    10.8 8.6e-05
variety:fert   2  38622   19311    59.7 1.9e-15
Residuals     65  21034     324
```

Note the small p-value for the between block sum of squares.

Use `summary.lm()` to show the effects:

```
round(signif(coef(summary.lm(ricebl.aov)), 3), 5)
```

```
                        Estimate Std. Error t value Pr(>|t|)
(Intercept)                129.0       8.21   15.80  0.00000
```

```
Block                       -14.0     4.24   -3.30  0.00156
varietyANU843              -101.0     7.34  -13.80  0.00000
fertNH4Cl                   -58.1     7.34   -7.91  0.00000
fertNH4NO3                  -35.0     7.34   -4.77  0.00001
varietyANU843:fertNH4Cl      97.3    10.40    9.37  0.00000
varietyANU843:fertNH4NO3     99.2    10.40    9.55  0.00000
```

```
with(summary.lm(ricebl.aov),
cat("Residual standard error: ", sigma, "on", df[2], "degrees of freedom"))
```

```
Residual standard error:  17.99 on 65 degrees of freedom
```

The above residual standard error, that is, 18.0 on 65 degrees of freedom, may be compared with a residual standard error of 19.3 on 66 degrees of freedom when there is no allowance for block effects.[1] The difference between blocks has, for this dataset, little consequence for treatment comparisons.

Because this was a complete balanced design, the function `model.tables()` can be used to obtain a convenient form of summary of treatment effects, thus:

```
model.tables(ricebl.aov, type="means", se=TRUE, cterms="variety:fert")
```

```
Tables of means
Grand mean

59.56

 variety:fert
        fert
variety  F10    NH4Cl  NH4NO3
  wt     108.33  50.25  73.33
  ANU843   7.33  46.58  71.50

Standard errors for differences of means
        variety:fert
               7.344
replic.           12
```

Note: Do not try to use `model.tables()` for anything other than complete balanced designs. Even for "balanced incomplete" designs such as will be discussed in Subsection 4.2.2, results will be incorrect.

4.2.2 A Balanced Incomplete Block Design

In tasting experiments, several products, for example, wines, are compared. If presented with too many specimens, tasters are likely to become confused. As well as taking care to wash the palette as a way to minimize carry-over effects, it is usual to limit to no more than three or four the number of products given to any one taster.

For the data that will now be analyzed, the products were different varieties of apple, identified by the numerical codes 298, 493, 649, and 937. The 20 tasters were

[1]
```
## AOV calculations, ignoring block effects
rice.aov <- aov(ShootDryMass ~ variety * fert, data=rice)
summary.lm(rice.aov)$sigma
```

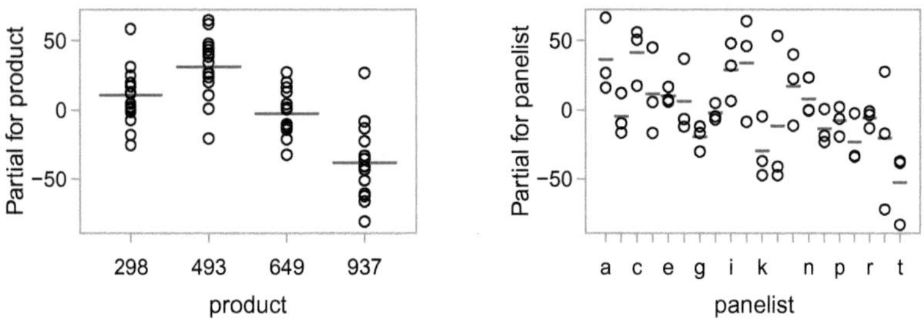

Figure 4.2 Plots show the respective contributions of the factors `panelist` and `product` to `aftertaste` scores, in an apple tasting experiment.

divided into four groups of five. For each group of five tasters, a different product was omitted. Panelists made a mark on a line that gave their rating of `aftertaste` (`0` for extreme dislike; `150` for extreme approval). The following summarizes the assignment of products to tasters:

```
appletaste <- DAAG::appletaste
with(appletaste, table(product, panelist))
```

```
         panelist
product  a b c d e f g h i j k l m n o p q r s t
    298  1 1 1 1 1 0 0 0 0 0 1 1 1 1 1 1 1 1 1 1
    493  1 1 1 1 1 1 1 1 1 1 0 0 0 0 0 1 1 1 1 1
    649  0 0 0 0 0 1 1 1 1 1 1 1 1 1 1 1 1 1 1 1
    937  1 1 1 1 1 1 1 1 1 1 1 1 1 1 1 0 0 0 0 0
```

This is a balanced incomplete block design (BIBD); each pair of products was tasted the same number of times by the same panelist.

The tasters play the role that blocks would play in a field design. In spite of differences in the way that different raters use the scale (some will tend to score low and some high), the careful choice and training of tasters can ensure a fair level of consistency in their comparative ratings. This does, at the same time, raise issues for generalizing results to the wider community!

The analysis specifies factors `panelist` and `product` as explanatory factors.

```
sapply(appletaste, is.factor) # panelist & product are factors
```

```
aftertaste    panelist     product
     FALSE        TRUE        TRUE
```

```
appletaste.aov <- aov(aftertaste ~ product + panelist, data=appletaste)
summary(appletaste.aov)
```

```
            Df  Sum Sq  Mean Sq  F value     Pr(>F)
product      3   32892    10964    15.08  0.0000014
panelist    19   31582     1662     2.29      0.015
Residuals   37   26892      727
```

The partial residual plot in Figure 4.2 gives a graphical summary of results. Notice that ratings seem generally lower for the final few raters. Was there deterioration over time? Simplified code is:

```
# Specify `partial=TRUE` to show partial residuals.
termplot(appletaste.aov, partial=TRUE, col.res="black")
```

The function `effects::effect()` can be used to obtain estimates of treatment means, standard errors, and confidence intervals:

```
as.data.frame(effects::Effect("product", appletaste.aov, confidence.level=0.95))
```

```
  product   fit   se  lower  upper
1     298 71.45 7.28 56.699  86.20
2     493 92.03 7.28 77.274 106.78
3     649 58.07 7.28 43.324  72.83
4     937 22.65 7.28  7.899  37.40
```

For comparing treatments, the standard errors should be multiplied by approximately $\sqrt{2}$. A direct comparison of treatments can be obtained from:

```
## NB that 'product' was first term in the model formula
## Thus, the 1st 4 coefficients have the information required
coef(summary.lm(appletaste.aov))[1:4, ]
```

```
            Estimate Std. Error t value     Pr(>|t|)
(Intercept)   107.74      16.69   6.455 0.0000001525
product493     20.57      10.44   1.971 0.0562961472
product649    -13.37      10.44  -1.281 0.2081800170
product937    -48.80      10.44  -4.674 0.0000384754
```

The "`(Intercept)`" is the mean for the first product (298) and the first panelist. The standard error of difference (SED) for comparisons with this as reference is 10.44. Because of the balance, this is also the SED for comparing any pair of treatments.[2]

The analysis has used only the within panelist information. Different panelists tasted different combinations of products. There is additional information in the comparison between panelists that, for BIB designs such as this, may allow a more precise comparison between products. See, for example, section 9.3 in Welham et al. (2014) for further details.

4.3 Fitting Multiple Lines

Multiple regression can be used to fit multiple lines. In the example that follows (Table 4.3), there are measurements of vapor pressure (`vapPress`) and of the difference between leaf and air temperature (`tempDiff`), for three different levels of carbon dioxide.

Possibilities we may want to consider are as follows.

- Model 1 (constant response): $y = a$.
- Model 2 (a single line): $y = a + bx$.

[2] Recall the warning, in the preceding Subsection 4.2.1, against use of `model.tables()` to obtain estimates of effects.

Table 4.3 *Values of* `CO2level`*,* `vapPress` *and* `tempDiff`*, from selected rows of the dataset* `leaftemp`.

CO2level	vapPress	tempDiff
low	1.88	1.36
low	2.20	0.60
...	...	...
medium	2.38	1.94
medium	2.72	0.83
...	...	...
high	2.56	1.50
high	2.55	0.85
...	...	...

Table 4.4 *Model matrix for fitting parallel lines (Model 3) to the data of Table 4.3, with y-values added in the right column.*

(Intercept)	Medium	High	vapPress	tempDiff
1	0	0	1.88	1.36
1	0	0	2.2	0.6
...	...	...	...	...
1	1	0	2.38	1.94
1	1	0	2.72	0.83
...	...	...	...	...
1	0	1	2.56	1.5
1	0	1	2.55	0.85
...	...	...	...	...

Table 4.5 *Model matrix for fitting three separate lines (Model 4), with y-values in the separate column to the right.*

(Intercept)	Medium	High	vapPress	Medium: vapPress	High: vapPress	tempDiff
1	0	0	1.88	0	0	1.36
1	0	0	2.2	0	0	0.6
...	...	...	...	...	...	...
1	1	0	2.38	2.38	0	1.94
1	1	0	2.72	2.72	0	0.83
...	...	...	...	...	...	...
1	0	1	2.56	0	2.56	1.5
1	0	1	2.55	0	2.55	0.85
...	...	...	...	...	...	...

- Model 3 (three parallel lines): $y = a_1 + a_2 z_2 + a_3 z_3 + bx$.
  (For the low CO_2 group ($z_2 = 0$ and $z_3 = 0$) the constant term is a_1; for the medium CO_2 group ($z_2 = 1$ and $z_3 = 0$) the constant term is $a_1 + a_2$, while for the high CO_2 group ($z_2 = 0$ and $z_3 = 1$) the constant term is $a_1 + a_3$.)
- Model 4 (three separate lines): $y = a_1 + a_2 z_2 + a_3 z_3 + b_1 x + b_2 z_2 x + b_3 z_3 x$.
  (Here, z_2 and z_3 are as in Model 3 (Panel B in Figure 4.3). For the low CO_2 group ($z_2 = 0$ and $z_3 = 0$) the slope is b_1; for the medium CO_2 group ($z_2 = 1$ and $z_3 = 0$) the slope is $b_1 + b_2$, while for the high CO_2 group ($z_2 = 0$ and $z_3 = 1$) the slope is $b_1 + b_3$.)

Selected rows from the model matrices for Model 3 and Model 4 are displayed in Tables 4.4 and 4.5, respectively.

The statements used to fit the four models are

```
## Fit various models to columns of data frame leaftemp (DAAG)
leaftemp <- DAAG::leaftemp
leaf.lm1 <- lm(tempDiff ~ 1 , data = leaftemp)
leaf.lm2 <- lm(tempDiff ~ vapPress, data = leaftemp)
leaf.lm3 <- lm(tempDiff ~ CO2level + vapPress, data = leaftemp)
leaf.lm4 <- lm(tempDiff ~ CO2level + vapPress
+ vapPress:CO2level, data = leaftemp)
```

Table 4.6 *Analysis of variance information. The initial model has only an intercept or "constant" term. The entries in rows 1–3 of the* `Df` *column and of the* `Sum of Sq` *column are then sequential decreases from fitting, in turn,* `vapPress`*, then three parallel lines, and then finally three separate lines.*

	Df	Sum of Sq	Mean square	F	Pr(<F)	
`vapPress` (variable)	1	5.27	5.27	11.3	0.0014	reduction in SS due to fitting one line
Three parallel lines	2	6.54	3.27	7.0	0.0019	additional reduction in SS due to fitting two parallel lines
Three different lines	2	2.13	1.06	2.3	0.1112	additional reduction in SS due to fitting two separate lines
Residuals	61	40.00	0.66			

The term `vapPress:CO2level` is, technically, an interaction between the factor `CO2level` and the variable `vapPress`. The effect of such a term is to allow different slopes for different levels of the factor, here for different levels of `CO2level`.

Now use an analysis of variance table to compare these models:

```
anova(leaf.lm1, leaf.lm2, leaf.lm3, leaf.lm4)
```

```
Analysis of Variance Table

Model 1: tempDiff ~ 1
Model 2: tempDiff ~ vapPress
Model 3: tempDiff ~ CO2level + vapPress
Model 4: tempDiff ~ CO2level + vapPress + vapPress:CO2level
  Res.Df  RSS Df Sum of Sq     F Pr(>F)
1     61 40.0
2     60 34.7  1      5.27 11.33 0.0014
3     58 28.2  2      6.54  7.03 0.0019
4     56 26.1  2      2.13  2.28 0.1112
```

This is a sequential analysis of variance table. Thus, the quantity in the sum of squares column (`Sum of Sq`) is the reduction in the residual sum of squares due to the inclusion of that term, given that earlier terms had already been included. The `Df` (degrees of freedom) column gives the change in the degrees of freedom due to the addition of that term. Table 4.6 explains this in detail.

The analysis of variance table suggests use of the parallel line model, shown in panel B of Figure 4.3. The reduction in the mean square from Model 3 (Panel B in Figure 4.3) to Model 4 (Panel C) in the analysis of variance table has a p-value equal to 0.1112 . The coefficients and standard errors for Model 3 are:

```
print(coef(summary(leaf.lm3)), digits=2)
```

```
                Estimate Std. Error t value Pr(>|t|)
(Intercept)         2.68       0.56     4.8 0.000012
CO2levelmedium      0.32       0.22     1.5 0.148615
CO2levelhigh        0.79       0.22     3.6 0.000582
vapPress           -0.84       0.26    -3.2 0.002129
```

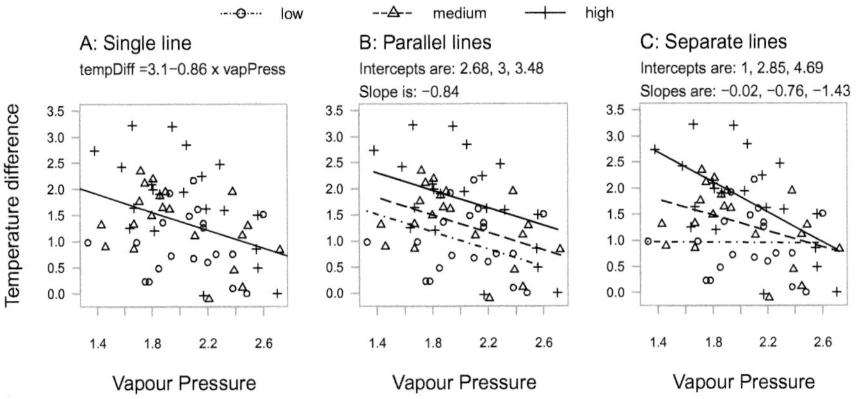

Figure 4.3 A sequence of models fitted to the plot of **tempDiff** versus **vapPress**, for low, medium, and high levels of **CO2level**. Panel A relates to Model 2, Panel B to Model 3, and Panel C to Model 4.

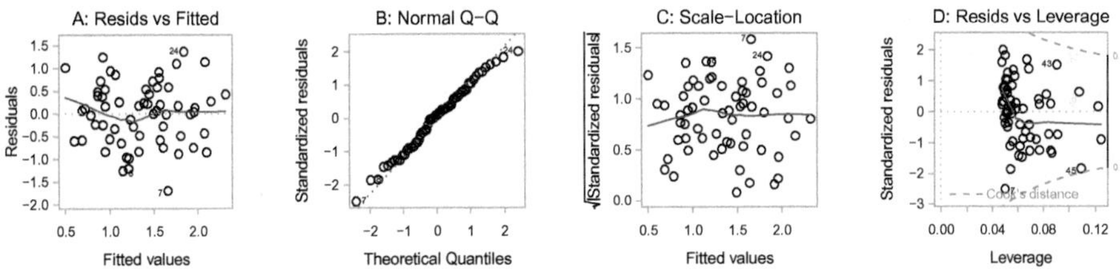

Figure 4.4 Diagnostic plots for the parallel line model of Figure 4.3.

The coefficients in the equations for this parallel line model are given in the annotation for Figure 4.3B. For the first equation (low CO_2), the constant term is 2.68, for the second equation (medium CO_2) the constant term is $2.68 + 0.32 = 3.00$, while for the third equation the constant term is $2.68 + 0.79 = 3.47$.

In addition, we examine a plot of residuals against fitted values, and a normal quantile-quantile plot of residuals (Figure 4.4). These plots seem unexceptional.

4.4 Methods for Fitting Smooth Curves

A first set of methods rely on including a term or terms in the model formula that generate a suitable model matrix. As with other models that can be fitted using the `lm()` function, they can alternatively be handled using the *mgcv* function `gam()`, which has much wider ranging abilities than `lm()`.

Simple forms of polynomial regression can be effective where the response curve has a simple convex (valley-like) or concave (hill) shape. Such shapes can often be modeled quite well using quadratic, that is, polynomial with degree 2, regression. Calculations formally identical to those for multiple regression can be handled by using x^2 as well as x as explanatory variables. Addition of a cubic (x^3) term may allow some limited asymmetry.

More generally, the columns of the model matrix that are generated from a variable x can be any suitably chosen functions. They could even be curves that have been drawn freehand and then digitized! They define a collection of curves that can be combined as required to generate a fitted curve. The number of basis terms, m for a polynomial of degree m (or $m+1$ if the constant term is counted), determines the complexity.

A generally better choice than a polynomial basis, for modeling anything more complex than a curve with a cubic shape, is a *spline* basis. Two types of spline basis functions and corresponding fitted spline curves will be described – *thin plate* regression splines and *cubic regression* splines. These can be used with a user choice of basis terms, or used with the roughness penalty methods, implemented using `mgcv::gam()`, that will be discussed in Subsection 4.4.2.

Roughness penalty methods extend the linear model framework by imposing a roughness (or wiggliness) penalty on curves fitted using a linear model. The *mgcv* package implements methods that allow automatic choice of parameters that control the amount of penalization. A key assumption, for the use of `gam()` is that errors are independent with homogeneous variance. The *mgcv* function `gamm()` allows, in place of the independence assumption, use of one of the correlation structures that are available in the *nlme* package. These include the Box–Jenkins type sequential correlation structures that will be described in Chapter 6. The function `bam()`, designed to work efficiently for large datasets, allows use of a much more restricted sequential correlation structure.

The functions `loess()` and `lowess()`, used in several places earlier in this text, implement a methodology that does not readily fit within the linear model framework. Subsection 4.4.10 gives further details.

4.4.1 Polynomial Regression

Use of a quadratic curve to fit the points shown in Figure 4.5 is not the most sensible choice. It carries the implication that yield will stop decreasing and start increasing once seeding rate is increased beyond a certain point. As will later be demonstrated, it makes better sense to fit a line, with both variables transformed logarithmically. The quadratic fit is used here to start a conversation.

The following fits the quadratic:

```
seedrates <- DAAG::seedrates
form2 <- grain ~ rate + I(rate^2)
# Without the wrapper function I(), rate^2 would be interpreted
# as the model formula term rate:rate, and hence as rate.
quad.lm2 <- lm(form2, data = seedrates)
## Alternative, using gam()
## quad.gam <- mgcv::gam(form2, data = seedrates)
```

Figure 4.5 shows number of grains per head (averaged over eight replicates), for different seeding rates of barley, with a fitted quadratic curve as well as a fitted line. The quadratic regression appears from visual inspection a good fit to the data. Fitting the x^2 term leaves only two degrees of freedom for error, which means

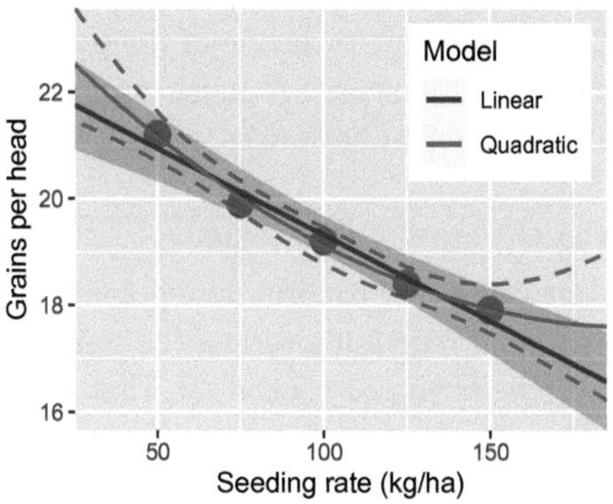

The first three columns form the model matrix for the quadratic curve model. The final column holds outcome variable values.

Intercept	rate	rate^2	
1	50	2 500	21.2
1	75	5 625	19.9
1	100	10 000	19.2
1	125	15 625	18.4
1	150	22 500	17.9

Figure 4.5 Number of grains per head versus barley seeding rate, for the data shown to the right of the figure, with fitted line and quadratic curve, in both cases with 95 percent confidence bounds added. Data relate to McLeod (1982).

that p-values or other forms of statistical summary depend strongly on normality assumptions

The fitted model may be written

$$\widehat{y} = a + b_1 x_1 + b_2 x_2,$$

where $x_1 = x$, and $x_2 = x^2$. Thus, the model matrix has a column of 1s, a column of values of x, and a column that has values of x^2. Coefficients, standard errors, and correlations between coefficient estimates, are:

```
quad.lm2 <- lm(grain ~ rate + I(rate^2), data = DAAG::seedrates)
print(coef(summary(quad.lm2)), digits=2)
cat("\nCorrelation matrix\n")
print(summary(quad.lm2, corr=TRUE)$correlation, digits=2)
```

```
            Estimate Std. Error t value Pr(>|t|)
(Intercept) 24.06000   0.455694    52.8  0.00036
rate        -0.06669   0.009911    -6.7  0.02138
I(rate^2)    0.00017   0.000049     3.5  0.07294

Correlation matrix
            (Intercept)  rate I(rate^2)
(Intercept)        1.00 -0.98      0.94
rate              -0.98  1.00     -0.99
I(rate^2)          0.94 -0.99      1.00
```

Correlations between the coefficients are all 0.94 or more. The large negative correlation between `rate` and `I(rate2̂)` implies that forcing the coefficient for `rate` to be high would lead to a low coefficient for `I(rate2̂)`, and vice versa.

Given a choice between fitted values from the linear model and those from the quadratic model, the quadratic may well, for a short distance beyond the final data point, give the better estimate. The much wider confidence bounds beyond a rate of about 160 are more realistic than the very narrow bounds for the line.

More than a short distance beyond the limits of the data, neither the line nor the curve should be given much credence. For `rate` $\geq$ 194.5 the fitted quadratic shows a pattern of increase in values of `grain` that is a mirror image of the pattern of decrease up to that point. This makes no scientific sense. A much preferable alternative is to work with logarithmic transformations on both axes, and fit a line.

*An Alternative Formulation Using Orthogonal Polynomials

Orthogonal polynomial regression offers an alternative way to formulate polynomial regression models. For fitting orthogonal polynomial regression terms, the separate terms `rate` and `I(rate2̂)` are replaced by the single term `poly(rate,2)`, that is, an orthogonal polynomial of degree 2 in `rate`. The fitted values will be identical, but the coefficients are then coefficients of the orthogonal polynomials, not coefficients of `rate` and `I(rate2̂)` For the `seedrates` data, the model is:

```
seedratesP.lm2 <- lm(grain ~ poly(rate,2), data = seedrates)
print(coef(summary(seedratesP.lm2)), digits=2)
```

```
                 Estimate Std. Error t value Pr(>|t|)
(Intercept)          19.3      0.051   376.8 0.000007
poly(rate, 2)1       -2.6      0.115   -22.3 0.001997
poly(rate, 2)2        0.4      0.115     3.5 0.072943
```

```
## Alternative, using mgcv::gam()
seedratesP.gam <- mgcv::gam(grain ~ poly(rate,2), data = seedrates)
```

An advantage of the orthogonal polynomial basis is that the coefficient(s) of lower-order terms (linear, ...) are uncorrelated and do not change when higher-order terms are added. One model fit, with the highest-order term present that is under consideration, provides the information needed to assess the order of polynomial required.

The orthogonal polynomial coefficients can be translated back into coefficients of powers of x (these are not, of course, independent), if required. Interested readers can use Exercise 4.7 at the end of the chapter as a starting point for investigating orthogonal polynomial regression. (In the early days of numerical computation, orthogonal polynomial regression was used to avoid potential numerical instability. With modern computational approaches, this is less of an issue.)

Quadratic Fit versus Transformed Variables

We could try other, single-parameter, models. Selecting a model from a number of choices that allow for the curvature may not, however, be much different in its implications for the effective degrees of freedom, from adding an x^2 term.

A better alternative is to model `log(grain)` (or possibly `grain`) as a linear function of `log(rate)`. The fitted value of `grain` then continues to decrease, but increasingly slowly, as `rate` increases beyond the highest rate used in the experiment. The following fits a model that is linear when both `grain` and `seed` are transformed to a logarithmic scale.

```
logseed.lm <- lm(log(grain) ~ log(rate), data=DAAG::seedrates)
coef(summary(logseed.lm))
```

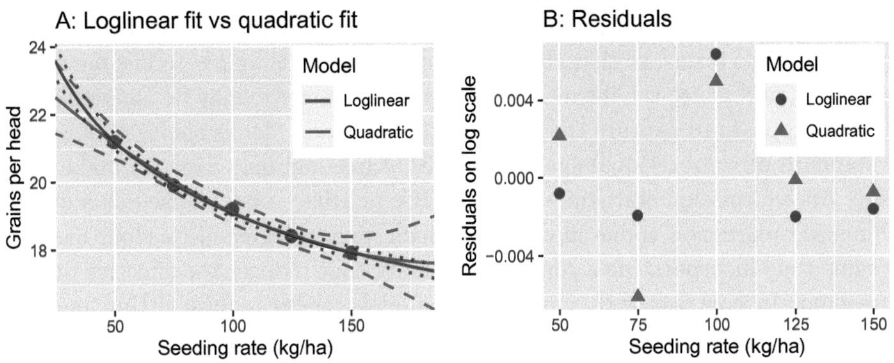

Figure 4.6 Panel A plots number of grains per head against seeding rate, with fitted line (blue) and (in red) fitted quadratic curve, both shown with 95 percent pointwise confidence bounds. Panel B shows residuals for the two models. For the loglinear model, residuals are calculated as `log(seedrates$grain)-log(fitted(quad.lm2)`.

```
              Estimate Std. Error t value     Pr(>|t|)
(Intercept)     3.6544   0.021702  168.39 0.0000004618
log(rate)      -0.1533   0.004768  -32.14 0.0000661863
```

Figure 4.6A shows the fit that results from a loglinear model, together with that for the quadratic model that was shown in Figure 4.5, in both cases with 95 percent confidence bounds. Panel B shows residuals.

Here quad.lm2 has 3+1 (for variance) parameters. This compares with 2+1 for logseed.lm. With the very small residual degrees of freedom (2 and 3), AIC statistics will be biased in favor of the more complex model. A further point is that use of the logarithmic scale for `rate` requires that `sum(2*log(seedrates$grain))`, here equal to 29.6, is added to the AIC statistic for the loglinear model in order to make it comparable. Here, for illustrative purposes, is the comparison:

```
aic <- AIC(quad.lm2, logseed.lm)
aic["logseed.lm",2] <- aic["logseed.lm",2] + sum(2*log(seedrates$grain))
round(aic,1)
```

```
           df  AIC
quad.lm2    4 -4.1
logseed.lm  3 -7.6
```

The observation that the loglinear model makes better scientific sense settles the choice of model.

4.4.2 Regression Spline Bases – Unpenalized and Penalized

Polynomial curves of degree greater than 3 or 4 can be problematic. High-degree polynomials tend to move up and down between data values in a snake-like manner. For anything not suitably fitted with a low-order polynomial, spline curves are in general a better choice. Spline curves are formed as linear combinations of spline basis functions.

Unpenalized regression spline models use spline basis curves in the same way as polynomial basis terms, so that the model can be fitted using `lm()`. The number of basis terms, and hence the degrees of freedom for the curve, may be chosen so that the curve appears to capture the trend in the data and "looks smooth." A plot of the standard error of residual against degrees of freedom may assist in making the choice. An information statistic – AIC or AICc or BIC – may be used as a guide.

Penalized regression spline models use much higher degree-of-freedom basis, at the same time incorporating a roughness penalty that reduces the effective degrees of freedom. In contrast with unpenalized models, these require fitting methods that go beyond what is available for `lm()`. Under independence and homogeneity of variance assumptions, the penalty can be chosen automatically. Choices still have to be made. Has the penalization been severe enough? Should one insist on a monotone smooth – changes always are up or always down.

As a starting point, consider smooths that are functions of one explanatory variable, that is, direct alternatives to the polynomial smooths discussed above. The ideas extend to the fitting of surfaces and higher dimensional responses.

For a k degrees of freedom regression spline fit, there will be basis functions $\phi_1(), \phi_2(), \ldots, \phi_k()$, where $\phi_1(x) = 1$, for all x. As with orthogonal polynomials, a k degrees of freedom regression spline fit chooses the coefficients $a_1, a_1, a_2, \ldots, a_k$ that, minimize, for an unpenalized fit

$$\sum_{i=1}^{n}(y_i - f(x_i))^2, \text{ where } f(x_i) = a_1\phi_1(x_i) - a_2\phi_2(x_i) - \cdots - a_k\phi_k(x_i).$$

Penalized fits use relatively high degree-of-freedom bases, and minimize a quantity that increases the residual sum of squares by a multiple λ of a roughness penalty that penalizes changes of slope.[3] Several alternative mechanisms, aiming to achieve much the same effect as the use of cross-validation, can be used to choose λ.

Among the spline bases implemented in *mgcv*, two will be noted here. *Thin plate regression splines*, used as the default for the function `mgcv::s()` that sets up smooths in model formulae, will be the main focus. These are implemented as computationally efficient low rank approximations to true thin plate spline fits. Beyond the boundary points, thin plate regression splines extrapolate (as do natural cubic splines) as straight lines. Wood (2017, pp. 215–221) discusses the theoretical motivations for thin plate splines.

Unlike the cubic spline bases that are noted in the next paragraph, but much in the style of polynomial bases, thin plate regression spline smooths of lower rank are nested within smooths of higher rank, so that thin plate spline fits of successively increasing degree correspond to successively more complex curves. The first basis function is (if an intercept is included) a constant, the second basis function included is a line, the third typically looks much like a quadratic, and so on. Thin plate regression splines readily generalize to allow the fitting of smooth surfaces, in an arbitrary number of dimensions.

[3] The penalty is $\int f''(x)^2 dx$, over the range of values of x. A cruder alternative might be to take the sum of squared differences between slopes for neighboring pairs of points.

Cubic regression splines, which predate thin plate regression splines, have a more straightforward motivation. Cubic regression spline basis terms combine to generate piecewise cubics, that is, two or more cubic curves join smoothly at points that have the name "knots." The internal knots, by default placed at equally spaced quantiles of the data, are supplemented by boundary "knots," usually placed at the limits of the data. Natural cubic regression splines are a special case – beyond the boundary knots these extrapolate as straight lines. (Degrees of freedom for a fit that uses natural cubic regression splines are the number of internal knots, plus 2. One degree of freedom is for the intercept.) For other smooth classes that are available in *mgcv*, see `?mgcv::smooth.terms`.

The following demonstrates alternative fits of degree-2 curves (+1 for the intercept) to the `DAAG::seedrates` data:

```
seedrates<-DAAG::seedrates
quad.lm2 <- lm(grain ~ poly(rate,degree=2), data=seedrates)
ns.lm2 <- lm(grain ~ splines::ns(rate,df=2), data=seedrates)
tps.gam2 <- mgcv::gam(grain ~ s(rate, k=3, fx=T), data=seedrates)
```

The three sets of model matrices are:

(Int)	poly2.1	poly2.2	(Int)	ns2.1	ns2.2	(Int)	s3.1	s3.2
1	−0.6325	0.5345	1	0.0000	0.0000	1	−0.3040	−1.4142
1	−0.3162	−0.2673	1	0.3570	−0.2172	1	0.1413	−0.7071
1	0.0000	−0.5345	1	0.5663	−0.2108	1	0.3255	0.0000
1	0.3162	−0.2673	1	0.5291	0.1681	1	0.1413	0.7071
1	0.6325	0.5345	1	0.3441	0.7706	1	−0.3040	1.4142

Note that, for the *mgcv* smoothing spline term `s()`, one degree of freedom is added for the intercept. The two `lm()` fits could equally well use `gam()`.

The *splines* package offers, as well as the natural cubic spline basis (`ns()`), the B-spline basis (`bs()`). Unlike other spline bases noted here, fits do not extrapolate as straight lines at the boundaries of the fitted curve. Degrees of freedom (`df`) must be at least 2. Note also `?stats::smooth.spline`.

GAM Models versus Models Fitted Using `lm()`

Generalized additive models (GAMs), as implemented in the *mgcv* package, generalize linear (and GLM) models to provide wide-ranging abilities for fitting smooth curves and surfaces. Smoothing terms are added as required to an `lm()` or `glm()` type model formula. The `scam()` function in the *scam* package that will be discussed in Subsection 4.4.5 provides also, among other possibilities, for fitting monotone smooths.

Differences in the diagnostic functions that are available, for models fitted with `gam()` as opposed to `lm()`, are as follows.

- For `lm()` models, use `plot()` to get diagnostic plots. For GAM models, `plot()` shows plots for the separate smooth (*semiparametric*) terms only.
- For `lm()`, use `termplot()` to get plots that show the contributions of the separate terms, albeit (as currently implemented) only for main effect terms that do not

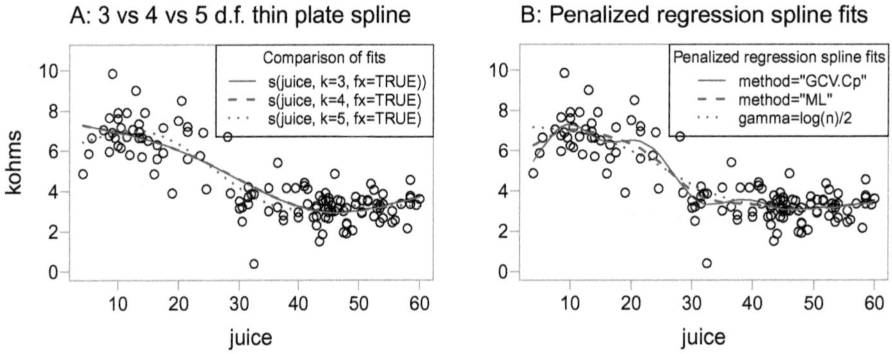

Figure 4.7 Resistance (in kiloohms) versus apparent juice content. The fits in Panel A are from thin plate spline regression (tprs) bases. Specifying `bs="cs"` in place of the default `bs="cs"` gives fits that are visually indistinguishable from the tprs fits. Panel B uses penalized spline models. The first uses the default penalization, the second uses a maximum likelihood estimate, and the third multiplies the effective degrees of freedom by `gamma=log(n)/2`, to give a smoother model.

have any modifying interaction terms. This function can be used, also, to show the contributions of parametric terms in GAM models. For GAM models,

- The function `mgcv::gam.check()` gives diagnostic plots, together with statistical details that can help in judging whether the fit has done the job expected of it.

Alternative Fits – What Is the Best Choice?

The dataset `DAAG::fruitohms`, giving apparent juice content and resistance (in ohms) for 128 slabs of fruit (Harker and Maindonald, 1994), will be used to illustrate the methodology. Unpenalized and penalized spline fits will be tried, then moving to a monotone decreasing fit.

Figure 4.7A shows 3-, 4-, and 5-degrees of freedom regression spline fits, using the default thin plate regression spline bases. Panel B uses penalized spline models. The first uses the default penalization, the second penalizes more strongly, and the third multiplies the effective degrees of freedom by `gamma=log(n)/2`, giving a smoother fit, equivalent to using the BIC for model comparison in preference to AIC.[4]

The `gam()` function's default `method="GCV.Cp"` for choosing λ uses a variant of generalized cross-validation that relies on an analytical approximation to the expected value of the cross-validation estimate of the residual sum of squares. It is used as the default because it is less computationally demanding than alternatives that are less prone to over-fitting. These include `method="ML"` (maximum likelihood) and `method="REML"` (restricted maximum likelihood). Whichever criterion is used, the result is a choice of curve or surface where the constraints that are of consequence arise directly from the data, under the assumption that observations are independent with homogeneous variance.

[4] See `www.maths.ed.ac.uk/~swood34/mgcv/tampere/mgcv-advanced.pdf`.

The inflation factor `gamma=log(n)/2` used in the `ohms.tpBIC` model may, at least in part, be correcting for some limited clustering or sequential correlation in the data. Readings that were taken at around the same time or by the same technician may have been relatively more similar. There may be systematic effects from fruit-to-fruit differences in the slabs used that were not reflected in the apparent juice content. Diagnostic plots will be examined below.

Code that fits the curves shown in Panel A is:

```
fruitohms <- within(DAAG::fruitohms, kohms <- ohms/1000)
## Panel A: 3, 4 and 5 d.f. tprs (cubic spline fits are almost identical)
ohms.tp3 <- gam(kohms~s(juice, bs="tp", k=3, fx=T), data=fruitohms)
ohms.tp4 <- gam(kohms~s(juice, bs="tp", k=4, fx=T), data=fruitohms)
ohms.tp5 <- gam(kohms~s(juice, k=5, fx=T), data=fruitohms)
```

For Panel B, the following gives the model fits:

```
## Fits with automatic choice of smoothing parameter
ohms.tp <- gam(kohms~s(juice, bs="tp"), data=fruitohms)
ohms.tpML <- gam(kohms ~ s(juice, bs="tp"), data=fruitohms, method="ML")
ohms.tpBIC <- gam(kohms ~ s(juice, bs="tp"), data=fruitohms,
                  gamma=log(nrow(fruitohms))/2, method="ML")
```

It is of little consequence what basis is used for the regression spline fits in Panel A, or for the first two fits in Panel B with automatic choice of smoothing parameter. The following checks this for the first fit in Panel B:

```
ohms.tp <- gam(kohms~s(juice, bs="tp"), data=fruitohms)
ohms.cs <- gam(kohms~s(juice, bs="cs"), data=fruitohms)
range(fitted(ohms.tp)-fitted(ohms.cs))
```

```
[1] -0.07957  0.12794
```

Summary output, for the `ohms.tp` model, is:

```
summary(ohms.tp)
```

```
Family: gaussian
Link function: identity

Formula:
kohms ~ s(juice, bs = "tp")

Parametric coefficients:
            Estimate Std. Error t value Pr(>|t|)
(Intercept)   4.3600     0.0795    54.8   <2e-16

Approximate significance of smooth terms:
           edf Ref.df    F p-value
s(juice) 8.37   8.89 47.1  <2e-16

R-sq.(adj) =  0.766   Deviance explained = 78.2%
GCV = 0.87286  Scale est. = 0.80897   n = 128
```

Summary output for the Panel B fit that used `gamma=log(n)/2` as an inflation factor to penalize the degrees of freedom for a `method=GCV.Cp"` fit is:

```
summary(ohms.tpBIC)
```

```
Family: gaussian
Link function: identity

Formula:
kohms ~ s(juice, bs = "tp")

Parametric coefficients:
            Estimate Std. Error t value Pr(>|t|)
(Intercept)   4.3600     0.0852    51.2   <2e-16

Approximate significance of smooth terms:
          edf Ref.df    F p-value
s(juice) 3.37    4.2 81.4  <2e-16

R-sq.(adj) =  0.731   Deviance explained = 73.8%
-ML = 77.941  Scale est. = 0.9295     n = 128
```

Graphs will now be shown that tease apart the contributions of the several basis curves to the k=3 ($= 2 + 1$) and k=4 ($= 3 + 1$) thin plate regression spline fits in Panel A. The equivalent graphs for the penalized fits in Panel B would have 10 panels of basis functions and 10 panels for the contributions to the fit.

4.4.3 The Contributions of Basis Curves to the Fit

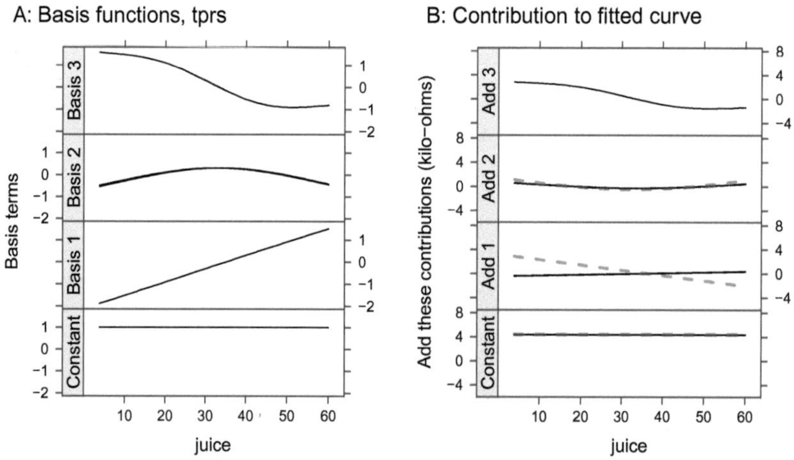

Figure 4.8 Panel A shows thin plate spline basis curves as obtained using the function *mgcv::s()* with the argument **fx=TRUE**. For the degree-3 ($= 2 + 1$) fit, the basis 3 is not used. Panel B shows the contributions of the basis functions to the fitted curve, in the regression of **kiloohms** on **juice**.

Figure 4.8A shows thin plate regression spline basis (tprs) curves, as generated by the *mgcv::s()*. The curves for three degrees of freedom (3 d.f.) are shown with dashes, while the 4 d.f. curves are shown as solid lines. The move from a 3 d.f. tprs curve to a 4 d.f. tprs curve adds one further basis function to those for the 3 d.f. tprs

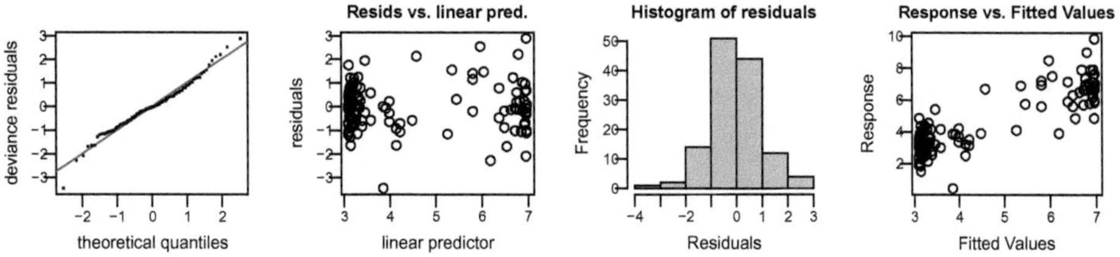

Figure 4.9 Diagnostic graphs from `gam.check()`, for the model `ohms.tpBIC` with inflated degrees of freedom.

curve. The basis curves follow a natural hierarchy, starting with a line and moving to more complex shapes. Figure 4.8B shows the contributions of the several basis functions to the fitted curve.

The breakdown of the fitted curve according to the contribution of the separate basis curves, as in Figure 4.8B, is important for understanding the mechanics of fitting the final curve. For use of the results, it may be of secondary interest.

Penalized fits work with linear combinations of a set of basis functions that allow the fitting of any of a large class of curves. The penalized sum that is minimized adds to the residual sum of squares a multiple λ of a roughness penalty that penalizes changes of slope.[5]

If Figure 4.8B is repeated for the penalized fits that use `gam()`, each of Figures 4.8A and B will have 10 panels. The roughness penalty gives a smoother curve (or surface) with an *effective degrees of freedom* (edf) that is less (and may be much less) than the dimension of the basis space. For the `ohms.tpBIC` model effective degrees of freedom were reduced to 3.3718.

See Wood (2010) for comments on the rationale for the maximum likelihood fit (`method="ML"`) with the penalization term set to correspond to that for the BIC.

4.4.4 Checks on the Fitted Model

The function `gam.check()` supplements statistical summary information with diagnostic graphs. The help page `?gam.check` has extensive detailed commentary on how the output should be understood and used.

Figure 4.9 shows the output for the `ohms.tpBIC` model.

```
## Figure 4.9, using 'mgcv' function
ohms.tpBIC <- gam(kohms ~ s(juice, bs="tp"), data=fruitohms,
                  gamma=log(nrow(fruitohms))/2, method="ML") # Work with a REML  fit
gam.check(ohms.tpBIC, tcl=-0.5, cex.main=1.25)
## Alternative: `mgcViz::check.mgcViz()`
ohms.gamViz <- mgcViz::getViz(ohms.tpBIC)  # Convert to a `gamViz` object
obj <- mgcViz::check.gamViz(ohms.gamViz, a.hist=list(bins=20))
plot(obj)        # Plot the ('ggplot2') graphics object.
```

Exercise 4.16 at the end of the chapter is intended as a starting point for trying out other functions in the *mgcViz* package.

[5] Given $y = f(x)$, the roughness penalty is $\lambda \int f''(x)^2 dx$, evaluated over the range of x.

```
Method: REML   Optimizer: outer newton
full convergence after 5 iterations.
Gradient range [-0.000000004967,0.00000000002727]
(score 79.88 & scale 0.9104).
Hessian positive definite, eigenvalue range [0.6127,25.46].
Model rank =  10 / 10

Basis dimension (k) checking results. Low p-value (k-index<1) may
indicate that k is too low, especially if edf is close to k'.

            k'  edf k-index p-value
s(juice) 9.00 3.78    0.89     0.1
```

The value `k'` is the number of degrees of freedom used for the basis (here this is one less than the default of `k=10`, while `edf` is the effective number of degrees of freedom used in fitting the model (this adjusts for the effect of penalization)). If the *p*-value in the final line is small, and especially if `edf` is close to `k'`, this may indicate that the basis space is too small. In that case, the fit should be repeated specifying a larger `k` in the call to the constructor function `s()`. For example, specify `s(juice, k=18)` in place of the default `s(juice, k=10)`. There is no strong case for that with the present example.

The default $k = 10$ (here, 1 for the intercept, plus 9) basis degrees of freedom for the smooth term constructor `s()` is well short of the full 127 basis functions (there are 127 distinct observations) that would allow maximum flexibility. This limits scope for very local changes of pattern in the fitted curve. The restriction to a $k = 10$ total degrees of freedom basis did, even so, allow the bumpiness that is apparent in the solid red curve in Figure 4.7B.

4.4.5 Monotone Curves

The *scam* package has provision for a variety of what are termed "shape constrained additive models." This includes monotone increasing responses (specify `s(...,bs="mpi")`) and monotone decreasing responses (specify `s(...,bs="mpd")`).

Summary output from fitting a monotonic decreasing smooth is:

```
ohms.scam <- scam::scam(kohms ~ s(juice,bs="mpd"), data=fruitohms)
summary(ohms.scam)
```

```
Family: gaussian
Link function: identity

Formula:
kohms ~ s(juice, bs = "mpd")

Parametric coefficients:
            Estimate Std. Error t value Pr(>|t|)
(Intercept)    6.916      0.214    32.4   <2e-16

Approximate significance of smooth terms:
```

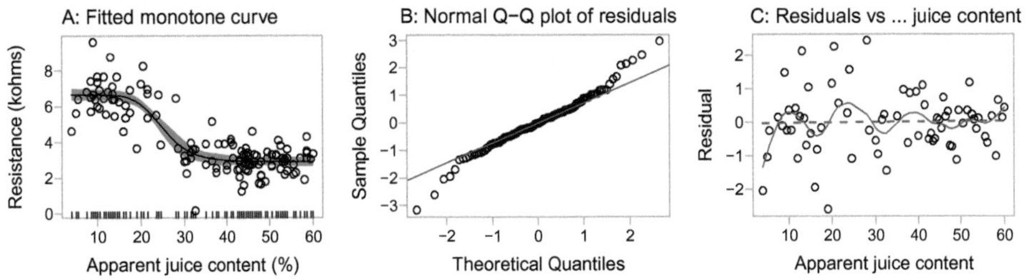

Figure 4.10 Panel A shows the fit from a monotonic decreasing spline curve, Panel B shows the normal quantile–quantile (Q-Q) plot for residuals. Panel C plots residuals against apparent juice content. The solid red line is from a smooth obtained with the default penalization, while the dashed red line is from the BIC-like penalization that had `penalty=log(nrow(fruitohms))/2`.

```
            edf Ref.df   F p-value
s(juice) 2.55    2.95 127   <2e-16

R-sq.(adj) =   0.7443    Deviance explained = 74.9%
GCV score = 0.90949   Scale est. = 0.88428    n = 128
```

Figure 4.10A shows the fitted curve. Unless there is clear evidence that the response is other than monotonic, this is the model that is likely to be preferred. A comparison using the AIC statistic favors the unconstrained fit, whereas the BIC statistic strongly favors the monotonic fit.

```
AIC(ohms.scam, ohms.tp)
```

```
BIC(ohms.scam, ohms.tp)
```

```
              df    AIC
ohms.scam  4.548  353.0
ohms.tp   10.369  347.1
```

```
              df    BIC
ohms.scam  4.548  366.0
ohms.tp   10.369  376.7
```

4.4.6 Different Smooths for Different Levels of a Factor

The dataset `MASS::whiteside` holds data that record weekly gas consumption and average external temperature at a house in south-east England for two heating seasons, one for 26 weeks before, and one for 30 weeks after, cavity-wall insulation was installed. Plots indicate that the response with temperature is not, at least for what was observed after insulation, a line or simple form of polynomial. Figure 4.11 shows weekly gas consumption as a function of external temperature, for the two time periods. The following fits the model:

```
whiteside <- MASS::whiteside
gas.gam <- gam(Gas ~ Insul+s(Temp, by=Insul), data=whiteside)
```

Specifying `by=Insul` ensures that separate curves are fitted for the two different levels of `Insul`. These smooths are centered, so that `Insul` has to be added, also, as a main effect. Summary output is:

```
summary(gas.gam)
```

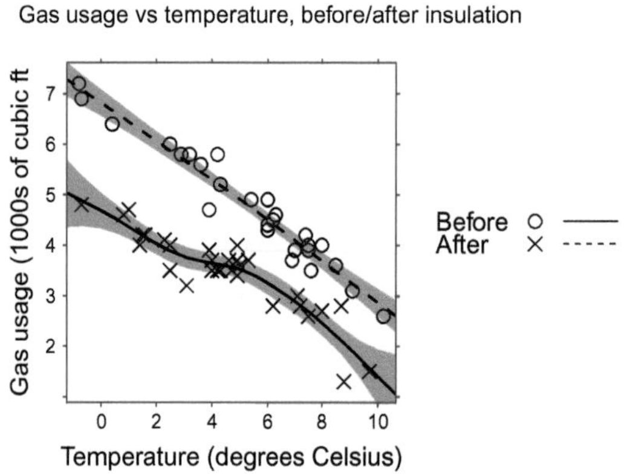

Figure 4.11 Gas consumption versus average external temperature at a house in south-east England for two heating seasons, one for 26 weeks before, and one for 30 weeks after, cavity-wall insulation was installed.

```
Family: gaussian
Link function: identity

Formula:
Gas ~ Insul + s(Temp, by = Insul)

Parametric coefficients:
             Estimate Std. Error t value Pr(>|t|)
(Intercept)    4.9394     0.0590    83.8   <2e-16
InsulAfter    -1.5650     0.0816   -19.2   <2e-16

Approximate significance of smooth terms:
                     edf Ref.df     F p-value
s(Temp):InsulBefore 1.35   1.63 228.7  <2e-16
s(Temp):InsulAfter  3.84   4.75  39.1  <2e-16

R-sq.(adj) =  0.936   Deviance explained = 94.3%
GCV = 0.10011  Scale est. = 0.087248   n = 56
```

The pattern of response with `Temp` that followed insulation shows a pattern that is different and less consistent than before insulation. This suggests influence(s) from other factor(s). Outside wind conditions may have been an issue, or there may have been changes in the amount of time spent at home. This one example, for one house and household, is generalizable only to the extent that it provides a broad indication of what insulation can achieve.

As both the "before" and "after" data appear to have been collected in successive weeks, it makes sense to check for short term sequential correlation in the residuals, perhaps using the *Box–Pierce* test thus:

```
Box.test(resid(gas.gam)[whiteside$Insul=='Before'], lag=1)
Box.test(resid(gas.gam)[whiteside$Insul=='After'], lag=1)
```

We leave the reader to verify that, at least as indicated by this test, there is no indication of sequential correlation.

4.4.7 The Remarkable Reach of mgcv and Related Packages

Chapter 5 will introduce generalized linear models (GLMs), in the first place fitted using the function `glm()` from base R. The `gam()` function has provision for fitting everything that can be handled using `glm()`, and more besides. See `?family.mgcv`. The function `gamm()` extends the range of models further, to include time series and other correlation and/or random effect error structures that are implemented in the *nlme* package.

Section 4.5 will introduce the use of functions in the `qgam` package to fit smooth quantiles of the data, using the function `s()`, in the same way as for fits using `gam()`, to set up the smooth or smooths. Smoothed quantiles of residuals from regression fits allow a much more finessed level of scrutiny in regression diagnostics than provided by quantile–quantile plots. They provide a check on whether the pattern of change of selected quantiles, as values of one or more explanatory variables change, is consistent with distributional assumptions.

Note also the function `bam()`, designed for use with large datasets, which uses as default a method that can be explicitly specified as `method="fREML"`. The function `gamm4()` in the *gamm4* package extends these abilities further, but using the *lme4* package as the underlying fitting engine in place of *nlme*.

Departures from Independence Assumptions

For data recorded in time sequence, serial correlation structures (see Chapter 6) are a common type of departure from independent errors. Where there is a sequential or spatial correlation structure in the data, the software will, if not instructed differently, try to use a smooth curve or surface to account for it. The function `gamm()` can be used to fit various alternative forms of correlation structure.

For spatial smoothing, the surface formed using `gam()` may be effective for spatial interpolation. The pattern that is thus extracted will not be reproducible under a rerun of the process – a different time or region with the same temporal or spatial correlation structure. Exercise 4.15 at the end of the chapter is designed to illustrate this point.

4.4.8 Multiple Spline Smoothing Terms – Dewpoint Data

The dataset `DAAG::dewpoint` has data on monthly averages of minimum temperature, maximum temperature, and dewpoint. For the background to these data, see Linacre (1992) and Linacre and Geerts (1997). The dewpoint is the maximum temperature at which the relative humidity reaches 100 percent. Monthly data were obtained for a number of sites worldwide. For each combination of minimum and maximum temperature the average dewpoint was then determined.

Figure 4.12 has used an additive model with two spline smoothing terms.

```
## Code
dewpoint <- DAAG::dewpoint
ds.gam <- gam(dewpt ~ s(mintemp) + s(maxtemp), data=dewpoint)
plot(ds.gam, resid=TRUE, pch=".", se=2, cex=2, fg="gray")
```

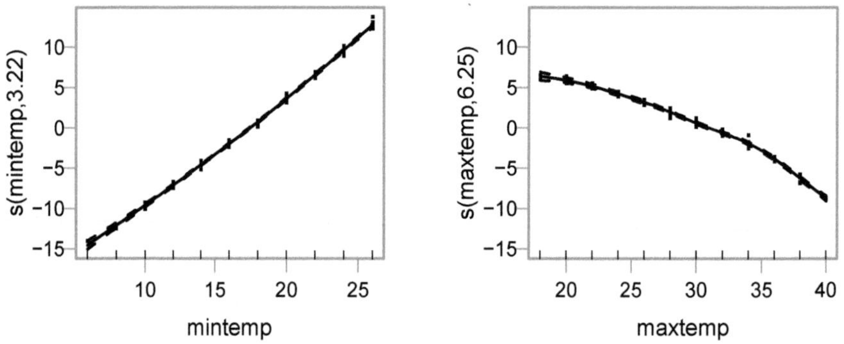

Figure 4.12 Representation of average dewpoint (**dewpt**) as the sum of an effect due to minimum temperature (**mintemp**), and an effect due to maximum temperature (**maxtemp**). (Data are from **DAAG::dewpoint**.) The dashed lines are 2SE pointwise confidence bounds.

We can write the model as

$$y = \mu + f_1(x_1) + f_2(x_2) + \varepsilon,$$

where y = **dewpt**, x_1 = **mintemp**, and x_2 = **maxtemp**. Both $f_1(x_1)$ and $f_2(x_2)$ are determined, in the model **ds.gam**, using the roughness penalty method that was described in Subsections 7.5.2 and 7.5.3.

Here μ is estimated by the mean of y, so that the estimates of $f_1(x_1)$ and $f_2(x_2)$ give differences from this overall mean. The left panel is a plot of the estimate of $f_1(x_1)$ against x_1, while the right panel plots $f_2(x_2)$ against x_2.

It is not obvious why the additive model should work so well. In general, we might expect an interaction term, that is, we might expect that $f_1(x_1)$ would be different for different values of x_2, or equivalently that $f_2(x_2)$ would be different for different values of x_1. Even where the effects are not additive, an additive model is often a good starting approximation. We can fit the additive model, and then check whether there are departures from it that require examination of the dependence of y upon x_1 and x_2 jointly.

Using Residuals as a Check for Nonadditive Effects

Figure 4.13 is designed as a coarse check on possible nonadditive effects. Plots of residuals against $x2$ = **maxtemp** are shown for each of "low," "medium," and "high" ranges of values of $x1$ = **mintemp**. (Some overlap has been allowed in the ranges.) There is no obvious indication that the pattern of the points and associated smooth changes systematically in the progression from "low" to "medium" to "high."[6]

[6]
```
library(lattice)
## Residuals vs maxtemp, for different mintemp ranges
mintempRange <- equal.count(dewpoint$mintemp, number=3)
ds.xy <- xyplot(residuals(ds.gam) ~ maxtemp|mintempRange, data=dewpoint,
                layout=c(3,1), scales=list(tck=0.5), aspect=1, cex=0.65,
```

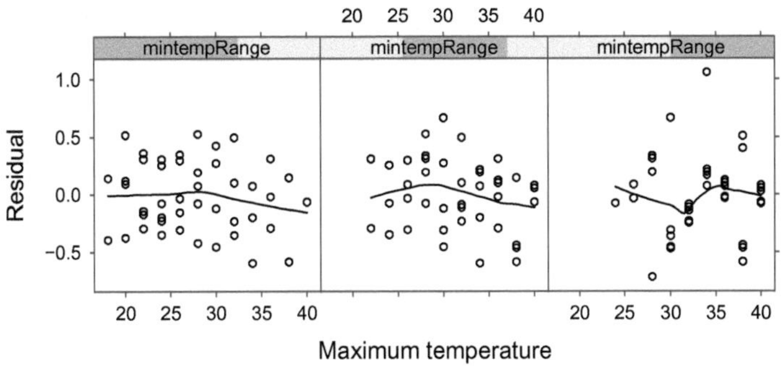

Figure 4.13 Plot of residuals versus maximum temperature, for three different ranges of values of minimum temperature. Panel strips are shaded to show the range of values of the conditioning variable.

*A Smooth Surface

A refinement of the additive model is to fit a surface, with a thin plate regression spline basis for `mintemp` and `maxtemp` jointly:

```
ds.tp <- gam(dewpt ~ s(mintemp, maxtemp), data=DAAG::dewpoint)
vis.gam(ds.tp, plot.type="contour")  # gives a contour plot of the
# fitted regression surface
vis.gam(ds.gam, plot.type="contour") # cf, model with 2 smooth terms
```

Three-dimensional perspective plots can also be obtained with the argument `plot.type="persp"`.

4.4.9* Atlantic Hurricanes That Made Landfall in the USA

Working with the dataset `hurricNamed`, Subsection 3.3.5 investigated the dependence of `deaths` on `BaseDam2014` and `LF.PressureMB`. The strategy used there led to the use of `log(BaseDam2014)` as the explanatory variable, with a power transform of `deaths` with $\lambda = -0.2$ as the outcome variable, in a regression that was linear in the transformed variables. The use of `LF.PressureMB` as a further explanatory variable added only marginal explanatory power to the model.

As a check that the linear model is adequate, the following fits smooth terms in `log(BaseDam2014)` and in `LF.PressureMB`.

```
hurricNamed <- DAAG::hurricNamed
hurricS.gam <- gam(car::yjPower(deaths, lambda=-0.2) ~
  s(log(BaseDam2014)) + s(LF.PressureMB),
  data=hurricNamed, method="ML")
anova(hurricS.gam)
```

```
Family: gaussian
Link function: identity

Formula:
car::yjPower(deaths, lambda = -0.2) ~ s(log(BaseDam2014)) +
                                      s(LF.PressureMB)

Approximate significance of smooth terms:
                    edf Ref.df     F p-value
s(log(BaseDam2014))   1      1 36.30  <2e-16
s(LF.PressureMB)      1      1  3.05   0.084
```

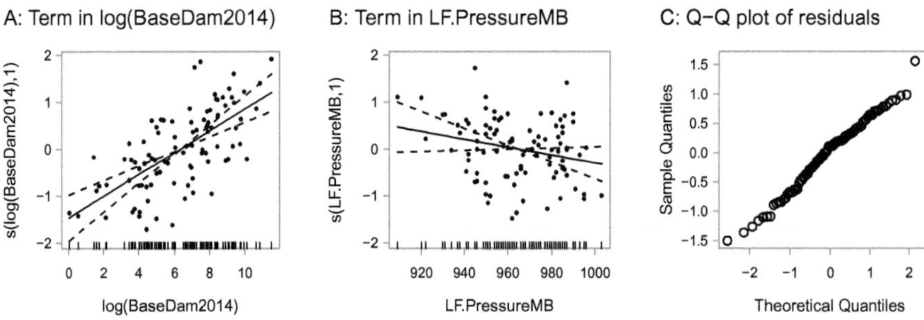

Figure 4.14 Panels A and B show the contributions of the separate terms. Panel C is a normal probability plot of residuals.

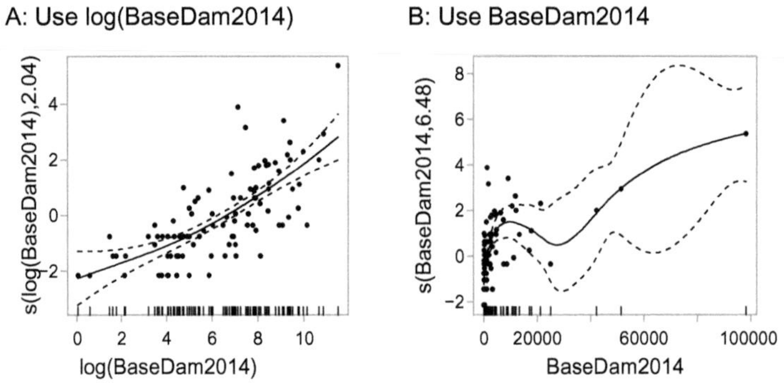

Figure 4.15 In Panel A, a logarithmic transformation removes most of the skewness in the explanatory variable. Panel B uses the untransformed variable. Fits are with the default method (`method="GCV.Cp"`). Use of `method="ML"` would give a somewhat better result for Panel B.

There is then no improvement on the model identified in Subsection 3.3.5. The p-value for the `LF.PressureMB` has increased somewhat. This is to be expected, as the model has been chosen in an analysis that allowed for a much wider range of possibilities.

Figure 4.14 shows the contributions of the separate terms, together with a normal quantile–quantile plot of residuals. The reader may care to check that the two points that stand out as outliers are for Audrey and Katrina.

Code for Figure 4.14 is:

```
plot(hurricS.gam, resid=TRUE, pch=16, cex=0.5, select=1, fg="gray")
plot(hurricS.gam, resid=TRUE, pch=16, cex=0.5, select=2, fg="gray")
qqnorm(resid(hurricS.gam), main="", fg="gray")
```

An Explanatory Variable with an Overly Long-Tailed Distribution

It is desirable to use explanatory variables with distributions that are not overly long-tailed. Figure 4.15 compares the fit from the model where a logarithmic transformation of the explanatory variable has resulted in a more symmetric distribution with a fit that uses the untransformed variable.

Here, `log(deaths+1)` will be used as the outcome variable. The change from a power transform of `deaths` with $\lambda = -0.2$ to use of `log(deaths+1)` as the explanatory variable means that we no longer expect a linear relationship with `log(BaseDam2014)`. The models are:

```
hurricSlog1.gam <- gam(log(deaths+1) ~ s(log(BaseDam2014)), data=hurricNamed)
hurricSlog2.gam <- gam(log(deaths+1) ~ s(BaseDam2014), data=hurricNamed)
```

The footnote has code for the plots.[7]

In Panel B, relatively few data points occupy a large part of the range on the right. The basis curves give undue attention to this part of the range. The accidents of what sampling variation may have done to these few points strongly affects the calculated roughness penalty. A distribution of data values that is strongly skewed calls for prior use of a transformation that will alleviate the skewness.

In general, fits with `method="ML"` are preferred. The default `method="GCV.Cp"` is faster, and a useful recourse with models that take a long time to run, but may give a less dependable result.

4.4.10 Other Smoothing Methods

As we have seen, simple forms of smooth can be handled by incorporating low degrees of freedom spline terms into a model that can be fitted using `lm()`. More general forms of spline smooth require the use of a relatively high degrees of freedom spline basis, with a penalty term then added to the residual sum of squares to prevent over-fitting.

The discussion will now move to methods that use a sequence of local fits to generate the overall fit. Note first locally weighted regression methods, implemented in different ways and with different functionality in the R functions `lowess()` and `loess()`. The method is *local*, in the sense that the fitted value $m(x)$ at a point x uses only the data within a specified neighborhood of x, with weights that reduce as the distance from x increases. The fitting process uses an iterative method, with the residual at the previous iteration determining the weight at the current iteration. Figure 3.14 is one of several examples of its use that appear elsewhere in this text.

By contrast with `lowess()`, which can only fit curves, `loess()` can fit surfaces as well as curves. It takes up to four numerical predictors. The default for `loess()` is a nonresistant smooth; for a resistant smooth, specify `family=symmetric`. Pointwise confidence bounds can be obtained from a fitted `loess` object. See `?predict.loess`.

Kernel smoothing methods further widen the range of possibilities for estimating a function $g(x)$. These are weighted polynomial regression methods with a model matrix centered at each point x where the estimated value of $g(x)$ is to be evaluated. For more information, see the help page `?KernSmooth::locpoly()`.

On lowess smoothing, see Cleveland (1981). Venables and Ripley (2002) have a useful brief discussion of smoothing methods. Fan and Gijbels (1996) discuss kernel smoothing, splines, and lowess.

[7]
```
plot(hurricSlog1.gam, resid=TRUE, pch=16, cex=0.5, adj=0, fg="gray")
plot(hurricSlog2.gam, resid=TRUE, pch=16, cex=0.5, fg="gray")
```

4.5 * Quantile Regression

Working with a linear model framework, the discussion has until now focused almost exclusively on models for the expected value or mean of the response variable as a function of (or conditioned on) one or more covariates. Models for the quantiles of the response (for example, 25 percent or lower quartile, median, 75 percent or upper quartile) are a further important and useful extension of the linear model framework. Here, we take a look at the interesting possibilities offered by the *qgam* package (Fasiolo et al., 2021).

2020 World Bank Data on Fertility and Life Expectancy

There is a close correlation, across countries, between fertility rate (number of children born per female) and life expectancy. Figure 4.16, from 2020 World Bank data on fertility and life expectancy, is designed to explore the connection.[8] The same drivers that lead to smaller family sizes lead also, it appears, to higher life expectancies.

Both in Panel A and in Panel B, a logarithmic scale has been used, in order to spread fertility rate values out more evenly. Degrees of freedom for the fitted smooth curve were chosen automatically. In Panel A, 2 SE bounds either side of the fitted curve have been added. Panel B shows the fitted curves, without standard error bounds, for 10 percent and 90 percent as well as for the 50 percent quantile. The function `qgam::qgam()` fits one quantile at a time, while the function `qgam::mqgam()` is designed to fit several quantiles with the one function call.

```
load("wdi.RData") # Needs `wdi.RData` in working directory; see footnote
library(qgam)
wdi[, "ppop"] <- with(wdi, population/sum(population))
wdi[,"logFert"] <- log(wdi[,"FertilityRate"])
form <- LifeExpectancy ~ s(logFert)
## Panel A model
fit.qgam <- qgam(form, data=wdi, qu=.5)
```

```
Estimating learning rate. Each dot corresponds to a loss evaluation.
qu = 0.5........done
```

```
## Panel B: Multiple (10%, 90% quantiles; unweighted, then weighted
fit19.mqgam <- mqgam(form, data=wdi, qu=c(.1,.9))
```

```
Estimating learning rate. Each dot corresponds to a loss evaluation.
qu = 0.1............done
qu = 0.9.........done
```

```
wtd19.mqgam <- mqgam(form, data=wdi, qu=c(.1,.9),
                     argGam=list(weights=wdi[["ppop"]]))
```

```
Estimating learning rate. Each dot corresponds to a loss evaluation.
qu = 0.1........................done
qu = 0.9............done
```

[8] Note that data collated by other agencies may differ somewhat from the World Bank data.

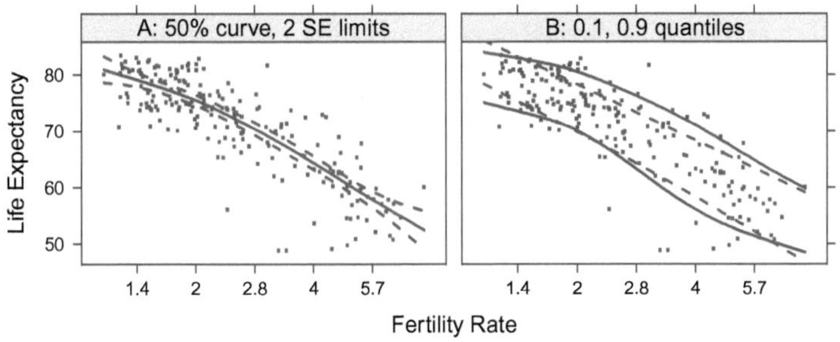

Figure 4.16 Panel A shows a fitted 50 percent quantile curve, with 2 SE bounds added. Panel B shows fitted 10 percent and 90 percent quantile curves. In both panels, a logarithmic scale has been used on the x-axis. Solid curves are for unweighted fits, while dashed curves are from weighting by population.

For the solid curves, all countries were given equal weight, while the dashed curves were from use of populations as weights, that is, each fertility rate was in effect repeated by the number in the population when calculating the quantile. The four largest populations and fertility rates were:

```
               China India United States Indonesia
billions        1.35  1.26          0.31      0.25
FertilityRate   1.55  2.51          1.88      2.50
LifeExpectancy 75.39 67.29         78.74     68.52
```

The population sizes of around 1.4 billion each for China and India are more than four times those of any other country. For a fertility rate close to 2, China's life expectancy will strongly weight the calculation for all three quantiles, while for a fertility rate close to 3, India's life expectancy will strongly weight the calculation. A consequence is that the quantiles from a weighted fit are quite different if the regression is on `FertilityRate` instead of `logFert`. For this dataset, the quantiles from the unweighted fit make better sense.

The footnote has code that, with a live internet connection, can be used to download the data.[9] Code for fitting the models for the quantiles is:

```
load("wdi.RData") # Needs `wdi.RData` in working directory; see footnote
library(qgam)
wdi[, "ppop"] <- with(wdi, population/sum(population))
wdi[,"logFert"] <- log(wdi[,"FertilityRate"])
form <- LifeExpectancy ~ s(logFert)
## Panel A model
fit.qgam <- qgam(form, data=wdi, qu=.5)
## Panel B: Multiple (10%, 90% quantiles; unweighted, then weighted
```

[9]
```
## If necessary, install the 'WDI' package & download data
inds <- c('SP.DYN.TFRT.IN','SP.DYN.LE00.IN', 'SP.POP.TOTL')
indnams <- c("FertilityRate", "LifeExpectancy", "population")
wdi2020 <- WDI::WDI(country="all", indicator=inds, start=2020, end=2020,
                    extra=TRUE)
wdi2020 <- na.omit(droplevels(subset(wdi2020, !region %in% "Aggregates")))
wdi <- setNames(wdi[order(wdi[, inds[1]]),inds], indnams)
save(wdi, file="wdi.RData")
```

```
fit19.mqgam <- mqgam(form, data=wdi, qu=c(.1,.9))
wtd19.mqgam <- mqgam(form, data=wdi, qu=c(.1,.9),
                     argGam=list(weights=wdi[["ppop"]]))
```

Plots for the individual quantiles, using base graphics rather than *lattice* and *latticeExtra* as in Figure 4.16, can be obtained thus:

```
## Panel A
plot(fit.qgam, shift=mean(predict(fit.qgam)))
## Panel B, 10% quantile
fitm10 <- qdo(fit19.mqgam, qu=0.1)
plot(fitm10, resid=T, shift=mean(predict(fitm10)),
    ylim=range(wdi$LifeExpectancy), cex=2)
wfitm10 <- qdo(wtd19.mqgam, qu=0.1)
plot(wfitm10, resid=T, shift=mean(predict(wfitm10)),
    ylim=range(wdi$LifeExpectancy), cex=2)
```

4.6 Further Reading and Remarks

On the design of experiments, and associated data analysis, see Cox (1958) and Cox and Reid (2000). Chapter 7 will extend the discussion in the present chapter.

Wood's website has extensive tutorial and explanatory material; help pages for functions in the *mgcv* package, and references given therein, should be consulted for more detailed explanatory information. Wood (2017) is the definitive reference for the *mgcv* package. It has extensive coverage of linear models and generalized linear models, then proceeding to an account of generalized additive models and generalized additive mixed models that has regard to a wide choice of spline bases. Later chapters make strong technical demands. The package *mgcViz* has extensive visualization functions for use with generalized additive models. Accompanying vignettes give detailed instructions on the use of the functions that are included.

Eubank (1999) gives a comprehensive and readable introduction to the use of spline smooths. Maindonald (1984) has an elementary introduction to B-splines, starting with piecewise linear functions. Faraway (2016) is a wide-ranging and practically oriented account that starts with generalized linear models.

Note the *gam* package (not to be confused with the `gam()` function in *mgcv*), which is for some purposes an alternative to *mgcv*. For brief comments on the comparison between the two packages, type `?mgcv::gam` and see under "Details."

4.7 Exercises

4.1. Reanalyze the sugar weight data of Subsection 4.1.1 using `log(weight)` in place of `weight`. Which model should be preferred, and why?

4.2. Use `anova()` to compare the two models:

```
roller.lm <- lm(depression~weight, data=roller)
roller.lm2 <- lm(depression~weight+I(weight^2), data=roller)
```

Is there any justification for including the squared term?

4.3. For each of the datasets `DAAG::elastic1` and `DAAG::elastic2`, determine the regression of `stretch` on `distance`. Use the method of Section 4.3 to compare, formally, the two regression lines.

4.4. The data frame `toycars` consists of 27 observations on the distance (in meters) traveled by one of three different toy cars on a smooth surface, starting from rest at the top of a 16-inch-long ramp tilted at varying angles (measured in degrees). Because of differing frictional effects for the three different cars, we seek three regression lines that relate distance traveled to angle. Start by plotting the data:

```
toycars <- DAAG::toycars
lattice::xyplot(distance ~ angle, groups=factor(car), type=c('p','r'),
                data=toycars, auto.key=list(columns=3))
```

a. Fit the following models:

```
parLines.lm <- lm(distance ~ 0+factor(car)+angle, data=toycars)
sepLines.lm <- lm(distance ~ factor(car)/angle, data=toycars)
```

Compare the AIC statistics for the two models. Examine the diagnostic plots carefully. Is there a systematic pattern of departure from linear relationships?

b. Fit the model

```
sepPol3.lm <- lm(distance ~ factor(car)/angle+poly(angle,3)[,2:3], data=toycars)
```

Compare the AIC statistics with those for the two models that fitted straight line relationships. Compare the diagnostic plots, with the diagnostic plots for one or other of the straight line models.

c. Repeat the comparison using the code:

```
sapply(list(parLines.lm, sepLines.lm, sepPol3.lm), AICcmodavg::AICc)
```

Comment on the result.

d. A plausible physical model suggests that the three lines should have the same intercept (close to 0), and possibly differing slopes, where the slopes are inversely related to the coefficient of dynamic friction for each car. Is that consistent from what is apparent here? Comment.

e. Extract the adjusted R^2 statistics for the three models

```
setNames(sapply(list(parLines.lm, sepLines.lm, sepPol3.lm),
  function(x)summary(x)$adj.r.squared), c("parLines","sepLines","sepPol3"))
```

Repeat for R^2. This illustrates why neither of these statistics should be taken too seriously. In neither case does maximizing the statistic give the best model!

4.5. The data frame `cuckoos` holds data on the lengths and breadths of eggs of cuckoos, found in the nests of six different species of host birds. Fit models for the regression of length on breadth that have:

a. a single line for all six species,
b. different parallel lines for the different host species,
c. separate lines for the separate host species.

Use the `anova()` function to print out the sequential analysis of variance table. Which of the three models is preferred? Print out the diagnostic plots for this model. Do they show anything worthy of note? Examine the output coefficients from this model carefully, and decide whether the results seem grouped by host species. How might the results be summarized for reporting purposes?

4.6. Fit the three models (a), (b), and (c) from the previous exercise, but now using the robust regression function `rlm()` from the *MASS* package. Do the diagnostic plots look any different from those from the output from `lm()`? Is there any substantial change in the regression coefficients?

4.7. *Compare the two results

```
seedrates.lm <- lm(grain ~ rate + I(rate^2), data=seedrates)
seedrates.pol <- lm(grain ~ poly(rate,2), data=seedrates)
```

Check that the fitted values and residuals from the two calculations are the same, and that the t-statistic and p-value are the same for the coefficient labeled `poly(rate, 2)` in the polynomial regression as for the coefficient labeled `I(rate^2)` in the regression on `rate` and `rate^2`.
Check that replacing `rate + I(rate^2)` by `poly(rate, 2, raw=TRUE)` in the calculation of `seedrates.lm` leaves the coefficients unchanged.
Regress the second column of `model.matrix(seedrates.pol)` on `rate` and `I(rate2̂)`, and similarly for the third column of `model.matrix(seedrates.pol)`. Hence, express the first and second orthogonal polynomial terms as functions of `rate` and `rate^2`.

4.8. The `DAAG::wages1833` data frame holds data on the wages of Lancashire cotton factory workers in 1833. Plot male wages against age and fit a smooth curve. Repeat using the numbers of male workers as weights. Do the two curves seem noticeably different? Repeat the exercise for female workers. (See Boot and Maindonald (2008) for background information on these data.)

4.9. Clutton-Brock et al. (1999), in a study conducted in the Kalahari Gemsbok Park in South Africa, recorded the time that adult meerkats spent on guarding for different sizes of group. Approximate percentages, read off from a graph, were:
Group size 1:50,47; 2:26; 3:26; 4:24,23; 5:19; 6:13; 7:3.
Model the percentage of time as a function of group size.

4.10. The seismic timing data in the data frame `geophones` gives measured thicknesses of a layer of Alberta substratum as measured by a line of geophones.

a. Fit the model:

```
geo.gam <- gam(thickness ~ s(distance), data=DAAG::geophones)
```

Use `plot()` with `resid=T` and perhaps `pch=1` to show the fit. Examine the diagnostic information given by `gam.check()`. Is the default `k=10` set large enough?

b. Use `scam::scam()`, with smoothing term `s(distance, bs="mpd")`, to fit a monotonic decreasing smooth to the `DAAG::geophones` data. Use `plot()`, as in Item a, to show the fit.

Use `AIC()` to compare the models from items (a) and (b). Which model appears best? Compare also the GCV scores (smaller is better) and the scale estimates. Is this a context to which the large sample properties of the AIC statistic are relevant? What is the relevant n/p ratio? (Check back to Figure 3.17 in Subsection 3.5.1.)

4.11. Use the functions `acf()` and `Box.test()` to check residuals from the GAM model for a sequential correlation with distance:

```
plot(DAAG::geophones$distance, acf(resid(geo.gam), lag.max=55)$acf)
Box.test(resid(geo.gam), lag=10)
Box.test(resid(geo.gam), lag=20)
Box.test(resid(geo.gam), lag=20, type="Ljung")
```

As often, what one sees depends on what one looks for! The initial plot shows a very clear pattern of spatial linear correlation.

4.12. Apply `lowess()` to the `geophones` data in the previous two exercises. You will need to experiment with the `f` argument, since the default value oversmooths this data. Small values of `f` (less than 0.2) give a very rough plot, while larger values give a smoother plot. A value of about 0.25 seems a good compromise.

4.13. In the data frame `worldRecords` (*DAAG*): (i) Fit `log(Time)` as a linear function of `log(Distance)`; (ii) fit `log(Time)` as a polynomial of degree 4 in `log(Distance)`; (iii) fit `log(Time)` as a natural spline function of degree 4 in `log(Distance)`.

a. Use `anova()` to compare the fits (i) and (ii).
b. Compare the R^2 statistics from the fits (i), (ii), and (iii). Do they convey useful information about the adequacy of the models?
c. For each of (i), (ii), and (iii), plot residuals against $\log(Distance)$. Which model best accounts for the pattern of change of time with $\log(Distance)$? For what range(s) of distances does there seem, for all three models, to be some apparent residual bias?

4.14. The `ozone` data frame holds data, for nine months only, on ozone levels at the Halley Bay station between 1956 and 2000. (See Christie (2000) and Shanklin (2001) for the scientific background.) Up-to-date data are available from the website given under `?DAAG::ozone`. Replace zeros by missing values. Determine, for each month, the number of missing values. Plot the October levels against Year, and fit a smooth curve. At what point is clear evidence of a decline apparent? Plot the data for other months and examine whether they show a similar pattern of decline.

4.15. *The following fits a `gam` model to data that have a strong sequential correlation:

```
library(mgcv)
xy <- data.frame(x=1:200, y=arima.sim(list(ar=0.75), n=200))
df.gam <- gam(y ~ s(x), data=xy)
plot(df.gam, residuals=TRUE)
```

a. Run the code several times. (Be sure, on each occasion, to simulate a new data frame `xy`.) Is the function `gam()` over-fitting? What is over-fitting in this context? Compare with the result from rerunning the code with `ar=0`.
b. Repeat, now with `ar=-0.75` in the code that generates the sequentially correlated series. Why is the result so different? (See Section 6.1 for the relevant time series concepts.)

4.16. The following fits the same **gam** model as in Subsection 4.4.4, then converting it into a **gamViz** object and creating a plot equivalent to Figure 4.11:

```
library(mgcViz)
ohms.tpBIC <- gam(kohms ~ s(juice, bs="tp"), data=fruitohms,
                 gamma=log(nrow(fruitohms))/2, method="REML")
ohms.gamViz <- mgcViz::getViz(ohms.tpBIC)  # Convert to a `gamViz` object
gl <- plot(sm(ohms.gamViz, 1)) # Graphics object for term 1 (of 1)
gl + l_fitLine(colour = "red") + l_rug(mapping = aes(x=x, y=y), alpha = 0.4) +
  l_ciLine(mul = 2, colour = "blue", linetype = 2) +  # Multiply SE by `mul`
  l_points(shape = 19, size = 1, alpha = 0.5)
```

a. The following does 20 simulations of data from the fitted model and fits one smooth curve for each simulation:

```
plot(sm(ohms.gamViz, 1), nsim = 20) + l_ciLine() + l_fitLine() + l_simLine()
```

What does this indicate for the higher levels of juice content (more than perhaps 50 percent)? What is gained and what is lost by leaving out the points and showing the fits to the simulated data?

b. Repeat the simulations of fits to data simulated from the fitted model, for the **whiteside** data of Figure 4.11 in Subsection 4.4.6:

```
gam(Gas ~ Insul+s(Temp, by=Insul), data=MASS::whiteside) |>
  getViz() -> gas.gamViz
plot(sm(gas.gamViz,1), nsim = 20) + l_ciLine() + l_fitLine() + l_simLine()
```

Repeat with `sm(gas.gamViz,1)` as the first argument to `plot()`. Again, what is gained and what is lost relative to Figure 4.11?

5

Generalized Linear Models, and Survival Analysis

Generalized linear models (GLMs), introduced in the 1970s, give a unified theoretical and computational approach to models that had previously been treated as distinct. They have been a powerful addition to the data analyst's armory of statistical tools.

The present chapter will limit attention to a few important special cases but also extending the discussion beyond models that fit strictly within the generalized linear model framework as implemented by R's `glm()` function. Note in particular the abilities implemented using the *mgcv* `gam()` and related functions. These are able to handle everything handled by `glm()`, and much more besides. Use will be made also of abilities in the *gamlss* package, which include helpful diagnostic plots.

The chapter ends with a discussion of survival models, a methodology which has a strong theoretical connection with that of generalized linear models but which has features that necessitate a different approach.

5.1 Generalized Linear Models

Section 2.5 introduced the linear regression model

$$y = \alpha + \beta x + \varepsilon,$$

where y is the outcome or response variable, x is a covariate or explanatory variable, and ε represents random or chance variation in the response y. Under the linear model assumptions, ε follow a mean-zero (approximately) normal distribution, so for a fixed value of x, the outcome variable also has a normal distribution but with expected value

$$\mathrm{E}[y] = \alpha + \beta x.$$

GLMs allow distributions for y other than the normal, and they allow for certain types of nonlinear relationship between $E[y]$ and any covariate(s). Logistic regression models which have a binomial-distributed outcome variable are perhaps the most widely used GLMs.

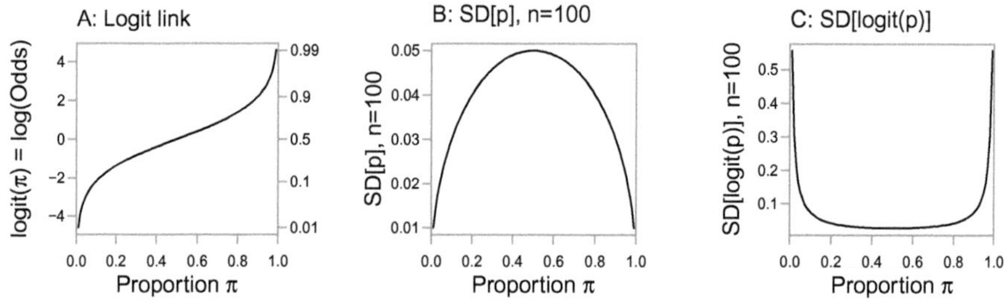

Figure 5.1 Panel A plots $\text{logit}(\pi)$ against proportion π, as for the logit link function. Notice how the range on the vertical axis is stretched out at both ends. Panel B shows how, for samples of size $n = 100$ from a binomial distribution with probability π, the standard deviation of p changes as the expected value of p varies between 0.01 and 0.99. Panel C shows how the standard deviation $\text{SD}[p]$ from Panel B translates to the logit scale of the linear predictor.

5.1.1 Linking the Expected Value to the Covariate

GLMs require the specification of a transformation $f()$, the *link function*, such that $f(\text{E}[y])$ is linearly related to the covariate (or, more generally, covariates). Thus,

$$f\,(\text{E}[y]) = \alpha + \beta x;\ \text{E}[y] = g(\alpha + \beta x), \text{ where } g() \text{ is the inverse link.}$$

The expression $\alpha + \beta x$ is referred to as the *linear predictor*. The link function $f()$ transforms from the scale of the response to the scale of the linear predictor.

Consider the `logit` link, used when y is the number of *successes* in a binomial distribution with *size* n. Setting $\pi = \text{E}[y]/n$,

$$f(\text{E}[y]) = \text{logit}(\pi) = \log\left(\frac{\pi}{1-\pi}\right), \quad \text{with inverse link } g(\ell) = \frac{\exp(\ell)}{1+\exp(\ell)}.$$

Figure 5.1A, shows the logit() link function for logistic regression.[1] Panel B shows how, for samples of size $n = 100$ from a binomial distribution with probability π, the standard deviation of p changes as π (the expected value of p) varies between 0.01 and 0.99. Panel C shows how the standard deviation $\text{SD}[p]$ from Panel B translates to the logit scale of the linear predictor. Observe the change from an upside-down U shape to a U shape.

Other widely used link functions are: $f(x) = x$, $f(x) = 1/x$, $f(x) = \log(x)$, and $f(x) = \text{sqrt}(x) = \sqrt{x}$. Observe that these functions (and their inverses) are all monotonic, that is, they increase or (in the case of $1/x$) decrease with increasing values of x.

[1]
```
## Simplified plot showing the logit link function
p <- (1:39)/40
logitp <- log(p/(1 - p))
plot(p, logitp, xlab = "Proportion", ylab = "logit(p)", type = "l", pch = 1)
```

5.1.2 Noise Terms Need Not Be Normal

Given

$$y = \mathrm{E}[y] + \varepsilon, \text{ where } f(\mathrm{E}[y]) = \alpha + \beta x,$$

the elements of y may have a distribution different from the normal. Common distributions are the binomial, where y is the number responding out of a given total n, and the Poisson, where y is a count. Recall that these distributions were discussed in Subsection 1.4.1.

5.1.3* Variation That Is Greater Than Binomial or Poisson

For use of *quasi* models, the model is fitted as for a binomial or Poisson model, but the theoretical binomial or Poisson variance estimates are replaced by a variance that is estimated from the residuals from the fitted model. The name *dispersion* is used in the help pages for modeling that uses the function `glm()`, for the factor Φ by which the theoretical binomial or Poisson variance is multiplied. Elsewhere in this text, in the context of specific models for extra-binomial and extra-Poisson variation, Φ is referred to as a dispersion index.

A widely implemented distributional form that accounts for extra-binomial variance is the betabinomial, introduced earlier in Subsection 2.3.2. The most widely used specific distributional form that accounts for extra-Poisson variation is the negative binomial. For details of implementations, and of several alternatives, see `?gamlss.dist::gamlss.family`, `?glmmTMB::family_glmmTMB`, and `?VGAM` (search for "Distribution").

For data with a 0/1 response, neither the `quasibinomial` nor the betabinomial or other such model is relevant, unless the 0/1 responses can be grouped to give repeated x out of n sets of results. With a 0/1 response, the residual deviance is a function of the fitted parameters, and gives no information on Φ. See McCullagh and Nelder (1989, section 4.5.1).

Least Squares versus Logistic Regression

Table 5.1 relates terminology used for logistic regression to that for least squares regression. The comparison extends to models that use other link functions. The deviance has a role very similar to that of the sum of squares about fitted values in least squares regression. For data are normally distributed, the two quantities are equivalent.

5.1.4 Log Odds in Contingency Tables

With proportions that range from less than 0.1 to greater than 0.9, it is not reasonable to expect that the expected proportion will be a linear function of x. A link function such as the logit is required. A good way to think about logit models is that they work on a log(odds) scale. If p is a probability (e.g., that horse A will

Table 5.1 *Terminology used for logistic regression (or more generally for generalized linear models), compared with normal theory linear model terminology.*

Regression	Logistic regression
Degrees of freedom	Degrees of freedom
Sum of squares (SS)	Deviance (D)
Mean sum of squares (divide by degrees of freedom)	Mean deviance (divide by degrees of freedom)
Fit models by minimizing the residual sum of squares.	Fit models by use of iteratively weighted least squares to minimize the deviance.

win the race), then the corresponding odds are $p/(1-p)$, and

$$\log(\text{odds}) = \log(p/(1-p)) = \log(p) - \log(1-p).$$

Logistic regression provides a framework for analyzing contingency table data. In the fictitious admissions data presented in Exercise 2.3 in Section 2.12, the observed proportion of students (male and female) admitted into Engineering was $40/80 = 0.5$. For Sociology, the admission proportion was $15/60 = 0.25$. Thus:

$$\log(\text{odds}) = \log(0.5/0.5) = 0 \text{ for Engineering,}$$
$$\log(\text{odds}) = \log(0.75/0.25) = 1.0986 \text{ for Sociology.}$$

Using logistic regression, log(odds of admission) to either department can be modeled as a function of any explanatory variable(s) for which data are available.

For such data, we may write

$$\log(\text{odds}) = \text{constant} + \text{effect due to faculty} + \text{effect due to gender}.$$

This now has the form of a linear model.

5.1.5 Logistic Regression with a Continuous Explanatory Variable

The likelihood is the joint probability of the observed data values, given the model parameters. The deviance is minus twice the logarithm of the likelihood. Maximizing the likelihood is equivalent to minimizing the *deviance*.

The data frame `DAAG::anesthetic` has the data for the example that now follows. Thirty patients were given an anesthetic agent that was maintained at a predetermined (alveolar) concentration for 15 minutes before a surgical incision was made. It was then noted whether the patient moved, that is, jerked or twisted. The interest is in estimating how the probability of jerking or twisting varies with increasing concentration of the anesthetic agent.

We take the response as `nomove`, because the proportion then increases with increasing concentration. The totals and proportions, for each of the six concentrations, can be calculated thus:

```
anestot <- aggregate(DAAG::anesthetic[, c("move","nomove")],
by=list(conc=DAAG::anesthetic$conc), FUN=sum)
## The column 'conc', because from the 'by' list, is then a factor.
```

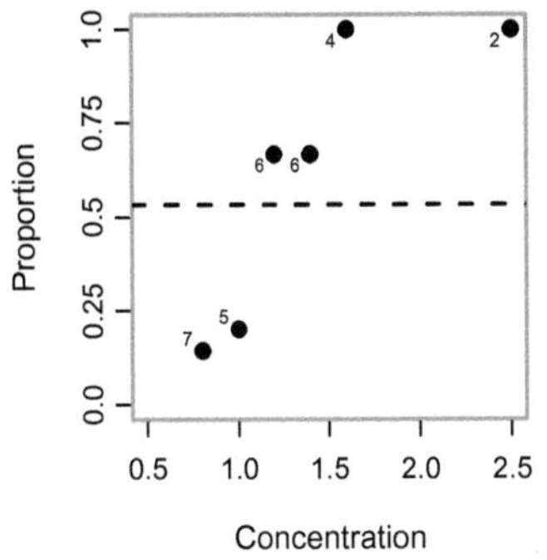

	Value of nomove		
conc	0 (move)	1 (no move)	prop
0.8	6	1	0.17
1	4	1	0.20
1.2	2	4	0.67
1.4	2	4	0.67
1.6	0	4	1.00
2.5	0	2	1.00

Figure 5.2 Plot, versus concentration, of proportion of patients not moving, for each of six different alveolar concentrations. The horizontal line is the proportion of no-moves over the data as a whole. Data are displayed to the right of the plot.

```
## The next line recovers the numeric values
anestot$conc <- as.numeric(as.character(anestot[["conc"]]))
anestot$total <- apply(anestot[, c("move","nomove")], 1 , sum)
anestot$prop <- anestot$nomove/anestot$total
```

Figure 5.2 plots the proportions. The table that is shown to the right of Figure 5.2 gives the information in the data frame `anestot` that has just been calculated. It gives, for each concentration, the respective numbers with `nomove` equal to 0 (i.e., movement) and `nomove` equal to 1 (i.e., no movement).

We can fit the logit model either directly to the binary outcome data, or to the proportions in the table that appears to the right of Figure 5.2:

```
## Fit model directly to the 0/1 data in nomove
anes.glm <- glm(nomove ~ conc, family=binomial(link="logit"),
                data=DAAG::anesthetic)
## Fit model to the proportions; supply total numbers as weights
anes1.logit <- glm(prop ~ conc, family=binomial(link="logit"),
weights=total, data=anestot)
```

The analysis assumes that individuals respond independently with a probability, estimated from the data, that on a log odds scale is a linear function of the concentration. For any fixed concentration, the assumption is that we have Bernoulli trials, namely, that individual binary responses are drawn at random from the same population. Figure 5.3 is a graphical summary. Given the small sample size, a convincing check of model adequacy is not possible.

A condensed version of output from use of `summary()` is:

```
Coefficients:
            Estimate Std. Error z value Pr(>|z|)
(Intercept)    -6.47       2.42   -2.67   0.0075
conc            5.57       2.04    2.72   0.0064

(Dispersion parameter for binomial family taken to be 1)

    Null deviance: 41.455  on 29  degrees of freedom
Residual deviance: 27.754  on 28  degrees of freedom
```

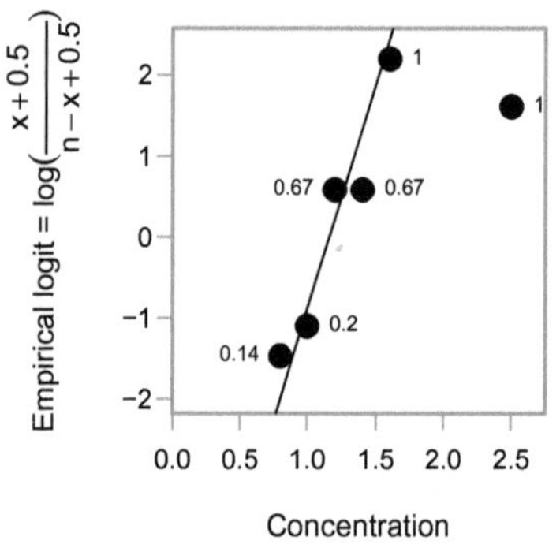

Figure 5.3 With x = number not moving, and n as the total, the empirical log(odds) has been calculated as $\log\left(\frac{x+0.5}{n-x+0.5}\right)$, which is then plotted against concentration. Labels on the points show the observed proportions. Notice that the transformation from $\frac{x}{n}$ to $\frac{x+0.5}{n-x+0.5}$ changes the order from that for the untransformed proportions. The line gives an estimate of the proportion of moves, based on the fitted logit (or log(odds)) model.

A Note on Model Output

An iterative procedure is used to fit the model, with no more than five or six iterations usually required. The default, for the *DAAG* function `sumry()`, is to print this information only if the number exceeds 10, hinting at a possible problem in fitting the model.

Output choices that are available using the function `summary()` are:

```
## Get coefficients, SEs, and associated statistics, specify:
print(coef(summary(anes.glm)), digits=2)
## Get full default output
summary(anes.glm, digits=2)
```

5.2 Logistic Multiple Regression

We now consider data on the distribution of the Southern Corroboree frog, that occurs in the Snowy Mountains area of New South Wales, Australia (data are from Hunter, 2000). In all, 212 sites were surveyed. In Figure 5.4, points for sites where frogs were found have been filled and over-plotted with a white "+".

The following extracts the data:

```
frogs <- DAAG::frogs
```

The variables are `pres.abs` (were frogs found?), `altitude` (in meters), `distance` (distance in meters to the nearest extant population), `easting` and `northing` (location reference), `NoOfPools` (number of potential breeding pools), `NoOfSites` (number of potential breeding sites within a 2 km radius), `avrain` (mean rainfall for Spring period), `meanmin` (mean minimum Spring temperature), and `meanmax` (mean maximum Spring temperature).

A first step is to check relationships among explanatory variables, where transforming makes sense so that those relationships are close to linear. If we can so

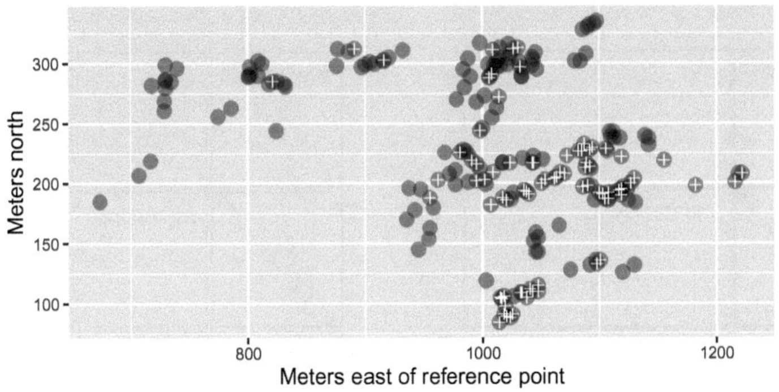

Figure 5.4 Location of sites, relative to reference point, that were examined for frogs. The sites are all in the Snowy Mountains region of New South Wales, Australia. Points for sites where frogs were found have been over-plotted with a white "+".

transform the variables, this gives, as noted earlier in connection with classical multiple regression, access to a theory that can be highly helpful in guiding the process of regression modeling.

An aim is to explain frog distribution as a function of the other variables. Because we are working within a quite restricted geographic area, we do not expect that the distribution will change as a function of latitude and longitude *per se*, so that `easting` and `northing` will not be used as explanatory variables. They have the potential to be important for accounting for spatial correlation. Figure 5.5A shows an initial plot for the untransformed variables:

```
## Pairs plot; frogs data
car::spm(~distance+NoOfPools+NoOfSites+avrain+altitude+meanmin+meanmax,
         data=frogs, regLine=FALSE, lwd=0.5,
         smooth=list(spread=FALSE, col.smooth='red', lwd.smooth=1))
```

The plot shows a very high correlation between the variables `altitude`, `meanmin`, and `minmax`. Figure 5.6, which appears later, has the relevant panels. In that figure, some variables other than the three noted have been transformed.

The high correlation between `meanmin` and `meanmax` is readily dealt with by using, instead, the variables `maxSubmin` = `meanmax-meanmin` and `maxAddmin` = `meanmax+meanmin`. Differences between minimum and maximum temperature do not to any large extent change with changes in the overall average. We have then:

```
frogs <- within(frogs, {maxSubmin <- meanmax-meanmin
                        maxAddmin <- meanmax+meanmin})
```

The two panels in Figure 5.5 show the difference that the change of variables makes.

The reductions in correlation between `maxSubmin` and the other two variables, while it appears small, has large implication for the effect on the variance inflation factor, with major implications for understanding how variables and factors in the regression drive the response.

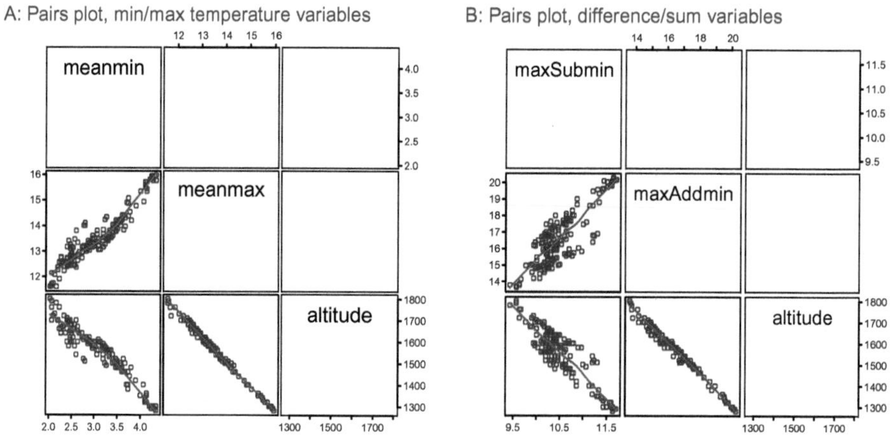

Figure 5.5 Panel A shows the scatterplot matrix for the three variables **meanmin** **meanmax** and **altitude**. Panel B shows the scatterplot matrices for **maxAddmin** = **meanmax+meanmin**, textttmaxSubmin = **meanmax-meanmin** and **altitude**.

Implications for the Variance Inflation Factor

The variance inflation factor (VIF) for `altitude` and for `maxAddmin` will be at least $(1 - 0.9933^2)^{-1} \simeq 74.9$ (the squared correlation between, e.g., `altitude`, and any one other explanatory variable, is a lower bound for the squared multiple correlation with all other explanatory variables). Inclusion of both of these as explanatory variables would result in such large standard errors for their coefficients that the estimated values are meaningless. The variable `altitude` will then at this point be omitted, but later checking the effect of replacing `maxAddmin` by `altitude` on the AIC statistic.

With both `meanmin` and `meanmax` included as explanatory variables, the VIF for their coefficients will be at least $(1-0.946^2){-}1 = 9.5$. The reduction to $(1-0.873^2)$ $= 4.2$ when these are replaced by `maxSubmin` and `maxAddmin` is a useful gain. The variable `maxAddmin` (or `meanmax`, if that were used instead) has to be regarded as for all practical purposes equivalent to `altitude`.

5.2.1 Choose Explanatory Terms, and Fit Model

The distributions for `distance` and `NoOfSites` are strongly skewed, so that points on the right tails of the distribution have an overly large say in determining the shape of the smooth curves, in the plots where `distance` appears on one axis and `NoOfSites` on the other.

The table now shown gives values of the power λ (`Pwr`) for the Box–Cox (or, for `NoOfSites` where there are some zero values, Yeo–Johnson) transforms that the function `car::powerTransform` chooses as optimal:

```
yjPower Transformations to Multinormality
           Est Power Rounded Pwr Wald Lwr Bnd Wald Upr Bnd
distance     -0.1583       -0.16      -0.2742      -0.0423
NoOfPools    -0.0232        0.00      -0.1592       0.1128
```

```
NoOfSites     0.5052        0.50        0.2966        0.7138
avrain       -1.6102       -1.00       -2.5681       -0.6523
maxAddmin     0.0131        1.00       -1.1070        1.1332
maxSubmin    -1.8787       -1.00       -3.7077       -0.0498

 Likelihood ratio test that all transformation parameters are
 equal to 0
                                    LRT df             pval
LR test, lambda = (0 0 0 0 0 0) 62.11  6 0.000000000017
```

```
## Code
useCols <- c('distance','NoOfPools','NoOfSites','avrain','maxAddmin','maxSubmin')
tfrogs <- car::powerTransform(frogs[,useCols], family="yjPower")
## Create, for later use, a matrix with variables transformed as suggested
transY <- car::yjPower(frogs[,useCols], coef(tfrogs, round=TRUE))
summary(tfrogs, digits=2)
```

The confidence limits do not directly indicate what difference it would make to choose one or other value of λ (`Pwr`) for the transformation used in the regression equation. For this reason, and because the confidence intervals rely on asymptotic approximations that can be quite inaccurate, the suggested values and confidence intervals should be treated as rough guides only. The suggested transforms for `avrain` and `maxSubmin` are awkward attempts to cope with bimodal distributions – they will be left untransformed.

We will use a logarithmic transformation, both (as suggested) for `NoOfPools`, and for `distance` where the upper bound for λ is close to 0. We will use the suggested square root transformation for `NoOfSites`. Figure 5.6 shows the scatterplot matrix for the transformed variables:

The initial choice of model is:

```
frogs0.glm <- glm(formula = pres.abs ~ log(distance) + log(NoOfPools)+
                  sqrt(NoOfSites) + avrain + maxAddmin + maxSubmin,
                  family = binomial, data = frogs)
DAAG::sumry(frogs0.glm, digits=1)
```

```
Coefficients:
                 Estimate Std. Error z value  Pr(>|z|)
(Intercept)      17.17957   16.17715    1.06    0.2883
log(distance)    -0.71934    0.25898   -2.78    0.0055
log(NoOfPools)    0.57057    0.21522    2.65    0.0080
sqrt(NoOfSites)   0.08379    0.30578    0.27    0.7841
avrain            0.00336    0.04118    0.08    0.9349
maxAddmin         1.51097    0.31609    4.78 0.0000018
maxSubmin        -3.85559    1.27594   -3.02    0.0025

(Dispersion parameter for binomial family taken to be 1)

    Null deviance: 279.99  on 211  degrees of freedom
Residual deviance: 197.58  on 205  degrees of freedom
```

The p-values should be used with more than usual caution. There has been no regard to spatial clustering, and there are questions about the adequacy of the asymptotic approximations used. What is clear is a separation of the explanatory variables into two groups. The variables `sqrt(NoOfSites)` and `avrain` have large p-values,

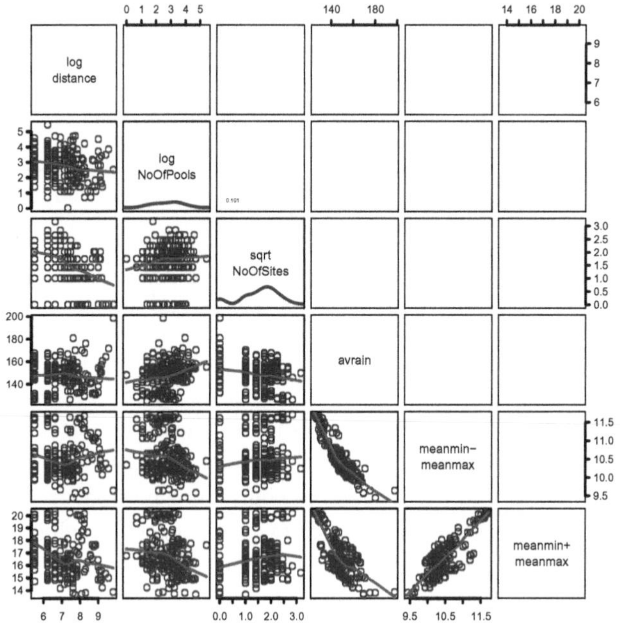

Figure 5.6 Scatterplot matrix, with suggested transformations.

while other p-values are all small. We can almost certainly omit both `NoOfSites` and `avrain`, as will now be checked. We will investigate, also, the further step of replacing `maxAddmin` by `altitude`:

```
## Check effect of omitting sqrt(NoOfSites) and avrain from the model
## ~ . takes the existing formula. Precede terms to be
## omitted by '-'.  (For additions, precede with '+')
frogs.glm <- update(frogs0.glm, ~ . -sqrt(NoOfSites)-avrain)
frogsAlt.glm <- update(frogs.glm, ~ . -maxAddmin+altitude)
AIC(frogs0.glm, frogs.glm,frogsAlt.glm)
```

```
             df   AIC
frogs0.glm    7 211.6
frogs.glm     5 207.7
frogsAlt.glm  5 208.2
```

The models have similar coefficients for the variables that they have in common.

```
            log(distance) log(NoOfPools) maxAddmin maxSubmin
frogs0.glm        -0.7193         0.5706     1.511    -3.856
frogs.glm         -0.7547         0.5707     1.498    -3.881
```

```
coef(frogsAlt.glm)[c('log(distance)','log(NoOfPools)','altitude','maxSubmin')]
```

```
 log(distance) log(NoOfPools)        altitude       maxSubmin
       -0.7711         0.5674         -0.0222         -4.4830
```

Coefficients for `frogs.glm` are:

```
coef(summary(frogs.glm))
```

	Estimate	Std. Error	z value	Pr(>|z|)
(Intercept)	18.5268	5.2673	3.517	0.000435900
log(distance)	-0.7547	0.2261	-3.338	0.000844459
log(NoOfPools)	0.5707	0.2152	2.652	0.007998691
maxAddmin	1.4985	0.3088	4.853	0.000001219
maxSubmin	-3.8806	0.9002	-4.311	0.000016273

5.2.2 Fitted Values

The function `fitted()` calculates fitted values that are on the scale of the response. The values that are returned by the linear predictor are back-transformed to give the fitted values. For logistic regression, the inverse of the logit, used for the back-transformation, is:

$$g(u) = \frac{\exp(u)}{1 + \exp(u)}.$$

The default action of the function `predict()` is to return fitted values on the scale of the linear predictor. Possibilities include:

```
fitted(frogs.glm)   # Fitted values' scale of response
predict(frogs.glm, type="response") # Same as fitted(frogs.glm)
predict(frogs.glm, type="link")     # Scale of linear predictor
## For approximate SEs, specify
predict(frogs.glm, type="link", se.fit=TRUE)
```

Figure 5.7 allows a comparison of model predictions with observed occurrences of frogs, with respect to geographical coordinates. Because the modeling has taken no account of spatial correlation, examination of such a plot is more than ordinarily desirable. It would be concerning if there were geographical regions where frogs were predicted with high probability but few were found; or with low probability but appeared with some frequency. There is little overt evidence of such clusters.

For models with a binary outcome, plots of residuals are not, in general, very useful. At each point the residual is obtained by subtracting the fitted value from either 0 or 1. As a consequence, the residual can take just one of two possible values. For the `frogs.glm` model it makes sense, as noted above, to look for patterns in the spatial arrangement of points where there seems a discrepancy between observations of frogs and predicted probabilities of occurrence.

5.2.3 Plots That Show the Contributions of Explanatory Variables

The fitted equation adds contributions from `log(distance)`, `log(NoOfPools)`, `meanmin`, and `meanmax`. Figure 5.8 shows the change due to each of these variables in turn, when other terms are held at their means. The code is:

```
termplot(frogs.glm, transform.x=TRUE, col.term=1, fg='gray')
```

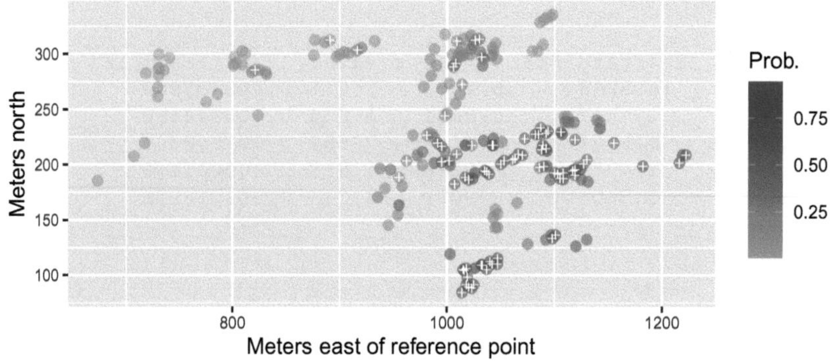

Figure 5.7 Fitted values (model predictions of the probability of finding a frog) are shown on a color density scale. For details of the model, see Subsection 5.2.1. A white "+" has been overlaid onto points where frogs were found.

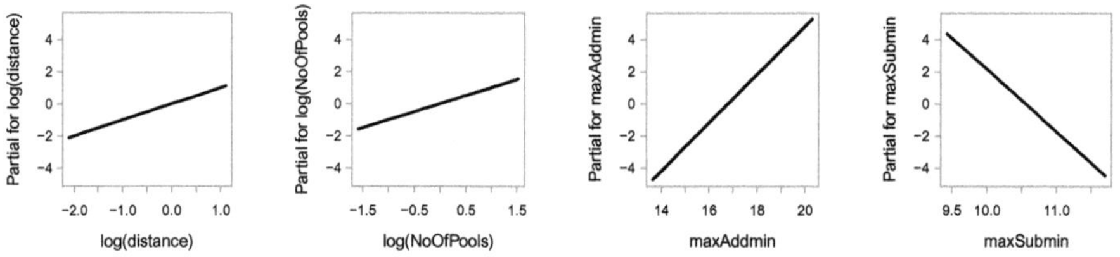

Figure 5.8 Contributions of the explanatory variables to the fitted values, on the scale of the linear predictor.

The y-axis in Figure 5.8 shows values of the linear predictor. As the link is the logit, zero corresponds to a probability of 0.5. Probabilities for other vertical axis labels are -4: 0.02, -2: 0.12, 2: 0.88, and 4: 0.98. The ranges on the vertical scale indicate that easily the largest effects are for `maxAddmin` (`meanmax+meanmin`) and `maxSubmin` (`meanmax-meanmin`). A large `maxAddmin` greatly increases the probability of finding frogs, while a large difference `maxSubmin` greatly reduces that probability. The contributions from log(`distance`) and log(`NoOfPools`) are, relatively, much smaller.

5.2.4 Cross-Validation Estimates of Predictive Accuracy

The function `DAAG::CVbinary()` calculates cross-validation estimates of predictive accuracy for these models. Folds are numbered according the part of the data that are used, at that fold, for testing. Once the cross-validation calculations are complete, each observation has been a member of a test set at one of the folds only. Thus, predictions are available for all observations that are derived independently of those observations. The cross-validation measure is the proportion that are correct:

```
DAAG::CVbinary(frogs.glm)
```

```
Fold:  1 6 2 4 7 10 5 3 9 8
Internal estimate of accuracy = 0.778
Cross-validation estimate of accuracy = 0.783
```

The training estimate assesses the accuracy of prediction for the data used in deriving the model. Cross-validation estimates the accuracy that might be expected for a new sample.

The cross-validation estimates can be highly variable. It is advisable to run the cross-validation routine several times. Also, for an accurate comparison, the cross-validation runs for the two models should be matched. For this, make a random assignment of observations to folds. Then call the cross-validation function, first with the full model and then with the reduced model. Six sets of matched accuracy estimates are:

```
                               [,1]  [,2]  [,3]  [,4]  [,5]  [,6]
frogs (all variables)         0.797 0.769 0.769 0.778 0.788 0.788
frogs0 (selected variables) 0.792 0.774 0.764 0.778 0.783 0.788
```

The pairwise comparisons do not show a consistent difference.[2]

5.2.5 Cholera Deaths in London – 1849 to 1855

Farr, who worked as statistician in the UK Registrar General's office, collected the 1848–1849 cholera death data that will now be examined. An earlier 1832 outbreak in London had killed more than 6500 people. There had been an ongoing debate on the mode of transmission. Coleman (2019) and Smith (2002) give detailed commentary on the background.

The prevailing medical opinion blamed "miasma" or noxious air, associated with the stink from rotting garbage, feces, and pollution in the Thames. Poor areas had higher rates of cholera, thought to be a result of worse smell that was a result of crowding and poorer sanitation. More directly to the point, people were older, houses were poorly heated, and the water supply was more likely to be contaminated. Human excreta went into cesspits, with night-soil periodically taken away.[3]

Chadwick (1842), in his report "The sanitary conditions of the labouring population" (Science Museum, 2019), showed a direct link between poor living conditions,

[2]
```
set.seed(19)
frogs.acc <- frogs0.acc <- numeric(6)
for (j in 1:6){
  randsam <- sample(1:10, 212, replace=TRUE)
  ## Sample 212 values (one per pbservation) from 1:10
  frogs.acc[j] <- DAAG::CVbinary(frogs.glm, rand=randsam,
                              print.details=FALSE)$acc.cv
  frogs0.acc[j] <- DAAG::CVbinary(frogs0.glm, rand=randsam,
  print.details=FALSE)$acc.cv
}
print(rbind("frogs (all variables)" = frogs.acc,
            "frogs0 (selected variables)" = frogs0.acc), digits=3)
```

[3] Anon (2016) *Cholera epidemics in Victorian London.*

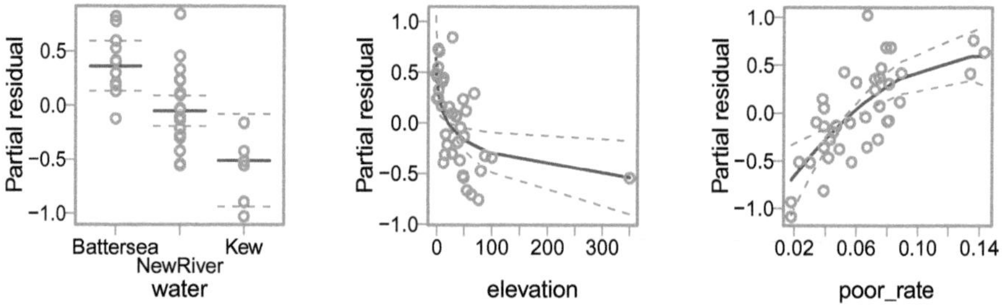

Figure 5.9 The panels show, in turn, the estimated contributions of terms relative to the mean contribution from other model terms. Changes in deaths are on a "log" scale, so that an increase by one unit multiplies the odds of death by close to 2.7, around an overall mean of just over six per 1000.

disease and life expectancy. Like others who accepted the "miasma" theory of disease, Chadwick did not understand that cholera, along with some other major diseases, was water-borne.[4] In 1848 the "Nuisances Removal and Diseases Prevention Act" was passed with the aim of preventing transmission of cholera. An outcome was the dumping of the contents of cesspools and raw sewage pits into the Thames, which was London's main source of drinking water. This only served to exacerbate the problem. The 1848–1849 epidemic followed shortly after the cesspits were banned. Hassall (1850), in a careful microbiological study, commented that:

> ... a portion of the inhabitants are made to consume ... a portion of their own excrement, and ... to pay for the privilege.

By Air, or by Water – the 1849 Epidemic

Farr classified districts into three groups thus, according to the source of the water for most of the householders:

1. Thames between Battersea Bridge and Waterloo Bridge, coded as `Battersea`;
2. New River/Rivers Lea and Ravensbourne (sources away from the Thames), coded as `NewRiver`;
3. Thames between Kew and Hammersmith, that is, further up the Thames than the first group, where the water was less polluted by sewage, coded as `Kew`.

Figure 5.9 summarizes results from a regression analysis that used Farr's data. None of the terms stands out as substantially more important than any other. Higher rates for the poor, where crowded conditions would often make it difficult to maintain hygiene, were to be expected. Code is:

```
Cholera <- HistData::Cholera
fitP2.glm <- glm(cholera_deaths ~ offset(log(popn)) + water +
             log(elevation+3) + poly(poor_rate,2) +I(elevation==350),
             data=Cholera, family=quasipoisson)
Cholera[["water"]] <- factor(Cholera[["water"]], labels=c("Battersea",
                      "NewRiver","Kew"))
termplot(fitP2.glm, partial=T, se=TRUE, pch =1,
```

[4] By comparison, COVID-19 is indeed spread through the air, but primarily from person-to-person contact, and without an association with stink from rotting garbage or faeces.

```
ylabs=rep("Partial residual",3), terms='water', fg="gray")
axis(1, at=2, labels="NewRiver", lwd=0, line=0.75)
termplot(fitP2.glm, partial=T, se=TRUE, pch =1,
        ylabs=rep("Partial residual",3), terms='log(elevation + 3)', fg="gray")
termplot(fitP2.glm, partial=T, se=TRUE, pch =1,
        ylabs=rep("Partial residual",3), terms='poly(poor_rate, 2)', fg="gray")
```

Snow (1855) argued that those living close to the Thames, and especially in the South, were more likely to be getting their water from or via sources that were contaminated with human excreta. The piping of water to higher ground gave contaminants more chance to settle, with less chance of exposure to human excreta. He gave examples that he had observed directly, where the means of transmission of the infection appeared to be a water source, or poor hygiene.

Farr gave Snow's arguments some credence, but discussed ways that the air might be the main source of transmission of an organism responsible for the disease, which multiplied in a process akin to fermentation that was presumed to take place in putrefying matter. The perspective brought by germ theory would come later, with the work of Pasteur in the late 1850s and Koch in the 1880s.

Regression calculations do not, on their own, prove anything. They require a context in which they can be understood and interpreted. Causal diagrams (DAGs) such as were discussed in Subsection 3.2.6 can be helpful in representing graphically what is known or surmised from that wider context.

While Snow had a better understanding of the contextual information, it was not comprehensive enough to persuade other medical specialists at the time. Data from the 1854 epidemic will now be examined. This allowed a comparison between death rates for two different sources of water supply – from the highly polluted lower Thames as against the less polluted higher Thames. This seems in retrospect to clinch the issue.

The 1854 Epidemic – a Natural Experiment

Both water companies – Lambeth, and Southwark and Vauxhall, had been taking water from the same polluted source, in both cases with high death rates. An 1852 act required water supply companies to move water intake upriver by 1855. By the time of the 1854 epidemic, Lambeth had moved the intake 22 miles upriver, where the water was not contaminated by London sewage. The Southwark and Vauxhall intake was unchanged until 1855. Data on the distribution of cholera in the 1854 epidemic then allowed Snow to test the claims made in his 1849 study:

	#houses	#Deaths	Rate per 10,000
Southwark & Vauxhall	40046	1263	315
Lambeth	26107	98	37
Rest of London	256423	1422	59

Snow wrote:

The experiment, too, was on the grandest scale. No fewer than 300,000 people ..., from gentlefolks down to the very poor, were divided into two groups without their choice, and, in most cases, without their knowledge; one group being supplied with water containing the sewage of London, and, amongst it, whatever might have come from the cholera patients,

the other group having water quite free from such impurity.
(Snow, 1855)

A further clue came from Snow's observation that:

Within 250 yards of the spot where Cambridge Street joins Broad Street there were upwards of 500 fatal attacks of cholera in 10 days ....

By contrast, none of the employees of a local Soho brewery developed cholera. The reason, he judged, was that they drank water from the brewery (which had a different source from the Broad Street pump) or just drank beer alone. It took a further 10 years for the medical establishment to begin to accept Snow's conclusions.

London was one of many different places worldwide that were similarly affected by widespread outbreaks of water-borne diseases in the nineteenth century. New Zealand cities had similar issues from the 1840s and 1850s through until the end of the century, arising from failures to install proper drainage systems. Conditions in Dunedin were so bad in 1889 that a cartoonist could refer to the city as "Stinkapool" (Dann, 2022).

5.3 Logistic Models for Categorical Data – an Example

The array `UCBAdmissions` (`datasets` package) has dimensions:
`Admit` (Admitted/Rejected) × `Gender` (Male/Female) × `Dept` (A, B, C, D, E, F).

A first step is to create a data frame whose columns hold the information in the observations by variables format that will be required for the use of `glm()`:

```
## Create data frame from multi-way table UCBAdmissions (datasets)
## dimnames(UCBAdmissions)  # Check levels of table margins
UCB <- as.data.frame.table(UCBAdmissions["Admitted", , ], responseName="admit")
UCB$reject <- as.data.frame.table(UCBAdmissions["Rejected", , ])$Freq
UCB$Gender <- relevel(UCB$Gender, ref="Male")
## Add further columns total and p (proportion admitted)
UCB$total <- UCB$admit + UCB$reject
UCB$pAdmit <- UCB$admit/UCB$total
```

We use a loglinear model to model the probability of admission of applicants. It is important, for present purposes, to fit `Dept`, thus adjusting for different admission rates in different departments, before fitting `Gender`:

```
UCB.glm <- glm(pAdmit ~ Dept*Gender, family=binomial, data=UCB, weights=total)
## Abbreviated `anova()` output:
anova(UCB.glm, test="Chisq") |>
 capture.output() |> tail(8) |> (\(x)x[-c(2,3)])() |> cat(sep='\n')
```

```
Terms added sequentially (first to last)
            Df Deviance Resid. Df Resid. Dev Pr(>Chi)
NULL                           11        877
Dept         5      855         6         22   <2e-16
Gender       1        2         5         20   0.2159
Dept:Gender  5       20         0          0   0.0011
```

After allowance for overall departmental differences in admission rate (but not for the `Dept:Gender` interaction; this is a sequential table), there is no detectable main effect of Gender. The significant interaction term suggests that there are department-specific gender biases, which average out to reduce the main effect of Gender to close to zero.

We now examine the individual coefficients in the model:

```
round(signif(coef(summary(UCB.glm)),4), 3)
```

```
                     Estimate Std. Error z value Pr(>|z|)
(Intercept)             0.492      0.072   6.859    0.000
DeptB                   0.042      0.113   0.368    0.713
DeptC                  -1.028      0.136  -7.584    0.000
DeptD                  -1.196      0.126  -9.462    0.000
DeptE                  -1.449      0.177  -8.196    0.000
DeptF                  -3.262      0.231 -14.110    0.000
GenderFemale            1.052      0.263   4.005    0.000
DeptB:GenderFemale     -0.832      0.510  -1.630    0.103
DeptC:GenderFemale     -1.177      0.300  -3.929    0.000
DeptD:GenderFemale     -0.970      0.303  -3.206    0.001
DeptE:GenderFemale     -1.252      0.330  -3.791    0.000
DeptF:GenderFemale     -0.863      0.403  -2.144    0.032
```

The first six coefficients relate to overall admission rates, for males, in the six departments. The strongly significant positive coefficient for GenderFemale, (females relative to males as reference), is increased by 1.052 in department A, and reduced by amounts in the range between 0.863 and 1.252 in departments C, D, E, and F.

5.4 Models for Counts – Poisson, Quasipoisson, and Negative Binomial

5.4.1 Data on Aberrant Crypt Foci

The data frame DAAG::ACF1 has the two columns: count and endtime. The column count has the counts of simple aberrant crypt foci (ACFs) – these are aberrant aggregations of tube-like structures – in the rectal end of 22 rat colons after administration of a dose of the carcinogen azoxymethane. Each rat was sacrificed after 6, 12, or 18 weeks (recorded in the column endtime). For further background information, see McLellan et al. (1991).

The argument is that there are a large number of sites where ACFs might occur, in each instance with the same low probability. Because "site" does not have a precise definition, the total number of sites is unknown, but it is clearly large. If we can assume independence between sites, then we might expect a Poisson model, for the total number of ACF sites. The output from fitting the model will include information that indicates whether a Poisson model was, after all, satisfactory. If a Poisson model does not seem satisfactory, then a quasipoisson model, consistent with clustering in the appearance of ACFs, may be a reasonable alternative. Clustering might occur because some rats are more prone to ACFs than others, or because ACFs tend to appear in clusters within the same rat. Figure 5.10 provides plots of the data. A logarithmic x-scale is appropriate on the x-axis because the Poisson model will use a log link.

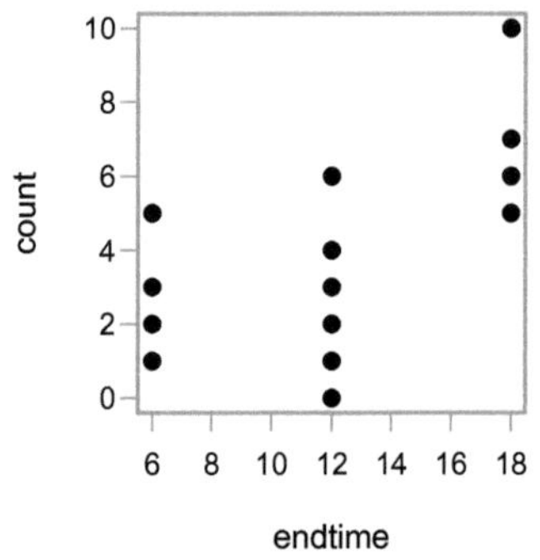

Figure 5.10 Plot of number of simple aberrant crypt foci (**count**) versus **endtime**. Means for each location are shown as large "+" symbols.

In order to accommodate the apparent quadratic effect, we try including an endtime2̂ term. The code and output summary is:

```
ACF.glm <- glm(formula = count ~ endtime + I(endtime^2),
            family = poisson(link="identity"), data = DAAG::ACF1)
DAAG::sumry(ACF.glm, digits=2)
```

```
Coefficients:
               Estimate  Std. Error  z value  Pr(>|z|)
(Intercept)      6.3393      2.4334     2.61    0.0092
endtime         -1.0952      0.4771    -2.30    0.0217
I(endtime^2)     0.0620      0.0211     2.94    0.0033

(Dispersion parameter for poisson family taken to be 1)

    Null deviance: 51.105  on 21  degrees of freedom
Residual deviance: 24.515  on 19  degrees of freedom
```

Notice the use of an `identity` link, where the default is `log`.

The fitted values are:

```
unique(round(predict(ACF.glm),2))
```

```
[1] 2.00 2.12 6.71
```

Observe that the residual mean deviance is $24.515/19 = 1.29$. For a Poisson model this should, unless a substantial proportion of fitted values are small (e.g., less than about 2), be close to 1. The residual mean deviance may be used as an estimate of the *dispersion*, in this context defined as the factor by which the variance is increased relative to the expected variance for a Poisson model. A better estimate (it has a smaller bias) is, however, that based on the Pearson chi-squared measure of lack of fit. This can be obtained as follows:

```
sum(resid(ACF.glm, type="pearson")^2)/19
```

```
[1] 1.254
```

This suggests that standard errors should be increased, and t-statistics reduced by a factor of $\sqrt{1.25} \simeq 1.12$ relative to those given above for the Poisson model. The following fits a quasipoisson model, which incorporates this adjustment to the variance. As the increased residual variance will take the quadratic term even further from the conventional 5 percent significance level, we do not bother to fit it:

```
ACFq.glm <- glm(formula = count ~ endtime + I(endtime^2),
family = quasipoisson, data = DAAG::ACF1)
print(coef(summary(ACFq.glm)), digits=2)
```

```
              Estimate Std. Error t value Pr(>|t|)
(Intercept)      1.722     1.2234     1.4     0.18
endtime         -0.262     0.2236    -1.2     0.26
I(endtime^2)     0.015     0.0089     1.7     0.11
```

Notice that `z value` has now become `t value`, suggesting that it should be referred to as a t-distribution (with 19 d.f., as 19 d.f. were available to estimate the dispersion).

There are enough small expected counts that the dispersion estimate and resultant t-statistics should be treated with modest caution. Additionally, does the same dispersion estimate apply to all values of `endtime`? This can be checked with:

```
sapply(split(residuals(ACFq.glm), DAAG::ACF1$endtime), var)
```

```
     6     12     18
0.9968 2.2571 0.3557
```

Under the assumed model, these should be approximately equal. The following approximate test for homogeneity ignores the small extent of dependence in the residuals:

```
fligner.test(resid(ACFq.glm) ~ factor(DAAG::ACF1$endtime))
```

```

        Fligner-Killeen test of homogeneity of variances

data:  resid(ACFq.glm) by factor(DAAG::ACF1$endtime)
Fligner-Killeen:med chi-squared = 4, df = 2, p-value = 0.1
```

The differences in estimated variance may well be due to chance effects.

5.4.2 Moth Habitat Example

The `moths` data are from a study of the effect of habitat on the densities of two species of moth. Transects were set out across the search area. Within transects, sections were identified according to habitat type. There were

- 41 different lengths (`meters`) of transect ranging from 2 m to 233 m,
- grouped into eight habitat types within the search area – `Bank`, `Disturbed`, `Lowerside`, `NEsoak`, `NWsoak`, `SEsoak`, `SWsoak`, `Upperside`
- with records taken at 20 different times (morning and afternoon) over 16 weeks.

The variables `A` and `P` give the numbers of moths of the two different species.

Here is a tabular summary, by habitat:

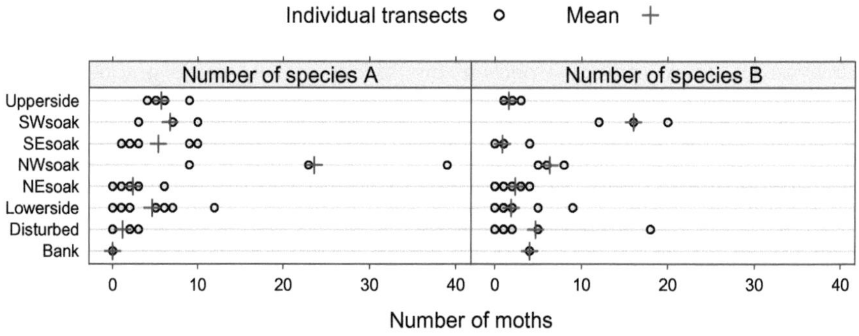

Figure 5.11 Dotplot summaries of the numbers of moths of each of the two species, by habitat type.

```
## Number of moths by habitat: data frame DAAG::moths
moths <- DAAG::moths
tab <- rbind(Number=table(moths[, 4]),
          sapply(split(moths[, -4], moths$habitat), apply, 2, sum))
```

`Number` is the number of transects for that habitat, while `meters` is the total length. Figure 5.11 gives a visual summary. There are a number of zero counts, thus:

```
## Number of zero counts, by habitats
with(droplevels(subset(moths, A==0)), table(habitat))
```

```
habitat
     Bank Disturbed Lowerside    NEsoak
        1         4         1         1
```

There is no reason why moths should appear independently, as assumed for the Poisson family. The following are means and variances for the species A counts, by `habitat`. We note, also, the mean lengths of the transects:

```
Astats <- with(DAAG::moths, sapply(split(A, habitat),
function(x)c(Amean=mean(x),Avar=var(x))))
avlength <- with(DAAG::moths, sapply(split(meters, habitat), mean))
round(rbind(Astats, avlen=avlength),1)
```

```
       Bank Disturbed Lowerside NEsoak NWsoak SEsoak SWsoak Upperside
Amean     0       1.1       4.6    2.3   23.7    5.3    6.7       5.6
Avar     NA       2.1      14.0    4.3  225.3   14.9   12.3       4.3
avlen    21       7.0      21.2   42.3   21.7   27.6   38.7     190.4
```

The variance is generally much larger than the mean, with the variance to mean ratio largest when the mean is largest. Differences in the lengths of transepts do not appear to account for the differences.

A `quasipoisson` *Model*

For species A, the assumption of a `quasipoisson` is problematic if the one transect for `Bank`, where no moths were found, is included in the analysis. The mean will be estimated as zero on the basis of just one count. Multiplication of a Poisson variance that is also zero by the dispersion estimate will not change the variance from zero. It is, however, instructive to see what happens if we proceed blindly and fit such a model. The use of a logarithmic link function, so that the model works with log(expected number of moths), is the default. The model then takes the form

$$y = \text{habitat effect} + \beta \log(\text{length of section}),$$

where y = log(expected number of moths). Effects are multiplicative, and the model allows for the possibility that the number of moths per meter might be relatively lower or higher for long than for short sections.

For the default parameterization, categorical effects are comparisons with the first factor level, used as a reference (or baseline). If not set explicitly, perhaps using the function `relevel()`, this is the first in alphanumeric order of level names. The zero count results in meaningless standard errors, as will now be apparent:

```
A.glm <- glm(A ~ habitat + log(meters), family=quasipoisson,
data=DAAG::moths)
DAAG::sumry(A.glm, digits=1)
```

```
Coefficients:
                  Estimate Std. Error t value Pr(>|t|)
(Intercept)        -15.696   2096.588   -0.01     0.99
habitatDisturbed    15.622   2096.588    0.01     0.99
habitatLowerside    16.906   2096.588    0.01     0.99
habitatNEsoak       16.084   2096.588    0.01     0.99
habitatNWsoak       18.468   2096.588    0.01     0.99
habitatSEsoak       16.968   2096.588    0.01     0.99
habitatSWsoak       17.137   2096.588    0.01     0.99
habitatUpperside    16.743   2096.588    0.01     0.99
log(meters)          0.129      0.153    0.85     0.40

(Dispersion parameter for quasipoisson family taken to be 2.701)

    Null deviance: 257.108  on 40  degrees of freedom
Residual deviance:  93.991  on 32  degrees of freedom
AIC: NA

Number of Fisher Scoring iterations: 13
```

The row of the data frame that has the information for `Bank` is:

```
subset(DAAG::moths, habitat=="Bank")
```

```
   meters A P habitat
40     21 0 4    Bank
```

The estimate for `(Intercept)` is −15.70. This is on a logarithmic scale. The expected number of moths, according to the fitted model, is then:

$$\exp(-15.7 + 0.13 \log(21)) = -2.26 \times 10^{-7}.$$

This is an approximation to zero! A tightening of the convergence criteria gives an even smaller intercept and an expected value that is closer still to the observed zero value.[5]

[5]
```
## Analysis with tighter convergence criterion
A.glm <- update(A.glm, epsilon=1e-10)
print(coef(summary(A.glm)), digits=2)
```

The huge standard errors, and the `NA` for the AIC statistic, are strong hints that the output should not be taken at face value. A further indication comes from comparing the standard error of the predicted value for `Bank` with the range of predicted values for other habitats:

```
AfitSE <- predict(A.glm, se=TRUE)$se.fit
cfSE <- with(DAAG::moths, c(AfitSE[habitat=="Bank"],
range(AfitSE[habitat!="Bank"])))
round(setNames(cfSE, c("SEbank", "SEotherMIN", "SEotherMAX")), digits=2)
```

```
 SEbank SEotherMIN SEotherMAX
2096.59       0.20       0.63
```

The approximation used to calculate a standard error breaks down when, as here, the fitted value for the reference level is zero. It is not possible, from this output, to say anything about the accuracy of comparisons with `Bank` or between other types of habitat. More generally, the approximation would fail for any comparison where the ratios of relevant fitted values are large. Subsection 5.6.2 comments on this issue as it translates to models with a binomial or quasibinomial error.

A More Satisfactory Choice of Reference Level

Output that is more useful is obtained if we take, for example, `Lowerside` as the reference:

```
moths <- DAAG::moths
moths$habitat <- relevel(moths$habitat, ref="Lowerside")
Alower.glm <- glm(A ~ habitat + log(meters),
                  family = quasipoisson, data = moths)
print(coef(summary(Alower.glm)), digits=1)
```

```
                 Estimate Std. Error t value Pr(>|t|)
(Intercept)          1.21        0.5   2.657  0.01219
habitatBank        -16.91     2096.6  -0.008  0.99362
habitatDisturbed    -1.28        0.6  -1.982  0.05610
habitatNEsoak       -0.82        0.5  -1.530  0.13580
habitatNWsoak        1.56        0.3   4.674  0.00005
habitatSEsoak        0.06        0.4   0.161  0.87299
habitatSWsoak        0.23        0.5   0.484  0.63161
habitatUpperside    -0.16        0.6  -0.278  0.78292
log(meters)          0.13        0.2   0.845  0.40414
```

The part of the summary output that has been omitted is the same as for the model where `Bank` was the reference. As before, the dispersion estimate is 2.7, where the expected value for a Poisson distribution is 1. Use of a quasipoisson model, rather than a Poisson model, has increased standard errors by a factor of $\sqrt{2.7} = 1.64$. For determining p-values, the ratio of estimate to standard error is referred to as a t-distribution with degrees of freedom as used for estimating the dispersion.

The estimates are on a logarithmic scale. Thus the model predicts, after adjusting for differences in transect length, `exp(-1.283)` $= 0.277$ times as many moths on `Disturbed` as on `Lowerside`. The fitted values remain the same as when `Bank` was the reference.

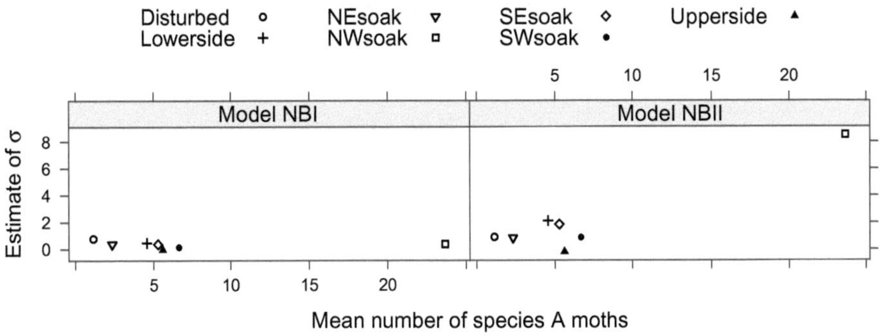

Figure 5.12 Estimates of the dispersion are plotted against the mean, as given by the formulae that give the variance for each the models NBI and NBII.

In general, the approximation used to calculate a standard error for a difference of categorical effects will break down when the difference corresponds to large ratios of fitted values. One recourse is to use a square root link. The linear model then predicts the square root of the Poisson or quasipoisson rate. On this scale, variances are the same (= 0.25 × dispersion) for any nonzero (> 0) Poisson rate constant. The resulting model will give a plausible values for the standard error of difference from `Bank`.

5.4.3 Models with Negative Binomial Errors*

As discussed in Section 2.3, the *gamlss* package offers several several distributions that are designed to accommodate extra-Poisson variance. Here, we compare negative binomial types I and II fits.

`NBI`: Mean $= \mu$; Variance $= \mu(1 + \mu\sigma)$
`NBII`: Mean $= \mu$; Variance $= \mu(1 + \sigma)$

Note that in the *glmmTMB* package, the parameter $\phi = \sigma^{-1}$ appears in place of σ. In modeling counts of organisms, a decrease in σ towards zero reflects decreasing aggregation, with a Poisson distribution where organisms are distributed independently as the limit. An increase towards infinity reflects increasing aggregation.

Given the mean and variance estimates obtained above, estimates of σ can be calculated, for each habitat except `Bank`, for each of the models `NBI` and `NBII`. Thus, for the model `NBI`, Variance = $= \mu(1 + \mu\sigma)$. It follows that $\sigma =$ (Variance $- \mu$) μ^{-2}, while for `NBII`, the final μ^{-2} is replaced by μ^{-1}. Figure 5.12 then plots these estimates against the estimate of μ.

We then proceed to fit two models with an `NBII` error, one keeping θ constant, and the other allowing a separate *theta* for each different habitat:

```
library(gamlss, quietly=TRUE)
noBank <- subset(moths, habitat!='Bank')
mothsCon.lss <- gamlss(A ~ log(meters)+habitat, family=NBI(), data=noBank,
                       trace=F)
mothsVary.lss <- gamlss(A ~ log(meters)+habitat, family=NBI(),
                        sigma.formula=~habitat, trace=FALSE, data=noBank)
```

The following uses a likelihood ratio test to compare the two models:

```
LR.test(mothsCon.lss, mothsVary.lss)
```

```
Likelihood Ratio Test for nested GAMLSS models.
(No check whether the models are nested is performed).

      Null model: deviance= 189.2 with  9 deg. of freedom
Altenative model: deviance= 184.6 with  15 deg. of freedom

LRT = 4.643 with 6 deg. of freedom and p-value= 0.5904
```

There is no convincing reason to allow for a scale parameter that varies between habitats. The main part of the output summary is:

```
## mothsCon.lss <- gamlss(A ~ log(meters)+habitat,family=NBI(),data=noBank)
## summary(mothsCon.lss, type="qr")   ## Main part of output
```

```
*******************************************************************
Family:  c("NBI", "Negative Binomial type I")
Mu link function:  log
Mu Coefficients:
                 Estimate Std. Error t value Pr(>|t|)
(Intercept)          1.18       0.40     3.0    0.006 **
log(meters)          0.15       0.14     1.1    0.298
habitatDisturbed    -1.29       0.47    -2.7    0.010 *
habitatNEsoak       -0.86       0.44    -2.0    0.058 .
habitatNWsoak        1.54       0.39     4.0   0.0004 ***
habitatSEsoak        0.05       0.35     0.1    0.895
habitatSWsoak        0.20       0.45     0.4    0.656
habitatUpperside    -0.21       0.54    -0.4    0.698
---
Signif. codes:  0 '***' 0.001 '**' 0.01 '*' 0.05 '.' 0.1 ' ' 1

-------------------------------------------------------------------
Sigma link function:  log
Sigma Coefficients:
            Estimate Std. Error t value Pr(>|t|)
(Intercept)     -1.4        0.5      -3     0.01 *
---
Signif. codes:  0 '***' 0.001 '**' 0.01 '*' 0.05 '.' 0.1 ' ' 1

-------------------------------------------------------------------
No. of observations in the fit:  40
Degrees of Freedom for the fit:  9
      Residual Deg. of Freedom:  31
                      at cycle:  3

Global Deviance:     189.2
            AIC:     207.2
            SBC:     222.4
*******************************************************************
```

The argument `type="qr"` is supplied because, for this model, the default method used to calculate the variance–covariance matrix fails.

```
*******************************************************************
        Summary of the Randomised Quantile Residuals
                               mean   =  0.01809
                           variance   =  0.985
                   coef. of skewness  =  -0.09571
                   coef. of kurtosis  =  2.282
Filliben correlation coefficient      =  0.9917
*******************************************************************
```

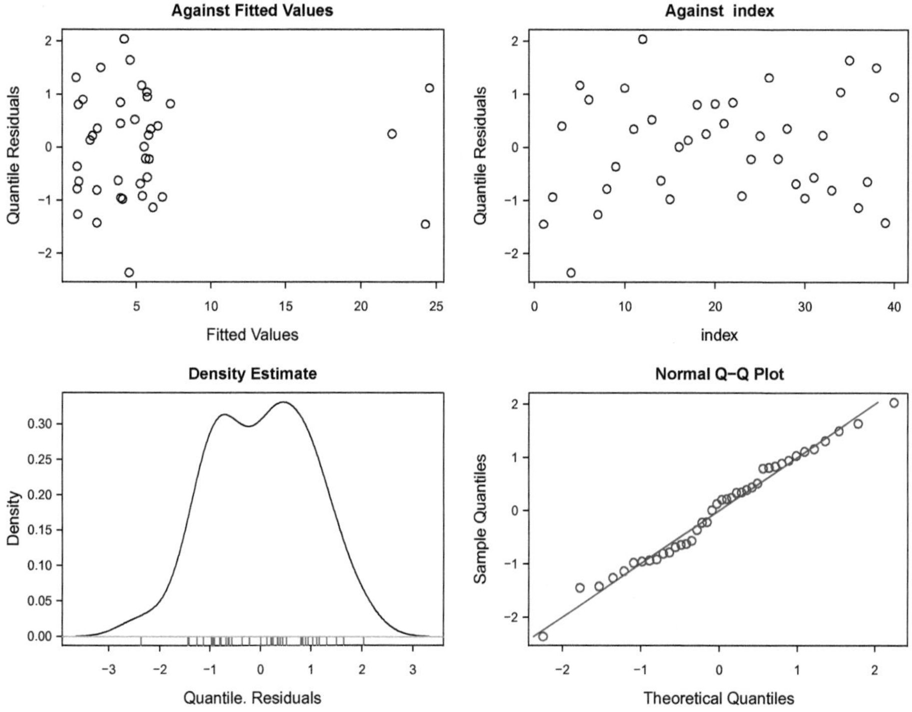

Figure 5.13 Diagnostic plots for modeling the `A` (number of moths of species A) as a function of `habitat` and `log(meters)`, for habitats other than `Bank`

Diagnostic Plots

Note, in particular, that the normal quantile–quantile (Q-Q) plot appears consistent with approximate normality. The scale–location plot appears consistent with the assumption of constant dispersion, independent of the predicted value.

Use of the Square Root (`sqrt`) *Link Function*

Both with a quasipoisson model and with a negative binomial model, the use of a logarithmic link causes problems for the case when the estimated mean count is zero, as for the habitat `Bank`. A suitable recourse is to use a square root link, then using `sqrt(meters)` in place of `log(meters)` as explanatory variable, thus:

```
Asqrt.lss <- gamlss(A ~ habitat + sqrt(meters), trace=FALSE,
                family = NBI(mu.link='sqrt'), data = moths)
```

The coefficient estimates and standard errors are:

```
## Asqrt.lss <- gamlss(A ~ habitat + sqrt(meters),
##                     family = NBI(mu.link='sqrt'), data = moths)
```

```
## summary(Asqrt.lss, type="qr")   ## Main part of output
```

```
*******************************************************************
Family:  c("NBI", "Negative Binomial type I")
Mu link function:  sqrt
Mu Coefficients:
                  Estimate Std. Error t value  Pr(>|t|)
(Intercept)           1.89       0.31     6.2 0.0000008 ***
habitatBank          -2.19       0.75    -2.9     0.006 **
habitatDisturbed     -1.00       0.32    -3.1     0.004 **
habitatNEsoak        -0.80       0.39    -2.1     0.046 *
habitatNWsoak         2.67       0.78     3.4     0.002 **
habitatSEsoak         0.09       0.38     0.2     0.818
habitatSWsoak         0.28       0.54     0.5     0.606
habitatUpperside     -0.41       0.69    -0.6     0.563
sqrt(meters)          0.07       0.06     1.2     0.248
---
Signif. codes:  0 '***' 0.001 '**' 0.01 '*' 0.05 '.' 0.1 ' ' 1

-------------------------------------------------------------------
Sigma link function:  log
Sigma Coefficients:
             Estimate Std. Error t value Pr(>|t|)
(Intercept)      -1.4        0.5      -3    0.004 **
---
Signif. codes:  0 '***' 0.001 '**' 0.01 '*' 0.05 '.' 0.1 ' ' 1

-------------------------------------------------------------------
No. of observations in the fit:  41
Degrees of Freedom for the fit:  10
      Residual Deg. of Freedom:  31
                      at cycle:  3

Global Deviance:     188.8
            AIC:     208.8
            SBC:     226
*******************************************************************
```

The t-statistic Bank, which is really for the comparison of Bank with the reference level, that is, with Lowerside, is now believable.

5.4.4* Negative Binomial versus Alternatives – Hurricane Deaths

Subsection 3.3.5 investigated the use of a least squares regression model for the hurricane deaths data in the hurricNamed dataset, in the *DAAG* package. Recall that this used as outcome variable a power transform of deaths+1 with $\lambda = -0.2$, using log(log(BaseDamage2014)) as explanatory variable.

A negative binomial fit, now with deaths as outcome variable will be compared with the fit on the power transform scale. For purposes of comparison, both fits will be plotted on a log(deaths+1) scale.

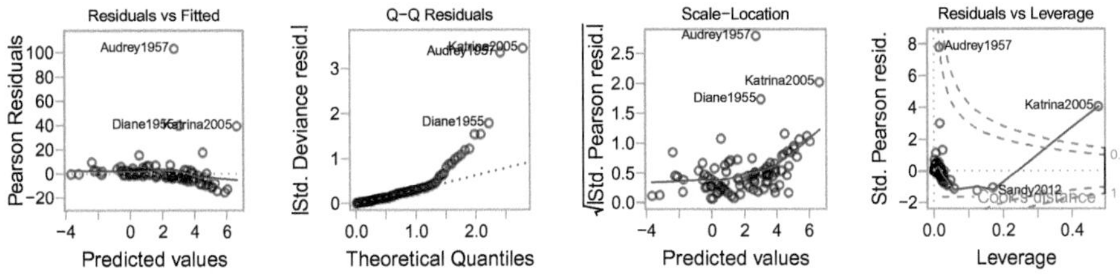

Figure 5.14 Diagnostic plots, for **quasipoisson** model fitted to the **DAAG::hurricNamed** data.

Aside – a Quasibinomial Binomial Fit

Figure 5.14 shows diagnostic plots from a quasipoisson model. They effectively rule this model out. Note especially the strong upward trend in the scale parameter with increasing predicted values.

Code is:

```
ordx <- with(DAAG::hurricNamed, order(BaseDam2014))
hurric <- DAAG::hurricNamed[ordx,]
# Ordering a/c values of BaseDam2014 simplifies later code
hurr.glm <- glm(deaths ~ log(BaseDam2014), family=quasipoisson, data=hurric)
plot(hurr.glm, col=adjustcolor('black', alpha=0.4),
     cex.caption=0.95, sub.caption=rep("",4), fg="gray")
```

Note that hurricane Audrey is a very clear outlier. It will be left out in subsequent fits, but still shown on the plots.

Negative Binomial versus Power-Transformed Scale

Under negative binomial model assumptions, fitted values are unbiased on a scale of $\mu = \mathrm{E}[\text{deaths}]$. The distribution of **deaths** around the mean is, however, highly skew. The distribution on the power-transform scale is, because this transformation is designed to match the distribution as close as possible to the normal, much closer to symmetric. This difference in distributions has implications for the positioning of the fitted values relative to quantiles of the data, as will be demonstrated graphically.

Fit a Negative Binomial (NBI) Model

Now use the **gamlss::gamlss()** function to fit a negative binomial model. The following fits the model and extracts both the usual residuals and the corresponding equivalent normal quantiles (z-scores):

```
library(gamlss)
hurrNB.gamlss <- gamlss::gamlss(deaths ~ log(BaseDam2014), family=NBI(),
                               data=hurric[-56,])
mures <- resid(hurrNB.gamlss, what="mu")
zres <- resid(hurrNB.gamlss, what="z-scores") ## equivalent normal quantiles
```

The distribution of **deaths** is highly skewed to the right, with the consequence that there are many more negative than positive residuals:

```
table(sign(mures))
```

```
-1  1
64 29
```

Thus, $64/93 \simeq 64.5$ percent of the residuals are negative.

Fit Linear Model to Power-Transformed Responses

The following fits a linear model to the power transformed values of `deaths+1`, using the power transform indicated in Subsection 3.3.5:

```
hurr.lm <- lm(car::yjPower(deaths,-0.2) ~ log(BaseDam2014), data=hurric[-56,])
## Use the following function to transform from power scale to log scale
powerTOlog <- function(z, lambda)log(lambda*z+1)/lambda
## Calculate fitted values, and transform to log(deaths+1) scale
hatPower <- powerTOlog(predict(hurr.lm), lambda=-0.2)
resPower <- log(hurric[-56,"deaths"]+1) - hatPower
```

With this model, less than 50 percent of the residuals are negative. As a symmetric error distribution has been fitted, this reflects a bias in the data.

```
table(sign(resPower))
```

```
-1  1
38 55
```

Thus, $38/93 \simeq 40.9$ percent of the residuals are negative.

Compare NBI and Power-Transform Fits with Smoothed Quantiles

The code that now follows uses the function `qgam::qgam()`, with automatically chosen smoothing parameters, to fit smooth 64.5 percent and 40.9 percent quantile curves as functions of `log(BaseDAm2014)`. The interest is to compare these with, respectively, the negative binomial (NBI) fit and the power-transform fit.

```
library(qgam, quietly=TRUE)
hat68.8 <- predict(qgam(log(deaths+1) ~ s(log(BaseDam2014)), qu=.648,
                   data=hurric[-56,]))
```

```
Estimating learning rate. Each dot corresponds to a loss evaluation.
qu = 0.648........done
```

```
hat40.9 <- predict(qgam(log(deaths+1) ~ s(log(BaseDam2014)), qu=.409,
                   data=hurric[-56,]))
```

```
Estimating learning rate. Each dot corresponds to a loss evaluation.
qu = 0.409........done
```

The quantile residuals used for Figure 5.15B are residuals that have been transformed into equivalent normal quantiles ("z-scores"). As a consequence, the usual normal distribution diagnostics can be used to check whether they have the expected distributional properties. Figure 5.15B shows, at higher quantiles, a nonlinear relationship that is inconsistent with a negative binomial distribution.

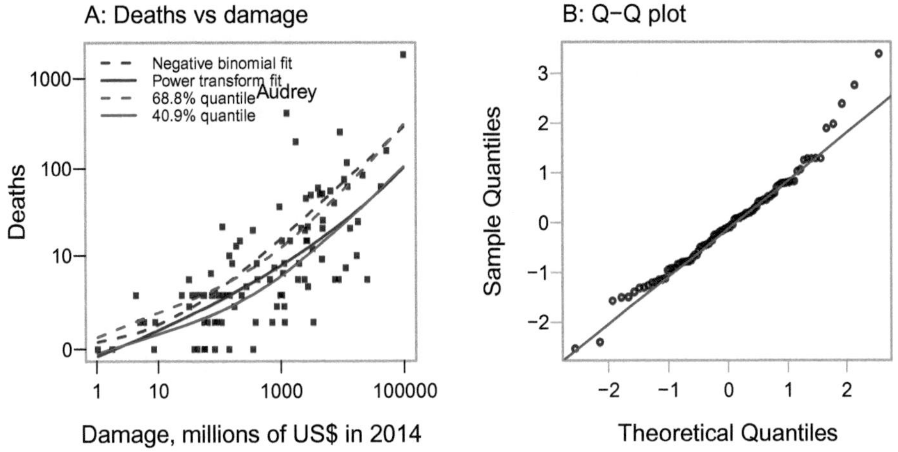

Figure 5.15 Panel A shows, as a dashed blue curve, the fitted values for the negative binomial model. Values on the y-scale are plotted on a scale of log(deaths+1). The solid blue curve is for a power-transform fit. Panel B shows a quantile–quantile (Q-Q) plot for quantile residuals for the negative binomial model. The very large residual is for hurricane Audrey (1955).

Notice that the fitted values for the negative binomial fit is a rough match to the 64.5 percent quantile curve. By contrast, the power-transformed values of `deaths` closer to symmetrically distributed. The fitted values for a linear least squares regression on the power-transformed scale are, when mapped onto the `log(deaths+1)` scale, a rough match to the 40.9 percent quantile curve shown in Figure 5.15A. The plots serve as a warning that, when the error distribution is strongly asymmetric, fitted values may be some distance from the distributional median.

Using Centiles for a More-Detailed Comparison

A detailed comparison between selected centiles of the fitted distribution and the data-based counts will help tease out the mismatch between the sample quantiles and the theoretical quantiles that is apparent in Panel B. The following compares centiles of the predicted number of deaths with the observed number of deaths for low (under \$150 million), medium, and high (\$150 million or higher) damage categories. If the model is fitting well, values in the 5 (fifth centile) column should be around 5, those in the tenth centile column around 10, and so on.

```
## a) Fitted and empirical centiles from hurrNB.gamlss
pc <- t(centiles.split(hurrNB.gamlss, xvar=log(hurric$BaseDam2014)[-56],
  cent=c(5,10,25,50,75,90,95), xcut.points=log(c(150, 1500)),
  plot=FALSE))
rownames(pc) <- c("up to 150M", "150M to 1500M", "above 1500M")
round(pc,2)
```

```
                   5    10    25    50    75     90     95
up to 150M     28.12 28.12 34.38 50.00 81.25  93.75  93.75
150M to 1500M   4.17 12.50 33.33 66.67 79.17 100.00 100.00
above 1500M     2.70  5.41 27.03 51.35 81.08  91.89  91.89
```

In the "up to 150 million dollars" range, 28.1 percent of the deaths occurred under the theoretical distribution's fifth centile limit. In the above 1500 million dollars range, no deaths were under the fifth centile limit, while 91.9 percent of deaths occurred under the theoretical 75th centile limit.

Now examine the corresponding numbers for the model that was fitted in Subsection 3.3.5. This model, referred to as model (b) in the further comparison that follows, used least squares to model a power transform of `deaths+1`, with $\lambda = -0.2$, as a linear function of `log(BaseDam2014)`. Recall that there was just one obvious outlier. A first step is to fit the model as a `gamlss` model with normal errors:

```
hurrP.gamlss <- gamlss(car::yjPower(deaths, -0.2) ~ log(BaseDam2014), data=hurric)
```

```
## Fitted and empirical centiles from hurrP.gamlss
pc <- t(centiles.split(hurrP.gamlss, xvar=log(hurric$BaseDam2014),
cent=c(5,10,25,50,75,90,95),
xcut.points=log(c(150, 1500)), plot=FALSE))
rownames(pc) <- c("up to 150M", "150M to 1500M", "above 1500M")
round(pc,2)
```

```
                  5    10    25    50    75    90    95
up to 150M     6.25 18.75 25.00 40.62 81.25 93.75 96.88
150M to 1500M  8.00 16.00 32.00 60.00 76.00 92.00 96.00
above 1500M    5.41  8.11 21.62 37.84 70.27 91.89 97.30
```

The centiles are much better aligned than for the negative binomial model.

The *gamlss* package has several alternatives to the negative binomial that are intended for use with count data. See `?gamlss::gamlss.family` for details. We have not found any that give a really satisfactory fit to the hurricane death data.

5.5 Fitting Smooths

The function `mgcv::gam()` can be used to fit GLM-type models that include smoothing terms, with automatic choice of smoothing parameter. All error families can be specified, and several more. See `?mgcv::family.mgcv`.

5.5.1 Handedness of First-Class Cricketers in the UK

The dataset `DAAG::cricketer` relates to British male first-class cricketers with year of birth 1840–1960. Total numbers by handedness, broken down by whether `live` or `dead` in 1992, with proportions shown on the right, are as follows.

	Number			Proportion	
	live	dead	Sum	live	dead
right	2104	2755	4859	0.433	0.567
left	469	632	1101	0.426	0.574

Several articles in medical journals have used such data to suggest that left-handers (those who used their left hand for bowling) had shorter lifespans than

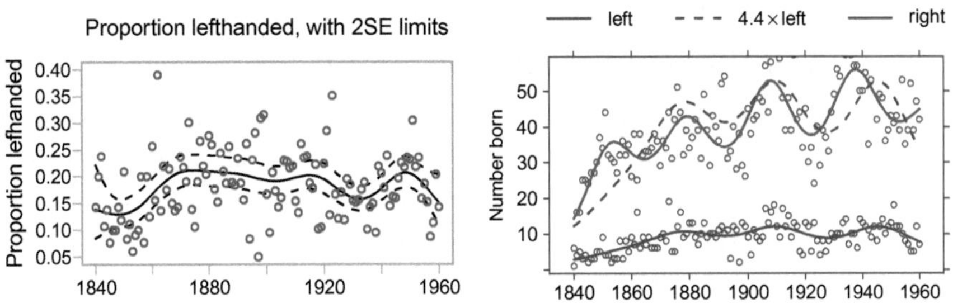

Figure 5.16 Proportion of lefthanders, as a smooth function of year of birth. Dashed lines are approximate pointwise 2 SE limits.

righthanders. Those articles did not account for changes over time in the proportions of lefthanders. Similar claims for basketballers have likewise ignored systematic changes over time in the proportions of lefthanders.

A GAM model, assuming binomial errors, will examine how the proportion of lefthanders has changed over time. Here, the independence assumption is plausible. An occasional father-and-son succession of lefthanders can be expected to make only a small contribution to the total data. Useful additional insight is provided by a plot that shows how numbers of lefthanders and righthanders changed over time.

The following gives the plot in the left panel of Figure 5.16:

```
library(mgcv)
DAAG::cricketer |> dplyr::count(year, left, name="Freq") -> handYear
names(handYear)[2] <- "hand"
byYear <- tidyr::pivot_wider(handYear, names_from='hand', values_from="Freq")
hand.gam <- gam(cbind(left,right) ~ s(year), data=byYear, family=binomial)
const <- attr(predict(hand.gam, type='terms'), "constant")
  ## `const` is the mean on the scale of the linear predictor
plot(hand.gam, shift=const, trans=function(x)exp(x)/(1+exp(x)),
    ylab="Proportion lefhanded")
  ## Add `const`, then apply inverse link function.
  ## Plots estimated proportions (i.e., on the scale of the response)
```

The right panel gives an alternative view of the data:

```
leftrt.gam <- gam(Freq ~ hand + s(year, by=factor(hand)), data=handYear,
                  family=poisson)
leftrt.pred <- predict(leftrt.gam, se=T, type='response')
handYear <- cbind(handYear, as.data.frame(leftrt.pred))
col2 <- DAAG::DAAGtheme(color=T)$superpose.symbol$col[c(2,2,1)]
gph.key <- list(lines=list(lty=c(1,2,1), col=col2, lwd=2), space="top",
                columns=3, text=list(c("left","4.4*left","right")))
gph <- xyplot(leftrt.pred$fit ~ year, groups=hand, ylab="Number born",
              type="l", col=col2[c(3,1)], data=handYear, key=gph.key, lwd=2)
gph1 <- xyplot(Freq~year, groups=hand, data=handYear, col=col2[c(3,1)])
gph+as.layer(gph1)+as.layer(xyplot(I(4.4*fit) ~ year, type="l", lty=2, lwd=2,
    data=subset(handYear, hand=="left"), col=col2[2]))
```

Exercise 5.7 at the end of the chapter looks further at the analysis, and at differences between lefthanders and righthanders.

5.6 Additional Notes on Generalized Linear Models

5.6.1 Residuals, and Estimating the Dispersion*

The R function `residuals.glm()`, which is called when `residuals()` is used with a `glm` object as its argument, offers a choice of three different types of residuals – deviance residuals (`type="deviance"`), Pearson residuals (`type="pearson"`), and working residuals (`type="working"`). For models with discrete error families (binomial, poisson, ...), the randomized quantile residuals that were introduced in Subsection 2.3.1 are in most contexts now to be preferred.

Even where randomized quantile residuals are used, plots of residuals can be hard to interpret. This is an especially serious problem for models that have a binary (0/1) response, where a suitable form of smooth curve is an essential aid to visual interpretation.

Other Choices of Link Functions for Binomial Models

Perhaps the most important alternative to the logit is the complementary log–log link. This has $f(x) = \log(-\log(1-x))$. For an argument from extreme value theory that motivates the use of the complementary log–log link, see Maindonald et al. (2001). It is often appropriate when p is a mortality that increases with time. For p close to 0, this behaves like the logit. For values of p close to 1, it is a much milder transformation than the probit or logit.

Also used is the probit, which is the normal quantile function, that is, the inverse of the cumulative normal distribution. This is slightly less severe than the logit, and hard to distinguish from it. Extensive data are required, and differences are likely to be evident only in the extreme tails.

Quasi Models – Estimating the Dispersion

For `quasibinomial` and `quasipoisson` models, the default estimate for the dispersion comes from dividing the sum of squares of the Pearson residuals by the degrees of freedom of the residual. This is a less-biased estimate of the dispersion than given by the residual mean deviance, and hence more appropriate for use in the calculation of standard errors. Such bias as it has is in most cases small enough to be ignored (McCullagh and Nelder, 1989, section 4.5.2). An alternative that is the default for use with models fitted using the *mgcv* function `gam()` is the "fletcher" estimate, which is a modified version of the Pearson estimate. See `?mgcv::gam.scale`.

In `lm` models, which are equivalent to GLMs with identity link and normal errors, the dispersion and the residual mean deviance both equal the mean residual sum of squares, and have a chi-squared distribution with degrees of freedom equal to the degrees of freedom of the residual. This is a good approximation for quasipoisson models with suitably large fitted values (e.g., at least 2), and for some binomial models. In other cases, it can be highly unsatisfactory.

The difference in deviance between two nested models has a distribution that is often well approximated by a chi-squared distribution. Where there are two such models, with nesting such that the mean difference in deviance (i.e., difference in deviance divided by degrees of freedom) gives a plausible estimate of the source of variation that is relevant to the intended inferences, this may be used to estimate the dispersion. For example, see McCullagh and Nelder (1989, section 4.5.2). A better alternative may be use of the `lme4::glmer()` function, specifying a binomial link and specifying the random part of the model appropriately. McCullagh and Nelder (1989, Chapter 9) discuss theoretical issues for the use of ideas of quasilikelihood.

5.6.2 Standard Errors and z- or t-Statistics for Binomial Models

The z- or t-statistics are sometimes known as the Wald statistics. They are based on an asymptotic approximation to the standard error. For binomial models, this approximation can be seriously inaccurate when the fitted proportions are close to 0 or 1, to the extent that an increased difference in an estimated proportion can be associated with a smaller t-statistic. Where a reasonably accurate p-value is important, this is suitably obtained from an analysis of deviance that compares models with and without the term.

The following demonstrates the effect:

```
fac <- factor(LETTERS[1:4])
p <- c(73, 30, 11, 2)/500
n <- rep(500,4)
round(signif(coef(summary(glm(p ~ fac, family=binomial, weights=n))), 6), 6)
```

```
             Estimate Std. Error z value Pr(>|z|)
(Intercept)   -1.7663     0.1267 -13.946 0.000000
facB          -0.9852     0.2269  -4.341 0.000014
facC          -2.0281     0.3301  -6.143 0.000000
facD          -3.7511     0.7198  -5.212 0.000000
```

The `z value` for level D is smaller than the `z value` for level C, even though the difference from level A (the reference) is greater.

The phenomenon is discussed in Hauck and Donner (1977).

5.6.3 Leverage for Binomial Models

In an `lm` model with a single predictor and with homogeneous errors, the points that are furthest from the mean inevitably have the largest leverages. For models with binomial errors, this is not the case. The leverages are functions of the fitted values. Figure 5.17 shows the pattern of change of the leverage, for the three common link functions, when points are symmetrically placed, on the scale of the response, about a fitted proportion of 0.5. The optimal placement of points for a `probit` link is slightly further apart than for a `logit` link.

Use the function `hatvalues()` to calculate leverages. The following plots leverages, as in Figure 5.17 for a logit link, against fitted proportions.

```
p <- (1:99)/100
toy.glm <- glm(p ~ log(p/(1-p)), family=binomial(link="logit"),
weights=rep(100,99))
plot(fitted(toy.glm), hatvalues(toy.glm), ylim=c(0, 0.027), type="l")
```

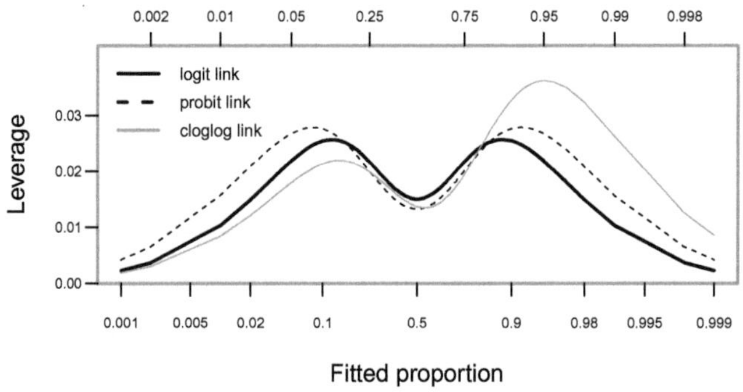

Figure 5.17 Leverage versus fitted proportion, for the three common link functions. Points that all have the same binomial totals were symmetrically placed, on the scale of the response, about a fitted proportion of 0.5. The number and location of points will affect the magnitudes, but for the symmetric links any symmetric configuration of points will give the same pattern of change. The x-axis is shown on a logit scale.

Table 5.2 *Data from a randomized trial – assessments of the clarity of the instructions provided for an inhaler.*

	Easy (category 1)	Needed rereading (category 2)	Not clear (category 3)
Inhaler 1	99	41	2
Inhaler 2	76	55	13

5.7 Models with an Ordered Categorical or Categorical Response

These further extend the generalized linear model framework. Here, the main focus will be ordinal regression models. Loglinear models, which may be appropriate when there is a qualitative (i.e., unordered) categorical response, will get brief mention.

5.7.1 Ordinal Regression Models

We will demonstrate how logistic and related generalized linear models that assume binomial errors can be used for an initial analysis. The particular form of logistic regression that we will demonstrate is *proportional odds logistic regression.*

Ordinal logistic regression is relevant when there are three or more ordered outcome categories that might, for example, be (1) complete recovery, (2) continuing illness, (3) death. Here, in Table 5.2, we give an example where patients who were randomly assigned to two different inhalers were asked to compare the clarity of leaflet instructions for their inhaler (data, initially published with the permission of 3M Health Care Ltd., are adapted from Ezzet and Whitehead (1991)).

Table 5.3 *Odds ratios, and logarithms of odds ratios, for two alternative choices of cutpoint in Table 5.2.*

	Easy versus some degree of difficulty		Clear after study versus not clear	
	Odds	Log odds	Odds	Log odds
Inhaler 1	99/43	log(99/43) = 0.83	140/2	log(140/2) = 4.25
Inhaler 2	76/68	log(76/68) = 0.11	131/13	log(131/13) = 2.31

Exploratory Analysis

A split of the outcomes into two categories can either contrast "easy" with the remaining two responses (some degree of difficulty), or can contrast the first two categories (clear, perhaps after study) with "not clear." Table 5.3 presents, side by side in parallel columns, odds based on these two splits. Values for log(odds) are given alongside.

Wherever we make the cut, the comparison favors the instructions for inhaler 1. The picture is not as simple as we might have liked. The log(odds ratio), namely, the difference on the log(odds) scale, differs between the two cutpoints.

* *Proportional Odds Logistic Regression*

The function `VGAM::vglm()` will be used to fit a formal model. We begin by fitting a separate models for the two rows of data in Table 5.2.

```
library(VGAM)
inhaler <- data.frame(freq=c(99,76,41,55,2,13),
  choice=rep(c("inh1","inh2"), 3),
  ease=ordered(rep(c("easy","re-read","unclear"), rep(2,3))))
inhaler1.vglm <- vglm(ease ~ 1, weights=freq, data=inhaler,
  cumulative(link="logitlink"), subset=inhaler$choice=="inh1")
inhaler2.vglm <- vglm(ease ~ 1, weights=freq, data=inhaler,
  cumulative(link="logitlink"), subset=inhaler$choice=="inh2")
```

The dependent variable `ease` specifies the categories, while frequencies are specified as weights. The part of the output that is of immediate interest is

```
## Inhaler 1
round(coef(summary(inhaler1.vglm)),3)
```

```
               Estimate Std. Error z value Pr(>|z|)
(Intercept):1     0.834      0.183   4.566        0
(Intercept):2     4.248      0.712   5.966        0
```

```
## Inhaler 2
round(coef(summary(inhaler2.vglm)),3)
```

```
               Estimate Std. Error z value Pr(>|z|)
(Intercept):1     0.111      0.167   0.666    0.505
(Intercept):2     2.310      0.291   7.945    0.000
```

For interpreting the output, observe that the intercepts for inhaler 1 are $0.834 = \log(99/43)$ and $4.248 = \log(140/2)$. For inhaler 2 they are $0.111 = \log(76/68)$ and $2.310 = \log(131/13)$.

Both sets of coefficients can be obtained in a single fit.

```
inhaler.vglm <- vglm(ease ~ choice, weights=freq, data=inhaler,
cumulative(link="logitlink", parallel=FALSE))
round(coef(summary(inhaler.vglm)),3)
```

```
                Estimate Std. Error z value Pr(>|z|)
(Intercept):1      0.834      0.183   4.566    0.000
(Intercept):2      4.248      0.712   5.966    0.000
choiceinh2:1      -0.723      0.247  -2.921    0.003
choiceinh2:2      -1.938      0.769  -2.520    0.012
```

The intercepts for inhaler 2 are $0.834 - 0.723 = 0.111$ and $4.248 - 1.938 = 2.310$, in agreement with the result above.

Is it reasonable to insist that both intercepts change by the same amount? This can be checked by comparing the `parallel=FALSE` model just fitted with a model that has `parallel=TRUE`:

```
inhalerP.vglm <- vglm(ease ~ choice, weights=freq, data=inhaler,
cumulative(link="logitlink", parallel=TRUE))
round(coef(summary(inhalerP.vglm)),3)
```

```
                Estimate Std. Error z value Pr(>|z|)
(Intercept):1      0.863      0.183   4.716    0.000
(Intercept):2      3.353      0.307  10.904    0.000
choiceinh2        -0.790      0.245  -3.226    0.001
```

The intercepts for inhaler 2 are $0.863 - 0.790 = 0.073$, $3.353 - 0.790 = 2.563$.

The function `predict()` can be used to get estimates of both sets of intercepts directly, with SEs if required:

```
pred <- predict(inhalerP.vglm, se.fit=TRUE, newdata=inhaler[1:2,])
colnames(pred$se.fit) <- paste("SE", colnames(pred$se.fit))
fitvals <- with(pred, cbind(fitted.values, se.fit))
colnames(fitvals) <- gsub('link', '', colnames(fitvals))
round(fitvals, 2)
```

```
  logit(P[Y<=1]) logit(P[Y<=2]) SE logit(P[Y<=1]) SE logit(P[Y<=2])
1           0.86           3.35              0.18              0.31
2           0.07           2.56              0.17              0.28
```

There is one less parameter for the nonparallel model than for the nonparallel model. The difference in deviance is:

```
d <- deviance(inhalerP.vglm) - deviance(inhaler.vglm)
## Refer to chi-squared distribution with 1 degree of freedom
c(Difference=d, "p-Value"=pchisq(3.416, df=1, lower.tail=FALSE))
```

```
Difference    p-Value
   3.41615    0.06457
```

Table 5.4 summarizes fitted values for the parallel model.

An alternative to the cumulative model is the adjacent category model. For comparing the log odds for adjacent categories, specify `family=acat(link="loge")`,

Table 5.4 *The entries are log(odds) and odds estimates for the proportional odds logistic regression model that was fitted to the parallel model.*

	log(odds). Odds in parentheses	
	Easy versus some degree of difficulty	Clear after study versus not clear
Inhaler 1	0.863 (exp(0.863) = 2.37)	3.353 (28.6)
Inhaler 2	0.0723 (1.075)	2.56 (13.0)

perhaps also supplying the argument `parallel=TRUE`. A further possibility is the "continuation ratio" or "stage" model. This focuses on the probability of progression beyond category ('stage') j, conditional on having reached stage j.

5.7.2 Loglinear Models*

Loglinear models specify expected values for the frequencies in a multiway table directly. For the model-fitting process, all margins of the table have the same status. However, one of the margins has a special role for interpretative purposes; it is known as the *dependent* margin. For the `UCBAdmissions` data that we discussed in Section 5.3, the interest was in the variation of admission rate with `Dept` and with `Gender`. A loglinear model, with `Admit` as the dependent margin, offers an alternative way to handle the analysis. Loglinear models are, however, generally reserved for use when the dependent margin has more than two levels, so that logistic regression is not an alternative. The help page `?MASS::loglm()` has examples that demonstrate the fitting of loglinear models.

5.8 Survival Analysis

Survival analysis involves concepts that are seldom encountered in the regression methods discussed earlier. Also referred to as time-to-event analysis, it is principally concerned with the time-duration of a given condition. The methodology is elegant though relatively unknown outside of the fields of medicine, actuarial science, and engineering. It answers questions such as: How long will a terminally ill patient survive when subjected to one of a collection of possible treatments? It is used to study the distribution of time to onset of disease symptoms after infection, and it is also possible to study the time to recurrence of an illness or other medical condition.

In nonmedical contexts, it is referred to as failure time or reliability analysis. Applications include the failure times of industrial machine components, electronic equipment, kitchen toasters, light bulbs, businesses, and loan defaults. The time may be time to any event of interest, not necessarily failure. For example, a diploma certification program may have interest in studying and promoting the length of time it takes for graduates to land their first job.

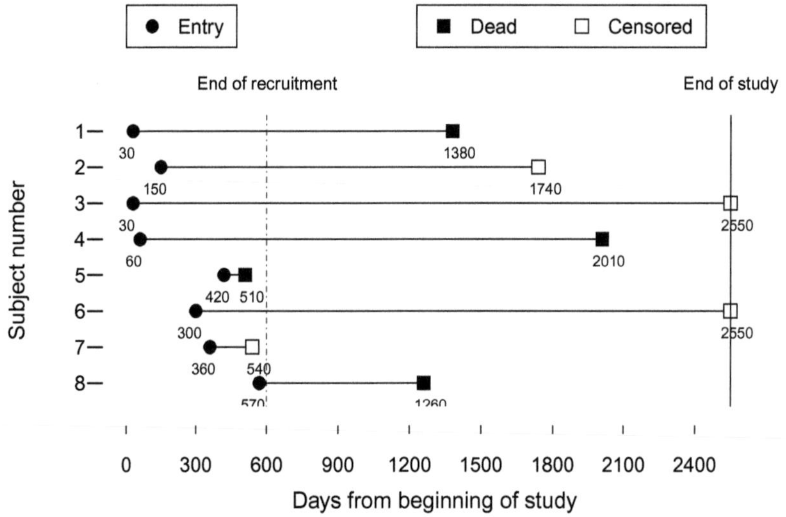

Figure 5.18 Outline of the process of collection of data that will be used in a survival analysis.

An important concept in the study of failure-time data is *censoring*. Censoring implies that information about the outcome is incomplete in some respect, but not completely missing. Where the subject has survived beyond the endtime of the study, the failure time is said to be "right censored." If it is only known that the failure event occurred prior to a known time instant, the event time is said to be left censored. Data of this type feature in the study of lightning-caused wildfire occurrences, where the time of fire ignition is usually unobserved, and the fire is discovered at some time after ignition.

Thus, for each observation there are two pieces of information: a time, and censoring information. The censoring information may indicate either right censoring denoted by a 0, or failure denoted by a 1. Figure 5.18 shows a common pattern for the collection of survival analysis data.

Many of the issues that arise in more classical forms of regression analysis also arise here. Diagnostic checking of the underlying model assumptions remains important. There have been considerable advances in this methodology in recent years. Model choice and variable selection share commonalities with regression and generalized linear models, but the handling of censored data requires new approaches.

A good introductory account of survival analysis can be found in the book by Klein and Moeschberger (2003). The computations that follow will use the *survival* package.

5.8.1 Analysis of the `Aids2` *Data*

In the study that provided the `Aids2` (`MASS` package) data, recruitment continued until the day prior to the end of the study. Once recruited, subjects were followed until either they were *censored*, that is, were not available for further study, or until they died from an AIDS-related, cause. The time from recruitment to death or censoring will be used for analysis.

Note the different types of right censoring. Subjects were censored because they died from a cause that was not AIDS-related, or because they could no longer be traced. Additionally, subjects who are still alive at the end of the study could not at that point be studied further, and thus said to be censored.

Details of the different columns are:

```
str(MASS::Aids2, vec.len=2)
```

```
'data.frame':   2843 obs. of  7 variables:
 $ state   : Factor w/ 4 levels "NSW","Other",..: 1 1 1 1 1 ...
 $ sex     : Factor w/ 2 levels "F","M": 2 2 2 2 2 ...
 $ diag    : int  10905 11029 9551 9577 10015 ...
 $ death   : int  11081 11096 9983 9654 10290 ...
 $ status  : Factor w/ 2 levels "A","D": 2 2 2 2 2 ...
 $ T.categ: Factor w/ 8 levels "hs","hsid","id",..: 1 1 1 5 1 ...
 $ age     : int  35 53 42 44 39 ...
```

Note that **death** really means "final point in time at which status was known."

The analyses that will be presented will use two different subsets of the data – individuals who contracted AIDS from contaminated blood, and male homosexuals. The extensive data in the second of these datasets makes it suitable for explaining the notion of *hazard*.

A good starting point for any investigation of survival data is the survival curve or (if there are several groups within the data) survival curves. The survival curve estimates the proportion who have survived at any time. The analysis will work with "number of days from diagnosis to death or removal from the study," and this number needs to be calculated.

The following extracts the subset of the data that contracted AIDS from contaminated blood.

```
bloodAids <- subset(MASS::Aids2, T.categ=="blood")
bloodAids$days <- bloodAids$death-bloodAids$diag
bloodAids$dead <- as.integer(bloodAids$status=="D")
```

All subjects in this subset were followed through until the end of the study. Censored patients were those that were still alive at the end of the study. Figure 5.19 compares, for this subset, females with males, with pointwise 95 percent confidence intervals placed around the estimated survival curves. These assume independence between the individuals in the study group.

```
## Code
plot(survfit(Surv(days, dead) ~ sex, data=bloodAids),
col=c(2,4), conf.int=TRUE)
legend("top", legend=levels(bloodAids$sex), lty=c(1,1),
col=c(2,4), horiz=TRUE, bty="n")
```

The function **Surv()** brings together the time and the censoring (alive = 0, dead = 1) information. The **survfit()** function then estimates the survival curve.

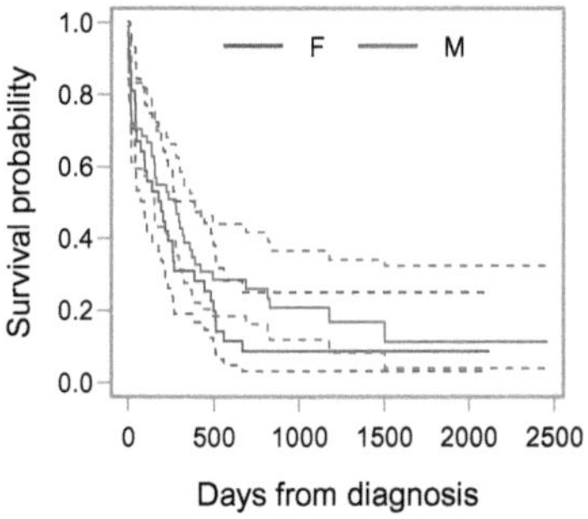

Figure 5.19 Survival curves compare females with males, for those who contracted AIDS from contaminated blood. Dashed curves show pointwise 95 percent confidence limits.

5.8.2 Right Censoring Prior to the Termination of the Study

This might happen in (at least) two ways.

- The subject may have died from a cause that is thought unlikely to be AIDS-related, for example, a traffic accident.
- The subject may have disappeared from the study, with efforts to trace them unsuccessful.

A common assumption is that, subject to any predictor effects, the pattern of risk after the time when the subject was last known to be alive remained the same as for individuals who were not censored. In technical language, the censoring was "noninformative." Censoring would be informative if it gave information on the risk of that patient. For example, some patients may, because of direct or indirect effects of their illness or of the associated medication, be at increased risk of such accidents. Such possibilities make it unlikely that it will be strictly true that censoring has been noninformative, though this can be a reasonable working approximation, especially if a relatively small number of subjects have been censored.

In order to illustrate the point, we will examine the pattern of censoring for males where the mode of transmission (`T.categ`) was homosexual activity. (These data will be used in the later discussion to illustrate the notion of *hazard*.)

```
hsaids <- subset(MASS::Aids2, sex=="M" & T.categ=="hs")
hsaids$days <- hsaids$death-hsaids$diag
hsaids$dead <- as.integer(hsaids$status=="D")
table(hsaids$status,hsaids$death==11504)
```

```
   FALSE TRUE
A     16  916
D   1531    1
```

Recall that `death` (i.e., time of death) really means "final point in time at which status was known." The interpretation of this output is as follows.

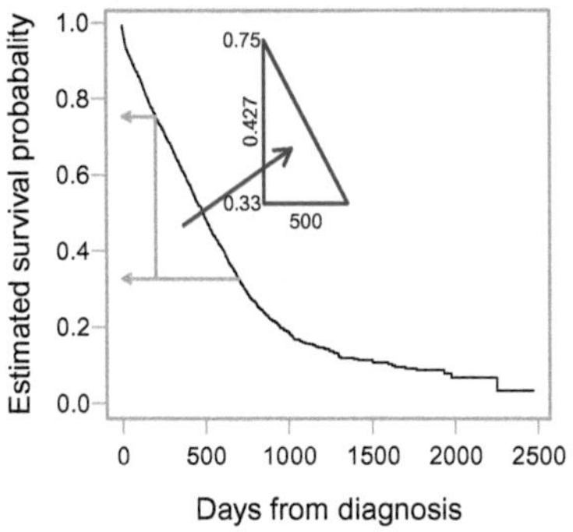

Figure 5.20 Survival curve for males for whom the mode of transmission was sexual activity. There are two sets of arrows that show how the estimated survival probability decreased over a 400-day period.

Alive at some time prior to end of study (16 censored at time < 11504)	Alive at end of study (916 censored on day 11504)
Dead at some time prior to end of study (1531 not censored)	Dead at end of study (1 not censored)

Just 16 individuals were censored prior to the end of the study, probably not enough to cause a serious bias, even if their censoring was to an extent informative.

5.8.3 The Survival Curve for Male Homosexuals

Figure 5.20 shows the survival curve for these data, with dashed curves showing 95 percent pointwise confidence limits. Annotation has been added that will be used to help illustrate the notion of *hazard.* The triangle on the upper left shows the change between 200 days and 700 days, from a survival of 0.75 at day 200 to a survival of 0.33 at day 700. The difference in survival is 0.42, or more precisely 0.427, which is a reduction of 0.000854 per day. The code is:

```
## Survival curve for male homosexuals
hsaids.surv <- survfit(Surv(days, dead) ~ 1, data=hsaids)
plot(hsaids.surv)
```

5.8.4 Hazard Rates

The hazard rate is obtained by dividing the mortality per day by the survival to that point. Over a short time interval, multiplication of the hazard by the time interval gives the probability of death over that interval, given survival up to that time. In Figure 5.20, hazard rates at days 200 and 700 are, approximately, the following.

Day 200	$0.00854/0.752 \simeq 0.11$
Day 700	$0.00854/0.326 \simeq 0.026$

More generally, the hazard rate can be determined at any point by fitting a smooth function to the survival curve, and dividing the slope of the tangent by the survival at that point. The above calculations of hazard are rough. More-refined estimates can be obtained by using the function `muhaz::muhaz()`. For precise estimates of the hazard, large sample sizes are needed.

5.8.5 The Cox Proportional Hazards Model

The Cox proportional hazards model requires the assumption that the ratio is constant between two groups that are to be compared. In the example now considered, the assumption will be that the hazard for males who contracted AIDS from contaminated blood was, relative to that for females, a constant.

The function `cox.zph()` can be used to check on the assumption. It replaces a constant β by a time dependent $\beta(t)$, and checks whether $\beta(t)$ can be plausibly regarded as constant. Where data are sufficiently extensive to make such a check effective, it often turns out that the ratio is not constant over the whole time period. Several available alternative transformations of the survival times can be checked. If it finally appears that the ratio is not truly constant over the whole time period, it may be reasonable to treat the estimated ratio as an average.

Using females as the baseline, we now examine the hazard ratios for males who contracted AIDS from contaminated blood. Code, with summary output is:

```
bloodAids.coxph <- coxph(Surv(days, dead) ~ sex, data=bloodAids)
print(summary(bloodAids.coxph), digits=6)
```

```
Call:
coxph(formula = Surv(days, dead) ~ sex, data = bloodAids)

  n= 94, number of events= 76

          coef exp(coef)  se(coef)         z Pr(>|z|)
sexM -0.275975  0.758832  0.232934 -1.18478  0.23611

     exp(coef) exp(-coef) lower .95 upper .95
sexM  0.758832    1.31782  0.480697    1.1979

Concordance= 0.52  (se = 0.031 )
Likelihood ratio test= 1.38  on 1 df,   p=0.24
Wald test            = 1.4  on 1 df,   p=0.24
Score (logrank) test = 1.41  on 1 df,   p=0.23
```

Let $h_0(x)$ be the hazard function for females. Then the model assumes that the hazard function $h_m(x)$ for males can be written:

$$h_m(x) = h_0(x)\exp(\beta).$$

In the above output, `coef` is what, in this formula, is β. There are several ways to examine the comparison of males with females.

- The confidence interval for β includes 0, so that the t-test for the test $\beta = 0$ has a p-value equal to 0.24.
- The confidence interval for $\exp(\beta)$ includes 1.

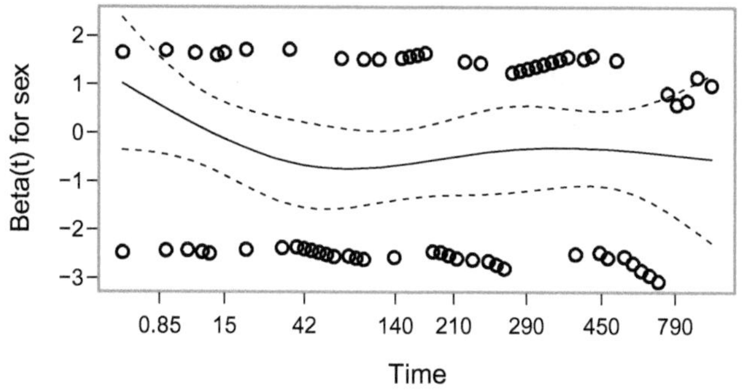

Figure 5.21 Time-dependent coefficients for the Cox proportional hazards model.

- The three test statistics are returned are in close agreement – likelihood ratio test ($p = 0.24$), Wald ($p = 0.24$), score (logrank ($p = 0.23$).

In general, β may be a function of predictors, and there may be several groups. Confidence intervals will then be given for the separate coefficients in this model. The likelihood ratio test, the Wald test, and the log-rank test are all then tests for the null hypothesis that the groups have the same hazard function.

5.8.6 Diagnostics for the Cox Proportional Hazards Model

Concordance

The concordance statistic is a measure of how effectively the model is predicting risk. At each event time the current risk score of the subject who failed is compared to the current scores of all those still at risk. A concordance of 0.5 implies that the model is doing no better than chance. Here, with a concordance that equals 0.52 (SE = 0.031), the model is performing only slightly better than chance. This improves slightly if `age` is added as an explanatory variable, to 0.524 (SE = 0.039). Code for this is:

```
bloodAids.coxph1 <- coxph(Surv(days, dead) ~ sex+age, data=bloodAids)
```

Constant versus Time-Dependent Coefficient $\beta(t)$

The function `cox.zph()` provides checks, for each covariate included in the Cox model and for the model as a whole, the proportional hazards (PH) assumption that the hazard ratio is a constant. For each covariate, statistical tests check whether the corresponding time-dependent estimate can be regarded as constant with time, rather than linearly increasing or decreasing. Additionally, it performs a global check for the model as a whole. The summary statistical information should be checked along with an accompanying plot (or plots) that shows how the time-dependent estimate varies with time, with pointwise confidence intervals shown. See `?plot.coxph` for the wide range of possibilities. Note also the references given there.

To check the PH assumption, we can type the following R code:

```
## Code
plot(cox.zph(bloodAids.coxph))
```

Printed output is:

```
cox.zph(bloodAids.coxph)
```

```
        chisq df    p
sex      1.24  1 0.27
GLOBAL   1.24  1 0.27
```

The graph suggests that the hazard ratio may have been greater for males for the first 40 days or so after diagnosis. However, the difference from a constant β cannot be distinguished from statistical error. In samples of this size, the difference from a constant ratio must be large to allow much chance of detection.

5.8.7 Did Lefthanded Cricketers Have Shorter Life Spans?

Subsection 5.5.1 used historical data in the dataset `DAAG::cricketer` to fit smooth curves to to the change in the proportion of lefthanders, and the numbers from each hand, among British first class cricketers born between 1840 and 1960. Here, we fit Cox proportional hazards models to compare the risk between lefthanders and righthanders. The main interest is in the comparison of risk of death (`kia=1`) in military action. For this, as the only information provided is on whether of not each individual was killed in action (not on which were in the military), it is necessary to assume that the numbers in the military were a similar fraction of both types of handedness. The following model was chosen after some preliminary investigation.

```
cricketer <- DAAG::cricketer
kia4.coxph <- coxph(Surv(life, kia) ~ left/poly(year,4),
                    data = cricketer, model=T)
kia6.coxph <- update(kia4.coxph, . ~ left/poly(year,6),
                     data = cricketer, model=T)
# Type `plot(cox.zph(kia6.coxph))` to plot the two graphs
# Perhaps check also `AIC(kia4.coxph, kia6.coxph)`
cox.zph(kia6.coxph)
```

```
                     chisq df                p
left                  1.99  1             0.16
left:poly(year, 6)   79.42 12 0.0000000000053
GLOBAL               80.83 13 0.0000000000077
```

Clearly the term `left:poly(year , 6)` is needed. Figure 5.22 plots the time-dependent coefficient estimates for the model `cox.zph(kia6.coxph)`.

5.9 Transformations for Proportions and Counts

It was at one time common to apply transformations directly to proportion or count data, then applying normal theory methods to the resulting values. Generalized linear models, where it is the expected value of the proportion or count that is transformed, have reduced the need for such approaches. They remain, as for

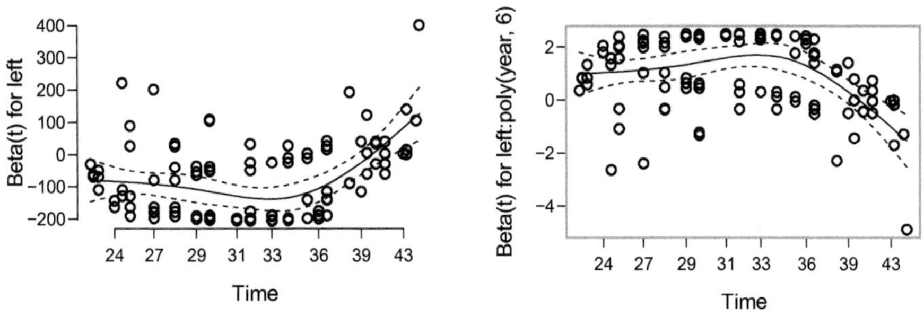

Figure 5.22 Time-dependent coefficient estimates, one set for each of two explanatory terms, for the Cox proportional hazards model.

the hurricane deaths data in Subsection 5.4.4, a recourse that can sometimes be useful. In addition to the link functions that are commonly used in GLMs, note the following.

- **The angular transformation:** $y = \arcsin(\sqrt{p})$, where p is a proportion. If proportions have been generated from a binomial distribution, the angular transformation will "stabilize the variance." The R function `asin()` gives values in radians. If values that run from 0 to 90 are preferred, multiply radians by $180/\pi = 57.3$.
- **Power transformations:** A version of the power transformation may, as discussed in Subsection 2.5.6, be applied to either proportions or counts.

For proportions that result from dividing a number x of "successes" by a total n, the transformation may be applied to $\frac{x+c}{n+2c}$ rather than to $\frac{x}{n}$, where c is a suitable positive constant (1, 0.5, and $\frac{1}{6}$ have been suggested). For the logit transformation, $c = \frac{1}{6}$ gives the version of the flog (folded logarithm) transformation proposed in Tukey (1992). Use of c as an offset bounds the transformation away from $-\infty$ when $x = 0$, and from ∞ when $x = 1$, more strongly for larger values of c.

For proportions where there is extra-binomial variation, an assumption of constant variance on a transformed scale may be more appropriate than the quasibinomial constant dispersion assumption. For count data, it may sometimes, as the use of the Yeo–Johnson variant of the Box–Cox power transformation in Subsections 3.3.5 and 5.4.3 illustrated, be more effective to work with transformed count data rather than to use a model that is specifically intended for count data.

The Poisson parameter λ is the mean for a distribution that, for small values of λ, is strongly skewed to the right. For a Poisson x, the distribution of $\log(x+c)$ is then closer to symmetric than is that for x. As a consequence, $\mathrm{E}[\log(x+c)]$ may be much smaller than $\log(\lambda+c)$. Similar comments apply to negative binomial models.

5.10 Further Reading

Dobson and Barnett (2008) is an elementary introduction to generalized linear models. See also Faraway (2016). Chapter 3 of Wood (2017) is a succinct, insightful and practically oriented summary of the theory of generalized linear models. A classic reference on generalized linear models is McCullagh and Nelder (1989); for quasibinomial and quasipoisson models, see pp. 200–208. Harrell (2015) gives a comprehensive account of both generalized linear models and survival analysis that includes extensive practical advice. See also Venables and Ripley (2002).

Collett (2014) is a basic introduction to elementary uses of survival analysis. Therneau and Grambsch (2001) describes extensions to the Cox model, with extensive examples that use the abilities of the *survival* package. Bland and Altman (2005) is an interesting example of the application of survival methods.

There are many ways to extend the models that we have discussed. Multiple levels of variation, such as are discussed in Chapter 7, are a further potential complication.

5.11 Exercises

5.1. The following table shows numbers of occasions when inhibition (i.e., no flow of current across a membrane) occurred within 120 s, for different concentrations of the protein peptide-C (data are used with the permission of Claudia Haarmann, who obtained these data in the course of her Ph.D. research). The outcome `yes` implies that inhibition has occurred.

```
conc 0.1 0.5  1 10 20 30 50 70 80 100 150
no   7.0 1.0 10  9  2  9 13  1  1   4   3
yes  0.0 0.0  3  4  0  6  7  0  0   1   7
```

Use logistic regression to model the probability of inhibition as a function of protein concentration.

5.2. In the dataset (an artificial one of 3121 patients, that is similar to a subset of the data analyzed in Stiell et al., 2001) `DAAG::headInjury`, obtain a logistic regression model relating `clinically.important.brain.injury` to other variables. Patients whose risk is sufficiently high will be sent for CT (computed tomography). Using a risk threshold of 0.025 (2.5 percent), turn the result into a decision rule for use of CT.

5.3. Consider again the `moths` dataset of Section 5.4.

a. What happens to the standard error estimates when the `poisson` family is used in `glm()` instead of the `quasipoisson` family?

b. Do an analysis for the `P` moths, following steps similar to those for the `A` moths. Comment on the effect of transect length.

5.4. *The factor `dead` in the dataset `DAAG::mifem` gives the mortality outcomes (`live` or `dead`), for 1295 female subjects who suffered a myocardial infarction. (See Subsection 8.3.1 for further details.) Determine ranges for `age` and `yronset` (year of onset), and determine tables of counts for each separate factor. Decide how to handle cases for which the outcome, for one or more factors, is not known. Fit a logistic regression model, beginning by comparing the model that includes all two-factor interactions with the model that has main effects only.

5.5. Use the function `DAAG::logisticsim()` to simulate data from a logistic regression model to study the `glm()` function, thus:

a. Simulate 100 observations from the model

$$\text{logit}(x) = 2 - 4x$$

for $x = 0, 0.01, 0.02, \ldots, 1.0$. (This is the default setting for `logisticsim()`.)

b. Plot the responses (y) against the "dose" (x). Note how the pattern of 0s and 1s changes as x increases.

c. Fit the logistic regression model to the simulated data, using the `binomial` family. Compare the estimated coefficients with the true coefficients. Are the estimated coefficients within about 2 SEs of the truth?

d. Compare the estimated logit function with the true logit function. How well do you think the fitted logistic model would predict future observations? For a concrete indication of the difference, simulate a new set of 100 observations at the same x values, using a specified pseudorandom number generator seed and the true model. Then simulate some predicted observations using the estimated model and the same seed.

5.6. As in the previous exercise, the function `poissonsim()` allows for experimentation with Poisson regression. In particular, `poissonsim()` can be used to simulate Poisson responses with log-rates equal to $a + bx$, where a and b are fixed values by default.

a. Simulate 100 Poisson responses using the model

$$\log \lambda = 2 - 4x$$

for $x = 0, 0.01, 0.02, \ldots, 1.0$. Fit a Poisson regression model to these data, and compare the estimated coefficients with the true coefficients. How well does the estimated model predict future observations?

b. Simulate 100 Poisson responses using the model

$$\log \lambda = 2 - bx,$$

where b is normally distributed with mean 4 and standard deviation 5. (Use the argument `slope.sd=5` in the `poissonsim()` function.) How do the results using the `poisson` and `quasipoisson` families differ?

5.7. Refer back to the discussion in Subsection 5.5.1 that used historical data in the dataset `DAAG::cricketer` to fit smooth curves to the change in the proportion of lefthanders, and the numbers from each hand, among British first-class cricketers born between 1840 and 1960.

a. Is the assumption of independence between cricketers, for these data, reasonable? Check, in each case, fitting a "quasi-" model, and check the dispersion estimate. (For example, `summary(hand.gam)$dispersion`, here, for binomial family, set to 1.0.)

b. What might explain the clear dip in the proportion of lefthanders with birth years in the decade or so leading up to 1934?

6

Time Series Models

Common time series models allow for a correlation between observations that is likely to be largest for points that are close together in time. Variation in a single spatial dimension may have characteristics akin to those of time series, and comparable models find application there. The present treatment will be introductory and restricted in scope. We now list the models noted in the section that follows.

Autoregressive (AR) These models make good intuitive sense, and are simple to describe.

Autoregressive moving average (ARMA) These allow for moving average as well as autoregressive terms.

Autoregressive-integrated-moving average (ARIMA) These extend ARMA models to allow for the use of preliminary difference to remove a systematic trend.

Examples will be given of the use of models fitted using the function `gamm()` in the *mgcv* package. Use of `gamm()` with time series errors will often be preferable to differencing.

Exponential smoothing state space (ETS) Models of this type are an alternative to ARIMA models. They provide a theoretical framework for the exponential forecasting methodology that was initially developed and used because it was often effective in practice.

Section 6.1 will make extensive use of the `LakeHuron` data (*datasets* package) that has historical data on annual depth measurements at a specific site on Lake Huron, initially to motivate and explain autoregressive models, and then to fit and compare the alternative models just noted. The link of the AR component of ARIMA models into the regression modeling of earlier chapters makes AR models, and their extension into ARMA and ARIMA models, a good context for the discussion of ideas and issues that are important for time series models more generally.

The discussion of ETS models will be brief, intended as a starting point for further study. They are extensively used for forecasting in a wide range of business and industrial time series applications, in a largely automated manner.

Section 6.2 will model a regression where the error term has a time series structure. The chapter will close with a brief discussion of "nonlinear" time series models, such as have been widely used for financial time series.

The analyses will use functions in the packages *stats* (included with binary distributions) and *forecast*. The brief discussion of nonlinear time series (ARCH and GARCH models) will require access to the *tseries* package.

The interested reader is directed to books listed in the references. Especially if the main interest is in forecasting, a good place to start is Hyndman and Athanasopoulos (2021), which has the use of ETS models as its main focus.

6.1 Time Series – Some Basic Ideas

The time series object `LakeHuron` (*datasets*) has annual depth measurements at a specific site on Lake Huron. This will be used both to illustrate ideas of sequential dependence, and to demonstrate functions that allow automatic choice of model from within a broad class. Note especially the `ar()` in the *stats* package, and the functions `auto.arima()` and `ets()` in the *forecast* package.

6.1.1 Time Series Objects

Note first basic functions that may be important for setting up and manipulating time series:

```
class("lakeHuron")
```

```
[1] "character"
```

```
## Use `time()` to extract the `time` attribute
range(time(LakeHuron))
```

```
[1] 1875 1972
```

```
## Use `window()` to subset a time series
LHto1925 <- window(LakeHuron, from=1875, to=1925)
```

The dataset `DAAG::jobs` holds the number of workers in the Canadian labor force broken down by region for the 24-month period from January 1995 to December 1996. The following show some of the possibilities:

```
jobs <- DAAG::jobs
names(jobs)
```

```
[1] "BC"       "Alberta"  "Prairies"  "Ontario"  "Quebec"   "Atlantic"
[7] "Date"
```

```
allRegions <- ts(jobs[, -7])  # Create multivariate time series
time(allRegions)              # Times run from 1 to 24
```

```
Time Series:
Start = 1
End = 24
Frequency = 1
 [1]  1  2 3 4 5 6 7 8 9 10 11 12 13 14 15 16 17 18 19 20 21 22
[23] 23 24
```

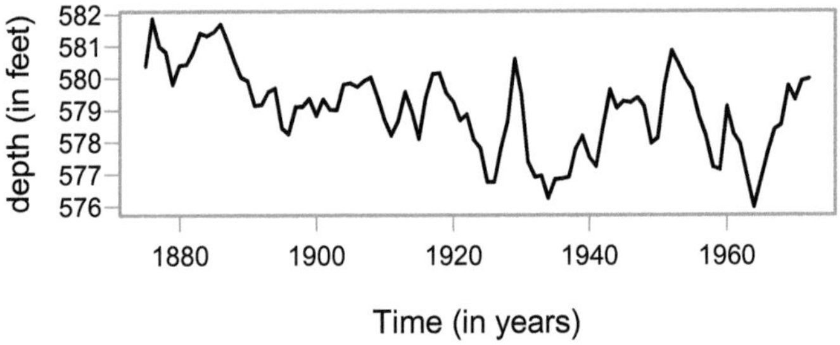

Figure 6.1 Trace plot of annual depth measurements of Lake Huron versus time.

```
allRegions <- ts(jobs[, -7], start=c(1995,1), frequency=12)
allRegions[,"BC"]              # Extract jobs data for British Columbia
```

```
      Jan  Feb  Mar  Apr  May  Jun  Jul  Aug  Sep  Oct  Nov  Dec
1995 1752 1737 1765 1762 1754 1759 1766 1775 1777 1771 1757 1766
1996 1786 1784 1791 1800 1800 1798 1814 1803 1796 1818 1829 1840
```

```
jobsBC <- ts(jobs[, "BC"], start=c(1995,1), frequency=12)
  # Obtain equivalent of `allRegions[,"BC"]` directly from `jobs` dataset
```

Most functions that work with nonseasonal time series will accept a numeric vector as argument, converting it to a time series object for analysis purposes. The analysis of multivariate time series is outside of the scope of the account that follows.

6.1.2 Preliminary Graphical Exploration

Figure 6.1 is a *trace* plot that shows depth measurements against year. The code is:

```
## Plot depth measurements: ts object LakeHuron (datasets)
plot(LakeHuron, ylab="depth (in feet)", xlab = "Time (in years)", fg="gray")
```

There is a slight downward trend for at least the first half of the series. Observe also that depth measurements that are close together in time are often close in value. Consistently with the sequential dependence that is typical in time series, these are not independent observations. The challenge is to find effective ways to model this dependence.

Lag plots may give a useful visual impression of the dependence. Suppose that our observations are $x_1, x_2, \ldots, x_n$. Then the lag 1 plot plots x_i against x_{i-1} ($i = 2, \ldots, n$), as follows.

y-value	x_2	x_3	$\ldots$	x_n
lag 1 (x-axis)	x_1	x_2	$\ldots$	x_{n-1}

For a lag 2 plot, x_i is plotted against x_{i-2} ($i = 3, \ldots, n$), and so on for higher lags. Notice that the number of points that are plotted is reduced by the number of lags.

Figure 6.2A shows the first four lag plots for the Lake Huron data. Code is:

```
lag.plot(LakeHuron, lags=3, do.lines=FALSE)
```

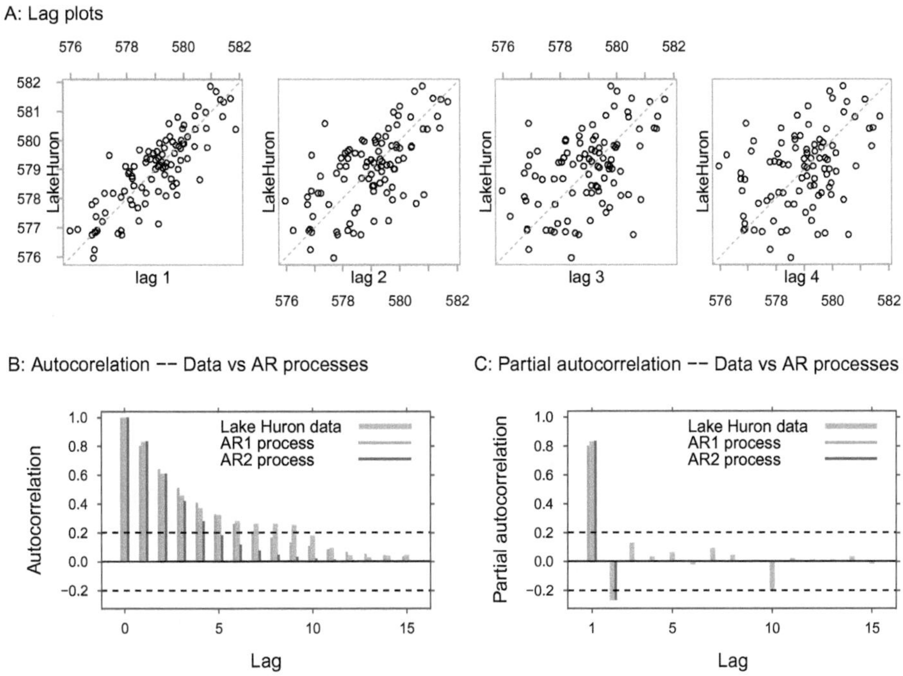

Figure 6.2 The top four panels (A) show the first four lag plots of the annual depth measurements of Lake Huron. Panel B compares the estimated autocorrelations with the autocorrelations for an AR(1) process, and for an AR(2) process. Panel C repeats the comparison, now for the partial autocorrelations. The dashed horizontal lines are approximate pointwise 5 percent critical values for the autocorrelations for a pure noise process, that is, for independent normal data with mean 0.

The scatter of points about a straight line in the first lag plot suggests that the dependence between consecutive observations has a linear component. The second, third and fourth lag plots show increasing scatter. As might be expected, points separated by two or three lags are successively less dependent. Note that the slopes, and therefore the correlations, are all positive.

6.1.3 The Autocorrelation and Partial Autocorrelation Function

The correlation that is evident in each of the lag plots in Figure 6.2A is an *autocorrelation* (literally, "self-correlation"), also referred to as the *serial* correlation. An autocorrelation function (ACF) plot, showing the autocorrelations at all successive lags, often gives useful insight. Figure 6.2B plots the first 19 autocorrelations. Code is:

```
acf(LakeHuron)
## pacf(LakeHuron) gives the plot of partial autocorrelations
```

The autocorrelation at lag 0 is included by default; this always takes the value 1, since it is the correlation between the data series and itself. Interest is in the autocorrelations at lag 1 and later lags. As inferred from the lag plots, the largest autocorrelation is at lag 1 (sometimes called the serial correlation), with successively smaller autocorrelations at lags 2, 3, ... There is no obvious linear association among observations separated by lags of more than about 10.

Autocorrelations at lags greater than 1 are in part a flow-on from autocorrelations at earlier lags. The *partial autocorrelation* at a particular lag measures the strength of linear correlation between observations separated by that lag, after adjusting for correlations between observations separated by fewer lags. Figure 6.2B indicates partial autocorrelations that may be greater than statistical error at lags 1, 2, and 10. Other autocorrelations are mostly a flow-on effect from the large autocorrelations at lag 1. Figure 6.2C shows the autocorrelation and partial autocorrelation function for a theoretical AR(1) model that, while accounting for a large part of the correlation structure in Figure 6.2B, does not account for the lag 2 partial autocorrelation that is indicated in Figure 6.2B.

As discussed in Subsection 6.1.4, autocorrelation in a time series complicates the estimation of such quantities as the standard error of the mean. There must be appropriate modeling of the dependence structure. If there are extensive data, it helps to group the data into sets of k successive values, and take averages. The serial correlation then reduces to ρ_1/k approximately. See Miller (1986) for further comment.

6.1.4 Autoregressive (AR) Models

We have indicated earlier that, whenever possible, the rich regression framework provides additional insights, beyond those available from the study of correlation structure. This is true also for time series. Autoregressive models move beyond attention to correlation structure to the modeling of regressions relating successive observations.

The AR(1) Model

Figures 6.2B and C showed the autocorrelation and partial autocorrelation plots for AR(1) and AR(2) processes. The autoregressive model of order 1 (AR(1)) for a time series $X_1, X_2, \ldots,$ has the recursive formula

$$X_t = \mu + \alpha(X_{t-1} - \mu) + \varepsilon_t, \quad t = 1, 2, \ldots,$$

where μ and α are parameters. Figure 6.2C had $\alpha = 0.8$. The discussion will focus, initially, on the AR(1) process.

Usually, α takes values in the interval $(-1, 1)$; this is the so-called *stationary* case. Nonstationarity, in the sense used here, implies that the properties of the series are changing with time. The mean may be changing with time, and/or the variances and covariances may depend on the time lag. Any such time nonstationarity will require attention.

For series of positive values, a logarithmic transformation will sometimes bring the series closer to stationarity and/or make it simpler to model any trend. Discussion of standard ways to handle trends will be deferred to Subsection 6.1.5.

The error term ε_t is the familiar independent noise term with constant variance σ^2. In this context the ε_t values are suitably described as *innovations*. These are changes ("shocks") that cannot be predicted from previous observations. The distribution of X_0 is assumed fixed and will not be of immediate concern.

For the AR(1) model, the ACF at lag i is α^i, for $i = 1, 2, \ldots$. If $\alpha = 0.8$, then the observed autocorrelations should be 0.8, 0.64, 0.512, 0.410, 0.328, ..., a geometrically decaying pattern, as in Figure 6.2C and not too unlike that in Figure 6.2B.

The correlation structure has important implications for estimating the standard error of the estimate for the mean μ. Under the AR(1) model, a large sample approximation to the standard error for the mean is

$$\frac{\sigma}{\sqrt{n}} \frac{1}{(1-\alpha)}.$$

For a sample of size 100 from an AR(1) model with $\sigma = 1$ and $\alpha = 0.5$, the standard error of the mean is 0.2. This is exactly twice the value that results from the use of the usual $\sigma/\sqrt{n}$ formula. Use of the usual standard error formula will result in misleading and biased confidence intervals for time series where there is substantial autocorrelation.

There are several alternative methods for estimating for the parameter α. The *method of moments* estimator uses the autocorrelation at lag 1, here equal to 0.8319. The maximum likelihood estimator, equal to 0.8376, is an alternative.[1]

The General AR(p) Model

It is possible to include regression terms for X_t against observations at greater lags than one. The autoregressive model of order p (the AR(p) model regresses X_t against $X_{t-1}, X_{t-2}, \ldots, X_{t-p}$:

$$X_t = \mu + \alpha_1(X_{t-1} - \mu) + \cdots + \alpha_p(X_{t-p} - \mu) + \varepsilon_t, \quad t = 1, 2, \ldots,$$

where $\alpha_1, \alpha_2, \ldots, \alpha_p$ are additional parameters that would need to be estimated. The parameter α_i is the partial autocorrelation at lag i. The output when using `ar()` or `arima()` labels the estimate of μ the *intercept*; but it is close to the sample mean of the time series.

The base R function `ar()` can be used, assuming an autoregressive process, to estimate the AR order. It uses the AIC that was introduced in Subsection 1.7.1. Use of this criterion, with models fitted using maximum likelihood, gives:

```
ar(LakeHuron, method="mle")
```

[1]
```
## Yule-Walker autocorrelation estimate
LH.yw <- ar(LakeHuron, order.max = 1, method = "yw")  # autocorrelation estimate
# order.max = 1 for AR(1) model
LH.yw$ar                     # autocorrelation estimate of alpha
## Maximum likelihood estimate
LH.mle <- ar(LakeHuron, order.max = 1, method = "mle")
LH.mle$ar                    # maximum likelihood estimate of alpha
LH.mle$x.mean                # estimated series mean
LH.mle$var.pred              # estimated innovation variance
```

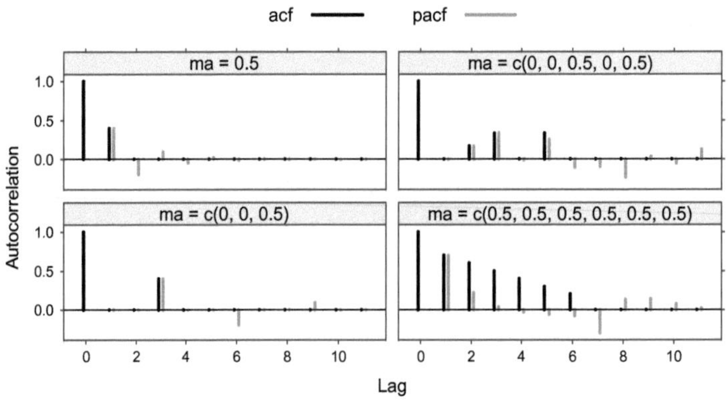

Figure 6.3 Theoretical autocorrelations for a moving average process, with the parameters shown. The thin gray lines are the partial autocorrelations.

```
Call:
ar(x = LakeHuron, method = "mle")

Coefficients:
     1       2
 1.044  -0.250

Order selected 2  sigma^2 estimated as  0.479
```

This suggests use of an AR(2) model. Figures 6.2B and C indicated that this does a reasonable job of modeling the correlation structure.

Is an AR(2) model adequate, or is something more needed? We now move to investigating use of an autoregressive moving average (ARMA) model, which adds one or more *moving average* terms, to examine whether this makes any worthwhile improvement.

* *Moving Average (MA) Processes*

In a moving average (MA) process of order q, the *error* term is the sum of an *innovation* ε_t that is specific to that term, and a linear combination of earlier *innovations* $\varepsilon_{t-1}, \varepsilon_{t-2}, \ldots, \varepsilon_{t-q}$. The equation is

$$X_t = \mu_t + \varepsilon_t + b_1\varepsilon_{t-1} + \cdots + b_q\varepsilon_{t-q}, \tag{6.1}$$

where ε_1, ε_2, …, ε_q are independent random normal variables, all with mean 0. The autocorrelation between terms that are more than q time units apart is zero. Moving average terms can be helpful for modeling autocorrelation functions that are spiky, or that have a sharp cutoff.

Figure 6.3 shows the autocorrelation functions for simulations of several moving average models. Notice that

- with $b_1 = 0.5$ ($q = 1$) there is a spike at lag 1,
- with $b_1 = b_2 = 0$, $b_3 = 0.5$ ($q = 3$) there is a spike at lag 3,
- with $b_1 = b_2 = 0$, $b_3 = 0.5$, $b_4 = 0, b_5 = 0.5$ ($q = 5$) there are spikes at lags 2, 3, and 5,
- with $b_i = 0.5$ ($i = 1, \ldots, 5$), there are spikes at the first five lags.

6.1.5* Autoregressive Moving Average (ARMA) Models – Theory

An autoregressive moving average (ARMA) model is an extension of an autoregressive model to include "moving average" terms. Autoregressive integrated moving average (ARIMA) models allow even greater flexibility. As an alternative to applying the model (AR or MA or ARMA) to the series itself, the model can be applied to a *differenced* series, where the differencing process may be repeated more than once. There are three parameters: the order p of the autoregressive component, the order d of differencing (in our example 0), and the order q of the moving average component.

Differencing of order 1 removes a linear trend, effectively replacing a time series `series` by `dseries = diff(series)` for the analysis. Differencing of order 2 repeats the differencing a second time, thus removing a quadratic trend. While differencing can be done explicitly, it is simplest to let the time series functions do any differencing that is required internally, then fitting the required ARMA model to the differenced series. For analysis results that apply to the undifferenced series, the relevant functions then reverse the differencing process as necessary. A downside of differencing is that it can complicate the correlation structure. Thus, it turns an uncorrelated series into an MA series of order 1. See further `?arima`.

Note: A point of contention is whether to allow a term that corresponds to μ in the differenced series. The function `arima()` (*stats*) does not allow such a term. The function `forecast::Arima()` has an argument `include.drift`, by default set to `TRUE`, which includes such a term when the order of differencing is $d = 1$ (but omits it for $d > 1$). If included, it is identified as a drift term.

6.1.6 Automatic Model Selection?

The function `forecast::auto.arima()` uses as a default the AICc criterion (with AIC and BIC as alternatives) in an automatic model selection process, thus removing some of the inevitable arbitrariness involved in model choice. What is important is to account for the major part of the correlation structure. A search for finesse in the detail may be pointless, with scant practical consequence. Of more consequence, in many applications can be the choice of order of difference: $d = 0$, or 1, or $d > 1$. The `LakeHuron` dataset is an interesting case, in this respect.

The algorithm looks for the optimal AR order p, the optimal order of differencing, and the optimal MA order q, within limits set by `max.p`, `max.d`, `max.q`, and `max.order` (= `p+q` for models that do not have a seasonal term.) Additionally, the algorithm checks for possible "drift." Drift allows forecasts to increase or decrease over time, with the amount set to the average change in the historical data, For data where there may be seasonal effects, the algorithm follows the same process to find, at the same time, the optimum choice of parameters P, D, and Q for fitting an ARIMA model to the seasonal effects. Subsection 6.1.7 has an example.

An exhaustive (nonstepwise) search can be very slow. The `auto.arima()` default is a stepwise search. At each iteration, the search is limited to a parameter space that is "close" to the parameter space of the current model, and similarly for seasonal and other parameters. Unless computation time is an issue, perhaps because the series is long and/or the seasonal period is long and/or there are many time series, the function should be called with the explicitly setting both of the arguments `approximation` and `stepwise` to `TRUE`, in place of the default `FALSE`.

Depending on previous experience with comparable series, there may be a case for checking the partial autocorrelation plot for clear "spikes" that may indicate high-order MA terms, before proceeding to a stepwise search. Note that, in a plot that shows lags 1 to 20 of a pure noise process, one can expect, on average, one spike that extends beyond the 95 percent pointwise limits.

Application of `auto.arima()` to the `LakeHuron` data gives the following:

```
library(forecast, quietly=TRUE)
(aaLH <- auto.arima(LakeHuron, approximation=F, stepwise=F))
```

```
Series: LakeHuron
ARIMA(2,1,1)

Coefficients:
        ar1     ar2     ma1
      0.971  -0.292  -0.911
s.e.  0.114   0.103   0.071

sigma^2 = 0.5:  log likelihood = -102.5
AIC=213.1   AICc=213.5   BIC=223.4
```

Now try

```
## Check that model removes most of the correlation structure
acf(resid(aaLH, type="innovation"))  # `type="innovation"` is the default
```

The function `auto.arima()` chose an ARIMA(2,1,1) model; that is, the order of the autoregressive terms is $p = 2$, the order of the differencing is $d = 1$, and the order of the moving average term is $q = 1$. Compare this with the result when the arguments `approximation` and `stepwise` are left at their defaults:

```
auto.arima(LakeHuron)
```

```
Series: LakeHuron
ARIMA(0,1,0)

sigma^2 = 0.559:  log likelihood = -109.1
AIC=220.2   AICc=220.3   BIC=222.8
```

Notice that `d=0`, that the information statistics AIC and AICc have increased substantially, and that BIC has decreased slightly.

Keeping `d=0`, we can do better than a stepwise fit:

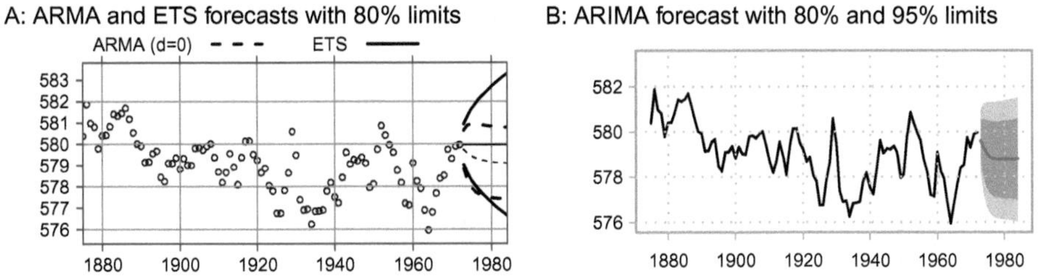

Figure 6.4 Predictions 12 years ahead, with pointwise confidence limits, are compared. Panel A shows predictions and 80 percent limits for the ARMA model (d=0) chosen as "best" overall, and for the default exponential time series (ETS) model. Panel B shows the graph that results, with 80 percent and 95 percent limits, when the fitted ARIMA(2,1,1) model is supplied as argument to the `plot()` function.

```
(aaLH0 <- auto.arima(LakeHuron, d=0, approximation=F, stepwise=F))
```

```
Series: LakeHuron
ARIMA(1,0,1) with non-zero mean

Coefficients:
        ar1     ma1     mean
      0.745   0.321   579.05
s.e.  0.078   0.114     0.35

sigma^2 = 0.49:  log likelihood = -103.2
AIC=214.5   AICc=214.9   BIC=224.8
```

The mean is a maximum likelihood estimate, and will differ slightly from the mean of the observed depths.

For all three information statistics, there is only a minor increase from that for the ARIMA(2,1,1) model. The difference in AIC from the overall "best" model is 214.5 − 213.1, which translates, if the formula used can be applied in this context, to a "relative likelihood" that equals 2.03. This is likely, because the overall "best" model resulted from a search within a much larger parameter space, to exaggerate the relative likelihood. It makes, at best, a very weak case for preferring the model for the undifferenced series. The difference in the predicted values (compare the blue dashed limits in Figure 6.4A with the darker gray shaded limits in Panel B) is not of great consequence, relative to year-to-year variation or to the 95 percent confidence limits. Also shown in Panel A is the forecast and much wider limits obtained by supplying a time series directly as an argument to `forecast()`, giving the exponential time series (ETS) prediction. The wider prediction intervals reflect a greater discounting of observations from the more distant past.

Plots for each of the three forecasts separately can be obtained thus:

```
plot( forecast (aaLH0, h=12)) ## `level=c(80,95)` is the default
fcETS <- forecast(LakeHuron, h=12)
plot(fcETS)
plot( forecast (aaLH, h=12, level=c(80,95)))  # Panel B; ARIMA(2,1,1)
```

Compare also with the AR model that was considered earlier:

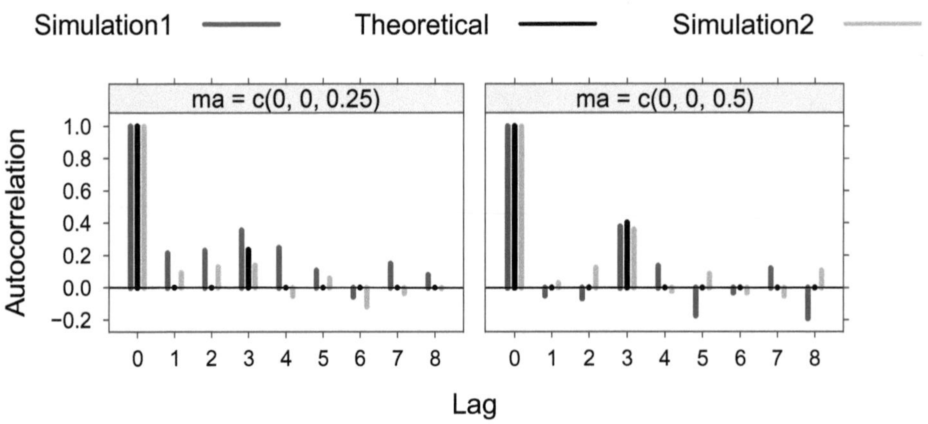

Figure 6.5 Results of two simulation runs (in different shades of gray), for an MA process of order 3, with $b_1 = b_2 = 0$, in Panel A with $b_3 = 0.25$, and in Panel B with $b_3 = 0.5$. The theoretical autocorrelation is shown, in each case, in black.

```
auto.arima(LakeHuron, d=0, max.Q=0, approximation=F, stepwise=F)
```

```
Series: LakeHuron
ARIMA(1,0,1) with non-zero mean

Coefficients:
        ar1     ma1     mean
      0.745   0.321   579.05
s.e.  0.078   0.114     0.35

sigma^2 = 0.49:  log likelihood = -103.2
AIC=214.5   AICc=214.9   BIC=224.8
```

Use of Simulation as a Check

Simulations can be insightful for the insight that they give into the extent to which MA or other coefficients are, for a given length of series, detectable. The simulations that now follow are for series of length $n = 98$, generated by a moving average process of order 3, with $b_1 = 0$, $b_2 = 0$, initially for Figure 6.5 for two runs each with $b_3 = 0.25$ and $b_3 = 0.5$.

Code that plots results from a single set of simulation runs is:

```
for(i in 1:2){
  simts <- arima.sim(model=list(order=c(0,0,3), ma=c(0,0,0.25*i)), n=98)
  acf(simts, main="", xlab="")
  mtext(side=3, line=0.5, paste("ma3 =", 0.25*i), adj=0)
}
```

Now do 20 simulation runs, noting in each case the order of MA process that is detected, for each of $b_3 = 0.125$, 0.25, 0.375, and 0.5:

```
set.seed(29)        # Ensure that results are reproducible
estMAord <- matrix(0, nrow=4, ncol=20)
for(i in 1:4){
```

```
  for(j in 1:20){
    simts <- arima.sim(n=98, model=list(ma=c(0,0,0.125*i)))
    estMAord[i,j] <- auto.arima(simts, start.q=3)$arma[2] }
}
detectedAs <- table(row(estMAord), estMAord)
dimnames(detectedAs) <- list(ma3=paste(0.125*(1:4)),
Order=paste(0:(dim(detectedAs)[2]-1)))
```

The following table summarizes the result of this calculation:

```
print(detectedAs)
```

```
        Order
ma3      0  1  2  3  4
  0.125 18  2  0  0  0
  0.25  11  3  0  6  0
  0.375  7  2  2  7  2
  0.5    1  1  0 13  5
```

With $b_3 = 0.5$, the MA component was detected as order 3 in just 13 of the 20 runs.

6.1.7 Seasonal Effects

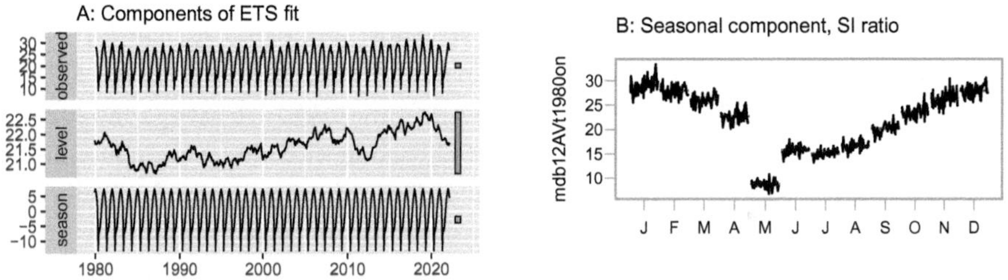

Figure 6.6 Panel A shows the original and adjusted series. Panel B shows the seasonal (monthly) component.

The functions `auto.arima()` and `ets()` from the *forecast* package can both be used with time series that have a seasonal component. Note also the extensive abilities in the *seasonal* package, which provides an R interface to software that was developed in the first place for use with official statistics.

Data shown in Figure 6.6 are monthly average temperatures, for the Murray–Darling Basin area of Australia, from January 1950 through to March 2022, downloaded from the Australian Bureau of meteorology website.[2]

Selected code is:

```
suppressPackageStartupMessages(library(ggplot2))
mdb12AVt1980on <- window(DAAG::mdbAVtJtoD, c(1980,1))
AVt.ets <- ets(mdb12AVt1980on)
autoplot(AVt.ets, main="", fg="gray") +
  ggplot2::ggtitle("A: Components of ETS fit") +
    theme(plot.title = element_text(hjust=0, vjust=0.5, size=11))
monthplot(mdb12AVt1980on, col.base=2,  fg="gray")
```

[2] `www.bom.gov.au/climate/change/index.shtml`.

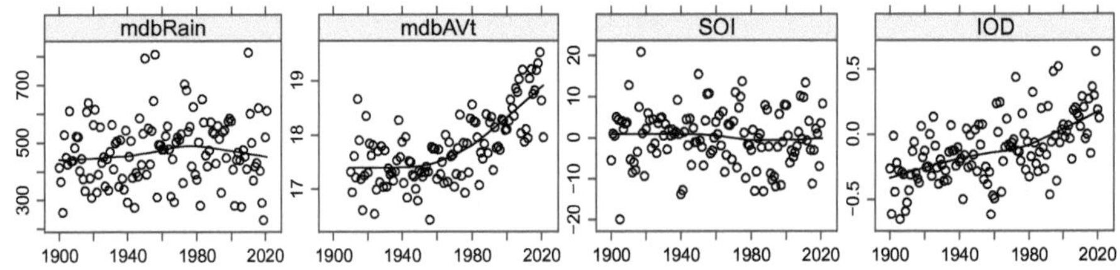

Figure 6.7 Plots of **mdbRain**, **mdbAVt** (in Australia's Murray–Darling Basin), **SOI** (Southern Oscillation Index), and **IOD** (Indian Ocean Dipole) against year.

6.2* Regression Modeling with ARIMA Errors

We will use the *mgcv* functions **gam()** and **gamm()** as required where there seems a need for smooths, reducing the need to resort to differencing. The strategy will be to first fit a model assuming independent errors, then using the function **forecast::auto.arima()** to check the residuals for autocorrelation and refitting as necessary. In the examples used here, it will in several instances turn out that the independent errors assumption appears acceptable.

The Southern Oscillation Index (SOI) is the difference in barometric pressure at sea level between the Pacific island of Tahiti and Darwin close to the northernmost tip of Australia. (See Nicholls et al. (1996) for background.) Another such index is the Indian Ocean Dipole (**IOD**); see the relevant Wikipedia article for details. Rainfall and temperature data for various parts of Australia over 1900–2021, together with **SOI** and **IOD** data, are in the data frame **DAAG::bomregions2021**. To what extent do these indices, along with global carbon dioxide levels, contribute to explaining rainfall and temperature levels in one or other region of Australia? The discussion will focus on data for the Murray–Darling Basin (**mdbRain**).

The Murray–Darling Basin takes its name from its two major rivers, the Murray and the Darling, which together account for 70 percent of Australia's irrigation resources. It is Australia's most significant agricultural area.[3]

Figure 6.7 plots the four series. The code is

```
bomreg <- DAAG::bomregions2021
## Plot time series mdbRain, SOI, and IOD: ts object bomregions2021 (DAAG)
gph <- xyplot(ts(bomreg[, c("mdbRain", "mdbAVt", "SOI", "IOD")], start=1900),
              xlab="", type=c('p','smooth'), scales=list(alternating=rep(1,3)))
update(gph, layout=c(4,1), par.settings=DAAG::DAAGtheme(color=F))
```

Use of a square root or cube root transformation, reducing skewness, is common practice for analysis of rainfall data (Stidd, 1953). Here, the square-root-transformed rainfall measure will be used. The following fits a GAM model, then checks for a sequential correlation structure:

```
suppressPackageStartupMessages(library(mgcv))
bomreg <- within(bomreg, mdbrtRain <- mdbRain^0.5)
## Check first for a sequential correlation structure, after
## fitting smooth terms s(CO2), s(SOI), and s(IOD)
library(mgcv)
```

[3] The help page for **bomregions2021** gives a link to a map that identifies these regions.

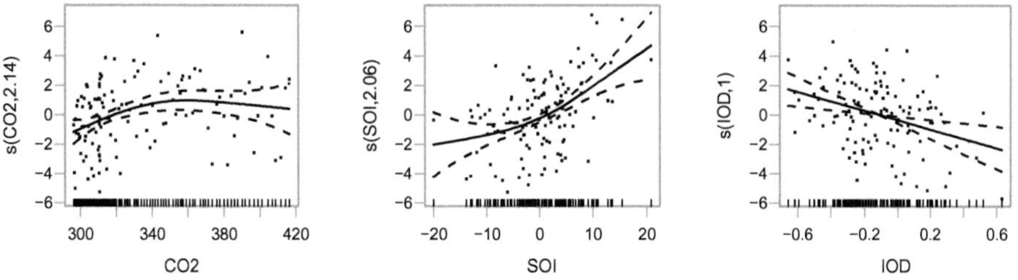

Figure 6.8 Contributions to the GAM model are shown for the separate smooth terms in CO2, SOI, and IOD.

```
mdbrtRain.gam <- gam(mdbrtRain~s(CO2) + s(SOI) + s(IOD), data=bomreg)
auto.arima(resid(mdbrtRain.gam))
```

```
Series: resid(mdbrtRain.gam)
ARIMA(0,0,0) with zero mean

sigma^2 = 4.42:  log likelihood = -263.8
AIC=529.6   AICc=529.7   BIC=532.4
```

Figure 6.8 shows the contributions of the separate terms. Code is:

```
plot(mdbrtRain.gam, residuals=T, cex=2, fg="gray")
## Do also `gam.check(mdbrtRain.gam)` (Output looks fine)
```

The anova() function returns, for gam models, or for the gam component of gamm models, the effect of leaving out each separate term from the full model. It does what drop1() does for lm models, and may be viewed as an analytic equivalent of Figure 6.8.

```
anova(mdbrtRain.gam)
```

```
Family: gaussian
Link function: identity

Formula:
mdbrtRain ~ s(CO2) + s(SOI) + s(IOD)

Approximate significance of smooth terms:
        edf Ref.df     F   p-value
s(CO2) 2.14   2.67  4.35    0.0109
s(SOI) 2.06   2.64 12.58 0.0000027
s(IOD) 1.00   1.00  9.70    0.0023
```

The Box.test() function can be used for a so-called *portmanteau* test of whiteness (i.e., lack of autocorrelation) that checks for evidence of correlation in the residuals at one or more lags up to and including the specified lag m. The test statistic (we use the Ljung–Box version where the default is Box–Pierce) is a weighted sum of squares of the first m sample autocorrelation estimates. If there is no autocorrelation among the residuals, it has an approximate chi-squared distribution on m degrees of freedom. Note that the default for the maximum lag m is 1, not usually what is wanted). The output is:

```
Box.test(resid(mdbrtRain.gam), lag=10, type="Ljung")
```

```

        Box-Ljung test

data:  resid(mdbrtRain.gam)
X-squared = 12, df = 10, p-value = 0.3
```

Outliers and other types of departure from normality (including outliers) have the potential to complicate estimation of the ARIMA modeling structure. A graphical check on normality is therefore desirable:

```
## Examine normality of estimates of "residuals"
qqnorm(resid(mdbrtRain.gam))
```

The `mdbAVt` *Series*

As before we fit smooth terms in s(CO2), s(SOI), and s(IOD), then checking for a sequential correlation structure:

```
mdbAVt.gam <- gam(mdbAVt ~ s(CO2)+s(SOI)+s(IOD), data=bomreg)
auto.arima(resid(mdbAVt.gam))
```

```
Series: resid(mdbAVt.gam)
ARIMA(0,0,0) with zero mean

sigma^2 = 0.169:  log likelihood = -59.33
AIC=120.7   AICc=120.7   BIC=123.4
```

```
anova(mdbAVt.gam)
```

```

Family: gaussian
Link function: identity

Formula:
mdbAVt ~ s(CO2) + s(SOI) + s(IOD)

Approximate significance of smooth terms:
        edf Ref.df    F p-value
s(CO2) 1.85   2.31 41.8  <2e-16
s(SOI) 1.00   1.00 10.7  0.0015
s(IOD) 1.00   1.00  0.0  0.9440
```

Clearly the `s(IOD)` term is redundant. Omitting it gives:

```
mdbAVt1.gam <- gam(mdbAVt ~ s(CO2)+s(SOI), data=bomreg)
```

Figure 6.9 shows the contributions of the separate terms. Simplified code is:

```
plot(mdbAVt1.gam, residuals=TRUE)
```

Figure 6.10 shows the fitted values for both rainfall and temperature. Code for Figure 6.10 is:

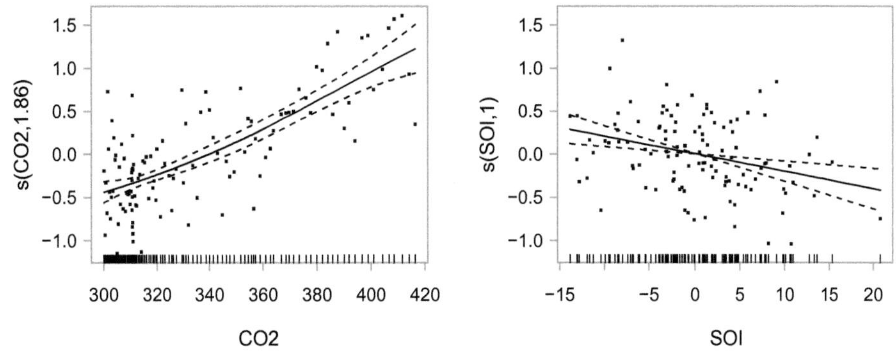

Figure 6.9 Contributions to the **gam** model for **mdbAVt** of the separate smooth terms in **CO2**, and **SOI**.

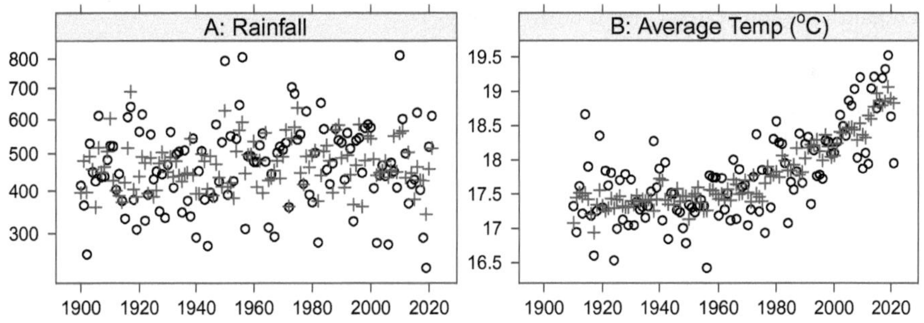

Figure 6.10 Panel A plots rainfall (on a square root scale) against year. Panel B plots average temperature. Points shown with a colored + are fitted values.

```
faclevs <- c("A: Rainfall", expression("B: Average Temp ("^o*"C)"))
fitrain <- fitted(mdbrtRain.gam)
fitAVt <- c(rep(NA,10), fitted(mdbAVt1.gam))
gph <- xyplot(mdbrtRain+mdbAVt~Year,data=bomreg, outer=T, xlab="", ylab="",
  scales=list(y=list(relation='free',
             at=list(sqrt((3:8)*100),(33:39)/2),
             labels=list((3:8)*100,(33:39)/2)), x=list(alternating=rep(1,2))),
  strip=strip.custom(factor.levels=faclevs))
gph + latticeExtra::as.layer(xyplot(fitrain+fitAVt~Year, outer=T,
                             scales=list(y=list(relation='free')),
                             data=bomreg, pch=3, col=2))
```

Note also the possibility of including regression terms in an `arima()` or `Arima()` fit, then using `forecast::auto.arima()` to automate the model selection process:

```
## Use `auto.arima()` to choose the ARIMA order:
aaFitCO2 <- with(bomreg[-(1:10),], auto.arima(mdbAVt, xreg=cbind(CO2,SOI)))
## Try including a degree 2 polynomial term
aaFitpol2CO2 <- with(bomreg[-(1:10),],
                 auto.arima(mdbAVt, xreg=cbind(poly(CO2,2),SOI)))
cbind(AIC(aaFitCO2, aaFitpol2CO2), BIC=BIC(aaFitCO2, aaFitpol2CO2))
```

```
               df   AIC BIC.df BIC.BIC
aaFitCO2        7 125.4      7   144.4
aaFitpol2CO2    5 129.0      5   142.6
```

There is little to choose between the fits.

The default for the use of `resid()` with `arima` or `Arima` models is to return the innovations, which should be uncorrelated if the model is correct.

6.2.1 The gamm() Function, with a Correlated Errors Model

The `mgcv::gamm()` function uses correlation structures from *nlme*, by default assuming uncorrelated errors. Suppose now we look for an equation that models the variation of `SOI` with `day`. The default normal (*gaussian*) error structure for the `gamm` model means that it should give the same overall fit as the `gam` model, but split into a `gam` and an `lme` component.

```
SOI.gam <- gam(SOI~s(Year), data=bomreg)
auto.arima(resid(SOI.gam))            # sigma^2 = 43.4
```

```
Series: resid(SOI.gam)
ARIMA(0,0,2) with zero mean

Coefficients:
        ma1     ma2
      0.207  -0.156
s.e.  0.094   0.101

sigma^2 = 43.4:  log likelihood = -402.2
AIC=810.4   AICc=810.6   BIC=818.8
```

```
## The following breaks the model into two parts -- gam and lme
SOI.gamm <- gamm(SOI~s(Year), data=bomreg)
res <- resid(SOI.gamm$lme, type="normalized")
auto.arima(res)                       # sigma^2 = 0.945
```

```
Series: res
ARIMA(0,0,2) with zero mean

Coefficients:
        ma1     ma2
      0.207  -0.156
s.e.  0.094   0.101

sigma^2 = 0.945:  log likelihood = -168.7
AIC=343.4   AICc=343.6   BIC=351.8
```

```
## Extract scale estimate for `gam` component of SOI.gamm
summary(SOI.gamm$gam)[['scale']]      # 45.98
```

```
[1] 45.98
```

```
  # Note that 45.98 x .945 ~= 43.4
```

If the model is correct *normalized* residuals should be approximately normally distributed with mean 0 and variance 1.

Now fit a model with MA2 errors and, for comparison, a model with AR2 errors:

```
SOIma2.gamm <- gamm(SOI~s(Year), data=bomreg, correlation=corARMA(q=2))
coef(SOIma2.gamm$lme$modelStruct$corStruct, unconstrained = FALSE) # MA2 ests
```

```
Theta1  Theta2
0.2070 -0.1557
```

```
SOIar2.gamm <- gamm(SOI~s(Year), data=bomreg, correlation=corARMA(p=2))
coef(SOIar2.gamm$lme$modelStruct$corStruct, unconstrained = FALSE) # AR2 ests
```

```
  Phi1    Phi2
0.2258 -0.2098
```

```
cbind(AIC(SOI.gam, SOIma2.gamm$lme, SOIar2.gamm$lme),
    BIC=BIC(SOI.gam, SOIma2.gamm$lme, SOIar2.gamm$lme)[,2])
```

```
                 df   AIC   BIC
SOI.gam           3 819.3 827.7
SOIma2.gamm$lme   6 816.4 833.2
SOIar2.gamm$lme   6 815.5 832.3
```

The three-parameter difference between the uncorrelated errors model changes the penalty function from `2 x 3 = 6` to `log(122) x 3` = 14.41, a difference of `8.41`. A difference of 3.75 in favor of the `SOIar2.gamm` changes to a difference of 4.66 in favor `SOI.gam`.

The Dataset `airquality` *(153 Days, New York, 1972)*

As another example, consider the data frame `airquality` from the *datasets* package. This has data collected over 153 days in New York in 1972, starting on May 1. A first step is to add day number starting from May 1 as a time variable:

```
## Add time in days from May 1 to data.
airq <- cbind(airquality[, 1:4], day=1:nrow(airquality))
  # Column 5 ('day' starting May 1) replaces columns 'Month' & 'Day')
## Check numbers of missing values    # Solar.R:7; Ozone:37
mice::md.pattern(airq, plot=FALSE)  # Final row has totals missing.
```

```
    Wind Temp day Solar.R Ozone
111    1    1   1       1     1  0
35     1    1   1       1     0  1
5      1    1   1       0     1  1
2      1    1   1       0     0  2
       0    0   0       7    37 44
```

Figure 6.11 plots the data. Note the presence of missing values that are clustered in time. It is no surprise that temperatures increase from spring into midsummer, and decrease again as autumn approaches. The trends in several of the smooths are inevitably far from linear.

```
smoothPars <- list(col.smooth='red', lty.smooth=2, spread=0)
car::spm(airq, cex.labels=1.2, regLine=FALSE, oma=c(1.95,3,4,3), gap=.15,
       col=adjustcolor('blue', alpha.f=0.3), smooth=smoothPars, fg="gray")
```

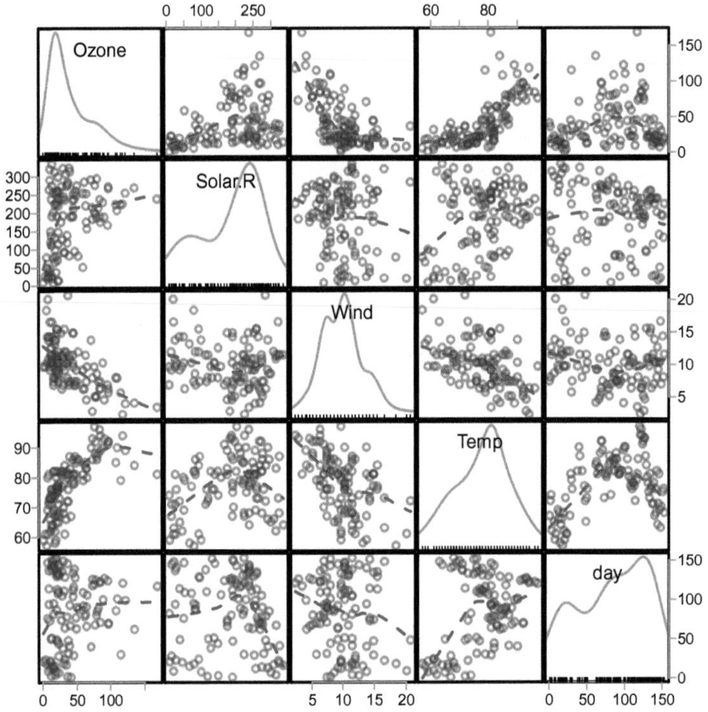

Figure 6.11 Scatterplot matrix for air quality data.

We now look at possibilities for modeling `Ozone` as a function of `Solar.R`, `Wind`, `Temp`, and perhaps `day`. We first look for a power transformation that, after accounting for explanatory variables, can be used to bring the distribution of `Ozone` closer to normality and symmetry. Failure to account for sequential correlation should not for this purpose matter greatly.

```
car::powerTransform(gam(Ozone ~ s(Solar.R)+s(Wind)+s(Temp)+s(day), data=airq))
```

```
Estimated transformation parameter
    Y1
0.2307
```

```
airq$rt4Ozone <- airq$Ozone^0.25
```

Now fit the following GAM model, and fit GAMM models for further checks:

```
Ozone.gam <- gam(rt4Ozone ~ s(Solar.R)+s(Wind)+s(Temp)+s(day), data=airq)
auto.arima(resid(Ozone.gam)) # Independent errors model appears OK
```

```
Series: resid(Ozone.gam)
ARIMA(0,0,0) with zero mean
```

```
sigma^2 = 0.059:  log likelihood = -0.4
AIC=2.79   AICc=2.83   BIC=5.5
```

```
## Check model terms
anova(Ozone.gam)  # For GAM models, this leaves out terms one at a time
```

```
Family: gaussian
Link function: identity

Formula:
rt4Ozone ~ s(Solar.R) + s(Wind) + s(Temp) + s(day)

Approximate significance of smooth terms:
            edf Ref.df     F  p-value
s(Solar.R) 2.28   2.87  7.70  0.00016
s(Wind)    2.45   3.10  9.50 0.000013
s(Temp)    4.28   5.29 13.30  < 2e-16
s(day)     1.00   1.00  0.49  0.48351
```

```
## The term in `day` has no explanatory, and will be removed
Ozone1.gam <- update(Ozone.gam, formula=rt4Ozone ~ s(Solar.R)+s(Wind)+s(Temp))
```

Thus, this equation predicts `Ozone` independently of time.

6.2.2 A Calibration Problem with Time Series Errors

The frosted flakes data (`DAAG::frostedflakes`) has measurements, made on 100 successive days, of the sugar concentration (percent) as measured by two different methods. The `Lab` values were measured by high performance liquid chromatography (a slow accurate laboratory method), while the `IA400` values were from a quick method using the infra-analyzer 400. We would like to obtain a calibration equation for future use, that will estimate values of `Lab`, given values of `IA400`.

Prediction of `Lab` given `IA400` runs into the errors in (predictor) variables problem with bias that was discussed in Section 3.7. One possible strategy, if it can be assumed that the regression of `IA400` on `Lab` has independent errors, has been to work from that equation.

```
flakes <- DAAG::frostedflakes
calib.arima <- with(flakes, auto.arima(IA400, xreg=Lab))
calib.arima
```

```
Series: IA400
Regression with ARIMA(0,0,1) errors

Coefficients:
        ma1  intercept   xreg
      0.388      6.923  0.832
s.e.  0.086      2.563  0.068

sigma^2 = 3.28:  log likelihood = -199.8
AIC=407.6   AICc=408   BIC=418
```

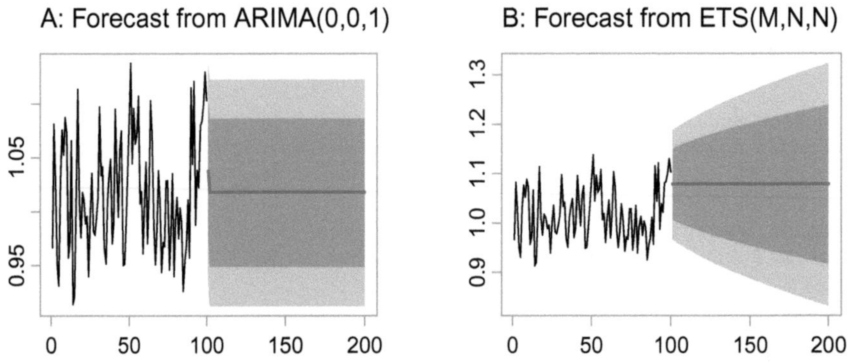

Figure 6.12 Panel A shows predicted values and 80 percent and 95 percent confidence intervals 100 days ahead, from a fitted ARIMA model. Panel B is for a fitted ETS model, with default settings.

The size of the `ma1` term relative to its standard error strongly suggests that errors are not independent.

Other possibilities, under the plausible assumption that values of the ratio are centered on 1, or that the difference is centered on 0, are to work with `IA400/Lab` or with `IA400-Lab`. The error structures that are identified are, in the two cases:

```
with(flakes, coef(auto.arima(IA400/Lab, approximation=F, stepwise=F)))
```

```
     ma1 intercept
  0.3718    1.0173
```

```
with(flakes, coef(auto.arima(IA400-Lab, approximation=F, stepwise=F)))
```

```
     ma1 intercept
  0.3839    0.6202
```

Again, in both cases, values appear to be dependent.

For putting the relationship between the two measures to use, predictions are required, with an accuracy measure, that can be used in the future. Figure 6.12 shows what one or other choice of time series model predicts for the 100 days that immediately follow the original measurements. The width of the confidence interval is, for this series, quite strongly dependent on what time series model is fitted, whether an ARIMA model or an ETS model.

```
calib.arima <- with(flakes, auto.arima(IA400/Lab))
fcast1 <- forecast(calib.arima, h=100)
plot(fcast1, fg='gray', main="A: Forecast from ARIMA(0,0,1)",
    adj=0, font.main=1)
## Alternative, ETS forecast
fcast2 <- with(flakes, forecast(IA400/Lab, h=100))
plot(fcast2, fg='gray', main="B: Forecast from ETS(M,N,N)",
    adj=0, font.main=1)
```

The time series errors, and uncertainty about which form of time series is appropriate, mean that there is no clear way to use the data for calibration. A further variable may be at work, perhaps related to humidity or temperature, that is affecting the relationship. As often, further research is required!

6.3* Nonlinear Time Series

In the ARMA models so far considered, the error structures have been constructed from linear combinations of the innovations, and the innovations have been iid normal random variables. Such models are unable to capture the behavior of series where the variance fluctuates widely with time, as happens for many financial and economic time series.

ARCH (autoregressive conditionally heteroscedastic) and GARCH (generalized ARCH) models have been developed to meet these requirements. The key idea underpinning a GARCH model is that there is an underlying (or hidden) process which governs the variance of the noise term (i.e., ε_t). The noise term is assumed uncorrelated between times. Market participants will, it is argued, quickly identify and take advantage of any correlation patterns that appear more than transient, thus negating them.

Perhaps the simplest example is a model with normal ARCH(1) errors. In such a model, the error term at the current time step is normally distributed with mean 0 and with a variance linearly related to the square of the error at the previous time step. Thus, squares of noise terms form an autoregressive process of order 1. An AR(1) process with ARCH(1) errors is given by

$$X_t = \mu + \alpha(X_{t-1} - \mu) + \varepsilon_t,$$

where ε_t is normal with mean 0 and variance $\sigma_t^2 = \alpha_0 + \alpha\varepsilon_{t-1}^2$. The error terms ε_t are uncorrelated, while their squares have serial correlations with the squares of historical values of the error term.

GARCH models are an extension of ARCH models. In a GARCH model of order (p, q), σ_t^2 is the sum of two terms: (1) a linear function both of the previous p squares of earlier errors, as for an ARCH model of order p, and (2) a linear function of the variances of the previous q error terms.

The function `tseries::garch()`, allows for estimation of the mean and the underlying process parameters for a given time series by maximum likelihood, assuming normality. Note also the function `white.test()` which can be used to test for nonlinearity, either in the dependence of the error term on earlier errors, or in residuals from a regression that includes a time series term. Be aware that the results of such tests should be interpreted with care. Nonlinearity can manifest itself in many different ways, and any one test used will not necessarily be sensitive to the particular type of nonlinearity that is present.

The following code may be used to simulate an ARCH(1) process with $\alpha_0 = 0.25$ and $\alpha_1 = 0.95$:

```
x <- numeric(999) # x will contain the ARCH(1) errors
x0 <- rnorm(1)
```

```
for (i in 1:999){
x0 <- rnorm(1, sd=sqrt(.25 + .95*x0^2))
x[i] <- x0
}
```

(Note that because the initial value is not quite set correctly, a "burn-in" period is required for this to settle down to a close approximation to an ARCH series.)

We can use the `garch()` function to estimate the parameters from the simulated data. Note that the `order` argument specifies the number of MA and AR terms, respectively. With a longer time series, we would expect the respective estimates to converge towards 0.25 and 0.95.

```
suppressPackageStartupMessages(library(tseries))
garch(x, order = c(0, 1), trace=FALSE)
```

```
Call:
garch(x = x, order = c(0, 1), trace = FALSE)

Coefficient(s):
   a0      a1
0.280   0.963
```

The *fSeries* package, which is part of the Rmetrics suite (Würtz, 2004), substantially extends the abilities in `tseries`.

6.4 Further Reading

Chatfield (2003) is a relatively elementary introduction to time series. For forecasting, Hyndman and Athanasopoulos (2021) is a good place to start. Brockwell and Davis (2002) is an excellent and practically oriented introduction, with more mathematical detail than Chatfield. More-advanced practically oriented texts are Cowpertwait and Metcalfe (2009), and Shumway and Stoffer (2006).

State space models provide a theoretical framework for the exponential forecasting approaches that have been widely used since the 1950s. See Ord et al. (1997), Hyndman and Athanasopoulos (2021), and Hyndman and Khandakar (2008). Methods of this type do well in the comparison, in Hyndman et al. (2008), of a number of alternative forecasting approaches. Methods of this type are implemented in the `StructTS()` and `HoltWinters()` functions in the *stats* package, as well as in the *forecast* package.

On ARCH and GARCH models, see Gourieroux (1997), the brief introduction in Venables and Ripley (2002, pp. 414–418), and references given therein. See also the references given on the help page for the `garch()` function.

Spatial Statistics

We have noted that time series ideas can be applied without modification to spatial series in one dimension. The ideas can be extended to higher-dimensional spatial data. Geostatistics, and spatial modeling in general, is concerned with notions of spatial autocorrelation. Kriging is a widely used multidimensional smoothing method. This gives best linear unbiased estimates in a spatial context. We direct the interested reader to the *spatial* package and to the references given therein.

Other Time Series Models and Packages

Consult the CRAN *TimeSeries* Task View for time series analysis for summary details of the extensive range of time series packages that are available. The abilities extend far beyond what has been described in this chapter. The following is a limited selection: *zoo*, for irregular time series; *fracdiff*, for "fractionally differenced" ARIMA "long memory" processes (where the correlation between time points decays slowly as the points move apart in time); *strucchange*, for estimating and testing for change points; and *dse*, for multivariate ARMA, state space modeling, and associated forecasting.

The R package *imputeTS* has a range of abilities for imputation with univariate time series. On multiple imputation for time series cross-sectional data, see Honaker and King (2010).

6.5 Exercises

6.1. A time series of length 100 is obtained from an AR(1) model with $\sigma = 1$ and $\alpha = -0.5$. What is the standard error of the mean? If the usual $\sigma/\sqrt{n}$ formula were used in constructing a confidence interval for the mean, with σ defined as in Section 6.1.4, would it be too narrow or too wide?

6.2. Use the `ar()` function to fit the second order autoregressive model to the Lake Huron time series.

6.3. Repeat the analysis of Section 6.2, replacing `mdbRain` by: (i) `southRain`, that is, annual average rainfall in Southern Australia; (ii) `northRain`, that is, annual average rainfall in Northern Australia.

6.4. *Use the `arima.sim()` (base: *stats*) to simulate 100 000 values from an AR(1) process with $\alpha = -0.5$. Now break this up in to 1000 series of length 100. If `x` is the series, a straightforward way to do this is to set

```
xx <- matrix(x, ncol=1000)
```

Now use the function `apply()` to find the means for each of these series of length 100. Compare

$$\frac{\sum(x_t - \bar{x})^2}{n-1} \text{ with } \mathrm{var}(\bar{x}) = \frac{\sigma^2}{n(1-\alpha)}.$$

For comparison, check the effect of using $\frac{\mathrm{rmvar}(x)}{n}$ to estimate the variance. First calculate the ordinary sample variance for each of our 1000 series. Then compute the average of these variance estimates and divide by the sample size, 100. (This gives a value that is also close to that predicted by the theory, roughly three times larger than the value that was obtained using the correct formula.)

6.5. Sugar content in cereal is monitored in two ways: a lengthy lab analysis (`Lab`) and by using quick, inexpensive high performance liquid chromatography (`IA400`). The data in `frostedflakes` (*DAAG*) are from 100 daily samples of measurements taken using the two methods.

a. Plot the sample autocorrelation function of the vector of differences `IA400-Lab`.
b. Check that `forecast::auto.arima()` selects an MA(1) model.
c. Compare the mean and SEM for the series, as estimated under the independence assumption and as estimated under the MA(1) assumption. Compare the two sets of 95 percent confidence intervals.

6.6. Repeat, for each of the remaining regional rainfall series in the data frame `bomregions2021`, an analysis of the type presented in Section 6.2.

6.7. *Take first differences of the logarithms of the first component of the time series object `tseries::ice.river`, that is

```
library(tseries)
data(ice.river)
river1 <- diff(log(ice.river[, 1]))
```

Use `arima()` to fit an ARMA(1,2) model to `river1`. Plot the residuals. Do they appear to have a constant variance? Test the residuals for nonlinearity.

6.8. Repeat, for each of the regional temperature series in Section 6.2, an the analysis of the type presented in Section 6.2. Is there a comparable dependence on `SOI`?
(Note: It will be necessary to omit the first 10 rows of the data frame, where there are no temperature data.)

6.9. Capability to fit a single-layer feed-forward neural network to univariate time series is afforded by the function `forecast::nnetar`. An illustration of its use in modeling the DAX stock market data in `EuStockmarkets` is given below.

```
library(forecast)
Eu1 <- window(EuStockMarkets[,1], end = c(1996, 260))
Eu1nn <- nnetar(Eu1)
Eu1f <- forecast(Eu1nn, end=end(EuStockMarkets[,1]))
plot(Eu1f, ylim=c(1400, 7000))
lines(EuStockMarkets[,1])
```

Specifically, the closing prices prior to 1997 are fit using the neural network, and then the remaining prices are forecast. A comparison of the actual prices and the forecast prices is displayed in the resulting plot.

a. How far into the future are the forecasts reasonably accurate?
b. Apply a time series bootstrap method, such as the block method employed by `boot::tsboot` to the data in `Eu1` to obtain 999 resampled time series. To each of these new series, fit the neural network model and obtain the corresponding forecasts. Obtain a 95 percent prediction interval for the price for January 1, 1998, and compare with the actual value.
c. Apply the technique to obtain similar forecasts for the other three time series in `EuStockMarkets`.

6.10. The following investigates, for modeling 'Temp' as a smooth function of 'day' for the dataset 'airquality' (_datasets_), the difference made by (wrongly) assuming independent errors:

a. Compare the following two plots, one from a GAM smooth that assumes independent observations, and the other from a smooth that allows for a sequential AR1 correlation:

```
airq <- cbind(airquality[, 1:4], day=1:nrow(airquality))
  # Column 5 ('day' starting May 1) replaces columns 'Month' & 'Day')
library(mgcv)
temp.gam <- gam(Temp~s(day), data=airq)
tempAR1.gamm <- gamm(Temp~s(day), data=airq, correlation=corAR1())
plot(temp.gam, res=T, cex=2)
plot(tempAR1.gamm$gam, res=T, cex=2)
```

Why is the pattern in the first plot so different? How does it differ?

b. The parameter `Phi` for the fitted AR1 process can be obtained thus:

```
(Phi <- coef(tempAR1.gamm$lme$modelStruct$corStruct,
             unconstrained = FALSE) )
Sigma <- sqrt(tempAR1.gamm$gam$sig2)
## Simulate an AR1 process with this parameter
AR1.sim <- arima.sim(model=list(ar=Phi), n=nrow(airq), sd=Sigma)
simSeries <- AR1.sim+fitted(tempAR1.gamm$gam)
plot(I(1:nrow(airq)), simSeries)
## Compare with initial series
plot(I(1:nrow(airq)), airq$Temp)
```

Repeat the simulation several times. What do the various series have in common?

7

Multilevel Models, and Repeated Measures

This chapter further extends the discussion of models that are a marked departure from the independent errors models of Chapters 2 to 5. In the models that will be discussed in this chapter, there is a hierarchy of variation that corresponds to groupings within the data. The groups are nested. For example, students might be sampled from different classes, which in turn are sampled from different schools. Or, crop yields might be measured on multiple parcels of land at each of a number of different sites.

After fitting such models, predictions can be made at any of the different levels. For example, crop yield could be predicted at new sites, or new parcels. Prediction for a new parcel at one of the existing sites is likely to be more accurate than a prediction for a totally new site. Multilevel models, that is, models which have multiple *error* (or *noise*) terms, are able to account for such differences in predictive accuracy.

Repeated measures models are multilevel models where measurements consist of multiple profiles in time or space; each profile can be viewed as a time series. Such data may arise in a clinical trial, and animal or plant growth curves are common examples; each "individual" is measured at multiple times. Typically, the data exhibit some form of time dependence that the model should accommodate.

By contrast with the data that typically appear in a time series model, repeated measures data consist of multiple profiles through time. Relative to the length of time series that is required for a realistic analysis, each individual repeated measures profile can and often will have values for a few time points only. Repeated measures data have, typically, multiple time series that are of short duration.

Ideas that will be central to the discussion of these different models are:

- fixed and random effects,
- variance components, and their connection, in special cases, with expected values of mean squares,
- the specification of mixed models with a simple error structure,
- sequential correlation in repeated measures profiles.

The discussion will start with an example where the data has the *balance* needed to allow the use of the function `aov()` from the base R *stats*) package, comparing and contrasting the output with that from the function `lmer()` from the *lme4*

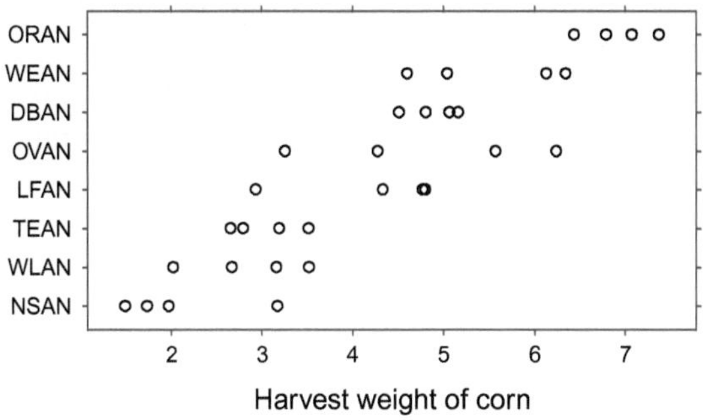

Figure 7.1 Corn yields for four parcels of land in each of eight sites on the Caribbean island of Antigua. Data are in Table 7.1. They are a summarized version (parcel measurements are block means) of a subset of data given in Andrews and Herzberg (1985, pp. 339–353). Sites are ordered according to the magnitude of the site means.

package which is designed to handle more general designs. Other packages that will be used include *afex*, *nlme*, *glmmTMB*, *gamlss*, and *DHARMa*.

The dataset `Orthodont` that is used for the analyses of Subsection 7.8.2, and several datasets that are used in the exercises, are in the *MEMSS* package.

Corn Yield Measurements Example

An especially simple multilevel model is the random effects model for the one-way layout. Thus, consider the data frame `ant111b` in the *DAAG* package, based on an agricultural experiment on the Caribbean island of Antigua. Corn yield measurements were taken on four parcels of land within each of eight sites. Figure 7.1 is a visual summary.

Code for Figure 7.1 is:

```
ant111b <- within(DAAG::ant111b, Site <- reorder(site, harvwt, FUN=mean))
gph <- lattice::stripplot(Site ~ harvwt, data=ant111b,
                          xlab="Harvest weight of corn")
update(gph, par.settings=DAAG::DAAGtheme(color=FALSE), scales=list(tck=0.5))
```

Figure 7.1 suggests that, as might be expected, parcels on the same site will be relatively similar, while parcels on different sites will be relatively less similar. A farmer whose farm was close to one of the experimental sites might take data from that site as indicative of what he/she might expect. In other cases it may be more appropriate for a farmer to regard his/her farm as a new site, distinct from the experimental sites, so that the issue is one of generalizing to a new site. Prediction for a new parcel at one of the existing sites is more accurate than prediction for a totally new site.

There are two levels of random variation. They are site, and parcel within site. Variation between sites may be caused, for example, by differences in elevation or proximity to bodies of water. Within a site, one might expect different parcels to be somewhat similar in terms of elevation and climatic conditions; however, differences in soil fertility and drainage may still have a noticeable effect on yield.

(Use of information on such effects, not available as part of the present data, might allow more accurate modeling.)

The model will need: (a) a random term that accounts for variation within sites, and (b) a second superimposed random term that allows variability between parcels that are on different sites to be greater than variation between parcels within sites. The different random terms are known as *random effects.*

The model can be expressed as:

$$\text{yield} = \text{overall mean} + \begin{matrix}\text{site effect}\\ \text{(random)}\end{matrix} + \begin{matrix}\text{parcel effect (within site)}\\ \text{(random)}\end{matrix}. \qquad (7.1)$$

The balance in the data (there are four parcels per site) makes this a suitable example for analysis of variance using `aov()`, as Section 7.1 will demonstrate.

It will then be instructive, in Subsection 7.2, to set results from use of `aov()` alongside results from the function `lme4::lmer()`. The comparison is between a traditional analysis of variance approach, which is fine for data from a balanced experimental design, and a general multilevel modeling approach that can in principle handle both balanced and unbalanced designs.

7.1 Corn Yield Data – Analysis Using aov()

In the above model, the overall mean is assumed to be a fixed constant, while the site and parcel effects are both assumed to be random. In order to account for the two levels of variation, the model formula must include an `Error(site)` term, thus:

```
ant111b <- DAAG::ant111b
ant111b.aov <- aov(harvwt ~ 1 + Error(site), data=ant111b)
```

Explicit mention of the "within-site" level of variation is unnecessary. (Use of the error term `Error(site/parcel)`, which explicitly identifies parcels within sites, is, however, allowed.) Output is:

```
summary(ant111b.aov)
```

```
Error: site
          Df Sum Sq Mean Sq F value Pr(>F)
Residuals  7   70.3    10.1

Error: Within
          Df Sum Sq Mean Sq F value Pr(>F)
Residuals 24   13.9   0.578
```

The analysis of variance (*anova*) table breaks the total sum of squares about the mean into two parts – variation within sites, and variation between site means. Since there are eight sites, the variation between sites is estimated from seven degrees of freedom, after estimating the overall mean. Within each site, estimation of the site mean leaves three degrees of freedom for estimating the variance for that site. Three degrees of freedom at each of eight sites yields 24 degrees of freedom for estimating within-site variation.

Table 7.1 *The leftmost column has harvest weights (`harvwt`), for the parcels in each site, for the Antiguan corn data. Each of these harvest weights can be expressed as the sum of the overall mean (= 4.29), site effect (fourth column), and residual from the site effect (final column). The information in the fourth and final columns can be used to generate the sums of squares and mean squares for the analysis of variance table.*

Site	Parcel measurements	Site means	Site effects	Residuals from site mean
DBAN	5.16, 4.8, 5.07, 4.51	4.88	+0.59	0.28, −0.08, 0.18, −0.38
LFAN	2.93, 4.77, 4.33, 4.8	4.21	−0.08	−1.28, 0.56, 0.12, 0.59
NSAN	1.73, 3.17, 1.49, 1.97	2.09	−2.2	−0.36, 1.08, −0.6, −0.12
ORAN	6.79, 7.37, 6.44, 7.07	6.91	+2.62	−0.13, 0.45, −0.48, 0.15
OVAN	3.25, 4.28, 5.56, 6.24	4.83	+0.54	−1.58, −0.56, 0.73, 1.4
TEAN	2.65, 3.19, 2.79, 3.51	3.03	−1.26	−0.39, 0.15, −0.25, 0.48
WEAN	5.04, 4.6, 6.34, 6.12	5.52	+1.23	−0.49, −0.93, 0.81, 0.6
WLAN	2.02, 2.66, 3.16, 3.52	2.84	−1.45	−0.82, −0.18, 0.32, 0.68

Interpreting the Mean Squares

The division of the sum of squares into two parts mirrors the two different types of prediction that can be based on these data.

First, suppose that measurements are taken on four new parcels at one of the existing sites. How much might the mean of the four measurements be expected to vary, between one such set of measurements and another? For this, the only source of uncertainty is parcel-to-parcel variation within the existing site. Recall that standard errors of averages can be estimated by dividing the (within) residual mean square by the sample size (in this case, four), and taking the square root. Thus, the relevant standard error is $\sqrt{0.578/4} = 0.38$. (Note that this is another form of the pooled variance estimate discussed in Subsection 1.3.5.)

Second, for prediction of an average of four parcels at some different site, distinct from the original eight, the relevant standard error can be calculated in the same way, but using the between site mean square; it is $\sqrt{10.05/4} = 1.6$.

Details of the Calculations

Table 7.1 contains the data and has details of the mean square calculations used to produce the anova table. First, the overall mean is calculated. It is 4.29 for this example. Then site means are calculated using the parcel measurements. Site effects are calculated by subtracting the overall mean from the site means. The parcel effects are the residuals after subtracting the site means from the individual parcel measurements.

The between-site sum of squares is obtained by squaring the site effects, summing, and multiplying by four. This last step reflects the number of parcels per site. Dividing by the degrees of freedom ($8 - 1 = 7$) gives the mean square.

The within site sum of squares is obtained by squaring the residuals (parcel effects), summing, and dividing by the degrees of freedom ($8 \times (4 - 1) = 24$).

Practical Use of the Analysis of Variance Results

Treating site as random when we do the analysis does not at all commit us to treating it as random for purposes of predicting results from a new site. Rather, it allows us this option, if this seems appropriate. Consider how a person who plans to come to the island might assess the prospects of a farming property that they are considering for purchase. The following are extremes in the range of possibilities.

1. The property is similar to one of the sites for which data are available, so similar in fact that yields would be akin to those from adding new parcels that together comprise the same area on that site.
2. It is impossible to say with any assurance where the new property should be placed within the range of results from experimental sites. The best that can be done is to treat it as a random sample from the population of all possible sites on the island.

Local knowledge, such as may be available from a well-informed local adviser, will be helpful in the attempt to decide where the property fits, relative to sites for which data are available. The standard error (for the mean of four parcels) may then be much less than 1.6, and if the match is close, nearer to 0.38.

Random Effects versus Fixed Effects

The random effects model bears some resemblance to the one-way model considered in Subsection 2.7.1. The important difference is that in Subsection 2.7.1 the interest was in differences between the *fixed* levels of the nutrient treatment that were used in the experiment. Generalization to other possible nutrient treatments was not of interest, and would not have made sense. The only predictions that were possible were for nutrient treatments considered in the study.

The random effects model allows for predictions at two levels: (1) for agricultural yield at a new location within an existing site, or (2) for locations in sites that were different from any of the sites that were included in the original study.

Nested Factors – a Variety of Applications

Random effects models apply in any situation where there is more than one level of random variability. In many situations, one source of variability is *nested* within the other – thus parcels are nested within sites.

Other examples include: variation between houses in the same suburb, as against variation between suburbs; variation between different clinical assessments of the same patients, as against variation between patients; variation within different branches of the same business, as against variation between different branches; variations in the bacterial count between subsamples of a sample taken from a lake, as opposed to variation between different samples; variation between the drug-prescribing practices of clinicians in a particular specialty in the same hospital, as against variation between different clinicians in different hospitals; and so on. In all these cases, the accuracy with which predictions are possible will depend on which of the two levels of variability is involved. These examples can all be extended in fairly obvious ways to include more than two levels of variability.

Sources of variation can also be *crossed.* For example, different years may be crossed with different sites. Years are not nested in sites, nor are sites nested in years. In agricultural yield trials these two sources of variation may be comparable; see, for example, Talbot (1984).

7.1.1 A More-Formal Approach

Consider now a formal mathematical description of the model. The model is:

$$y_{ij} = \mu + \underset{\text{(site, random)}}{\alpha_i} + \underset{\text{(parcel, random)}}{\beta_{ij}} \quad (i = 1, \ldots, 8; j = 1, \ldots, 4) \qquad (7.2)$$

with $\text{var}(\alpha_i) = \sigma_L^2$, $\text{var}(\beta_{ij}) = \sigma_W^2$. The quantities σ_L^2 (L = location, another term for site) and σ_W^2 (W = within) are referred to as *variance components.*

Variance components allow inferences that are not immediately available from the information in the analysis of variance table. Importantly, the variance components provide information that can help design another experiment.

Relations between Variance Components and Mean Squares

The expected values of the mean squares are, in suitably balanced designs such as this, linear combinations of the variance components. The discussion that now follows demonstrates how to obtain the variance components from the analysis of variance calculations. In an unbalanced design, this is not usually possible.

Consider, again, prediction of the average of four parcels within the ith existing site. This average can be written as

$$\bar{y}_i = \mu + \alpha_i + \bar{\beta}_i,$$

where $\bar{\beta}_i$ denotes the average of the four parcel effects within the ith site. Since μ and α_i are constant for the ith site (in technical terms, we *condition* on the site being the ith), $\text{var}(\bar{y}_i)$ is the square root of $\text{var}(\bar{\beta}_i)$, which equals $\sigma_W/\sqrt{4}$.

In the `aov()` output, the expected mean square for `Error: Within`, that is, at the within-site (between packages) level, is σ_W^2. Thus $\widehat{\sigma_W^2} = 0.578$ and $\text{SE}(\bar{y}_i)$ is estimated as $\widehat{\sigma_W}/\sqrt{4} = \sqrt{0.578/4} = 0.38$.

Next, consider prediction of the average yield at four parcels within a new site. The expected mean square at the site level is $4\sigma_L^2 + \sigma_W^2$, that is, the between-site mean square, which in the `aov()` output is 10.05, estimates $4\sigma_L^2 + \sigma_W^2$. The standard error for the prediction of the average yield at four parcels within a new site is

$$\sqrt{\sigma_L^2 + \sigma_W^2/4} = \sqrt{(4\sigma_L^2 + \sigma_W^2)/4}.$$

The estimate for this is $\sqrt{10.05/4} = 1.59$.

Finally, note how, in this balanced case, σ_L^2 can be estimated from the analysis of variance output. Equating the expected between-site mean square to the observed mean square:

$$4\widehat{\sigma_L^2} + \widehat{\sigma_W^2} = 10.05, \tag{7.3}$$

$$\text{that is, } 4\widehat{\sigma_L^2} + 0.578 = 10.05, \tag{7.4}$$

so that $\widehat{\sigma_L^2} = (10.05 - 0.578)/4 = 2.37$.

Interpretation of Variance Components

In summary, here is how the variance components can be interpreted, for the Antiguan data. Plugging in numerical values $\left(\widehat{\sigma_W^2} = 0.578 \text{ and } \widehat{\sigma_L^2} = 2.37\right)$, take-home messages from this analysis are as follows.

- For prediction for a new parcel at one of the existing sites, the standard error is $\widehat{\sigma_W} = \sqrt{0.578} = 0.76$.
- For prediction for a new parcel at a new site, the standard error is $\sqrt{\sigma_L^2 + \sigma_W^2} = \sqrt{2.37 + 0.578} = 1.72$.
- For prediction of the mean of n parcels at a new site, the standard error is $\sqrt{\sigma_L^2 + \sigma_W^2/n} = \sqrt{2.37 + 0.578/n}$.
  (Notice that while σ_W^2 is divided by n, σ_L^2 is not. This is because the site effect is the same for all n parcels.)
- For prediction of the total of n parcels at a new site, the standard error is $\sqrt{\sigma_L^2 n + \sigma_W^2} = \sqrt{2.37n + 0.578}$.

Additionally, we have the following.

- The variance of the difference between two such parcels at the same site is $2\sigma_W^2$. (Both parcels have the same site effect α_i, so that $\text{var}(\alpha_i)$ does not contribute to the variance of the difference.)
- The variance of the difference between two parcels that are in different sites is

$$2\left(\sigma_L^2 + \sigma_W^2\right).$$

Thus, where there are multiple levels of variation, the predictive accuracy can be dramatically different, depending on what is to be predicted. Similar issues arise in repeated measures contexts, and in time series.

Intra-class Correlation

According to the model, two observations at different sites are uncorrelated. Two observations at the same site are correlated. The measure used has the name *intra-class correlation*, and is the proportion of residual variance explained by differences between sites. Here, it equals $\sigma_L^2/\left(\sigma_L^2 + \sigma_W^2\right)$.

Plugging in the variance component estimates, the intra-class correlation for the corn yield data is $2.37/(2.37 + 0.578) = 0.804$. Roughly 80 percent of the yield variation is due to differences between sites.

7.2 Analysis Using `lme4::lmer()`

In output from the function `lmer()`, the assumption of two nested random effects, that is, a hierarchy of three levels of variation, is explicit. Variation between sites (this appeared first in the anova table in Subsection 7.1) is the "lower" of the two levels. Here, the *nlme* convention will be followed, and this will be called level 1. Variation between parcels in the same site (this appeared second in the anova table, under "Residuals") is at the "higher" of the two levels, conveniently called level 2.

The modeling command takes the form:

```
library(lme4)
ant111b.lmer <- lmer(harvwt ~ 1 + (1 | site), data=ant111b)
```

The only fixed effect is the overall mean. The `(1 | site)` term fits random variation between sites. Variation between the individual units that are nested within sites, that is, between parcels, are by default treated as random. Here is the default output:

```
## Note that there is no degrees of freedom information.
print(ant111b.lmer, ranef.comp="Variance")
```

```
Linear mixed model fit by REML ['lmerMod']
Formula: harvwt ~ 1 + (1 | site)
   Data: ant111b
REML criterion at convergence: 94.42
Random effects:
 Groups   Name        Variance
 site     (Intercept) 2.368
 Residual             0.578
Number of obs: 32, groups:  site, 8
Fixed Effects:
(Intercept)
       4.29
```

Observe that, according to `lmer()`, $\widehat{\sigma_W^2} = 0.578$, and $\widehat{\sigma_L^2} = 2.368$. Observe also that $\widehat{\sigma_W^2} = 0.578$ is the mean square from the analysis of variance table. The mean square at level 1 does not appear in the output from the `lmer()` analysis.

The Processing of Output from `lmer()`

The function `coef()` with output from `summary()` as argument, gives estimates of fixed effect coefficients and their standard errors. For the model `ant111b.lmer`, we obtain:

```
coef(summary(ant111b.lmer))
```

```
            Estimate Std. Error t value
(Intercept)    4.292     0.5604   7.659
```

Users who require approximate p-values for comparison with the reference level of a factor (not relevant for the present model) can use the function `afex::mixed()`. A call to `mixed()`, which in turn calls `lmer()`, replaces the direct call to `lmer()`. If called with `method="KR"`, the Kenward–Roger approximation is used to calculate degrees of freedom for statistics in the `t value` column in the output from `lmer()`.

With degrees of freedom thus given, the t-values are treated as t statistics and approximate p-values are determined. Subsection 7.3.1 has an example of its use.

Objects returned by the `lmer()` have the class `merMod`. Objects returned by the `summary()` method for `merMod` objects have class `summary.merMod`. Objects returned by `VarCorr()`, used in the sequel for extracting variance component estimates, have class `VarCorr.merMod`.

See `?lme4::merMod` for details of methods for `merMod` and `summary.merMod` objects. Note in particular the `print()` methods, with arguments that control the details of what is printed.[1]

Fitted Values and Residuals in `lmer()`

In hierarchical multilevel models, fitted values can be calculated at each level of variation that the model allows. Corresponding to each level of fitted values, there is a set of residuals that is obtained by subtracting the fitted values from the observed values.

The default, and at the time of writing the only option, is to calculate fitted values and residuals that adjust for all random effects except the residual. Here, these are estimates of the site expected values. They differ slightly from the site means, as will be seen below. Such fitted values are known as BLUPs (best linear unbiased predictors). Among linear unbiased predictors of the site means, the BLUPs are designed to have the smallest expected error mean square.

Relative to the site means $\bar{y}_{i.}$, the BLUPs are pulled in toward the overall mean $\bar{y}_{..}$. The most extreme site means will, on average, because of random variation, be more extreme than the corresponding "true" means for those sites.

For the simple model considered here, the fitted value $\widehat{\alpha}_i$ for the ith site is:

$$\widehat{y_{i\cdot}} = \bar{y}_{..} + \frac{n\widehat{\sigma_L^2}}{n\widehat{\sigma_L^2} + \widehat{\sigma_W^2}}(\bar{y}_{i.} - \bar{y}_{..}).$$

Shrinkage is substantial, that is, a shrinkage factor much less than 1.0, when $n^{-1}\widehat{\sigma_W^2}$ is large relative to $\widehat{\sigma_L^2}$. (For the notation, refer back to Equation (7.2).)

In practice, the BLUPs are likely to be calculated, either as fitted values, or by adding site random effects to the overall mean. The following shows the three ways to calculate the BLUPs:

```
s2W <- 0.578; s2L <- 2.37; n <- 4
sitemeans <- with(ant111b, sapply(split(harvwt, site), mean))
grandmean <- mean(sitemeans)
shrinkage <- (n*s2L)/(n*s2L+s2W)
## Check  that fitted values equal BLUPs, and compare with site means
BLUP <- grandmean + shrinkage*(sitemeans - grandmean)
BLUP <- fitted(ant111b.lmer)[match(names(sitemeans), ant111b$site)]
BLUP <- grandmean + ranef(ant111b.lmer)$site[[1]]
```

Now compare the BLUPs with the grand mean:

[1] Thus, for use of `print()` with `merMod` and `summary.merMod` objects, the argument `ranef.comp` can be set to any combination of `comp="Variance"` and `comp="Std.Dev."`. For use of `print()` with `VarCorr.merMod` objects, the same alternatives are available for the `comp` argument.

```
          DBAN  LFAN  NSAN  ORAN  OVAN  TEAN  WEAN  WLAN
BLUP      4.851 4.212 2.217 6.764 4.801 3.108 5.455 2.925
sitemeans 4.885 4.207 2.090 6.915 4.833 3.036 5.526 2.841
```

Observe that, for site means below the overall mean (4.29), the fitted values are slightly larger (closer to the overall mean). For site means above the overall mean, the fitted values are smaller.

The function `fitted()` has given the fitted values at level 1, that is, it adjusts for the single random effect. The fitted value at level 0 is the overall mean, given by `fixef(ant111b.lmer)`. Residuals can be also defined on several levels. At level 0, they are the differences between the observed responses and the overall mean. At level 1, they are the differences between the observed responses and the fitted values at level 1 (which are the BLUPs for the sites).

**Uncertainty in the Parameter Estimates – Profile Likelihood and Alternative*

The limits of acceptance of a likelihood ratio test for the null hypothesis of no change in a parameter value can be used as approximate 95 percent confidence limits for that parameter. Where the likelihood is a function of more than one parameter, the profile likelihood may be used. For any parameter ψ, the profile likelihood is the function of ψ that is obtained by maximizing the likelihood, for each value of ψ, over values of other parameters.

The function `confint()` can be used to pull together the profile information, calculated using the profile method for `merMod` objects, to create approximate confidence intervals:[2]

```
prof.lmer <- profile(ant111b.lmer)
CI95 <- confint(prof.lmer, level=0.95)
rbind("sigmaL^2"=CI95[1,]^2, "sigma^2"=CI95[2,]^2)
```

```
           2.5 % 97.5 %
sigmaL^2 0.7965  6.936
sigma^2  0.3444  1.079
```

A 95 percent confidence interval for the intercept is:

```
CI95[3,]
```

```
 2.5 % 97.5 %
 3.128  5.456
```

The function `confint()`, as used here, returned confidence intervals for σ_L (row label `.sig01`, random), for σ (row label `.sigma`, random), and for `(Intercept)` (fixed). The `(Intercept)` is for the fitted model, and estimates the overall mean.

The profile likelihoods, scaled so that the lower 2.5 percent limit transforms to −1.96 and the upper lower 97.5 percent limit, are shown in Figure 7.2. Code is:

[2] Be aware that convergence problems will sometimes generate warning messages.

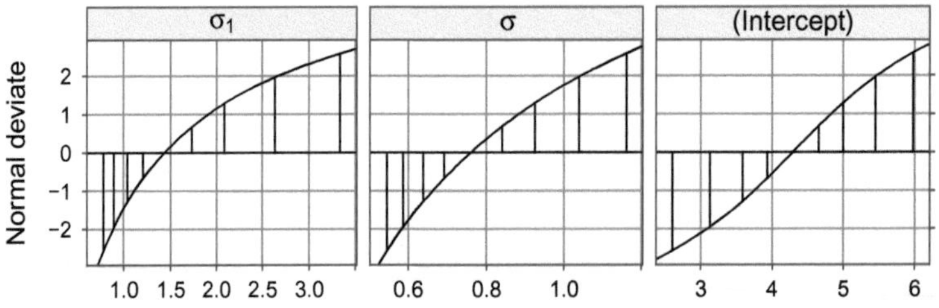

Figure 7.2 Profile likelihoods for the two random and one fixed parameters in the model `ant111b.lmer`. The horizontal scales are $\sigma_1 = \sigma_L$, $\sigma = \sigma_W$, and `(Intercept)`. On the vertical scale, the confidence interval limits are labeled according to the equivalent normal deviates. The 95% confidence interval limits are thus at -1.96 and 1.96. The vertical bars are placed at 50%, 80%, 95%, and 99% limits.

```
library(lattice)
gph <- xyplot(prof.lmer, conf=c(50, 80, 95, 99)/100,
              aspect=0.8, between=list(x=0.35))
```

For variances, the horizontal scales show `Std.Dev.` $= \sqrt{\text{Variance}}$. For details of this and other displays that can be used for the output from the `profile()` method for `merMod` objects, see `?lme4::xyplot.thpr`.

See `?lme4::confint.merMod` for details of the `confint` method for `merMod` objects. Alternatives to the default argument `method="profile"` are `method="Wald"` or `method="boot"`. The `Wald` method is fast but uses approximations that will, if variances change sharply in the region of the estimate, be quite inaccurate. The `boot` method uses repeated fits to suitably constructed bootstrap samples, and can be time consuming. The trustworthiness of results from this method may be in question if more than an occasional fit fails. For further details of use of the argument `method="boot"`, see `?lme4::bootMer`. and `?lme4::simulate.merMod`.

Modeling More Than Two Levels of Random Variation

There can be variation at each of several nested levels. In the example in the next section, attitude to science scores, on a scale that measured extent of `like`, were obtained for 1385 year 7 students, divided between 66 classes which in turn were divided between 41 schools.

The analysis in Section 7.3 will treat both school and class as random effects. Using the terminology of the *nlme* package, there are then three levels of random variation – level 3 is pupil, level 2 is class, and level 1 is school. (Note, however, that the `lmer()` function is not limited to the hierarchical models to which this terminology applies, and does not make formal use of the "levels" terminology.)

The model will also take account of two "fixed effects." One of these accounts for a possible difference between sexes, and the other for a possible differences between public and private schools. Much of the interest is in the implications of the random effects for the accuracy of the fixed effect estimates.

The random effects are in each case assumed to be independent normal variables – one set for schools, one for classes, and one for pupils, operating independently. Careful analysts will watch for any indication that failure in a part of this framework of assumptions may compromise the analysis.

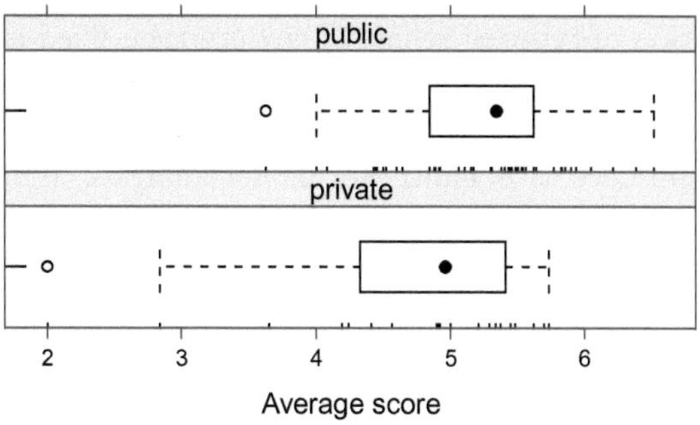

Figure 7.3 Average scores for class, compared between public and private schools.

7.3 Survey Data, with Clustering

The data that will now be explored are from the data frame `science` (*DAAG*). They are measurements of attitudes to science, from a survey where there were results from 20 classes in 12 private schools and 46 classes in 29 public (i.e., state) schools, all in and around Canberra, Australia. Results are from a total of 1385 year 7 students. The variable `like` is a summary score based on two of the questions. It is on a scale from 1 (dislike) to 12 (like). The number in each class from whom scores were available ranged from 3 to 50, with a median of 21.5. Figure 7.3 compares results for public schools with those for private schools.[3]

7.3.1 Alternative Models

Within any one school, we might have

$$y = \text{ class effect } + \text{ pupil effect,}$$

where y represents the attitude measure.

Within any one school, we might use a one-way analysis of variance to estimate and compare class effects. However, this study has the aim of generalizing beyond the classes in the study to all of some wider population of classes, not just in the one school, but in a wider population of schools from which the schools in the study were drawn. In order to be able to generalize in this way, we treat school (`school`), and class (`class`) within school, as random effects. We are interested in possible differences between the sexes (`sex`), and between private and public schools (`PrivPub`). The two sexes are not a sample from some larger population of possible

[3]
```
## Means of like (data frame science: DAAG), by class
science <- DAAG::science
classmeans <- with(science, aggregate(like, by=list(PrivPub, Class), mean))
# NB: Class identifies classes independently of schools
#     class identifies classes within schools
names(classmeans) <- c("PrivPub", "Class", "avlike")
gph <- bwplot(~avlike|PrivPub, layout=c(1,2), xlab="Average score",
              panel=function(x,y,...){panel.bwplot(x,y,...)
              panel.rug(x,y,...)}, data=classmeans)
```

sexes (!), nor are the two types of school (for this study at least) a sample from some large population of types of school. They are then fixed effects. The interest is in the specific fixed differences between males and females, and between private and public schools.

The preferred approach is a multilevel model analysis. While it is sometimes possible to treat such data using an approximation to the analysis of variance as for a balanced experimental design, the adequacy of the approximation may be in doubt. We specify sex (`sex`) and school type (`PrivPub`) as fixed effects, while school (`school`) and class (`class`) are specified as random effects. Class is *nested* within school; within each school there are several classes. The model is:

$$y = \underset{\text{(fixed)}}{\text{sex effect}} + \underset{\text{(fixed)}}{\text{type (private or public)}} + \underset{\text{(random)}}{\text{school effect}} + \underset{\text{(random)}}{\text{class effect}} + \underset{\text{(random).}}{\text{pupil effect}}$$

The following are questions we might ask.

- Are there differences between private and public schools?
- Are there differences between females and males?
- Clearly there are differences among pupils. Are there differences between classes within schools, and between schools, greater than pupil-to-pupil variation within classes would lead us to expect?

The following fits an initial model:

```
science <- DAAG::science
science.lmer <- lmer(like ~ sex + PrivPub + (1 | school) +
                     (1 | school:class), data = science,
                     na.action=na.exclude)
```

```
boundary (singular) fit: see help('isSingular')
```

The components of variance estimates are:

```
print(VarCorr(science.lmer), comp="Variance", digits=2)
```

```
 Groups       Name        Variance
 school:class (Intercept) 0.32
 school       (Intercept) 0.00
 Residual                 3.05
```

Note that the variance components form a nested hierarchy. The order is `Residual` (variation between students), `school:class`, and `school`. Variation between students (3.052) contributes to variation between classes. Once variation between students within classes (0.321) and between classes within schools has been accounted for, there is nothing left for variation between schools to explain. The warning message indicates that the estimate might, if allowed, have gone negative. If owing to more than random variation, this will indicate a failure of model assumptions. Teachers and the teaching environment explain or (if there really is an issue with model assumptions) over-explain the variation in responses that has been observed.

The table of estimates and standard errors for the coefficients of the fixed component is:

```
print(coef(summary(science.lmer)), digits=2)
```

```
              Estimate Std. Error t value
(Intercept)       4.72      0.162    29.1
sexm              0.18      0.098     1.9
PrivPubpublic     0.41      0.186     2.2
```

Groups within the 1383 observations that are included are:

```
summary(science.lmer)$ngrps
```

```
school:class       school
          66           41
```

Degrees of freedom are as follows.

- Between types of school: 41 (number of schools) − 2 = 39.
- Between sexes: 1383 − 1 (overall mean) − 1 (differences between males and females) − 65 (differences between the 66 `school:class` combinations) = 1316.

The comparison between types of schools compares 12 private schools with 29 public schools, comprising 41 algebraically distinct items of information. Because the numbers of classes and class sizes differ between schools, the three components of variance contribute differently to these different accuracies, and the 39 degrees of freedom are for a statistic that has only an approximate t-distribution. On the other hand, schools are made up of mixed males and female classes. The between-pupils level of variation, where the only component of variance is that for the `Residual` in the output above, is thus the relevant level for the comparison between males and females. The t-test for this comparison is, under model assumptions, an exact test with 1316 degrees of freedom.

Omission of the between-school random effect leads to the following simpler model, with variance component estimates that are, to three decimal places, the same as before:

```
science1.lmer <- lmer(like ~ sex + PrivPub + (1 | school:class),
                      data = DAAG::science, na.action=na.exclude)
```

Estimates of random and fixed effects are:

```
print(VarCorr(science1.lmer), comp="Variance", digits=3)
```

```
 Groups       Name        Variance
 school:class (Intercept) 0.321
 Residual                 3.052
```

```
print(coef(summary(science1.lmer)), digits=2)
```

```
              Estimate Std. Error t value
(Intercept)       4.72      0.162    29.1
sexm              0.18      0.098     1.9
PrivPubpublic     0.41      0.186     2.2
```

Approximate p-values can be obtained thus:

```
opt <- options(contrasts=c("contr.sum","contr.poly"))
  # Change is otherwise made as and if required for individual factors
  # prior to fitting model, and a warning message is generated.
afex::mixed(like ~ sex + PrivPub + (1 | school:class), method="KR", type=2,
            data = na.omit(science), sig_symbols=rep("",4), progress=FALSE)
```

```
Mixed Model Anova Table (Type 2 tests, KR-method)

Model: like ~ sex + PrivPub + (1 | school:class)
Data: na.omit(science)
   Effect          df    F p.value
1     sex 1, 1379.49 3.44    .064
2 PrivPub    1, 60.44 4.91    .030
```

```
options(opt)      # Reset to previous contrasts setting
```

As there is no interaction term, a type 2 (or type 3) test checks for the contribution of each main effect given the other. This contrasts with a type 1 sequential test. (This use of the word type should not be confused with its use in connection with type 1 and type 2 errors.) Subsection 7.8.2 will briefly discuss `afex::mixed()` test type distinctions more generally.

More-Detailed Examination of the Output

Now use the function `confint()` to get approximate 95 percent confidence intervals for the variance components:

```
## Use profile likelihood
pp <- profile(science1.lmer, which="theta_")
# which="theta_": all random parameters
# which="beta_": fixed effect parameters
var95 <- confint(pp, level=0.95)^2
# Square to get variances in place of SDs
rownames(var95) <- c("sigma_Class^2", "sigma^2")
signif(var95, 3)
```

```
              2.5 % 97.5 %
sigma_Class^2 0.178  0.511
sigma^2       2.830  3.300
```

To what extent do differences between classes affect the attitude to science? The *intra-class correlation*, which is the proportion of variance that is explained by differences between classes, is $0.321/(0.321 + 3.052) = 0.095$. The main influence comes from outside the class that the pupil attends, for example, from home, television, friends, inborn tendencies, etc.

Do not be tempted to think that, because 0.321 is small relative to the within-class component variance of 3.05, it is of little consequence. The variance for the mean of a class that is chosen at random is $0.321 + 3.05/n$. Thus, with a class size of 20, the between-class component makes a bigger contribution than the within-class component. If all classes were the same size, then the standard error of the difference

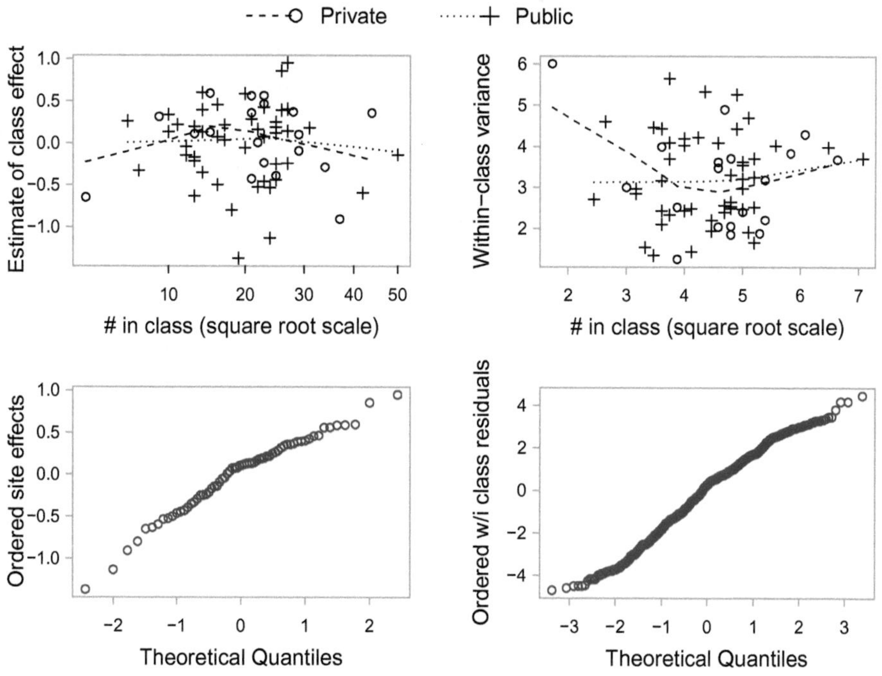

Figure 7.4 Panel A plots class effects against number in the class. Panel B plots within-class variance against number in the class. Panels C and D show normal quantile–quantile plots, for the class effect and for the level 1 residuals (adjusting for the class effect) respectively.

between class means for public schools and those for private schools would, as there were 20 private schools and 46 public schools, be

$$\sqrt{(0.321 + 3.05/n)\left(\frac{1}{20} + \frac{1}{46}\right)}.$$

From the output table of coefficients and standard errors, we note that the standard error of difference between public and private schools is 0.1857. For this to equal the expression just given, we require $n = 19.1$. Thus, the sampling design is roughly equivalent to a balanced design with 19.1 pupils per class.

Figure 7.4 displays information that may be helpful in the assessment of the model.

```
## Fit model and generate quantities that will be plotted
science1.lmer <- lmer(like ~ sex + PrivPub + (1 | school:class),
data = science, na.action=na.omit)
## Panel A: random site effects vs number in class
ranf <- ranef(obj = science1.lmer, drop=TRUE)[["school:class"]]
flist <- science1.lmer@flist[["school:class"]]
privpub <- science[match(names(ranf), flist), "PrivPub"]
num <- unclass(table(flist)); numlabs <- pretty(num)
## Panel B: Within class variance estimates vs numbers
res <- residuals(science1.lmer)
```

```
vars <- tapply(res, INDEX=list(flist), FUN=var)*(num-1)/(num-2)
## Panel C: Normal probability of random site effects (`ranf`)
## Panel D: Normal probability of residuals (`res`)
```

Panel A does not show clear trend. Panel B perhaps suggests that variances may be larger for those few classes that had more than about 30 students. Panels C and D show distributions that seem acceptably close to normal. The interpretation of panel C is complicated by the fact that the different effects are estimated with different accuracies.

7.3.2 Instructive, Though Faulty, Analyses

Ignoring Class as the Random Effect

It is important that the specification of random effects be correct. It is enlightening to do an analysis that is not quite correct, and investigate the scope that it offers for misinterpretation. We fit `school`, ignoring `class`, as a random effect. The estimates of the fixed effects change little.

```
science2.lmer <- lmer(like ~ sex + PrivPub + (1 | school),
data = science, na.action=na.exclude)
print(coef(summary(science2.lmer)), digits=3)
```

```
              Estimate Std. Error t value
(Intercept)      4.738      0.163   29.00
sexm             0.197      0.101    1.96
PrivPubpublic    0.417      0.185    2.25
```

The estimated variance components are:

```
## NB: Output is misleading
print(VarCorr(science2.lmer), comp="Variance", digits=3)
```

```
 Groups   Name        Variance
 school   (Intercept) 0.166
 Residual             3.219
```

This analysis suggests, wrongly, that the between schools component of variance is substantial. From our earlier investigation, it is clear that the difference is between classes, not between schools!

Ignoring the Random Structure in the Data

Here is the result from a standard regression (linear model) analysis, with `sex` and `PrivPub` as fixed effects:

```
## Faulty analysis, using lm
science.lm <- lm(like ~ sex + PrivPub, data=science)
round(coef(summary(science.lm)), digits=4)
```

```
              Estimate Std. Error t value Pr(>|t|)
(Intercept)     4.7402     0.0996  47.616   0.0000
sexm            0.1509     0.0986   1.531   0.1261
PrivPubpublic   0.3951     0.1051   3.759   0.0002
```

Do not believe this analysis! The SEs are too small, and the number of degrees of freedom for the comparison between public and private schools is much too large. The contrast is more borderline than this analysis suggests.

7.3.3 Predictive Accuracy

The variance of a prediction of the average for a new class of n pupils, sampled in the same way as existing classes, is $0.32 + 3.05/n$. If classes were of equal size, we could derive an equivalent empirical estimate of predictive accuracy by using a resampling method with the class means. With unequal class sizes, use of the class means in this way will be a rough approximation. There were 60 classes. If the training/test set methodology is used, the 60 class means would be divided between a training set and a test set.

An empirical estimate of the within class variation can be derived by applying a resampling method (cross-validation, or the bootstrap) to data for each individual class. The variance estimates from the different classes would then be pooled.

The issues here are important. Data do often have a hierarchical variance structure comparable with that for the attitudes to science data. As with the Antiguan corn yield data, the population to which results are to be generalized determines what estimate of predictive accuracy is needed. There are some generalizations, for example, to another state, that the data cannot support.

7.4 A Multilevel Experimental Design

Figure 7.5, based on a similar figure in Maindonald (1992), shows the field layout for a kiwifruit shading trial that generated the data in in `DAAG::kiwishade`. Further details may be found in Snelgar et al. (1992). The two papers have different shorthands (e.g., Sept.–Nov. versus Aug.–Dec.) for describing the time periods for which the shading was applied. In summary, we can say the following.

- This is a balanced design with four vines per plot, four plots per block, and three blocks.
- There are three levels of variation that will be assumed random – between vines within plots, between plots within blocks, and between blocks.
- The experimental unit is a plot; this is the level at which the treatment was applied. We have four results (vine yields) per plot.
- Within blocks, treatments were randomly allocated the four plots.

The northernmost plots were grouped together because they were similarly affected by shading from the sun in the north. For the remaining two blocks, shelter effects, whether from the west or from the east, were thought more important. Table 7.2 displays a breakdown of the data.

The `aov()` function allows calculation of an analysis of variance table that accounts for the multiple levels of variation, and allows the use of variation at the plot level to compare treatments. Variance components can be derived, should they be required, from the information in the analysis of variance table. The section will conclude by demonstrating the use of `lmer()` to calculate the variance components directly, and provide information equivalent to that from the use of `aov()`.

The model is

$$\text{yield} = \text{overall mean} + \begin{array}{c}\text{block effect}\\ \text{(random)}\end{array} + \begin{array}{c}\text{shade effect}\\ \text{(fixed)}\end{array} + \begin{array}{c}\text{plot effect}\\ \text{(random)}\end{array} + \begin{array}{c}\text{vine effect}\\ \text{(random).}\end{array}$$

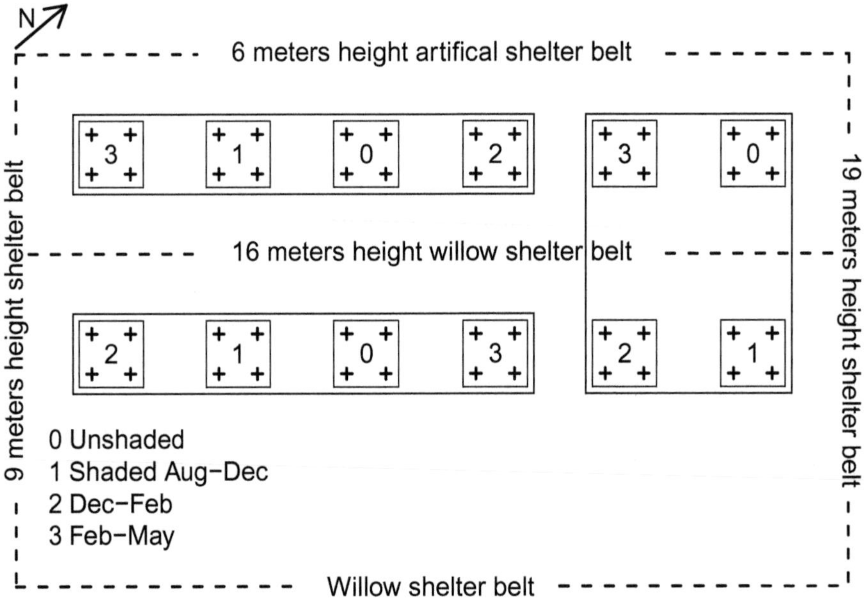

Figure 7.5 Field layout for the kiwifruit shading trial.

We characterize the design as follows.

Fixed effect: shade (treatment).
Random effect: vine (nested) in plot in block, or block/plot/vine.

Although block is included as a random effect, the estimate of the block component of variance has limited usefulness. On the one hand, the common location of the three blocks has exposed them to similar soil and general climate effects. On the other hand, their different orientations (north, west, and east) to sun and prevailing wind will lead to systematic differences. At best, the estimate of the block component of variance will give a rough hint on the likely accuracy of predictions for other blocks.

There is some limited ability to generalize to other plots and other vines. When horticulturalists apply these treatments in their own orchards, there will be different vines, plots, and blocks. Thus, vines and plots are treated as random effects. A horticulturalist will, however, reproduce, as far as possible, the same shade treatments as were used in the scientific trial, and these are taken as fixed effects. A caveat is that these effects may well operate differently in the different conditions (climate, soil, and other) of a different site.

7.4.1 The Analysis of Variance (`anova`) *Table*

The model formula that is supplied to `aov()` is an extension of an `lm()` style of model formula that includes an `Error()` term. Observe that each different plot within a block has a different shading treatment, so that the `block:shade` combination can be used to identify plots. Thus the two error terms that need to be specified

Table 7.2 *Data from the* **kiwishade** *data is broken down by plot means, and differences of yields for individual vines from the plot mean. The level names for the factor* `shade` *are mnemonics for the period during which shading was applied. Thus,* `none` *implies no shading,* `Aug2Dec` *means "August to December," and similarly for* `Dec2Feb` *and* `Feb2May`. *Yields are in kilograms.*

block	shade	Mean	vine1	vine2	vine3	vine4
east	none	99.03	1.285	−2.025	−0.975	1.715
east	Aug2Dec	105.55	3.315	−2.415	2.765	−3.665
east	Dec2Feb	88.92	−3.520	−7.490	5.020	5.990
east	Feb2May	95.88	−3.430	1.690	1.270	0.470
north	none	104.03	−2.915	3.995	2.645	−3.725
north	Aug2Dec	103.59	−0.495	−1.075	0.425	1.145
north	Dec2Feb	93.70	−1.528	0.112	1.062	0.352
north	Feb2May	92.03	0.545	1.415	−1.745	−0.215
west	none	97.56	−4.918	5.932	3.123	−4.138
west	Aug2Dec	100.55	5.220	0.860	−2.950	−3.130
west	Dec2Feb	87.15	−0.495	3.605	−0.085	−3.025
west	Feb2May	90.41	−3.138	4.582	−1.347	−0.097
Grand mean = 96.53						

can be written `block` and `block:shade`. There is a shorthand way to specify both of these together. Write `block/shade`, which expands into `block+block:shade`. Suitable code is:

```
## Analysis of variance: data frame kiwishade (DAAG)
kiwishade <- DAAG::kiwishade
kiwishade.aov <- aov(yield ~ shade + Error(block/shade),
data=kiwishade)
summary(kiwishade.aov)
```

```
Error: block
          Df Sum Sq Mean Sq F value Pr(>F)
Residuals  2    172    86.2

Error: block:shade
          Df Sum Sq Mean Sq F value Pr(>F)
shade      3   1395     465    22.2 0.0012
Residuals  6    126      21

Error: Within
          Df Sum Sq Mean Sq F value Pr(>F)
Residuals 36    439    12.2
```

Notice the use of `summary()` to give the information that is required. The function `anova()` is, in this context, unhelpful.

Table 7.3 structures the output, with a view to making it easier to follow. The final column will be discussed later, in Subsection 7.4.2.

Table 7.3 *Mean squares in the analysis of variance table. The final column gives expected values of mean squares, as functions of the variance components.*

	Df	Sum of Sq	Mean sq	E[Mean sq]
`block` level	2	172.35	86.17	$16\sigma_B^2 + 4\sigma_P^2 + \sigma_V^2$
`block.plt` level				
`shade`	3	1394.51	464.84	$4\sigma_P^2 + \sigma_V^2$ + treatment component
`residual`	6	125.57	20.93	$4\sigma_P^2 + \sigma_V^2$
`block.plt.vines` level	36	438.58	12.18	σ_V^2

7.4.2 Expected Values of Mean Squares

The final column of Table 7.3 shows how the variance components combine to give the expected values of mean squares in the analysis of variance table. In this example, calculation of variance components is not necessary for purposes of assessing the effects of treatments. We compare the `shade` mean square with the `residual` mean square for the `block.plt` level. The ratio is

$$F\text{-ratio} = \frac{464.84}{20.93} = 22.2, \text{ on 3 and 6 d.f. } (p = 0.0024).$$

As this is a complete balanced design, the treatment estimates can be obtained using `model.tables()`:

```
model.tables(kiwishade.aov, type="means", cterms="shade")
```

```
Tables of means
Grand mean

96.53

 shade
shade
   none Aug2Dec Dec2Feb Feb2May
 100.20  103.23   89.92   92.77
```

The footnote gives an alternative way to calculate these means.[4]

Treatment differences are estimated within blocks, so that σ_B^2 does not contribute to the standard error of the differences (SED) between means. The SED is, accordingly, $\sqrt{2}\times$ the square root of the residual mean square divided by the sample size: $\sqrt{2} \times \sqrt{(20.93/12)} = 1.87$. The sample size is 12, since each treatment comparison is based on differences between two different sets of 12 vines.

Subsection 7.4.3 will demonstrate calculation of the sums of squares in the analysis of variance table, based on a breakdown of the observed yields into components that closely reflect the different terms in the model. Readers who do not at this point wish to study Subsection 7.4.3 in detail may nevertheless find it helpful to examine Figure 7.6, taking on trust the scalings used for the effects that they present.

[4]
```
## Calculate treatment means
with(kiwishade, sapply(split(yield, shade), mean))
```

Table 7.4 *Each plot mean is expressed as the sum of overall mean (= 96.53), block effect, shade effect, and residual for the* `block:shade` *combination (or* `plt`*).*

`block`	`shade`	Mean	Block effect	Shade effect	`block:shade` residual
east	none	99.02	0.812	3.670	−1.990
east	Aug2Dec	105.56	0.812	6.701	1.509
east	Dec2Feb	88.92	0.812	−6.612	−1.813
east	Feb2May	95.88	0.812	−3.759	2.294
north	none	104.02	1.805	3.670	2.017
north	Aug2Dec	103.60	1.805	6.701	−1.444
north	Dec2Feb	93.70	1.805	−6.612	1.971
north	Feb2May	92.04	1.805	−3.759	−2.545
west	none	97.56	−2.618	3.670	−0.027
west	Aug2Dec	100.55	−2.618	6.701	−0.066
west	Dec2Feb	87.15	−2.618	−6.612	−0.158
west	Feb2May	90.41	−2.618	−3.759	0.251
			square, add, multiply by 4, divide by df=2, to give ms	square, add, multiply by 4, divide by df=3, to give ms	square, add, multiply by 4, divide by df=6, to give ms

*7.4.3** ***The Analysis of Variance Sums of Squares Breakdown***

This subsection shows how to calculate the sums of squares and mean squares. These details are not essential to what follows, but do give useful insight. The breakdown extends the approach used in the simpler example of Sections 7.1 and 7.2.

For each plot, we calculate a mean, and differences from the mean. See Table 7.2.[5] Note that whereas we started with 48 observations we have only 12 means. Now we break the means down into overall mean, plus block effect (the average of differences, for that block, from the overall mean), plus treatment effect (the average of the difference, for that treatment, from the overall mean), plus residual.

Table 7.4 uses the information from Table 7.2 to express each plot mean as the sum of a block effect, a shade effect and a residual for the `block:shade` combination. The notes in the last row of each column show how to determine the mean squares in Table 7.3. Moreover, we can scale the values in the various columns so that their standard deviation is the square root of the error mean square, and plot them. Figure 7.6 plots all this information. It shows the individual values, together with one standard deviation limits either side of zero. The chief purpose of these plots is to show the much greater variation at these levels than at the `plot(plt)` and vine level.

[5]
```
## For each plot, calculate mean, and differences from the mean
vine <- paste("vine", rep(1:4, 12), sep="")
vine1rows <- seq(from=1, to=45, by=4)
kiwivines <- unstack(kiwishade, yield ~ vine)
kiwimeans <- apply(kiwivines, 1, mean)
kiwivines <- cbind(kiwishade[vine1rows,  c("block","shade")],
Mean=kiwimeans, kiwivines-kiwimeans)
kiwivines <- with(kiwivines, kiwivines[order(block, shade), ])
mean(kiwimeans)       # the grand mean
```

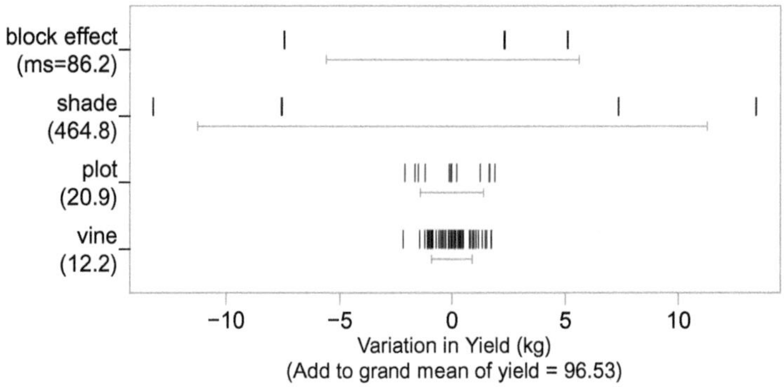

Figure 7.6 Variation at the different levels, for the kiwifruit shading data. The individual data values are given, together with one standard deviation limits either side of zero.

The estimate of between plot variance in Table 7.3 was 20.93. While larger than the between vine mean square of 12.18, it is not so much larger that the evidence from Figure 7.6 can be more than suggestive. Variation between treatments does appear much greater than can be explained from variation between plots, and the same is true for variation between blocks.

We now explain the scaling of effects in Figure 7.6. Consider first the 48 residuals at the vine level. As 12 degrees of freedom were expended when the 12 plot means were subtracted, the 48 residuals share 36 degrees of freedom and are positively correlated. To enable the residuals to present the appearance of uncorrelated values with the correct variance, we scale the 48 residuals so that the average of their squares is the between vine estimate of variance σ_V^2; this requires multiplication of each residual by $\sqrt{(48/36)}$.

At the level of plot means, we have six degrees of freedom to share between 12 plot effects. In addition, we need to undo the increase in precision that results from taking means of four values. Thus, we multiply each plot effect by $\sqrt{(12/6)} \times \sqrt{(4)}$. If the between-plot component of variance is zero, the expected value of the average of the square of these scaled effects will be σ_V^2. If the between-plot component of variance is greater than zero, the expected value of the average of these squared effects will be greater than σ_V^2.

In moving from plot effects to treatment effects, we have a factor of $\sqrt{(4/3)}$ that arises from the sharing of three degrees of freedom between four effects, further multiplied by $\sqrt{(12)}$ because each treatment mean is an average of 12 vines. For block effects, we have a multiplier of $\sqrt{(3/2)}$ that arises from the sharing of two degrees of freedom between three effects, further multiplied by $\sqrt{(16)}$ because each block mean is an average of 16 vines. Effects that are scaled in this way allow visual comparison, as in Figure 7.6.

7.4.4 The Variance Components

The mean squares in an analysis of variance table for data from a balanced multilevel model can be broken down further, into variance components. The variance components analysis gives more detail about model parameters. Importantly, it provides information that will help design another experiment. Here is the breakdown for the kiwifruit shading data.

- Variation between vines in a plot is made up of one source of variation only. Denote this variance by σ_V^2.
- Variation between vines in different plots is partly a result of variation between vines, and partly a result of additional variation between plots. In fact, if σ_P^2 is the (additional) component of the variation that is due to variation between plots, the expected mean square equals

$$4\sigma_P^2 + \sigma_V^2.$$

(Note: The 4 comes from 4 vines per plot.)

- Variation between treatments is

$$4\sigma_P^2 + \sigma_V^2 + T,$$

where T (> 0) is due to variation between treatments.

- Variation between vines in different blocks is partly a result of variation between vines, partly a result of additional variation between plots, and partly a result of additional variation between blocks. If σ_B^2 is the (additional) component of variation that is due to differences between blocks, the expected value of the mean square is

$$16\sigma_B^2 + 4\sigma_P^2 + \sigma_V^2 \qquad \text{(16 vines per block; 4 vines per plot).}$$

We do not need estimates of the variance components in order to do the analysis of variance. The variance components are helpful for designing another experiment. We calculate the estimates thus:

$$\widehat{\sigma}_V^2 = 12.18,$$
$$4\widehat{\sigma}_P^2 + \widehat{\sigma}_V^2 = 20.93, \text{ that is, } 4\widehat{\sigma}_P^2 + 12.18 = 20.93.$$

This gives the estimate $\widehat{\sigma}_P^2 = 2.19$. We can also estimate $\widehat{\sigma}_B^2 = 4.08$.

We are now able to estimate how much the precision would change if we had eight (or, say, 10) vines per plot. With n vines per plot, the variance of the plot mean is

$$(n\widehat{\sigma}_P^2 + \widehat{\sigma}_V^2)/n = \widehat{\sigma}_P^2 + \widehat{\sigma}_V^2/n = 2.19 + 12.18/n.$$

We could also ask how much of the variance, for an individual vine, is explained by vine-to-vine differences. This depends on how much we stretch the other sources of variation. If the comparison is with vines that may be in different plots, the proportion is $12.18/(12.18 + 2.19)$. If different blocks are in mind, the proportion is $12.18/(12.18 + 2.19 + 4.08)$.

7.4.5 The Mixed Model Analysis

For a mixed model analysis, we specify that treatment (`shade`) is a fixed effect, that `block` and `plot` are random effects, and that `plot` is nested in `block`. The software works out for itself that the remaining part of the variation is associated with differences between vines.

For using `lmer()`, the command is

```
kiwishade.lmer <- lmer(yield ~ shade + (1|block) + (1|block:plot),
data=kiwishade)
# block:shade is an alternative to block:plot
```

The following agree with results from the preceding section:

```
print(kiwishade.lmer, ranef.comp="Variance", digits=3)
```

```
Linear mixed model fit by REML ['lmerMod']
Formula: yield ~ shade + (1 | block) + (1 | block:plot)
   Data: kiwishade
REML criterion at convergence: 252
Random effects:
 Groups     Name        Variance
 block:plot (Intercept)  2.19
 block      (Intercept)  4.08
 Residual               12.18
Number of obs: 48, groups:  block:plot, 12; block, 3
Fixed Effects:
 (Intercept)  shadeAug2Dec  shadeDec2Feb  shadeFeb2May
      100.20          3.03        -10.28         -7.43
```

Residuals and Estimated Effects

In this hierarchical model there are three levels of variation: level 1 is between blocks, level 2 is between plots, and level 3 is between vines. The function `fitted()` adjusts for all levels of random variation except between individual vines, that is, fitted values are at level 2. Unfortunately, `lmer()`, which was designed for use with crossed as well as hierarchical designs, does not recognize the notion of levels. The function `ranef()` can, however, be used to extract the relevant random effect estimates.

Figure 7.7A shows residuals. Figure 7.7B is a normal quantile–quantile plot that shows the plot effects. The locations of the four plots that suggest departure from normality are printed in the top left of the panel. Figure 7.7C shows overlaid normal quantile–quantile plots from three simulations. As the present interest is in the normality of the effects, not in variation in standard deviation (this would lead, in Figure 7.7C, to wide variation in aspect ratio), the effects are in each case standardized.

It is the plot effects that are immediately relevant to assessing the validity of assumptions that underlie statistical comparisons between treatment means, not the residuals. The plot effect estimates seem clearly inconsistent with the assumption of normal plot effects. Note, however, that each treatment mean is an average over three plots. This averaging will take the sampling distribution of the treatment means closer to normality.

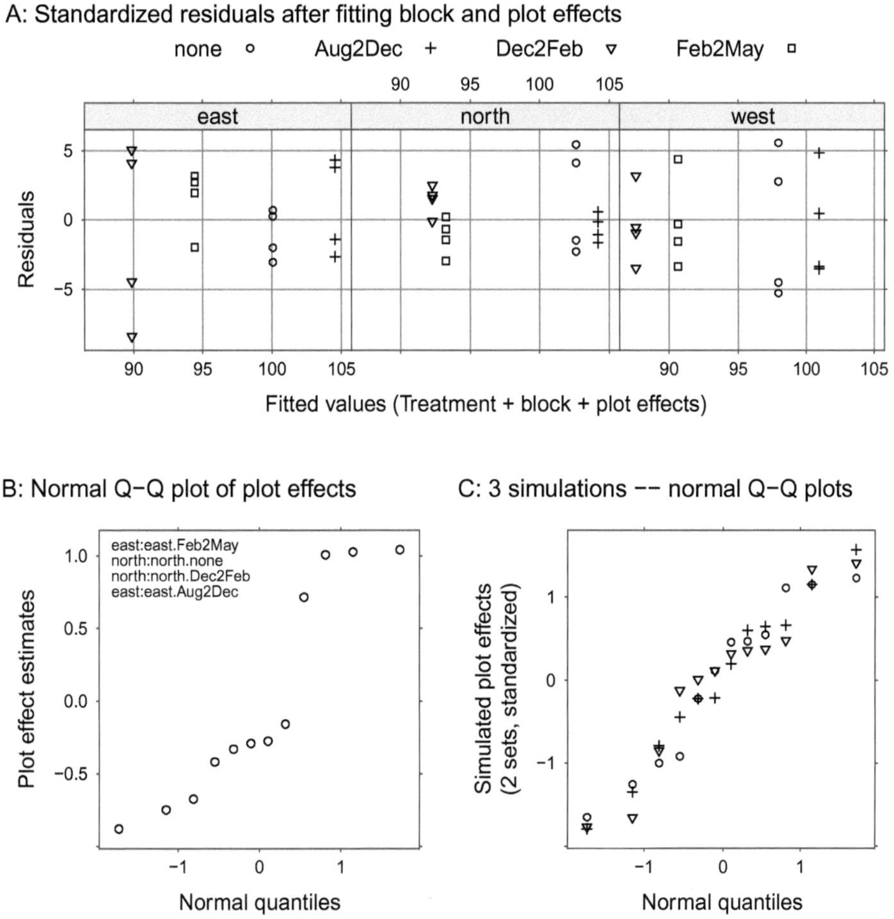

Figure 7.7 Panel A shows standardized residuals after fitting block and plot effects, plotted against fitted values. There are 12 distinct fitted values, one for each plot. Panel B is a normal probability plot that shows the plot effects. The names in the top left-hand corner identify the plots with the largest residuals. Panel C shows overlaid normal quantile–quantile plots of plot effects from three simulations.

The plot effects are estimates from a calculation that involves the estimation of a number of parameters. Before deciding that normality assumptions are in doubt, it is desirable to examine normal quantile–quantile plots, such as are shown in Panel C, from data that have been simulated according to the normality and other model assumptions.

Stripped down code for Panel A is:

```
## Panel A: Residuals
res <- residuals(kiwishade.lmer)
xyplot(res ~ fitted(kiwishade.lmer)|block, data=kiwishade,
groups=shade, layout=c(3,1), par.settings=list(pch=1:4),
grid=TRUE, aspect=1, auto.key=list(space='top', columns=4))
```

As background to Figure 7.7B, note that the treatment means are, in order:

```
with(kiwishade, sapply(split(yield, shade), mean))
```

```
   none  Aug2Dec  Dec2Feb  Feb2May
 100.20   103.23    89.92    92.77
```

Observe that the plot-specific effects go in opposite directions, relative to the overall treatment means, in the `east` and `north` blocks.

Code for Panel B is:

```
## Panel B: Observed plot effects (stripped down code)
ploteff <- ranef(kiwishade.lmer, drop=TRUE)[[1]]
qqmath(ploteff, ylab="Plot effect estimates", aspect=1)
```

The footnote has stripped down code for Panel C:[6]

7.4.6 Predictive accuracy

We have data for one location on one site only. We thus cannot estimate a between location component of variance for different locations on the current site, let alone a between site component of variance. Use of resampling methods will not help; the limitation is inherent in the experimental design.

Where data are available from multiple sites, the site to site component of variance will almost inevitably be greater than zero. Given adequate data, the estimate of this component of variance will then also be greater than zero, even in the presence of explanatory variable adjustments that attempt to adjust for differences in rainfall, temperature, soil type, etc. (Treatment differences are often, but by no means inevitably, more nearly consistent across sites than are the treatment means themselves.)

Where two (or more) experimenters use different sites, differences in results are to be expected. Such different results have sometimes led to acrimonious exchanges, with each convinced that there are flaws in the other's experimental work. Rather, assuming that both experiments were conducted with proper care, the implication is that both sets of results should be incorporated into an analysis that accounts for site to site variation. Better still, plan the experiment from the beginning as a multi-site experiment!

7.5 Within- and Between-Subject Effects

The data frame `tinting` is from an experiment that aimed to model the effects of the tinting of car windows on visual performance. (For more information, see Burns et al. (1999).) Interest was focused on visual recognition tasks that would be performed when looking through side windows.

[6]
```
## Panel C: Random effects from fits to simulated data
## For more simulations, change nsim as required, and re-execute
simvals <- simulate(kiwishade.lmer, nsim=3)
simranef <- function(y)ranef(lme4::refit(kiwishade.lmer, y))[[1]]
simeff <- apply(simvals, 2, function(y) scale(simranef(y)))
simeff <- as.data.frame(simeff)
qqmath(~ sim_1+sim_2+sim_3, data=simeff, aspect=1)
```

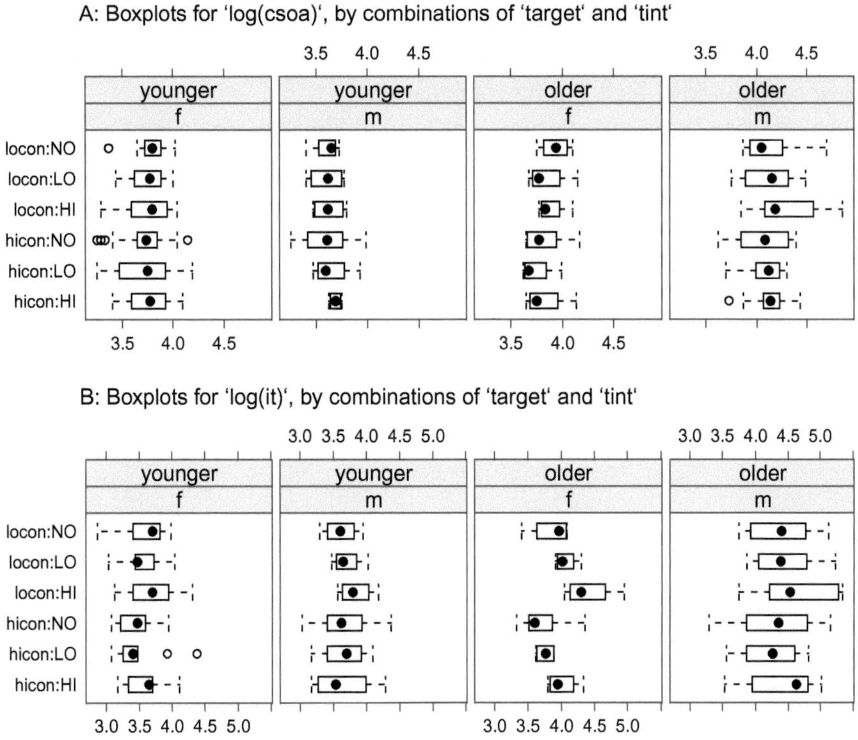

Figure 7.8 Panel A shows boxplots `log(csoa)`, for each combination of `target` and `tint`. Panel B repeats the boxplots, now for `log(it)`. Notice that, for purposes of labeling in this graph, levels of `tinting` are in upper case.

Data were collected in two sessions, with half the individuals undertaking the `csoa` task in the first session and the `it` task in the second session, and the other half doing the two types of task in the reverse order. Within each session, the order of presentation of the two levels of target contrast were balanced over participants. For each level of target contrast the levels of `tint` were in the order `no` (100 percent VLT = visible light transmittance), `lo` (81.3 percent VLT = visible light transmittance) and `hi` (35 percent VLT = visible light transmittance). Each participant repeated the combination of high contrast with no tinting (100 percent VLT) at the end of the session, thus allowing a check on any change in performance through the session. The analysis that follows will focus on `it`.

The variables are `csoa` (critical stimulus onset asynchrony, that is, the time in milliseconds required to recognize an alphanumeric target), `it` (inspection time, i.e., the time required for a simple discrimination task) and `age`, while `tint` (three levels) and `target` (two levels) are ordered factors. The variable `sex` has levels `f` and `m`, while the variable `agegp` has levels `Younger` (all in their 20s) and `Older` (all in their 70s).

Figures 7.8A and B show that, even after logarithmic transformation, there is substantial heterogeneity, mainly affecting older males, and especially obvious for the low contrast with high tinting combination.

There are two levels of variation – within individuals (who were each tested on each combination of `tint` and `target`), and between individuals. Thus, we need to specify `id` (identifying the individual) as a random effect.

Model Fitting Criteria

The function `lmer()` allows use of one of two criteria: restricted (or residual) maximum likelihood (REML), which is the default, and maximum likelihood (ML). The parameter estimates from the REML method are generally preferred to those from ML, as more nearly unbiased. Use of `anova()` to compare models fitted using `lmer()` relies on maximum likelihood theory, and the models should be fitted using ML.

7.5.1 Model Selection

A good principle is to limit initial comparisons between models to several alternative models within a hierarchy of increasing complexity. Thus, consider main effects only, main effects plus all first-order interactions, main effects plus all first- and second-order interactions, as far on up this hierarchy as seems reasonable. This makes for conceptual clarity, and limits the influence of selection effects. As the number of candidate models increases, selection effects become an increasing concern.

Three models will be considered.

1. All possible interactions (this is likely to be more complex than is needed):

```
## Capitalize tinting$agegp
levels(tinting$agegp) <- R.utils::capitalize(levels(tinting$agegp))
## Fit all interactions: data frame tinting (DAAG)
it3.lmer <- lmer(log(it) ~ tint*target*agegp*sex + (1 | id),
                 data=DAAG::tinting, REML=FALSE)
```

2. All two-factor interactions (this is a reasonable guess; two-factor interactions may be all we need):

```
it2.lmer <- lmer(log(it) ~ (tint+target+agegp+sex)^2 + (1 | id),
                 data=DAAG::tinting, REML=FALSE)
```

3. Main effects only (this is a very simple model):

```
it1.lmer <- lmer(log(it)~(tint+target+agegp+sex) + (1 | id),
                 data=DAAG::tinting, REML=FALSE)
```

The use of `REML=FALSE`; is advisable for the `anova()` (likelihood ratio) comparison that now follows:

```
anova(it1.lmer, it2.lmer, it3.lmer)
```

```
Data: DAAG::tinting
Models:
it1.lmer: log(it) ~ (tint + target + agegp + sex) + (1 | id)
it2.lmer: log(it) ~ (tint + target + agegp + sex)^2 + (1 | id)
it3.lmer: log(it) ~ tint * target * agegp * sex + (1 | id)
```

```
          npar   AIC  BIC logLik deviance Chisq Df Pr(>Chisq)
it1.lmer     8  1.14 26.8   7.43    -14.9
it2.lmer    17 -3.74 50.7  18.87    -37.7 22.88  9     0.0065
it3.lmer    26  8.15 91.5  21.93    -43.9  6.11  9     0.7288
```

Notice that `Df` is now used for degrees of freedom, where `DF` was used in connection with `summary.aov()`. earlier.

The p-value for comparing model 1 with model 2 is 0.73, while that for comparing model 2 with model 3 is 0.0065. This suggests that the model that limits attention to two-factor interactions is adequate. (Note also that the AIC statistic favors model 2. The BIC statistic favors the model that has main effects only.)

Note that the different standard errors are based on variance component information at more than one level of the design, so that the critique in Vaida and Blanchard (2005) perhaps makes the use of either of the statistics AIC or BIC problematic. See Spiegelhalter et al. (2002) for various alternatives to AIC and BIC that may be better suited for use with models with "complex" error structures. Analysts are advised to use all such statistics with caution, and to consider carefully implications that may arise from the intended use of model results. The theory on which use of these statistics relies applies in the large sample limit, in a context where account has to be taken of sample sizes at more than one level of variation.

The analysis of variance table indicated that main effects together with two-factor interactions were enough to explain the outcome. Interaction plots, looking at the effects of factors two at a time, are therefore an effective visual summary of the analysis results. In the table of coefficients that appears below, the highest t-statistics for interaction terms are associated with `tint.L:agegpOlder`, `targethicon:agegpOlder`, `tint.L:targethicon`, and `tint.L:sexm`. It makes sense to look first at those plots where the interaction effects are clearest, that is, where the t-statistics are largest. The plots may be based on either observed data or fitted values, at the analyst's discretion.[7]

7.5.2 Estimates of Model Parameters

For exploration of parameter estimates in the model that includes all two-factor interactions, we refit the model used for `it2.lmer`, but now setting `REML=TRUE` (restricted maximum likelihood estimation), and examine the estimated effects. The parameter estimates that come from the `REML` analysis are in general preferable, because they avoid or reduce the biases of maximum likelihood estimates. (See, for example, Diggle et al. (2002). The difference from likelihood can, however, be of little consequence.)

```
it2.reml <- update(it2.lmer, REML=TRUE)
print(coef(summary(it2.reml)), digits=2)
```

[7]
```
## Code that gives the first four such plots, for the observed data
interaction.plot(tinting$tint, tinting$agegp, log(tinting$it))
interaction.plot(tinting$target, tinting$sex, log(tinting$it))
interaction.plot(tinting$tint, tinting$target, log(tinting$it))
interaction.plot(tinting$tint, tinting$sex, log(tinting$it))
```

```
                       Estimate Std. Error t value
(Intercept)              3.6191      0.130   27.82
tint.L                   0.1609      0.044    3.64
tint.Q                   0.0210      0.045    0.46
targethicon             -0.1181      0.042   -2.79
agegpolder               0.4712      0.233    2.02
sexm                     0.0821      0.233    0.35
tint.L:targethicon      -0.0919      0.046   -2.00
tint.Q:targethicon      -0.0072      0.048   -0.15
tint.L:agegpolder        0.1308      0.049    2.66
tint.Q:agegpolder        0.0697      0.052    1.34
tint.L:sexm             -0.0979      0.049   -1.99
tint.Q:sexm              0.0054      0.052    0.10
targethicon:agegpolder  -0.1389      0.058   -2.38
targethicon:sexm         0.0779      0.058    1.33
agegpolder:sexm          0.3316      0.326    1.02
```

```
# NB: The final column, giving degrees of freedom, is not in the
# summary output. It is our addition.
```

Because `tint` is an ordered factor with three levels, its effect is split up into two parts. The first, which always carries a `.L` (linear) label, checks if there is a linear change across levels. The second part is labeled `.Q` (quadratic), and as `tint` has only three levels, accounts for all the remaining sum of squares that is due to `tint`. A comparable partitioning of the effect of `tint` carries across to interaction terms. The t-statistics for interactions involving `tint.Q` are 0.46, −0.15, 1.34 and 1.10, all at a level that can be ascribed to statistical variation.

Comparisons that relate to `agegp` and `sex` are made relative to variation between individuals. Standard errors for such comparisons, in the output, are in the range 0.23–0.32. A conservative estimate for the degrees of freedom is then $8+3+3+8 = 22$. (There are nine younger and four older females, against four younger and nine older males, each contributing one less than the number in the group to the degrees of freedom count.)[8] Given the large number of coefficient estimates, only the largest of the individual t-statistics warrant attention. Thus, note `tint.L:agegpOlder` ($t = 2.66$, two-sided $p = 0.007$) and perhaps `targethicon:agegpOlder` ($t = -2.38$, two-sided $p = 0.026$). These seem broadly consistent with the pattern that is apparent in Figure 7.8B for older males.

Comparisons between levels of `tint` or `target` are made several times for each of the 26 individuals, and are relatively consistent from one individual to another. Standard errors for these comparisons are small – in the range 0.042–0.058. The main effects `tint.L` and `targethicon` are thus able to stand out clearly in the table, with t-statistics equal to 3.64 and −2.79 respectively.

Heterogeneity of variance, as it affects older males, is apparent in the plots. This calls for more attention than we have given it.

[8] `subs <- with(tinting, match(unique(id), id))`

7.6 A Mixed Model with a Betabinomial Error

7.6.1 The Betabinomial Distribution

Data that have the form required for analysis as binomial (e.g., x insects dead out of n) often fail to satisfy binomial assumptions. An immediate indication of this is a variance that is larger than the variance for a binomial distribution with the same mean. The betabinomial distribution, discussed in Subsection 5.1.3, is the most widely implemented distribution that can be considered for data of this type. The total number of "successes" out of n is modeled as the sum from n Bernoulli trials (each has a 0/1 outcome), with the probability varying from one trial to another according to a beta distribution.

The function `glmmTMB`, as implemented in the *glmmTMB* package, gives further flexibility by allowing the modeling of the scale parameter as a function of explanatory variables. This will be important for the insect mortality data considered here, and for other comparable datasets where the dispersion index Φ appears high at midrange mortalities and close to 1 (i.e., close to what would be expected for a binomial distribution) at high mortalities.

In the sequel, it will be necessary to have the *qra* (quantal response analysis) and *glmmTMB* packages installed. If not available from CRAN, the *qra* package can be installed from Github, thus:

```
devtools::install_github("jhmaindonald/qra")
```

Notation

For present purposes, it is the scale parameter that is of interest. Take the location parameter π, with observed value P, to be the expected mortality. Then, in notation consistent with that used in `glmmTMB()`:

$$\text{var}[P] = \frac{\pi(1-\pi)}{n}(1 + (n-1)\rho), \text{ where } \rho = (1 + e^{\eta})^{-1}.$$

The parameter ρ is the intra-class correlation. It can be used, as an alternative to η, as the scale parameter. The function `glmmTMB()` has provision to model variation in η, and hence ρ, as a function of one or more explanatory variables and/or factors.

The dispersion index is $\Phi = 1 + (n-1)\rho$. An important difference from the "dispersion" as defined for quasibinomial models (see `?quasibinomial`) is that it is now a function of n, rather than constant as n varies.

The variance can never be less than $\pi(1-\pi)\rho$. The fraction by which it is increased above this minimum is $(1-\rho)n^{-1}$. If $\rho > 0$, then as the sample size n increases, there comes a point at which any further increase in n gives only a very slight further increase in the variance. It may be that the betabinomial model is in this respect too pessimistic. In the present state of the art, packaged code appears not to offer good alternatives, such as perhaps the mixture of binomial and betabinomial that is described in Morgan and Ridout (2008).

Source of Data

Disinfestation is the removal or disabling of insect pests or pathogens from produce, for transportation across international or other boundaries. Cold storage, usually applied while the produce is in transit, is now a common and effective approach that avoids the use of chemical fumigants (Follett and Neven, 2006). For the data used here, see Follett et al. (2018).

The dataset `qra::HawCon` is from experimental work that was designed to assess the lengths of cold storage times that, for the species/lifestage combinations investigated, appear effective, as a prelude to setting up large-scale commercial trials. We thank Dr. Peter Follett for use of this dataset. Data are for four lifestages of each of two species, as follows.

- Species are: Mediterranean fruit fly (MedFly); and Melon fly (MelonFly)
- Lifestages are: Egg, L1 (Larval 1), L2, L3
  - There is one replicate of L1, 3 replicates of others
- Mortality is for varying times in cool storage at 1.5–2 °C
  Code that provides the `HawCon` data, in the form required, is:

```
HawCon <- within(as.data.frame(qra::HawCon), {
  trtGp <- gsub("Fly", "", paste0(CN,LifestageTrt))
  trtGp <- factor(trtGp, levels=sort(unique(trtGp))[c(1,5,2,6,3,7,4,8)])
  trtGpRep <- paste0(CN,LifestageTrt,":",RepNumber)
  scTime <- scale(TrtTime)  # Centering and scaling can help model fit
  })
```

Fit `glmmTMB` Model – Fruitfly Data

```
## Load packages that will be used
suppressMessages(library(lme4)); suppressMessages(library(glmmTMB))
```

Choice of Model

For both the complementary log–log link and logit links, we now try the alternatives:

- separate lines for each treatment group;
- separate lines for each treatment group, plus a a common quadratic adjustment across all treatment groups. (For this "added curve" model, the suffix "2s" is added to the model name.)

The scale parameter is in each case modeled as a two-degree polynomial function of time in cool storage, with a different multiplier for each different treatment group. (Effects are additive on the logarithmic link scale, multipliers when unlogged.)

```
library(splines)
form <- cbind(Dead,Live)~0+trtGp/TrtTime+(1|trtGpRep)
## Add the quadratic term from a degree 2 orthogonal polynomial
form2s <- update(form, . ~ . + scale(scTime^2))
  ## Scale "corrections" to reduce risk of potential numerical problems
HCbb.cll <- glmmTMB(form, dispformula=~trtGp+ns(scTime,2),
                family=glmmTMB::betabinomial(link="cloglog"), data=HawCon)
HCbb2s.cll <- update(HCbb.cll, formula=form2s)
HCbb.logit <- glmmTMB(form, dispformula=~trtGp+ns(scTime,2),
                family=glmmTMB::betabinomial(link="logit"), data=HawCon)
HCbb2s.logit <- update(HCbb.logit, formula=form2s)
```

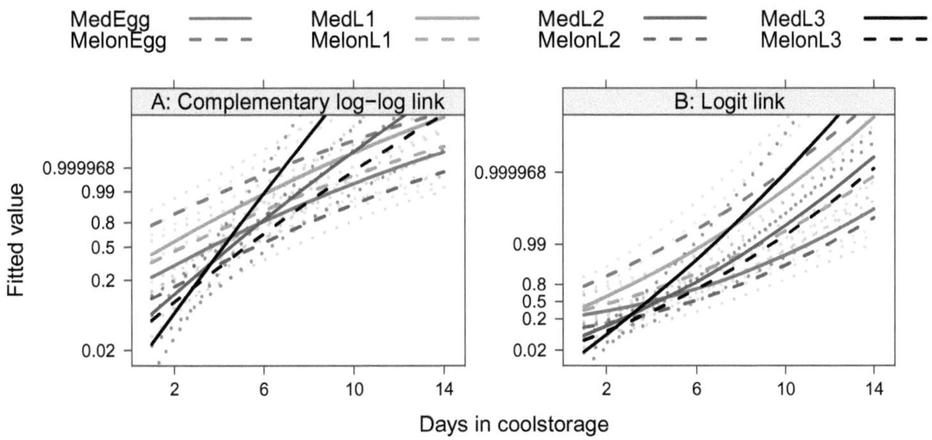

Figure 7.9 Fitted quadratic curves, and 95% pointwise confidence bounds (shown as dotted lines) for the model where the curve shifts up/down a/c variety. Panel A is for a complementary log-log (cloglog) link, while Panel B is for a logit link.

Now check whether the quadratic "corrections" appear to account for more than statistical variation:

```
summary(HCbb2s.cll)$coefficients$cond["scale(scTime^2)",]    ## CLL
```

```
Estimate Std. Error    z value    Pr(>|z|)
-0.09130    0.06143   -1.48629    0.13720
```

```
summary(HCbb2s.logit)$coefficients$cond["scale(scTime^2)",]  ## Logit
```

```
Estimate Std. Error    z value    Pr(>|z|)
 0.43219    0.17766    2.43268    0.01499
```

The quadratic adjustment term is, for the complementary log–log link, well within the bounds of plausible statistical error. The case for such a departure for the logit link is a little weaker than the *p*-value might suggest. Use of the normal as the reference distribution gives a *p*-value that is likely to be overly small.

The following shows AIC-based model comparisons:

```
             df   AIC                         Details
HCbb2s.cll   28 709.9             BB: Compl. log-log
HCbb.cll     27 710.0 BB: Compl. log-log, added curve
HCbb2s.logit 28 717.2          BB: Logit, added curve
HCbb.logit   27 721.7                       BB: Logit
```

In Figure 7.9A, unlike Figure 7.9B, the curves are close to straight lines. Curves in Panel A mostly have a mildly cup down shape. In replacing the curves by lines, the corresponding lines will predict too rapid an approach to high mortality. In Panel B, curves have a mild to strong cup up shape. Replacing them by lines will predict an overly slow approach to high mortality. The AIC based comparison points in the same direction, but indicates that for the complementary log–log model, the allowance for curvature makes little difference.

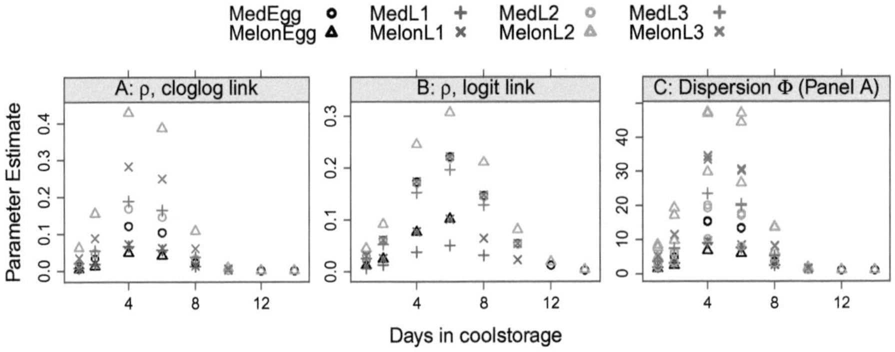

Figure 7.10 Panels A and B show intra-class correlation estimates for, respectively, a complementary log–log link and a logit link. Both models assume a beta binomial error. Panel C shows the dispersion estimate Φ for the Panel A model.

The attempt to add any more-complex form of adjustment than an overall quadratic departure from the line is likely to generate warnings of problems with numerical convergence. It can nonetheless sometimes be useful to examine such fits, if they appear reasonable.

It would be useful to check and compare models over a wide range of data from comparable studies, for example over a wide range of cold storage fruitfly mortality data. There are to our knowledge no publicly available repositories that hold such data.

We will now proceed to compare the fitted pattern of variation of the parameter ρ between the models with the two different link functions, when there is no underlying smooth.

Patterns of Variation of Intra-class Correlation and of Dispersion Index Φ

Figures 7.10A (with a complementary log–log link) and B (with a logit link) show estimates of the intra-class correlation ρ for the model where an overall quadratic curve is added to a straight line response that is different for each different treatment group. Figure 7.10C shows the dispersion estimates that correspond to the estimates of ρ in Panel A.

Figure 7.10A plots the estimates of ρ, with the dispersion index estimates Φ for the *cloglog* model in Panel C.

7.6.2 Diagnostic Checks

Randomized quantile residuals provide what can be effective checks. For any residual, the corresponding quantile residual is the proportion of residuals expected, under model assumptions, to be less than or equal to it. If the distributional assumptions are satisfied, the quantile residuals should have a distribution that differs only by statistical error from a uniform distribution. The simulation of residuals that can be used as a reference distribution for calculation of *quantile* residuals can be handled using the function `DHARMa::simulateResiduals()`.

- For each observation, the quantile residual is the proportion of simulated residuals that are greater than the observed residual.
  - Thus, a value of 0 means that all simulated residuals are larger than the observed value, and a value of 0.5 means half of the simulated residuals are larger than the observed value.
- For a correctly specified model, the quantile residuals should be uniformly distributed on the unit interval.
  - For the data as a whole, this can be checked by plotting the quantile residuals against the corresponding quantiles of the assumed distribution.
  - A second check plots quantile residuals against quantiles of predicted values. Quantile regression is then used to fit curves at 25%, 50%, and 75% quantiles of the quantile residuals. If the model is correctly specified, these should all be, to within statistical error, horizontal lines.

Figure 7.11 shows diagnostic plots for the linear model with a complementary log–log link. The function `DHARMa::simulateResiduals()` returns repeated (by default, 250) simulations of residuals from the fitted model. These are then used to replace the residuals from the model with quantile residuals. The functions `plotQQunif()` and `plotResiduals()` (both in the *DHARMa* package) are then used to give the plots that are shown in Panels A to D.

```
## Code for plots, excluding main titles
set.seed(29)
simRef <- DHARMa::simulateResiduals(HCbb.cll, n=250, seed=FALSE)
DHARMa::plotQQunif(simRef)
DHARMa::plotResiduals(simRef, form=HawCon$trtGp)
DHARMa::plotResiduals(simRef)
DHARMa::plotResiduals(simRef, form=HawCon$Total)
```

The quantile–quantile (Q-Q) plot looks fine. In Panel D, the quantile residuals from the data are well away from their respected reference horizontal lines. The model is underestimating the residual variance for low totals, and giving underestimates at midrange total numbers.

7.6.3 Lethal Time Estimates and Confidence Intervals

The estimated time that is required to kill 99 percent of insects (lethal time 99, or LT99) is commonly used as a starting point for assessing what time might be effective in commercial practice. Thus, for the model that used a complementary log–log link, and setting:

$$y = \log(-\log(1 - 0.99)) = 1.53,$$

one solves for $x = \text{LT99}$ in an equation of the form $y = a + bx$. Thus:

$$\text{LT99} = x = \frac{y - a}{b}.$$

The determination of confidence intervals for such ratios is one of a much wider class of problems. The Fieller's formula approach (Morgan, 1992), implemented in

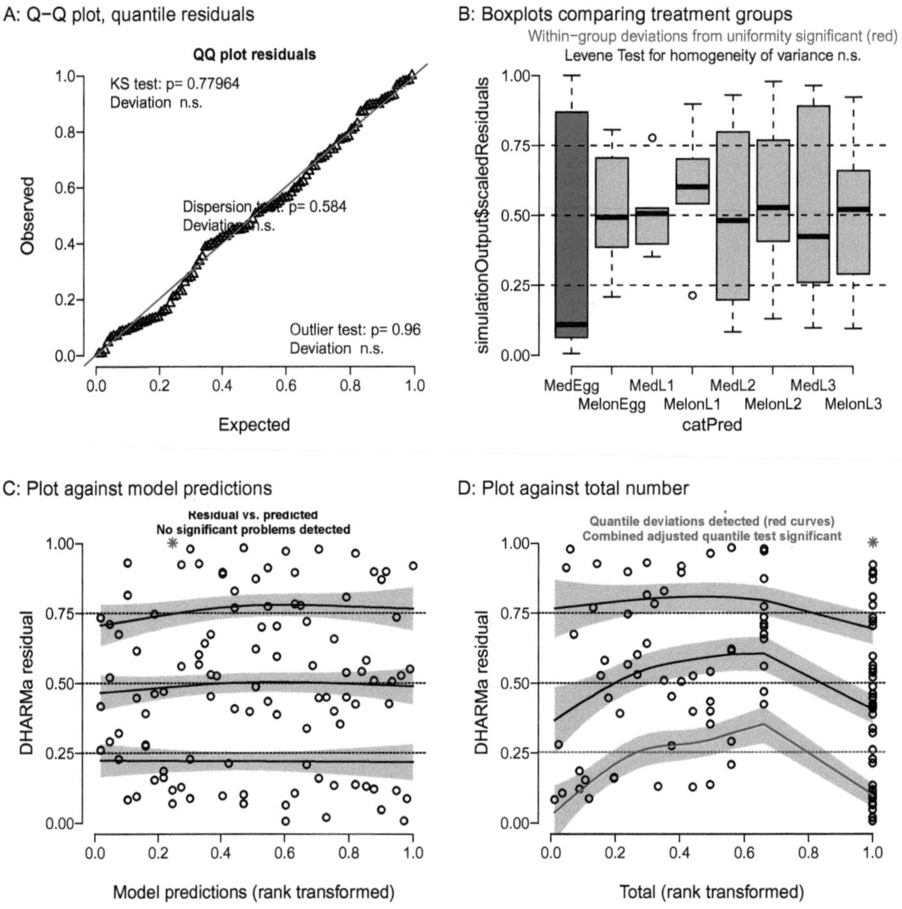

Figure 7.11 Panel A shows quantile–quantile plots for the quantile residuals. Panel B shows boxplots that compare residuals between treatment groups. Panel C compares estimated quantiles with model predictions, while Panel D plots estimated quantiles against number of insects. In Panels C and D, 2 SE pointwise limits are shown for each of the quantiles.

the *qra* package, makes the common assumption that $(y - a, b)$ has been sampled from a distribution for which the bivariate normal is an adequate approximation.

The sampling distribution of the calculated value x is typically, unless var$[b]$ is small relative to b, long-tailed. As a consequence, the *Delta* method, which uses an approximate variance as the basis for inference, is in general unreliable. See `?qra::fieller`.

The Fieller's formula approach cannot in general be adapted to give confidence intervals for differences of LT99s or other such ratio statistics, unless the denominators of the statistics that are compared happen to be the same. A usable implementation of the simulation approach, which seems needed for the calculation of confidence

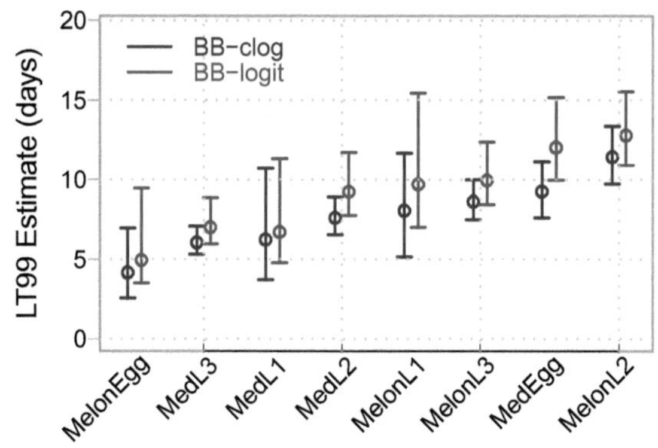

Figure 7.12 LT99 95 percent confidence intervals are compared between the model with a complementary log–log link, and the model with a logit link, in both cases with a betabinomial error.

intervals for LT99 differences, requires adaptation of the function `lme4::bootMer()` to work with objects that have been fitted using `glmmTMB::glmmTMB`.

Figure 7.12 compares confidence intervals, calculated using Fieller's formula, from use of a complementary log–log link, with intervals from use of a logit link. In each case a polynomial with two degrees of freedom was used to model the parameter that determines scale, and hence ρ.

Code to extract LT99 estimates and confidence intervals for the complementary log–log model is:

```
LTbb.cll <- qra::extractLT(p=0.99, obj=HCbb.cll, link="cloglog",
                a=1:8, b=9:16, eps=0, df.t=NULL)[,-2]
rownames(LTbb.cll) <- gsub("trtGp|Fly|:", '', rownames(LTbb.cll), perl=T)
```

If one fits a model with binomial error, error that would otherwise be accounted for in the individual data points is transferred to the between replicates component of error. No account is taken of the relatively lower variation at low and high mortalities that is evident in Figure 7.10C. As a result, variation at low and high mortalities is inflated.

The following fits a model with binomial errors, with complementary log–log link, and calculates LT99 confidence intervals:

```
HCbin.cll <- glmmTMB(cbind(Dead,Live)~0+trtGp/TrtTime+(scTime|trtGp),
                  family=binomial(link="cloglog"), data=HawCon)
LTbin.cll <- qra::extractLT(p=0.99, obj=HCbin.cll,
                  a=1:8, b=9:16, eps=0, df.t=NULL)[,-2]
```

Warnings are likely to be generated – a common problem with fitting such models. In this instance, this may well happen because the model is not effectively accounting for variation in the data. Suggestions on reasons for such warnings, and on possible ways to avoid them, are given in the vignette that can be accessed by entering `vignette("troubleshooting", package="glmmTMB")` at the R command line.

A Warning against Over-interpretation

Figure 7.11 made it clear that the attempt to bring all treatment groups together in the one model had not worked well. Results for groups other than MedEgg would be better based on the model that results when MedEgg is left out. Such an analysis is left for the reader. Separate analysis of the MedEgg data would leave, unfortunately, too few degrees of freedom to allow a usable estimate of between replicate variation. For this treatment group, the result from the overall analysis may be the best that can be done, with the proviso attached that heavy reliance should not be placed on the result.

In commercial practice, LT99 estimates such as were plotted in Figure 7.12 are used to guide the choice of treatment regimes that will then be checked out in large-scale trials. The model or models that should be preferred are those that perform well across multiple comparable datasets. For this purpose, data should as a matter of course be collected into a common database, with results from large-scale trials also included.

7.7 Observation-Level Random Effects – the `moths` Dataset

Consider again the `moths` data of Subsection 5.4.2. An alternative to use of a quasipoisson or negative binomial model to account for extra-Poisson variation is to allow for a random between-transects error that is additive on the scale of the linear predictor. The model incorporates a term that allows for normally distributed random variation, additional to the Poisson variation at each observation. The model then incorporates what are termed "observation-level random effects."

The attempt to fit a model that uses the default log link generates, if data for the habitat `Bank` are included, a warning that the model is nearly unidentifiable. Use of a square root link avoids this problem. Once again, `lowerside` will be used as reference level.

```
moths <- DAAG::moths
moths$transect <- 1:41  # Each row is from a different transect
moths$habitat <- relevel(moths$habitat, ref="Lowerside")
A.glmer <-  glmer(A~habitat+sqrt(meters)+(1|transect),
family=poisson(link=sqrt), data=moths)
print(summary(A.glmer), show.resid=FALSE, correlation=FALSE, digits=3)
```

```
Generalized linear mixed model fit by maximum likelihood (Laplace
  Approximation) [glmerMod]
 Family: poisson  ( sqrt )
Formula: A ~ habitat + sqrt(meters) + (1 | transect)
   Data: moths

     AIC      BIC   logLik deviance df.resid
   212.6    229.7    -96.3    192.6       31

Random effects:
 Groups   Name        Variance Std.Dev.
 transect (Intercept) 0.319    0.564
Number of obs: 41, groups:  transect, 41
```

```
Fixed effects:
                  Estimate Std. Error z value   Pr(>|z|)
(Intercept)         1.7322     0.3513    4.93 0.00000082
habitatBank        -2.0415     0.9377   -2.18      0.029
habitatDisturbed   -1.0359     0.4071   -2.54      0.011
habitatNEsoak      -0.7319     0.4323   -1.69      0.090
habitatNWsoak       2.6787     0.5101    5.25 0.00000015
habitatSEsoak       0.1178     0.3923    0.30      0.764
habitatSWsoak       0.3900     0.5260    0.74      0.458
habitatUpperside   -0.3135     0.7549   -0.42      0.678
sqrt(meters)        0.0675     0.0631    1.07      0.285
```

The Poisson component of the variance, on the square root scale of the linear predictor, is 0.25. The observation-level random effect, labeled **transect** in the above output, increases this by 0.319 to 0.569, that is, by a factor of 2.28. Compare this with the increase by a factor of 2.7 for the quasipoisson model.

Now compare predicted values for habitats and standard errors of difference from **Lowerside**, between the three models: quasipoisson, negative binomial, and observation-level random effects. The two models are:

```
suppressPackageStartupMessages(library(gamlss))
A1quasi.glm <- glm(A~habitat, data=moths, family=quasipoisson(link=sqrt))
Asqrt.lss <- gamlss(A ~ habitat + sqrt(meters), trace=FALSE,
                    family = NBI(mu.link='sqrt'), data = moths)
A1.glmer <- glmer(A~habitat+(1|transect), data=moths, family=poisson(link=sqrt))
```

The following compares the three sets of differences and SEs of differences from `Lowerside`:[9]

	quasi-Coef	quasi-SE	NBI-Coef	NBI-SE	glmer-Coef	glmer-SE
Bank	-2.13	0.86	-2.19	0.94	-1.99	0.95
Disturbed	-1.07	0.41	-1.00	0.41	-1.13	0.40
NEsoak	-0.61	0.43	-0.80	0.43	-0.57	0.41
NWsoak	2.73	0.54	2.67	0.51	2.73	0.51
SEsoak	0.16	0.41	0.09	0.39	0.19	0.39
SWsoak	0.45	0.54	0.28	0.53	0.54	0.51
Upperside	0.23	0.45	-0.41	0.75	0.36	0.43

Observe that the standard errors for comparisons with **Lowerside** are similar for the two models. The fitted values in the observation level random effects model are pulled in towards zero, relative to the quasipoisson model.

It is left as an exercise for the reader to compare the plots of residuals versus fitted values between the models.

7.8 Repeated Measures in Time

Repeated measures models adapt the multilevel modeling approach to handle models for longitudinal data, that is, data where the measurements were repeated at

[9]
```
Cglm <- coef(summary(A1quasi.glm))
Cglmer <- coef(summary(A1.glmer))
fitAll <- cbind("quasi-Coef"=Cglm[-1,1], "quasi-SE"=Cglm[-1,2],
  "NBI-Coef"=coef(Asqrt.lss)[2:8], "NBI-SE"=c(0.94,.41,.43,.51,.39,.53,.75),
  "glmer-Coef"=Cglmer[-1,1], "glmer-SE"=Cglmer[-1,2])
rownames(fitAll) <- substring(rownames(fitAll),8)
round(fitAll, 2)  # NB, all SEs are for the difference from 'Lowerside'
```

different times. There is a close link between a wide class of repeated measures models and time series models. In the time series context, there is usually just one realization of the series, which may however be observed at many time points. In the repeated measures context, there may be many realizations of a series that is typically quite short.

Perhaps the simplest case is where there is no apparent trend with time. Thus, consider data from a clinical trial of a drug (progabide) used to control epileptic fits. (For an analysis of data from the study to which this example refers, see Thall and Vail (1990).) The analysis assumes that patients were randomly assigned to the two treatments – placebo and progabide. After an eight-week run-in period, data were collected, both for the placebo group and for the progabide group, in each of four successive two-week periods. The outcome variable was the number of epileptic fits over that time.

One way to do the analysis is to work with the total number of fits over the four weeks, perhaps adjusted by subtracting the baseline value. It is possible that we might obtain extra sensitivity by taking account of the correlation structure between the four sets of fortnightly results.

Where there is a trend with time, working with a mean over all times will not usually make sense. Any or all of the following can occur, both for the overall pattern of change and for the pattern of difference between one profile and another.

1. There is no trend with time.
2. The pattern with time may follow a simple form, for example, a line or a quadratic curve.
3. A general form of smooth curve, for example, a curve fitted using splines, may be required to account for the pattern of change with time.

The Theory of Repeated Measures Modeling

A key idea is that there are (at least) two levels of variability – between subjects and within subjects. In addition, there is measurement error. For the moment, profiles (or subjects) are assumed independent. The analysis should allow for dependencies between the results of any one subject at different times. For a balanced design, we will assume n subjects ($i = 1, 2, \ldots, n$) and p times ($j = 1, 2, \ldots, p$), though perhaps with missing responses (gaps) for some subjects at some times. The plot of response versus time for any one subject is that subject's *profile*.

The simplest commonly used model has a between-subjects variance component denoted by ν^2, while there is a within-subjects variance at any individual time point that is denoted by σ^2. The measurement error may be bundled in as part of σ^2. The variance of the response for one subject at a particular time point is $\nu^2 + \sigma^2$.

In the special case just considered, the variance of the difference between two time points for one subject is $2\sigma^2$. Comparisons "within subjects" are more accurate than comparisons "between subjects."

*Correlation Structure

The simple model just described takes no account of the common occurrence by which the separation of points in time is reflected in a correlation between time points that decreases as the time separation increases. The variance for differences between times will then increase as points move further apart in time.

There is a contrast between the role of correlation structure in repeated measures, and its role in time series analysis. In time series analysis the structure must typically be estimated from just one series, by assuming that the series is in some sense part of a repeating pattern. In repeated measures there may be many realizations, allowing a more-direct estimate of the correlation structure.

While we are typically better placed than in time series analysis to estimate the correlation structure, there is, for most of the inferences that we may wish to make, less need to know the correlation structure. Typically interest is in the consistency of patterns between individuals. Thus, we may want to know: "Do patients on treatment A improve at a greater rate than patients on treatment B?"

There is a broad distinction between approaches that model the profiles, and approaches that focus more directly on the correlation structure. Direct modeling of the profiles leads to random coefficient models, which allow each individual to follow their own profile. Variation between profiles may largely account for the sequential correlation structure. Direct modeling of the correlation structure is most effective when there are no evident systematic differences between profiles.

For further discussion of repeated measures modeling, see Diggle et al. (2002) and Pinheiro and Bates (2000). The Pinheiro and Bates book is based around the S-PLUS version of the *nlme* package.

Different Approaches to Repeated Measures Analysis

Methods that have been used include the following.

- A simple way to analyze repeated measures data is to form one or more summary statistics for each subject, and then use these summary statistics for further analysis.
- An assumption that is, in general, unrealistic is that the correlation between results is the same for all pairs of times. Assuming also that the variance is the same at all times, the variance of the difference is the same for all pairs of time points. The data can then in principle be analyzed using an analysis of variance model that allows for two components of variance: (1) between subjects, and (2) between times.
- Various adjustments adapt the analysis of variance approach to allow for the possibility that the variance of time differences are not all equal. These should be avoided now that there are good alternatives to the analysis of variance approach.
- Multivariate comparisons accommodate all possible patterns of correlations between time points. This approach accommodates the time series structure, but does not take advantage of it to find an economical parameterization of the correlation structure.

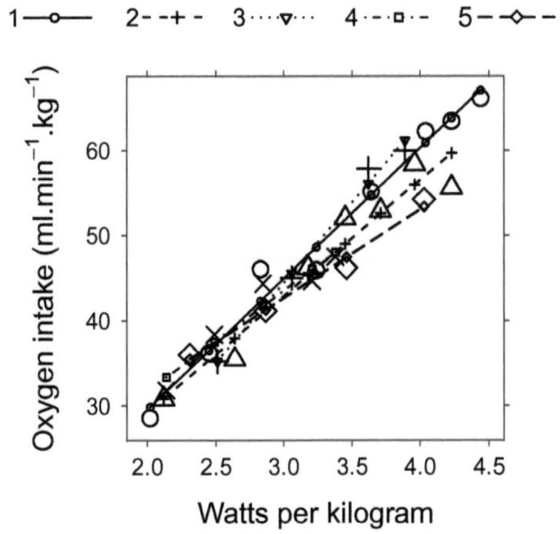

Figure 7.13 Oxygen intake, plotted against power output, for each of five athletes who participated in investigations designed to assess the feasibility of a proposed *Daedalus* 119 km human-powered flight.

- Repeated measures models aim to reflect the sequential structure, in the fixed effects, in the random effects, and in the correlation structure. They do this in two ways: by modeling the overall pattern of difference between different profiles, and by direct modeling of the correlation structure. This modeling approach often allows insights that are hard to gain from approaches that ignore or do not take advantage of the sequential structure.

7.8.1 Example – Random Variation between Profiles

The data frame `humanpower1` has data from investigations (Bussolari, 1987, Nadel and Bussolari, 1988) designed to assess the feasibility of a proposed 119 km human-powered flight from the island of Crete – in the initial phase of the *Daedalus* project. After an initial five-minute warm-up period and five-minute recovery period, the power requirements from the athletes were increased, at two-minute intervals, in steps of around 30 W, oxygen intake was measured at each time point. Figure 7.13 gives a visual summary of the data.

The following places the data frame `humanpower1` in the workspace:

```
humanpower1 <- DAAG::humanpower1
```

We leave it as an exercise to verify, using a fixed effects analysis such as was described in Section 4.3, that separate lines are required for the different athletes, and that there is no case for anything more complicated than straight lines. The separate lines fan out at the upper extreme of power output, consistent with predictions from a random slopes model.

Separate Lines for Difference Athletes

The model is

$$y_{ij} = \alpha + \beta x_{ij} + a + bx_{ij} + e_{ij},$$

where i refers to individual, and j to observation j for that individual, α and β are fixed, a and b have a joint bivariate normal distribution, each with mean 0, independently of the e_{ij} which are iid normal. Each point in Figure 7.13 is a realization of an $(\alpha + a, \beta + b)$ pair.

The intercepts and slopes for the five lines can be calculated thus:

```
## Calculate intercepts and slopes; plot Slopes vs Intercepts
## Uses the function lmList() from the lme4 package
humanpower1 <- DAAG::humanpower1
hp.lmList <- lmList(o2 ~ wattsPerKg | id, data=humanpower1)
coefs <- coef(hp.lmList)
round(coefs,3)
```

```
  (Intercept) wattsPerKg
1      -1.155      15.35
2       1.916      13.65
3     -12.008      18.81
4       8.029      11.83
5      11.553      10.36
```

```
c("Correlation between intercept and slope"=cor(coefs[,1],coefs[,2]))
```

```
Correlation between intercept and slope
                                -0.9975
```

The function `lmList()`, given the formula `o2 ~ wattsPerKg | id` as argument, regresses `o2` on `wattsPerKg` for each level of the factor `id`, with the summary information stored in the object `hp.lmList`.

A Random Coefficients Model

Possible reasons for modeling the variation between slopes as a random effect are as follows.

- There may be an interest in generalizing to further similarly selected athletes – what range of responses is it reasonable to expect?
- The fitted lines from the random slopes model may be a better guide to performance than the fitted "fixed" lines for individual athletes. The range of the slopes for the fixed lines will on average exaggerate somewhat the difference between the smallest and largest slope, an effect which the random effects analysis corrects.

Here, the chief reason for working with these data is that they demonstrate a relatively simple application of a random effects model. Depending on how results will be used, a random coefficients analysis may well, for these data, be overkill!

The attempt to fit a model that allows both a random slope (for `wattsPerKg`) and a random intercept for each different athlete generates a warning:

```
hp.lmer <- lmer(o2 ~ wattsPerKg + (wattsPerKg | id), data=humanpower1)
```

```
boundary (singular) fit: see help('isSingular')
```

The model shows a correlation of 1.0 between the two sets of random effects. The following allows only for random slopes – one might equally fit only random intercepts.

```
hp.lmer <- lmer(o2 ~ wattsPerKg + (0+wattsPerKg | id), data=humanpower1)
print(summary(hp.lmer), digits=3)
```

```
Linear mixed model fit by REML ['lmerMod']
Formula: o2 ~ wattsPerKg + (0 + wattsPerKg | id)
   Data: humanpower1

REML criterion at convergence: 129.7

Scaled residuals:
    Min      1Q  Median      3Q     Max
-1.9117 -0.8978  0.0598  0.7854  1.5382

Random effects:
 Groups   Name       Variance Std.Dev.
 id       wattsPerKg 0.211    0.46
 Residual            5.776    2.40
Number of obs: 28, groups:  id, 5

Fixed effects:
            Estimate Std. Error t value
(Intercept)    1.299      2.220    0.59
wattsPerKg    14.204      0.715   19.88

Correlation of Fixed Effects:
           (Intr)
wattsPerKg -0.936
```

The random slope effects (variations about a mean of 14.2041) are:

```
sort(coef(lmList(o2 ~ wattsPerKg | id, data=humanpower1))[,1])
```

```
[1] -12.008  -1.155   1.916   8.029  11.553
```

Random effects relate to the particular population from which the five athletes were sampled. Almost certainly, the pattern of variation would be different, and greater, for five people who were drawn at random from a wider population of recreational sportspeople.

Here, the mean response pattern was assumed linear, with random changes, for each individual athlete, in the slope. More generally, the mean response pattern will be nonlinear, and random departures from this pattern may be nonlinear.

7.8.2 Orthodontic Measurements on Children

The `MEMSS::Orthodont` data frame has measurements on the distance between two positions on the skull, at two-yearly intervals from ages 8 until 14, for 16 males and 11 females. Does the pattern of growth differ between males and females? The following places the data in the workspace, and adds a column that has the logarithms of the distance:

```
Orthodont <- within(MEMSS::Orthodont, logdist <- log(Orthodont$distance))
```

Figure 7.14 shows the pattern of change for each of the 27 individuals. Lines have been added; overall the pattern of growth seems close to linear.

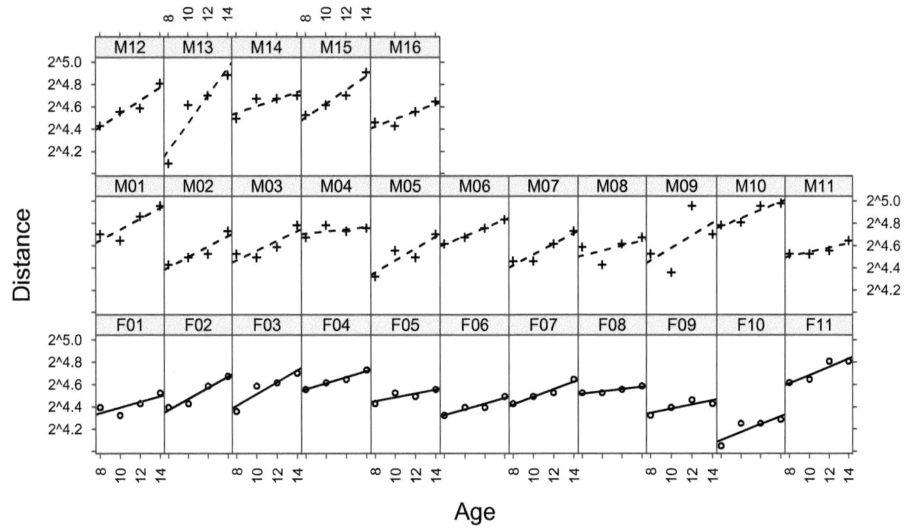

Figure 7.14 Distance between two positions on the skull for each of 27 children, on a scale of $\log_2$, plotted against age.

Preliminary Data Exploration

The following uses the function `lmlist()` to extract the slopes:

```
ab <- cbind(coef(lmList(distance ~ age | Subject, Orthodont)),
            coef(lmList(logdist ~ age|Subject, data=Orthodont)))
names(ab) <- c("a", "b","alog","blog")
## Obtain intercept at x=11, for each subject.
## (For each subject, this is independent of the slope)
ab <- within(ab, {ybar = a + b*11; b=b; ylogbar = alog + blog * 11;
                  blog=blog; sex = substring(rownames(ab), 1 ,1) } )
bySex <- sapply(split(ab, ab$sex), function(z)range(z$b))
extremes <- with(ab, ybar %in% range(ybar) | b %in% bySex)
```

Figures 7.15A (with untransformed data) and B (log transformed data) plot slopes against intercepts at the mean age of 11. A two-sided t-test will now compare Panel B male with female slopes. As the largest male slope (M13) is a clear outlier, it and (to make the comparison fair) the smallest (M04) male slope will be omitted. As the slopes are for logged distances, we are effectively comparing relative changes.[10] The part of the output that is of chief interest is:

```
t = -2.3, df = 23, p-value = 0.03
alternative hypothesis: true difference in means is not equal to 0
95 percent confidence interval:
 -0.0160529 -0.0009191
mean of x mean of y
  0.02115   0.02963
```

10
```
extreme.males <- match(c("M04","M13"), rownames(ab))
t_out <- capture.output(with(ab[-extreme.males,],
              t.test(blog[sex=="F"], blog[sex=="M"], var.equal=TRUE)))
# Specify var.equal=TRUE, to allow comparison with anova output
```

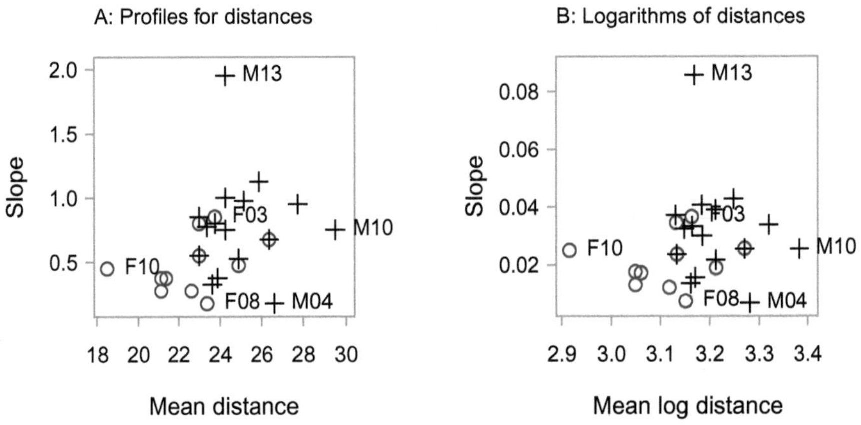

Figure 7.15 Slopes of profiles, plotted against means of distance (Panel A) or log(distance) (Panel B). Females are shown with open circles, males with + symbols.

The higher average slope for males is on the borderline of what might comfortably be attributed to statistical error.

A Random Coefficients Model

Now consider a random coefficients model. We will omit the same two males as before. If we allow different slopes for males and females, with the slope for individual children varying randomly about the slope for their sex, we get a warning:

```
keep <- !(Orthodont$Subject%in%c("M04","M13"))
Orthodont$scAge <- with(Orthodont, age-11)  ## Center values of age
orthdiffx.lmer <- lmer(logdist ~ Sex * scAge + (scAge | Subject),
                       data=Orthodont, subset=keep)
```

```
boundary (singular) fit: see help('isSingular')
```

The message indicates that the random effects variance–covariance matrix is near singular. The function `rePCA` uses a principal components decomposition of the variance–covariance matrix to check for singularity.

```
rePCA(orthdiffx.lmer)
```

```
$Subject
Standard deviations (1, .., p=2):
[1] 1.632 0.000

Rotation (n x k) = (2 x 2):
          [,1]     [,2]
[1,] -0.99993 -0.01153
[2,] -0.01153  0.99993

attr(,"class")
[1] "prcomplist"
```

The variance of the second principal component is detected to be 0. The *rotation* matrix results in components that differ only slightly from the negative of the intercept coefficient and the coefficient of `scAge`.

The case is, then, to simplify the random effects formula, removing the `scAge` slope component, so that it becomes `(1 | Subject)`. The code and output is:

```
orthdiff.lmer <- lmer(logdist ~ Sex * scAge + (1 | Subject),
                      data=Orthodont, subset=keep)
summary(orthdiff.lmer)
```

```
Linear mixed model fit by REML ['lmerMod']
Formula: logdist ~ Sex * scAge + (1 | Subject)
   Data: Orthodont
 Subset: keep

REML criterion at convergence: -232

Scaled residuals:
   Min     1Q Median     3Q    Max
-3.312 -0.510  0.014  0.543  3.945

Random effects:
 Groups   Name        Variance Std.Dev.
 Subject  (Intercept) 0.00633  0.0796
 Residual             0.00238  0.0488
Number of obs: 100, groups:  Subject, 25

Fixed effects:
              Estimate Std. Error t value
(Intercept)    3.11451    0.02510  124.11
SexMale        0.09443    0.03354    2.82
scAge          0.02115    0.00329    6.42
SexMale:scAge  0.00849    0.00440    1.93

Correlation of Fixed Effects:
            (Intr) SexMal scAge
SexMale     -0.748
scAge        0.000  0.000
SexMal:scAg  0.000  0.000 -0.748
```

The standard errors are functions of more than one variance component. As a consequence, the values in the column headed `t value` are not true *t*-statistics.

The function `afex::mixed()` can be used to refit the model, and use one of several methods (the default is the Satterthwaite method) that modify the degrees of freedom to provide approximations that do account for random effects. The following is suitable code:

```
Orthodont2 <- droplevels(subset(Orthodont, keep))
opt <- options(contrasts=c("contr.sum","contr.poly"))
orthdiff.mixed <- afex::mixed(logdist ~ Sex * scAge + (1 | Subject), type=2,
                              method='S', data=Orthodont2)
```

```
Fitting one lmer() model. [DONE]
Calculating p-values. [DONE]
```

```
  ## NB `type` refers to type of test, NOT `error` type.
options(opt)      # Reset to previous contrasts setting
orthdiff.mixed
```

```
Mixed Model Anova Table (Type 2 tests, S-method)

Model: logdist ~ Sex * scAge + (1 | Subject)
Data: Orthodont2
      Effect        df          F p.value
1        Sex 1, 23.00    7.93 **     .010
2      scAge 1, 73.00 140.72 ***   <.001
3 Sex:scAge 1, 73.00     3.72 +     .058
---
Signif. codes:  0 '***' 0.001 '**' 0.01 '*' 0.05 '+' 0.1 ' ' 1
```

Notice that factor contrasts are set to `contr.mixed`. This avoids a message that otherwise appears, warning that the setting has been changed. An alternative to making the change globally is to make it for the specific factors in the model:

```
contrasts(Orthodont2[['Subject']]) <- 'contr.sum'
contrasts(Orthodont2[['Sex']]) <- 'contr.sum'
```

Type 2 and type 3 tests are variants of what is commonly termed a test for a main effect in the presence of an interaction involving that main effect. A type 3 test checks for setting the average effect, taken over all levels of the factor, to zero. With a type 2 test, the average that is set to zero is weighted according to the number of observations for the relevant factor level. Think carefully, in any specific study context, whether either variant makes sense. Type 1 tests are sequential, according to the order of the terms in the analysis of variance table. See the discussion of the three types of tests in Singmann and Kellen (2019, p. 10), included in the *afex* package as a vignette that can be displayed by entering `vignette('introduction-mixed-models',package='afex')` at the command line. (Go to p. 10.)

The AIC statistic favors a model that has the same slope for males and females:

```
orthdiffa.lmer <- update(orthdiff.lmer, formula=. ~ . -Sex:scAge)
AIC(orthdiffa.lmer,orthdiff.lmer)
```

```
               df    AIC
orthdiffa.lmer  5 -227.4
orthdiff.lmer   6 -220.1
```

The interaction is best omitted, so that the type 2/3 distinction ceases to matter.

Correlation between Successive Times

We can use the function `forecast::auto.arima()` to check the individual sequences for a standard form of sequential correlation structure.

```
res <- resid(orthdiff.lmer)
Subject <- factor(Orthodont$Subject[keep])
orth.arma <- sapply(split(res, Subject),
                    function(x)forecast::auto.arima(x)$arma[c(1,6,2)])
orthsum <- apply(orth.arma,2,sum)
orth.arma[, orthsum>0]
```

```
      F08  M06
[1,]    1    1
[2,]    0    0
[3,]    1    1
```

Thus, an identifiable structure was detected for just two of the 15 individuals.

Fitting a Sequential Correlation Structure

While there seems no case for it here, it is useful to note how a simple correlation structure can be fitted, using the function `lme()` from the *nlme* package. While the choice of starting value (here 0.1) for the value for order 1 autocorrelation should not matter, it is sometimes wise to try several alternatives.

```
library(nlme)
keep <- !(Orthodont$Subject%in%c("M04","M13"))
Orthodont2 <- droplevels(subset(Orthodont,keep))
orthdiff.lme <- lme(logdist ~ Sex * scAge, random = ~1|Subject,
                    cor=corCAR1(0.1, form=~1|Subject), data=Orthodont2)
## For AR1 models `phi` is the sequential correlation estimate
orthdiff.lme$modelStruct$corStruct
```

```
Correlation structure of class corCAR1 representing
              Phi
0.0000000003311
```

Aside from giving the estimate of `phi`, the output is very little changed.

**The Variance for the Difference in Slopes*

This can be calculated from the components of variance information. The sum of squares about the mean, for one line, is $\sum(x - \bar{x})^2 = 20$. The sum of the two components of variance for an individual line is then: $1.19 \times 10^{-12} + 0.002383/20 = 0.00011915$. The standard error of the difference in slopes is then:

$$\sqrt{0.00011915(1/14 + 1/11)} = 0.00440.$$

Compare this with the value given against the fixed effect `SexMale:I(age - 11)` in the output above. The numbers are, to within rounding error, the same. Degrees of freedom for the comparison are 23, as for the *t*-test.

7.9 Further Notes on Multilevel Models

7.9.1 Sources of Variation – Complication or Focus of Interest?

In the discussion of multilevel models, the main interest was in the parameter estimates. The different sources of variance were a complication. In other applications, the variances may be the focus of interest. Where there is substantial genetic variability, breeding programs have the best chance of creating improved varieties.

Investigations into the genetic component of human intelligence, as measured by standard types of IQ tests, have generated fierce debate. Most such studies have used data from identical twins who have been adopted out to different homes, comparing them with non-identical twins and with siblings who have been similarly adopted out. An important limitation is that the adopting homes for any pair of siblings are in general likely to be more similar, within the range from extreme social disadvantage to extreme privilege, than two homes chosen at random from the general population. Results apply, then, only within this limited context rather than to the general population. A further issue is that both siblings grow up with parents that are not their biological parents, making their experience untypical of that of children more generally. It is not obvious how this might affect results. A further issue is that there has not, until recently, been allowance for the substantial effects that arise from simultaneous or sequential occupancy of the maternal womb (Bartholemew, 2004, Daniels et al., 1997). A possibility that has to be taken seriously is that reversible "epigenetic" changes that control gene expression may carry through from one generation to the next in a manner that adjusts biological offspring to the conditions in which their parents lived.

The modeling does not account for the Flynn effect (Bartholemew, 2004, pp. 138-140), by which measured IQs in many parts of the world have in recent times increased by about 15 IQ points per generation. Clearly strong social conditioning effects are at work, which have changed between generations, in different ways for different communities.

Interactions between genetic and environmental effects have the consequence that there is no clear division between the two – what we see is "Nature via Nurture" as in the title for Ridley and Pierpoint (2003). The simple models used in the attempt to tease out the relative contributions of genetics and environment are simplistic to an extent that the numbers obtained have to be regarded with a level of skepticism. Zimmer (2019) has a detailed discussion of the competing views. See also Kaminski et al. (2018).

7.9.2 Predictions from Models with a Complex Error Structure

Here, "complex" refers to models that assume something other than an iid (usually normal) error structure. Most of the models considered in this chapter can be used for different predictive purposes, and give standard errors for predicted values that differ according to the intended purpose. Accurate modeling of the structure of variation allows, as for the Antiguan corn yield data in Section 7.1, these different inferential uses. As has been noted, shortcuts are sometimes possible. Thus, for using the kiwifruit shading data to predict yields at any level other than the individual vine, there is no loss of information from basing the analysis on plot means.

Consequences from Assuming an Overly Simplistic Error Structure

In at least some statistical application areas, analyses that assume an overly simplistic error structure (usually, an iid model) are relatively common in the literature. Inferences may be misleading, or not, depending on how results are used. Where there are multiple levels of variation, all variation that contributes to the sampling error of fixed effects must be modeled correctly. Otherwise, the standard errors of model parameters that appear in computer output will almost inevitably be wrong, and should be ignored.

In data that have appropriate balance, predicted values will ordinarily be unbiased, even if the error structure is not modeled appropriately. The standard errors will almost certainly be wrong, usually optimistic. A good understanding of the structure of variation is typically required in order to make such limited inferences as are available when an overly simplistic error structure is assumed!

7.9.3 An Historical Perspective on Multilevel Models

The inventor of the analysis of variance was R. A. Fisher. Many of the analysis of variance calculations that he demonstrated were, in the terminology now in use, analyses of specific forms of multilevel models. The particular characteristic of the experimental design models that generated the data was one or other form of "balance" that made it possible to use analysis of variance methods to handle the analysis. The variance estimates that are needed for different comparisons can be taken from the different lines of an analysis of variance table, circumventing the need to estimate the variances of the random effects that appear in analysis approaches that can be used more generally

Until the modern computing era, multilevel data whose structure did not follow one of the standard designs, and thus did not fit the analysis of variance framework, required some form of approximate analysis. Such approximate analyses, if they were possible at all, often demanded a high level of skill. Statistical analysts who used Fisher's experimental designs and methods of analysis followed Fisher's rules, and those of his successors, for the calculations. Each different design had its own recipe. Among books that gave instructions on how to do the analyses, the most comprehensive was Cochran and Cox (1957).

The Genstat system (Payne et al., 1997) was the first major system to implement general methods for the analysis of multilevel models that had a suitable "balance." Its coherent and structured approach to the analysis of data from suitably balanced designs took advantage of the balance to simplify and structure the output.

General-purpose software that can be used with unbalanced data, in the style of the `lme4` package, made its appearance relatively recently. The analyses that resulted from earlier approaches were relatively inflexible in their ability to handle quirks in the data, and often less insightful and informative than what is now available within a multilevel modeling framework. Attention to experimental design is as important as ever. The power of modern software can be a trap. There may be inadequate care in the design of data collection, in the expectation that computer software will take care of any problems. The result may be data whose results are hard to interpret or cannot be interpreted at all, or that make poor use of resources.

Regression models are another starting point for consideration of multilevel models. Both the fixed effects parts of the model have a structure, thus moving beyond the models with a single random (or "error") term that have been the stock in trade of courses on regression modeling. Even now, regression texts may give scant recognition of the implications of structure in the random part of the model. Yet data do often have structure – students within classes within institutions, nursing staff within hospitals within regions, managers within local organizations within regional groupings, and so on.

As has been noted, models have not always been written down. Once written down, there was a preoccupation with models that had a single error term. These had only a very limited connection into the practical analysis of experimental designs, where most analysts were content to follow Cochran and Cox and avoid formal mathematical description of the models that underpinned their analyses.

7.9.4 Meta-analysis

Meta-analysis is a name for analyses that bring together into a single analysis framework data from, for example, multiple agricultural trials, or from multiple clinical trials, or from multiple psychological laboratories. Multilevel modeling, and extensions of multilevel modeling such as repeated measures analysis, make it possible to do analyses that take proper account of site-to-site or center-to-center or study-to-study variation. If treatment or other effects are consistent relative to all identifiable major sources of variation, the result can be compelling for practical application.

Meta-analysis is uncontroversial when data are from a carefully planned multilocation trial, or from multiple such trials. More problematic is the bringing together into one analysis of data from quite separate investigations, including perhaps observational studies. Such analyses challenge the critical acumen of the analyst. A range of methodologies have been developed to handle the issues that arise. Gaver et al. (1992) is a useful summary. See also the comprehensive account in Turner et al. (2009).

7.9.5 Functional Data Analysis

Much of the art of repeated measures modeling lies in finding meaningful statistical summaries, both of the individual profiles and of variation between those profiles. Spline curves are widely used in this context. Chapter 9 will discuss the use of principal components to give a low-dimensional representation of multivariate data. A similar methodology can be used to find representations of curves in terms of a few basis functions. See Ramsay and Silverman (2002) for further details.

7.9.6 Error Structure in Explanatory Variables

This chapter has discussed error structure in response variables. There may also be a structure to error in explanatory variables. Studies of the health effects of dietary components, such as were described in Section 3.7, provide interesting and important examples, with major implications for the design of such studies.

7.10 Recap

Multilevel models account for multiple levels of random variation. The random part of the model is a sum of distinct random components. In setting up an analysis for these models it is necessary to

- identify which are fixed and which random effects,
- correctly specify the nesting of the random effects.

Predictions based on multilevel models will differ depending on the population to which the predictions apply.

In repeated measures designs, it is necessary to specify or otherwise model the pattern of correlation within profiles. A further generalization is to the modeling of random coefficients, for example, regression lines that vary between different subsets of the data.

7.11 Further Reading

Fisher (1935) is a nonmathematical account that takes the reader step by step through the analysis of important types of experimental design. It is useful background for reading more modern accounts. Williams et al. (2002) is similarly example-based, with an emphasis on tree breeding. See also Cox (1958) and Cox and Reid (2000). Cox and Reid is an authoritative account of the area, with a more practical focus than its title might seem to imply. On multilevel and repeated measures models see Gelman and Hill (2006), Snijders and Bosker (2011), Diggle et al. (2002), Goldstein (2010), Pinheiro and Bates (2000), and Venables and Ripley (2002).

Talbot (1984) is an interesting example of the use of multilevel modeling, with important agricultural and economic implications. It summarizes a extensive information on yields for ctops that are widely grown in the UK, giving assessments both of center-to-center and of year-to-year variation.

The relevant chapters in Payne et al. (1997), while directed to users of the Genstat system, have helpful commentary on the use of the methodology and on the interpretation of results. Pinheiro and Bates (2000) describes the use of the *nlme* package for handling multilevel analyses.

On meta-analysis see Chalmers and Altman (1995), Gaver et al. (1992), and Turner et al. (2009).

7.12 Exercises

7.1. Repeat the calculations of Subsection 7.4.5, but omitting results from two vines at random. Here is code that will handle the calculation:

```
n.omit <- 2
take <- rep(TRUE, 48)
take[sample(1:48,2)] <- FALSE
kiwishade.lmer <- lmer(yield ~ shade + (1|block) + (1|block:plot),
                       data = kiwishade,subset=take)
vcov <- VarCorr(kiwishade.lmer)
print(vcov, comp="Variance")
```

Repeat this calculation five times, for each of `n.omit` = 2, 4, 6, 8, 10, 12, and 14. Plot (i) the plot component of variance and (ii) the vine component of variance, against number of points omitted. Based on these results, for what value of `n.omit` does the loss of vines begin to compromise results? Which of the two components of variance estimates is more damaged by the loss of observations? Comment on why this is to be expected.

7.2. Repeat the previous exercise, but now omitting 1, 2, 3, 4 complete plots at random.

7.3. The dataset `MEMSS::Gun` gives the numbers of rounds fired per minute by each of nine teams of gunners, each tested twice using each of two methods. In the nine teams, three were made of men with slight build, three with average, and three with heavy build. Is there a detectable difference, in number of rounds fired, between build type or between firing methods? For improving the precision of results, which would be better – to double the number of teams, or to double the number of occasions (from two to four) on which each team tests each method?

7.4. *The dataset `MEMSS::ergoStool` has data on the effort needed to get up from a stool, for each of nine individuals who each tried four different types of stool. Analyze the data both using `aov()` and using `lme()`, and reconcile the two sets of output. Was there any clear winner among the types of stool, if the aim is to keep effort to a minimum?

7.5. *In the dataset `MEMSS::MathAchieve`, the factors `Minority` (levels `yes` and `no`) and `sex`, and the variable `SES` (socioeconomic status) are clearly fixed effects. Discuss how the decision whether to treat `School` as a fixed or as a random effect might depend on the purpose of the study? Carry out an analysis that treats `School` as a random effect. Are differences between schools greater than can be explained by within school variation?

7.6. *The data frame `sorption` (*DAAG*) includes columns `ct` (concentration–time sum), `Cultivar` (apple cultivar), `Dose` (injected dose of methyl bromide), and `rep` (replicate number, within `Cultivar` and `year`). Fit a model that allows the slope of the regression of `ct` on `Dose` to be different for different cultivars and years. and to vary randomly with replicate. Consider the two models:

```
cult.lmer <- lmer(ct ~ Cultivar + Dose + factor(year) +
                  (-1 + Dose | gp), data = sorption, REML=TRUE)
cultdose.lmer <- lmer(ct ~ Cultivar/Dose + factor(year) +
                  (-1 + Dose | gp), data = sorption, REML=TRUE)
```

Explain (i) the role of the each of the terms in these models, and (ii) how the two models differ. Which model seems preferable? Write a brief commentary on the output from the preferred model.

(Note: The factor `gp`, which has a different level for each different combination of `Cultivar`, `year` and replicate, associates a different random effect with each such combination.)

8

Tree-Based Classification and Regression

Tree-based methods are radically different from those discussed in previous chapters. They are relatively easy to use, with relevance to a wide class of problems. As with the new machine learning methods, construction of a tree, or (in the random forest approach, trees) follows an algorithmic process. The methods were motivated, historically, by the informal methods of dendrogram construction that have been in use for centuries for botanical classification trees. Social scientists began automating tree-based procedures for classification in the 1940s and 1950s, using methods akin to some current partitioning methods. See Belson (1959).

Single-tree methods, as implemented in the *rpart* (Therneau and Atkinson, 1997) package, will occupy the first part of this chapter. The details of the way that the tree is generated and predictive accuracy assessed are not readily described in a few sentences. The *rpart.plot* package will be used for plotting trees.

By generating a separate tree for each of a large number of bootstrap random samples (the default is 500), and taking a simple majority vote across the multiple trees, the random-forests methodology that occupies Section 8.4 can often greatly improve on the predictive accuracy of a single tree. The methodology operates more as a black box, but with implementation details that are simpler to describe than for single-tree methods. The choice of number of splits for individual trees is not of great consequence. In large sample classification problems, the methodology has often proved superior to other contenders. The error rate is assessed by comparing, for each observation, the outcome with a simple majority vote of the predictions made for all trees whose bootstrap sample did not include that observation.

In large datasets, the random-forests methodology has the potential to reflect relatively complex forms of dependence, of a kind that conventional regression modeling might miss. As described here, both types of method (single tree and random forest) make limited use of the ordering of values of continuous or ordinal explanatory variables. A further issue is the strong assumption that the sample data can for predictive purposes be treated as a random sample of the population to which results will be applied. See in this connection the brief note in Subsection 8.4.3.

The primary focus will be on binary classification, noting also possibilities for use in a regression context more generally. Other possibilities include tree-based survival analysis.

When Are Tree-Based Methods Appropriate?

In small datasets, parametric models that build in quite strong assumptions commonly work best. Any bias introduced because the model is overly simple is the price that is paid for obtaining good predictive power. Tree-based methods may work well for datasets that are large enough that very limited assumptions will allow useful inference. For the methodology of the first three sections, which generates splits sequentially to obtain a single tree, a serious limitation is that while each local split is optimal, the final tree may be far from optimal.

As will be discussed in Section 8.5, tree-based methods can sometimes be used in tandem with more classical approaches, in ways that combine the strengths of the different approaches. Exploration of a new dataset with tree-based regression or classification may give helpful clues on which variables have major effects on the outcome.

Section 8.3, which will conclude the discussion of single-tree methodology, will focus on classification with two outcomes. The primary example, with 11 explanatory variables, examines the mortality of hospitalized female heart attack patients. For such binary outcomes, the use of a classification tree is a competitor to a logistic or related regression. Unordered classification with multiple outcomes is a straightforward extension, for which, however, this chapter has not found room.

8.1 Tree-Based Methods – Uses and Basic Notions

Examples That Will Be Used to Demonstrate the Methodology

We will use a dataset on email spam to start the discussion, building a classification tree that is designed to distinguish legitimate messages from spam. (Development and use of such a tree in practice would, of course, require up-to-date data.) Several simple toy datasets, that is, datasets that have been constructed for use for demonstration, will then be used to help explain the methodology. Also used for illustrative purposes is a dataset that gives mileage versus weight, for cars described in US April 1990 *Consumer Reports.*

8.1.1 Detecting Email Spam – an Initial Look

Data, collected by researchers at Hewlett–Packard Laboratories, consisted of 4601 email items, of which 1813 items were identified as spam. See `?DAAG::spam7` and Blake and Merz (1998). The simplest possible classification tree, involving only the *root node* (i.e., before taking account of any explanatory variables) would be to predict nonspam every time, since proportion of nonspam ($= 1 - 0.394$) exceeds the proportion of spam. This gives a root node error rate of 1813/4601 or 0.394.

For simplicity, we will work with six of the 57 explanatory variables that are available in the full dataset. The choice is based on the first author's intuition, educated by his exposure to email spam! Figure 8.1 shows boxplots of the six chosen variables (untransformed in Figure 8.1A; log transformed with an offset of 1.0 in Figure 8.1B), based in each instance on 500-row samples.[1]

[1]
```
## Obtain 500-row sample; repeat the first plot (of crl.tot)
spam.sample <- spam7[sample(seq(1,4601), 500, replace=FALSE), ]
lattice::bwplot(crl.tot ~ yesno, data=spam.sample, horizontal=F)
```

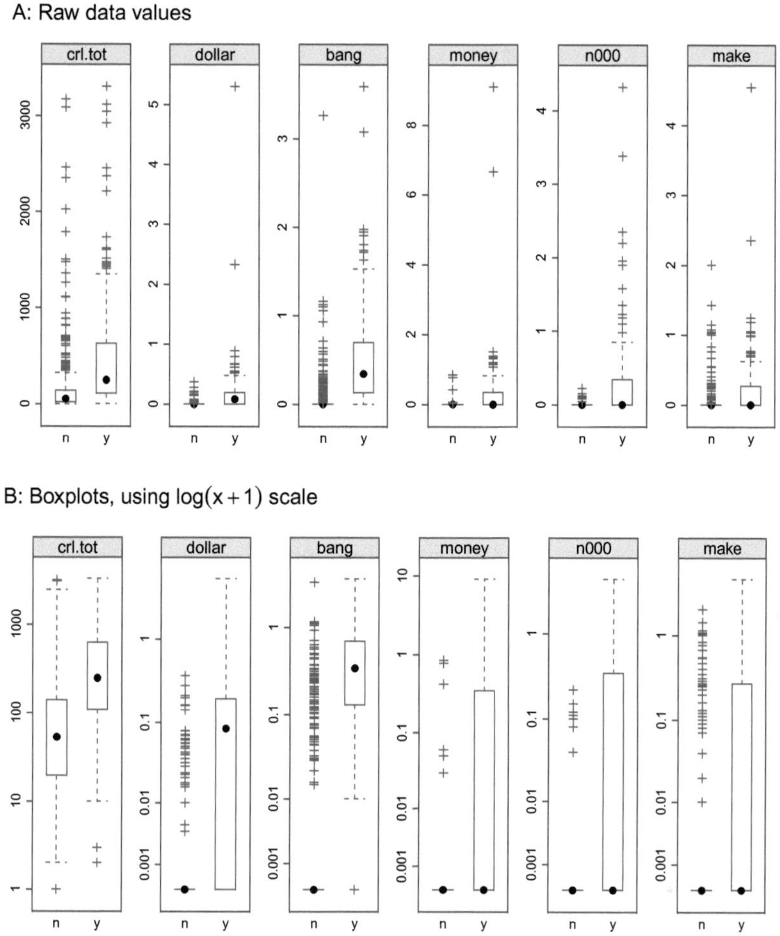

Figure 8.1 Boxplots for the six selected explanatory variables, in a random sample of 500 out of 4601 rows (email messages) in the SPAM database. (Data are subsampled, to make it easier to see the patterns of outliers.) The series A panels are for untransformed data, while the series B panels use $\log(x + 0.001)$ scales.

The explanatory variables are:

- `crl.tot`, total length of words that are in capitals,
- `dollar`, the frequency of the "\$" symbol, as a percentage of all characters,
- `bang`, the frequency of the "`!`" symbol, as a percentage of all characters,
- `money`, frequency of the word "`money`", as a percentage of all words,
- `n000`, frequency of the character string "`000`", as a percentage of all words,
- `make`, frequency of the word "`make`", as a percentage of all words.

The outcome is the factor `yesno`, which is `n` for nonspam and `y` for spam.

The distributions of variable values are so different between nonspam and spam email that it is hard to see how logistic regression or another parametric technique could be used effectively. For tree-based regression, the distributions of the explanatory variables are of relatively minor consequence.

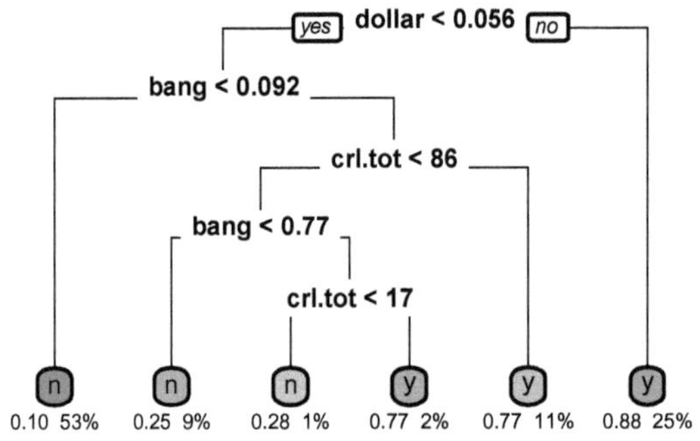

Figure 8.2 Graphical representation of output from the function `rpart()`, with `method="class"`, for classification with the email spam dataset, using the six explanatory variables noted in the text. At each splot, observations for which the condition is satisfied take the branch to the left.

Figure 8.2 shows the tree obtained when these six variables are used as predictors, with default settings of control parameters. The argument `method="class"`, here explicitly specified, is the default when, as here, the outcome is a factor. Code is:

```
suppressMessages(library(rpart))
set.seed(31)    ## Reproduce tree shown in text
spam.rpart <- rpart(formula = yesno ~ crl.tot + dollar + bang + money + n000 +
                    make, method="class", model=TRUE, data=DAAG::spam7)
rpart.plot::rpart.plot(spam.rpart, type=0, under=TRUE, branch.lwd=0.4,
                       nn.lwd=0.4, box.palette="auto", tweak=1.25)
```

Reading the tree is done as follows. If the condition that is specified at a node is satisfied, then we take the branch to the left. Thus, `dollar` (!) < 0.056 and `bang >= 0.091` leads to the prediction that the email is not spam. Under each node, the first number (fraction) is the predicted probability that the email is spam, while the second is the percentage of observations at the node.

Now use `printcp(spam.rpart)` to display predictive accuracy information:

```
printcp(spam.rpart, digits=3)
```

```
Classification tree:
rpart(formula = yesno ~ crl.tot + dollar + bang + money + n000 +
    make, data = DAAG::spam7, method = "class", model = TRUE)

Variables actually used in tree construction:
[1] bang    crl.tot dollar

Root node error: 1813/4601 = 0.394

n= 4601

      CP nsplit rel error xerror   xstd
1 0.4766      0     1.000  1.000 0.0183
2 0.0756      1     0.523  0.547 0.0154
3 0.0116      3     0.372  0.388 0.0135
4 0.0105      4     0.361  0.384 0.0134
5 0.0100      5     0.350  0.382 0.0134
```

The final row gives information on the performance of the decision tree in Figure 8.2. Earlier rows show the performances of trees with fewer splits.

There are two types of error rate, both expressed as multiples of the root node error rate: the relative error rate, and the cross-validation error rate. The relative error rate compares the error rate for a given tree with the null tree consisting only of the root node. The resubstitution or training data error rate is the misclassification error rate when applying the tree to the data used in its construction. In general,

$$\text{relative error rate} = \frac{\text{resubstitution error rate}}{\text{root node error rate}}.$$

For the rates given in the final row of the table, details are as follows.

1. The final row of the column headed `rel error` gives the *resubstitution* error rate. This is the relative error rate for predictions for the data that generated the tree, here 35 percent. Multiplication by the root node error gives an absolute error rate of $0.394 \times 0.35 = 0.138$, or 13.8 percent. This can never increase as tree size increases, gives an optimistic assessment of relative error in a new sample, and is of no use in deciding tree size.
2. The column headed `xerror` presents the more useful measure of performance. The `x` in `xerror` is an abbreviation for cross-validated. The absolute cross-validated error rate is $0.394 \times 0.379 = 0.15$, or 15 percent.

The cross-validated error rate, in the column headed `xerror`, suggests that five splits may be marginally better than three splits. Recall that this estimates the error rate for use of the prediction tree with new data that are sampled in the same way as the data used to derive the tree. The use of six or more splits will be investigated later, in Subsection 8.3.4.

8.1.2 Choosing the Number of Splits

In classical regression, the inclusion of too many explanatory variables may lead to a loss of predictive power, relative to a more parsimonious model. With tree-based methods, the more immediate issue is the number of splits, rather than the number of explanatory variables. Choice of a tree whose cross-validation error is close to the minimum protects against choosing too many splits. The email spam example will be the basis for a later, more extended, investigation.

Section 8.2 will explain the terminology and the methodology for forming trees. From there, the discussion will move to showing the use of cross-validation for assessing predictive accuracy and for choosing the optimal size of tree. Calculations are structured to determine a sequence of splits, to get unbiased assessments of predictive accuracy for a range of sizes of tree, and to allow an assessment of optimal tree size.

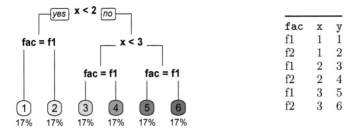

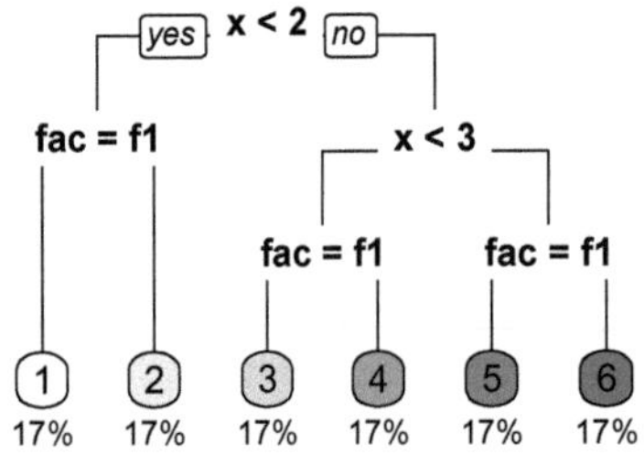

fac	x	y
f1	1	1
f2	1	2
f1	2	3
f2	2	4
f1	3	5
f2	3	6

Figure 8.3 This illustrative tree is generated from one explanatory factor (`fac`) and one explanatory variable (`x`). The toy data used to generate the tree are shown to the right of the tree. For factors, the levels that lead to a branch to the left are given. For variables, the range of values is given that leads to taking the left branch. Terminal nodes (the *leaves*) are numbered 1,...,5.

8.2 Splitting Criteria, with Illustrative Examples

The tree in Figure 8.3 illustrates basic nomenclature and labeling conventions.[2] In order to illustrate the methodology, it has been generated as a regression tree, treating the outcome `y` as a continuous variable.

There is an explanatory factor (`fac`) that has two levels, and an explanatory variable (`x`) that has three values. Each *split* carries a label that gives the decision rule (`fac=f1` or `x`<2 or `x`<3), either the factor levels or a range of variable values, that leads to split going to the left branch. We have arranged, for this toy example, that the outcome value is 1 for level `a`, 2 for level `b`, etc.

There are nine *nodes* in total, made up of four splits and five terminal nodes or *leaves*. In this example, the leaves are labeled 1, 2, ..., 5. The number of splits is always one less than the number of leaves. Output from `rpart()` uses the number of splits as a measure of tree size.

Choosing the Split – Regression Trees

The use of `method="anova"` is the default when the outcome variable is a continuous or ordinal variable. The anova splitting rule minimizes the residual sum of squares, calculated in the manner that will now be described, and termed *deviance* in the output from `rpart()`. Reasonable homogeneity of variance is important for ensuring the consistency of the measure of "error" across the whole range of values of the outcome variable.

Let $\mu_{[j]}$ be the mean for the cell to which y_j is currently assigned. Then the residual sum of squares is

$$D = \sum_j (y_j - \mu_{[j]})^2.$$

[2]
```
tree.df <- data.frame(fac = factor(rep(c('f1','f2'), 3)),
x = rep(1:3, rep(2, 3)), Node = 1:6)
u.tree <- rpart(Node ~ fac + x, data = tree.df,
                control = list(minsplit = 2, minbucket = 1, cp = 1e-009))
rpart.plot::rpart.plot(u.tree, type=0, under=TRUE, branch.lwd=0.25,
                       nn.lwd=0.25, box.palette="Grays", tweak=1.6)
```

Table 8.1 *Comparison of candidate splits at the* root *(first split).*

	Overall mean	Cell means	"Within" sum of squares	"Between" sum of squares
`fac=="a"` (`y==1,3,5`) vs `fac=="b"` (`y==2,4,6`)	3.5	3, 4	$8 + 8 = 16$	$3 \times (3 - 3.5)^2 + 3 \times (4 - 3.5)^2 = 1.5$
`x==1` (`y==1,2`) vs `x==2` or `3` (`y==3,4,5,6`)	3.5	1.5, 4.5	$0.5 + 5.0 = 5.5$	$2 \times (1.5 - 3.5)^2 + 4 \times (4.5 - 3.5)^2 = 12$
`x==1` or `2` (`y=1,2,3,4`) vs `x==3` (`y==5, 6`)	3.5	2.5, 5.5	$5.0 + 0.5 = 5.5$	$4 \times (2.5 - 3.5)^2 + 2 \times (5.5 - 3.5)^2 = 12$

Calculations proceed as in forward stepwise regression. At each step, the split is chosen that gives the maximum reduction in D. Observe that D is the sum of the "within-cells" sums of squares.

Prior to the first split, the deviance is

$$D = \sum_j (y_j - \bar{y})^2.$$

The split will partition the set of subscripts j into two subsets – a set of j_1s (write $\{j_1\}$) and a set of j_2s (write $\{j_2\}$). For any such partition,

$$D = \sum_j (y_j - \bar{y})^2 = \sum_{j_1} (y_{j_1} - \bar{y}_1)^2 + \sum_{j_2} (y_{j_2} - \bar{y}_2)^2 + n_1(\bar{y}_1 - \bar{y})^2 + n_2(\bar{y}_2 - \bar{y})^2,$$

where the first two terms comprise the new "within-group" sum of squares, and the final two terms make up the "between-group" sum of squares. If the values y_j are ordered, then the partition between $\{j_1\}$ and $\{j_2\}$ must respect this ordering, that is, the partitioning is defined by a cutpoint. If the outcome variable is an unordered factor, that is, if the values are unordered, then every possible split into $\{j_1\}$ and $\{j_2\}$ must in principle be considered.

The split is chosen to minimize the sum of the first two terms, and to maximize the sum of the final two terms. The criterion is equivalent to maximizing the between-groups sum of squares, as in a one-way analysis of variance. For later splits, each of the current cells is considered as a candidate for splitting, and the split is chosen that gives the maximum reduction in the residual sum of squares.

8.2.1 Within and Between Sums of Squares

The toy example of Figure 8.3 had one explanatory factor (with levels "`left`" and "`right`") and one explanatory variable `x`. The dependent variable is `y`, with values $y_j = j$ ($j = 1, 2, \ldots, 6$). Table 8.1 shows the sums of squares calculations for the candidate splits at the root.

The split between `fac=="f1"` and `fac=="f2"` gives a between sum of squares = 1.5, and a 'within' sum of squares = 16. Either of the splits on `x` (between `x` = `1` and `x > 1`, or between `x` $<$ 3 and `x` = 3) give a within sum of squares equal to 5.5. As the split on `x` leads to the smaller within sum of squares, it is the first of the splits on `x` that is chosen. (The second of the splits on `x` might equally well be taken. The tie must be resolved somehow!)

The algorithm then looks at each of the subcells in turn, and looks at options for splits within each subcell. The split chosen is the one that gives the largest "between" sum of squares, for the two new subcells that are formed.

8.2.2 Choosing the Split – Classification Trees

The argument `method="class"` in the `rpart()` call specifies a classification tree, This is the default when the outcome is a factor, but is best stated explicitly.

The classes (indexed by k) are the categories of the classification. Then n_{ik} is the number of observations at the ith leaf who are assigned to class k. The n_{ik} are used to estimate the proportions p_{ik}. Each leaf becomes, in turn, a candidate to be the node for a new split.

For classification trees, different software programs may offer different selections of splitting criteria. The `rpart()` default is `gini`, which uses a modified version of the Gini index as its default measure of "error," or "impurity." This takes the form

$$\sum_{j \neq k} p_{ij} p_{ik} = 1 - \sum_{k} p_{ik}^2.$$

An alternative is `information`, or deviance. The `rpart()` documentation and output use the generic term *error*, irrespective of the measure used.

The `information` criterion, or deviance, is

$$D_i = \sum_{\text{classes } k} n_{ik} \log(p_{ik}).$$

This differs only by a constant from the entropy measure that is used elsewhere, and thus would give the same tree if the same stopping rule were used. For the two-class problem (a binary classification), the Gini index and the deviance will almost always choose the same split as the deviance or entropy.

The splitting rule, if specified, is set by specifying, for example, `parms=list(split =gini)` or `parms=list(split=information)`.

8.2.3 Tree-Based Regression versus loess Regression Smoothing

The scatterplot of gas mileage versus vehicle weight in Figure 8.4 suggests a non-linear relationship. Useful insights may be gained from comparing predictions from tree-based regression with predictions from the more conventional and (for these data) more appropriate use of a `loess()` or similar regression smoothing approach.

To fit a regression tree to the car mileage data shown in Figure 8.4, the model formula is `Mileage ~ Weight` (i.e., predict `Mileage` given `Weight`), just as for the use of `lm()` or `loess()`. Figure 8.5A used the default split criteria, while split criteria for Figure 8.5B were chosen to give finer-grained splits.

The code for Figure 8.4, which uses `scatter.smooth()` to perform a `loess` type smooth, is:

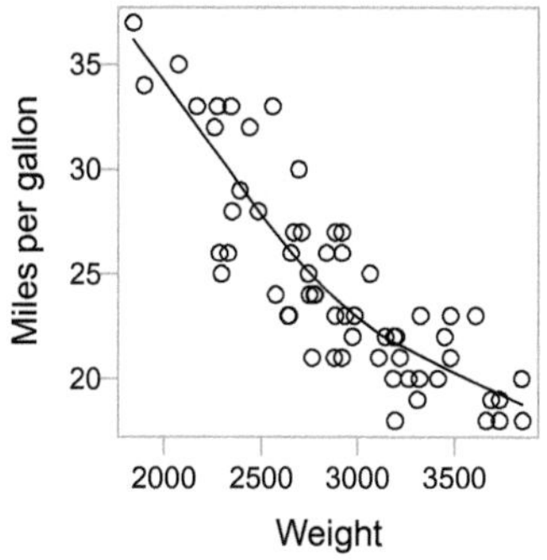

Figure 8.4 `Mileage` (mpg) versus `Weight`, for 60 cars from the US April 1990 *Consumer Reports.* A *loess* curve is overlaid.

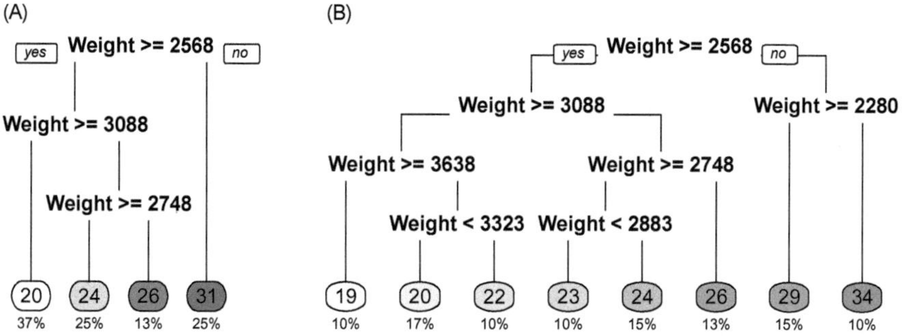

Figure 8.5 Tree-based model for predicting `Mileage` given `Weight`, for cars described in US April 1990 *Consumer Reports.* Panel A used the `rpart()` default split criteria, giving relatively coarse-grained splits. For Panel B, split criteria were set that gave more and finer-grained splits.

```
## loess fit to Mileage vs Weight: data frame car.test.frame (rpart)
with(rpart::car.test.frame, scatter.smooth(Mileage ~ Weight))
```

Code for Figures 8.5A and B is:

```
## Panel A: Split criteria were left a their defaults
car.tree <- rpart(Mileage ~ Weight, data = car.test.frame)
rpart.plot::rpart.plot(car.tree, type=0, under=TRUE)
## Panel B: Finer grained splits
car2.tree <- rpart(Mileage ~ Weight, data=car.test.frame, method="anova",
                   control = list(minsplit = 10, minbucket = 5, cp = 0.0001))
## See `?rpart::rpart.control` for details of control options.
```

Setting `minsplit=10` (the default is 20) allows splitting at any node that has at least 10 observations, while `minbucket=5` reduces to five the minimum number of observations at a terminal node. Setting `cp=0.0001` (the default is `cp=0.01`) greatly reduces the penalty that increases with the number of splits.

Table 8.2 compares the three sets of predictions. The first two are from the tree-based models of Figures 8.5A and B, while the third is from the `loess()` model of Figure 8.4. Notice the anomaly in Figure 8.5B's finer-grained prediction, where increased `Weight` has not given a reduction in predicted `mileage`.

Table 8.2 *Predictions from the regression trees of Figures 8.5A (coarse) and 8.5B (fine), and (a range of values) from the loess curve in Figure 8.4.*

Range of `Weight`	Predicted `Mileage`		Range of predictions
	A: Default	B: Fine-grained	(loess curve)
1845 – 2279	30.9	34.0	36.2 – 30.7
2280 – 2567	30.9	28.9	30.7 – 27.1
2568 – 2747	25.6	25.6	27.1 – 25.1
2748 – 2882	23.8	23.3	25.1 – 23.8
2883 – 3087	23.8	24.1	23.8 – 22.3
3088 – 3322	20.4	20.5	22.3 – 21.1
3323 – 3637	20.4	22.0	21.1 – 19.7
3638 – 3855	20.4	18.7	19.7 – 18.8

8.2.4 Predictive Accuracy, and the Cost–Complexity Tradeoff

Each new split adds to model complexity, with the new model selected from an increasingly wide range of candidate models. Realistic estimates of the predictive power of a model must take account of the extent of effects from this selection process, as an aid to judging when splitting should stop. The `rpart()` function makes available results from a form of on-the-fly use of cross-validation as calculations proceed, for use in deciding how complex a model is justified.

The cross-validation error is relevant to predictions for the population from which the data were sampled. Testing performance under conditions of actual use, if different from the conditions that generated the initial data, requires a validation set that is separate from any of the data used to generate the model. See also the further comments in Subsection 8.4.3.

8.2.5 Cross-Validation

As explained in the earlier discussion in Subsection 2.6.1, the cross-validation process proceeds by splitting of the data into k subsets, where for `rpart()` the default choice is $k = 10$. In a sequence of k *folds*, each of the k subsets of the data is left out in turn. At each fold the model is then fitted to the remaining data, and the result used to predict the outcome for the subset that has been left out. The k sets of predictive accuracies that result are then combined to give an overall cross-validation accuracy. Thus, at each fold, the subset that is left out has the role of a test set, with the remaining data having the role of a training set. The data that for the time being form the test set have a role that is somewhat akin to that of the "out-of-bag" data in the bootstrap aggregation approach in the random-forests methodology that will be discussed in Section 8.4.

In a regression model, prediction error is usually taken as the sum of differences between observed and predicted, that is, the criterion is the same as that used for the splitting rule. In a classification model, prediction error is usually determined by counting 1 for a misclassification and 0 for a correct classification. The crucial feature of cross-validation is that each prediction is independent of the data to which it is applied. As a consequence, cross-validation gives an unbiased estimate of predictive power, albeit for a model that uses, on average, a fraction $(k-1)/k$ of the data. An estimate of average error is found by summing the measure of "error" over all observations and dividing by the number of observations. Once predictions are available in this way for each of the subsets, the average error is taken as (total error)/(total number of observations). This process is repeated for each new split.

In order to determine the optimal number of splits, it is necessary to continue splitting until the cross-validation error starts to increase, giving a tree object that has more splits than are optimal. A final step is to prune it back to a tree that has close to the minimum cross-validated prediction error.

8.2.6 The Cost–Complexity Parameter

Rather than controlling the number of splits directly, this is controlled indirectly, via the quantity `cp` (complexity parameter, c_p) that puts a cost on each additional split. A large `cp` gives a small tree (additional cost quickly offsets the decrease in the lack-of-fit measure), while a small value gives a complex tree. For details, see section 4 of the vignette that can be displayed by typing:

```
vignette("longintro", package="rpart")
```

Previous experience in use of tree-based methods with similar problems may suggest a suitable setting for `cp` for an initial run of the calculations. Otherwise, the rpart default can be used. If the cross-validation error has not obviously reached a minimum, this will indicate that the tree is too small, and calculations need to be rerun with a smaller `cp`.

Having fitted a tree that is more complex than is optimal, we then plot the cross-validated relative error against c_p (or equivalently, against number of splits), and determine the value of c_p for which the tree seems optimal.

It can be shown that there is a sequence of prunings from the constructed tree back to the root, such that

- at each pruning the complexity reduces,
- each tree has the smallest number of nodes possible for that complexity, given the previous tree.

This is true even if the lack-of-fit measure used for pruning is different from that used in the formation of the tree. See, for example, Ripley (1996). For classification trees, it is common to use fraction or percent misclassified when trees have been pruned.

For the final choice of tree, an alternative to use of the cross-validation estimate of error is to examine the error rate for a new set of data.

In summary, we have the following.

- The parameter `cp` is a proxy for the number of splits. For the initial `rpart()` model, it should be set small enough that the cross-validation error rate achieves a minimum.
- Having identified the optimal tree (with the minimum cross-validation error rate), later splits are then pruned off.

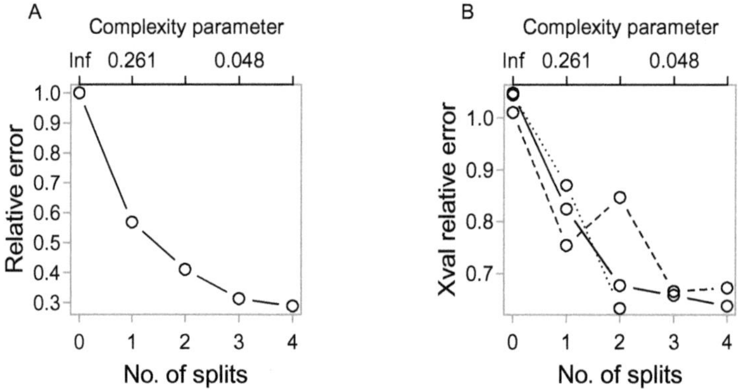

Figure 8.6 While the relative error (A) must inevitably decrease as the number of splits increases, the cross-validation relative error (X-val relative error, shown in B) is likely, once the number of splits is large enough, to increase. Results from three cross-validation runs are shown. Plots are for the car mileage data of Figure 8.4 and Table 8.2.

8.2.7 Prediction Error versus Tree Size

Figure 8.6 returns to the car mileage data of Figure 8.4 and Table 8.2. Figures 8.6A and 8.6B plot, against tree size, different assessments of the relative error. As we have a continuous outcome variable (`Mileage`), the relative error is the sum of squares of residual divided by the total sum of squares.

Figure 8.6A plots the resubstitution assessment of relative error, which shows the performance of the tree-based prediction on the data used to form the tree. Figure 8.6B shows estimates from three cross-validation runs, with the data split into $k = 10$ subsets (or *folds*) at each run. The plot gives an indication of the variability that can be expected, for these data, from one cross-validation run to another.

The optimal tree, in Figure 8.6, is the smallest tree that has near-minimum cross-validated relative error. Use of several cross-validation runs, as in Figure 8.6, gives an indication of the effect of sampling variation in the cross-validation process. The three runs suggest different optimal tree sizes. The defaults for the arguments `minsplit` and `minbucket` (see `?rpart::rpart.control`) have limited the number of splits to four. Between two and four splits may be optimal.

8.3 The Practicalities of Tree Construction – Two Examples

The subsection that follows will examine data on the outcome for female heart attack patients, in the data frame `DAAG::mifem`. A detailed analysis of the data on email spam will follow.

8.3.1 Data for Female Heart Attack Patients

The data are for the mortality (`live` or `dead`) of 1295 female heart attack patients. The following is a summary:

```
mifem <- DAAG::mifem
summary(mifem)    # data frame mifem (DAAG)
```

```
 outcome          age            yronset        premi     smstat    diabetes
 live:974   Min.   :35.0   Min.   :85.0   y :311   c :390   y :248
 dead:321   1st Qu.:57.0   1st Qu.:87.0   n :928   x :280   n :978
            Median :63.0   Median :89.0   nk: 56   n :522   nk: 69
            Mean   :60.9   Mean   :88.8            nk:103
            3rd Qu.:66.0   3rd Qu.:91.0
            Max.   :69.0   Max.   :93.0
 highbp   hichol   angina   stroke
 y :813   y :452   y :472   y :  153
 n :406   n :655   n :724   n :1063
 nk: 76   nk:188   nk: 99   nk:   79
```

(Technically, these are patients who have suffered a *myocardial infarction*. Data are from the Newcastle (Australia) center of the Monica project; see the website given under `?DAAG::monica`.)

In order to fit the tree, we specify

```
set.seed(29)     # Make results reproducible
mifem.rpart <- rpart(outcome ~ ., method="class", data = mifem, cp = 0.0025)
```

The dot (`.`) on the right-hand side of the formula has the effect of including all available explanatory variables. A choice of `cp` = 0.0025 continues splitting to the point where the cross-validated relative error has started to increase. The following shows the change in cross-validated error rate as a function of tree size.

```
## Tabular equivalent of Panel A from `plotcp(mifem.rpart)`
printcp(mifem.rpart, digits=3)
```

```
. . .
Root node error: 321/1295 = 0.248

n= 1295

        CP nsplit rel error xerror   xstd
1 0.20249      0     1.000  1.000 0.0484
2 0.00561      1     0.798  0.829 0.0453
3 0.00467     13     0.717  0.875 0.0462
4 0.00312     17     0.698  0.860 0.0459
5 0.00250     18     0.695  0.863 0.0460
```

Notice the increase in the cross-validated error rate when there are more than two splits. Any value for `cp` that is less than the value in the first line of the table, that is, less than ~0.2, causes splitting to continue beyond the root node. The cross-validated error rate is $0.248 \times 0.832 = 0.206$. For this tree, the optimum is a single split, that is, two leaves.

Figure 8.7A shows the change in cross-validated error rate as a function of tree size. Panel B shows the tree, with two leaves, that was chosen as optimal. Note that the levels of `angina` are `y`, `n`, and `nk`. The single split is between the 92 percent of all patients at the left leaf whose angina level was known and who are predicted to live, and the 8 percent at the right leaf whose angina status was unknown and were

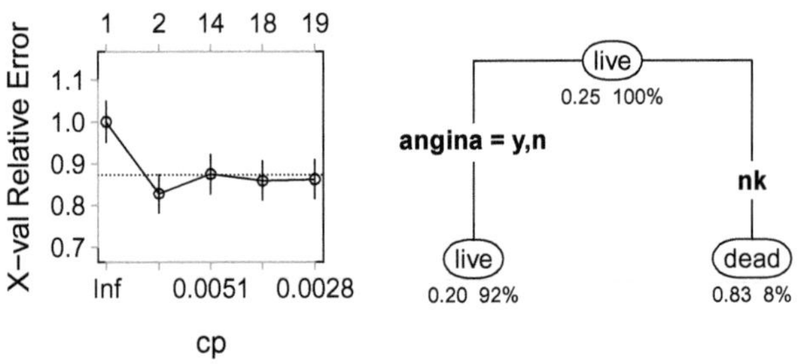

Figure 8.7 The left panel shows the cross-validated error versus cp, for the female heart attack data. The top side of the bounding box is labeled with the size of tree, that is, the number of leaves. Panel B shows the tree of size 2 that results from pruning back to just two leaves.

predicted to die. Out of these totals, the probability of `dead` is 0.2 or 20 percent for the left leaf (angina status known), and 0.83 or 83 percent for the right leaf (angina status not known). The high death rate for the right node may well have arisen because many of these were already dead or unconscious when they presented, and could not be asked to give their status.

Code for Figure 8.7 is:

```
plotcp(mifem.rpart, fg="gray", tcl=-0.25)
mifemb.rpart <- prune(mifem.rpart, cp=0.01)  ## Prune tree back to 2 leaves
rpart.plot::rpart.plot(mifemb.rpart, under=TRUE, type=4,
                       box.palette=0, tweak=1.0)
```

8.3.2 The One-Standard-Deviation Rule

The function `rpart()` calculates, for each tree, both the cross-validated estimate of "error" and a standard deviation for that error. Where the interest is in which splits are likely to be meaningful, users are advised to choose the smallest tree whose error is less than

$$\text{minimum error } + 1 \text{ standard deviation.}$$

Figure 8.7 has a horizontal line at a height of `xerror` $= 0.855$ $(= 0.810 + 0.045)$, that shows where this error level is attained. Here the one-standard-error rule leads to the same choice of tree size as for the absolute minimum. The rule is in general conservative, and the predictive power will on average be slightly reduced.

8.3.3 Printed Information on Each Split

We will now examine output that is available from printing the `rpart` object for the very simple tree that is shown in Figure 8.7:

```
print(mifemb.rpart)
```

```
n= 1295

node), split, n, loss, yval, (yprob)
```

```
      * denotes terminal node

1) root 1295 321 live (0.7521 0.2479)
  2) angina=y,n 1196 239 live (0.8002 0.1998) *
  3) angina=nk 99  17 dead (0.1717 0.8283) *
```

Predictions are as follows.

- At the *root* node (no splits) the prediction is `live` (probability 0.75), with the 25 percent who are `dead` misclassified. Here the `loss` (number misclassified) is 321.
- Take the left branch from node 1 if the person's angina status is `y` or `n`, that is, if it is known (1196 persons). The prediction is `live` (probability 0.80), with the 239 who die misclassified.
- Take the right branch from node 1 if the angina status is unknown (99 persons). The prediction is `dead`, probability 0.83), with the 17 who are `live` misclassified.

The function `summary.rpart()` gives information on alternative splits.

8.3.4 Detecting Email Spam – the Optimal Tree

In Figure 8.2, where `cp` had its default value of 0.01, splitting did not continue long enough for the cross-validated relative error to reach a minimum. In order to find the minimum, we now repeat the calculation, this time with `cp` = 0.002. (This choice followed some limited experimentation.)

```
set.seed(59)
spam7a.rpart <- rpart(formula = yesno ~ crl.tot + dollar + bang +
                  money + n000 + make, method="class", cp = 0.002,
                  model=TRUE, data = DAAG::spam7)
```

The choice `cp` = 0.002 in place of `cp` = 0.01 has carried the splitting far enough that the cross-validated error starts to increase.

In this instance, the output from `plotcp(spam7.rpart)` is not very useful. The changes are so small that it is not visually clear, from the graph, where the minimum falls. Instead, the printed output will be used:

```
printcp(spam7a.rpart, digits=3)
```

```
Classification tree:
rpart(formula = yesno ~ crl.tot + dollar + bang + money + n000 +
    make, data = DAAG::spam7, method = "class", model = TRUE,
    cp = 0.002)

Variables actually used in tree construction:
[1] bang    crl.tot dollar  money   n000

Root node error: 1813/4601 = 0.394

n= 4601

        CP nsplit rel error xerror   xstd
1  0.47656      0      1.000  1.000 0.0183
```

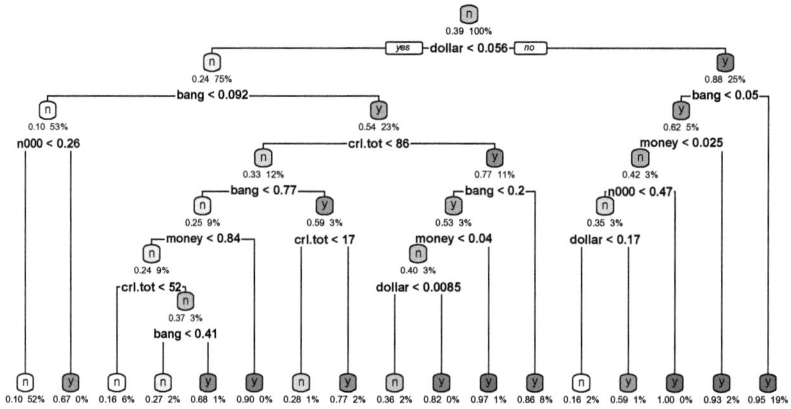

Figure 8.8 Decision tree for the email spam data. The one-standard-error rule was used to choose the size (= 16).

```
2  0.07557    1   0.523  0.550 0.0154
3  0.01158    3   0.372  0.390 0.0135
4  0.01048    4   0.361  0.386 0.0134
5  0.00634    5   0.350  0.374 0.0133
6  0.00552   10   0.317  0.360 0.0130
7  0.00441   11   0.311  0.357 0.0130
8  0.00386   12   0.307  0.352 0.0129
9  0.00276   16   0.291  0.339 0.0127
10 0.00221   17   0.288  0.339 0.0127
11 0.00200   18   0.286  0.336 0.0127
```

Choice of the tree that minimizes the cross-validated error leads to **nsplit**=11 with **xerror**=0.336. Again, note that different runs of the cross-validation routine will give slightly different results.

Observe that changes in the **xerror** for the last several splits are smaller than the standard errors. The one-standard-deviation rule suggests taking **nsplit**=16. (From the table, minimum + standard error = 0.336 + 0.0127 = 0.3487. The smallest tree whose **xerror** is less than or equal to this has **nsplit** = 16.)

Figure 8.8 plots this tree. Any value of CP that is between that for 12 splits and that for 16 splits can be used to prune back to 0, 1, 2, 3, 4 splits. Here take **cp** = **cpval** = 0.0033.

Code to prune the tree, and plot the pruned tree, is:

```
spam7b.rpart <- prune(spam7a.rpart, cp=cpval)
rpart.plot::rpart.plot(spam7b.rpart, under=TRUE, box.palette="Grays", tweak=1.65)
```

The absolute error rate is estimated as $0.328 \times 0.394 = 0.129$ if the one-standard-error rule is used, or $0.320 \times 0.394 = 0.126$ if the tree is chosen that gives the minimum cross-validated error.

How Does the One-Standard-Error Rule Affect Accuracy of Estimates?

The function `DAAG::compareTreecalcs()` can be used to assess how accuracies are affected, on average, by use of the one standard error rule. Data are split into two nearly equal subsets I and II, and the following accuracies are calculated:

1. the estimated cross-validation error rate when `rpart()` is run on the training data (I), and the one-standard error rule is used;
2. the estimated cross-validation error rate when `rpart()` is run on subset I, and the model used that gives the minimum cross-validated error rate;
3. the error rate when the model fitted in item 1 is used to make predictions for subset II;
4. the error rate when the model fitted in item 2 is used to make predictions for subset II.

See `?DAAG::compareTreecalcs`. An example of the function's use, for just one run of the calculations, is:

```
DAAG::compareTreecalcs(data=DAAG::spam7, fun="rpart")
```

```
rpSEcvI     rpcvI rpSEtest    rptest  nSErule    nREmin
 0.1396    0.1387   0.1269    0.1217   7.0000    8.0000
```

The calculations need to be repeated for many splits of the data, in order to get differences between the different "accuracies" that stand out above statistical variation. The following generates results for 100 splits:

```
acctree.mat <- matrix(0, nrow=100, ncol=6)
spam7 <- DAAG::spam7
for(i in 1:100)
acctree.mat[i,] <- DAAG::compareTreecalcs(data=spam7, fun="rpart")
```

In a run of the code just given (results will of course differ from run to run), we obtained the following results: The prediction accuracy for subset II was indeed similar to the cross-validated accuracy when the model was fit to subset I. There was a small average loss of accuracy (0.45 percent, SE = 0.07 percent), from use of the one-standard-error rule.

How Is the Standard Error Calculated?

For classification trees, using number misclassified, the standard deviation is, assuming independent errors, approximately equal to the square root of the number misclassified.

When Are Tree-Based Methods Appropriate?

Exploration of a new dataset with tree-based regression or classification can sometimes yield a quick handle on which variables have large effects on the outcome variable. There is, however, a risk of missing interesting structure because assumptions have been too weak. Parametric models have a better chance of capturing such structure; they are almost always more appropriate for small datasets. A further issue is optimality; while the local splits are optimal, the overall tree may be far from optimal.

8.4 From One Tree to a Forest – a More Global Optimality

The function `randomForest()` in the *randomForest* package is an attractive alternative to `rpart()` that, for relatively complex trees, is likely to give an improved predictive accuracy. For each of many bootstrap samples (by default, 500), drawn using simple random sampling (with replacement) from the rows of the data frame, trees are independently grown. A new random sample of variables is chosen for use with each new tree, $\sqrt{p}$ variables for a classification tree or $p/3$ for a regression tree (in each case rounded down), where p is the number of variables. The "out-of-bag" (OOB) prediction for each observation is determined by a simple majority vote across trees whose bootstrap sample did not include that observation.

Trees are grown to their maximum extent, limited only by `nodesize` (minimum number of trees at a node), and optionally by setting `maxnodes` to limit the number of nodes. The main tuning parameter is the number `mtry` of variables that are randomly sampled at each split. It may seem surprising that it is (usually) beneficial to take a random sample of variables. Essentially, `mtry` controls the tradeoff between the amount of information in each individual tree, and the correlation between trees. A very high correlation limits the ability of an individual tree to convey information that is specific to that tree.

The following uses `randomForest()` with the data frame `spam7`:

```
suppressPackageStartupMessages(library(randomForest))
spam7.rf <- randomForest(yesno ~ ., data=spam7, importance=TRUE)
spam7.rf
```

```
Call:
 randomForest(formula = yesno ~ ., data = spam7, importance = TRUE)
               Type of random forest: classification
                     Number of trees: 500
No. of variables tried at each split: 2

        OOB estimate of  error rate: 11.56%
Confusion matrix:
     n    y class.error
n 2651  137     0.04914
y  395 1418     0.21787
```

Use of the OOB error rate is crucial for calculating realistic error rates, unless separate test data are available. Notice that the error rate that was achieved here is slightly better than the 13.0 percent error rate achieved by `rpart()`.

The function `tuneRF()` makes it straightforward to find the optimal value of `mtry`, thus:

```
z <- tuneRF(x=spam7[, -7], y=spam7$yesno, plot=FALSE)
```

The result is:

```
         mtry=1     2     4
OOBError  0.127 0.118 0.118
```

The value of `OOBerror` is smallest for `mtry=2`, which is the default when there are six variables. The result will vary somewhat from one run of `tuneRF()` to another.

Two "importance" measures can be calculated for each variable. The first, available if the argument `importance=TRUE` is supplied in the call to `randomForest()`, is a "leave-one-out" type assessment of its contribution to prediction accuracy, calculated as the average decrease in prediction accuracies in the OOB portions of the data from permuting values of the variable. The second, available by default, is the average decrease in lack-of-fit from splitting on the variable, averaged over all trees. For the present data, the values are:

```
importance(spam7.rf)
```

```
            n      y MeanDecreaseAccuracy MeanDecreaseGini
crl.tot 46.73  54.19                70.57           248.10
dollar  56.21  55.35                76.13           431.75
bang    91.66 100.46               115.95           588.53
money   33.09  51.87                53.49           206.51
n000    58.25  15.74                62.29           115.46
make    13.67  21.76                26.72            41.13
```

Observe that the first measure gives roughly equal importance to the first three and fifth variables, while the second measure rates `bang` as easily the most "important." Is a variable important? It depends on how importance is measured.

Exercise 8.9 at the end of the chapter demonstrates the power of the random-forest approach to obtain accurate predictions for data for which it would be hard to find an effective `lm` or GAM model.

8.4.1 Prior Probabilities

In the randomForest() implementation, there is no direct provision for varying prior probabilities from the relative group frequencies. It is unclear what the argument `classwt` does in the R implementation, but the effect is not equivalent to the specifying of prior probabilities.

The effect of specifying prior probabilities can, however, be achieved by varying the sample size (`sampsize`) between groups. As an example, consider the dataset `MASS::Pima.tr`. The 200 sample points divide up as follows:

```
Pima.tr <- MASS::Pima.tr
table(Pima.tr$type)
```

```

 No Yes
132  68
```

The default is to take a bootstrap sample of size 200 from the total data. On average each bootstrap sample will have 34 percent of type `Yes`, that is, these are diabetics, but this proportion will vary from sample to sample. Here are error rates for the default settings:

```
set.seed(41)    # This seed should reproduce the result given here
Pima.rf <- randomForest(type ~ ., data=Pima.tr)
## The above is equivalent to:
## Pima.rf <- randomForest(type ~ ., data=Pima.tr, sampsize=200)
round(Pima.rf$confusion,3)
```

```
     No Yes class.error
No  110  22       0.167
Yes  32  36       0.471
```

The overall error rate is $0.66 \times 0.167 + 0.34 \times 0.471$, which equals 0.27. This varies from run to run. Thus, in one set of five different runs, the variation was between 27 percent and 30 percent. Note the much greater accuracy for classifying the larger number in the `No` group, as opposed to the `Yes` group.

Sample sizes can be set at fixed values within groups, with numbers that are in each no larger than the number in the respective groups. Thus, sample sizes can be set so that they give the effect of a relevant prior relative probability, For equal prior probabilities, the first sample size can be reduced to be the same size as the smaller of the two groups, that is, `sampsize=c(68,68)`:

```
Pima.rf <- randomForest(type ~ ., data=Pima.tr, sampsize=c(68,68))
```

The following insists on choosing bootstrap samples separately at the maximum for each of the two groups, giving exactly 132 that are `No` and 68 that are `Yes`.

```
Pima.rf <- randomForest(type ~ ., data=Pima.tr, sampsize=c(132,68))
```

One source of variation, that is, in the relative numbers of `Yes` and `No` in the bootstrap samples, has been removed. Thus, one might expect less variability in the error rates, with the average rate the same as before.

Taking smaller samples can sometimes increase accuracy, or may not reduce it very much. Reduced accuracy for individual trees is traded against reduced correlation between trees.

8.4.2 A Low-Dimensional Representation of Observations

The proportion of trees in which both members of a pair of observations appear in the same terminal node gives a measure of proximity, or nearness. Methods that will be described in Subsection 9.1.3 can then be used to derive a low-dimensional representation of the points. See Figure 9.24, and the accompanying discussion, for an example.

8.4.3 Models with a Complex Error Structure

Tree-based models, as implemented in current software, are less than ideal for use with data where there is correlation in time or space (as in Chapters 6 and 7), or where there is more than one level of variation (as in Chapter 7). If tree-based models are nevertheless used with such data, accuracy should be assessed at the level of variation that is relevant for any use of model predictions.

As a focus to the discussion, consider the `Vowel` dataset in the *mlbench* package.[3] The help page describes this dataset as intended for "Speaker independent recognition of the eleven steady state vowels of British English". For each utterance, there are values of 10 continuous measures, repeated at least 6 times for each of 15

[3] Note that the package `mlbench` does not export its datasets. Use the function `data()` to make them available, for example, `data(Vowel, package="mlbench")`.

speakers. Use of the `randomForest()` function with the built-in bootstrap sampling of observations yields high predictive accuracy, albeit with results which apply to new observations for the same 15 speakers. To assess accuracy for a new speaker, it is necessary to take bootstrap samples of speakers. The `randomForest()` function has no provision for this. See, however, `?gamclass::RFcluster`. Repeated calls to `randomForest()` ensure that predictions are checked on OOB clusters. Predictive accuracy is very substantially reduced, for example, in one comparison, from 0.978 to 0.556.

If there is clustering in the data, and the size of the clusters varies widely, the naive use of a tree-based method will lead to predictions that are biased.

8.5 Additional Notes – One Tree, or Many Trees?

8.5.1 Differences between `rpart()` *and* `randomForest()`

As noted earlier, accuracy is in most cases markedly better for `randomForest()` than for `rpart()`. Use of `randomForest()` is largely automatic, with limited need or opportunity for tuning. There is no equivalent to the complexity parameter `cp` for `rpart()`, and no possibility or need for pruning. The attraction of `rpart()` is that it yields a single tree that provides insight on the decision making process. Differences in syntax are:

- `rpart()` requires a model formula, whereas `randomForest()` allows, alternatively, specification of a matrix whose columns are used as predictors;
- `randomForest()` does not have a direct equivalent of `rpart()`'s `method` argument that can be used to distinguish between regression, classification, and other models. Instead, `randomForest()` assumes a classification model if the response is a factor, and otherwise assumes a regression model.

Error Rates – `rpart()` *versus* `randomForest()`

In the following, the `spam7` will be repeatedly split at random into two nearly equal subsets: subset I has 2300 observations, and subset II has 2301 observations. Models with be fit (1) using `rpart()` and (2) using `randomForest()`. Figure 8.9A is designed to check that `randomForest()` did not overfit. Figure 8.9B shows that the model fitted using `randomForest()` has given an average reduction in the error rate, relative to `rpart()`, of 0.9 percent [SE = 0.1 percent].

The calculations are handled thus:

```
acctree.mat <- matrix(0, nrow=100, ncol=8)
colnames(acctree.mat) <- c("rpSEcvI", "rpcvI", "rpSEtest", "rptest",
                           "n.SErule", "nre.min.12", "rfcvI", "rftest")
for(i in 1:100)acctree.mat[i,] <- DAAG::compareTreecalcs(data=spam7,
                                    fun=c("rpart", "randomForest"))
## Panel A: Plot `rfOOBI` against `rftest`
## Panel B: Plot `rptest` against `rftest`
```

The difference between `rpart()` and `randomForest()` is much larger if the full spam database, with 57 explanatory variables, is used. In that case, in three runs,

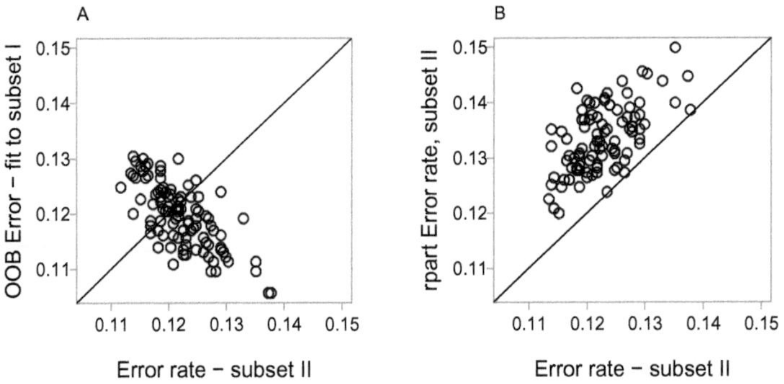

Figure 8.9 For each of 100 random splits of **spam7** into two nearly equal subsets I and II, random-forest models were fitted to subset I, keeping a record both of the OOB error rate on subset I and the error rate on predictions for subset II. Panel A compares the two error rates. Panel B compares the error rate from use of `rpart()` with the second of the error rates for the random-forest model.

`rpart()` gave error rates of 8.45%, 8.34%, and 8.24%, whereas `randomForest()` gave error rates of 4.56%, 4.41%, and 4.54%.

Times Required for Computation

The following times were for the full spam database (dimension 4601 × 58), on a 2.16 GHz MacBook Pro with 2 GB of memory. Elapsed times were:

- `rpart()` with `cp=0.00025`: 6.4 s (here there is no alternative to use of a model formula, typically with variables taken from the columns of a data frame);
- `randomForest()`: 27.3 s when a model formula and data frame were specified, reduced slightly when explanatory variable columns were supplied as a matrix.

8.5.2 Tree-Based Methods, versus Other Approaches

The following comments match tree-based methods against linear models, generalized additive models, and parametric discriminant methods. Strengths of tree-based regression include the following.

- Results are invariant to a monotone reexpression of explanatory variables.
- The methodology is readily adapted to handle missing values, without omission of complete observations.
- Tree-based methods are adept at capturing nonadditive behavior. Interactions are automatically included.
- It handles regression, and in addition unordered and ordered classification.
- Results from single-tree methods are in an immediately useful form for classification or diagnosis, providing they are not, as for the 2000+ leaf tree for the `ggplot2:diamonds` dataset in Exercise 8.8b at the end of the chapter, unreasonably complex.
- A simplified tree may be useful, as perhaps with the `diamonds` data, for getting an initial rough assessment.

Weaknesses of methods that yield a single tree include the following.

- The overall tree may not be optimal.
- Large trees make poor intuitive sense; their predictions must be used as black boxes.
- Low-order interaction effects do not take precedence over higher-order interactions, which may be an issue for ease of interpretation.
- Limited notions of what to look for may result in failure to find useful structure.
- Assumptions of monotonicity or continuity across the boundaries created by successive splits are lost. This risks obscuring insights that would be available from parametric modeling, for example, a steadily increasing risk of cancer with increasing exposure to a carcinogen.

Ensemble methods, including random forests, yield more optimal trees. They are more open than single trees to the complaint that their predictions must be treated as black boxes.

Tree-Based Methods May Usefully Complement Other Approaches

Tree-based approaches can sometimes be used in tandem with parametric approaches, in ways that combine the strengths of the different approaches. Thus, tree-based regression may suggest interaction terms that ought to appear in a parametric model. We might also apply tree-based regression analysis to residuals from conventional parametric modeling, in order to check whether there is residual structure that the parametric model has not captured. Another variation is to apply tree-based regression to fitted values of a parametric model, in order to cast predictions in the form of a decision tree.

Subsection 9.7.5 will use `randomForest()` to provide a two-dimensional representation of points in a seven-dimensional space.

8.5.3 Further Notes

Pruning as Variable Selection

Venables and Ripley (2002) suggest that pruning might be regarded as a method of variable selection. This suggests using an AIC-like criterion as the criterion for optimality. We refer the reader to their discussion for details.

8.6 Further Reading and Extensions

Venables and Ripley (2002) has a good brief overview. Ripley (1996), Berk (2008), and Hastie et al. (2009) are more comprehensive. Berk (2008) has extensive insightful comments on the properties, practical use, and usefulness of these and related technologies.

The *rpart* package allows two types of tree, additional to those discussed in this chapter. The `poisson` splitting method adapts `rpart` models to event rate data. See Therneau and Atkinson (1997, pp. 35–41). The `survival` splitting method is intended for use with survival data, where each subject has either 0 or 1 events. (The underlying model is a special case of the Poisson event rate model.) See again Therneau and Atkinson (1997, pp. 41–46).

Boosting is an extension of tree-based methodology that, in contrast to the `randomForest()` "bagging" approach, uses an approach known as "boosting" to build a large number of trees. Trees are built in sequence, with extra weight given to points that were incorrectly predicted by earlier trees. A weighted vote is finally taken to get a consensus prediction. Relative to random forests, the statistical properties of boosting methods are not well understood, and they can overfit. The function `adaboost.M1()` in the *adabag* package implements the Adaboost.M1 algorithm. Note also the *gbm* Generalized Boosted Regression Models package.

Therneau and Atkinson (1997, pp. 50–52) give comparisons between `rpart` methodology and other software. Lim and Loh (2000) investigated 10 decision tree implementations, not, however, including `rpart`. Several of these implementations offer a choice of algorithms. For a biostatistical perspective, including a discussion of survival modeling and analysis of longitudinal data, see Zhang and Singer (1999). The CRAN *MachineLearning* task view lists several R packages that implement refinements or adaptations of tree-based methodology.

Tree-based methodology is designed to investigate a potentially unlimited variety of models, in the style of machine learning. A crucial challenge in the development of tree-based methods has been the finding of ways to avoid over-fitting and to generate realistic accuracy estimates. These issues have an importance that has not always had the attention required in machine learning approaches more generally.

There are refinements on tree-based models that build in less structure than classical regression modeling, but more structure than classification and regression trees.

8.7 Exercises

8.1. Refer to the `headInjury` data frame.

   a. Use the default setting in `rpart()` to obtain a tree-based model for predicting occurrence of clinically important brain injury, given the other variables.
   b. How many splits gives the minimum cross-validation error?
   c. Prune the tree using the one-standard-error rule.

8.2. The dataset `mifem` is part of the larger dataset in the data frame `DAAG::monica`. Use tree-based regression to predict mortality in this larger dataset. What is the most immediately striking feature of the analysis output? Should this be a surprise?

8.3. Use tree-based regression to predict `re78` in the data frame `DAAG::nswpsid1`. Compare the predictions with the multiple regression predictions in Chapter 3.

8.4. The complete email spam dataset is available from `https://archive.ics.uci.edu/dataset/94/spambase`, or from the *bayesreg* package. Carry out a tree-based regression using all 57 available explanatory variables. Determine the change in the cross-validation estimate of predictive accuracy.

8.5. This exercise will compare alternative measures of accuracy from `randomForest()` runs. First, 16 rows where data (on `V6`) is missing will be omitted:

```
sapply(MASS::biopsy, function(x)sum(is.na(x)))  ## Will omit rows with NAs
```

```
   ID    V1    V2    V3    V4    V5    V6    V7    V8    V9 class
    0     0     0     0     0     0    16     0     0     0     0
```

```
biops <- na.omit(MASS::biopsy)[,-1]            ## Omit also column 1 (IDs)
## Examine list element names in randomForest object
names(randomForest(class ~ ., data=biops))
```

```
 [1] "call"              "type"              "predicted"
 [4] "err.rate"          "confusion"         "votes"
 [7] "oob.times"         "classes"           "importance"
[10] "importanceSD"      "localImportance"   "proximity"
[13] "ntree"             "mtry"              "forest"
[16] "y"                 "test"              "inbag"
[19] "terms"
```

a. Compare repeated `randomForest()` runs:

```
## Repeated runs, note variation in OOB accuracy.
for(i in 1:10) {
  biops.rf <- randomForest(class ~ ., data=biops)
  OOBerr <- mean(biops.rf$err.rate[,"OOB"])
  print(paste(i, ": ", round(OOBerr, 4), sep=""))
  print(round(biops.rf$confusion,4))
}
```

b. Compare OOB accuracies with test set accuracies:

```
## Repeated train/test splits: OOB accuracy vs test set accuracy.
for(i in 1:10){
  trRows <- sample(1:dim(biops)[1], size=round(dim(biops)[1]/2))
  biops.rf <- randomForest(class ~ ., data=biops[trRows, ],
    xtest=biops[-trRows,-10], ytest=biops[-trRows,10])
  oobErr <- mean(biops.rf$err.rate[,"OOB"])
  testErr <- mean(biops.rf$test$err.rate[,"Test"])
print(round(c(oobErr,testErr),4))
}
```

Plot test set accuracies against OOB accuracies. Add the line $y = x$ to the plot. Is there any consistent difference in the accuracies? Given a random training/test split, is there any reason to expect a consistent difference between OOB accuracy and test accuracy?

c. Calculate the error rate for the training data:

```
randomForest(class ~ ., data=biops, xtest=biops[,-10], ytest=biops[,10])
```

Explain why use of the training data for testing leads to a zero error rate.

8.6. Starting in turn with samples of sizes n = 25, 50, 100, 200, 400, 800, take a bootstrap sample of the relevant size n. In each case, determine the number of observations that are repeated. The expected number is $(1 - n^{-1})^n$, with limiting value exp(−1) for infinite n.[4]

a. Plot the observed number of repeats against the expected number of repeats.
b. Plot, against $\log(n)$, the difference $\exp(-1) - (1 - n^{-1})^n$.

8.7. *Apply `randomForest()` to give predictions for `type` in the dataset `MASS::Pima.tr`, then comparing the error rate with that from a fit to a bootstrap sample of rows of `Pima.tr`:

```
## Run model on total data
randomForest(as.factor(type) ~ ., data=Pima.tr)
rowsamp <- sample(dim(Pima.tr)[1], replace=TRUE)
randomForest(as.factor(type) ~ ., data=Pima.tr[rowsamp, ])
```

Compare the two error rates. Why is the error rate from the fit to the bootstrap sample of rows so (spuriously) low?

8.8. This exercise will focus on the `ggplot2::diamonds` dataset that has more than 54,000 observations on nine variables.

a. Use the following and any other graphs that you think useful to check out the `ggplot2::diamonds` dataset:

```
d500 <- ggplot2::diamonds[sample(1:nrow(ggplot2::diamonds), 500),]
unlist(sapply(d500, class)) # Check the class of all 10m columns
car::spm(d500)      # If screen space is limited do two plots, thus:
 # 1) variables 1 to 5 and 7 (`price`); 2) variables 6 to 10
plot(density(d500[, "price", drop = T]))        # Distribution is very skew
MASS::boxcox(price~., data=ggplot2::diamonds) # Suggests log transform
```

Comment on what the graphs show. Which variables appear from the scatterplot to have, individually, the largest effect on price?

b. Use `rpart::rpart()` to create a tree object:

```
diamonds <- ggplot2::diamonds; Y <- diamonds[,"price", drop=T]
library(rpart)
d7.rpart <- rpart(log(Y) ~ ., data=diamonds[,-7], cp=5e-7) # Complex tree
d.rpart <- prune(d7.rpart, cp=0.0025)
printcp(d.rpart)  # Relative to `d7.rpart`, simpler and less accurate
nmin <- which.min(d7.rpart$cptable[,'xerror'])
dOpt.rpart <- prune(d7.rpart, cp=d7.rpart$cptable[nmin,'CP'])
print(dOpt.rpart$cptable[nmin])
(xerror12 <- dOpt.rpart$cptable[c(nrow(d.rpart$cptable),nmin), "xerror"])
 ## Subtract from 1.0 to obtain R-squared statistics
```

Cross-validated relative errors are 0.0593 for `cp=0.0025`, with a minimum of 0.0107 for `cp=0` giving 2314 leaves. The root node error is 1.0295, giving an absolute "error" (here variance, but with divisor n) that equals 0. Check the vignette `vignette("longintro",package="rpart")` for details of the variable importance statistic. Compare the variable importance statistics between the two trees. The following code converts these to percentages of the total:

[4] The probability that any particular point (observation) will be excluded is $(1 - n^{-1})^n$, where n is the sample size. Summing over all points, the expected number excluded is $n(1 - n^{-1})^n$, that is, a fraction $(1 - n^{-1})^n$ of the number of points n.

```
rbind("d.rpart"=d.rpart[['variable.importance']],
      "dOpt.rpart"=dOpt.rpart[['variable.importance']]) |>
  (\(x)100*apply(x,1,function(x)x/sum(x)))() |> round(1) |> t()
```

What differences do you notice between the two sets of percentages? What do those differences indicate? Consider earlier versus later splits, and the handling of what would be interaction effects in linear models.

c. Modify the code in (b) to give the tree object that results when the one-standard-error rule is used.

8.9. Now proceed to use `randomForest::randomForest()` with the `diamonds` data. (Be warned that the calculations may be challenging for computers that have limited memory and/or slow processing units.)

For an initial fit, work with a subset of perhaps 5000 rows:

```
Y <- ggplot2::diamonds[,"price", drop=T]
samp5K <- sample(1:nrow(diamonds), size=5000)
(diamond5K.rf <- randomForest(x=diamonds[samp5K,-7], y=log(Y[samp5K]),
                xtest=diamonds[-samp5K,-7], ytest=log(Y[-samp5K])))
## Omit arguments `xtest` and `ytest` if calculations take too long
```

Note how "% Var explained" compares with the R^2 statistic from `dOpt.rpart` in the previous exercise. If calculations complete within reasonable time, repeat several times. Try also with `sampR5K` replaced by a set of row numbers `sampR10K` that selects 10,000 rows. Does this lead to a noticeable increase in "% Var explained"? Show the importance measure that is available from `diamond5K.rf`, and note any differences from those calculated previously for `dOpt.rpart`.

```
sort(importance(diamond5K.rf)[,1], decreasing=T) |>
  (\(x)100*x/sum(x))() |> round(1) |> t()
```

a. Repeat the calculations in the previous item, but working with `price` as the outcome variable

```
(diamond5KU.rf <- randomForest(x=diamonds[samp5K,-7], y=Y[samp5K],
                xtest=diamonds[-samp5K,-7], ytest=Y[-samp5K]))
```

What change do you notice in "% Var explained"?

9

Multivariate Data Exploration and Discrimination

Earlier chapters have made extensive use of exploratory graphs that have examined variables and their pairwise relationships, as a preliminary to regression modeling. This chapter will move from regression to methods that focus on the pattern presented by multiple variables, albeit with applications in regression analysis.

A starting point will be the use of principal components analysis (PCA) to project the data on to a low-dimensional space, usually two or three dimensions, with the aim of obtaining insightful "views" of the data. New derived "orthogonal" (i.e., uncorrelated) variables that are linear combinations of the original variables, called *principal components*, are extracted and ordered according to the amount of variation that they explain when points are projected onto them. The most insightful plots are often, but not at all inevitably, those for the first few principal components. It may happen, but is by no means guaranteed, that simple modifications of the components will give new variables that are readily interpretable. In a regression context, the hope may be to replace a large number of candidate explanatory variables with a smaller number of principal components, with minimal loss of information.

Cluster analysis, or clustering, describes the exploratory process of grouping alike observations. Like many exploratory methods, these analyses may flag interesting patterns within multivariate data that beg further investigation. Importantly, the results of a cluster analysis may be further used as an explanatory variable in a regression, or similar, context – in essence generating a latent variable from patterns within the data. We will consider several popular approaches.

Discriminant analysis methods, for data where observations belong to one of several "known" classes or groups, are another focus. The aim is to find a rule, based on values of explanatory variables, that will as far as possible assign observations to their correct classes. This rule may then be used to classify new observations whose class is unknown or unclear. An obvious way to evaluate classification rules is to examine their *predictive accuracy*, that is, the accuracy with which they can be expected to assign new observations.

Discriminant analysis methodology is important in its own right. Much as with PCA, it may be used as a data reduction technique. One or several "discriminant components", namely, linear combinations of the candidate variables that for discrimination purposes sum up the information in those variables, may replace explanatory variables, for example, finding use as explanatory variables in a regression analysis. Plots of such components may be useful for data exploration.

Sections that follow discuss issues for the analysis of data, such as from high-throughput genomics, where the aim is to determine, from among large numbers of variables (in the examples considered, thousands or tens of thousands), which are shifted in value between groups in the data.

A section on the role of balance and matching in making inferences from observational data then follows. The chapter ends with a brief introduction to methods for *multiple imputation*, a methodology that aims to use relationships between variables to fill in missing values in observations that are incomplete, allowing those observations can have at least some role in a regression or other further analysis.

9.1 Multivariate Exploratory Data Analysis

Preliminary exploration of the data is as important for multivariate analysis as for classical regression. Examination of relevant scatterplot matrices is often a good starting point. Unexpected features may be apparent in the data. Gross errors will often show up as outliers.

```
## Make the lattice package and the possum dataset available
library(latticeExtra)
possum <- DAAG::possum
```

9.1.1 Scatterplot Matrices

The dataset `possum` was described in Subsection 1.1.5. The interest is in comparing morphometric characteristics between possums at the different Australian sites. Which sites stand out as different, for some or all of the variables? For reasons of simplicity and ease of fitting the plots onto the page, Figures 9.1A and B show only three of the nine variables. Figure 9.1A shows a scatterplot matrix, while Figure 9.1B shows a three-dimensional perspective plot (cloud plot). The footnote has code.[1]

The choice of the particular set of three variables anticipates results of a later analysis, designed to identify the variables that discriminate the populations most effectively. Observe that there are two clusters of points, with each of six sites pretty much restricted to one or other of the clusters. Readers might create for themselves, on a screen or a large sheet of paper, a scatterplot matrix that has all nine variables.

[1]
```
## Colors distinguish sexes; symbols distinguish sites
sitenames <- row.names(DAAG::possumsites)[c(1,2,4:6,3,7)]
key <- list(points = list(pch=0:6), text=list(sitenames),
            columns=4, between=1, between.columns=2)
colr <- c("red","blue")
vnames <- c("tail\nlength","foot\nlength", "conch\nlength")
gphA <- with(possum, splom(~ possum[, 9:11], pch=(0:6)[site], col=colr[sex],
            xlab="",  varnames=vnames, key=key, axis.line.tck=0.6))
gphB <- with(possum, cloud(earconch~taill+footlgth, data=possum,
  col=colr[sex], key=key, pch = (0:6)[site],
  zlab=list("earconch", rot=90), zoom=0.925))
update(c("A: Scatterplot matrix"=gphA, "B: Cloud plot"=gphB),
       between=list(x=1))
```

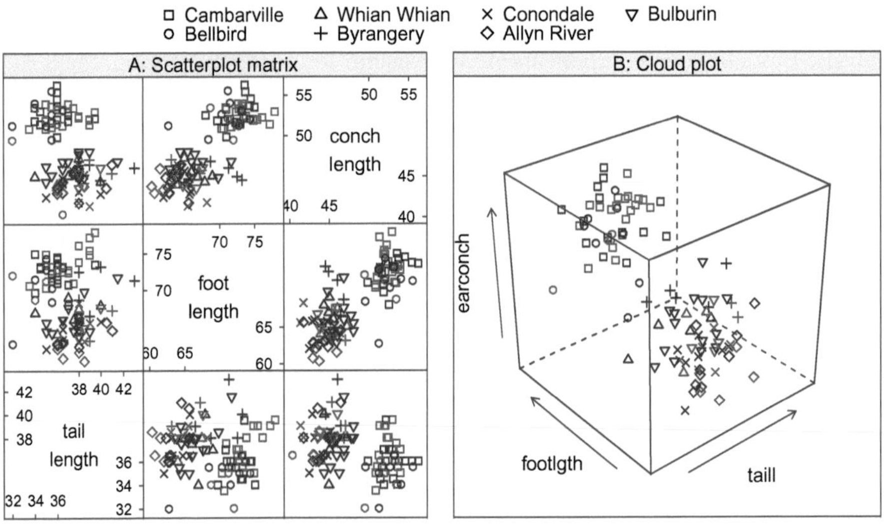

Figure 9.1 Panel A shows the scatterplot matrix for three morphometric measurements on the mountain brushtail possum. Females are in red, and males in blue. Panel B shows a three-dimensional perspective plot (cloud plot), for the same three variables.

9.1.2 Principal Components Analysis

As noted at the beginning of the chapter, the idea is to replace the original variables by one or several "principal components" that are linear combinations of the initial variables and together may account for most of the variation in the data. A useful starting point for thinking about principal component analysis is to imagine a two-dimensional scatterplot of data that has, roughly, the shape of an ellipse. Then the first principal component coincides with the longer axis of the ellipse. For example, if we had just the two variables `footlgth` (foot length) and `earconch` (ear conch length) from the `possum` dataset, then the first principal component would have the direction of a line from the bottom left to the top right of the scatterplot in the first row and second column of Figure 9.1A. (We might equally well examine the plot in the second row and third column, where the x- and y-axes are interchanged.)

In three dimensions the scatter of data has the shape of an ellipsoidal object, for example, the shape of a mango or marrow or other similarly shaped fruit or vegetable, but perhaps flattened on one side. The first principal component is the longest axis. If the first principal component accounts for most of the variation, then the object will be long and thin.

Figure 9.1B gave a three-dimensional representation of the variables shown in Figure 9.1A. Notice that the data form into two clusters – the mango has separated into two parts! One use for principal components and associated plots is to potentially give a visual identification of such clusters.

The scaling of variables is important as those with the highest variance will tend to form the principal axes on their own. If the variables are measured on comparable scales, then unstandardized data may be appropriate. If the scales are not comparable, and especially if the ranges of variables are very different, then standardization may be appropriate. Use of the logarithms of measurements is usually desirable for morphometric (shape and size) data such as in the `possum` data frame, thus placing all variables on a scale on which equal distances correspond to equal relative changes. The first component is often an overall measure of size. This may be of less interest than later principal components that capture differences in relative body dimensions.

For the `possum` data frame, interest will be in using principal components, created from the morphometric data in columns 6 to 14, to investigate differences between sites and sexes. Changes with age, which also require attention, will be investigated here only to the extent of comparing the distributions of ages between sites.

Preliminary Data Scrutiny

Ratios of largest to smallest value are, for all variables, 1.6 or less:

```
## Ratios of largest to smallest values: possum[, 6:14] (DAAG)
possum <- DAAG::possum
sapply(na.omit(possum[, 6:14]), function(x)round(max(x)/min(x),2))
```

```
 hdlngth    skullw totlngth      taill footlgth earconch         eye
    1.25      1.37     1.29       1.34     1.29     1.36        1.39
   chest     belly
    1.45      1.60
```

As a consequence, taking logarithms would make little difference to the appearance of the scatterplots.

The underlying trends in these morphometric measurements are close to linearly related, so that examination of the linear combinations that emerge from a principal components analysis makes good sense. The first principal component, when there are m variables, is given by the line that minimizes the average squared distance from the line in the m-dimensional space spanned by the (perhaps scaled) variables. At the same time the variance of the projected data, calculated as the variance of the distance of points along the line, is maximized. The second principal component is the component that, among linear combinations of the variables that are uncorrelated with the first principal component, explains the greatest part of the remaining variation, and so on.

Different pairs of principal components allow different two-dimensional views of the data. A usual first step is to plot the second principal component against the first principal component. Or, a scatterplot matrix form of presentation can be used to examine all the pairwise plots for the first three or four principal components.

Calculations will use the function `prcomp()`. This is preferred to the older function `princomp()` which uses a generally less accurate algorithm. In order to obtain coefficients that are unique to within multiplication by ±-1, the `prcomp()` function scales them so that their squares sum to one. The function `prcomp()` uses the usual $n-1$, not n as for `princomp()`, as the divisor for calculating the variances.

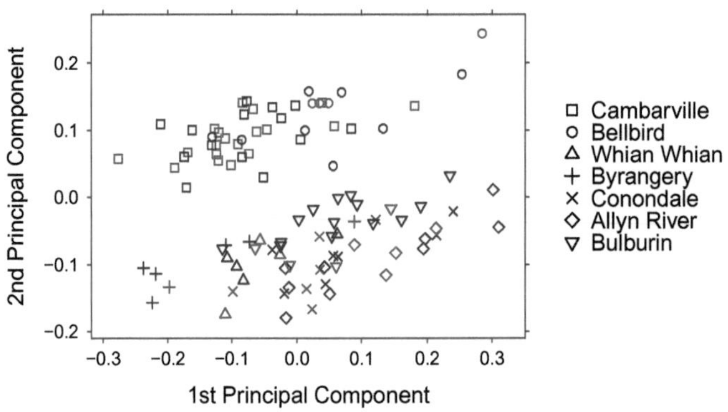

Figure 9.2 Second versus first principal component, for variables in columns 6 to 14 of the `possum` data frame, after logarithmic transformation. Females are in red, males in blue. Scales have been chosen so that units are the same on both axes.

The coefficients for the principal components are referred to as `rotations` rather than "loadings," and the values that result are stored in a list element that has the name `x`, otherwise known as "scores."

The following calculates the principal component scores, after logarithmic transformation, for variables 6 to 14 in the `possum` data:

```
## Principal components calculations: possum[, 6:14] (DAAG)
here <- complete.cases(possum[, 6:14])
possum.prc <- prcomp(log(possum[here, 6:14]))
scores <- cbind(predict(possum.prc), possum[here, c('sex', 'site')])
```

Figure 9.2 plots the second principal component against the first. The main part of the code is:

```
## For parset, key and colr; see code for Fig 9.1
pchr <- c(3,4,0,8,2,10,1)
parset <- list(fontsize=list(text=10, points=6), cex=0.75, pch=pchr, alpha=0.8)
key <- modifyList(key, list(columns=1, space="right"))
gph <- with(scores, xyplot(PC2 ~ PC1, aspect="iso", key = key,
          col = colr[sex], pch = (0:6)[site]))
```

Use of the argument `aspect="iso"` gives units that are the same on both axes.

Here are further details of the principal components output:

```
print(summary(possum.prc),digits=2)
## By default, blanks are shown for loadings < 0.1 in magnitude
```

```
Importance of components:
                        PC1  PC2   PC3   PC4   PC5   PC6   PC7   PC8    PC9
Standard deviation     0.13 0.10 0.064 0.054 0.051 0.035 0.027 0.025 0.0186
Proportion of Variance 0.42 0.26 0.105 0.074 0.066 0.032 0.019 0.016 0.0089
Cumulative Proportion  0.42 0.68 0.784 0.859 0.925 0.956 0.975 0.991 1.0000

Rotations (otherwise called Loadings)
           PC1    PC2   PC3    PC4    PC5    PC6     PC7    PC8    PC9
hdlngth  -0.24 -0.068 0.067 -0.146  0.024 -0.294 -0.0048 -0.463  0.782
skullw   -0.30 -0.133 0.079 -0.325  0.277 -0.703  0.2093  0.319 -0.253
totlngth -0.30 -0.082 0.022 -0.321 -0.387  0.034 -0.0140 -0.628 -0.506
```

```
taill    -0.11 -0.315 -0.073 -0.351 -0.631  0.196  0.2189  0.462  0.249
footlgth -0.32  0.416  0.119 -0.099 -0.198 -0.081 -0.7644  0.260  0.034
earconch -0.23  0.752  0.162  0.077 -0.149  0.049  0.5671  0.029  0.039
eye      -0.18 -0.283  0.897  0.186  0.061  0.203  0.0165  0.047 -0.019
chest    -0.52 -0.037 -0.223 -0.283  0.529  0.563  0.0252  0.059  0.036
belly    -0.55 -0.228 -0.297  0.718 -0.170 -0.114  0.0338  0.039 -0.040
```

Most of the variation is in the first three or four principal components. Components 5 and 6 each explain only 3 percent of the variance, and later components, individually, even less. The variation in these later components is so small that it may well mostly represent noise in the data.

The loadings are the multiples of the original (logged) variables that add to form a principal component. To a close approximation, the first component (`PC1`) is:

-0.24×`hdlngth`-0.30×`skullw`-0.30×`totlngth`-0.11×`taill`
-0.32×`footlgth`-0.23×`earconch`-0.18×`eye`-0.52×`chest`-0.55×`belly`

This first component can be interpreted as a weighted sum of the magnitudes of the logarithms of the variables – it is a size component. The negative signs are an accident of the computations – they might equally well have all been positive. It will be large in magnitude (and, here, negative) for animals that are overall large in body dimensions.

The Stability of the Principal Components Plot

Figure 9.2 shows a clear separation into two groups, distinguishing Bellbird and Cambarville from the other sites. Bootstrap methodology offers a means to check the stability, relative to statistical variation, of the clusters that are apparent. A dataset in which each of the sample observations is repeated an infinite number of times is used to represent the population from which the `possum` dataset was taken. Sampling with replacement from the original sample, otherwise called bootstrap sampling, is used to choose a new sample of the same size as the original sample, from this infinite population. This is done for each of the seven sites, thus giving a bootstrap sample data frame `bsample1.possum` that replaces the original data. The process is repeated several times, giving further such data frames `bsample2.possum`, `bsample3.possum`, etc.

The steps that led to Figure 9.2 are then repeated for each of these bootstrap sample data frames, and plots obtained that reproduce Figure 9.2 for each of these bootstrap sample data frames. Figure 9.3 presents three such plots. The graphs are simplified so that they distinguish the two Victorian sites (Cambarville and Bellbird) from the other five sites. All three panels show a similar distinction between the two sets of sites, indicating that the view given by the principal components is reasonably stable with respect to sampling variation.

The following gives a slightly stripped down version of Figure 9.3:

```
suppressPackageStartupMessages(library(ggplot2))
## Bootstrap principal components calculations: possum (DAAG)
## Sample from rows where there are no missing values
rowsfrom <- (1:nrow(possum))[complete.cases(possum[, 6:14])]
logpossum6to14 <- log(possum[rowsfrom, 6:14])
sexPop <- possum[rowsfrom, c("sex","Pop")]
n <- length(rowsfrom); ntimes <- 3
```

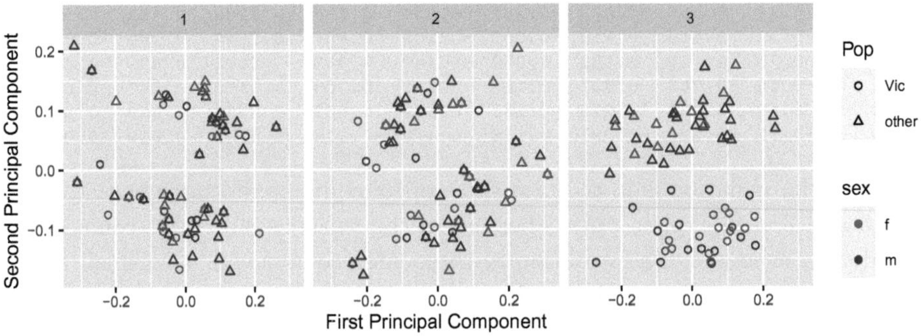

Figure 9.3 This repeats Figure 9.2, now for logarithms of variables in columns 6 to 14 of the three bootstrap versions of the `possum` data.

```
bootscores <- data.frame(scores1=numeric(ntimes*n), scores2=numeric(ntimes*n))
for (i in 1:ntimes){
  samprows <- sample(1:n, n, replace=TRUE)
  bootscores[n*(i-1)+(1:n), 1:2] <-
  prcomp(logpossum6to14[samprows, ])$x[, 1:2]
}
bootscores[, c("sex","Pop")] <- sexPop[samprows, ]
bootscores$sampleID <- factor(rep(1:ntimes, rep(n,ntimes)))
gph <- quickplot(x=scores1, y=scores2, colour=sex, size=I(1.0),
  asp=1, shape=Pop, facets=.~sampleID, data=bootscores) +
  scale_shape_discrete(solid=F)
```

The PCA form of mathematical representation has applications in many contexts aside from those discussed here. As used here, PCA is a special case of a much wider class of multidimensional scaling (MDS) methods. Subsection 9.1.3 is a brief introduction to this wider class of methods.

9.1.3 Multidimensional Scaling

We noted above that PCA, in the use made of it here, is a special case of a much wider class of multidimensional scaling (MDS) methods. MDS starts with a matrix of "distances" between points. Classical MDS with Euclidean distance (in three-dimensional space this is just the usual "distance") is equivalent to a principal components representation, working with the unscaled variables. MDS thus allows a choice of a distance measure that can in principle more closely match the scientific requirements. Computational demands can be severe, relative to principal components approaches.

Distance Measures

For some commonly used non-Euclidean distances, see `?dist`, or, for a more extensive range of possibilities, the help page for the function `?cluster::daisy`. The function `cmdscale()` implements classical MDS.

A simple example of a non-Euclidean distance (a 'metric') is the `"manhattan"`. In two dimensions this is the smallest walking distance between street corners,

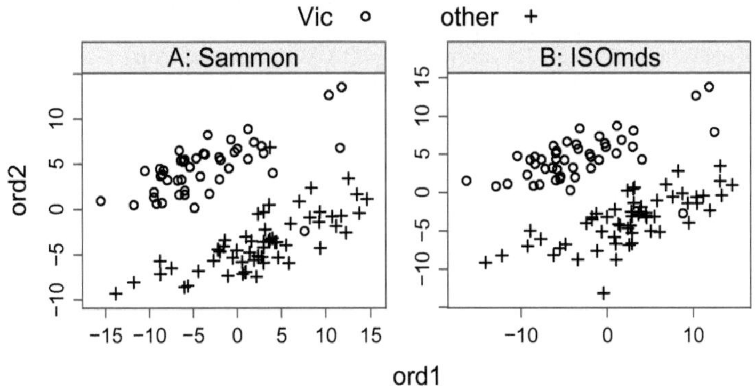

Figure 9.4 Two-dimensional representations have been obtained from Euclidean distances in a nine-dimensional space. Panel A used Sammon scaling, while Panel B used Kruskal's Nonmetric Multidimensional Scaling.

taking a succession of left and/or right turns along streets that are laid out in a two-dimensional grid.

In some applications, a distance measure arises naturally from the way that the data are believed to have been generated. Thus, for gene sequences, the function `ape::dist.dna()` has several different measures of distance that arise from different models for the evolutionary process.

Ordination

In classical ("metric") MDS the distances, however derived, are treated as Euclidean. The function `cmdscale()` implements this methodology, seeking a configuration of points in a low-dimensional space that as far as possible preserves the distances. Nonmetric methods typically use classical MDS to derive a starting configuration.

The propensity scores that will be discussed in Subsection 9.7.4 (see Figure 9.24), which lie between 0 and 1, are an example of a separation measure that it is not appropriate to treat as Euclidean distances. Or it may be appropriate to treat small distances as more accurate and give greater weight to small distances. The Sammon method (see `?MASS::sammon`), described as a "semimetric" method, minimizes a weighted sum of squared differences between the supplied and the fitted distances, with weights inversely proportional to the distance. At the other extreme from fully metric methods are nonmetric methods such as Kruskal's, which the function `MASS::isoMDS()` implements. Nonmetric MDS is a challenge for optimization algorithms, and calculations may take a long time.

Figure 9.4 demonstrates the use of `sammon()` (Panel A), and `isoMDS()` (Panel B) to obtain two-dimensional representations from Euclidean distances in a nine-dimensional space: The plots are closely aligned. A rotation and a reflection will bring them into remarkably close alignment with Figure 9.2.

```
## Code that will display individual graphs
d.possum <- dist(possum[,6:14]) # Euclidean distance matrix
MASS::sammon(d.possum, k=2, trace=FALSE)$points |> as.data.frame() |>
```

```
  setNames(paste0("ord",1:2)) |> cbind(Pop=DAAG::possum$Pop) -> sammon.possum
MASS::isoMDS(d.possum, k=2, trace=FALSE) |> as.data.frame() |>
  setNames(paste0("ord",1:2)) |> cbind(Pop=DAAG::possum$Pop) -> mds.possum
gph1 <- xyplot(ord2~ord1, groups=Pop, aspect="iso", data=sammon.possum)
gph2 <- xyplot(ord2~ord1, groups=Pop, aspect="iso", data=mds.possum)
```

For further details, see Venables and Ripley (2002), Gordon (1999), Cox and Cox (2000), and Izenman (2008).

Binary Data

Binary data raise special issues, both for the choice of distance measure and for the choice of MDS methodology. For the "binary" measure, the number of bits where only one is "on" (i.e., equal to one) is divided by the number where at least one is on. If it turns out that distances of 1.0 are a substantial proportion of the total data, they may then not be very informative. Points that are at distances of 1.0 from each other and from most other points cannot, if there are many of them, be accurately located in the low-dimensional space.

It is then undesirable to give much weight to distances close to or equal to 1.0. Use of `sammon()` or `isoMDS()` is then much preferable to use of `cmdscale()`. The plots may have a striking visual appearance, with points for which distances from most other points are close to 1.0 lying on a circle around the boundary of the total configuration of points.

9.2 Principal Component Scores in Regression

The dataset `socsupport`, from a survey that was designed to collect from students information on social and other kinds of support, has the following columns.

1, 2. `gender` (male, female); `age` (18-20, 21-24, 25-30, 31-40, 40+)
3. `country`: Australia, other
4, 5. `marital` (married, single, other); `livewith` (alone, friends, parents, partner, residences, other)
6. `employment`: full-time, part-time, govt assistance, parental support, other
7, 8. `firstyr` (first year, other); `enrolment` (full-time, part-time, blank)
9, 10. `emotional`, `emotionalsat`: availability of emotional support, and associated satisfaction (5 questions each)
11, 12. `tangible`, `tangiblesat`: availability of tangible support and associated satisfaction (4 questions each)
13, 14. `affect`, `affectsat`: availability of affectionate support sources and associated satisfaction (3 questions each)
15, 16. `psi`, `psisat`: availability of positive social interaction and associated satisfaction (3 questions each)
17, 18, 19. `esupport` (emotional), `psupport` (practical), `socsupport` (social): extent of support sources (4 questions each)
20. `BDI`: Score on the Beck depression index (total over 21 questions)

The Beck depression index (`BDI`) is a standard psychological measure of depression (see, for example, Streiner et al. (2014)). The data are from individuals who were generally normal and healthy. One interest was in studying how the support measures (columns 9 to 19 in the data frame) may affect `BDI`, and in what bearing the information in columns 1 to 8 may have. Pairwise correlations between the 11 measures range from 0.28 to 0.85. In the regression of `BDI` on all the variables 9 to 19, nothing appears significant, though the F-statistic makes it clear that, overall, there is a statistically detectable effect. It is not possible to disentangle the effects of these various explanatory variables. Attempts to take account of variables 1 to 8 will only make matters worse. Variable selection has the difficulties noted in Chapter 3.

Additionally, any attempt to interpret individual regression coefficients focuses attention on specific variables, where a careful account will acknowledge that we observe their combined effect. Hence, the attraction of a methodology that, prior to any use of regression methods, has the potential to reduce the 11 variables to some smaller number of variables that together account for the major part of the variation. Surveys of this type are often devised, as here, with a view to an analysis that works with principal components scores.

The number of questions whose scores were added varied, ranging from 3 to 5. This makes it more than usually desirable to base the principal components calculation on the correlation matrix rather than the variance–covariance matrix.

These were the steps followed in the analysis.

1. Scores for the first six principal components were taken from a principal components calculation on variables 9 through to 19.
2. A regression analysis that had `BDI` as the response variable then used the six sets of scores as explanatory variables. The first run of this regression calculation identified an outlier, which was then omitted and the calculation repeated.
3. Loadings on the one component in the regression output that appeared important were then checked.

Code to do the initial analysis is:

```
## Principal components: data frame socsupport (DAAG)
socsupport <- DAAG::socsupport
ss.pr1 <- prcomp(as.matrix(na.omit(socsupport[, 9:19])), retx=TRUE, scale=TRUE)
```

Figure 9.5 shows the scatterplot matrix for the first three principal component scores. There is one clear outlier on the first component, which we can identify thus:

```
summary(sort(ss.pr1$rotation[,1]))
```

```
   Min. 1st Qu.  Median    Mean 3rd Qu.    Max.
 -0.351  -0.314  -0.294  -0.301  -0.286  -0.262
```

```
## Note the very large maximum value
which.max(ss.pr1$x[,1])
```

```
36
34
```

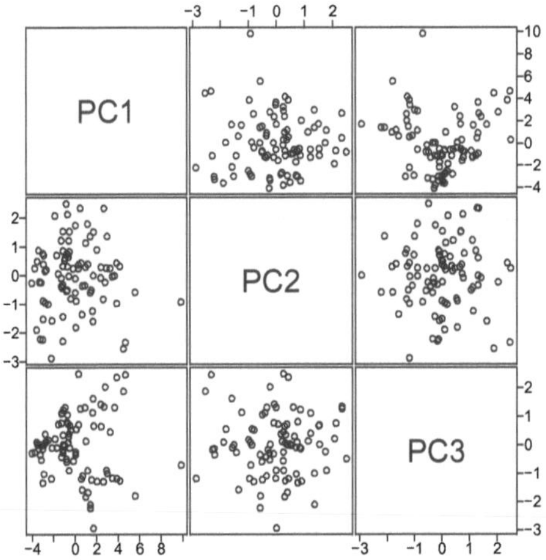

Figure 9.5 Pairs plot of first three principal components.

```
## Try also boxplot(ss.pr1$x[,1])
## ss.pr1$x["36",1]  ## Check that this returns 42
```

The name "36" for the point that we have identified as an outlier is the row name in the initial file. We omit this point and repeat the calculation.

```
use <- complete.cases(socsupport[, 9:19])
use[36] <- FALSE
ss.pr <- prcomp(as.matrix(socsupport[use, 9:19]))
```

The output from `summary(ss.pr)` is

```
Importance of components:
                       PC1 PC2 PC3  PC4  PC5  PC6  PC7  PC8  PC9  PC10  PC11
Standard deviation     6.7 3.7 3.2 2.47 1.96 1.82 1.32 1.20 0.99 0.901 0.587
Proportion of Variance 0.5 0.2 0.1 0.07 0.04 0.04 0.02 0.02 0.01 0.009 0.004
Cumulative Proportion  0.5 0.7 0.8 0.86 0.90 0.94 0.96 0.98 0.99 0.996 1.000
```

Now regress BDI on the first six principal components. Because the successive columns of scores are uncorrelated, the coefficients are independent. Extraneous terms that contribute little except noise will have little effect on residual mean square, and hence to the standard errors. Thus, there is no reason to restrict the number of terms that we choose for initial examination. The coefficients in the regression output are:

```
comp <- as.data.frame(ss.pr$x[,1:6])
ss.lm <- lm(socsupport[use, "BDI"] ~ ., data=comp)
signif(round(coef(summary(ss.lm)),5), digits=3)
```

```
            Estimate Std. Error t value Pr(>|t|)
(Intercept)  10.5000      0.892  11.700  0.00000
PC1           0.4260      0.134   3.190  0.00203
PC2          -0.2150      0.239  -0.899  0.37100
PC3           0.0974      0.278   0.350  0.72800
PC4          -0.5950      0.363  -1.640  0.10500
```

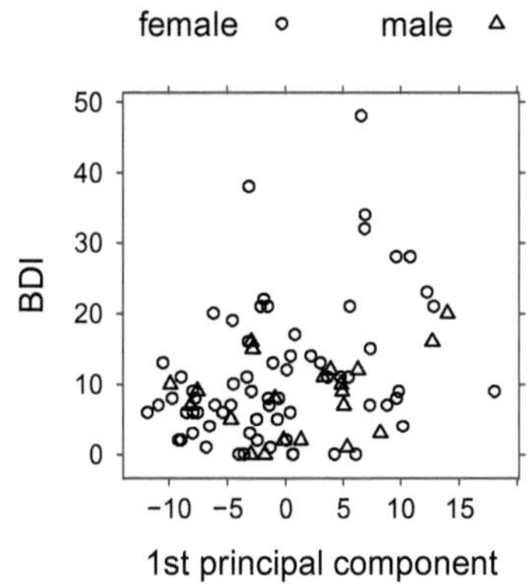

Figure 9.6 Plot of BDI against scores on the first principal component.

```
PC5           0.6330     0.457   1.390  0.16900
PC6          -0.9880     0.493  -2.010  0.04820
```

Components other than the first do not make an evident contribution to prediction of BDI. Compare $p = 0.00007$ for scores on the first component with p-values for later sets of scores. For component 5, $p > 0.07$; otherwise $p > 0.18$.

Loadings for the first component are:[2]

```
print(ss.pr$rotation[, 1], digits=2)
```

```
 emotional emotionalsat     tangible  tangiblesat       affect    affectsat
     -0.39        -0.31        -0.36        -0.31        -0.32        -0.27
       psi       psisat     esupport     psupport  supsources
     -0.29        -0.25        -0.24        -0.32        -0.22
```

The first component is, in this analysis, akin to an average of the 11 measures, albeit multiplied by -1 because of an accident of the algorithmic processes. Figure 9.6 plots BDI against the scores on the first principal component, using different colors and symbols for females and males. This should be repeated for each of the other seven factors represented by columns 1 to 8 of the data frame `socsupport`.

Two observations appear anomalous, with BDI indices that are high relative to their scores on the first principal component. Both are females. We leave it as an exercise for the reader to recalculate the principal components with these points omitted, and repeat the regression.

Regression on principal component scores has identified a clear effect from the social support variables. It is not possible to ascribe these effects, with any confidence, to individual variables. The attempt to ascribe effects to individual social support variables, independently of other support variables, can anyway be misguided. They exercise their effects in combination.

[2] The vector is unique up to multiplication by -1. It is an accident of the algorithmic processes that, in this instance, all coefficients are negative.

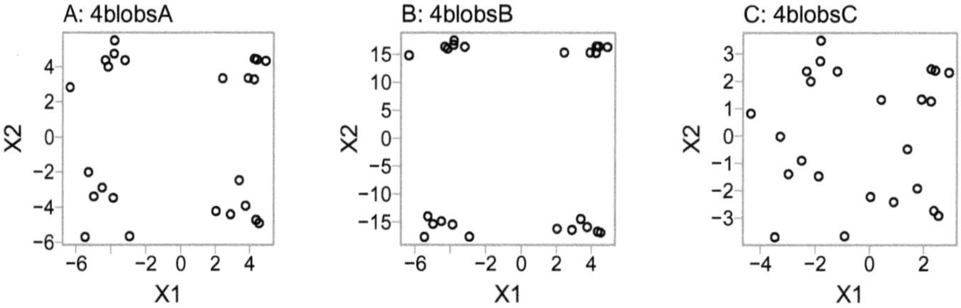

Figure 9.7 In Panel A, the four "blobs" of uncorrelated multivariate normal data have mean values (centers) that are set nearly equidistant from each other. In Panel B, the blobs from Panel A have been pulled vertically. In Panel C, centers have been shifted to be closer together, better reflecting what might be expected with real data.

9.3 Cluster Analysis

The word "clusters" was used in the previous section to describe the visual separation within the `possum` dataset. Cluster analysis, or just clustering, describes automated approaches for seeking these types of separations in, potentially high-dimension, multivariate data. Common approaches for cluster analysis, or clustering, include hierarchical (both agglomerative and divisive), *k*-means, and mixture model-based.

9.3.1 Hierarchical Clustering

Hierarchical methods operate in an iterative manner on pairwise distance/similarity measures/metrics, which provides a degree of flexibility for the user in small-to-moderate sample sizes as these methods remain applicable regardless of the variable types observed in the data – if a sensible pairwise distance measure can be computed, then clustering can commence. The three panels in Figure 9.7 show three different patterns of separation of the means of four blobs of uncorrelated multivariate normal data. These will feature in the discussion that follows.

```
library(mvtnorm)
makeClust <- function(n=6, d1=4, d2=4, sigs=c(1, 1, 1, 1), seed=NULL){
  if(!is.null(seed))set.seed(seed)
  g1 <- rmvnorm(n, mean = c(-d1,d2), sigma=sigs[1]*diag(2))
  g2 <- rmvnorm(n, mean = c(d1,d2), sigma=sigs[2]*diag(2))
  g3 <- rmvnorm(n, mean = c(-d1,-d2), sigma=sigs[3]*diag(2))
  g4 <- rmvnorm(n, mean = c(d1,-d2), sigma=sigs[4]*diag(2))
  rbind(g1,g2,g3,g4)
}
```

```
## Code for the plots
datA <- makeClust(seed=35151)
datB <- makeClust(d2=16, seed=35151)
datC <- makeClust(d1=2,d2=2, seed=35151)
plot(datA, xlab="X1", ylab="X2", fg="gray")
title(main="A: 4blobsA", adj=0, line=0.5, font.main=1)
## Repeat previous two lines for datB and datC
```

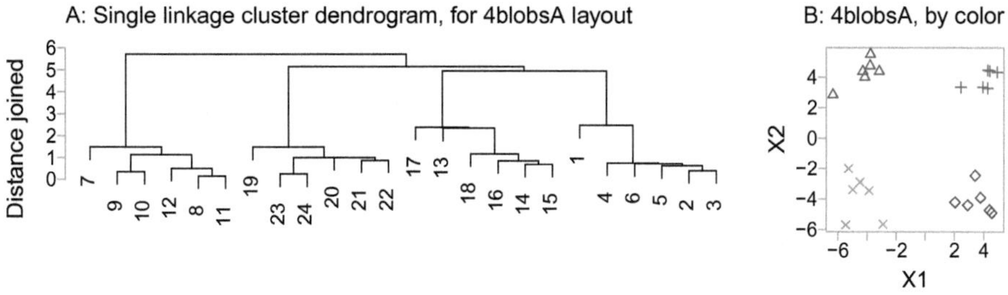

Figure 9.8 Panel A shows results from single linkage hierarchical clustering, for the data shown in Figure 9.7A. The four large vertical jumps in the dendrogram mark off four groups of points. Panel B distinguishes these four groups of points of points by color. Observe that these four groups coincide with the four blobs of points.

In the agglomerative approach to hierarchical clustering, each observation begins in its own "cluster." Next, the two closest observations are combined to form the first multiobservation cluster. Software traditionally provides several options for defining the distance between this new cluster and the remaining clusters, referred to as "linkage." We will shortly introduce three common linkage methods. Supposing for the moment that the distance between the new cluster and other clusters is defined, we then return to combining clusters together according to the minimum pairwise distance. This process is repeated until only one cluster remains, which then contains all observations in the data.

Returning to linkages, the (perhaps) most intuitive way to compute the distance between two groups of objects is by measuring the distance between the two closest points, usually referred to as "single linkage." "Average linkage" requires consideration of the pairwise distances between all observations across each cluster and subsequently averaging those values. Finally, "complete linkage" defines the distance between clusters as the distance between the two furthest points.

Interestingly, while single linkage certainly has its niche use cases, it tends to underperform most other linkage types in many practical applications. Before we see why, we must consider how we might visualize the process we just described as agglomerative clustering. Dendrograms provide the observations along the X-axis and graphically display the distance at which those observations (and subsequently as we move up vertically, those *clusters* of observations) are joined. As such, they provide a useful visualization of the entire clustering algorithm, including, importantly, a visual cue for a potential data-driven argument for the appropriate number of clusters within the data. As we move vertically upwards across the span of the dendrogram, there may exist a large "jump" wherein no observations (or clusters of observations) are being joined together.

```
## Code for single linkage plots: `?plot.hclust` gives help for the plot method
clusres_sing <- hclust(dist(datA), method="single")
par(fig=c(0,0.75,0,1))
plot(clusres_sing, sub="", xlab="", ylab="Distance joined", adj=0.5,
    main="", fg="gray")
mtext('A: Single linkage cluster dendrogram, for 4blobsA layout', side=3, adj=0,
    font=1, line=1, cex=1.15)
```

```
par(fig=c(0.72,1,0,1), new=TRUE)
membs <- cutree(clusres_sing, 4)
col4= RColorBrewer::brewer.pal(4,'Set1')
plot(datA, xlab="X1", ylab="X2", col=col4[membs], fg='gray', pch=membs+1)
mtext('B: 4blobsA, by color', side=3, adj=1.0, font=1, cex=1.15, line=1)
## To see plots from 'average' and 'complete' linkage methods,do:
# plot(hclust(dist(datB), method="average"))
# plot(hclust(dist(datC), method="complete"))
```

Figure 9.7A, where respective means for the four blobs are set nearly equidistant from each other, illustrates this. The resulting dendrograms are, because the blobs are clearly separated, quite similar across all linkages. Figure 9.8A shows the result for the first linkage type.

The largest "jump" where no groups are joined as we move vertically along the dendrogram occurs where four lines remain from left-to-right – this is also true for the other linkage types. This hints towards the existence of four groups for each solution, and sure enough these solutions agree on the group memberships therein. Figure 9.8B uses colors to distinguish the groups in the single linkage result.

Now, real data are rarely this well behaved, so it behooves us to consider how trivial changes to this simulation can affect the results. As we are using Euclidean distance by default via the "dist()" command, we can easily stir the pot by focusing changes on the scale of the axes. We simply pull the "blobs" vertically, as can be seen in Panel B in Figure 9.7.

Viewing the scatterplot in Figure 9.7B, it still seems apparent that four groups exist; however, the objective criterion we previously discussed for interpreting the dendrogram in Figure 9.9A now tells a consistently different story: that two groups appears to be preferred. This is because of the fact that observations are distinctly separated across the X2 axis due to the increased scale there. A simple fix is a change of distance measure, specifically using standardized Euclidean wherein each

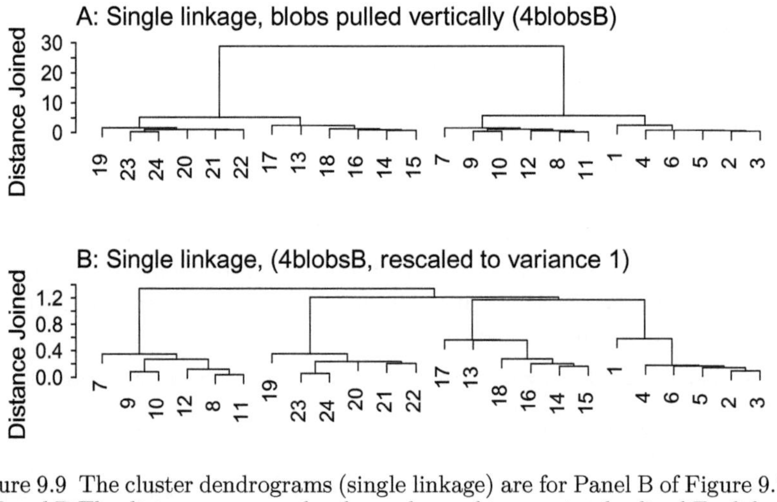

Figure 9.9 The cluster dendrograms (single linkage) are for Panel B of Figure 9.7. In Panel B The distance measure has been changed to use standardized Euclidean distances. Each variable is rescaled to have variance 1.

variable is rescaled to have variance 1. Figure 9.9B shows the result from using the scale() command on the data prior to computing the pairwise distances. The dendrogram has returned to approximately what we had seen in the original more well-behaved simulation.

For real data analyses where automated clustering methods are a necessity, clusters tend to be less well defined, often overlapping among a majority of variables. In Figure 9.7C, the centers have been shifted closer to one another. Figure 9.10 shows the resulting dendrograms, for the three clustering methods.

The average and complete linkage dendrograms are still relatively informative towards the four-group solution. The single-linkage dendrogram, on the other hand, at the very least suggests a group of one observation (13) in addition to the four groups that a seasoned dendrogram interpreter might see forming.

```
## Code. Follow each use of `hclust()` with a `plot()` command
clusres_sing2 <- hclust(dist(datC), method="single")
clusres_avg2 <- hclust(dist(datC), method="average")
clusres_comp2 <- hclust(dist(datC), method="complete")
```

To finish off our focus on hierarchical clustering, we note several pitfalls for this particular cluster analysis for practitioners. Computationally, large sample sizes pose a threat as pairwise ($n \times n$ symmetric) distance matrices become prohibitively expensive to calculate, store, and update. As we've hinted at in the simulations, clustering results can be quite sensitive to linkage method and distance measures, which may lack strong justification prior to the analysis being undertaken. Finally,

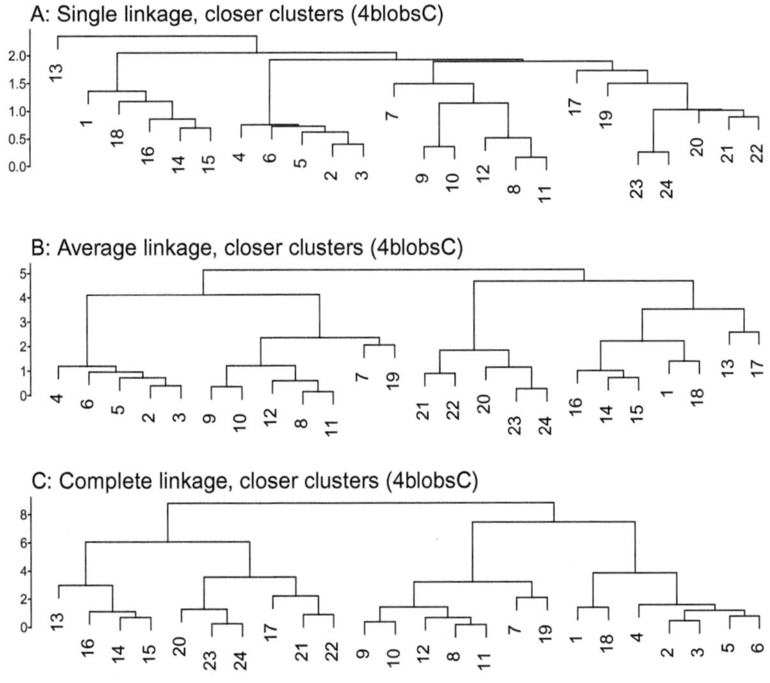

Figure 9.10 Dendrograms shown are from moving clusters closer together.

among the methods we will discuss, hierarchical clustering is uniquely suited to provide groups that consist of a solitary observation. The pessimistic view of this is that it runs somewhat counter to the *idea* of a "cluster," but an optimist would note that this may serve some purpose as an unsupervised form of outlier detection. It is worth reminding the reader, in light of the usage of simulations with known underlying groups, that a true cluster analysis is exploratory in nature.

9.3.2 k-Means Clustering

The k-means algorithm for clustering, and its countless variants, continues to be the cluster analysis of choice in many disciplines. This is despite the strong assumptions that a traditional k-means implementation makes on the underlying data. Through recursively minimizing the within-group sum of squares for a set number of groups, k-means contains an implicit assumption of equal-sized (in Euclidean space, not sample size) and spherical groups which then dictates the clustering boundaries. This further implicitly assumes local independence across the variables within the groups. The end result does not provide spherical-looking groups, necessarily, since the spheres will often overlap. We continue with our simulation theme, first noting that k-means would have no difficulty with the initial simulation shown in Figure 9.7. However, by merely varying the space that some of the clusters inhabit, we can show where these implicit assumptions go awry. The major change in the following code is providing a small variety in the variance for X1 and X2 in the groups. For clarity purposes, we increase sample sizes as well. The resulting groups shown in Figure 9.11 illustrate how the equal-sized groups assumption can negatively affect clustering results, as outlying points from the two larger groups on the bottom are scooped up by the smaller groups above, even though all four of the groups seem well separated.

```
set.seed(35151)
kdat <- makeClust(n=100, d1=5, d2=5, sigs=c(.5, .5, 6, 6))
plot(kdat, xlab="X1", ylab="X2", fg="gray")
kmres <- kmeans(kdat, 4, nstart=30)
plot(kdat, col=rainbow(4)[kmres$cluster], pch=kmres$cluster+1,
    xlab="X1", ylab="X2", fg="gray")
```

The continued popularity of k-means is almost certainly due to its computational efficiency versus most other clustering methods, as it requires only recursively computing distances between group centroids and the observations (as compared with, say, all pairwise distances among observations for hierarchical), making it skimp on resources as both the number of observations and the dimensionality grow as compared to almost any other sensible clustering methodology. Many useful extensions are available in the literature, including k-prototypes for mixed variable types (Huang, 1997) and fuzzy C-means (Bezdek et al., 1984) for soft cluster allocations.

Beyond pitfalls already stressed, it's noteworthy that k-means is sensitive to random initialization, but this is usually dealt with through brute force of using many random starts (as shown in the code just presented, via the `nstart` argument). Finally, we comment that a standard, Euclidean implementation should generally only be considered on continuous, or very nearly continuous, variables.

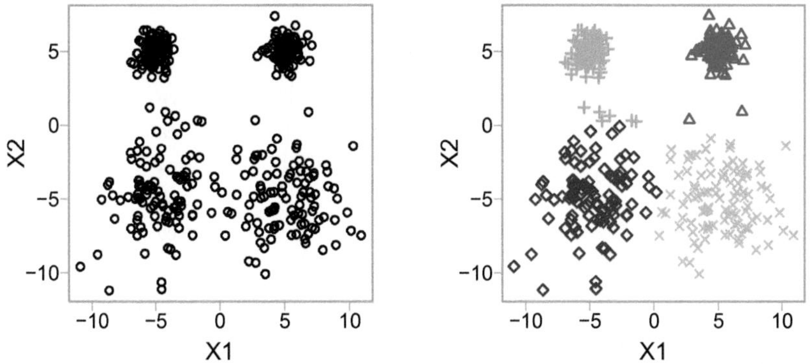

Figure 9.11 A four-group k-means example illustrating the implicit equal-sized assumption.

Comments on k-Means and Hierarchical Clustering

Both hierarchical methods and k-means-type methods assign each observation wholly to one, and only one, group (except for variants specifically built to do otherwise, such as fuzzy C-means). Both methods have suggestions in the literature for arguments related to the number of groups present in the data, some of which are objective and some of which are subjective. While we have not delved deeply into the underlying details of either sets of procedures, both approaches could be largely summarized as heuristic methods to generate feasible groupings for certain forms of observed datasets.

From a statistician's viewpoint, they remain largely unsatisfying as it is somewhat unclear what form of model is being assumed to generate the results of the cluster analysis. We will return to this thought after introducing mixture model-based clustering, as there is an argument for a familiar, though obfuscated, statistical model underlying k-means.

9.3.3 Mixture Model-Based Clustering

Finite mixture models are constructed via a convex combination (positively weighted sum, with weights constrained to sum to 1) of probability distributions. Of course, being a convex combination ensures that a finite mixture model itself *is* a probability distribution. Interestingly, if one simply assumes that the groups presumed to exist within a dataset have arisen under differing probability conditions, then *ipso facto* some form of mixture model provides the generative model for the data. This, in essence, serves as the underpinning for arguing that mixture model-based cluster analysis is the "only clustering technique that is entirely satisfactory from the mathematical point of view. It assumes a well-defined mathematical model, investigates it by well-established statistical techniques, and provides a test of significance for the results" (Marriott, 1974, pg. 70). For a mixture model to be a useful approach *to that extent* for cluster analysis, one still needs to assume the approximately correct form of the probability distributions and subsequently fit that model "blindly" to the observed data. Blindly here refers to the lack of knowledge

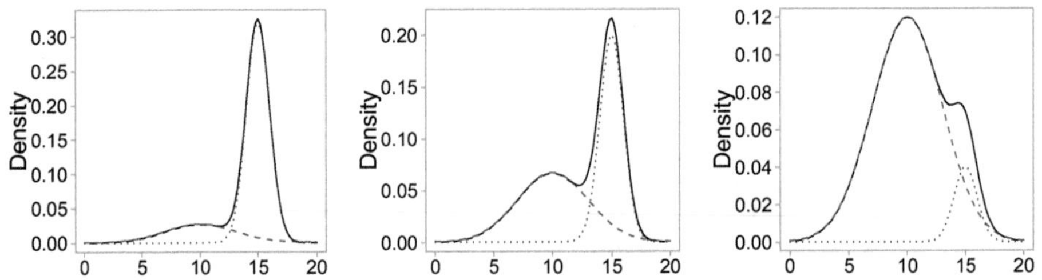

Figure 9.12 Two-component mixtures of univariate Gaussians with differing population proportions. The solid/black line is the mixture distribution, red/dashed line is component one, blue/dotted line is component two.

for which observations arose from which probability distribution. Clearly, these are large hurdles to overcome.

While finite mixture models in general are not constrained to particular probability densities, it is common practice to construct mixture models using a single parametric family. Far and away the most popular approach is finite mixtures of multivariate normal/Gaussian distributions, though many more flexible implementations have become available over the past decade (see, for example, McNicholas, 2016). Herein, we will utilize the *teigen* package (Andrews et al., 2018) which can implement both multivariate Gaussian and multivariate t mixtures. A random vector $\mathbf{X}_i$ is realized from a finite mixture of multivariate Gaussian distributions if its distribution takes the form

$$f(\mathbf{x}_i) = \sum_{g=1}^{G} \tau_g \Phi\left(\mathbf{x}_i \mid \boldsymbol{\mu}_g, \boldsymbol{\Sigma}_g\right), \tag{9.1}$$

where G underlying groups/components/clusters are assumed at a population proportion of τ_g with $\sum_{g=1}^{G} \tau_g = 1$, and Φ is the multivariate Gaussian distribution of equivalent dimension to the observation vector $\mathbf{x}_i$ with mean vector $\boldsymbol{\mu}_g$ and covariance $\boldsymbol{\Sigma}_g$ as the defining parameters. We illustrate several two-component univariate Gaussian mixtures in Figure 9.12.

```
## Code
plotMix2 <- function(taus=c(.5, .5), means=c(10,15), sds=c(3,1), xlims=c(0,20)){
  curve(taus[1]*dnorm(x, mean=means[1], sd=sds[1]) +
          taus[2]*dnorm(x, mean=means[2], sd=sds[2]),
        from=xlims[1], to=xlims[2], ylab="Density", fg="gray")
  curve(taus[1]*dnorm(x, mean=means[1], sd=sds[1]),
        from=xlims[1], to=xlims[2], col="red", lty=2, add=TRUE, fg="gray")
  curve(taus[2]*dnorm(x, mean=means[2], sd=sds[2]),
        from=xlims[1], to=xlims[2], col="blue", lty=3, add=TRUE, fg="gray")
}
plotMix2(taus=c(.2, .8))
plotMix2(taus=c(.5, .5))
plotMix2(taus=c(.9, .1))
```

While not without its flaws, the most common model-fitting approach makes use of the expectation maximization (EM) algorithm. We will avoid depth on notation and details, for those consider McLachlan and Krishnan (2008), but formally introducing the missing information (which observations belong to which group) helps greatly in summarizing how the EM algorithm operates. So, we introduce $Z_{ig} = 1$ when observation i belongs to group/cluster g, and $Z_{ig} = 0$ otherwise.

Consider assigning each observation to some number of underlying groups completely at random. If we then assume that grouping information is correct, we can easily estimate the parameters of a multivariate normal distribution ($\hat{\mu}_g$ and $\hat{\sigma}_g$) for each group, along with the relative proportions of each group ($\hat{\tau}_g$) – specifically using maximum likelihood estimators, in this case: the group sample means, (biased) sample covariances, and sample proportions. If we then assume those parameter estimates are correct, we can compute the expected value for our group memberships ($\hat{z}_{ig}$) using straightforward conditional probability rules. Namely, the updated group memberships are computed via

$$\hat{z}_{ig} = \frac{\hat{\tau}_g \Phi\left(\mathbf{x}_i \mid \hat{\boldsymbol{\mu}}_g, \hat{\boldsymbol{\Sigma}}_g\right)}{\sum_{k=1}^{G} \hat{\tau}_k \Phi\left(\mathbf{x}_i \mid \hat{\boldsymbol{\mu}}_k, \hat{\boldsymbol{\Sigma}}_k\right)}. \tag{9.2}$$

As a nontechnical summary, the EM algorithm simply iterates back and forth between these two steps: (1) assuming the group memberships are correct, update parameter estimates; (2) assuming parameter estimates are correct, update group memberships. After sufficient iterations, the algorithm will largely stabilize and thus provide a clustering result via $\hat{z}_{ig}$ as well as a probability density estimate for both the population and subpopulations.

As a monotonic "hill climbing" algorithm, the EM approach is quite susceptible to finding solutions that are only locally optimized rather than globally – and the optimization surface can be quite complex. Because of this (in tandem with the computational cost of the method, which we will discuss shortly), the initial random group-assigning step is often discarded for a "smart" initialization, such as one given by another clustering algorithm. A common choice for initialization is k-means, due to its speed.

To focus on the positives, consider again Equation (9.2) and specifically focus on the fact that Φ, being the multivariate normal distribution, is nonzero across its entire, real number domain. Thus, strictly speaking, $\hat{z}_{ig}$ are computed on the interval $(0, 1)$ with the bounds noninclusive; though often lack of machine precision may cloud this fact. From a clustering standpoint, mixture models differentiate greatly from traditional implementations of hierarchical and k-means clustering in this regard. We are provided *nuance* in the clustering results, wherein an observation is estimated as having arisen from a particular group/component/cluster with some level of *(un)certainty*.

An additional benefit from mixture model-based clustering is, as a proper statistical model, the ability to make use of model-fitting measures such as AIC or the BIC – the latter being particularly popular in the clustering literature. This allows an objective competition between different mixture models when applied to the same dataset. Perhaps most importantly, we can consider varying the number of groups/components/clusters for the mixture model and use the BIC to provide an argument for the number of underlying groups.

```
  G=1   G=2   G=3   G=4   G=5   G=6   G=7   G=8   G=9
-1522 -1472 -1505 -1546 -1544 -1582 -1618  -Inf  -Inf
```

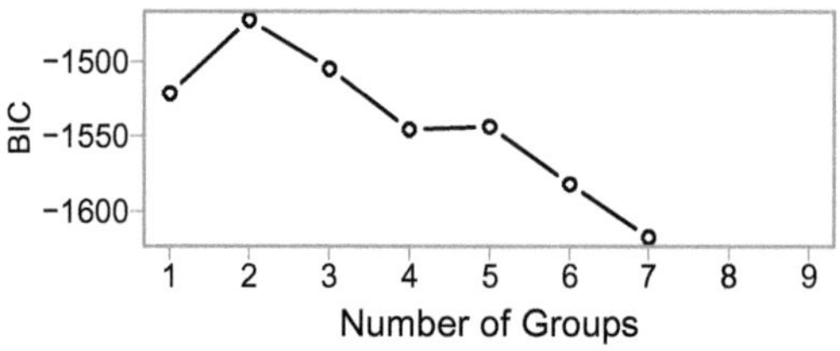

Figure 9.13 BIC values (−BIC as used elsewhere) are plotted against number of groups.

We return to the possum dataset and implement the clustering approaches introduced within this section, starting with mixture model-based. We consider the same set of three variables provided in Figure 9.1 and fit the multivariate Gaussian mixture model described in Equation (9.1).

```
library(teigen)
possml <- na.omit(DAAG::possum[,c(3,9:11)])
set.seed(513451)
gaus_fit <- teigen(possml[,2:4], models="UUUU", gauss=TRUE, verbose=FALSE,
                   scale=FALSE)
```

We will look into what we can make of the results, then move on to commenting on issues of parameterization and scaling.

Now return to the model fitted in the earlier code chunk and see some of the results. First, we note the default `teigen()` call will fit from 1 to 9 groups. Figure 9.13 shows the BIC values associated with each of these models.

```
## BIC values are plotted against number of groups
gaus_fit$allbic
plot(gaus_fit$allbic, type="b", ylab="", xlab="Number of Groups", fg="gray")
mtext(side=2, line=3.5, "BIC", las=0)
axis(1, at=1:9, fg="gray")
```

Note that the *teigen* package, and several others that relate to the mixture model literature, compute the BIC as $2\log\left(\hat{L}\right) - p\log(n)$ (in other words, the negative of the BIC that was introduced in Section 1.7.1). As such, we are seeking the *maximum* value of the BIC. The "missing value" in the plot for $G = 8$ corresponds to a `-Inf` entry for the BIC. This occurs when model-fitting fails – usually when the number of observations contributing to the estimation of a group covariance matrix falls below the number of free parameters in that covariance matrix.

Thus, we can see the BIC is recommending a two-group solution, which is promising given our earlier viewing of the possum data. A natural question would be: How close do these groups match to a known factor in the possum data? A good starting point is simply to cross-tabulate the discovered groups with some of the possum factors. In the end, the groups we appear to be discovering exactly match the `possum$Pop` factor.

```
table(possml$Pop, gaus_fit$classification)
```

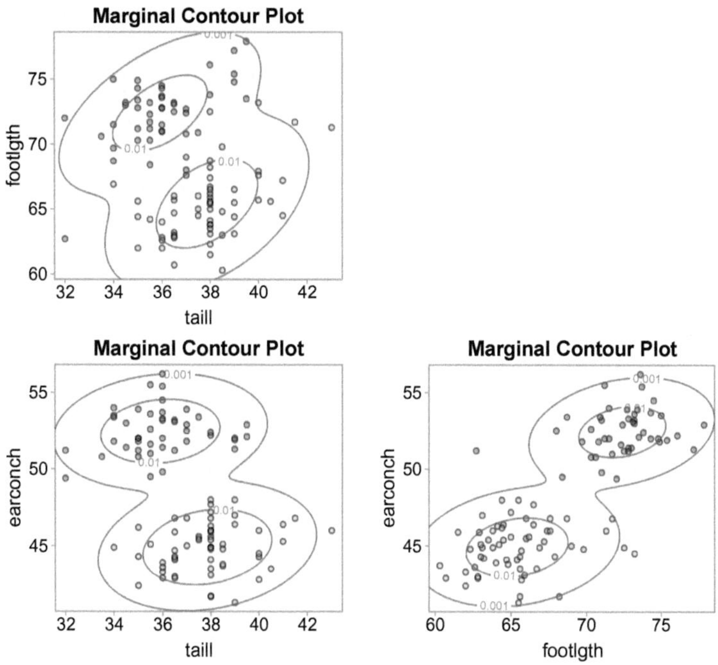

Figure 9.14 Density contours of the fitted mixture model.

```
        1  2
Vic    45  0
other   0 58
```

Figure 9.14 views the density contours of the fitted mixture model through joint marginal plots, placed in a similar fashion as a scatterplot matrix. Technically, marginal densities are computed by integrating out the remaining random variables within the multivariate distribution – hence, in general, a joint marginal for X_1 and X_2 would integrate out $X_3, \ldots, X_p$.

Code for Figure 9.14 is:

```
par(fig=c(0, 0.5, 0.5, 1))
plot(gaus_fit, what="contour", xmarg=1, ymarg=2, draw.legend=FALSE, fg="gray")
## See ?teigen::plot.teigen for details of the plot command used here.
par(fig=c(0, 0.5, 0, 0.5), new=TRUE)
plot(gaus_fit, what="contour", xmarg=1, ymarg=3, draw.legend=FALSE, fg="gray")
par(fig=c(0.5, 1, 0, 0.5), new=TRUE)
plot(gaus_fit, what="contour", xmarg=2, ymarg=3, draw.legend=FALSE, fg="gray")
par(fig=c(0,1,0,1))
```

Issues of High Parameterization and Scaling

The high parameterization in the covariance matrix $\mathbf{\Sigma}$ poses the biggest threat for a standard Gaussian mixture model EM implementation. The number of free parameters in these matrices grows quadratically with the number of variables used in the analysis, and they need to be inverted when computing the probability density function (which occurs at least once per iteration). From a practical standpoint, the user needs to thus ensure that they have sufficient sample sizes such that the sample covariance matrices are full rank, and sufficient computing power/patience for high-dimensional cases. It is therefore common to consider decompositions and subsequent constraints on these matrices in an effort to track down parsimonious models. We note that in our example above the `models="UUUU"` command is indicating a fully unconstrained covariance model. See the help page `?teigen::teigen` for further details on this particular family of models and the swath of constraints available. The `scale=FALSE` command is used to avoid transforming the data to have mean 0 and variance 1 on each variable. For the unconstrained mixture model, this may seem inconsequential as the *model* is scale invariant. However, even in the case of this particular package, the algorithm is initialized via k-means clustering, creating a potential for a scaling effect on the results. Furthermore, several of the constrained models implemented in packages like *teigen* are *not* scale invariant, and the user therefore may need to consider scale concerns such as noted for other clustering methods.

9.3.4 Relationship between k-Means and Mixture Models

The traditional k-means algorithm has a well-established (though sometimes overlooked) relationship to mixture models – see discussants of a 2011 manuscript by Steinley and Brusco, chiefly Vermunt (2011) who provides a concise argument and McLachlan (2011) who traces the literature as far as Scott and Symons (1971). In essence, k-means is a highly constrained Gaussian mixture model – specifically, where $\Sigma = \sigma^2 I$, where σ^2 is some positive scalar and I is a $p \times p$ identity matrix – fitted through a classification maximum likelihood approach (Celeux and Govaert, 1992). Basically, one restricts the conditional expectations for the Z_{ig} to be only 0s and 1s within the EM framework sketched in the previous subsection.

9.4 Discriminant Analysis

Discriminant analysis seeks a rule that will allow prediction of the class to which a new observation may belong. Using language that came originally from the engineering pattern recognition literature, the interest is in supervised learning. For example, the aim may be to predict, based on prognostic measurements and outcome information for previous patients, which future patients will remain free of disease symptoms for 12 months or more. Two methods will be demonstrated here – logistic discrimination and linear discriminant analysis using the function `MASS::lda()`. Among other methods, note the tree-based methods, including random forests, that were discussed in Chapter 8.

Cross-validation, and the training/test set methodology, introduced in earlier chapters as approaches for the assessing predictive accuracy, will have key roles in work with discriminant methods. Note again that resubstitution or training set accuracy, that is, prediction accuracy on the data used to derive the model, cannot

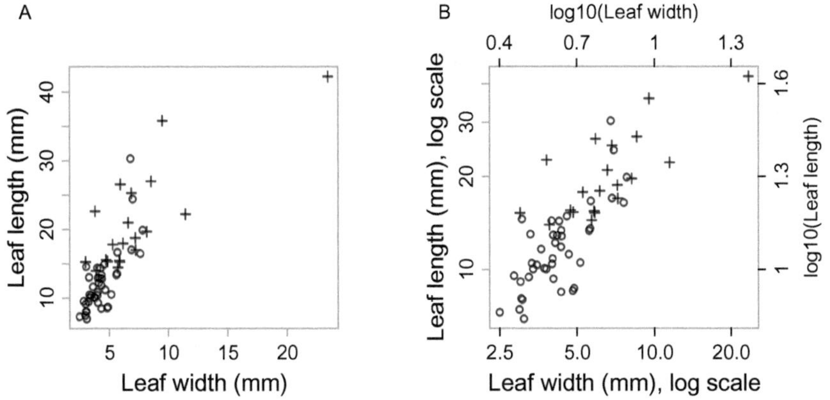

Figure 9.15 Leaf length versus leaf width (A) with untransformed scales, and (B) using logarithmic scales. The symbols are o = plagiotropic, and + = orthotropic. Data, in `DAAG::leafshape17`, are from an Australian North Queensland site.

decrease as the prediction model becomes more complex. The cross-validation estimate of predictive accuracy will, if the full model is over-fitted, begin to decrease at some point as model complexity increases. Predictive accuracy on test data that are separate from the data used to train the model will likewise commonly show the same pattern of increase to an optimum, followed by decrease.

Cross-validation assessments of accuracy, or assessments that are based on test data derived from splitting the sample data into two parts, do, however, have limitations. Cross-validation gives an estimate of predictive accuracy for the "source" population, that is, for the population from which the data have been sampled. With observational data, the target to which results will be applied is almost inevitably different, in time and/or space, from the "source." Accuracy estimates that are based on cross-validation, or on a training/test split of the sample data, must then be treated as provisional, until and unless test data become available from the population that is the true target.

9.4.1 Example – Plant Architecture

Data for our first example relate to the study of plant architecture that is reported in King and Maindonald (1999), limiting attention to data from a North Queensland site that was one of six sites that provided data. Orthotropic species have steeply angled branches, with leaves coming off on all sides. Plagiotropic species have spreading branches (a few intermediates and a third uncommon branching pattern are excluded). (King (1998) has diagrams that show the differences.) The interest is in comparing the leaf dimensions of species with the two different architectures. Is leaf shape a good discriminator? To what extent does leaf shape discriminate between the two architectures?

Figures 9.15A and B show alternative views of the data. Code that gives a stripped down version of Figure 9.15A is:

```
leafshape17 <- DAAG::leafshape17
```

```
plot(bladelen ~ bladewid, data=leafshape17, pch=c(1,3)[arch+1])
## For panel B, specify log="xy" in the call to plot()
```

A logarithmic scale is clearly preferable.

With two explanatory variables, a plot of the second versus first principal components scores from the log-transformed data would look much like a version of Figure 9.15B where the axes have been rotated so that the major axis of variation (running from the lower left to the upper right of Figure 9.15B) is horizontal.

The function `glm()`, and the predict method for `glm` objects, make no explicit assumptions about the prior frequencies of the classes. The expected proportions in the two (or more) classes can be important in finding a rule that will optimally assign a new sample to a cancer type.

More generally, different types of misclassification may have different costs that should be taken into account, in ways that have obvious importance in a medical context. In a screening test for a disease, some false positives are acceptable, while any false negative (failing to detect an instance of the disease) may have more serious consequences.

Logistic Regression, versus Linear Discriminant Analysis

Let π_0 and π_1 be the respective prior probabilities of plagiotropic (coded as 0) and orthotropic (coded as 1) architectures.

- For predictions from the logistic regression, π_0 and π_1 are each implicitly assumed equal to 0.5, so that $\frac{\pi_1}{\pi_0} = 1$ and $\log\left(\frac{\pi_1}{\pi_0}\right) = 0$. If another prior probability is appropriate, output from `glm()` must be adapted to accommodate this.
- In the call to `lda()`, π_0 and π_1 can be supplied, using the argument `prior`. They can also be changed, using an argument that again has the name `prior`, in a call to the predict method for an `lda` object. The default is that `lda()` takes π_0 and π_1 to be the frequencies in the data.

9.4.2 Logistic Regression

The model specifies log(odds orthotropic) as a linear function of the explanatory variables for the classification. We obtain the linear function thus:

```
## Fit logistic regression model
leafshape17 <- DAAG::leafshape17
leaf17.glm <- glm(arch ~ logwid + loglen, family=binomial(link=logit),
data=leafshape17)
print(DAAG::sumry(leaf17.glm)$coef, digits=2)
```

```
             Estimate Std. Error z value Pr(>|z|)
(Intercept)    -15.29        4.1   -3.70  0.00021
logwid           0.19        1.6    0.12  0.90622
loglen           5.27        2.0    2.68  0.00727
```

Thus, we have

$$\log(\text{odds orthotropic}) = -15.3 + 0.185\log(\text{width}) + 5.628\log(\text{length}).$$

Predictive Accuracy

The cross-validation estimate is an assessment of the accuracy that can be expected for a new set of data, sampled in the same way as the existing training data and from the same source population. The function `DAAG::CVbinary()` can conveniently be used for the cross-validation calculations. The list element `cvhat` returns the class probabilities that are predicted from the cross-validation, for each observation:

```
set.seed(29)
leaf17.cv <- DAAG::CVbinary(leaf17.glm)
```

```
Fold:  5 10 2 3 7 8 1 4 6 9
Internal estimate of accuracy = 0.82
Cross-validation estimate of accuracy = 0.803
```

```
tCV <- table(DAAG::leafshape17[["arch"]], round(leaf17.cv$cvhat))
rownames(tCV) <- colnames(tCV) <- c("0=Plagiotropic","1=Orthotropic")
cbind(tCV, "Proportion correct"=c(tCV[1,1], tCV[2,2])/(tCV[,1]+tCV[,2]))
```

```
               0=Plagiotropic 1=Orthotropic Proportion correct
0=Plagiotropic             36             5              0.878
1=Orthotropic               7            13              0.650
```

In the table, 0.878 (calculated as 36 out of 41) is the proportion of plagiotropic plants that were correctly classified as plagiotropic, while 0.65 is the proportion of orthotropic plants that were correctly classified as such. The overall predictive accuracy is $(36+13)/(36+5+7+13) = 0.803$. The results will vary somewhat from one run of `CVbinary()` to the next.

The following compares the training estimate, which is in general optimistic, with the cross-validation estimate of accuracy:

```
round(unlist(leaf17.cv[c("acc.training","acc.cv")]),3)
```

```
acc.training       acc.cv
       0.820        0.803
```

The cross-validation accuracy is, for the cross-validation run that is reported here and contrary to what might be expected, slightly lower than the training set assessment.

9.4.3 Linear Discriminant Analysis

The function `MASS::lda()` is set in an explicit Bayesian framework, as described in Ripley (1996, p. 36). For two classes it is a logistic regression, but the assumptions (notably, multivariate normal within group distributions with a variance–covariance matrix that is common across groups) are different from those for `glm()`. It yields posterior probabilities of membership of the several groups. The allocation which makes the smallest expected number of errors chooses, following the *Bayes* rule, the class with the largest posterior probability. Where there are $g > 2$ groups, there are $g - 1$ discriminant axes.

With two classes, the analysis yields a linear function $f(x, y)$ of $x = \log(\text{leaf width})$ and $y = \log(\text{leaf length})$, that has the form $a(x-\bar{x}) + b(y-\bar{y})$, where a and b must be estimated. If

$$f(x,y) < -\log\left(\frac{\pi_1}{\pi_0}\right), \quad \text{where } f(x,y) = a(x-\bar{x}) + b(y-\bar{y}),$$

the prediction is that the plant will be plagiotropic, while otherwise the plant is predicted to be orthotropic. The values of $f(x,y)$, one for each observation, are termed *scores*.

We first extract predictions, and then examine the discriminant function. The code is:

```
suppressPackageStartupMessages(library(MASS))
## Discriminant analysis; data frame leafshape17 (DAAG)
leaf17.lda <- lda(arch ~ logwid+loglen, data=DAAG::leafshape17)
print(leaf17.lda)
```

```
Call:
lda(arch ~ logwid + loglen, data = DAAG::leafshape17)

Prior probabilities of groups:
     0      1
0.6721 0.3279

Group means:
  logwid loglen
0  1.429  2.460
1  1.866  2.994

Coefficients of linear discriminants:
          LD1
logwid 0.1555
loglen 3.0658
```

The coefficient estimates are a = 0.156 and b = 3.066.

The prior probabilities should reflect the expected proportions, and where relevant misclassification costs, in the population to which the discriminant function will be applied. Both `lda()` and the `predict` method for `lda` objects accept the argument `prior`, allowing predictions to use prior probabilities that may be different from those that were assumed in the call to `lda()`.

Assessments of Predictive Accuracy

Use of `predict(leaf17.lda)` gives predictions for the data used to train the model. An alternative, which allows the comparison of predicted values with data that have not been used to fit the model, is to rerun the calculation with the argument `CV=TRUE`. Predictions are then based on leave-one-out cross-validation, that is, observations are left out one at a time, the model is fitted to the remaining data, and a prediction is made for the omitted observation:

```
set.seed(29)
leaf17cv.lda <- lda(arch ~ logwid+loglen, data=leafshape17, CV=TRUE)
## the list element 'class' gives the predicted class
```

```
## The list element 'posterior' holds posterior probabilities
tab <- table(leafshape17$arch, leaf17cv.lda$class)
rownames(tab) <- colnames(tab) <- c("0=Plagiotropic","1=Orthotropic")
cbind(tab, "Proportion correct"=c(tCV[1,1], tCV[2,2])/(tCV[,1]+tCV[,2]))
```

```
               0=Plagiotropic 1=Orthotropic Proportion correct
0=Plagiotropic             37             4              0.878
1=Orthotropic               8            12              0.650
```

```
cbind(tab, c(tab[1,1], class.acc=tab[2,2])/(tab[,1]+tab[,2]))
```

```
               0=Plagiotropic 1=Orthotropic
0=Plagiotropic             37             4 0.9024
1=Orthotropic               8            12 0.6000
```

```
cat("Overall proportion correct =", sum(tab[row(tab)==col(tab)])/sum(tab), "\n")
```

```
Overall proportion correct = 0.8033
```

The Function `qda()`*, and Other Alternatives to* `lda()`

The function `MASS::qda()` allows for different variance–covariance matrices in different groups. A restriction is that, for use of p features, each group must have at least $p+1$ observations. Unlike `lda()`, it does not lead to discriminant axes that are common across all groups.

Among other possibilities, note `nnet::multinom()`, which is, however, less suited for use for prediction.

9.4.4 An Example with More Than Two Groups

We present discriminant analysis calculations for the `possum` data frame. The methods followed here are similar to those used in Lindenmayer et al. (1995), with these same data, in making a case for the identification of a new possum species. (The species is named *Trichodurus cunninghami* for the statistician whose analysis led to this identification. See Hall (2003).) We will use the same nine variables as before.

```
## Linear discriminant calculations for possum data
possum <- DAAG::possum
possum.lda <- lda(site ~ hdlngth + skullw + totlngth + taill + footlgth +
                  earconch + eye + chest + belly, data=na.omit(possum))
# na.omit() omits any rows that have one or more missing values
```

Figure 9.16 shows the scatterplot matrix for the first three discriminant scores, which together account for 98.4 percent of the between class variance. Code that shows the layout of points, without the key, is:

```
plot(possum.lda, dimen=3, col=1:9)
# Scatterplot matrix - scores on 1st 3 canonical variates
# See `?plot.lda` for details of the generic lda plot function
```

Printed output from the analysis now follows:

```
## Linear discriminant calculations for possum data
print(possum.lda, digits=3)
```

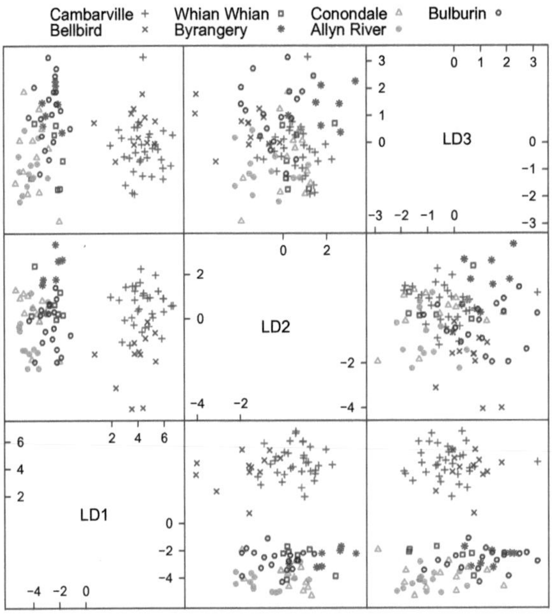

Figure 9.16 Scatterplot matrix for the first three canonical variates, based on use of linear discriminant analysis for the **possum** data.

```
Call:
lda(site ~ hdlngth + skullw + totlngth + taill + footlgth + earconch +
    eye + chest + belly, data = possum)

Prior probabilities of groups:
    1     2     3     4     5     6     7
0.320 0.117 0.068 0.068 0.126 0.126 0.175

Group means:
  hdlngth skullw totlngth taill footlgth earconch  eye chest belly
1    93.7   57.2     89.7  36.4     73.0     52.6 15.0  27.9  33.3
2    89.8   55.1     81.7  34.7     70.8     52.1 14.4  26.3  31.2
3    94.6   58.9     88.1  37.2     66.6     45.3 16.1  27.6  34.9
4    97.6   61.7     92.2  39.7     68.9     45.8 15.5  29.6  34.6
5    92.2   56.2     86.9  37.7     64.7     43.9 15.4  26.7  32.0
6    89.2   54.2     84.5  37.7     63.1     44.0 15.3  25.2  31.5
7    92.6   57.2     85.7  37.7     65.7     45.9 14.5  26.1  31.9

Coefficients of linear discriminants:
              LD1     LD2     LD3     LD4     LD5     LD6
hdlngth  -0.15053  0.0583  0.2557 -0.0124 -0.0819  0.1871
skullw   -0.02653  0.0399  0.2498  0.1245 -0.1365 -0.1438
totlngth  0.10696  0.2792 -0.3052 -0.1849 -0.1390  0.0892
taill    -0.45063 -0.0896  0.4458 -0.1730  0.3242 -0.4951
footlgth  0.30190 -0.0360  0.0391  0.0756  0.1191  0.1261
earconch  0.58627 -0.0436  0.0731 -0.0882 -0.0638 -0.2802
eye      -0.05614  0.0892 -0.7845  0.4644  0.2848 -0.2972
chest     0.09062  0.1042 -0.0498  0.1275  0.6475  0.0787
belly     0.00997 -0.0517 -0.0936  0.1672 -0.2903 -0.1939
```

```
Proportion of trace:
   LD1    LD2    LD3    LD4    LD5    LD6
0.8927 0.0557 0.0365 0.0082 0.0047 0.0022
```

The "proportion of trace" figures are the proportions of the between class variance that are explained by the successive linear combinations. For these data, the first linear discriminant does most of the discriminating. The variables that seem important are `hdlngth`, and `taill`, contrasted with `totlngth` and `footlgth`.

We invite the reader to repeat the analysis with the argument `CV=TRUE` in the call to `lda()`, in order to obtain a realistic predictive accuracy estimate.

9.5* High-Dimensional Data – RNA-Seq Gene Expression

Subsection 2.7.3 demonstrated how, given numerous p-values that were generated in the same experiment or series of experiments, false discovery rate (FDR) estimates could be obtained. Here, we resume that discussion, using data from an experiment where plants were exposed to one of three treatments. Data are from Peter Crisp, obtained in the course of his PhD work in the ARC Centre of Excellence in Plant Energy Biology at Australian National University. The treatments were:

- a control;
- light stress, namely, one hour of continuous exposure to light at 10 times the level that the plants are normally grown under;
- drought stress, namely, nine days without water, causing wilting of the leaves.

The interest is in how light stress and drought stress affect gene expression. Gene activity in the production of proteins was monitored by using RNA sequencing technology to determine, for each gene, the number of mRNA (messenger RNA) sequences, in a sample of plant tissue, that carry that gene's information. (Note that the mRNA counts measure only the activity of the cell machinery in production of protein. The relationship to protein production will be different for different genes, and affected also by other factors.)

After removing very sparse counts there were counts, for each of the three treatments, for 18,568 genes. On average, in the absence of any real effect, 5 percent or approximately 928 of the genes can be expected to show a difference at the 5 percent significance level. We can then note the number m of differences observed at the 5 percent level, and take those with the smallest m-928 p-values as probably real. This is the basis for the Benjamini–Hochberg false discrimination rate (FDR) approach that was introduced in Subsection 2.7.3.

Setup for Installing and Using Bioconductor Packages

Run the following code:

```
## For latest details, see: https://www.bioconductor.org/install/
if (!require("BiocManager", quietly = TRUE))
  install.packages("BiocManager")
BiocManager::install()
BiocManager::install('limma','multtest')
```

*Brief Note on mRNA Technical Issues

The role of the mRNA is to carry information encoded in the genes to the cell factories (ribosomes) that manufacture the proteins. Links on **https://ghr.nlm.nih.gov/handbook/hgp/genome**, or on another such site, can be consulted for more details on the biological mechanisms. The counts are, inevitably, sums over a very large number of plant cells.

9.5.1 Data and Design Matrix Setup

The counts are in the matrix `DAAGbio::plantStressCounts`. The column names identify the samples:

```
counts <- DAAGbio::plantStressCounts
colSums(counts)
```

```
    CTL1     CTL2     CTL3   Light1   Light2   Light3 Drought1 Drought2
  933573   943262   944871   946921   926570   931086   925995   915023
Drought3
  930588
```

The column sums are in each case close to a million.

The function `cpm()` (counts per million reads) standardizes counts for each gene by dividing by entries in the `lib.size` column and multiplying by 10^6. Here, the `lib.size` values are just the column totals. We retain the genes with a count per million of at least one in three of the nine samples:

```
## Require at least 3 counts per million that are > 1
keep <- rowSums(counts)≥3
counts <- counts[keep,]
```

The *limma* package (Ritchie et al., 2015) is set up to work with a design matrix that specifies the treatment structure. The following sets up the design matrix to have one column for each of the three treatments.

```
treatment <- factor(rep(c("CTL", "L", "D"), rep(3,3)))
design <- model.matrix(~0+treatment)
colnames(design) <- levels(treatment)
```

Note the use of L for light stress and D for drought stress.

A Two-Dimensional Representation

We now use the function *limma::voom()* to transform the counts counts to log(count + 1). At the same time it estimates, as a smooth curve, the mean–variance relationship. Optionally, it will output a plot, as in Figure 9.17A, that shows the fitted mean–variance relationship. The variance estimates will be used to determine weights (= inverses of variances) for individual genes that will be used in fitting the model. Stripped down code is:

```
library(limma)
v <- voom(counts, design, plot=TRUE)
```

Figure 9.17B then applies the function `plotMDS()` to the output from `voom()`. This uses multidimensional scaling to give a broad overall comparison of the nine samples.

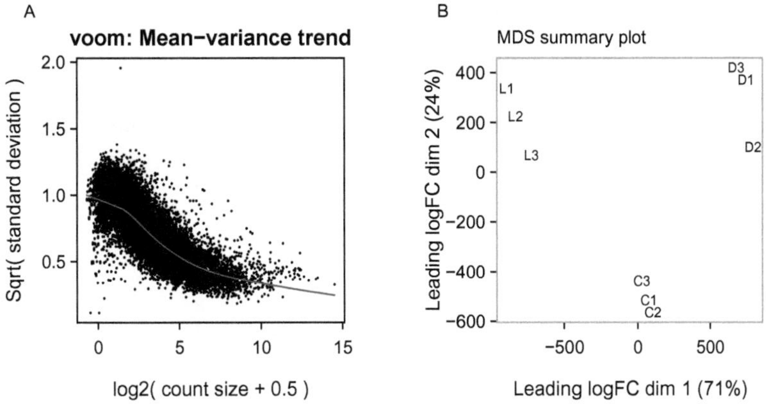

Figure 9.17 Panel A shows the mean–variance relationship. Panel B plots results from the use of multidimensional scaling to locate samples in two-dimensional space. By default, the "top" 500 genes are used. As there are three groups, two dimensions suffice.

```
v <- voom(counts, design, plot=TRUE)
firstchar <- substring(colnames(counts),1,1)
plotMDS(counts, labels=paste0(firstchar, rep(1:3,3)), cex=0.8)
```

Plots such as are shown in Figure 9.17B can be important in drawing attention to samples where something is clearly wrong. The limma user guide has an example where a batch effect appears to be associated with sequencing type and date. Under Section 18.2 on "Differential Splicing after Pasilla Knockdown", see Subsection 18.2.8 on "Scale Normalization". (The section and subsection numbers are for the June 12, 2020 version of the manual.)

Fitting the Model

We then proceed to fit the model:

```
fit <- lmFit(v, design)
```

We then specify the treatment contrasts in which we are interested, and extract information about these:

```
contrs <- c("D−CTL", "L−CTL", "L−D")
contr.matrix <- makeContrasts(contrasts=contrs,
levels=levels(treatment))
fit2 <- contrasts.fit(fit, contr.matrix)
efit2 <- eBayes(fit2)
```

Recall that `L` is light stress and `D` is drought stress. The function `eBayes()` uses an empirical Bayes method to shrink the probewise sample variances in towards a common value, with a consequent increase in the degrees of freedom for the individual variances. It is needed here as a preliminary to examining output from `efit2`.

9.5.2 From p-Values to False Discovery Rate (FDR)

The function `topTable()` sorts output according to whatever criterion is used to determine "top"; the default is to take first genes where p-values are smallest. Included in the output is a column `adj.P.val`. With the default argument `adjust.method="BH"`, this returns the Benjamini–Hochberg false discovery rate (FDR) estimates that were described in Subsection 2.7.3.

```
## First contrast only; Drought-CTL
print(round(topTable(efit2, coef=1, number=4),15), digits=3)
```

```
           logFC AveExpr    t P.Value adj.P.Val    B
Gene24491   3.69     9.6 35.5   0e+00  3.90e-14 32.2
Gene13749   2.23    10.3 28.4   0e+00  1.10e-12 28.4
Gene10904   2.62    10.6 26.3   0e+00  2.09e-12 27.1
Gene13210   2.58    10.0 26.1   1e-15  2.09e-12 26.9
```

The FDR estimates can alternatively be obtained by direct use of the function call `p.adjust()`. Thus, try the following:

```
round(sort(p.adjust(p=efit2$p.value[,1], method="BH"))[1:4], 15) # Not run
```

Note also the use of an ANOVA-like overall check, across all three contrasts, for differential expression, thus:

```
round(topTable(efit2, number=4), 15)
```

```
            D.CTL   L.CTL    L.D AveExpr     F P.Value adj.P.Val
Gene10714  -3.254  2.2083  5.462   8.693 864.7       0     6e-15
Gene24491   3.692 -0.1529 -3.845   9.595 857.9       0     6e-15
Gene11934  -1.027  3.3864  4.413   8.191 801.6       0     8e-15
Gene13377  -2.299  3.2733  5.573   8.585 763.7       0     9e-15
```

Notice that the p-values and "adjusted" p-values for the genes that appear first in what is now a new order, are now smaller. This is to be expected, because the F-statistic summarizes evidence for differential expression across all three contrasts.

The function `decideTests()` provides, by default with an adjusted p-value or FDR of 0.05, a matrix that scores each of the three contrasts as -1 (effect, in opposite direction to contrast), 0 (as judged by the chosen criterion, no effect), and 1 (effect, in same direction as the contrast). The first five rows of output are:

```
head(decideTests(fit2),5)
```

```
TestResults matrix
       Contrasts
        D-CTL L-CTL L-D
  Gene1     0     0   0
  Gene2     0     1   1
  Gene3     0     0   1
  Gene4     0     0   0
  Gene6     0     0   0
```

A summary is:

```
summary(decideTests(fit2))
```

```
       D-CTL L-CTL   L-D
Down    3215  2538  3162
NotSig 13445 15134 13156
Up      2291  1279  2633
```

```
## Try also
## summary(decideTests(fit2, p.value=0.001))
```

This very high level of differential expression is surely a comment on the plant's priorities.

The linear modeling approach of *lmFit*, and the statistical methods that are used are described in Phipson et al. (2016).

9.6 High-Dimensional Data from Expression Arrays

The technology that generated the data that will now be discussed is to an extent superseded by RNA-based approaches, or by more direct measurement of the protein created. The analyses nonetheless serve to make highly pertinent points of importance for many different types of high-dimensional data.

9.6.1 Molecular Classification of Cancer – an Older Technology

Each of the 7129 rows of the matrix `hddplot::Golub` holds "gene expression indices" (variables, or "features") that are measures of the biological activity of a gene. The dataset is the result of some further preprocessing of data from the *golubEsets* package. See Golub et al. (1999) for details of the work that generated the *golubEsets* data.

Following a terminology that is common for such data, the variables will be called features. Each of the 72 observations (columns of `Golub`) is from a tissue sample from a cancer patient. The 72 observations are classified into one of the three cancer types: ALL B-type (coded `allB`), ALL T-type (coded `allT`), and AML (coded `aml`). ALL is Acute Lymphoblastic Leukemia (lymphoblastic = producing lymph tissue), while AML is Acute Myoblastic Leukemia (myoblastic = producing muscle tissue).

The data frame `hddplot::golubInfo` has information on the tissue samples, which are the observations. As well as different sexes, there are two different body tissues (bone marrow and peripheral blood). There may also be variation because the tissues came from four different hospitals; this will not be pursued here. These differences within the cancer types are a complication for investigating differences between the cancers.

The presence of these other factors makes graphical exploration especially important, with the initial focus (and here, the only focus) on differences within cancer types. Finding suitable views of the data, inevitably low-dimensional, is a challenge. Views are required that may help reveal subgroups in the data, or points that may have been misclassified, or between group differences in the variance–covariance structure. Graphs should be revealing, without serious potential to mislead.

Note: One use for data of this general type might be the finding of a discrimination rule that, using a small subset of the features, will allow discrimination between the different cancer types. A diagnostic device (a "probe") could then be designed that, given a new sample, could determine the cancer type. Note, however, that any classification of cancers is likely to conceal large individual differences that, in many cancers, arise from random differences in the timing and outcome of trigger points in a cascade of genomic damage and disruption.

The papers Maindonald and Burden (2005), Ambroise and McLachlan (2002), and Zhu et al. (2006) are useful background reading for the discussion of this section.

Breakdown of ALL B-type Data, with One Observation Excluded

The frequencies in the two-way classification by `cancer` and `tissue.mf` are:

```
library(hddplot)
data(golubInfo)
with(golubInfo, table(cancer, tissue.mf))
```

```
        tissue.mf
cancer  BM:NA BM:f BM:m PB:NA PB:f PB:m
  allB      4   19   10     2    1    2
  allT      0    0    8     0    0    1
  aml      16    2    3     1    1    2
```

Observe that `allB` is predominately `BM:f`, while `aml` is predominately `BM` of unknown sex. If we compare `allB` with `aml` and ignore other factors, will any differences be due to cancer type, or to the sex of the patient, or to the tissue type?

The investigation here will be limited to the ALL B-type subset of the data. A factor `tissue.mfB` will be defined that classifies this subset according to tissue type and sex. (The single `allB` observation that is `PB:f` will be omitted.)

The following calculations separate out the `allB` subset (`GolubB`) of the data that will be used, and derive the factor `tissue.mfB` whose levels are `BM:f` (relabel to `b_f`), `BM:m` (`b_m`) and `PB:m` (`PBm`):

```
## Identify allB samples that are BM:f or BM:m or PB:m
subsetB <- with(golubInfo,
cancer=="allB" & tissue.mf%in%c("BM:f","BM:m","PB:m"))
## Separate off the relevant columns of the matrix Golub
## NB: variables (rows) by cases (columns)
GolubB <- with(golubInfo, Golub[, subsetB])
## Form vector that identifies these as BM:f or BM:m or PB:m
tissue.mfB <- with(golubInfo, tissue.mf[subsetB, drop=TRUE])
## Change the level names to leave out the colons
levels(tissue.mfB) <- list("b_f"="BM:f", "b_m"="BM:m", "PBm"="PB:m")
```

The argument `drop=TRUE` in `tissue.mf[subsetB, drop=TRUE]` causes the return of a factor that has only the levels that are present in the data subset.

9.6.2 Classifications and Associated Graphs

In the discussion that now follows, interest will be on the graphical view that can be associated with one or other discriminant rule, rather than in the discriminant rules themselves. The objective is to give a visual representation that shows one or other classification that is of interest. Different classifications will lead to different graphical views – what is seen depends, inevitably, on which clues are pursued. Overly complex classifications may force unsatisfactory compromises in the view that is presented. As noted above, care is required to ensure that graphs present a fair view of the data, not showing spurious differences between groups or exaggerating such differences as may exist.

Discrimination will use the relatively simple and readily understood linear discriminant function methodology that was introduced and used earlier, in Section 9.4.3. Analyses will, again, use the function `MASS::lda()`. Linear discriminant functions may be as complicated as is sensible, given the substantial noise in current expression array datasets. In any case, the emphasis will be on insight rather than on the use of methods that are arguably more optimal.

The statistical information given in the output from the function `lda()` assumes that the variance–covariance matrix is the same in all groups. Even where this is not plausible, the graph obtained remains useful, perhaps showing pronounced between group differences in the variance–covariance structure.

The methodology that will be described is not readily adaptable for use with `qda()`, which is designed to accommodate variance–covariance matrices that differ between groups.

Preliminary Data Manipulation

An observation on a tissue sample comes from a single "chip," possibly leading to systematic differences between observations. Preprocessing is needed to align the feature values for the different chips. For the dataset `hddplot::Golub`, data have been processed so that, in particular, the median and standard deviation are the same across the different slides.

As is standard practice with expression array data, the rows of `Golub` are features (variables), while the columns are observations. Transposition to an observations-by-features layout will be required for use of `lda()` or other modeling functions.

Before proceeding further, the distribution for individual observations across features, and the distribution for a selection of features across observations, should be checked.[3] Both distributions are positively skewed.

Flawed Graphs

Figure 9.18A is a flawed attempt at a graph that shows the separation of the 31 observations into the three specified groups. It uses discriminant axes that were determined using 15 features that individually gave the "best" separation into the three groups (see below). It is flawed because no account is taken of the effect of selecting the 15 features judged best, out of 7129. Figure 9.18B, which was obtained by applying the same procedure to random normal data, from 7129 independent normal variables that all had the same mean and variance, shows the potential for getting an entirely spurious separation into groups. In spite of its evident flaws, it is important to understand the procedure that was followed, as the later discussion will extend and adapt it to give graphs that are not similarly flawed.

In summary, Figure 9.18 was obtained as follows.

[3]
```
## Display distributions for the first 20 observations
boxplot(data.frame(GolubB[, 1:20]))  # First 20 columns (observations)
## Random selection of 20 rows (features)
boxplot(data.frame(GolubB[sample(1:7129, 20), ]))
```

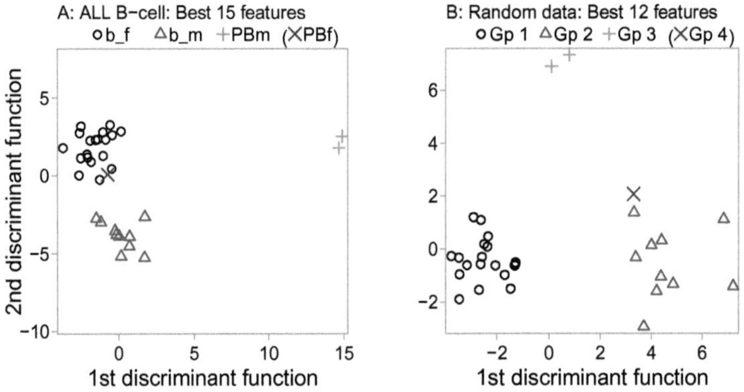

Figure 9.18 Panel A used the subset of ALL B-cell observations for which **Gender** was known. The one `PB:f` observation was excluded for purposes of analysis. An anova *F*-statistic calculation identified the 15 features that, individually, "best" separated the data into three groups. These 15 features were then used in a linear discriminant analysis. Scores were then determined for each of the two available discriminant axes. Additionally, a predicted score was determined for the `PB:f` observation. For Panel B, the same procedure was followed, but now using a matrix where the "expression values" were random normal data.

- The 15 features (from 7129) were selected that, as measured by an analysis of variance *F*-statistic, gave the best separation of the 31 observations into the three groups `BM:f`, `BM:m`, `PB:f`.[4]
- The two discriminant functions, and their associated discriminant scores, were calculated and the scores plotted.
- A predicted score was calculated for the one `PB:f` sample, for inclusion in the plot.[5]

Figure 9.18B used the same two steps, but with the input expression values replaced by random normal values.[6]

The function `simulateScores()` makes it straightforward, using different numbers of features, and different numbers of observations and groupings of those ob-

[4]
```
## Uses orderFeatures() (hddplot); see below
ord15 <- orderFeatures(GolubB, cl=tissue.mfB)[1:15]
```

[5]
```
## Panel A: Take 1st 15 features & transpose to observations by features
dfB15 <- data.frame(t(GolubB[ord15, ]))
dfB15.lda <-  MASS::lda(dfB15, grouping=tissue.mfB)
scores <- predict(dfB15.lda, dimen=2)$x
## Scores for the single PB:f observation
chooseCols <- with(golubInfo, tissue.mf=="PB:f"& cancer=="allB")
df.PBf <- data.frame(t(Golub[ord15, chooseCols, drop=FALSE]))
scores.PBf <- predict(dfB15.lda, newdata=df.PBf, dimen=2)$x
## Warning! The plot that now follows may be misleading!
## Use hddplot::scoreplot()
scoreplot(list(scores=scores, cl=tissue.mfB, other=scores.PBf, cl.other="PB:f"),
          fg="gray")
```

[6]
```
## Panel B: Repeat plot, now with random normal data
simscores <- simulateScores(nrow=7129, cl=rep(1:3, c(19,10,2)),
cl.other=4, nfeatures=15, seed=41)
# Returns list elements: scores, cl, scores.other & cl.other
scoreplot(simscores)
```

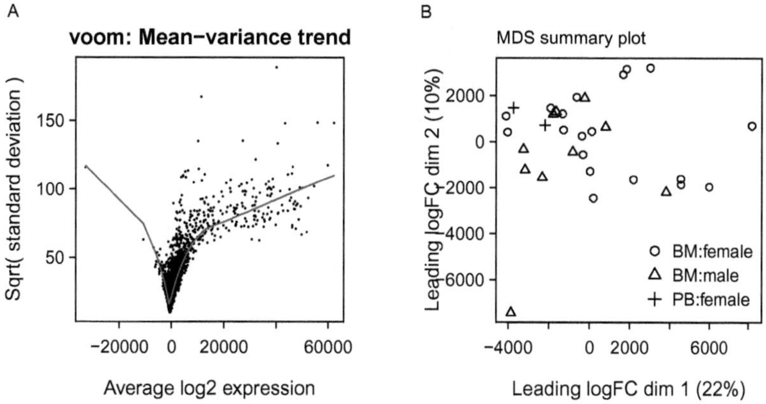

Figure 9.19 Panel A shows the mean–variance relationship. Panel B shows a plot from use of multidimensional scaling to locate samples in two-dimensional space.

servations, to examine the use of the procedure just described with different configurations of random data. Readers are encouraged to experiment, using the code in the footnote as a model.[6]

The selection of 15 features from a total of 7129, selected to have the largest F-statistics, makes it unwise to give much credence to the clear separation achieved with expression array data in Figure 9.18A. The extent of separation in Figure 9.18B from use of random normal data indicates the potential severity of the selection effect, for the data used for Figure 9.18A. The 15 most extreme F-statistics out of 7129, from a null distribution in which there is no separation between groups, will all individually show some separation. Choice of the "best" two discriminant axes that use these 15 features will achieve even clearer separation than is possible with any of the features individually. Clearer apparent separation, both for random data and for the Golub data, can be achieved by choosing more than 15 features.

9.6.3 The Mean–Variance Relationship

The function `limma::vooma()` is an analogue to `voom()`, for use with expression array data. Like `voom()`, it can be used to determine a mean–variance relationship, and weights for use with `lmFit()`. Figure 9.19 repeats Figure 9.17, now with expression array data. The groups are mot well separated in Figure 9.19B.

```
designG <- model.matrix(~0+tissue.mfB)
colnames(designG) <- levels(tissue.mfB)
vG <- vooma(GolubB, designG, plot=TRUE)         # Panel A
plotMDS(vG, pch=unclass(tissue.mfB), cex=0.8)  # Panel B
```

Cross-Validation to Determine the Optimum Number of Features

Note first the function `orderFeatures()` that will be used extensively in the sequel. It selects features that, as measured by an analysis of variance F-statistic, give, individually, the best separation between groups. The function takes as arguments

- `x`: the matrix of expression values, in the features-by-observations layout that is usual in work with expression arrays;
- `cl`: a factor that classifies the observations;
- `subset`: if changed from its default (`NULL`), this identifies a subset of observations (columns of `dset`) that will be used for calculating the statistics;
- `FUN`: currently the only available function (`aovFbyrow()`)uses the analysis of variance F-statistic as a measure of between group separation;
- `values`: by default the function returns the order. If set to `TRUE` the function returns the ordered F-statistic values as well as the order.

Selection of features that discriminate best individually, in an analysis of variance F-statistic sense, is not guaranteed to select the features that perform best in combination. It is akin to using, in a multiple regression, the variables that perform well when used as the only predictors. The development of defensible variable selection methods, applicable to the data such as in this section, is the subject of ongoing research.

Cross-Validation for a Range of Choices of Number of Features

We will demonstrate the use of 10-fold cross-validation, repeated for each choice of number of features in the range that is pertinent, to determine how many features to choose. There are 31 observations, divided into three groups, so that the maximum number of features that can be used for discrimination is 23. This is calculated as follows: At each fold, the training data consists of nine out of ten subsets in the 10-fold division of the data, that is, at least 27 out of the 31 points. (Each subset has three or four observations.) One degree of freedom is lost for each of the three subgroups, and at least one degree of freedom should be left for estimating the variance. Thus, at most 23 ($= 27 - 4$) degrees of freedom can be used for estimating linear discriminant parameters.

In order to choose the optimum number of features, the cross-validation must be repeated for each choice of g = number of features in the range 1, 2, ..., g_{max} = 23, calculating the cross-validation accuracy for each such choice. The number of features will be chosen to give an accuracy that is, or is close to, the maximum.

The full procedure is as follows.

For $g = 1, 2, \ldots, g_{max}$, do the following.

. For each fold $i = 1, \ldots k$ in turn (k = number of folds) do the following.

Split Take the ith set as the test data, and use the remaining data (all except the ith set) for training.

Select Choose the g features that have the largest anova between group F-statistics.

Classify Determine discriminant functions, using the chosen features and the current training data.

Predict Predict the groups to which observations in the current test set belong.

. Record, against the number g of features used, the proportion of correct predictions. (This is calculated across all folds, and hence for the total data.)

Accuracies are now available for all choices of number of features. Choose the smallest number of features that gives close to the maximum accuracy.

The 10-fold cross-validation will be repeated for each of four different splits into 10 subsets. Especially in the present context, where at each fold of each repeat of the cross-validation there is a variable selection step, such use of repeats is desirable for adequate sampling of the variability.

Computations are greatly reduced by determining the ordering of features, for each fold of the data, in advance. These orderings are stored in a matrix of character values, with as many columns as there are folds, and with number of rows equal to the maximum number of features under consideration. There is a rigid upper limit to the number of features that can be accommodated on the discriminant analysis. For this dataset, this is, as noted above, 23. When the preliminary calculations are finished, column i of the matrix will record the features that give the 23 highest F-statistics for the fold i training data. For selecting the "best" n_f features, one set for each different fold, the first n_f rows of this matrix ($f \leq 23$) will be taken.

Calculations will use the function `hddplot::cvdisc()`. For comparison, results are obtained both from the resubstitution measure of accuracy and from a defective use of cross-validation:

```
##  Cross-validation to determine the optimum number of features
## 10-fold (x4). Warning messages are omitted.
## Accuracy measure will be: tissue.mfB.cv$acc.cv
tissue.mfB.cv <- cvdisc(GolubB, cl=tissue.mfB, nfeatures=1:23,
nfold=c(10,4), print.progress=FALSE)
```

```
Accuracy             Best accuracy, less 1SD   Best accuracy
(Cross-validation) 0.85 (3 features)           0.9 (4 features)
```

```
## Defective measures will be in acc.resub (resubstitution)
## and acc.sel1 (select features prior to cross-validation)
tissue.mfB.badcv <- defectiveCVdisc(GolubB, cl=tissue.mfB,
foldids=tissue.mfB.cv$folds, nfeatures=1:23)
```

```
##
## Calculations for random normal data:
set.seed(43)
rGolubB <- matrix(rnorm(prod(dim(GolubB))), nrow=nrow(GolubB))
rtissue.mfB.cv <- cvdisc(rGolubB, cl=tissue.mfB, nfeatures=1:23,
nfold=c(10,4), print.progress=FALSE)
```

```
[1] "Input rows (features) are not named. Names"
[1] "1:7129 will be assigned."


Accuracy             Best accuracy, less 1SD   Best accuracy
(Cross-validation) 0.39 (1 features)           0.48 (9 features)
```

```
rtissue.mfB.badcv <- defectiveCVdisc(rGolubB, cl=tissue.mfB,
nfeatures=1:23,
foldids=rtissue.mfB.cv$folds)
```

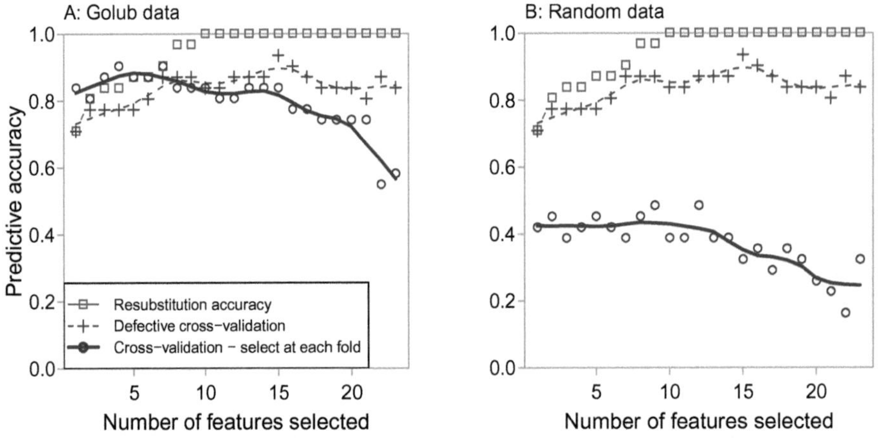

Figure 9.20 Panel A compares different accuracy measures, in the development of a discriminant rule for the classification, into the categories `BM:f`, `BM:m`, and `PB:m`, of the B-cell ALL data for which gender is known. The resubstitution measure (□) is a severely biased measure. Cross-validation, but with features selected using all the data (+), is less severely biased. An acceptable measure of predictive accuracy (∘) requires reselection of features at each fold of the cross-validation. Panel B shows the performance of each of these measures when the expression values were replaced by random data.

```
[1] "Input rows (features) are not named. Names"
[1] "1:7129 will be assigned."
```

The resubstitution and "defective CV" points show biased and therefore inappropriate accuracy measures. The resubstitution points show the proportion of correct predictions when the discrimination rule is applied to the data used to develop the rule. The "defective CV" points show the proportion of correct predictions when the same features, selected using all the data, are used at each fold, and do not change from one fold to the next.

Figure 9.20B applies the same calculations to random data. The bias in the two incorrect "accuracies" is now very obvious. The correct cross-validation estimates are now much worse than chance for more than three or four features, while the "defective CV" estimates continue to increase up to about 15 features. At each fold, the rule is tuned to be optimal for the quirks of the training data. It is therefore suboptimal for the test data at each fold.

Figure 9.20 appears as figure 5 (section 4.1) in the vignette `QUICKhddplot` in the `hddplot` package. Code that will recreate the figure may be found there.

Which Features?

It is of interest to see what features have been used at the different folds. This information is available from the list element `genelist`, in the object `tissue.mfB.cv` that the function `cvdisc()` returned. As the interest is in working with three features, it is the first three rows that are relevant. The following is a summary.

```
genelist <- matrix(tissue.mfB.cv$genelist[1:3, ,], nrow=3)
tab <- table(genelist, row(genelist))
ord <- order(tab[,1], tab[,2], tab[,3], decreasing=TRUE)
tab[ord,]
```

```
genelist         1  2  3
  M58459_at     32  4  0
  S74221_at      4  0  0
  U29195_at      4  0  0
  X54870_at      0 16  8
  U91327_at      0  8 16
  L08666_at      0  4  0
  U49395_at      0  4  0
  X00437_s_at    0  4  0
  X62654_rna1_at 0  0  8
  X53416_at      0  0  4
  X82494_at      0  0  4
```

Observe that `M58459_at` is the predominant first choice. There is much less consistency in the second and third choices.

9.6.4 Graphs Derived from the Cross-Validation Process

With a methodology available for choosing the number of features, it is now possible to look for an alternative to Figure 9.18A that does not run the same risk of bias. A possible approach is to divide the data in two, with the two halves successively used as the training data, and the remaining half as the test data. The function `hddplot::cvscores()` is designed to give one plot for all the data. It can be used with any data where there are enough groups in each subset of the classification that `hddplot::cvdisc()` can be used satisfactorily.

Consider first the creation of a plot for the subset of the `allB` data that formed classification 1. Figure 9.20A suggested that the optimum number of features is, conservatively, 3. Calculations will then be described that use three features.

Test scores can be calculated for the test data at each of the folds. As the different pairs of scores (with three groups, there can at most be two sets of scores) relate to different discriminant functions and to different choices of features, they are appropriately called "local" test scores. Local fold i training scores are similarly available, again with one set for each value of i.

The local training scores are used to make the connection between the test scores at the different folds. A vignette that gives details is included with the package *hddplot*. The methodology is a modification of that described in Maindonald and Burden (2005). Code for Figure 9.21 is:

```
## Uses tissue.mfB.acc from above
tissue.mfB.scores <-
cvscores(cvlist = tissue.mfB.cv, nfeatures = 3, cl.other = NULL)
scoreplot(scorelist = tissue.mfB.scores, cl.circle=NULL,
prefix="B—cell subset —", fg='gray')
```

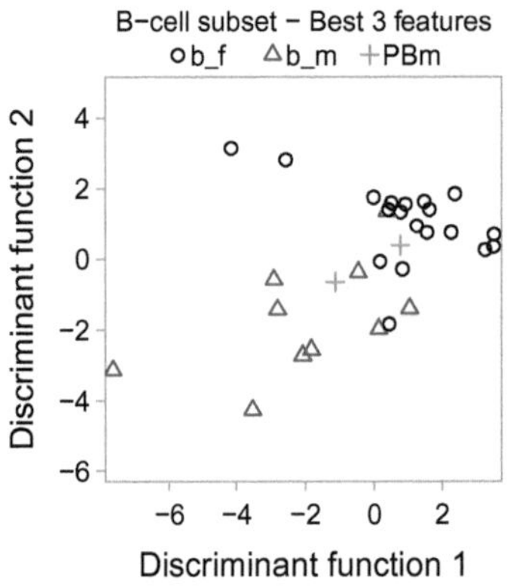

Figure 9.21 This plot of projections of linear discriminant analysis scores is designed to fairly reflect the performance of a linear discriminant in distinguishing known groups.

There are two clusters of points, with tissues from females mostly in one cluster and tissues from males in the other cluster.

The Key Role of Cross-Validation

The cross-validation methodology used above has far-reaching importance. The choice of variables, in Subsections 9.6.2 and 9.6.4, can be viewed as a form of model tuning. With more complicated models (really, families of models) such as neural nets and Support Vector Machines (SVMs), there are many more tuning choices and tuning parameters. Thus, for example, see the details of tuning parameters that are given on the help page for the function `e1071::svm()` (Meyer, 2001). Such tuning can interact in complex ways with feature selection. For valid accuracy assessment, such tuning (in principle, at least) must be repeated at each cross-validation fold.

The *randomForest* package seems an attractive alternative, for working with expression array data, to the methods that have been discussed here. Its function `MDSplot()` can be used to obtain a low-dimensional representation of the data, based as above on known prior groupings.

Better understanding of gene interactions may suggest better alternatives to using large numbers of features as discriminant variables. Such understanding seems certain to lead also, in the course of time, to more targeted data collection. There will be a greater use of studies that gather data on a few features of known relevance to the phenomena under investigation.

9.6.5 Estimating Contrasts, and Calculating False Discovery Rates

We now fit the model to the counts as transformed in Subsection 9.6.3 using the function `vooma()`. We then specify the treatment contrasts in which we are interested, extract information about these, and use the function `eBayes()` to shrink the probewise sample variances towards a common value:

```
fitG <- lmFit(vG, designG)
contrs <- c("b_f−b_m", "b_f−PBm", "b_m−PBm")
contr.matrix <- makeContrasts(contrasts=contrs,
levels=levels(tissue.mfB))
fit2 <- contrasts.fit(fitG, contr.matrix)
fit2 <- eBayes(fit2)
```

From p-Values to False Discovery Rate (FDR)

The following proceeds immediately to an ANOVA-like overall check for differential expression:

```
print(topTable(fit2, number=5), digits=2)
```

```
                    b_f.b_m b_f.PBm b_m.PBm AveExpr  F P.Value adj.PVal
U73379_at              1229    2801    1572  2369.4 24 5.0e-07   0.0035
HG371-HT26388_s_at     -238     756     995  -131.3 17 9.5e-06   0.0206
X56199_at               653    1011     358   -47.3 17 1.1e-05   0.0206
L25876_at               472    1305     833   470.0 17 1.2e-05   0.0206
U22963_at                59     897     838     5.3 16 1.6e-05   0.0235
```

An overall summary is:

```
summary(decideTests(fit2))
```

```
       b_f-b_m b_f-PBm b_m-PBm
Down         0       1       0
NotSig    7129    7043    7125
Up           0      85       4
```

```
## Try also
## summary(decideTests(fit2, p.value=0.001))
```

Distributional Extremes

The analysis in the third edition (Maindonald and Braun, 2010) used permutation methods, as implemented by the function `multtest::mt.maxT()`, to determine a reference distribution for *F*-statistics that were calculated without accounting for the mean–variance relationship. Without extensive simulations, it is not clear how the strong mean–variance relationship might affect results.

9.7 Balance and Matching – Causal Inference from Observational Data

We begin by examining approaches to checking on and adjusting for differences between groups in observational data. The hope is that, after adjustment, remaining differences will be entirely due to a further variable or factor, a "treatment" perhaps, whose causal or other explanatory role is under investigation. In medical applications, the groups are usually "treatment" group(s) and a "control." If there are two groups, an ideal is to find "propensity" scores that measure the probability of that an observation belongs in one or other group. There can be no guarantee that such a one-dimensional "ordination" will be effective for this purpose. It will not always be able to do the job required of it.

Explanatory variables ("confounders") must be available that can be used both to check matching between groups, and to adjust for group differences that do not result from the "treatment" or other intervention. An important assumption is that all relevant confounders are available. In all cases, checks on the effectiveness of the adjustment are essential. These approaches should not be regarded as a replacement for the use of randomized controlled trials.

9.7.1 Tools for the Task

The chief focus will be on comparing two groups, here identified as treatment and control. A strong theme is that, after covariate adjustments, groups that are to be compared must be closely matched. There are a number of R packages that provide graphical and other checks. A good place to start, for an overview of relevant R packages and of the checks that they offer, is the introductory vignette "Covariate balance tables and plots: A guide to the cobalt package" from the *cobalt* package. Several further vignettes in this and the *MatchIt* package include comment on methodological issues, on available functions, and give extensive references. Functions in the *MatchIt* package, with more limited use of functions in the *cobalt* package, will be key tools for the account that follows. The discussion here will cover only a limited range of the possibilities. Among papers that discuss the issues involved see, for example, Glass et al. (2013).

Often, as in the data that will be examined here, there will be many more control than treated observations, with the focus on mechanisms for matching control to treated observations. A balance has to be found between stricter matching that leads to the discarding or downweighting of unmatched controls, and coarser mechanisms where the larger adjustments needed to account for group differences become a larger source of uncertainty.

Propensity scores, typically obtained using logistic regression or an equivalent, attempt to provide a single variable that can account for group differences that are not due to the intervention, with the hope that one set of propensity scores can replace all confounders. Whether or not they are successful in this, propensity scores can be used for coarse checks on group differences. They are not a substitute for more detailed checks that compare individual variables and factors, or for two- or three-dimensional ordinations such as in Figure 9.24.

9.7.2 Regression with Propensity Scores – Labor Training Data

Attention will be limited to the case where two groups – labeled for convenience "treatment" and "control," that are to be compared. As noted at the start of this chapter, a propensity is a measure, determined by covariate values, aims to provide a measure of the probability that an observation will fall in the treatment rather than in the control group. Of particular interest is checking the extent of overlap between on propensity scores between different groups. This can be later supplemented by more detailed checks. See Rosenbaum and Rubin (1983) and Morgan and Winship (2015) for further comments on the methodology.

Table 9.1 *Proportion in the stated category, for each of the datasets indicated. Proportions for the experimental data are in the final two lines of the table.*

	Proportion					
	Black	Hispanic	Married	Dropout	re75> 0	re78> 0
psid1	0.25	0.03	0.87	0.31	0.90	0.89
psid2	0.39	0.07	0.74	0.49	0.66	0.66
psid3	0.45	0.12	0.70	0.51	0.39	0.49
cps1	0.07	0.07	0.71	0.30	0.89	0.86
cps2	0.11	0.08	0.46	0.45	0.82	0.83
cps3	0.20	0.14	0.51	0.60	0.69	0.77
nsw-ctl	0.80	0.11	0.16	0.81	0.58	0.70
nsw-treat	0.80	0.09	0.17	0.73	0.63	0.77

The experimental data are from a study, conducted under the aegis of the US National Supported Work (NSW) Demonstration program, of individuals who had a history of employment and related difficulties. Over 1975–1977, an experiment randomly assigned individuals who met the eligibility criteria either to a treatment group that participated in a 6–18 months training program, or to a control group that did not participate. The results for males, because they highlight methodological problems more sharply, have been studied more extensively than the corresponding results for females. Participation in the training gave an increase in male 1978 earnings, relative to those in the control group, by an average of \$886 (SE \$472).

Here, the experimental "treatment" data will be compared with several nonexperimental groups, with the aim of determining whether or to what extent comparable results can be obtained when the treatment group are matched to a nonexperimental control group that received no such training? The results highlight the difficulty in reaching secure conclusions from the use of observational data. The nonexperimental data are from:

1. The Panel Study of Income Dynamics study (PSID: 2490 males, data in `psid1`, with filtered data in `psid2` and `psid3`),
2. Westat's Matched Current Population Survey – Social Security Administration file (CPS: 16 289 males, data in `cps1`, with filtered data in `cps2` and `cps3`).

Published studies include Lalonde (1986) and Dehejia and Wahba (1999).

Table 9.1 has summary information on proportions for discrete categories that are of interest, for different choices of control group that have been investigated.[7] The variable `trt` has values 0 (`control`) or 1 (`treatment`). Other variables are:

[7]
```
library(DAAG)
## Columns 4:7 are factors; columns 9:10 (re75 & re78) are continuous
propmat <- matrix(0, ncol=6, nrow=8)
dimnames(propmat) <- list(c("psid1", "psid2", "psid3", "cps1", "cps2", "cps3",
"nsw-ctl", "nsw-trt"), names(nswdemo)[c(4:7, 9:10)])
for(k in 1:8){
  dframe <- switch(k, psid1, psid2, psid3, cps1, cps2, cps3,
  subset(nswdemo, trt==0), subset(nswdemo, trt==1))
  propmat[k,] <- c(sapply(dframe[,4:7], function(x){
                  z <- table(x); z[2]/sum(z)}),
                  sapply(dframe[,9:10], function(x)sum(x>0)/sum(!is.na(x))))
```

`age` (years); `educ` (years of education)
`black` (0=white 1=black); `hisp` (0=non-hispanic 1=hispanic)
`marr` (0 = not married 2=married)
`nodeg` (0=completed high-school 1=dropout); i.e., educ ≤ 11
`re74`, `re75`, `re78` (real earnings: 1974, 1975, 1978)
(`re74` is available for a subset of the experimental data only.)

The binary variables (`trt`, `marr`, `nodeg`, `black`, `hisp`) will be converted to factors, with `black` and `hisp` merged into the single factor `ethnicid`. With the default parameterization, the initial level becomes in each case the baseline, with coefficients for the subsequent levels giving differences from this baseline. Information on `re74` is complete for the nonexperimental sets of control data, but incomplete for the experimental data. We will take up the issue of how to handle `re74` below.

Notice the big differences, for `black`, `marr`, and `nodeg` (dropout), between the nonexperimental controls (first six lines) and both sets of experimental data (final two lines). Even in the filtered datasets (`psid2`, `psid3`, `cps2`, and `cps3`), the differences are substantial. The big changes that the filtering has made to the proportion with nonzero earnings is worrying. Notice particularly the huge differences between `psid3` and `psid1`, both for `re75` and `re78`.

Figure 9.22 compares the distributions of nonzero values, in the control and treatment groups, for the explanatory variables `log(re75)`, `log(re78)`, `age`, and `educ`, for each of the candidate sets of control data. There are large differences between treatment and controls, whichever set of nonexperimental controls is chosen. The very heavy tails in the distributions of `re75` and `re78` make use of a logarithmic transformation desirable.

The distributions of nonzero values of `log(re78)` are almost identical between experimental treated and control observations, just as similar as for `log(re75)`. A more careful comparison will use quantile–quantile (Q-Q) plots. The comparison can be repeated with several bootstrap samples, as a check that such small differences as are apparent are not maintained under bootstrap sampling. We will later check whether the differences that are apparent between nonexperimental controls and treatment are maintained after a propensity score adjustment.

The function `addControl()` will be used to match the experimental treatment with a specified set of control data. The factor `z75` is designed to account for the `re75` point mass at 0.

```
addControl <-
function(control, offset=30){
  nam <- deparse(substitute(control))
  if(nam=="nswdemo")nsw0 <- nswdemo else
    nsw0 <- rbind(control, subset(DAAG::nswdemo, trt==1))
  nsw0$z75 <- factor(nsw0$re75==0, labels=c("0",">0"))
  nsw0$ethnicid <- factor(with(nsw0, ifelse(black==1, "black",
    ifelse(hisp==1, "hisp", "other"))), levels=c("other","black","hisp"))
nsw0 <- nsw0[, -match(c("black","hisp"), names(nsw0))]
nsw0
}
```

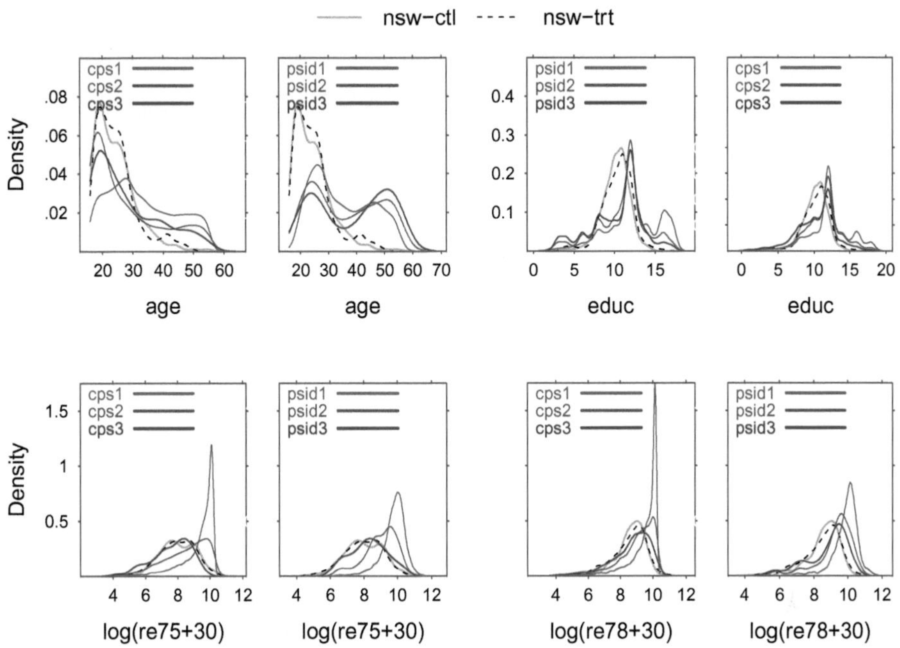

Figure 9.22 Overlaid density plots, comparing treatment groups with the experimental control data in **nswdemo** and with six different choices of nonexperimental control data, for the variables `log(re75)`, `log(re78)`, `age`, and `educ`. Nonexperimental control datasets are `cps1` `cps2`, `cps3`, `psid1`, `psid2`, and `psid3`. Variable values that are zero (`-Inf` on a logarithmic scale) are omitted.

The following creates a dataset `nsw` that combines the `psid1` control data with the experimental treatment data, for the same variables as shown in Figure 9.22. Log-transformed values, after adding an offset of 30, have been added for the variables `re75` and `re78`. This gives somewhat more symmetric distributions.

```
## Create dataset that will be used for later analyses
nsw <- addControl(psid1)
nsw <- within(nsw, {re75log <- log(re75+30);
                    re78log <- log(re78+30);
                    trt <- factor(trt, labels=c("Control","Treat"))})
## A treated values only dataset will be required below
trtdat <- subset(nsw, trt=="Treat")
trtdat$pres74 <- factor(!is.na(trtdat$re74), labels=c("<NA>","pres"))
table(trtdat$pres74)
```

```
<NA> pres
 112  185
```

In the experimental data, just over 40 percent of the values of the explanatory variable `re74` are missing. The minimum value of `re74` in the experimental data is 445 (dollars), which is close to six times the minimum of 74 for `re75`.

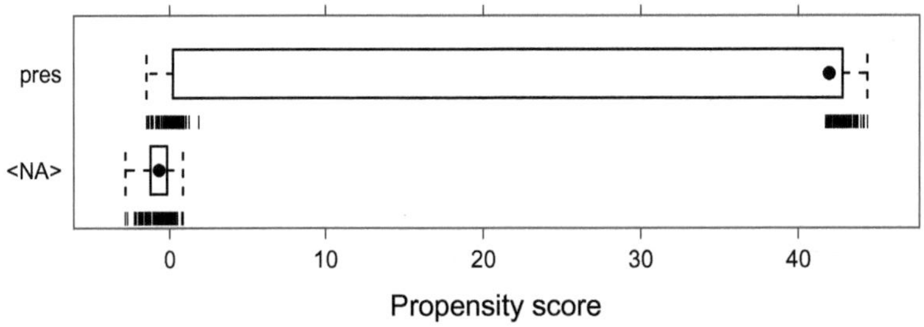

Figure 9.23 Comparison, between observations for which `re74` is available and those for which it is not, of propensity scores that use remaining variables to account for differences between the two subsets of the treatment data.

Figure 9.23 uses propensity scores based on variables other than `re74` to account for differences between observations for which `re74` is available and those for which it is not. The missing values clearly relate to a different subgroup within the data.

The points for individuals whose values are missing values all belong very clearly with a subset of the zero-earnings group. Note that a propensity value that is 0 corresponds to a probability of 0.5 of the value being missing. The table below provides the reason for the strong pattern. Primarily, the contrast is between individuals who had no earnings in 1975, and those for which earnings were greater than zero.

```
with(trtdat, table(pres74,z75))
```

```
       z75
pres74    0   >0
  <NA>  112    0
  pres   74  111
```

Thus, the use of `re74` for explanatory purposes risks introducing bias.

The *MatchIt* and *cobalt* packages both include the `lalonde` dataset. This combines a subset of the `psid1` data with those observations in the experimental (`nswdemo`) dataset for which values of `re74` are available. A consequence is that, when control observations are matched to the treatment subset of the `lalonde` dataset, the results apply to a population different from that for the experimental `nswdemo` dataset. Following analyses based on the `nsw` dataset that has just been created, we will comment on differences from analyses that use the `lalonde` dataset.

9.7.3 Regression Comparisons

One possibility is to use regression methods directly to compare the two groups, with variables other than `re78` used as explanatory variables. Issues for the use of regression methods, here and more generally, are as follows.

- Continuous variables almost certainly will often require some form of nonlinear transformation. Regression splines can be a reasonable way to proceed.
- Should interaction terms be included?

- The large number of explanatory variables, and interactions if they are included, complicates the use of diagnostic checks.
- A substantial proportion of the values of `re78` are zero. The distribution of nonzero values of `re78` is highly skew, in both of the experimental groups (treatment and nontreatment), and in all of the nonexperimental controls. A consequence is that the regression results will be strongly influenced by a few very large values. A $\log(\text{re78} + 30)$ transformation (the choice of offset, in a range of perhaps 20–200, is not crucial) gives values that may more reasonably be used for regression. (In spite of the evident skewness, both Lalonde (1986) and Dehejia and Wahba (1999) used `re78` as the response variable in their analyses.)
- Control and training groups can be made more comparable by some initial filtering on values of explanatory variables. The R *MatchIt* package[8] is one of several R packages that implement a range of alternative matching mechanisms. The choice of mechanism is inevitably to an extent subjective, and may bias results.
- Explanatory variables must at the same time model both within-group relationships and between-group differences. These two demands can be in conflict.

Taken together, these points raise such serious issues that claims that are based on results from any use of regression methods have to be carefully critiqued and treated with caution.

The complications of any use of regression analyses, and the uncertainties that remain after analysis, are in stark contrast to the relative simplicity of analysis for the experimental data. Experimental treatment and control distributions can be compared directly. Assuming that the randomization was properly done, this comparison avoids the complications that arise from the attempt to adjust for explanatory variable effects. For both types of study, it is important that observations can be treated as a random sample from the population that is of interest.

Regression Calculations

In the following regressions, smooths that use the `gam()` function in the *mgcv* package have been used for each of `log(re75+30)`, `age`, and `educ`. The following shows how the treatment effect estimates change with the choice of control group.

```
        Est.  exp(Est.) CIlower CIupper
psid1   0.13743     1.147  0.8802   1.496
psid2   0.17787     1.195  0.7124   2.003
psid3   0.62041     1.860  0.9790   3.533
cps1    0.13180     1.141  0.9013   1.444
cps2    0.01631     1.016  0.7299   1.416
cps3    0.31439     1.369  0.8724   2.150
nswdemo 0.34826     1.417  1.0549   1.902
```

These show modest variation, but do all point in the same direction as the experimental comparison in the final row. It is instructive to rerun the calculations with `re75` replacing $\log(\text{re75+30})$ and `re78` replacing $\log(\text{re78+30})$ as the outcome variable. The different results do not then all point in the same direction. The likely

[8] Note the spelling – *MatchIt* with an upper case `I`.

reason is that a few very large values of `re78` now have high leverage and a large influence. (An exercise at the end of the chapter is designed to check this out.)

The model fitted was, for the comparison with the `psid1` data:

```
nsw.gam <- gam(log(re78+30)~ trt + ethnicid + z75 + nodeg + s(age) +
               s(educ) + log(re75+30), data=nsw)
```

9.7.4 The Use of Scores to Replace Covariates

Several approaches for estimating the treatment effect will be tried and compared. One is to replace the explanatory variables by a single *propensity* score. This is justifiable on theoretical grounds if the distribution of the explanatory variables is, conditional on the propensity score, the same for treatment and control observations. Summary and information and plots can be checked to see whether this is plausible. Limited checks can be performed to determine whether this assumption is plausible. If these indicate problems, the analysis might still give reasonable results, but there will not be a sound basis for confidence in them.

For the analyses described here, we will start by using control observations from the dataset `psid1`. Analyses that work with control observations from one of the other datasets are left as exercises for the reader.

9.7.5 Two-Dimensional Representation Using randomForest Proximities

The function `randomForest()` from the *randomForest()* can be used to derive proximity scores. With the setting `proximity=TRUE`, it returns a matrix of "proximity" measures. These are "distances" between observations that are derived from the frequency with which pairs of data points appear in the same terminal nodes.

As calculations with the 2787 × 2787 matrix of distances between the rows of `nsw` would be very time consuming, the scores in an initial `randomForest` model are used to select a subset of observations, then proceeding to a second `randomForest()` fit that was used to calculate proximities for the reduced dataset.

Refer back to Subsection 9.1.3. Plots are shown for three ranges of scores – low, medium, and high. The text in the panel is labeled according to the equivalent range of probabilities. Figure 9.24 shows the result.

```
suppressPackageStartupMessages(library(randomForest))
form <- trt ~ age + educ + ethnicid + marr + nodeg + z75 + re75log
nsw.rf <- randomForest(form, data=nsw, sampsize=c(297,297))
p.rf <- predict(nsw.rf,type="prob")[,2]
sc.rf <- log((p.rf+0.001)/(1-p.rf+0.001))
```

Values of `p.rf` that are not 0 or 1 were in the range 0.0022, 0.9978. Hence the 0.001 offset for the probabilities for calculating the scores `sc.rf`.

There is a clear separation between points, even for those given the highest probability (more that 0.52) of belonging with the treatment group. Matching the data on the first ordinate might well do better than matching on the propensity score.

```
omitn <- match(c("PropScore","weights","subclass"), names(dat2RF), nomatch=0)
matchISO.rf <-matchit(trt ~ age + educ + ethnicid + marr + nodeg + z75 +
                      re75log, ratio=1, data=dat2RF[,-omitn], distance=isoScores[,1])
```

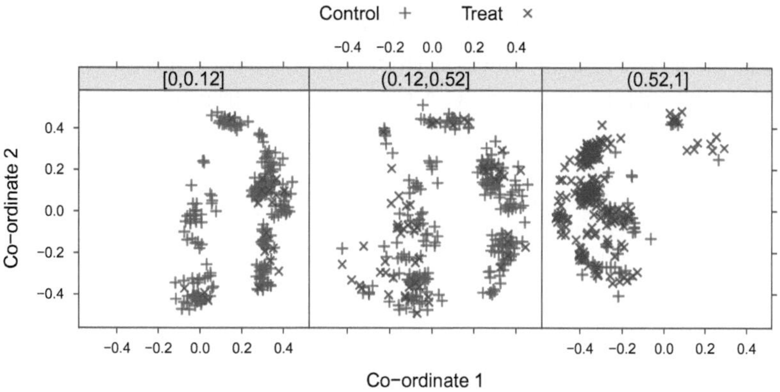

Figure 9.24 These plots check the extent to which random-forest propensity scores, used to account for explanatory variable differences, are comparable between treated and controls. The ranges shown are for the probabilities before use of the logit transformation to give scores. Cutpoints have been chosen so that the three ranges contain an approximately equal number of observations. Note that results will differ somewhat from one run to the next.

```
## summary(match.rf,un=F,improvement=F)
## summary(match.rf, un=F, interactions=T, improvement=F)$sum.matched[,1:4]
## In the first place, look only at the first 4 columns
```

The results obtained allow estimation of effects. More detailed explanation will be provided in the discussion of methods that use scores from other types of models, or that do not use scores for matching.

```
dat1RF <- match.data(matchISO.rf, distance="PropScore")
dat1RF.lm <- lm(re78log ~ trt, data = dat1RF, weights = weights)
library(sandwich)  # Allows use of `vcovCL()` from the `sandwich` package
lmtest::coeftest(dat1RF.lm, vcov. = vcovCL, cluster = ~subclass)
```

```
t test of coefficients:

            Estimate Std. Error t value Pr(>|t|)
(Intercept)    8.022      0.149   54.01   <2e-16
trtTreat      -0.644      0.207   -3.11   0.0019
```

```
## Check for increase in number with non-zero earnings
dat1RF.glm <- glm(I(re78>0) ~ trt, data = dat1RF, weights = weights,
                  family=binomial)
lmtest::coeftest(dat1RF.glm, vcov. = vcovCL, cluster = ~subclass)
```

```
z test of coefficients:

            Estimate Std. Error z value Pr(>|z|)
(Intercept)   1.2922     0.1414    9.14   <2e-16
trtTreat     -0.0588     0.2049   -0.29     0.77
```

On this analysis, the groups are for all practical purposes indistinguishable.

Derivation and Investigation of Scores

We now use the `mgcv::gam()` function to derive propensity scores. The following fits a GAM model with binomial error. A GLM model that is very nearly equivalent is fitted for comparison:

```
library(mgcv)
formG <- trt ~ ethnicid + marr+ z75 + s(age) + s(educ) + s(re75log)
nsw.gam <- gam(formG, family=binomial(link="logit"), data=nsw)
pred <- predict(nsw.gam, type='response')
table(nsw$trt, round(pred))
```

```
            0    1
  Control 2434   56
  Treat     84  213
```

```
## Alternative
library(splines) ## Fit normal cubic splines using splines::ns()
formNS <- trt ~ ethnicid + marr+ z75 + ns(age,2) +
ns(educ) + ns(re75log,3)
nsw.glm <- glm(formNS, family=binomial(link="logit"), data=nsw)
pred <- predict(nsw.glm, type='response')
table(nsw$trt, round(pred))
```

```
            0    1
  Control 2437   53
  Treat     93  204
```

```
cbind(AIC(nsw.glm,nsw.gam), BIC(nsw.glm, nsw.gam))
```

```
           df   AIC    df   BIC
nsw.glm 11.00 737.8 11.00 803.0
nsw.gam 18.61 711.3 18.61 821.7
```

A GAM model is the model of preference because functions in the *MatchIt* and *cobalt* packages that check for balance do not accommodate regression spline terms in `glm` models. As GAM models allow a much wider range of possibilities, including the use of regression spline terms that are closely equivalent to those in the GLM model, this is not a real limitation.

A GAM model that includes factor-by-factor interactions and some variable-by-factor interactions did give a slightly lower AIC. Given the large number of parameters estimated, the BIC statistic, which is very substantially increased, is the better criterion. (The variable-by-factor interactions appears problematic. On the author's computer, the fit failed when the same model formula was supplied to `matchit()`.) Suitable code, for readers who wish to investigate this model, is:

```
## Include factor by factor and variable interactions with ethnicid
## and marr (Result not shown)
formGx <- trt ~ (ethnicid+marr+z75)^2 + s(age, by=ethnicid)+
           s(educ, by=ethnicid) + s(re75log,by=ethnicid)+
           s(age, by=marr)+ s(educ, by=marr) + s(re75log,by=marr)
nswx.gam <- gam(formula = formGx, data = nsw, family=binomial(link = "logit"))
```

```
predx <- predict(nswx.gam, type='response')
table(nsw$trt, round(predx))
AIC(nsw.glm,nsw.gam,nswx.gam)
```

The `matchit()` function provides a framework for fitting the model and collecting together ancillary information. The `distance="gam"` argument indicates that "distances" (i.e., propensity scores) are to be calculated using the `gam()` function with the specified formula, and finally recalculated using the matched data:

```
library(MatchIt)
## Use data frame that omits re74. Otherwise matchit() will generate NAs
## where they occur in re74, even though re74 is not in the model formula.
nswG <- nsw[, c("trt","age","educ","ethnicid", "marr","nodeg","z75",
              "re75log","re78log","re78")]
formG <- trt ~ ethnicid + marr+ z75 + s(age) + s(educ) + s(re75log)
match.gam <- matchit(formula = formG, data = nswG, method = "nearest",
                    distance = "gam", link = "logit", reestimate=TRUE)
datG <- match.data(match.gam, distance="PropScore")
## Summary information
match.gam
```

```
A matchit object
 - method: 1:1 nearest neighbor matching without replacement
 - distance: Propensity score
             - estimated with GAM with a logit link
 - number of obs.: 2787 (original), 594 (matched)
 - target estimand: ATT
 - covariates: ethnicid, marr, z75, age, educ, re75log
```

```
## summary(match.gam,un=F,improvement=F)
## summary(match.gam, un=F, interactions=T, improvement=F)$sum.matched[,1:4]
## In the first place, look only at the first 4 columns
```

Clearly the data are not well matched. While adding in interaction terms may help, this leads to a very complex model if all possible interactions are to be accounted for. At the same time, it increases the risk (or likelihood) that the result will reflect quirks in the control data. Figure 9.25 compares the distributions of propensity scores between treatment and control groups after matching, noting also scores for unmatched observations.

In Figure 9.26, Panel A summarizes the extent to which the two groups have been matched on the covariates. Panel B plots differences between treatment and control, for matched observations, against scores. Clearly the matching has not been very successful. Code for Figure 9.26 is

```
suppressPackageStartupMessages(library(gridExtra))
suppressPackageStartupMessages(library(ggplot2))
suppressPackageStartupMessages(library(cobalt))
gg1<- cobalt::love.plot(match.gam, position="bottom", grid=TRUE,
                        star.char="",stars='raw') +
  ggtitle("A: Differences from balance") +
  theme(plot.title = element_text(hjust=0, vjust=0.5, size=11),
        plot.margin=unit(c(9,15,0,9), 'pt'))
sub <- match(with(subset(datG, trt=="Control"),subclass),
            with(subset(datG, trt=="Treat"),subclass))
datGpaired <- cbind(subset(datG, trt=="Treat"),
```

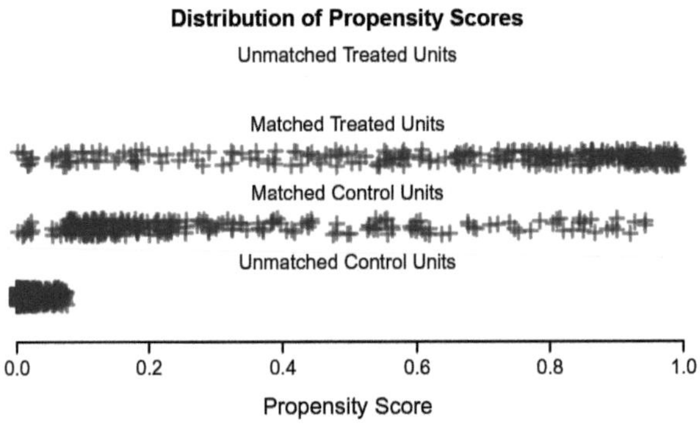

Figure 9.25 Distributions of propensity scores for treatment and control groups after matching.

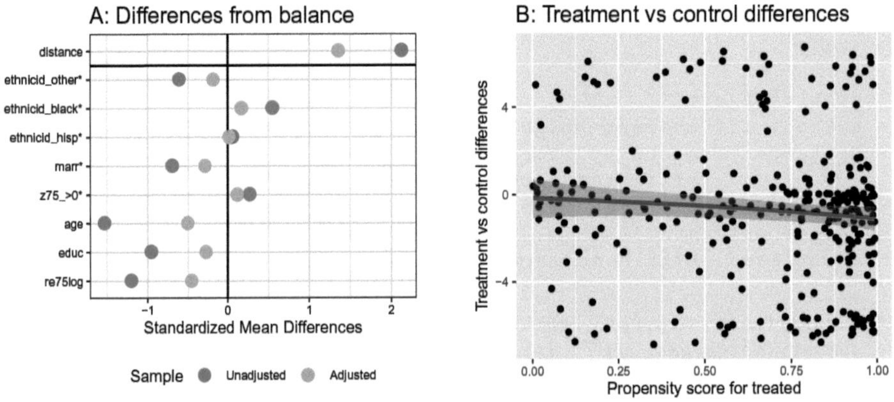

Figure 9.26 Panel A is a "love plot" that summarizes the extent to which the matching has, for the several covariates, led to a closer match between treatment and control. Differences for continuous variables are standardized. Factor effects, marked with an asterisk, are not. Panel B plots differences between treatment and control, for matched observations, against scores, with a smooth fitted.

```
                  with(subset(datG, trt=="Control")[sub,],
                  cbind("Cre78log"=re78log,"CPropScore"=PropScore)))
gg2 <- ggplot(datGpaired)+
  geom_point(aes(PropScore,I(re78log-Cre78log)), size=1)+
  geom_smooth(aes(PropScore,I(re78log-Cre78log)), method = "gam",
              formula = y ~ s(x, bs = "cs")) +
  xlab("Propensity score for treated")+
  ylab("Treatment vs control differences") +
  ggtitle("B: Treatment vs control differences") +
  theme(plot.title = element_text(hjust=0, vjust=0.5, size=11),
        plot.margin=unit(c(9,9,0,15), 'pt'))
grid.arrange(gg1, gg2, ncol=2)
```

Now use the matched data to investigate the treatment effect:

```
library(sandwich)
datG.lm <- lm(re78log ~ trt, data = datG, weights = weights)
```

```
## With 1:1 matching, the weights argument is not really needed
## Print first two coefficients only.
lmtest::coeftest(datG.lm, vcov. = vcovCL, cluster = ~subclass)[1:2,]
```

```
             Estimate Std. Error t value    Pr(>|t|)
(Intercept)    8.1631     0.1379  59.185 8.571e-251
trtTreat      -0.7857     0.1952  -4.025  6.427e-05
```

```
## Check number whose income was greater than 0
datG.glm <- glm(I(re78>0) ~ trt, data = datG, weights = weights, family=binomial)
lmtest::coeftest(datG.glm, vcov. = vcovCL, cluster = ~subclass)[1:2,]
```

```
             Estimate Std. Error z value  Pr(>|z|)
(Intercept)    1.5041     0.1507   9.981 1.852e-23
trtTreat      -0.2707     0.2054  -1.318 1.876e-01
```

Alternative Matching Approaches

The function `MatchIt::matchit()` offers several alternative ways to calculate the distance scores. See `?MatchIt::matchit` for details. Note in particular the use, in Figure 9.24, of scores generated using `randomForest()`. Random-forest models can in principle take account in an automatic manner of interactions and nonlinearities, and can provide a useful check on results from the fitting of GLM and other parametric models. A downside is that where numbers of observations are in hundreds rather than thousands, the random-forest approach may not do well in handling variables and ordered factors.

9.7.6 Coarsened Exact Matching

For coarsened exact matching, matches are sought within each of a number of categories. The following tries two settings of the `cutpoints` argument – 4 and 5. For factors, the default is to insist on exact matching. The effect is to omit the 112 treatment observations for which earnings in 1974 were unknown. The fact that earnings were not known is likely indicative of differences in circumstances, so that their omission, as well as changing the treatment population, may well compromise the comparison.

```
form <- trt ~ age + educ + ethnicid + marr + nodeg + z75 + re75log
match5.cem <- matchit(formula=form, data=nswG, method="cem", cutpoints=5)
datcem5 <- match.data(match5.cem)
match6.cem <- matchit(formula=form, data=nswG, method="cem", cutpoints=6)
datcem6 <- match.data(match6.cem)
## Show the effect of adding another cutpoint
match5.cem
```

```
A matchit object
 - method: Coarsened exact matching
 - number of obs.: 2787 (original), 837 (matched)
 - target estimand: ATT
 - covariates: age, educ, ethnicid, marr, nodeg, z75, re75log
```

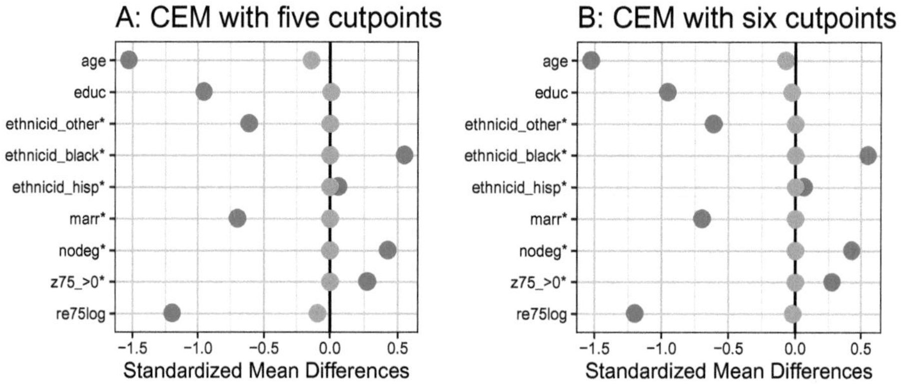

Figure 9.27 Panels A and B are love plots for `match5.cem` (five cutpoints) and `match6.cem` (six cutpoints) respectively. These summarize the extent to which the matching has, for the several covariates, led to a closer match between treatment and control. Differences for continuous variables are standardized. Factor effects, marked with an asterisk, are not standardized.

```
match6.cem
```

```
A matchit object
 - method: Coarsened exact matching
 - number of obs.: 2787 (original), 557 (matched)
 - target estimand: ATT
 - covariates: age, educ, ethnicid, marr, nodeg, z75, re75log
```

Increasing the number of cutpoints from five to six reduces the number of matched observations, but does bring the standardized differences for `age` and `re75log` closer to 0, and well under the difference of 0.1 in absolute value that is sometimes set as the largest standardized difference that should be tolerated. Further calculations will be based on `match6.cem`. The matched data in `nswMatch6` includes weights that use the mean weighting through stratification (MMWS) approach (Hong, 2010).

The love plots in Figure 9.27 show the extent of matching. There has been a large improvement over Figure 9.26, but at the expense of subsetting the treatment dataset so that it is no longer representative of the treatment population.

We can supply the weights that are in the output from `match.data()` to a call to `lm()` to perform weighted least squares regression. The weights argument ensures that account is taken of the breakdown into subclasses.

```
library(sandwich)
datcem5.lm <- lm(re78log ~ trt, data = datcem5, weights = weights)
## The function vcovHC() provides cluster robust standard errors
lmtest::coeftest(datcem5.lm, vcov. = vcovHC)
```

```

t test of coefficients:

            Estimate Std. Error t value Pr(>|t|)
(Intercept)  7.34523    0.39687   18.51   <2e-16
```

```
trtTreat      -0.00416     0.43036    -0.01       0.99
```

```
## Estimate treatment effect on number with some earnings:
datcem6.glm <- glm(I(re78>0) ~ trt, data = datcem6, weights = weights,
family=binomial)
lmtest::coeftest(datcem6.glm, vcov. = vcovHC)
```

```
z test of coefficients:

            Estimate Std. Error z value Pr(>|z|)
(Intercept)    1.375      0.334    4.12 0.000038
trtTreat      -0.297      0.373   -0.80     0.43
```

The warning is a result of the use of noninteger weights. The function is being used in a context different from that for which it was specifically developed.

The results indicate that, after matching, no convincing case can be made from comparison between the chosen control data and the experimental treatment data. At least in this instance, the observational data is not an effective substitute for the experimental data.

9.8 Multiple Imputation

Multiple imputation approaches all use what are in essence multivariate methods, in order to fill in gaps created by missing values. Several different R packages, some offering a choice of methods, are available for this purpose. The discussion that follows is introductory, designed to highlight some of the important issues that arise. There is a large and growing literature.

The strongest assumption is "missing completely at random" (MCAR) missingness. The assumption that usually underpins multiple imputation is the weaker "missing at random" (MAR) assumption, that missingness can be explained by variables on which full information is available. Bhaskaran and Smeeth (2014) give as an example blood pressure measures, for which it might be reasonable to make the MAR assumption that individuals of similar age and of the same sex are all equally likely to have missing blood pressure information.

The MAR assumption is not testable. The analyses that follow reflect, relative to contexts in which missing data is found in practice, a best case situation. The imputation process inevitably relies on the modeling of relationships between variables, and may rely also on modeling of patterns of change over space and/or time. Available checks are inevitably limited.

The discussion that follows will demonstrate use of the packages *mice* and *Amelia*. Note also the package *miceadds*, which implements methods for some types of summary information, including correlations, that are not available in *mice*. The *Amelia* package relies, with some room for adaptation, on multivariate normal assumptions, but claims to work well more generally. It has tailoring that is specifically directed at use with time series cross-sectional data. See Honaker and King

(2010). Both *mice* and *Amelia* implement plots that provide useful diagnostic checks.

The `Amelia` package has several vignettes that provide step by step introductions to *multiple imputation* and to associated diagnostics, with examples that users can work through as they read. A series of 10 vignettes that relate to the *mice* package, with vignettes 1 to 4 and 6 recommended as a starting point, are available from `www.gerkovink.com/miceVignettes/`.

Imputation has the consequence that information for rows that contain missing values has a greater uncertainty than rows that are complete. Unless the number of imputed values is small, and/or values can be imputed with high accuracy, any subsequent analysis should account for these differing uncertainties. A regression that involves one or more variables that has imputed values should, if a substantial proportion of rows have missing values, be done separately for each of the `m` sets of imputed values, with the results subsequently combined.

```
suppressPackageStartupMessages(library(mice))
Boys <- with(subset(mice::boys, age>=9),
             data.frame(age=age, loghgt=log(hgt), logbmi=log(bmi), loghc=log(hc)))
(Pattern <- md.pattern(Boys, plot=F))
```

```
    age loghgt logbmi loghc
382   1      1      1     1  0
34    1      1      1     0  1
1     1      0      0     1  2
1     1      0      0     0  3
      0      2      2    35 39
```

For purposes of obtaining a complete data frame to work with, we will use the function `mice::ampute()` to greatly increase the number of missing values. In practice, this can be a useful way, given a dataset A with a small number of rows with missing values, and a dataset B with many such rows, to create a dataset Aimp whose missing value pattern is roughly equivalent to to that of B. A comparison between results for Aimp and A can then be used to help in judging the effectiveness of the imputation process for dataset B.

We now generate a data frame where a large fraction of the rows have missing values. Here, the choice of pattern is pretty much arbitrary:

```
set.seed(31)        # Set to reproduce result shown
PatternB <- rbind(Pattern[-c(1,nrow(Pattern)), -ncol(Pattern)],
             c(0,1,1,1), c(0,1,0,0), c(0,0,1,0))
boys <- rbind(ic(Boys),
              ampute(cc(Boys), pattern=PatternB, freq=c(.3,.15,.15,.2,.1,.1),
                     prop=0.75)$amp)
md.pattern(boys, plot=FALSE)
```

```
    age logbmi loghgt loghc
84    1      1      1     1  0
120   1      1      1     0  1
53    1      0      0     1  2
43    1      0      0     0  3
61    0      1      1     1  1
30    0      1      0     0  3
```

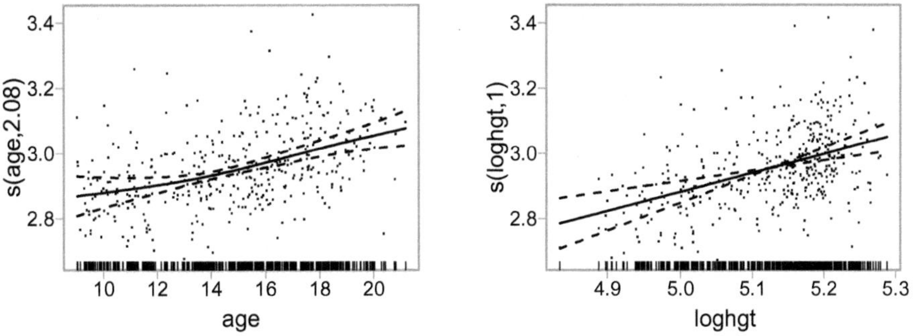

Figure 9.28 Term plots for a GAM model. Notice that fits appear close to linear. At this point, this is used only to check that a model with straight line terms is likely to be adequate.

```
27     0      0      1     0   3
     118    123    126   220 587
```

Now impute the missing values, and average over the imputations:

```
set.seed(17)     # Set to reproduce result shown
out <- capture.output(     # Evaluate; send screen output to text string
  boys.mids <- mice(boys, method='pmm', m=8)  )
impDFs <- complete(boys.mids, action='all')  # Returns a list of m=8 data frames
## Average over imputed data frames (use for exploratory purposes only)
impArray <- sapply(impDFs, function(x)as.matrix(x), simplify='array')
boysAv <- as.data.frame(apply(impArray, 1:2, mean))
```

A next step is to fit a GAM model with the explanatory terms age and loghgt, and check that straight-line terms appear adequate. Figure 9.28 shows the term plots.

Now impute the missing values, fit a regression for each imputation, and use `mice::pool()` to combine results to give a single set:

```
fits <- with(boys.mids, lm(logbmi~age+loghgt))
pool.coef <- summary(pool(fits))  # Include in table below
```

For comparison with: (1) the coefficients obtained from pooling the fits to the individual data frame, now examine what difference made if coefficients are calculated: (2) from the data frame that leaves out rows with missing values, and (3) from the data frame `boysAv` obtained by averaging over the $m = 8$ imputations. For checking the extent to which the procedure is able to recover the information in the original data frame, with just 36 out of 418 rows with one or more values missing, we will also report (4) the regression result from using that data:

```
## 2) Regression that leaves out rows with NAs
omitNArows.coef <- coef(summary(lm(logbmi~age+loghgt, data=boys)))
## 3) Regression fit to average over data frames after imputation
boysAv.coef <- coef(summary(lm(logbmi~age+loghgt, data=boysAv)))
## 4) Fit to original data, with 36 rows had missing data
Orig.coef <- coef(summary(lm(logbmi ~ age+loghgt, data=Boys)))
```

The following sets the three sets of results side by side:

```
ctab <- cbind(summary(pool(fits))[,2:3], omitNArows.coef[,1:2], boysAv.coef[,1:2],
     Orig.coef[,1:2])
tab <- setNames(cbind(ctab[,c(1,3,5,7)], ctab[,c(2,4,6,8)]),
          paste0(rep(c('Est','SE'), c(4,4)), rep(1:4, 2)))
round(tab,3)
```

```
              Est1  Est2  Est3  Est4   SE1   SE2   SE3   SE4
(Intercept) -0.155 0.063 0.042 0.425 0.832 0.791 0.561 0.534
age          0.016 0.016 0.020 0.021 0.005 0.005 0.004 0.004
loghgt       0.559 0.517 0.511 0.433 0.177 0.167 0.119 0.113
```

In the regression (3) with the average over the imputed datasets, the analysis has no way to know which data are observed and which are missing, and treats all data values as real. Just as when the GAM model was fitted, it underestimates the uncertainty of the parameters. The coefficients and standard errors for the pooled regression results, while they can in general be expected to do a better job than (2) or (3), do rely on assumptions of their own. Careful checking is needed.

Time Series Cross-Sectional Data – an Example

The data frame `airquality`, from the *datasets* package, was the basis for examples in Section 6.2. Refer back to Figure 6.11, and note the presence of missing values. The following sets up the data:

```
airquality <- datasets::airquality
airq <- cbind(airquality[, 1:4], day=1:nrow(airquality))
  # 'day' (starting May 1) replaces columns 'Month' & 'Day')
## Replace `Ozone` with `rt4ozone`:
airq <- cbind(rt4ozone=airq$Ozone^0.25, airq[,-1])
```

The following code can be used to reproduce a modified version of the scatterplot matrix that was shown in Figure 6.11:

```
## Generate the scatterplot matrix, now with `rt4ozone` replacing `Ozone`
smoothPars <- list(col.smooth='red', lty.smooth=2, spread=0)
car::spm(airq, cex.labels=1.2, regLine=FALSE, col='blue',
       oma=c(1.95,3,4, 3), gap=.25, smooth=smoothPars)
```

The increase in temperature from spring into midsummer that was evident in Figure 6.11, and decrease as autumn approached, was to be expected. The trends in several of the smooths are inevitably far from linear. This creates, as will be seen, problems for multiple imputation.

The following shows a simple-minded approach to imputing the missing values for `rt4ozone` and `Solar.R`:

```
set.seed(31)        # Needed to reproduce exact following figure
airq.imp <- mice(airq, m=20, print=FALSE) # Set m=20 to demonstrate
  ## For meaningful CIs, set m≥100  (takes a long time to run)
```

Figure 9.29 shows results from the function `overimpute()` from the *micemd* package, here with just 20 of the 100+ recommended imputations. For both variables, low values tend to be too high, and some high values appear low. At least for `Solar.R`, the model obtained when rows with missing values are omitted appears a better choice than the model obtained from use of imputed values.

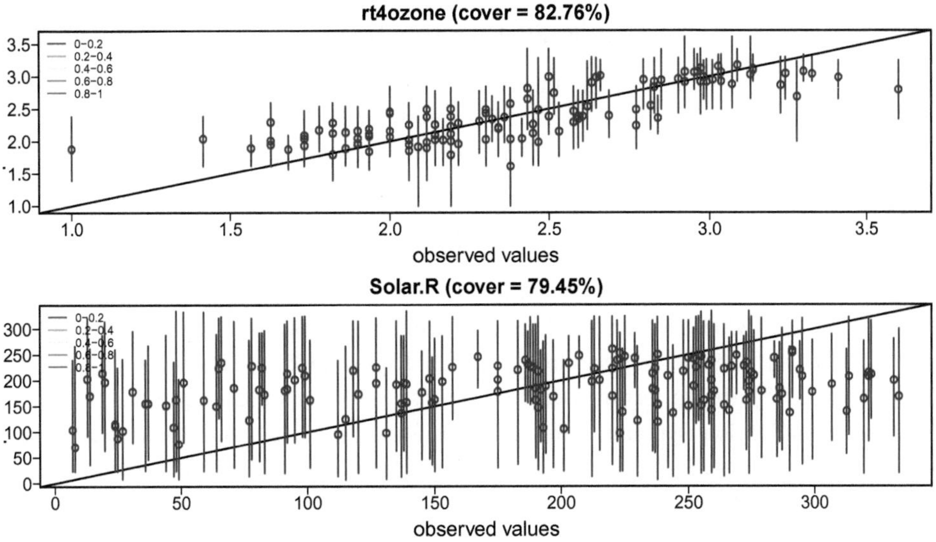

Figure 9.29 Means of the overimputations (solid points) are shown with lower and upper 90 percent confidence bounds. Colors (here all blue, i.e., interval 0–0.2) relate to the proportion of missing values for the individual profile.

```
## Code for figure
suppressPackageStartupMessages(library(micemd))
out <- overimpute(airq.imp)
```

As the dependence pattern for the model `Ozone.gam` that was fitted in Section 6.2 showed no indication of change with time, there seems a strong case, if interest is in predicting `Ozone` levels, for working directly with that model. An ideal would be to obtain complete data from New York in another year in the 1970s, insert missing values into the same dates and variables as for the `airquality` data, and check how well the GAM model does in reproducing the omitted values.

Some Further Points

Blackwell et al. (2017) argue that multiple imputation should be treated as an extreme form of measurement error. The methodology that they offer is designed to be relatively easy to use, to be statistically robust, to address both imputation error and errors in variables, and to handle a wide range of applications. The R package *NAsImput*, available from github (`https://github.com/OmegaPetrazzini/NAsImpute`), has code that is designed to assist in the comparison of different multiple imputation methods on user datasets. Van Buuren (2018) gives a detailed and comprehensive account of missing data imputation using `mice`.

Jakobsen et al. (2017) make detailed recommendations on the handling of missing values in randomised clinical trials. A 5 percent proportion of observations with missing values is suggested as a threshold below which, unless missing values are concentrated in specific groups such as the well or sick, analysis may reasonably proceed with those observations omitted.

9.9 Further Reading

There is a large literature on the methodologies discussed, and a large and growing range of abilities available in R and in other software. See the CRAN Task Views for Machine Learning and Multivariate Analysis. Krzanowski (2000) is a comprehensive and accessible overview of the methodology of classical multivariate analysis.

Machine learning and data-mining specialists have brought to these problems a research perspective that has been different from that of academic statisticians. Useful insights have been mixed with highly exaggerated claims. See the discussion in Maindonald (2006). Recently, there has been extensive interchange between the two streams of methodological development. Ripley (1996), Hastie et al. (2009), and Berk (2008) are important contributions to the ongoing dialogue.

Data visualization systems offer many different tools beyond those that have been described here. Note especially the R package `rggobi`, which provides an R interface to the GGobi system (Cook and Swayne, 2007). Note also the *rgl* package.

Streiner et al. (2014) discuss important considerations for the collection and analysis of multivariate data in medicine, in the health social sciences, and in psychology.

Data with More Variables than Observations

Data where there are many times more variables ("features") than observations are now common, creating new challenges. There are new opportunities for gaining information that, in a classical regression or classification problem, is unlikely to be available. Variables that have little or no effect on the outcome variable may nevertheless give important clues about the dependence structure between observations, as described in Leek and Storey (2007). Exaggerated predictive accuracy claims are common; see Ambroise and McLachlan (2002) for examples.

Sections 9.5 and 9.6 introduced the analysis of gene expression data. This is just one of the many areas of bioinformatics that have grown rapidly in importance since a human genome reference sequence was initially released in 2001. It soon became clear that the 21,000 human protein-coding genes that were identified were on their own, far from enough to account for the developmental and physiological complexity of humans. See Frazer (2012) for comment.

The Bioconductor project (Bickel et al. 2022), coordinating the development of what is now an extensive suite of R packages, has become an important source of computational tools in response to the computational challenges. The Bioconductor website (`www.bioconductor.org/`) has extensive details on what is available in other systems as well as for R. It has extensive tutorial and other resource material.

Causal Inference

Cunningham (2021) is a very readable overview. See also Rosenbaum (2002) and Imbens (2015). The labor training data of Subsection 9.7.2 is one of three sets of data on which Imbens provides commentary and analysis. Refer back, also, to the comments on causal inference in Section 3.10.

Multiple Imputation

Sangari and Ray (2021) list and discuss 10 different imputation approaches, and compare the performance of six of them on a specific dataset. Honaker and King (2010) comment on issues that are specific to time series cross-sectional data. See also Harrell (2015) and the seminal work Rubin (1987).

9.10 Exercises

9.1. Carry out the principal components analysis of Subsection 9.1.2, separately for males and females. For each of the first and second principal components, plot the rotations for females against the rotations for all data combined, and similarly for males. Are there any striking differences?

9.2. In the discriminant analysis for the `possum` data (Subsection 9.4.4), determine, for each site, the means of the scores on the first and second discriminant functions. Plot the means for the second discriminant function against the means for the first discriminant function. Identify the means with the names of the sites.

9.3. The data frame `DAAG::possumsites` holds latitudes, longitudes, and altitudes for the seven sites. The following code, which assumes that the *oz* package is installed, locates the sites on a map that shows the eastern Australian coastline and nearby state boundaries:

```
library(DAAG)
oz::oz(sections=c(3:5, 11:16))
names(possumsites)[1:2] <- c("long", "lat")
with(possumsites, {
points(long, lat);
text(long, lat, row.names(possumsites), pos=c(2,4,2,2,4,2,2))
})
```

Do the site means that were calculated in Exercise 9.2 relate in any obvious way to geographical position, or to altitude?

9.4. Determine two-dimensional representations of the data in the `MASS::painters` dataset using (1) classical metric scaling, (2) Sammon scaling, (3) Kruskal's nonmetric scaling. On each graph show the school to which the painter belonged.

9.5. Repeat the principal components calculation omitting the points that appear as outliers in Figure 9.6, and redo the regression calculation. What differences are apparent, in loadings for the first two principal components and/or in the regression results?

9.6. Create a version of Figure 9.15B that shows the discriminant line. In the example of Subsection 9.4.1, investigate whether use of `logpet`, in addition to `logwid` and `loglen`, improves discrimination.

9.7. The following uses the difference of the correlation from 1.0 as a distance measure:

```
data(wine, package='gclus')
mat <- with(wine,
  round(1-cor(cbind(Alcohol, Malic, Magnesium, Phenols, Flavanoids)),2))
colnames(mat) <- rownames(mat) <- 1:5
print(mat)
```

```
  1    2    3    4    5
1 0.00 0.91 0.73 0.71 0.76
2 0.91 0.00 1.05 1.34 1.41
3 0.73 1.05 0.00 0.79 0.80
4 0.71 1.34 0.79 0.00 0.14
5 0.76 1.41 0.80 0.14 0.00
```

Under hierarchical clustering, which two observations would be joined first and which joined second

a. under single linkage,
b. under complete linkage?

9.8.* The dataset `DAAG::leafshape` has three leaf measurements – `bladelen` (blade length), `bladewid` (blade width), and `petiole` (petiole length). These are available for each of two plant architectures, in each of six locations. (The dataset `leafshape17` that we encountered in Subsection 9.4.1 is a subset of the dataset `leafshape`.) Use logistic regression to develop an equation for predicting architecture, given leaf dimensions and location. Compare the alternatives: (i) different discriminant functions for different locations; (ii) the same coefficients for the leaf shape variables, but different intercepts for different locations; (iii) the same coefficients for the leaf shape variables, with an intercept that is a linear function of latitude; (iv) the same equation for all locations. Interpret the equation that is finally chosen as discriminant function.

9.9. The data frame `Vehicle` from the *mlbench* package has values of 18 features that were extracted from the images of silhouettes of four different "Corgie" model vehicles. (Note that the package *mlbench* does not export its datasets. Use the function `data()`, as in the code that follows, to make them available.)

a. Compare the performance of `lda()`, `qda()` and `randomForest()` in classifying the vehicle types.

```
`confusion` <-
function(actual, predicted, digits=4){
  tab <- table(actual, predicted)
  confuse <- apply(tab, 1, function(x)x/sum(x))
  print(round(confuse, digits))
  acc <- sum(tab[row(tab)==col(tab)])/sum(tab)
  invisible(print(c("Overall accuracy" = round(acc,digits))))
}
data(Vehicle, package="mlbench")
lhat <- MASS::lda(Class ~ ., data=Vehicle, CV=TRUE)$class
qhat <- MASS::qda(Class ~ ., data=Vehicle, CV=TRUE)$class
DAAG::confusion(Vehicle$Class, lhat)
DAAG::confusion(Vehicle$Class, qhat)
randomForest::randomForest(Class ~ ., data=Vehicle, CV=TRUE)
```

b. What proportion of the trace do the first two linear discriminants explain? (For this, refit with `CV=FALSE`.)

c. Plot the first discriminant function against the second discriminant function, adding also density contours. The function `ggplot2::quickplot()` offers an easy way to do this:

```
Vehicle.lda <- MASS::lda(Class ~ ., data=Vehicle)
twoD <- predict(Vehicle.lda)$x
ggplot2::quickplot(twoD[,1], twoD[,2], color=Vehicle$Class,
                   geom=c("point","density2d"))
```

What hints does the plot give that might explain the difference between the `lda()` and `qda()` results?

9.10. Run the following code:

```
library(ape); library(MASS)
library(DAAGbio)
primates.dna <- as.DNAbin(primateDNA)
primates.dist <- dist.dna(primates.dna, model="K80")
primates.cmd <- cmdscale(primates.dist)
eqscplot(primates.cmd)
rtleft <- c(4,2,4,2)[unclass(cut(primates.cmd[,1], breaks=4))]
text(primates.cmd, labels=row.names(primates.cmd), pos=rtleft)
```

Do the following calculations and comment on the result:

```
d <- dist(primates.cmd)
sum((d-primates.dist)^2)/sum(primates.dist^2)
```

9.11. Run the following code:

```
library(DAAG)
pacific.dist <- dist(x = as.matrix(rockArt[-c(47,54,60,63,92),28:641]),
                     method = "binary")
sum(pacific.dist==1)/length(pacific.dist)
plot(density(pacific.dist, to = 1))
## Check that all columns have at least one distance < 1
symmat <- as.matrix(pacific.dist)
table(apply(symmat, 2, function(x) sum(x<1)))
pacific.cmd <- cmdscale(pacific.dist)
pacific.sam <- sammon(pacific.dist)
```

Why were rows 47, 54, 60, 63, and 92 omitted? Compare the plot from `pacific.cmd` with that from `pacific.sam$points`. Why are they so different?

9.12. Examine the implications that the use of the logarithms of the income variables in the analysis of the dataset `nswpsid1` has for the interpretation of the results. Determine predicted values for each observation. Then exp(predicted values) gives predicted incomes in 1978. Take exp(estimated treatment effect) to get an estimate of the factor by which a predicted income for the control group must, after adding the offset, be multiplied to get a predicted (income + offset) for the treatment group, if explanatory variable values are the same.

9.13. Investigate the sensitivity of the regression results in Subsection 9.7.4 to the range of values of the scores that are used in filtering the data. Try the effect of including data where: (a) the ratio of treatment to control numbers, as estimated from the density curve, is at least 1:40; (b) the ratio lies between 1:40 and 40; (c) the ratio is at least 1:10.

9.14. Subsection 9.7.3 defined a function `nswlm()`, then using it to create a table that gives treatment effect estimates. Rerun the calculations that generated the table entries, now supplying the argument `log78=FALSE`. Comment on changes in the treatment effect estimates.

9.15. This exercise returns to work with the data frame `wine` of Exercise 9.7. Start by comparing boxplots for the different measures:

```
Wine <- setNames(cbind(stack(wine, select=2:14), rep(wine[,-1], 13)),
                 c("value", "measure", "Class"))
bwplot(measure ~ value, data=Wine)
```

The measures are clearly on totally different scales.

a. Run the following code:

```
wine.pr <- prcomp(wine[,-1], scale=TRUE)
round(wine.pr$sdev,2)
t(round(wine.pr$rotation[,1:2],2))
scores <- as.data.frame(cbind(predict(wine.pr), Class=wine[,1]))
xyplot(PC2 ~ PC1, groups=Class, data=scores, aspect='iso',
       par.settings=simpleTheme(pch=16), auto.key=list(columns=3))
```

What are the major differences in the rotations betweeen PC1 and PC2?

b. Try also with the default `scale=FALSE` in the first line above. What does the comparison between the two sets of results tell you?

c. Now use linear discriminant analysis to compare the groups:

```
library(MASS)
wine.lda <- lda(Class ~ ., data=wine)
wineCV.lda <- lda(Class ~ ., data=wine, CV=T)
t(round(wine.lda$scaling,2))
tab <- table(wine$Class, wineCV.lda$class,
             dnn=c('Actual', 'Predicted'))
tab
setNames(round(1-sum(diag(tab))/sum(tab),4), "CV error rate")
scores <- as.data.frame(cbind(predict(wine.lda)$x, Class=wine[,1]))
xyplot(LD2 ~ LD1, groups=Class, data=scores, aspect='iso',
       par.settings=simpleTheme(pch=16), auto.key=list(columns=3))
```

Comment on the comparison between the linear discriminants and first two principal components from the use of `prcomp()`.

d. Use `randomForest()` from the *randomForest* package to fit a model that accounts for differences between groups, thus:

```
wine$Class <- factor(Wine$Class)
wine.rf <- randomForest(x=wine[,-1], y=wine$Class)
```

Compare the OOB estimate of error rate with that from use of `MASS::lda()` with `CV=TRUE`.

Epilogue

The discussion has progressed from simple models that make strong assumptions, to models that allow for an increasingly wide range of possibilities. Always, the assumptions made limit the range of problems to which methods can reasonably be applied.

Models that are not strictly correct, or even perhaps badly broken, may nevertheless be useful, giving acceptably accurate predictions. The validity of model assumptions remains an important issue. We need to know the limits of the usefulness of our models. Comparing results from a simple model with results from a model that takes better account of the data can help in developing intuition. Somewhat ironically, Chapters 4 to 9 could be viewed as essential background for those who hope to do a good job of the analyses described in Chapters 2 and 3! An understanding of multilevel and repeated measures models seems particularly important, since these models bring attention to structure in the noise component that has implications for generalization of results beyond the specific circumstances that generated the data.

Whether or not faulty assumptions matter will depend on the circumstances. For simpler models, the assumption of independently and identically distributed errors often makes little difference to estimates of model parameters and to fitted values, but can have a large effect on standard errors. For example, a better model for the frogs data in Chapter 5 would account for spatial correlations. Because we did not take account of spatial autocorrelation in our more standard logistic regression analysis, the standard errors are not very reliable; the best we could do was to make a tentative distinction between coefficients that seemed clearly statistically significant, and those that were not. Modeling the correlation structure would have given us a description that should generalize better to sites in the vicinity of those that were studied, with more believable indications of the accuracy of such a description. For generalizing in time, for example, to a subsequent year, the benefits are more doubtful. If data from multiple years were available, then for predictive purposes the modeling of the temporal structure should be the priority.

The emphasis in this text has been on careful modeling of the data, using both fixed and random effects as appropriate. This allows maximum flexibility in the subsequent use of the fitted model whether the aim is scientific understanding or prediction. Predictive accuracy measurement makes its own modeling demands. In general, there may be two models. First, there is a model for the population from which the data have been drawn and the sampling mechanism. Second, there must be a model for the population and associated sampling mechanism when predictions are made. The AIC, BIC, and cross-validation error rates that relate to the data used to develop the model, all assume that the two populations and associated sampling mechanisms are the same.

The following situations all occur in practice.

1. The data used to develop the model are, to a close approximation, a random sample from the population to which predictions will be applied. If this can be assumed, a simple use of a resampling method will give an estimate of the score function that is unbiased with respect to the population that is the target for predictions.
2. Test data are available from the target population, with a sampling mechanism that reflects the intended use of the model. The test data can then be used to derive a realistic estimate of predictive accuracy.
3. The sampling mechanism for the target data differs from the mechanism that yielded the data in situation 1, or yielded the test data in situation 2. However, there is a model that predicts how predictive accuracy will change with the change in sampling mechanism. Thus, in the attitudes to science data considered in Chapter 7, the predictive accuracy for the mean of a new class depends on the number in the class.
4. The connection between the population from which the data have been sampled and the target population may be weak or tenuous. It may be so tenuous that a confident prediction of the score function for the target population is impossible. In other words, a realistic test set and associated sampling mechanism may not be available. An informed guess may be the best that is available.

These four possibilities are not completely distinct; they overlap at the boundaries. A modeling approach offers a framework of understanding from which to make an informed judgement in all these situations.

Appendix A

The R System: a Brief Overview

The notes that follow are offered as a starting point for gaining skills that will be helpful for use of the R code included in the text. As readers work through the text, they may find it useful to refer back to these notes, at the same time checking relevant R help pages and referring to the wealth of tutorial material that is available online. Refer back to Section 1.11 for suggestions for online content.

A.1 Getting Started with R

A.1.1 An overview of R

An up-to-date version of R may be downloaded from a Comprehensive R Archive Network (CRAN) mirror site. There are links at `http://cran.r-project.org/`. Installation instructions are given for installing R under Windows, Unix, Linux, and MacOS X. Contributed packages extend the capabilities of R. A number of these are included in the "recommended" packages that are in the standard R distribution. These are just a few of the thousands of packages that are available for download and installation. Many datasets that are mentioned in this book have been collected into our *DAAG* package that is available from CRAN sites. The CRAN Task Views web page can be a good place to start when looking for abilities of a particular type. The Task Views that are available at the time of writing include, for example: Bayesian inference, Cluster analysis, Finance, Graphics, and Time series. Go to `http://cran.at.r-project.org/web/views/`

Users are encouraged to install the RStudio IDE (Interactive Display Environment: `https://posit.co/products/open-source/rstudio/`), and to run R from within RStudio. Packages and package updates can be conveniently installed from the RStudio menu.

A.1.2 Learn by Typing Code at the Command Line

The command line prompt (`>`) is an invitation to type commands or expressions. Once the command or expression is complete, and the Enter key is pressed, R evaluates the result. If not assigned to a variable name, it goes to the command line and is printed in the console window.

Practice in the evaluation of arithmetic expressions will help develop needed conceptual and keyboard skills. Look up relevant R help pages, or check other sources of help, for further explanation of any of the code now shown:

```
> ## Arithmetic calculations.  See the help page `?Arithmetic`
> 2*3+10          # The symbol `*` denotes 'multiply'
```

```
[1] 16
```

The first element is labeled "[1]" even when there is just one element!

```
> ## Use the `c()` function to join results into a numeric vector
> c(sqrt(10), 2*3+10, sqrt(10), 2^3)  # 2^3 is 2 to the power of 3
```

```
[1]  3.162 16.000  3.162  8.000
```

```
> ## R knows about pi
> 2*pi*6378        # Approximate circumference of earth at equator (km)
```

```
[1] 40074
```

Notice that anything that follows a # on the command line is taken as comment and ignored by R. For extra emphasis, ## is sometimes used in place of #. In code that now follows, the command line prompt (>) will be omitted.

The following all display help pages:

```
?help            # Get information on the use of `help()`
?sqrt            # Or, type help(sqrt)
?Arithmetic        # See, in similar vein ?Syntax
?'<'             # `?Comparison` finds the same help page
```

Further examples of arithmetic calculations are:

```
## Two commands on one line; Use ';' as separator
2*3*4+10; sqrt(10)        ## Try also `cat(2*3*4+10, sqrt(10), sep='n')
## Convert CO2 carbon emissions from tonnes of carbon to tonnes of CO2
3.664*c(.53, 2.56, 9.62)  ## Data are for 1900, 1960 & 2020
```

In each case, the result is returned to the command line. This then automatically invokes the function print(), so that the result is printed. The alternative is to assign the result to a named object.

The function cat() allows the printing of several suitably simple objects, with control of the formatting:

```
## Use `cat()` to print several items, with control of formatting
cat(2*3*4+10, sqrt(10), '\n')
```

```
34 3.162
```

Assignment

Assignment is usually to the left, using <- or =:

```
## Convert from amounts of carbon to amounts of CO2 (billions of tonnes)
## and assign result to a named object
fossilCO2vals <- c(.53, 2.56, 9.62)*3.664 # Amounts in 1900, 1960, and 2020
  # Equivalently `fossilCO2vals <- c(.53, 2.56, 9.62)*rep(3.664,3)`
## To assign and print, enclose in round brackets
(fossilCO2vals <- c(.53, 2.56, 9.62)*3.664)
```

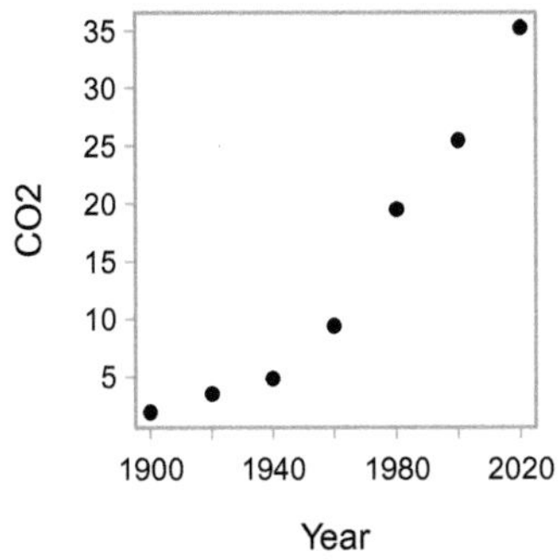

Year	CO2
1900	1.94
1920	3.52
1940	4.84
1960	9.38
1980	19.49
2000	25.46
2020	35.25

Figure A.1 Estimated worldwide annual totals of carbon dioxide emissions from fossil fuel use (but excluding use for carbonated drinks) and cement production, in billions of tonnes. Data are due to Friedlingstein et al. (2022).

```
[1]  1.942  9.380 35.248
```

Operations such as * and + are designed to operate on vectors. So also are functions such as `log()`.

Assignment can alternatively be to the right, with the arrow pointing right:

```
3.664*c(.53,2.56, 9.62) -> fossilCO2vals
```

The right pointing assignment is best reserved for use with the pipe syntax that will be discussed in Subsection A.3.4.

Entry of Data at the Command Line, a Graphics Formula, and a Graph

Figure A.1 shows the estimates, by 40-year intervals, of worldwide totals of carbon emissions from fossil fuel use, taken from the web page `https://github.com/owid/co2-data`. To enter and plot the data, proceed thus:

```
Year <- c(1900, 1920, 1940, 1960, 1980, 2000, 2020)
CO2 <- c(.53,.96,1.32,2.56,5.32,6.95,9.62)*3.664
## Now plot Carbon Dioxide emissions as a function of Year
plot(CO2 ~ Year, pch=16, fg="gray")
```

Note the following.

- The construct `CO2 ~ Year` is a graphics formula. The `plot()` function interprets this formula to mean "Plot `Carbon` as a function of `Year`" or "Plot `CO2` on the y-axis against `Year` on the x-axis."
- The setting `pch=16` (where `pch` is "plot character") gives a solid black dot.
- Case is significant for names of R objects or commands. Thus, `CO2` is different from `co2`.

This basic plot could be improved by adding more-informative axis labels, adding a title, and so on. See examples in Chapter 1.

Once created, the objects `Year` and `CO2` are stored in the *workspace*, which holds the user's working collection of R objects. Users have the copy or "image" of the workspace upon quitting the session, so that it can be restored later. RStudio users can set the default behavior, globally or for an individual project, by going to Tools|Project Options... or to Tools|Global Options... on the main RStudio menu, then setting defaults as required. The default setting for `q()` can be over-ridden by supplying the argument `save="yes"` or `save="no"`, as required.

Grouping Vectors Together into Data Frames

The two vectors `Year` and `CO2` are matched, element for element. It is convenient to group them together into a *data frame* object, and use the data frame columns to create the plot.

```
CO2byYear <- data.frame(year=Year, co2gas=CO2)
CO2byYear       # Display the contents of the data frame.
rm(Year, CO2)    # Optionally, remove `Year` and `Carbon` from the workspace
plot(co2gas ~ year, data=CO2byYear, pch=16)
```

The objects `Year` and `CO2` become, respectively, the columns `year` and `co2gas` in the data frame. The axis labels (these can be changed from the default) now change to `year` (x-axis) and `co2gas` (y-axis). Section A.2 will discuss character and logical vectors, dates, and factors. These, likewise, can all appear as columns in data frames.

Section A.5 will comment on graphics packages and graphs more generally.

Setting the Number of Digits in Output

Often, calculations will, by default, give more decimal places of output than are useful. In the output that we give, we often reduce the number of decimal places below what R gives by default. The `options()` function can be used to make a global change to the number of significant digits that are printed. For example:

```
sqrt(10)         # Number of digits is determined by current seting
```

```
[1] 3.162
```

```
options(digits=2) # Change until further notice,
sqrt(10)
```

```
[1] 3.2
```

Note that `options(digits=2)` expresses a wish, which R will not always obey!

Rounding will sometimes introduce small inconsistencies. For example, with rounding to two decimal places:

$$\sqrt{\frac{2}{3}} = 0.82; \quad 2 \times \sqrt{\frac{2}{3}} = 1.63.$$

Note, however, that $2 \times 0.82 = 1.64$

Wide-Ranging Information Access and Searches

The function `help.start()` opens a browser interface to help information, manuals, and helpful links. It takes practice, and time, to learn to navigate the wealth of information that is on offer.

The function `RSiteSearch()` initiates (assuming a live internet connection) a search of R manuals and help pages, and of the R-help mailing list archives, for key words or phrases. The argument `restrict` allows some limited targeting of the search. See `?RSiteSearch` for details.

The help pages, while not an encyclopedia on statistical methodology, have wide-ranging information that includes: insightful and helpful examples, references to related functions, and references to papers and books that give the relevant theory. Some abilities will bring pleasant surprises. It is wise, before launching into the use of an unfamiliar R function, to check the relevant help page!

A.2 R Data Structures

Data structures that will be discussed are vectors, dates, factors, data frames, matrices and arrays, and lists. Refer back to Chapter 6 for commentary on time series.

A.2.1 Vectors, Dates, and Arrays

The term *vector* is in general used to refer to "atomic" vectors, whose elements cannot be further subsetted. Lists, which may also be classed as vectors, will be discussed separately, in Subsection A.2.7.

The common vector "modes," basically storage types, are *numeric* (or *double*), *character*, and *logical.*

```
vehicles <- c("Compact", "Large", "Midsize", "Small", "Sporty", "Van")
c(T, F, F, F, T, T, F)  # A logical vector, assuming F=FALSE and T=TRUE
```

```
[1]  TRUE FALSE FALSE FALSE  TRUE  TRUE FALSE
```

The global variables `F` (`FALSE`) and `T` (=`TRUE`) are a convenient shorthand when working at the command line, providing that the default settings have not been messed with!

In addition to numeric vectors, note *factor*s and *date*s, both of which have mode numeric, but are not formally vectors. Factors (class `factor`), which are important when fitting models for identifying groups within data, will be discussed separately, in Subsection A.2.7. Dates have class `Date`.

Examples of vectors are:

```
## Character vector
mammals <- c("Rat", "Pig", "Rat", "Mouse", "Pig")
## Logical vector
rodent <- c("TRUE", "FALSE", "TRUE", "FALSE", "TRUE", "FALSE")
## From character vector `mammals`, create factor
mfac <- factor(mammals)
levels(mfac)
```

```
[1] "Mouse" "Pig"   "Rat"
```

```
table(mfac)
```

```
mfac
Mouse   Pig   Rat
    1     2     2
```

The values of `mfac` are stored as c(3, 2, 3, 1, 2), where 1="Mouse", 2="Pig", 3="Rat".

Dates

Dates are by default stared as the number of days since January 1, 1978.

```
day1 <- as.Date(c("2022-01-01", "2022-02-01", "2022-03-01"))
as.numeric(day1)  # Days since 1 January 1970
```

```
[1] 18993 19024 19052
```

```
day1[3] - day1[2]
```

```
Time difference of 28 days
```

The Use of Square Brackets to Extract Subsets of Vectors

Note three ways to extract subsets of vectors. In each case, the subscripting information (in the simplest case, a vector of subscript indices) is enclosed in square brackets.

```
## Specify the indices of the elements that are to be extracted
x <- c(3, 11, 8, 15, 12,18)
x[c(1,4:6)]        # Elements in positions 1, 4, 5, and 6
```

```
[1]  3 15 12 18
```

```
## Use negative indices to identify elements for omission
x[-c(2,3)]         # Positive and negative indices cannot be mixed
```

```
[1]  3 15 12 18
```

```
## Specify a vector of logical values.
x > 10             # This generates a vector of logical values
```

```
[1] FALSE  TRUE FALSE  TRUE  TRUE  TRUE
```

```
x[x > 10]
```

```
[1] 11 15 12 18
```

Elements of vectors can be given names. Elements can then be extracted by name.

```
bodywt <- c(Cow=465, Goat=28, Donkey=187, Pig=192)
bodywt[c("Goat", "Pig")]
```

```
Goat  Pig
  28  192
```

Matrices and Arrays

An array is stored as a vector, but with a dimension attribute. Internally, a matrix (a two-dimensional array) is a vector in which columns are stored one following another. In a three-dimensional array, the vectors that form the row-by-column matrices are stacked one following another.

Matrices (two subscripts) and arrays more generally, can be subscripted in the same way as vectors. Thus, consider:

```
arr123 <- array(1:24, dim=c(2,4,3))
## This prints as three 2 by 4 matrices.  Print just the first of the three.
arr123[, 2, 1]    # Column 2 and index 1 of 3rd dimension
```

```
[1] 3 4
```

```
attributes(arr123)
```

```
$dim
[1] 2 4 3
```

A.2.2 Factors

Factors, used for categorical data, are fundamental to the use of many of the R modeling functions. Ordered factors are appropriate for use with ordered categorical data. For both factors and ordered factors, the order of levels determines the order of cells within a table, or the default order of panels when used for conditioning in a *lattice* plot.

Consider a survey that has data on 691 females and 692 males. If the first 691 are females and the next 692 males, we can create a vector of strings that holds the values, then turning this vector into a factor, thus:

```
gender <- c(rep("male",691), rep("female",692))
gender <- factor(gender)  # From character vector, create factor
levels(gender)            # Notice that `female` comes first
```

```
[1] "female" "male"
```

Internally, the factor `gender` is stored as 691 2s, followed by 692 1s. It has stored with it the levels vector. By default, the levels are in sorted order for the data type from which the factor was formed, so that `"female"` precedes `"male"`.

To cause `male` to come before `female`, use:

```
Gender <- factor(gender, levels=c("male", "female"))
```

This syntax can also be used to change the order in a case where `gender` is an existing factor. Take care to spell the level names correctly. Specifying `"Male"` in place of `"male"` in the `levels` argument will cause all values that were `"male"` to be coded as missing.

The `labels` argument to `factor()` can be used to change the level names from the values in the data:

```
mf1 <- factor(rep(c('male','female'),c(2,3)), labels=c("f", "m"))
## The following has the same result
mf2 <- factor(rep(c('male','female'), c(2,3)))
levels(mf2) <- c("f","m")  # Assign new levels
if(all(mf1==mf2))print(mf1)
```

In graphs and tables, the order of the levels determines the order in which the levels will appear. In most contexts that seem to demand a character string, the 1 is translated into `"female"` and the 2 into `"male"`, that is, into the levels of the factor. For example:

```
sum(gender=="male")
```

```
[1] 691
```

Assignment of a new set of levels can be used to combine levels:

```
table(chickwts$feed)  # feed is a factor
```

```

   casein horsebean   linseed  meatmeal   soybean sunflower
       12        10        12        11        14        12
```

```
source <- chickwts$feed
levels(source) <- c("milk","plant","plant","meat","plant","plant")
table(source)
```

```
source
 milk plant  meat
   12    48    11
```

The following are specific issues.

- Use, for example, `as.character(fac)`, to obtain a character vector in which factor levels replace the factor elements.
- Specify `unclass(fac)` to extract the integer values 1, 2, ...
- Use of `c()` to concatenate two or more factors yields an integer vector that concatenates the separate integer vectors.
- Subsection 5.1.5 had an example where use of the function `aggregate()` generated a factor `conc`, with levels `"0.8"`, `"1"`, `"1.2"`, `"1.4"`, `"1.6"`, and `"2.5"`). The syntax `as.numeric(levels(conc))[conc]` is recommended as the preferred to recover the original numeric values. (There may, in general, be small differences that are the result of rounding error.)

Ordered Factors

To create an ordered factor, or to turn a factor into an ordered factor, use `ordered()`. All factors, ordered or not, have an order for their levels! The special feature of ordered factors is that the levels are treated as positions on an ordinal scale. Their values can be compared using the relational operators `<`, `<=`, `>`, `>=`, and `==`.

As an example, consider:

```
stress <- rep(c("low","medium","high"), 2)
ord.stress <- ordered(stress, levels=c("low", "medium", "high"))
ord.stress
```

```
[1] low    medium high   low    medium high
Levels: low < medium < high
```

```
ord.stress >= "medium"
```

```
[1] FALSE  TRUE  TRUE FALSE  TRUE  TRUE
```

Ordered factors have (*inherit*) the attributes of factors, and have a further ordering attribute.

Missing Values in Values of Factors

When factors are formed, the missing value symbol is by default excluded from the levels vector. Use of the argument `exclude=NULL` (the default is `exclude=NA`) will make `NA` an extra level. One can, in addition, code an individual value as missing; see `?factor`.

A.2.3 Operations with Data Frames

Consider the data frame `DAAG::Cars93.summary`, created from the `Cars93` dataset in the *MASS* package. Its contents are:

```
Cars93sum <- DAAG::Cars93.summary # Create copy in workspace
Cars93sum
```

```
        Min.passengers Max.passengers No.of.cars abbrev
Compact              4              6         16      C
Large                6              6         11      L
Midsize              4              6         22      M
Small                4              5         21     Sm
Sporty               2              4         14     Sp
Van                  7              8          9      V
```

The first three columns are numeric. The fourth, which is a factor, could equally well be stored as a character variable.

The following demonstrates the extraction of subsets of rows and/or columns:

```
Cars93sum[4:6, 2:3]  # Extract rows 4 to 6 and columns 2 and 3
Cars93sum[6:4, ]     # Extract rows in the order 6, 5, 4
Cars93sum[, 2:3]     # Extract columns 2 and 3
## Or, use negative integers to specify rows and/or columns to be omitted
Cars93sum[-(1:3), -c(1,4)] # In each case, numbers must be all +ve or all -ve
## Specify row and/or column names
Cars93sum[c("Small","Sporty","Van"), c("Max.passengers","No.of.cars")]
```

The first three columns of `Cars93sum` could equally well be stored as a numeric matrix, and the same syntax used for subset extraction.

Data Frames versus Matrices

- Both for data frames and matrices, the function `nrow()` returns the number of rows, while `ncol()` returns the number of columns.
- The `names()` function shows the names of data frame columns, but returns `NULL` when the argument is a matrix. The functions `rownames()` and `colnames()` can be used either with data frames or matrices.

The functions `names()` (with data frames only), `rownames()`, and `colnames()` can also be used to assign new names, thus:

```
names(Cars93sum)[3] <- "numCars"
names(Cars9sum) <- c("minPass","maxPass","numCars","code")
```

Using a Data Frame as a Database: `with()` *and* `within()`

The function `with()` sets up its first argument as a *database* for use for its second argument:

```
## trees (datasets) has data on Black Cherry Trees
with(trees, round(c(mean(Girth), median(Girth), sd(Girth)),1))
```

```
[1] 13.2 12.9  3.1
```

Use curly brackets (braces) to extend the scope of `with()` over multiple lines:

```
with(DAAG::pair65,       # stretch of rubber bands
  {lenchange = heated−ambient
   c(mean(lenchange), median(lenchange))
})
```

```
[1] 6.3 6.0
```

Use of `with()` ensures that even if there is an object of the same name in the workspace, the specified data frame column is taken. A less satisfactory alternative is to use `attach()`, thus extending the *search list*, by default placing it at position 2 on the list of *databases* where R looks for objects. Once a data frame has been attached (e.g., `attach(DAAG::pair65)`), its columns can be referred to by name, without further need to give the name of the data frame. Note, however, that if a column name is the same as that of an object in the workspace, the object in the workspace will (unless the workspace has been moved from position 1 on the search list) be taken instead.

The function `within()` can be convenient for adding or modifying data frame columns. The following is from Subsection 3.2.1.

```
## Add variables `mph` and `gradient` to `DAAG::nihills`
nihr <- within(DAAG::nihills, {mph <- dist/time; gradient <- climb/dist})
```

Extracting Rows from Data Frames

`Cars93sum[1, ]` returns a data frame. Use of `unlist(Cars93sum[1, ])` returns a vector, but with the side effect that the factor value in the final column is coerced to numeric. This is not usually what is wanted.

```
unlist(Cars93sum[1, ])
```

```
Min.passengers Max.passengers        No.of.cars            abbrev
             4              6                16                 1
```

A.2.4 Data Manipulation Functions Used in Earlier Chapters

This text has only limited comments on a few of the wide range of data manipulation functions that are available in R packages. The following, used earlier in the text, are a very limited selection.

The function `sapply()` provides a convenient way to apply a function to all elements of a vector, or to all elements of a list, or to all columns of a data frame, then simplifying as relevant, to give a vector, matrix, or more general array.

```
## For columns of `DAAG::jobs`, show the range of values
sapply(DAAG::jobs, range)
```

```
       BC Alberta Prairies Ontario Quebec Atlantic Date
[1,] 1737    1366      973    5212   3167      941   95
[2,] 1840    1436      999    5360   3257      968   97
```

```
## Split egg lengths by species, calculate mean, sd, and number for each
with(DAAG::cuckoos, sapply(split(length,species),
                     function(x)c(av=mean(x), sd=sd(x), nobs=length(x))))
```

```
     hedge.sparrow meadow.pipit pied.wagtail robin tree.pipit  wren
av              23        22.29         22.9 22.56      23.08 21.12
sd               1         0.92          1.1  0.68       0.88  0.75
nobs            14        45.00         15.0 16.00      15.00 15.00
```

The function `apply()` is designed for use with matrices and arrays more generally. If used with the data frame, the data frame will first be coerced to a matrix form. The array `UCBAdmissions` has dimensions `Gender` (`Admitted` or `Rejected`), `Gender` (`Male` or `Female`), and `Dept` (one of `A`, `B`, `C`, `D`, `E`, `F`). The following calculates, for each `Dept` (dimension 3), the percentage of applicants of each gender admitted:

```
apply(UCBAdmissions, 3, function(x)(x[1,2]/(x[1,2]+x[2,2]))*100) # Females
```

```
 A  B  C  D  E  F
82 68 34 35 24  7
```

```
apply(UCBAdmissions, 3, function(x)(x[1,1]/(x[1,1]+x[2,1]))*100) # Males
```

```
   A    B    C    D    E    F
62.1 63.0 36.9 33.1 27.7  5.9
```

Check by looking at the first department separately, for example

```
UCBAdmissions[, , 1]
```

```
            Gender
Admit        Male Female
  Admitted   512     89
  Rejected   313     19
```

There has been very limited use of functions in the *tidyverse* collection of packages. Subsection 5.5.1 used the following code, first to count numbers of lefthanded and righthanded cricketers born in each year and then to create a data frame in which numbers of lefthanders and righthanders were shown side by side in separate columns.

```
DAAG::cricketer |> dplyr::count(year, left, name="Freq") -> handYear
names(handYear)[2] <- "hand"
byYear <- tidyr::pivot_wider(handYear, names_from='hand', values_from="Freq")
```

As with other *tidyverse* packages, both *tidyr* and *dplyr* come with a number of vignettes that demonstrate the use of the functions that are provided.

A.2.5 Writing Data to a File, and Reading Data from a File

The functions `write.table()` and `read.table()` (default is to use a tab or space as separator), and the related functions `write.csv()` and `read.csv()` (use a comma as separator), are designed for use for output and input of data frames.

```
CO2byYear <- data.frame(year = c(1900, 1920, 1940, 1960, 1980, 2000, 2020)
                    co2gas = c(1.94, 3.52, 4.84, 9.38, 19.49, 25.46, 35.25))
write.table(CO2byYear, file='gas.txt')    # Write data frame to file
CO2byYear <- read.table(file="gas.txt")  # Read data back in
write.csv(CO2byYear, file='gas.csv')              # Write data frame
CO2byYear <- read.csv(file="gas.csv", row.names=1)   # Read data back in
```

For available options, consult the help page for `read.table()`.

Readers who are working from the RStudio interface will often find this convenient for data input. Click on Tools, then on Import Dataset.

On Microsoft Windows systems, it is immaterial whether the file is called `fuel.txt` or `Fuel.txt`. Unix file systems may, depending on the specific file system in use, treat letters that have a different case as different.

Data Input from the RStudio Menu – Data Frames versus tibbles

For input of data that are set out in row-by-column format, the RStudio menu has as its first two options either the use of a base R function, or the use of a function from the package *readr* in the *tidyverse* collection of packages. Other available input types, in each case using a relevant tidyverse package, include Excel spreadsheet data, SPSS POR or SAV files, SAS XPT or SAS files, and Stata DTA files. Input of Excel spreadsheet data uses `readxl::read_excel()`, while input of SPSS, SAS, and Stata files is handled using functions from the *haven*) package. See `www.tidyverse.org/` for details of the *tidyverse* "opinionated collection of R packages designed for data science."

With an R base function, input is to a data frame. For *readr* and other *tidyverse* functions, input is to a data frame variant that has the name *tibble*. Among other differences, row names are not added, and character strings are not converted to factors. Conversion of any character string column to a factor, if required, must be done after input.

A.2.6 Issues for Working with Data Frames and tibbles

Extraction of Columns from Data Frames and tibbles

Where a single column is extracted from a data frame, the default action of the `[` operator, as in `cars[,2]` or `cars[, "dist"]` is to return the column vector, not the one-column data frame, thus:

```
sites <- DAAG::possumsites     # sites is then a data frame
sites[,3]                      # returns a vector
sites[,3, drop=FALSE]          # returns a 1-column data frame
```

The tibble data frame variant that is used in the tidyverse collection of packages has `drop=FALSE` as the default.

The preferred notation, when the column vector is required, is `sites[[3]]` or `sites[["altitude"]]`. This will return a vector, irrespective of whether `sites` is a data frame or a tibble, or a list, whose third element contains the vector `altitude`.

```
dplyr::as_tibble(sites)[,3]  # returns a 1-column tibble
dplyr::as_tibble(sites)[[3]] # returns a vector
sites[[3]]                   # returns a vector
```

Tidyverse packages offer a wide range of abilities, for data manipulation, and for plotting. In this text there has been occasional use of plotting functions from the *ggplot2* and related packages, with only occasional use of functions from other tidyverse packages.

**Conversion between Data Frames and tibbles*

For creation of a tibble, `tibble()` and `as_tibble()` are the respective counterparts of `data.frame()` and `as.data.frame()`. When a tibble is printed using the default print method, a row is added under the column names that shows the classes. The row is omitted if `print.data.frame()` is used to print the `tibble`.

When `read.table()` or an alias is used to input data, row names may be created. See `?read.table`. These are stored as an attribute, which can be inspected thus:

```
attributes(DAAG::possumsites)[['row.names']]
```

```
[1] "Cambarville" "Bellbird"    "Allyn River" "Whian Whian"
[5] "Byrangery"   "Conondale"   "Bulburin"
```

When the function `as_tibble()` is used to convert a data frame to a tibble, the default behavior is to silently remove row names. The `rownames` argument can be used to transfer the rownames to a column in the `tibble` with a specified row name. For example:

```
possumSites <- tibble::as_tibble(DAAG::possumsites, rownames="Site")
possumSites
```

A.2.7 Lists

Atomic vectors, to which the term "vector" usually refers, were introduced earlier in Subsection A.2.1. A list is a second and very different type of *vector*, which can join together an arbitrary collection of objects.

An important distinction is between list elements (which are themselves lists) and the contents of list elements. It can be helpful to think of list elements as holding, not the list element itself, but a pointer to the contents of the list element. A pointer to a pointer is a pointer!

A data frame is really a special type of list, in which all list elements (columns) have the same length. The contents of data frame list elements are, among other possibilities, atomic vectors, or factors, or dates. The interest in this subsection is in more general types of list.

Here is an example of a simple list:

```
## Summary statistics for 31 felled black cherry tree
## Median (middle value), range, number, units
htstats <- list(med=76, range=c(low=63,high=87), n=31, units="ft")
htstats[1:2]      # Show first two list elements only
```

```
$med
[1] 76

$range
 low high
  63   87
```

The `$` symbols that precede the list element names indicate that they are themselves lists of length one. The `[` operator extracts the specified list or lists. To extract the contents of an element, one has to use either the `[[` operator or the `$` operator. The syntax is different in the two cases:

```
## The following are alternative ways to extract the second list element
htstats[2]        # First list element (Can replace `2` by 'range')
```

```
$range
 low high
  63   87
```

```
htstats[2][1]     # A subset of a list is a list
```

```
$range
 low high
  63   87
```

Alternative ways to extract the contents of second list elements are:

```
htstats[[2]]; htstats$range; htstats[["range"]]
```

These all give the same result – notice that there is now no `$range` preceding the list element contents:

```
 low high
  63   87
```

Try also:

```
unlist(htstats[2]) # Contents of second list element, with composite names
```

```
range.low range.high
       63         87
```

```
unlist(htstats[2], use.names=F)  # Elements have no names
```

```
[1] 63 87
```

Lists are widely used in R for storing data analysis information. Thus, consider a *t*-test result that compares wear for two different types of shoe leather:

```
tstats <- with(MASS::shoes, t.test(B, A, paired=TRUE))
names(tstats)      ## Names of list elements. See `?t.test` for details.
```

```
 [1] "statistic"   "parameter"   "p.value"     "conf.int"
 [5] "estimate"    "null.value"  "stderr"      "alternative"
 [9] "method"      "data.name"
```

```
tstats[1]         ## Type tstats[1] to see the first list element
```

```
$statistic
  t
3.3
```

```
## Compact listing of contents list elements 1 to 5, which are all numeric
unlist(tstats[1:5]) ## With `unlist(tstats)` all elements become character
```

```
             statistic.t                parameter.df
                  3.3489                      9.0000
                 p.value                   conf.int1
                  0.0085                      0.1330
              conf.int2 estimate.mean difference
                  0.6870                      0.4100
```

The function `c()` can be used to join together, not just atomic vectors, but also lists and indeed any object for which there is a method. Subsection A.5.1 has code for the use of latticeExtra::c() to combine two separate *trellis* objects in the creation of Figure 1.1.

A.3 Functions and Operators

A.3.1 Common Useful Built-In Functions

```
## Data indices
length()     # number of elements in a vector or a list
order()      # x[order(x)] sorts x (by default, NAs are last)
which()      # which indices of a logical vector are `TRUE`
which.max()  # locates (first) maximum (NB, also: `which.min()`)
```

```
## Data manipulation
c()       # join together (`concatenate`) elements or vectors or lists
diff()    # vector of first differences
sort()    # sort elements into order, by default omitting NAs
rev()     # reverse the order of vector elements
t()       # transpose matrix or data frame
          # (a data frame is first coerced to a matrixwith()
with()    # do computation using columns of specified data frame
```

```
## Data summary
mean()        # mean of the elements of a vector
median()      # median of the elements of a vector
range()       # minimum and maximum value elements of vector
unique()      # form the vector of distinct values
## List function arguments
args()        # information on the arguments to a function
```

```
## Obtain details
head()        # display first few rows (by default 6) of object
ls()          # list names of objects in the workspace
```

```
## Print multiple objects
cat()         # prints multiple objects, one after the other
```

```
## Functions that return TRUE or FALSE?
all()         # returns TRUE if all values are TRUE
any()         # returns TRUE if any values are TRUE
is.factor()   # returns TRUE if the argument is a factor
is.na()       # returns TRUE if the argument is an NA
              # NB also is.logical(), etc.
```

Be sure to check, where this is relevant, the handling of missing values. In case of doubt, consult the relevant help page. Refer to Subsection A.4.1. Users may wish to add to or subtract from the above list, or to make their own list.

Where it does not lead to ambiguity, function arguments can usually be abbreviated. Thus, the following are equivalent:

```
seq(from =1, by=2, length.out=3)  # Unabbeviated arguments
```

```
[1] 1 3 5
```

```
seq(from =1, by=2, length=3)      # Abbreviate `length.out` to `length`
```

```
[1] 1 3 5
```

Many functions have a ... argument that allows the passing of optional arguments. Check the relevant help page for details in any specific case.

A.3.2 User-Written Functions

The Structure of Functions

The following shows code for a function that calculates the mean and standard deviation of a numeric vector, with descriptive information overlaid:

```
function name              argument(s)
mean.and.sd  <- function(x=rnorm(10))
           {
function    av <- mean(x)
  body      sdev <- sd(x)
return
 value      c(mean = av, SD = sdev)
           }
```

Having constructed the function, we can apply it to a numeric vector, thus:

```
distance <- c(148,182,173,166,109,141,166)
mean.and.sd(distance)
```

```
mean    SD
 155    25
```

The variables `av` and `sdev` are local to the function. They cannot be accessed outside of the internal function environment.

Note the specification of the default argument `x = rnorm(10)`. If an argument `x` is not supplied when the function is executed, a vector of 10 random numbers is generated to which the function is then applied.

```
## Execute the function with the  default argument:
mean.and.sd()
```

If the function body consists of just one statement that gives the return value, the curly braces ({ }) are unnecessary. The return value, which must be a single object, is given by the final statement of the function body. For returning several objects that are of different types, join them into a list.

```
## Thus, to return the mean, SD and name of the input vector
## replace c(mean=av, SD=sdev) by
list(mean=av, SD=sdev, dataset = deparse(substitute(x)))
```

A.3.3 Generic Functions, and the Class of an Object*

The printing of a data frame requires steps that are different from those for the printing of a vector of numbers. Yet, in R, the same `print()` function handles both tasks. All R objects have a *class* that is used to decide how the printing should be handled. The `print()` function calls the function, if any, that is designed for the specific *class* of object. The function `print.default()` handles the printing of objects (such as numeric vectors) that do not have a their own print method.

For simple objects such as numbers and text strings, the class is determined informally. More complex objects such as data frames carry a tag (an *attribute*) that shows the class. The function `class()` can be used to show the class.

A generic can have the same name as a standard R function. Typing `help(plot)` gives a choice of two help pages. The first, The Default Scatterplot Function, gives the help page for the `plot()` function from the *graphics* package that is one of the base R packages. Clicking instead on Generic X-Y Plotting brings up a help page with the information that `plot()` is a generic function that has methods for many different R objects. Type `methods(plot)` to get a (long) list.

A.3.4 Pipes – a "Do This, Then This, ... " Syntax

Contrast the two following ways of generating 20 random normal numbers, and then calculating their mean.

```
mean(rnorm(20, sd=2))
```

```
[1] 0.071
```

```
20 |> rnorm(sd=2) |> mean()
```

```
[1] 0.42
```

The first calculation uses the conventional R function syntax. The second uses the base R pipe syntax operator `|>` that was first introduced in R 4.1.0. The base R operator `|>` functions in a similar, but not identical, way to the pipe syntax operator `%>%` in the tidyverse *magrittr* package. Observe that the 20 was slotted in as the first argument to the function `rnorm()`, which is the number `n` or random numbers that are to be generated.

The user who wants to save the mean value that is generated can add in either a `<-` assignment at the start of the first line, or a `->` at the end of the final line.

```
logmammals <- MASS::mammals |> log() |> setNames(c("logbody","logbrain"))
## Alternatively, use the ability to reverse the assignment operator.
MASS::mammals |> log() |> setNames(c("logbody","logbrain")) -> logmammals
  ## This last is more in the spirit of pipes.
```

Relative to the syntax `mean(rnorm(20, sd=2))`, calculations start with the initial argument of the innermost bracket pair and move out. Use of the pipe syntax to set out the separate components the calculation in the order in which they occur can make it it easier to follow the sequence of operations.

A further tweak allows the creation on the fly of an unnamed (*anonymous*) function that is then executed. This greatly extends the functionality of pipes.

```
MASS::mammals |>
  log() |>
  setNames(c("logbody","logbrain")) |>
  (\(d)lm(logbrain ~ logbody, data=d))() |>
  coef()
```

```
(Intercept)      logbody
       2.13         0.75
```

Notice that the function definition has to be surrounded by either round brackets or parentheses (`{}`). The construct `(\(d)lm(logbrain ~ logbody, data=d))` returns the function that is created. Following it with `()` then executes the function, with the argument that resulted from the operation that preceded the previous pipe symbol. The function call operates in the same way as for a named function.

A.3.5 Operators

All operators are implemented as functions. Thus `2+4` can be written in the nonstandard form `"+"(2,4)`.

Arithmetic operators are `+`, `-`, `/`, `^` , `%%` , and `%/%`. The operator `^` is for exponentiation, while `%%` and `%/%` implement modular arithmetic.

```
## Multiple of divisor that leaves smallest non-negative remainder
c("Multiple of divisor" = 24 %/% 9, "Remainder after division" = 6)
```

```
     Multiple of divisor Remainder after division
                       2                        6
```

Logical operators include `!` (negation), `&`, `&&` (logical AND), `|`, `||` (logical OR). The shorter forms perform elementwise comparisons. See `?Logic` for the use of the longer (`&&` and `||`) forms. Note also `xor()` which asks whether one or the other, but not both, is `TRUE`.

A.4 Calculations with Matrices, Arrays, Lists, and Data Frames

Calculations in Parallel across all Elements of a Vector

Many of R's functions operate in parallel on all elements of atomic vectors, arrays, matrices, and data frames. For example:

```
x <- 1:6
log(x)                  # Natural logarithm of 1, 2, ... 6
log(x, base=10)         # Common logarithm (base 10)
log(64, base=c(2,10))  # Apply different bases to one number
log(matrix(1:6, nrow=2), base=2)  # Take logarithms of all matrix elements
```

Patterned Data

Recall the use of, for example, `5:15` to generate all integers between 5 and 15 inclusive. The function `seq()` allows a wider range of possibilities. For example:

```
seq(from=5, to=22, by=3)  # The first value is 5.
```

```
[1]  5  8 11 14 17 20
```

```
rep(c(2,3,5), 4)        #  Repeat the sequence (2, 3, 5) four times over
```

```
 [1] 2 3 5 2 3 5 2 3 5 2 3 5
```

```
rep(c("female", "male"), c(2,3))  # Use syntax with a character vector
```

```
[1] "female" "female" "male"   "male"   "male"
```

A.4.1 Missing Values

The missing value symbol is `NA`. As an example, consider the variable `branch` from the dataset `rainforest`:

```
nbranch <- subset(DAAG::rainforest, species=="Acacia mabellae")$branch
nbranch          # Number of small branches (2cm or less)
```

```
 [1] NA 35 41 50 NA NA NA NA NA  4 30 13 10 17 46 92
```

Any arithmetic expression that involves an `NA` generates `NA` as its result. Functions such as `mean()` allow the argument `na.rm=TRUE`, so that `NA`s are omitted before proceeding with the calculation. For example:

```
mean(nbranch, na.rm=TRUE)
```

```
[1] 34
```

Functions that behave similarly include `sum()`, `median()`, `range()`, and `sd()`.

Arithmetic and logical expressions in which NAs appear return NA, thus:

```
nbranch == NA    # This always equals `NA`
```

```
 [1] NA NA NA NA NA NA NA NA NA NA NA NA NA NA NA NA
```

The unknown values might in each case just possibly equal 35. This is a matter of strict logic, not probability. Thus, all results are NA. Use instead:

```
is.na(nbranch)   # Use to check for NAs
```

```
 [1]  TRUE FALSE FALSE FALSE  TRUE TRUE TRUE TRUE TRUE FALSE FALSE
[12] FALSE FALSE FALSE FALSE FALSE
```

To replace all NAs by −999 (rarely a good idea) use `is.na()`, thus:

```
nbranch[is.na(nbranch)] <- -999
  # `mean(nbranch)` will then be a nonsense value
```

NAs in Modeling Functions

The argument `na.action`, available for many of the modeling functions, has a global setting that can be inspected thus:

```
options()$na.action # Version 3.2.2, following startup
```

```
[1] "na.omit"
```

The argument `na.action=na.omit` causes omission of rows that hold NAs, prior to the analysis. A useful alternative, when it is available, can be `na.exclude`. This excludes rows that have NAs from the analysis, but returns values for all rows when fitted values, residuals, etc., are calculated, placing NAs in positions where no value can be calculated. Individual functions may have defaults that are different from the global setting. See `?na.action`, and help pages for individual modeling functions.

Counting and Identifying NAs – the Use of `table()`

The default action of `table()` is to exclude NAs and NaNs. Supply the argument `exclude=NULL` (exclude nothing) to tabulate both NAs and NaNs. More generally, `exclude` can be a vector that has any mix of NAs, NaNs, and factor levels.

An alternative, if NAs are the only concern, is the argument `useNA="ifany"`. The following indicates, for each treatment group in the data frame `DAAG::nswdemo`, whether `re74` is 0, greater than 0, or unknown:

```
with(DAAG::nswdemo, table(trt, re74>0, useNA="ifany"))
```

```

trt FALSE TRUE <NA>
  0   195   65  165
  1   131   54  112
```

Infinities and NaN*s*

Other legal values that may require special attention are NaN (not a number; e.g., 0/0), Inf (e.g., 1/0), and -Inf (e.g., -1/0). The expression 0/0 returns NaN, as does 0*Inf, or Inf-Inf, or log(-1).

The expression 1/0 returns Inf, while 1/(-0) returns -Inf. The rationale is that $1/x$ can be made arbitrarily large, and $1/(-x)$ can be made arbitrarily small, by taking x to be a small enough positive number. Similarly, log(0) returns -Inf. Note also that if n is a finite value, then n/Inf returns 0.

It can in some circumstances simplify coding to allow quantities that are Inf or NaN to propagate through an arithmetic calculation, dealing with the need to raise a flag at the endpoint of the calculation.

A.4.2 Access to Datasets and Functions in R Packages

The *DAAG* package follows the great majority of packages in allowing a *pkg-name*::*objname* form of reference, as in the following code:

```
summary(DAAG::primates)
```

This form of reference avoids any ambiguity over where to look for the object.

Where there will be repeated reference to the dataset primates, it can be copied into the workspace, thus:

```
primates <- DAAG::primates
```

While the dataset remains in the workspace, a reference to primates will suffice.

An alternative is to use library(DAAG) to load the package, that is, to add it to the session library. This makes available all of *DAAG*'s datasets and functions that are available for use outside the package, with no need for further reference If there is a dataset primates in the workspace, summary(primates) will give summary information for that object, which may not be what the user wants.

Where there is any risk of ambiguity, use the *function-name*::*objname* form of reference:

```
gplots::plotCI()   # `plotCI() function in package `gplots`
plotrix::plotCI()  # `plotCI() function in package `plotrix`
```

The *pkgname*::*objname* form of reference is not available for a small number of packages that do not enable the *lazy data* mechanism. In such cases, the function data() can be used to load the required dataset into the workspace. See ?data.

A limited number of packages are automatically attached at the beginning of a session. The following shows the names of base packages:

```
sessionInfo()[['basePkgs']]
```

```
[1] "stats"     "graphics"  "grDevices" "utils"     "datasets"
[6] "methods"   "base"
```

Functions that *base* and *stats* provide include such functions as print(), plot(), and mean(). Users can change the setup defaults, usually so that further packages are added at the start of a session.

Type search() to see which packages are attached at any point in time:

```
## List just the workspace and the first eight packages on the search list:
search()[1:9]
```

```
[1] ".GlobalEnv"         "tools:rstudio"      "package:stats"
[4] "package:graphics"   "package:grDevices"  "package:utils"
[7] "package:datasets"   "package:knitr"      "package:methods"
```

Technically, these are termed *databases.* The database `".GlobalEnv"` is the workspace.

For commands executed from the command line, and in the absence of any specific information on where an object is to be found, R starts its search at the first item in the search list and proceeds as necessary on towards the last.

Datasets That Accompany R Packages

Type `data()` to get a list of datasets (mostly data frames) in all packages that are in the current search path. To list datasets in the base *datasets* package, type

```
data(package="datasets")
```

Replace `"datasets"` by the name of any other installed package, as required (type `library()` to get the names of the installed packages).

A.5 Brief Notes on R Graphics Packages and Functions

Base graphics, using the *graphics* package, implements a relatively "traditional" style of graphics. Plots go directly to the graphics device that is open at the time. Functions divide between those that create a new plot, those that add to an existing plot, and a few that allow a choice between these possibilities. Type `library(help='graphics')` to obtain a full list of available functions. Commonly used functions that start a new plot include such functions as `plot()`, `dotchart()`, `boxplot()`, `hist()`, and `barplot()`. Among functions that add to existing plots, note in particular `points()`, `lines()`, `title()`, `mtext()`, and `rug()`.

The other graphics systems that have more than an occasional use in the text, whether directly or using packages that exploit their functionality, are:

1. the low-level *grid* package on which *lattice* and *ggplot2* are built;
2. lattice (trellis) graphics, using the *lattice* package;
3. *ggplot2*, which implements Wilkinson's *Grammar of Graphics.*

By contrast, *lattice* and *ggplot2* functions create graphics objects. If output to the command line, the effect is to *print* the graph, which for a graphics object creates a plot on the currently open graphics device. If assigned to a named object, the graphics object can then be updated, or one or more layers added, prior to printing. In the following, a graph obtained using the base graphics function `plot()` is followed by plots that demonstrate the greater functionality of the lattice `xyplot()` function.

The *ggplot2* package implements a rich graphics language. Extensive tutorial material is available from the Internet. Layering is a built-in feature of the *ggplot2* package, while *lattice* requires the add-on package *latticeExtra* for this purpose. R packages that adapt and/or extend *ggplot2* abilities include *GGally*, *ggridges*, *ggsci*, *mgcViz*, *plotly*, and *cobalt*. The package *gginnards* has abilities that may be helpful in working with *ggplot2* objects.

Note the point made in Section A.3.3, that `plot()` is one of several R functions that can operate either as a *generic* and invoke the plot method for the class of object supplied as argument, or invoke the default plot function in the base *graphics* package. Thus if `gph` is either a *lattice* or a *ggplot2* object, `plot(gph)` (an alternative is `print(gph)`) will generate a plot, usually on the screen if no other device has been opened. See `?device` for details.

A.5.1 Lattice Graphics – a Step Beyond Base Graphics

The discussion that follows includes code that readers can use to explore key features of lattice graphics, but leaving aside most details of labeling and annotation. We start, as a basis for comparison, with a plot that uses base graphics.

```
grog <- DAAG::grog
chr <- with(grog, match(Country, c('Australia', 'NewZealand')))
  # Australia: 1; matches 1st element of c('Australia', 'NewZealand')
  # NewZealand: 2; matches 2nd element
plot(Beer ~ Year, data=grog, ylim=c(0, max(Beer)*1.1), pch = chr)
with(grog, points(Wine ~ Year, pch=chr, col='red'))
legend("bottomright", legend=c("Australia", "New Zealand"), pch=1:2)
title(main="Beer consumption (l, pure alcohol)", line=1)
```

Contrast this with a roughly equivalent lattice plot:

```
library(latticeExtra)  ## Loads both lattice and the add-on latticeExtra
gph <- xyplot(Beer+Wine ~ Year, groups=Country, data=grog)
update(gph, par.settings=simpleTheme(pch=19), auto.key=list(columns=2))
```

```
## Or, condition on `Country`
xyplot(Beer+Wine+Spirit ~ Year | Country, data=grog,
       par.settings=simpleTheme(pch=19), auto.key=list(columns=3))
```

Use the arguments `xlab` and `ylab` to replace the default axis labels, and `main` to add a main title. To change the strip labels from the fault, specify, for example, for three panels, `strip=strip.custom(factor.levels=LETTERS[1:3]))`. The `scales` argument has provision for the use of logarithmic scales, for controlling whether or not all panels use the same scale, and for controlling the details of axis labels.

There can be multiple conditioning factors. The `DAAG::tinting` dataset is from an experiment that used two different measures of response time (`csoa` and `it`) to measure response, for three difference levels of tinting (`tint`: `low`, `medium`, `high`) of car side windows, for targets with two different levels of contrast (`target`: `locon`, `hicon`), and for two different age groups (`agegp`: `younger`, `older`) of subject. The following is a possible graph:

```
tinting <- DAAG::tinting
xyplot(csoa~it | tint*target, groups=agegp, data=tinting, auto.key=list(columns=2))
```

New features can be overlaid by adding a new layer to a graphics object. It is often easiest to create a further separate graphics object, and use the function `as.layer()` to add that as a new layer.

```
cuckoos <- DAAG::cuckoos
av <- with(cuckoos, aggregate(length, list(species=species), FUN=mean))
gph <- dotplot(species ~ length, data=cuckoos, alpha=0.4) +
  as.layer(dotplot(species ~ x, pch=3, cex=1.4, col="black", data=av))
update(gph, xlab="Length of egg (mm)")
```

The following code directly adds a new layer:

```
## Alternatives, using `layer()` or `as.layer()`
avg <- with(cuckoos, data.frame(nspec=1:nlevels(species),
                      av=sapply(split(length,species),mean)))
dotplot(species ~ length, data=cuckoos) +
  latticeExtra::layer(lpoints(nspec~av, pch=3, cex=1.25, col="black"), data=avg)
```

```
dotplot(species ~ length, data=cuckoos) +
  as.layer(dotplot(nspec~av, data=avg, pch=3, cex=1.25, col="black"))
```

A further possibility is to use the argument `panel` to specify a panel function. If preferred, the function can be defined prior to calling `dotplot()`:

```
## Specify panel function
dotplot(species ~ length, data=cuckoos,
  panel=function(x,y,...){panel.dotplot(x, y, pch=1, col="gray40")
    avg <- data.frame(nspec=1:nlevels(y), av=sapply(split(x,y),mean))
    with(avg, lpoints(nspec~av, pch=3, cex=1.25, col="black")) })
```

Combining Separately Created Graphics Objects

Use the function `c()`, which for trellis objects calls the function `c.trellis()`, for this purpose. Figure 1.1 showed the graph that results.

```
cuckoos <- DAAG::cuckoos
## Panel A: Dotplot without species means added
gphA <- dotplot(species ~ length, data=cuckoos)
## Panel B: Box and whisker plot
gphB <- bwplot(species ~ length, data=cuckoos)
update(c("A: Dotplot"=gphA, "B: Boxplot"=gphB), between=list(x=0.4),
     xlab="Length of egg (mm)", layout=c(2,1))
  ## `latticeExtra::c()` joins compatible plots together.
  ## `layout=c(2,1)` : join horizontally; `layout=c(1,2)` : join vertically
```

A.5.2 Dynamic Graphics – the rgl *Package*

The right-hand panel in Figure 3.15 in Subsection 3.4.2 used the interface to the three-dimensional dynamic graphics of the *rgl* package provided by the *car* functions `scatter3d()` and `Identify3d()` functions. The vignette `rgl` gives an overview of what is available.

Note also the wide-ranging abilities that are implemented in the *plot3D* package. A good starting point is the vignette that can be displayed by typing:

```
vignette('plot3D', package='plot3D')
```

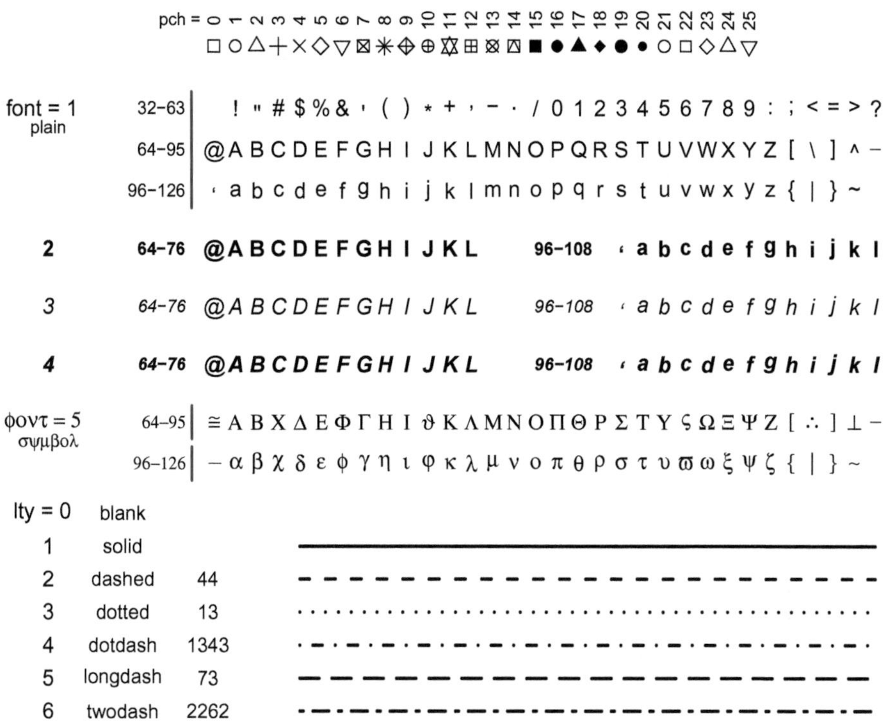

Figure A.2 Fonts, symbols, and line types, created using the default postscript/pdf encoding (see `?postscript` for details). For `pch` in the range 32–126, symbols may vary depending on the family and on the device. Here, the font family is the default sans-serif font **Helvetica**. Set (`par(family="")` or `par(family="sans")`) for a postscript or pdf device. Observe that the "y" in "symbol" has translated, in the symbol font, to ψ. Line types may be specified by number, by name (`lty="dashed"`, ...), or by code (`lty="44"`, ...).

A.6 Plotting Characters, Symbols, Line Types, and Colors

Setting `pch` to one of the numbers 0, 1, ..., 25 gives one of 26 different plotting symbols. In addition, assuming that a single-byte character set is in use, `pch` may be set to any value in the range 32–255. (Multibyte character sets are needed, e.g., for Asian languages.) Figure A.2 gives the full range of characters for `font=1`. An alternative is to use a quoted string, for example, `pch="a"`. For plotting, characters are centered vertically about their mid-position.

There are six line types that can be specified by number (0, 1, ..., 6) or by name (`"blank"`, `"solid"`, ...). Use of a number sequence that is enclosed in quotes allows a more flexible specification of line types. Thus, `"33"` describes a length of three units that is drawn, followed by three units that are skipped. Up to four (draw, skip) pairs are allowed, that is, a total of eight numbers. Units are, on most devices, line widths.

The base graphics function `symbols()` offers a choice of circles, squares, rectangles, stars, thermometers, and boxplots. Supply `fg` (foreground) to specify the color of the symbol outline, and `bg` (background) for the fill color. See `?symbols`.

Font Families

A font family is a collection of device-specific font faces. Within any font family, the numbers 1–4 identify, wherever possible, a specific face. Font 1 is plain text, font 2 is bold face, font 3 is italic, and font 4 is bold italic. Font 5 is a special setting that specifies the symbol font (in Adobe symbol encoding).

The `family` argument to the `par()` function accepts the generic names: `"sans"` (on an out-of-the-box setup, the default), `"serif"`, `"mono"`, and `"symbol"`. On devices that honor this setting, these are mapped to device-specific families. Thus, `"sans"` is mapped to `Helvetica` on postscript or pdf devices. Under Windows, using (`win.graph()`), it is mapped to `Arial`. Herschey font families are another possibility; see `?Hershey`.

Colors

Type `palette()` to see the names or codes for a set of colors that can be identified by number, starting with 1, in calls to base graphics functions. Palettes from the *RColorBrewer* package can be good alternatives. To change to the 12-color version of the *RColorBrewer* `Set3` palette, enter:

```
library(RColorBrewer)
palette(brewer.pal(12, "Set3"))
```

The help page `?heat.colors` gives details of several alternative palettes that give graduated colors. The function `colorRampPalette()` creates a function that interpolates a given set of colors. Note also *RColorBrewer*'s quantitative scales.

The function `rgb()` defines ("mixes") colors in a red/green/blue color space, `hcl()` in a hue/chroma/lightness space and `hsv()` in a hue/saturation/value space. See the relevant help pages.

The function `adjustcolor()` can be used to set the opacity `alpha` for the color that is returned. Thus, with `alpha=0.4`, 60 percent of the background shows through. Two overlapping points have a combined opacity of 80 percent, so that 20 percent of the background shows through. Lattice and ggplot2 functions accept the argument `alpha` directly.

The function `dichromat::dichromat()` offers several palettes that, for individuals with one of two common types of red–green color blindness, distinguish the colors. The color `"green3"`, which has replaced `"green"` in the default palette, does appear different from `"red"`.

References

Aitchison, J. (2003). *The Statistical Analysis of Compositional Data.* Blackburn Press. 416 pp. (cit. on p. 187).

Akaike, H. (1978). "On the likelihood of a time series model." *Journal of the Royal Statistical Society: Series D (The Statistician)* 27.3-4, pp. 217–235 (cit. on p. 223).

Aldrich (1995). "Correlations genuine and spurious in Pearson and Yule." *Statistical Science* 10, pp. 364–376 (cit. on p. 90).

Allison, D. B. et al. (2016). "Reproducibility: A tragedy of errors." *Nature* 530.7588, pp. 27–29. `https://doi.org/10.1038/530027a` (cit. on p. 79).

Ambroise, C. and G. J. McLachlan (2002). "Selection bias in gene extraction on the basis of microarray gene-expression data." *Proceedings of the National Academy of Sciences (PNAS)* 99, pp. 6262–6266 (cit. on pp. 434, 462).

Andersen, B. (1990). *Methodological Errors in Medical Research: an Incomplete Catalogue.* Blackwell Scientific. 288 pp. (cit. on p. 79).

Andrews, D. F. and A. M. Herzberg (1985). *Data. A Collection of Problems from Many Fields for the Student and Research Worker.* Springer-Verlag (cit. on p. 319).

Andrews, J. L. et al. (2018). "teigen: An R package for model-based clustering and classification via the multivariate t distribution." *Journal of Statistical Software* 83.1, pp. 1–32 (cit. on p. 418).

Anon (2016). *Cholera epidemics in Victorian London.* `www.thegazette.co.uk/all-notices/content/100519` (visited on 01/01/2021) (cit. on p. 257).

Aphalo, P. J. (2020). *Learn R: As a Language.* Chapman and Hall/CRC (cit. on p. 79).

Barnett, V. (2002). *Sample Survey: Principles & Methods.* 3rd ed. Wiley-Blackwell. (cit. on p. 3).

Bartholemew, D. (2004). *Measuring Intelligence. Facts and Fallacies.* Cambridge University Press. 186 pp. (cit. on p. 368).

Bates, D. M. and D. G. Watts (1988). *Nonlinear Regression Analysis and Its Applications.* Wiley. 392 pp. (cit. on p. 203).

Begley, C. G. (2013). "Reproducibility: Six red flags for suspect work." *Nature* 497.7450, pp. 433–434 (cit. on p. 76).

Begley, C. G. and L. M. Ellis (2012). "Drug development: Raise standards for preclinical cancer research." *Nature* 483.7391, pp. 531–533 (cit. on p. 76).

Belson, W. A. (1959). "Matching and prediction on the principle of biological classification." *Applied Statistics* 8, pp. 65–75 (cit. on p. 373).

Benjamin, D. J. et al. (2018). "Redefine statistical significance." *Nature Human Behaviour* 2.1, pp. 6–10 (cit. on p. 78).

Berk, R. A. (2008). *Statistical Learning from a Regression Perspective.* Springer. 360 pp. (cit. on pp. 395, 462).

Berkson, J. (1942). "Tests of significance considered as evidence." *Journal of the American Statistical Association* 37.219, pp. 325–335 (cit. on p. 58).

Bezdek, J. C., R. Ehrlich, and W. Full (1984). "FCM: The fuzzy c-means clustering algorithm." *Computers & Geosciences* 10.2-3, pp. 191–203 (cit. on p. 416).

Bhaskaran, K. and L. Smeeth (2014). "What is the difference between missing completely at random and missing at random?" *International Journal of Epidemiology* 43.4, pp. 1336–1339. https://doi.org/10.1093/ije/dyu080. https://academic.oup.com/ije/article-pdf/43/4/1336/9727786/dyu080.pdf (cit. on p. 457).

Bickel, P. J., E. A. Hammel, and J. W. O'Connell (1975). "Sex bias in graduate admissions: data from Berkeley." *Science* 187, pp. 398–403 (cit. on p. 89).

Bioconductor Open Source Software for Bioinformatics (2022). http://bioconductor.org/ (cit. on p. 462).

Blackwell, M., J. Honaker, and G. King (2017). "A unified approach to measurement error and missing data: overview and applications." *Sociological Methods & Research* 46.3, pp. 303–341. https://doi.org/10.1177/0049124115585360 (cit. on pp. 195, 461).

Blake, C. and C. Merz (1998). *UCI Repository of Machine Learning Databases.* www.ics.uci.edu/~mlearn/MLRepository.html (cit. on p. 374).

Bland, M. and D. Altman (2005). "Do the left-handed die young?" *Significance* 2, pp. 166–170 (cit. on pp. 196, 290).

Bolker, B. M. (2008). *Ecological Models and Data in R.* Princeton University Press. 408 pp. (cit. on pp. 137, 203).

Boot, H. M. and J. Maindonald (2008). "New estimates of age- and sex-specific earnings and the male–female earnings gap in the British cotton industry, 1833–1906." *Economic History Review* 61, pp. 380–408 (cit. on p. 242).

Bowman, A. W. et al. (2019). "Graphics for uncertainty." *Journal of the Royal Statistical Society, Series A (Statistics in Society)* 182. Pt 2, pp. 403–18 (cit. on p. 80).

Box, G. E. P. and D. R. Cox (1964). "An analysis of transformations (with discussion)." *Journal of the Royal Statistical Society* B 26, pp. 211–252 (cit. on p. 113).

Box, G. E., J. S. Hunter, and W. G. Hunter (2005). "Statistics for experimenters." In *Wiley Series in Probability and Statistics.* Wiley (cit. on p. 123).

Braun, W. J. (2012). "Naive analysis of variance." *Journal of Statistics Education* 20.2 (cit. on p. 123).

Braun, W. J. and D. J. Murdoch (2021). *A First Course in Statistical Programming with R.* 3rd ed. Cambridge University Press. 280 pp. (cit. on p. 79).

Breheny, P. J. (2019). "Marginal false discovery rates for penalized regression models." *Biostatistics* 20.2, pp. 299–314. https://academic.oup.com/biostatistics/article/20/2/299/4840255 (cit. on p. 186).

Breheny, P. and J. Huang (2011). "Coordinate descent algorithms for nonconvex penalized regression, with applications to biological feature selection." *Annals of Applied Statistics.* www.ncbi.nlm.nih.gov/pmc/articles/PMC3212875/ (cit. on pp. 186, 191).

Breiman, L. (2001). "Statistical modeling: The two cultures." *Statistical Science* 16, pp. 199–215 (cit. on p. 137).

Brillinger, D. R. (2002). "John W. Tukey: His life and professional contributions." *Annals of Statistics*, pp. 1535–1575 (cit. on p. xiv).

Brockwell, P. and R. A. Davis (2002). *Introduction to Time Series and Forecasting.* 2nd ed. Springer (cit. on p. 314).

Burns, N. R. et al. (1999). "Effects of car window tinting on visual performance: a comparison of elderly and young drivers." *Ergonomics* 42, pp. 428–443 (cit. on p. 344).

Bussolari, S. (1987). "Human factors of long-distance human-powered aircraft flights." *Human Power* 5, pp. 8–12 (cit. on p. 360).

Button, K. S. et al. (2013). "Power failure: Why small sample size undermines the reliability of neuroscience." *Nature Reviews Neuroscience* 14.5, pp. 365–376. https://doi.org/10.1038/nrn3475. www.projectimplicit.net/nosek/papers/BIMNFRM2013.pdf (cit. on pp. 55, 56, 79).

Camerer, C. F. et al. (2016). "Evaluating replicability of laboratory experiments in economics." *Science* 351.6280, pp. 1433–1436. http://science.sciencemag.org/content/351/6280/1433.full.pdf. https://authors.library.caltech.edu/64988/1/aaf0918-Camerer-SM.pdf (cit. on p. 76).

Carroll, R. (2004). *Measuring Diet.* Texas A & M Distinguished Lecturer series (cit. on p. 192).

Carroll, R. J., D. Ruppert, and L. A. Stefanski (2006). *Measurement Error in Nonlinear Models: A Modern Perspective.* 2nd ed. Chapman and Hall/CRC. 484 pp. (cit. on pp. 193, 203).

Celeux, G. and G. Govaert (1992). "A classification EM algorithm for clustering and two stochastic versions." *Computational Statistics and Data Analysis* 14.3, pp. 315–332 (cit. on p. 422).

Chadwick, E. (1842). *Report on the Sanitary Condition of the Labouring Population of Great Britain.* W. Clowes (cit. on p. 257).

Chalmers, I. and D. G. Altman (1995). *Systematic Reviews.* BMJ Publishing Group, London. 119 pp. (cit. on p. 371).

Chambers, J. M. (2008). *Software for Data Analysis: Programming 'with R.* Springer. 516 pp. (cit. on pp. xvi, 79).

Chang, W. (2013). *R Graphics Cookbook.* 1st ed. O'Reilly (cit. on p. 80).

Charig, C. R. (1986). "Comparison of treatment of renal calculi by operative surgery, percutaneous nephrolithotomy, and extracorporeal shock wave lithotripsy." *British Medical Journal* 292, pp. 879–882 (cit. on p. 19).

Chatfield, C. (2003). *The Analysis of Time Series: an Introduction.* 6th ed. Chapman and Hall. 352 pp. (cit. on p. 314).

Christie, M. (2000). *The Ozone Layer: a Philosophy of Science Perspective.* Cambridge University Press (cit. on p. 243).

Chu, I. et al. (1988). "Reproduction study of toxaphene in the rat." *Journal of Environmental Science and Health Part B. Pesticides and Food Contamination* 23, pp. 101–126 (cit. on p. 139).

Clarke, D. (1968). *Analytical Archaeology.* Methuen. 684 pp. (cit. on p. 137).

Cleveland, W. S. (1981). "LOWESS: a program for smoothing scatterplots by robust locally weighted regression." *The American Statistician* 35, p. 54 (cit. on p. 237).

Clutton-Brock, T. H. et al. (1999). "Selfish sentinels in cooperative mammals." *Science* pp. 1640–1644 (cit. on p. 242).

Clyde, M. et al. (2022). "An introduction to Bayesian thinking. A companion to the Statistics with R course." `https://statswithr.github.io/book/` (cit. on p. 62).

Cochran, W. G. and G. M. Cox (1957). *Experimental Designs.* 2nd ed. Wiley. 640 pp. (cit. on p. 369).

Cohen, P. (1996). "Pain discriminates between the sexes." *New Scientist* 2054, p. 16 (cit. on p. 196).

Coleman, T. (2019). "Causality in the time of cholera: John Snow as a prototype for causal inference." `https://papers.ssrn.com/sol3/papers.cfm?abstract_id=3262234` (cit. on p. 257).

Collett, D. (2014). *Modelling Survival Data in Medical Research.* 3rd ed. Chapman and Hall. 548 pp. (cit. on p. 290).

Cook, D. and D. F. Swayne (2007). *Interactive and Dynamic Graphics for Data Analysis.* Springer (cit. on p. 462).

Cook, R. D. and S. Weisberg (1999). *Applied Regression Including Computing and Graphics.* Wiley. 632 pp. (cit. on pp. 171, 202).

Cowpertwait, P. S. P. and A. V. Metcalfe (2009). *Introductory Time Series with R.* Springer (cit. on p. 314).

Cox, D. R. (1958). *Planning of Experiments.* Wiley. 320 pp. (cit. on pp. 79, 240, 371).

— (2006). *Principles of Statistical Inference.* Cambridge University Press (cit. on p. xiv).

Cox, D. R. and N. Reid (2000). *Theory of the Design of Experiments.* Chapman and Hall. 326 pp. (cit. on pp. 240, 371).

Cox, D. R. and N. Wermuth (1996). *Multivariate Dependencies: Models, Analysis and Interpretation.* Chapman and Hall. 272 pp. (cit. on pp. 30, 203).

Cox, T. F. and M. A. A. Cox (2000). *Multidimensional Scaling.* 2nd ed. Chapman and Hall/CRC. 328 pp. (cit. on p. 408).

Cunningham, S. (2021). *Causal Inference.* Yale University Press. `https://mixtape.scunning.com/index.html` (visited on 03/28/2022) (cit. on pp. 159, 202, 462).

Dalgaard, P. (2008). *Introductory Statistics with* R. 2nd ed. Springer. 364 pp. (cit. on p. 79).

Daniels, M., B. Devlin, and K. Roeder (1997). "Of genes and IQ." In *Intelligence, Genes and Success*. Ed. by B. Devlin, S. Fienberg, and K. Roeder. Chapter 3. Springer (cit. on p. 368).

Dann, C. (2022). "Sewage, water and waste – stinking cities." In *Te Ara – the Encyclopedia of New Zealand*. New Zealand Government. `https://teara.govt.nz/en/zoomify/24431/dunedin-renamed-stinkapool` (visited on 02/20/2022) (cit. on p. 260).

Davison, A. C. and D. V. Hinkley (1997). *Bootstrap Methods and Their Application*. Cambridge University Press. 594 pp. (cit. on p. 121).

Dehejia, R. H. and S. Wahba (1999). "Causal effects in non-experimental studies: reevaluating the evaluation of training programs." *Journal of the American Statistical Association* 94, pp. 1053–1062 (cit. on pp. 445, 449).

Diedenhofen, B. and J. Musch (2015). "cocor: A comprehensive solution for the statistical comparison of correlations." *PloS one* 10.4, e0121945 (cit. on p. 95).

Diggle, P. J. et al. (2002). *Analysis of Longitudinal Data*. 2nd ed. Clarendon Press (cit. on pp. 347, 359, 371).

Dobson, A. J. and A. Barnett (2008). *An Introduction to Generalized Linear Models*. Chapman and Hall/CRC. 320 pp. (cit. on p. 289).

Donner, A. and N. Klar (2000). *Design and Analysis of Cluster Randomization Trials in Health Research*. Wiley. 194 pp. (cit. on p. 3).

Donohue, J. J. and S. D. Levitt (May 2019). *The Impact of Legalized Abortion on Crime over the Last Two Decades*. Working Paper 25863. National Bureau of Economic Research. `https://doi.org/10.3386/w25863`. `www.nber.org/papers/w25863` (cit. on p. 202).

Doorn, J. van et al. (2021). "The JASP guidelines for conducting and reporting a Bayesian analysis." *Psychonomic Bulletin & Review* 28.3, pp. 813–826 (cit. on p. 137).

Edwards, D. (2000). *Introduction to Graphical Modelling*. 2nd ed. Springer. 335 pp. (cit. on p. 203).

Efron, B. and R. Tibshirani (1993). *An Introduction to the Bootstrap*. Chapman and Hall. 456 pp. (cit. on p. 69).

Efron, B. et al. (2003). *Least Angle Regression*. `www-stat.stanford.edu/~hastie/Papers/LARS/LeastAngle_2002.pdf` (cit. on p. 186).

Ellenberg, J. (2015). *How Not To Be Wrong*. 1st ed. Penguin Books (cit. on p. 80).

Errington, T. (2021). *Replication Study Results*. `https://osf.io/e81xl/wiki/home/` (visited on 12/07/2021) (cit. on p. 77).

Errington, T. M. et al. (2021). "Investigating the replicability of preclinical cancer biology." *Elife* 10, e71601 (cit. on p. 77).

Eubank, R. L. (1999). *Nonparametric Regression and Spline Smoothing*. 2nd ed. Marcel Dekker. 360 pp. (cit. on p. 240).

Ezzet, F. and J. Whitehead (1991). "A random effects model for ordinal responses from a crossover trial." *Statistics in Medicine* 10, pp. 901–907 (cit. on p. 278).

Fan, J. and I. Gijbels (1996). *Local Polynomial Modelling and Its Applications*. Chapman and Hall/CRC. 360 pp. (cit. on p. 237).

Faraway, J. J. (2014). *Linear Models with R*. 2nd ed. Taylor & Francis Ltd. 286 pp. (cit. on p. 202).

— (2016). *Extending the Linear Model with R*. 2nd ed. Taylor & Francis Inc. 413 pp. (cit. on pp. 240, 289).

Farmer, C. (2005). "Another look at Meyer and Finney's 'Who wants airbags?"' *Chance* 19, pp. 15–22 (cit. on pp. 23, 24).

Fisher, R. A. (1926). "The arrangement of field experiments." *Journal of Ministry of Agriculture of Great Britain* 33, pp. 503–513 (cit. on p. 56).

— (1935). *The Design of Experiments*. (7th ed, 1960). Oliver and Boyd (cit. on pp. 57, 371).

Follett, P. A. and L. G. Neven (2006). "Current trends in quarantine entomology." *Annual Review of Entomology* 51.1, pp. 359–385. `https://doi.org/10.1146/annurev.ento.49.061802.123314` (cit. on p. 350).

Follett, P. A., N. C. Manoukis, and B. Mackey (2018). "Comparative cold tolerance in Ceratitis capitata and Zeugodacus cucurbitae (Diptera: Tephritidae)." *Journal of Economic Entomology* 111.6, pp. 2632–2636 (cit. on p. 350).

Fox, J. and S. Weisberg (2018). *An R Companion to Applied Regression.* Sage Publications. `http://socserv.socsci.mcmaster.ca/jfox/Books/Companion` (cit. on pp. 176, 202).

Franco-Watkins, A., P. Derks, and M. Dougherty (2003). "Reasoning in the Monty Hall problem: Examining choice behaviour and probability judgements." *Thinking & Reasoning* 9.1, pp. 67–90 (cit. on p. 142).

Frazer, K. A. (2012). "Decoding the human genome." *Genome Research* 22.9, pp. 1599–1601 (cit. on p. 462).

Friedlingstein, P. et al. (2022). "Global carbon budget 2021." *Earth System Science Data* 14.4, pp. 1917–2005 (cit. on p. 471).

Galili, T. (2015). *Tutorials for learning R.* (Accessed on 02/03/2017) (cit. on p. 79).

Gaver, D. P. et al. (1992). *Combining Information: Statistical Issues and Opportunities for Research.* National Research Council, National Academy Press. 234 pp. (cit. on pp. 370, 371).

Gelman, A. and J. Carlin (2014). "Beyond power calculations assessing type S (sign) and type M (magnitude) errors." *Perspectives on Psychological Science* 9.6, pp. 641–651 (cit. on p. 56).

Gelman, A. and J. Hill (2006). *Data Analysis Using Regression and Multilevel/Hierarchical Models.* Cambridge University Press. 648 pp. (cit. on p. 371).

Gelman, A. B. et al. (2003). *Bayesian Data Analysis.* 2nd ed. Chapman and Hall/CRC. 690 pp. (cit. on p. 80).

Gelman, A., J. Hill, and A. Vehtari (2020). *Regression and Other Stories.* Cambridge University Press (cit. on p. 202).

Gigerenzer, G. (1998). "We need statistical thinking, not statistical rituals." *Behavioural and Brain Sciences* 21, pp. 199–200 (cit. on p. 79).

— (2002). *Reckoning with Risk: Learning to Live with Uncertainty.* Penguin Books. 320 pp. (cit. on p. 80).

Gigerenzer, G. et al. (1989). *The Empire of Chance.* Cambridge University Press. 360 pp. (cit. on pp. xv, 80).

Gihr, M. and G. Pilleri (1969). "Anatomy and biometry of Stenella and Delphinus." In *Investigations on Cetacea.* Ed. by G. Pilleri. Hirnanatomisches Institute der Universität Bern (cit. on p. 115).

Glass, T. A. et al. (2013). "Causal inference in public health." *Annual Review of Public Health* 34, pp. 61–75 (cit. on pp. 161, 444).

Goldstein, H. (2010). *Multilevel Statistical Models.* 4th ed. John Wiley & Sons. 384 pp. (cit. on p. 371).

Golub, T. R. et al. (1999). "Molecular classification of cancer: Class discovery and class prediction by gene expression monitoring." *Science* 286, pp. 531–537 (cit. on p. 433).

Gordon, A. D. (1999). *Classification.* 2nd ed. Chapman and Hall/CRC. 272 pp. (cit. on p. 408).

Gordon, N. C. et al. (1995). "Enhancement of morphine analgesia by the $GABA_B$ agonist baclofen." *Neuroscience* 69, pp. 345–349 (cit. on p. 196).

Gordon, W. (1894). *Our Country's Birds and How to Know Them.* Day and Son (cit. on p. 5).

Gourieroux, C. (1997). *ARCH Models and Financial Applications.* Springer. 229 pp. (cit. on p. 314).

Grasso, L. C. et al. (2008). "Microarray analysis identifies candidate genes for key roles in coral development." *BMC Genomics* 9, p. 540 (cit. on p. 126).

Greenland, S. et al. (2016). "Statistical tests, P values, confidence intervals, and power: A guide to misinterpretations." *European Journal of Epidemiology* 31.4, pp. 337–350. `https://doi.erg/10.1007/s10654-016-0149-3` (cit. on p. 79).

Greenwood, M. and H. M. Woods (1919). "A report on the incidence of industrial accidents upon individuals with special reference to multiple accidents." *Reports of the Industrial Fatigue Research Board* 4, pp. 3–28 (cit. on p. 98).

Guo, S. et al. (2021). "Improving Google flu trends for COVID-19 estimates using Weibo posts." *Data Science and Management* 3, pp. 13–21 (cit. on p. 74).

Guy, W. A. (1882). "Two hundred and fifty years of small pox in London, together with a supplement relating to England and Wales." *Journal of the Royal Statistical Society* 45, pp. 399–443 (cit. on p. 15).

Hales, S. et al. (2002). "Potential effect of population and climate change global, distribution of dengue fever: an emprical model." *The Lancet* 360, pp. 830–834 (cit. on p. 26).

Hall, P. (2003). "A possum's tale – how statistics revealed a new mammal species." *Chance* 16, pp. 8–13 (cit. on p. 427).

Hand, D. J. et al. (1993). *A Handbook of Small Data Sets.* CRC Press (cit. on p. 104).

Harker, F. R. and J. H. Maindonald (1994). "Ripening of nectarine fruit." In: *Plant Physiology* 106, pp. 165–171 (cit. on p. 226).

Harrell, F. E. (2015). *Regression Modeling Strategies, with Applications to Linear Models, Logistic and Ordinal Regression, and Survival Analysis.* 2nd ed. Springer. XXV + 581 pp. (cit. on pp. 184, 202, 203, 290, 463).

Hassall, A. H. (1850). "Memoir on the organic analysis or microscopic examination of water: Supplied to the inhabitants of London and the suburban districts." *The Lancet* 55.1382, pp. 230–235 (cit. on p. 258).

Hastie, T., R. Tibshirani, and J. Friedman (2009). *The Elements of Statistical Learning. Data Mining, Inference and Prediction.* 2nd ed. Springer. 745 pp. (cit. on pp. 202, 203, 347, 395, 462).

Hauck, W. W. J. and A. Donner (1977). "Wald's test as applied to hypotheses in logit analysis." *Journal of the American Statistical Association* 72, pp. 851–853 (cit. on p. 277).

Held, L. and M. Ott (2018). "On p-values and Bayes factors." *Annual Review of Statistics and Its Application* 5, pp. 393–419. `https://doi.org/10.5167/uzh-148600` (cit. on p. 132).

Hernán, M. A. and J. M. Robins (2020). *Causal inference. What if?* `https://cdn1.sph.harvard.edu/wp-content/uploads/sites/1268/2020/01/ci_hernanrobins_21jan20.pdf` (visited on 03/28/2022) (cit. on pp. 158, 202).

Hernández-Díaz, S., E. F. Schisterman, and M. A. Hernán (2006). "The birth weight paradox uncovered?" *American Journal of Epidemiology* 164.11, pp. 1115–1120 (cit. on pp. 160, 161).

Hoaglin, D. C. (2003). "John W. Tukey and Data Analysis." *Statistical Science* 18, pp. 311–318 (cit. on p. 10).

Hobson, J. A. (1988). *The Dreaming Brain.* Basic Books (cit. on p. 102).

Höfler, M. (2005). "The Bradford Hill considerations on causality: a counterfactual perspective." *Emerging Themes in Epidemiology* 2.1, pp. 1–9. `https://link.springer.com/article/10.1186/1742-7622-2-11` (cit. on p. 158).

Honaker, J. and G. King (2010). "What to do about missing values in time-series cross-section data." *American Journal of Political Science* 54.2, pp. 561–581. `https://citeseerx.ist.psu.edu/document?repid=rep1{&}type=pdf{&}doi=d927076009fc1d86676d5c2da5b11d9fae159bbf` (cit. on pp. 315, 457, 463).

Hong, G. (2010). "Marginal mean weighting through stratification: Adjustment for selection bias in multilevel data." *Journal of Educational and Behavioral Statistics* 35.5, pp. 499–531 (cit. on p. 456).

Hothorn, T., F. Bretz, and P. Westfall (2008). "Simultaneous inference in general parametric models." *Biometrical Journal* 50.3, pp. 346–363 (cit. on p. 124).

Huang, Z. (1997). "Clustering large data sets with mixed numeric and categorical values." In: *Proceedings of the 1st Pacific–Asia Conference on Knowledge Discovery and Data Mining (PAKDD).* Citeseer, pp. 21–34 (cit. on p. 416).

Hunter, D. (2000). "The conservation and demography of the southern corroboree frog *(Pseudophryne corroboree)*." MSc, University of Canberra (cit. on p. 250).

Hyndman, R. J. and G. Athanasopoulos (2021). *Forecasting: Principles and Practice.* 3rd ed. The second edition can be accessed online. OTexts. `https://otexts.com/fpp2/` (cit. on pp. 293, 314).

Hyndman, R. J. and Y. Khandakar (2008). "Automatic time series forecasting: The forecast package for R." *Journal of Statistical Software* 27.3, pp. 1–22 (cit. on p. 314).

Hyndman, R. J. et al. (2008). *Forecasting with Exponential Smoothing: The State Space Approach.* Springer. 360 pp. (cit. on p. 314).

Imbens, G. W. (2015). "Matching methods in practice: Three examples." *Journal of Human Resources* 50.2, pp. 373–419 (cit. on pp. 161, 462).

Ioannidis, J. P. (2005). "Why most published research findings are false." *PLoS Medicine* 2.8, e124 (cit. on pp. 55, 56, 79).

(2018). "The proposal to lower P value thresholds to .005." *JAMA* 319.14, pp. 1429–1430. `www.academia.edu/download/62536357/jama_Ioannidis_2018_vp_1800120200329-98596-ugfydf.pdf` (cit. on p. 78).

Izenman, A. J. (2008). *Modern Multivariate Statistical Techniques: Regression, Classification, and Manifold Learning.* Springer. 733 pp. (cit. on p. 408).

Jakobsen, J. C. et al. (2017). "When and how should multiple imputation be used for handling missing data in randomised clinical trials – a practical guide with flowcharts." *BMC Medical Research Methodology* 17.1, pp. 1–10. `https://rdcu.be/c9plG` (cit. on p. 461).

Johnson, D. H. (1995). "Statistical sirens: the allure of nonparametrics." *Ecology* 76, pp. 1998–2000 (cit. on p. 137).

Jung, K. et al. (2014). "Female hurricanes are deadlier than male hurricanes." *Proceedings of the National Academy of Sciences (PNAS)* 111, pp. 8782–8787. `www.pnas.org/cgi/doi/10.1073/pnas.1402786111` (cit. on p. 168).

Kahneman, D. (2013). *Thinking, Fast and Slow.* 1st ed. Farrar, Straus and Giroux (cit. on pp. 75, 79).

Kahneman, D., O. Sibony, and C. R. Sunstein (2021). *Noise: A Flaw in Human Judgment.* Little, Brown (cit. on p. 10).

Kaminski, J. A. et al. (2018). "Epigenetic variance in dopamine D2 receptor: A marker of IQ malleability?" *Translational Psychiatry* 8.1, pp. 1–11 (cit. on p. 368).

Kass, R. E. and A. E. Raftery (Mar. 1993). *Bayes Factors and Model Uncertainty.* Tech. rep. 254. Carnegie-Mellon University, Dept. of Statistics. `www.semanticscholar.org/paper/Bayes-factors-and-model-uncertainty-Kass-Raftery/42d671ae17a611ac474cb39f59f4cf31f65b51ef` (cit. on pp. 61, 62, 80).

(1995). "Bayes factors." *Journal of the American Statistical Association* 90.430, pp. 773–795 (cit. on p. 65).

King, D. A. (1998). "Relationship between crown architecture and branch orientation in rain forest trees." *Annals of Botany* 82, pp. 1–7 (cit. on p. 423).

King, D. A. and J. H. Maindonald (1999). "Tree architecture in relation to leaf dimensions and tree stature in temperate and tropical rain forests." *Journal of Ecology* 87, pp. 1012–1024 (cit. on p. 423).

Klein, J. P. and M. L. Moeschberger (2003). *Survival Analysis: Techniques for Censored and Truncated Data.* Vol. 2. Springer (cit. on p. 282).

Klein, R. A. et al. (2014). "Investigating variation in replicability: A 'many labs' replication project." *Social Psychology* 45.3, p. 142. `https://psycnet.apa.org/fulltext/2014-20922-002.html` (cit. on p. 77).

Krzanowski, W. J. (2000). *Principles of Multivariate Analysis. A User's Perspective.* Revised. Clarendon Press. 612 pp. (cit. on p. 462).

Lalonde, R. (1986). "Evaluating the economic evaluations of training programs." *American Economic Review* 76, pp. 604–620 (cit. on pp. 22, 445, 449).

Latter, O. H. (1902). "The egg of *Cuculus canorus*. An inquiry into the dimensions of the cuckoo's egg and the relation of the variations to the size of the eggs of the foster-parent, with notes on coloration, &c." *Biometrika* 1, pp. 164–176 (cit. on pp. 4, 5).

Law, C. W. et al. (2014). "voom: Precision weights unlock linear model analysis tools for RNA-seq read counts." *Genome Biol* 15.2, R29 (cit. on p. 126).

Lazer, D. et al. (2014). "The parable of Google Flu: Traps in big data analysis." *Science* 343.6176, pp. 1203–1205 (cit. on p. 74).

Lee, J. S. et al. (2017). "A local-EM algorithm for spatio-temporal disease mapping with aggregated data." *Spatial Statistics* 21, pp. 75–95. `https://doi.org/10.1016/j.spasta.2017.05.001`. `www.sciencedirect.com/science/article/pii/S2211675317300064` (cit. on p. 26).

Leek, J. T. and J. D. Storey (2007). "Capturing heterogeneity in gene expression studies by surrogate variable analysis." *PLoS Genetics* 3.9, e161 (cit. on p. 462).

Levitt, S. D. and S. J. Dubner (2005). *Freakonomics. A Rogue Economist Explores the Hidden Side of Everything.* William Morrow. 242 pp. `http://freakonomics.com/books/` (cit. on p. 202).

Lichtenstein, A. H. et al. (2021). "2021 Dietary guidance to improve cardiovascular health: A scientific statement from the American Heart Association." *Circulation* 144.23, e472–e487 (cit. on p. 159).

Lim, T.-S. and W.-Y. Loh (2000). "A comparison of prediction accuracy, complexity, and training time of thirty-three old and new classification algorithms." *Machine Learning* 40, pp. 203–228 (cit. on p. 396).

Linacre, E. (1992). *Climate Data and Resources. A Reference and Guide.* Routledge (cit. on p. 233).

Linacre, E. and B. Geerts (1997). *Climates and Weather Explained.* Routledge (cit. on p. 233).

Linde, K. et al. (2005). "Acupuncture for patients with migraine. A randomized controlled trial." *Journal of the American Medical Association* 293, pp. 2118–2125 (cit. on p. 137).

Linde, M. et al. (2021). "Decisions about equivalence: A comparison of TOST, HDI-ROPE, and the Bayes factor." *Psychological Methods* 28, pp. 740–755 (cit. on p. 62).

Lindenmayer, D. B. et al. (1995). "Morphological variation among columns of the, mountain brushtail possum, *Trichosurus caninus* Ogilby (Phalangeridae: Marsupiala)." *Australian Journal of Zoology* 43, pp. 449–458 (cit. on p. 427).

Maindonald, J. H. (1984). *Statistical Computation.* Wiley. 370 pp. (cit. on p. 240).

(1992). "Statistical design, analysis and presentation issues." *New Zealand Journal of Agricultural Research* 35, pp. 121–141 (cit. on pp. 79, 335).

(2003). *The Role of Models in Predictive Validation.* Invited Paper. ISI (cit. on p. 121).

(2006). "Data mining methodology weaknesses and suggested fixes." In *Fifth Australasian Data Mining Conference (AusDM2006).* Ed. by P. Christen et al. Vol. 61. CRPIT. Sydney, Australia: ACS, pp. 9–16 (cit. on p. 462).

Maindonald J. and J. Braun (2003). *Data Analysis and Graphics Using R.* Cambridge University Press. 386 pp. (cit. on p. xviii).

Maindonald, J. and W. J. Braun (2010). *Data Analysis and Graphics Using R.* 3rd ed. Cambridge University Press. 549 pp. (cit. on p. xxi).

Maindonald, J. H. and C. J. Burden (2005). "Selection bias in plots of microarray or other data that have been sampled from a high-dimensional space." In *Proceedings of 12th Computational Techniques and Applications Conference CTAC-2004.* Vol. 46, pp. C59–C74 (cit. on pp. 434, 441).

Maindonald, J. H., B. C. Waddell, and R. J. Petry (2001). "Apple cultivar effects on codling moth (Lepidoptera: Tortricidae) egg mortality following fumigation with methyl bromide." *Postharvest Biology and Technology* 22, pp. 99–110 (cit. on p. 276).

Marriott, F. (1974). *The Interpretation of Multiple Observations.* Academic Press (cit. on p. 417).

Matloff, N. (2011). *The Art of R Programming.* No Starch Inc. XXIV + 374 pp. (cit. on p. 79).

McCullagh, P. and J. A. Nelder (1989). *Generalized Linear Models.* 2nd ed. Chapman and Hall. 532 pp. (cit. on pp. 247, 276, 277, 290).

McLachlan, G. J. (2011). "Commentary on Steinley and Brusco (2011): Recommendations and cautions." *Psychological Methods* 16.1, pp. 80–81 (cit. on p. 422).

McLachlan, G. and T. Krishnan (2008). *The EM Algorithm and Extensions.* 2nd ed. John Wiley & Sons (cit. on p. 418).

McLellan, E. A., A. Medline, and R. P. Bird (1991). "Dose response and proliferative characteristics of aberrant crypt foci: putative preneoplastic lesions in rat colon." *Carcinogenesis* 12, pp. 2093–2098 (cit. on p. 261).

McLeod, C. C. (1982). "Effect of rates of seeding on barley grown for grain." *New Zealand Journal of Agriculture* 10, pp. 133–136 (cit. on p. 221).

McNicholas, P. D. (2016). *Mixture Model-Based Classification.* Chapman and Hall/CRC Press (cit. on p. 418).

Meyer, D. (2001). "Support Vector Machines." *R News* 1.3, pp. 23–26 (cit. on p. 442).

Meyer, M. (2006). "Commentary on 'Another look at Meyer and Finney's "Who wants airbags?"'" *Chance* 19, pp. 23–24 (cit. on p. 23).

Meyer, M. and T. Finney (2005). "Who wants airbags?" *Chance* 18, pp. 3–16 (cit. on p. 23).

Miller, R. G. (1986). *Beyond ANOVA, Basics of Applied Statistics.* Wiley. 318 pp. (cit. on pp. 93, 102, 137, 296).

Mitchell, B. R. (1988). *British Historical Statistics.* Cambridge University Press (cit. on p. 15).

Mogil, J. S. and M. R. Macleod (2017). "No publication without confirmation." *Nature* 542.7642, pp. 409–411. `https://doi.org/10.1038/542409a` (cit. on p. 79).

Mokdad, A. H. et al. (2018). "The state of US health, 1990–2016: burden of diseases, injuries, and risk factors among US states." *AMA* 319.14, pp. 1444–1472 (cit. on p. 160).

Morgan, B. J. T. (1992). *Analysis of Quantal Response Data.* Chapman & Hall (cit. on pp. 100, 353).

Morgan, B. J. T. and M. S. Ridout (2008). "A new mixture model for capture heterogeneity." *Journal of the Royal Statistical Society: Series C (Applied Statistics)* 57.4, pp. 433–446. `https://doi.org/10.1111/j.1467-9876.2008.00620.x` (cit. on pp. 100, 349).

Morgan, S. L. and C. Winship (2015). *Counterfactuals and Causal Inference: Methods and Principles for Social Research.* 2nd ed. Cambridge University Press (cit. on p. 444).

Murrell, P. (2011). *R Graphics.* 2nd ed. Chapman and Hall/CRC. 546 pp. `www.e-reading.org.ua/bookreader.php/137370/Murrell_-_R_Graphics.pdf` (cit. on p. 80).

Myers, R. H. (1990). *Classical and Modern Regression with Applications.* 2nd ed. Brooks Cole. 488 pp. (cit. on p. 203).

Nadel, E. and S. Bussolari (1988). "The Daedalus project: physiological problems and solutions." *American Scientist* 76, pp. 351–360 (cit. on p. 360).

Neath, A. A. and J. E. Cavanaugh (2012). "The Bayesian information criterion: background, derivation, and applications." *Wiley Interdisciplinary Reviews: Computational Statistics* 4.2, pp. 199–203 (cit. on p. 133).

Newton, A. and H. Gadow (1896). *A Dictionary of Birds.* A. and C. Black (cit. on pp. 4, 5).

Nicholls, N. et al. (1996). "Recent apparent changes in relationships between the El Niño – southern oscillation and Australian rainfall and temperature." *Geophysical Research Letters* 23, pp. 3357–3360 (cit. on p. 304).

Nosek, B. A. and T. M. Errington (2020). "The best time to argue about what a replication means? Before you do it." *Nature* 583, pp. 518–520 (cit. on p. 77).

Nosek, B. A. et al. (2015). "Promoting an open research culture." *Science* 348.6242, pp. 1422–1425 (cit. on p. 79).

O'Neil, C. (2016). *Weapons of Math Destruction.* 1st ed. Crown (cit. on pp. 73, 79).

Open Science Collaboration (2015). "Estimating the reproducibility of psychological science." *Science* 349.6251. Open Science Collaboration (Nosek, B. A. and others), 'aac4716-1'–'aac4716-7'. `https://osf.io/k9rnd/` (cit. on pp. 76, 207).

Ord, J. K., A. B. Koehler, and R. D. Snyder (1997). "Estimation and prediction for a class of dynamic nonlinear statistical models." *Journal of the American Statistical Association* 92, pp. 1621–1629 (cit. on p. 314).

Paluch, A. E. et al. (2021). "Steps per day and all-cause mortality in middle-aged adults in the Coronary Artery Risk Development in Young Adults study." *JAMA Network Open* 4.9, e2124516-e2124516 (cit. on p. 160).

Payne, R. W. et al. (1997). *Genstat 5 Release 3 Reference Manual.* Oxford University Press (cit. on pp. 369, 371).

Perrine, F. M. et al. (2001). "Rhizobium plasmids are involved in the inhibition or stimulation of rice growth and development." *Australian Journal of Plant Physiology* 28, pp. 923–927 (cit. on p. 129).

Phipson, B. et al. (2016). "Robust hyperparameter estimation protects against hypervariable genes and improves power to detect differential expression." *The Annals of Applied Statistics* 10.2, p. 946 (cit. on p. 433).

Pinheiro, J. C. and D. M. Bates (2000). *Mixed Effects Models in S and S-PLUS.* Springer (cit. on pp. 359, 371).

Prinz, F., T. Schlange, and K. Asadullah (2011). "Believe it or not: how much can we rely on published data on potential drug targets?" *Nature Reviews Drug Discovery* 10.9, pp. 712–712 (cit. on pp. 55, 76).

Ramsay, J. and B. Silverman (2002). *Applied Functional Data Analysis.* Springer. 191 pp. (cit. on p. 370).

Ridley, M. and G. Pierpoint (2003). *Nature via Nurture: Genes, Experience, and What Makes Us Human.* Vol. 19. HarperCollins (cit. on p. 368).

Ripley, B. D. (1996). *Pattern Recognition and Neural Networks.* Cambridge University Press. 416 pp. (cit. on pp. 383, 395, 425, 462).

Ritchie, M. E. et al. (2015). "limma powers differential expression analyses for RNA-sequencing and microarray studies." *Nucleic Acids Research* 43.7, e47 (cit. on p. 430).

Robbins, N. (2012). *Creating More Effective Graphs.* Wiley. (cit. on p. 80).

Robinson, G. K. (2000). *Practical Strategies for Experimenting.* Wiley. (cit. on p. 79).

Rodgers, P. and A. Collings (2021). "Reproducibility in cancer biology: What have we learned?" *Elife* 10, e75830 (cit. on p. 77).

Rosenbaum, P. R. (2002). *Observational Studies.* 2nd ed. Springer. 377 pp. (cit. on pp. 202, 462).

Rosenbaum, P. and D. Rubin (1983). "The central role of the propensity score in observational studies for causal effects." *Biometrika* 70, pp. 41–55 (cit. on p. 444).

Rouder, J. N. et al. (2009). "Bayesian t tests for accepting and rejecting the null hypothesis." *Psychonomic Bulletin & Review* 16.2, pp. 225–237. `https://link.springer.com/content/pdf/10.3758/PBR.16.2.225.pdf` (cit. on pp. 61, 133).

Rubin, D. B. (1987). *Multiple Imputation for Nonresponse in Surveys.* Wiley-Interscience (cit. on p. 463).

Rudin, C. et al. (2022). "Interpretable machine learning: Fundamental principles and 10 grand challenges." *Statistics Surveys* 16, pp. 1–85 (cit. on p. 73).

Sangari, S. and H. E. Ray (2021). "Evaluation of imputation techniques with varying percentage of missing data." *arXiv preprint arXiv:2109.04227.* `https://arxiv.org/pdf/2109.04227` (cit. on pp. 75, 463).

Schatzkin, A. et al. (2003). "A comparison of a food frequency questionnaire with a 24-hour recall for use in an epidemiological cohort study: results from the biomarker-based Observing Protein and Energy Nutrition (OPEN) study." *International Journal of Epidemiology* 32, pp. 1054–1062 (cit. on pp. 191, 192).

Scheel, A. M., M. R. Schijen, and D. Lakens (2021). "An excess of positive results: Comparing the standard psychology literature with registered reports." *Advances in Methods and Practices in Psychological Science* 4.2, p. 25152459211007467. `https://doi.org/10.1177/25152459211007467` (cit. on p. 78).

Schmidt-Nielsen, K. (1984). *Scaling. Why Is Animal Size So Important?* Cambridge University Press. 256 pp. (cit. on p. 115).

Science Museum (2019). *Cholera in Victorian London.* `www.sciencemuseum.org.uk/objects-and-stories/medicine/cholera-victorian-london` (visited on 01/01/2022) (cit. on p. 257).

Scott, A. J. and M. J. Symons (1971). "Clustering methods based on likelihood ratio criteria." *Biometrics*, pp. 387–397 (cit. on p. 422).

Sellke, T., M. Bayarri, and J. O. Berger (2001). "Calibration of ρ values for testing precise null hypotheses." *The American Statistician* 55.1, pp. 62–71 (cit. on pp. 63, 132, 133).

Senn, S. (2003). *Dicing with Death: Chance, Risk and Health.* Cambridge University Press. 261 pp. (cit. on p. 15).

Shanklin, J. (2001). *Ozone at Halley, Rothera and Vernadsky/Faraday.* `www.antarctica.ac.uk/met/jds/ozone/` (cit. on p. 243).

Sharp, S. J., S. G. Thompson, and D. G. Altman (1996). "The relation between treatment benefit and underlying risk in meta-analysis." *British Medical Journal* 313, pp. 735–738 (cit. on p. 195).

Shoesmith, G. L. (2017). "Crime, teenage abortion, and unwantedness." *Crime & Delinquency* 63.11, pp. 1458–1490 (cit. on p. 202).

Shumway, R. and D. Stoffer (2006). *Time Series Analysis and Its Applications.* Springer (cit. on p. 314).

Simpson, E. H. (1951). "The interpretation of interaction in contingency tables." *Journal of the Royal Statistical Society, Series B* 13, pp. 238–241 (cit. on p. 90).

Singmann, H. and D. Kellen (2019). "An introduction to mixed models for experimental psychology." *New Methods in Cognitive Psychology* 28.4, pp. 4–31 (cit. on p. 366).

Smith, G. (2014). *Standard Deviations: Flawed Assumptions, Tortured Data, and Other Ways to Lie with Statistics.* Duckworth Overlook. 304 pp. (cit. on pp. 75, 137).

Smith, G. D. (2002). "Commentary: Behind the Broad Street pump: aetiology, epidemiology and prevention of cholera in mid-19th century Britain." *International Journal of Epidemiology* 31.5, pp. 920–932 (cit. on p. 257).

Smyth, G. K. (2004). "Linear models and empirical Bayes methods for assessing differential expression in microarray experiments." *Statistical Applications in Genetics and Molecular Biology* 3. No. 1, Article 3 (cit. on p. 126).

Snelgar, W. P., P. J. Manson, and P. J. Martin (1992). "Influence of time of shading on flowering and yield of kiwifruit vines." *Journal of Horticultural Science* 67, pp. 481–487 (cit. on p. 335).

Snijders, T. and R. Bosker (2011). *Multilevel Analysis: An Introduction to Basic and Advanced Multilevel Modeling.* 2nd ed. Sage Publications. 354 pp. (cit. on p. 371).

Snow, J. (1855). *On the Mode of Communication of Cholera* 2nd ed. John Churchill. `www.ph.ucla.edu/epi/snow/snowbook.html` (cit. on pp. 259, 260).

Soyer, E. and R. M. Hogarth (2012). "The illusion of predictability: How regression statistics mislead experts." *International Journal of Forecasting* 28.3, pp. 695–711. `https://doi.org/10.1016/j.ijforecast.2012.02.002` (cit. on p. 181).

Spiegelhalter, D. J. et al. (2000). "Bayesian methods in health technology assessment: a review." *Health Technology Assessment* 4.38. `https://leicester.figshare.com/articles/report/Bayesian_methods_in_health_technology_assessment_a_review/10077032/files/18168374.pdf` (cit. on p. 137).

Spiegelhalter, D. J. et al. (2002). "Bayesian measures of model complexity and fit." *Journal of the Royal Statistical Society, Series B* 64. With following discussion, pp. 616–639, pp. 583–616 (cit. on p. 347).

Sprent, P. (1966). "A generalized least squares approach to linear functional relationships." *Journal of the Royal Statistical Society, Series B* 28. With following discussion, pp. 288–297, pp. 278–288 (cit. on p. 112).

Stewardson, C. L. et al. (1999). "Gross and microscopic visceral anatomy of the male Cape fur seal, *Arctocephalus pusillus pusillus* (Pinnipedia: Otariidae), with reference to organ size and growth." *Journal of Anatomy (Cambridge)* 195 (WWF project ZA-348), pp. 235–255 (cit. on p. 114).

Stewart, K. M., R. F. Van Toor, and S. F. Crosbie (1988). "Control of grass grub (Coleoptera: Scarabaeidae) with rollers of different design." *New Zealand Journal of Experimental Agriculture* 16, pp. 141–150 (cit. on p. 43).

Stidd, C. K. (1953). "Cube-root-normal precipitation distributions." *Transactions of the American Geophysical Union* 34, pp. 31–35 (cit. on p. 304).

Stiell, I. G. et al. (2001). "The Canadian CT head rule for patients with minor head injury." *The Lancet* 357, pp. 1391–1396 (cit. on p. 290).

Stocks, P. (1942). "Measles and whooping cough during the dispersal of 1939–1940." *Journal of the Royal Statistical Society* 105, pp. 259–291 (cit. on p. 15).

Streiner, D. L., G. R. Norman, and J. Cairney (2014). *Health Measurement Scales: A Practical Guide to their Development and Use.* Oxford University Press. xiii + 399 pp. (cit. on pp. 8, 408, 462).

Talbot, M. (1984). "Yield variability of crop varieties in the U.K." *Journal of the Agricultural Society of Cambridge* 102, pp. 315–321 (cit. on pp. 323, 371).

Thaler, R. H. (2015). *Misbehaving.* Allen Lane (cit. on p. 79).

Thall, P. F. and S. C. Vail (1990). "Some covariance models for longitudinal count data." *Biometrics* 46, pp. 657–671 (cit. on p. 358).

Therneau, T. M. and E. J. Atkinson (1997). *An Introduction to Recursive Partitioning Using the RPART Routines.* Tech. rep. 61. Department of Health Science Research, Mayo Clinic, Rochester, MN (cit. on pp. 373, 395, 396).

Therneau, T. M. and P. M. Grambsch (2001). *Modeling Survival Data: Extending the Cox Model.* Springer. 350 pp. (cit. on p. 290).

Tu, Y. and M. S. Gilthorpe (2011). *Statistical Thinking in Epidemiology.* CRC Press. 231 pp. (cit. on p. 202).

Tukey, J. W. (1953). "The growth of experimental design in a research laboratory." In *Research Operations in Industry.* Ed. by D. B. Hertz. Vol. 3. King's Crown Press, pp. 303–313 (cit. on p. xiv).

(1992). *Exploratory Data Analysis.* Note the comment in `www.sumsar.net/blog/2013/09/a-bayesian-twist-on-tukeys-flogs/` on Tukey's flog (folded logarithm) transformation. Addison-Wesley (cit. on p. 289).

(1997). "More honest foundations for data analysis." *Journal of Statistical Planning and Inference* 57.1, pp. 21–28 (cit. on pp. 9, 90).

Turner, R. M. et al. (2009). "Bias modelling in evidence synthesis." *Journal Of The Royal Statistical Society Series A* 172.1, pp. 21–47 (cit. on pp. 370, 371).

Vaida, F. and S. Blanchard (2005). "Conditional Akaike information for mixed-effects models." *Biometrika* 92, pp. 351–370 (cit. on p. 347).

Van Buuren, S. (2018). *Flexible Imputation of Missing Data.* CRC press (cit. on p. 461).

Venables, W. N. (1998). "Exegeses on linear models." In *Proceedings of the 1998 International S-PLUS User Conference* (cit. on pp. 203, 213).

Venables, W. N. and B. D. Ripley (2002). *Modern Applied Statistics with* S. 4th ed. (cit. on pp. 183, 202, 237, 290, 314, 371, 395, 408). (See also R Complements to Modern Applied Statistics with S. Springer.)

Vermunt, J. K. (2011). "K-Means may perform as well as mixture model clustering but may also be much worse: Comment on Steinley and Brusco (2011)." *Psychological Methods* 16.1, pp. 82–88 (cit. on p. 422).

Wainright, P., C. Pelkman, and D. Wahlsten (1989). "The quantitative relationship between nutritional effects on preweaning growth and behavioral development in mice." *Developmental Psychobiology* 22, pp. 183–193 (cit. on p. 157).

Wang, Z. et al. (2021). "Are deep learning models superior for missing data imputation in large surveys? Evidence from an empirical comparison." *arXiv preprint arXiv:2103.09316* (cit. on p. 74).

Welch, B. L. (1949). "Further note on Mrs. Aspin's tables and on certain approximations to the tabled function." *Biometrika* 36, pp. 293–296 (cit. on p. 93).

Welham, S. et al. (2014). *Statistical Methods in Biology: Design and Analysis of Experiments and Regression.* CRC Press. 608 pp. (cit. on p. 216).

Wickham, H. (2015). *Advanced R.* CRC Press. 476 pp. (cit. on p. 79).

(2016). *R for Data Science.* O'Reilly (cit. on p. 79).

Wilcox, A. J. (2006). "Invited commentary: the perils of birth weight – a lesson from directed acyclic graphs." *American Journal of Epidemiology* 164.11, pp. 1121–1123 (cit. on p. 161).

Wilkinson, L. and Task Force on Statistical Inference (1999). "Statistical methods in psychology journals: guidelines and, explanation." *American Psychologist* 54, pp. 594–604 (cit. on p. 79).

Williams, E. R., A. C. Matheson, and C. E. Harwood (2002). *Experimental Design and Analysis for Use in Tree Improvement.* Revised. CSIRO Information Services. 220 pp. (cit. on p. 371).

Williams, G. P. (1983). "Improper use of regression equations in the earth sciences." *Geology* 11, pp. 195–197 (cit. on p. 195).

Wonnacott, T. H. and R. Wonnacott (1990). *Introductory Statistics*. 5th ed. Wiley. 736 pp. (cit. on p. 80).

Wood, S. N. (2010). *More advanced use of mgcv*. `www.maths.ed.ac.uk/-swood34/mgcv/tampere/mgcv-advanced.pdf` (visited on 01/25/2022) (cit. on p. 229).

(2017). *Generalized Additive Models. An Introduction with R*. 2nd ed. Chapman and Hall/CRC. 410 pp. (cit. on pp. 224, 240, 289).

Würtz, D. (2004). *Rmetrics: An Environment for Teaching Financial Engineering and Computational Finance with R*. Rmetrics, ITP, ETH Zürich. Zürich, Switzerland (cit. on p. 314).

Xie, Y. and X. Cheng (Oct. 2008). "animation: A package for statistical animations." *R News* 8.2, pp. 23–27 (cit. on p. 40).

Yong, E. (2012). "Nobel laureate challenges psychologists to clean up their act." *Nat. News* 490 (cit. on p. 77).

Zeger, S. L. et al. (2000). "Exposure measurement error in time-series studies of air pollution: concepts and consequences." *Environmental Health Perspectives* 108. See also vol. 109, p. A517, pp. 419–426 (cit. on p. 194).

Zhang, H. and B. Singer (1999). *Recursive Partitioning in the Health Sciences*. Springer (cit. on p. 396).

Zhu, X., C. Ambroise, and G. J. McLachlan (2006). "Selection bias in working with the top genes in supervised classification of tissue samples." *Statistical Methodology* 3, pp. 29–41 (cit. on p. 434).

Zimmer, C. (2019). *She Has Her Mother's Laugh: The Powers, Perversions, and Potential of Heredity*. Dutton (cit. on p. 368).

References to R Packages

afex — Singmann, H. et al. (2022). *afex: Analysis of Factorial Experiments.* R package version 1.1-1.

AICcmodavg — Mazerolle, M. J. (2020). *AICcmodavg: Model Selection and Multimodel Inference Based on (Q)AIC(c).* R package version 2.3-1.

Amelia — Honaker, J., G. King, and M. Blackwell (2011). "Amelia II: A program for missing data." *Journal of Statistical Software* 45.7, pp. 1–47. `www.jstatsoft.org/v45/i07/`.

ape — Paradis, E. and K. Schliep (2019). "*ape:* ape 5.0: an environment for modern phylogenetics and evolutionary analyses in R." *Bioinformatics* 35, pp. 526–528.

Base R — R Core Team and contributors worldwide (2023). *R Base Packages: base, compiler, datasets, grDevices, graphics, grid, methods, parallel, splines, stats, stats4, tcltk, tools, and utils.* R Foundation for Statistical Computing. Vienna, Austria.

BayesFactor — Morey, R. D. and J. N. Rouder (2022). *BayesFactor: Computation of Bayes Factors for Common Designs.* R package version 0.9.124.4.

bayesplay — Colling, L. J. (2021). *bayesplay: The Bayes Factor Playground.* R package version 0.9.2.

BHH2 — Barrios, E. (2016). *BHH2: Useful Functions for Box, Hunter and Hunter II.* R package version 2016.05.31.

BiocManager — Morgan, M. (2022). *BiocManager: Access the Bioconductor Project Package Repository.* R package version 1.30.18.

boot — Canty, A. and B. D. Ripley (2021). *boot: Bootstrap R (S-Plus) Functions.* R package version 1.3-28.

car — Fox, J. and S. Weisberg (2019). *car: An R Companion to Applied Regression.* 3rd ed. Sage. `https://socialsciences.mcmaster.ca/jfox/Books/Companion/`.

cobalt — Greifer, N. (2022). *cobalt: Covariate Balance Tables and Plots.* R package version 4.3.2.

compositions — van den Boogaart, K. G., R. Tolosana-Delgado, and M. Bren (2022). *compositions: Compositional Data Analysis.* R package version 2.04.

DAAG Maindonald, J. H. and W. J. Braun (2011). *DAAG: Data analysis and graphics using R. An Example-Based Approach.* 3rd ed. The DAAG package was created to support this text. Cambridge University Press.

DAAGbio Maindonald, J. (2017). *DAAGbio: Data Sets and Functions, for Demonstrations with Expression Arrays and Gene Sequences.* R package version 0.63-3.

DHARMa Hartig, F. (2022). *DHARMa: Residual Diagnostics for Hierarchical (Multi-Level / Mixed) Regression Models.* R package version 0.4.5.

dichromat Lumley, T. (2022). *dichromat: Color Schemes for Dichromats.* R package version 2.0-0.1.

dplyr Wickham, H. et al. (2022). *dplyr: A Grammar of Data Manipulation.* R package version 1.0.9.

e1071 Meyer, D. et al. (2022). *e1071: Misc Functions of the Department of Statistics, Probability Theory Group (Formerly: E1071), TU Wien.* R package version 1.7-11.

effects Fox, J. and S. Weisberg (2018). "*effects:* Visualizing fit and lack of fit in complex regression models with predictor effect plots and partial residuals." *Journal of Statistical Software* 87.9, pp. 1–27. `https://doi.org/10.18637/jss.v087.i09`.

effectsize Ben-Shachar, M. S., D. Lüdecke, and D. Makowski (2020). "*effectsize*: Estimation of effect size indices and standardized parameters." *Journal of Open Source Software* 5.56, p. 2815. `https://doi.org/10.21105/joss.02815`.

forecast Hyndman, R. et al. (2022). *forecast: Forecasting functions for time series and linear models.* R package version 8.16. `https://pkg.robjhyndman.com/forecast/`.

leaps Fortran code by Alan Miller, T. l. based on (2020). *leaps: Regression Subset Selection.* R package version 3.1.

gamlss Rigby, R. A. and D. M. Stasinopoulos (2005). "*gamlss:* Generalized additive models for location, scale and shape (with discussion)." *Applied Statistics* 54, pp. 507–554.

gclus Hurley, C. (2019). gclus: *Clustering Graphics.* R package version 1.3.2.

ggdag Barrett, M. (2022). *ggdag: Analyze and Create Elegant Directed Acyclic Graphs.* R package version 0.2.6.

ggplot2 Wickham, H. (2016). *ggplot2: Elegant Graphics for Data Analysis.* Springer-Verlag. `https://ggplot2.tidyverse.org`.

glmmTMB Brooks, M. E. et al. (2017). "*glmmTMB*: glmmTMB balances speed and flexibility among packages for zero-inflated generalized linear mixed modeling." *The R Journal* 9.2, pp. 378–400. `https://journal.r-project.org/archive/2017/RJ-2017-066/index.html`.

gmodels	Warnes, G. R. et al. (2022). *gmodels: Various R Programming Tools for Model Fitting.* R package version 2.18.1.1.
gridExtra	Auguie, B. (2017). *gridExtra: Miscellaneous Functions for "Grid" Graphics.* R package version 2.3.
hddplot	Maindonald, J. H. and C. J. Burden (2005). "*hddplot:* Selection bias in plots of microarray or other data that have been sampled from a high-dimensional space." In *Proceedings of 12th Computational Techniques and Applications Conference CTAC-200).* Ed. by R. May and A. J. Roberts. Vol. 46, pp. C59–C74. `journal.austms.org.au/V46/CTAC2004/Main/home.html`.
Hmisc	Harrell Jr, F. E. (2022). *Hmisc: Harrell Miscellaneous.* R package version 4.7-1.
imputeTS	Moritz, S. and T. Bartz-Beielstein (2017). "*imputeTS*: Time series missing value imputation in R." *The R Journal* 9.1, pp. 207–218. `https://doi.org/10.32614/RJ-2017-009`.
investr	Greenwell, B. M. and C. M. S. Kabban (2014). "*investr*: An R package for inverse estimation." *The R Journal* 6.1, pp. 90–100. `https://doi.org/10.32614/RJ-2014-009`.
KernSmooth	Wand, M. (2021). *KernSmooth: Functions for Kernel Smoothing Supporting Wand & Jones (1995).* R package version 2.23-20.
knitr	Xie, Y. (2023). *knitr: A General-Purpose Package for Dynamic Report Generation in R.* R package version 1.42. `https://yihui.org/knitr/`.
lattice	Sarkar, D. (2008). *lattice: Lattice: Multivariate Data Visualization with R.* Springer. `http://lmdvr.r-forge.r-project.org`.
latticeExtra	Sarkar, D. and F. Andrews (2022). *latticeExtra: Extra Graphical Utilities Based on Lattice.* R package version 0.6-30.
limma	Ritchie, M. E. et al. (2015). "*limma:* limma powers differential expression analyses for RNA-sequencing and microarray studies." *Nucleic Acids Research* 43, e47. `https://doi.org/10.1093/nar/gkv007`. (Install using `Bioconductor::install()`.)
lme4	Bates, D. et al. (2015). "*lme4:* Fitting linear mixed-effects models using lme4." *Journal of Statistical Software* 67.1, pp. 1–48. `https://doi.org/10.18637/jss.v067.i01`.
lmtest	Zeileis, A. and T. Hothorn (2002). "*lmtest:* Diagnostic checking in regression relationships." *R News* 2.3, pp. 7–10.
locfdr	Efron, B., B. Turnbull, and B. Narasimhan (2015). *locfdr: Computes Local False Discovery Rates.* R package version 1.1-8.
MASS	Venables, W. N. and B. D. Ripley (2002). *MASS: Modern Applied Statistics with S.* 4th ed. Springer. `www.stats.ox.ac.uk/pub/MASS4/`.
MatchIt	Ho, D. E. et al. (2011). "*MatchIt:* Nonparametric preprocessing for parametric causal inference." *Journal of Statistical Software* 42.8, pp. 1–28. `https://doi.org/10.18637/jss.v042.i08`.
MCMCpack	Martin, A. D., K. M. Quinn, and J. H. Park (2011). "*MCMCpack:* Markov Chain Monte Carlo in R." *Journal of Statistical Software* 42.9, p. 22. `https://doi.org/10.18637/jss.v042.i09`.

MEMSS Bates, D., M. Maechler, and B. Bolker (2019). *MEMSS: Data Sets from Mixed-Effects Models in S.* R package version 0.9-3.

mgcv Wood, S. N. (2021). *mgcv Package – Resources.* `www.maths.ed.ac.uk/~swood34/mgcv/`.

mgcViz Fasiolo, M. et al. (2018). "Scalable visualisation methods for modern generalized additive models." *Arxiv preprint.* `https://arxiv.org/abs/1809.10632`.

mice van Buuren, S. and K. Groothuis-Oudshoorn (2011). "mice: Multivariate imputation by chained equations in R." *Journal of Statistical Software* 45.3, pp. 1–67. `https://doi.org/10.18637/jss.v045.i03`. `www.gerkovink.com/miceVignettes/`.

miceadds Robitzsch, A. and S. Grund (2023). *miceadds: Some Additional Multiple Imputation Functions, Especially for 'mice'.* R package version 3.16-18.

micemd Audigier, V. and M. Resche-Rigon (2021). *micemd: Multiple Imputation by Chained Equations with Multilevel Data.* R package version 1.8.0.

missForest Stekhoven, D. J. and P. Buehlmann (2012). "missForest: MissForest – non-parametric missing value imputation for mixed-type data." *Bioinformatics* 28.1, pp. 112–118. `https://academic.oup.com/bioinformatics/article/28/1/112/219101?`.

MPV Braun, W. J. and S. MacQueen (2022). *MPV: Data Sets from Montgomery, Peck and Vining.* R package version 1.58.

muhaz Hess, K. and R. Gentleman (2021). *muhaz: Hazard Function Estimation in Survival Analysis.* R package version 1.2.6.4.

multtest Pollard, K. S., S. Dudoit, and M. J. van der Laan (2005). "Multiple testing procedures: R multtest package and applications to genomics." In *Bioinformatics and Computational Biology Solutions Using R and Bioconductor.* Springer. (Install using `Bioconductor::install()`.)

mvtnorm Genz, A. et al. (2021). *mvtnorm: Multivariate Normal and t Distributions.* R package version 1.1-3.

nlme Pinheiro, J., D. Bates, and R Core Team (2022). *nlme: Linear and Nonlinear Mixed Effects Models.* R package version 3.1-158.

nnet Venables, W. N. and B. D. Ripley (2002). *nnet: Modern Applied Statistics with S.* 4th ed. Springer. `www.stats.ox.ac.uk/pub/MASS4/`.

oz Venables, W. N. and K. Hornik (2016). *oz: Plot the Australian Coastline and States.* R package version 1.0-21. S original by Bill Venables, R port by Kurt Hornik.

plyr Wickham, H. (2011). "plyr: The split-apply-combine strategy for data analysis." *Journal of Statistical Software* 40.1, pp. 1–29. `www.jstatsoft.org/v40/i01/`.

qgam	Fasiolo, M. et al. (2021). "qgam: Bayesian nonparametric quantile regression modeling in R." *Journal of Statistical Software* 100.9, pp. 1–31. `https://doi.org/10.18637/jss.v100.i09`.
qra	Maindonald, J. H. (2021). qra: *Quantal Response Analysis for Dose-Mortality Data.* R package version 0.2.7.
randomForest	Liaw, A. and M. Wiener (2002). "*randomForest:* Classification and regression by randomForest." *R News* 2.3, pp. 18–22.
Rcmdr	Fox, J. and M. Bouchet-Valat (2022). Rcmdr: *R Commander.* R package version 2.8-0. `https://socialsciences.mcmaster.ca/jfox/Misc/Rcmdr/`.
RColorBrewer	Neuwirth, E. (2022). RColorBrewer: *ColorBrewer Palettes.* R package version 1.1-3.
ReplicationSuccess	Held, L., C. Micheloud, and S. Pawel (2021). "*ReplicationSuccess*: The assessment of replication success based on relative effect size." *The Annals of Applied Statistics* 16.2, pp. 706–720. `https://doi.org/10.1214/21-AOAS1502`.
reshape2	Wickham, H. (2007). "*reshape2:* Reshaping data with the reshape package." *Journal of Statistical Software* 21.12, pp. 1–20. `www.jstatsoft.org/v21/i12/`.
rgl	Murdoch, D. and D. Adler (2021). *rgl: 3D Visualization Using OpenGL.* R package version 0.108.3.
robustbase	Maechler, M. et al. (2022). robustbase: *Basic Robust Statistics.* R package version 0.95-0. `http://robustbase.r-forge.r-project.org/`.
rpart	Therneau, T. and B. Atkinson (2022). rpart: *Recursive Partitioning and Regression Trees.* R package version 4.1.16.
rpart.plot	Milborrow, S. (2022). rpart.plot: *Plot 'rpart' Models: An Enhanced Version of 'plot.rpart'.* R package version 3.1.1.
statsr	Rundel, C. et al. (2021). statsr: *Companion Software for the Coursera Statistics with R Specialization.* R package version 0.3.0.
scam	Pya, N. (2021). scam: *Shape Constrained Additive Models.* R package version 1.2-12.
survival	Therneau, T. M. and P. M. Grambsch (2000). *Modeling Survival Data: Extending the Cox Model.* Springer.
teigen	Andrews, J. L. et al. (2018). "teigen: An R package for model-based clustering and classification via the multivariate t distribution." *Journal of Statistical Software* 83.7, pp. 1–32. `http://doi.org/10.18637/jss.v083.i07`.
tidyr	Wickham, H. and M. Girlich (2022). *tidyr: Tidy Messy Data.* R package version 1.2.0.
tseries	Trapletti, A. and K. Hornik (2022). tseries: *Time Series Analysis and Computational Finance.* R package version 0.10-51.
vcd	Meyer, D., A. Zeileis, and K. Hornik (2022). vcd: *Visualizing Categorical Data.* R package version 1.4-10.

VGAM Yee, T. W. (2023). *VGAM: Vector Generalized Linear and Additive Models.* R package version 1.1-8.

WDI Arel-Bundock, V. (2022). WDI: *World Development Indicators and Other World Bank Data.* R package version 2.7.7.

xtable Dahl, D. B. et al. (2019). xtable: *Export Tables to LaTeX or HTML.* R package version 1.8-4.

zoo Zeileis, A. and G. Grothendieck (2005). "zoo: S3 infrastructure for regular and irregular time series." *Journal of Statistical Software* 14.6, pp. 1–27. `https://doi.org/10.18637/jss.v014.i06`.

The following are other packages and package bundles mentioned in the text, or used only as a source for a single dataset.

adabag (Alfaro, E., Gamez, M., Garcia, N.), *agricolae* (de Mendiburu, F.), *animation* (Xie, Y.), *cocor* (Diedenhofen, B., Musch, J.), *coda* (Plummer, M., Best, N., Cowles, K.), *DAAGbio* (Maindonald, J.), *dr* (Weisberg, S.), *dse* (Gilbert, P.), *fracdiff* (Maechler, M.), *fSeries* (Wuertz, D.), *gam* (Hastie, T.), *gamm4* (Wood, S., Scheipl, F.), *gbm* (Greenwell, B., Boehmke, B., Cunningham, J., GBM Developers), *gginnards* (Aphalo, P.), *golubEsets* ((install using `Bioconductor::install()`)), *haven* (Wickham, H., Miller, E., Smith, D.), *learnr* (Schloerke, B., Allaire, J., Borges, B.), *magrittr* (Bache, S., Wickham, H.), *mlbench* (Newman, D., Hettich, S., Blake, C., Merz, C.), *ncvreg* (Breheny, P., Huang, J.), *nnet* (Venables, W. N., Ripley, B. D.), *rattle* (Williams, G. J.), *readr* (Wickham, H., Hester, J., Bryan, J.), *seasonal* (Sax, C., Eddelbuettel, D.), *spatial* (Venables, W. N., Ripley, B. D.), *strucchange* (Zeileis, A. et al).

For more complete citations, see the help pages for the individual packages and/or the information given by calling `citation()` with the package name as character string argument. To check for packages on the CRAN site, use the generic weblink `https://CRAN.R-project.org/package=DAAG`, substituting the relevant package name for *DAAG*.

Index of R Functions

The round brackets following the function name enclose, either the name of the package that has the function, or the function used to create the object that was supplied as argument. Selected appearances only are cited for the very common functions.

abbreviate (*base*), 11, 81, 82
abline (*graphics*), 44, ..., 85
abs (base), 85
acf (*stats*), 84, 136, 171, 243, 295, 300, 302
add1 (*stats*), 176, 178
addControl (*inline code*), 446, 447
addmargins (*stats*), 24
adjustcolor (*grDevices*), 86, 110, 310, 494
aggregate (*stats*), 11, 26, 86, 329, 476, 492
AIC (*stats*), 58–62, 66, 86, 107, 112, 155, 176–179, 207, 223, 226, 231, 241, 242, 288, 301, 347, 452, 468
AICc (*AICcmodavg*), 59, 60, 176–179, 241
ampute (*mice*), 458
anova (glm()), 260
anova (lm()), 106, 123, 125, 146, 176, 178, 205, 207, 218, 241, 243
anova (lme()), 212
anova (lmer()), 347
any (*base*), 484
aov (*stats*), 123, 209, 210, 212–214, 216
apply (*base*), 52, 82, 84, 87, 121, 138, 177, 178, 249, 264, 459, 464, 465, 479
ar (*stats*), 293, 297, 315
Arima (*forecast*), 299, 307
arima (*stats*), 297, 299, 307, 316
arima.sim (*stats*), 243, 302, 303, 315, 317
array (*base*), 475
as.character (*base*), 476
as.data.frame (*base*), 63, 64, 408, 411, 459, 481
as.Date (*base*), 17, 474
as.DNAbin (*ape*), 465
as.integer (*base*), 142
as.layer (*latticeExtra*), 275, 491, 492
as.matrix (*base*), 409, 410, 459, 465
as.numeric (*base*), 249, 474, 476
as.vector (*base*), 23, 91
as_tibble (*dplyr*), 481
auto.arima (*forecast*), 293, 299–306, 308, 309, 311, 312, 316, 367
avPlots (*car*), 197, 198

bestsetNoise (*DAAG*), 185
betabinomial (*glmmTMB*), 351
BIC (*stats*), 58, 62, 65, 107, 133, 134, 176–179, 189, 224, 226, 231, 299, 301, 307, 309, 347, 420, 452, 468
BIC (gam(), gamm()), 309
BIC (glm(), gam()), 452
binomial (*glm*), 355
binomial (*stats*), 424, 452
boot (*boot*), 68, 70, 119, 120, 139
boot.ci (*boot*), 69, 70, 139
box (*graphics*), 97
Box.test (*stats*), 232, 243, 305, 306
boxcox (*MASS*), 114
boxplot (*graphics*), 410, 435, 490
brewer.pal (*RColorBrewer*), 414, 494
bsnVaryNvar (*DAAG*), 186
bwplot (*lattice*), 492

c (*base*), 20, 34, ..., 470, 471, 474, 475, 483
capture.output (*utils*), 260
cat (*base*), 427, 470, 484
cbind (*base*), 308, 309, 317, 339, 351, 355, 357, 363, 404, 408, 425, 427, 452, 454, 460, 464
cc (*mice*), 459
chisq.test (*stats*), 101, 102
cloud (*lattice*), 401
cmdscale (*stats*), 406–408, 465
coef (*stats*), 411
col (*base*), 427, 464
colnames (*base*), 425, 427, 430, 431, 437, 464, 478
colSums (*base*), 430

compareTreecalcs (*DAAG*), 389, 393
complete (*mice*), 459
complete.cases (*stats*), 80, 404, 406, 410
confint (*lme4*), 327
contr.SAS (*stats*), 212
contr.sum (*stats*), 211, 212
contr.treatment (*stats*), 212
contrasts (*stats*), 211, 212, 366
cor (*stats*), 30, 70, 81, 94, 361, 464
cor.test (*stats*), 30, 95
corARMA (*nlme*), 309
corCAR1 (*nlme*), 367
cox.zph (*survival*), 286–288
coxph (*survival*), 288
crPlots (*car*), 152, 163
cumulative (*VGAM*), 279
curve (*graphics*), 82, 140, 418
cut (*base*), 465
cutree (*stats*), 414
CVbinary (*DAAG*), 256, 257, 414, 425
cvdisc (*hddplot*), 439–441
CVlm (*DAAG*), 117, 118
cvscores (*hddplot*), 442

data (*utils*), 187, 316, 392, 434, 464, 489, 490
dbinom (*stats*), 31, 96
decideTests (*limma*), 432, 433, 443
defectiveCVdisc (*hddplot*), 440
density (*stats*), 398, 447, 465
densityplot (*lattice*), 13
deparse (*base*), 485
deviance (*VGAM*), 280
dfbetas (*stats*), 171, 175, 176
diag (*base*), 413
diff (*base*), 16, 29
diff.ts (*stats*), 299, 316
dim (*base*), 303, 397, 398, 440
dimnames (*base*), 184, 260, 303, 445
dist (*stats*), 406, 408, 414, 415, 465
dist.dna (*ape*), 407, 465
dnorm (*stats*), 34, 418
dotplot (*lattice*), 492
dpois (*stats*), 32
drop1 (*stats*), 178, 305
droplevels (*base*), 366, 367
droplevels (*stats*), 239, 264
dummy.coef (*stats*), 212

eBayes (*limma*), 431, 442, 443
eqscplot (*MASS*), 465
errorsINx (*DAAG*), 192, 193, 206
ets (*forecast*), 293, 303
exp (*base*), 17, 39, 63, 100, 113, 134, 139
expand.grid (*base*), 87
expression (*base*), 84, 307
extractLT (*qra*), 355

factor (*base*), 25, 52, 81, 85, 120, 122, 406, 430, 447, 450, 474–477
fitted (glm()), 255
fitted (aov()), 210
fitted (gam()), 227, 307
fitted (gamm()), 317
fitted (lm()), 223
fitted (lmer()), 326, 327, 342, 343
forecast (*forecast*), 301, 316
format (*base*), 17
ftable (*stats*), 24

gam (*mgcv*), 208, 219, 220, 222, 225–227, 229, 231, 233–237, 240, 242–245, 274, 275, 304–306, 309–311, 317, 449, 452, 453
gam.check (*mgcv*), 226, 229, 242
gamlss (*gamlss*), 97, 98, 140, 268, 269, 271, 274, 357
gamm (*mgcv*), 220, 233, 304, 308, 309
garch (*tseries*), 313, 314
ggplot (*ggplot2*), 454
glm (*stats*), 99, 225, 233, 245, 247, 249, 253, 259, 260, 262, 263, 265, 266, 271, 278, 290, 357, 424, 425, 451, 452, 455, 457
glmer (*lme4*), 277, 357
glmmTMB (*glmmTMB*), 349, 351, 355
grid.arrange (*gridExtra*), 454
gsub (*base*), 350

hatvalues (*stats*), 174, 277
hclust (*stats*), 414, 415
head (*utils*), 432, 484
histogram (*lattice*), 35
HoltWinters (*stats*), 314

ic (*mice*), 459
ifelse (*base*), 447
importance (*randomForest*), 391, 399
interaction.plot (*stats*), 129, 347
IQR (*stats*), 86
is.factor (*base*), 484
is.na (*base*), 397, 445, 447, 484, 488
isoMDS (*MASS*), 407, 408

kmeans (*stats*), 416

layer (*latticeExtra*), 52, 61, 492
layout (*graphics*), 136
lda (*MASS*), 422, 424–429, 455, 456, 465, 466
legend (*graphics*), 491
length (*base*), 27, 50, 52, 54, 60, 84, 87, 91, 120, 127, 134, 142, . . . , 406, 465, 479, 484
levels (*base*), 430, 431, 434, 437, 443, 474–476
levels (*stats*), 283
library (*base*), 6, 39, 68, 87, 91, 119, 123, 135, 178, 186, 235, 239, 240, 243, 244, 268, 271, 272, 275, 279, 300, 303, 305, 314, 316, 317, 325, 328, 350, 351, 357, 367, 376, 390, 398, 489–491, 494
lines (*graphics*), 490
list (*base*), 482, 485, 491, 492

lm (*stats*), 43–47, 60, 61, 105–107, 110, 115, 119, 131, 134, 135, 140, ..., 486
lmBF (*BayesFactor*), 178
lme (*nlme*), 131, 367, 372
lmer (*lme4*), 131, 318, 320, 325, 326, 328, 330, 331, 334, 335, 342, 346, 361, 362, 364, 365, 372
lmFit (*limma*), 431, 437, 443
lmList (*lme4*), 361–363
lmrob (*robustbase*), 108
loess (*stats*), 105, 106, 220, 237, 380
log (*base*), 16–18, ..., 471, 486, 487, 489
log10 (*base*), 15, 422
log2 (*base*), 431
logLik {stats}, 60
love.plot (*cobalt*), 454
lowess (*stats*), 44, 220, 237
lqs (*MASS*), 108, 172, 173, 206

mad (*stats*), 28, 86
makeClust (*inline code*), 413, 416
makeContrasts (*limma*), 431, 443
margin.table (*base*), 20, 89, 90
match (*base*), 326, 334, 348, 363, 447, 451, 454, 491
match.data (*matchIt*), 451, 453, 456
matchit (*matchIt*), 451–453, 455, 456
matrix (*base*), 52, 54, 102, 103, 134, 136, 172, 184, 189, 441, 445, 487
max (*base*), 403, 491
MCMCregress (*MCMCpack*), 134
md.pattern (*mice*), 309, 458, 459
mean (*base*), 6, 11, 25, 26, 28, 39, ..., 478, 479, 484, 486–489
mean.and.sd (*inline code*), 485
median (*stats*), 68, 478, 484, 488
mice (*mice*), 459, 460
min (*base*), 403
mixed (*afex*), 325, 332, 366
model.matrix (*stats*), 47, 147, 174, 210, 242, 430, 437
modifyList (*utils*), 404
monthplot (*stats*), 303
mqgam (*qgam*), 238, 239
mtext (*graphics*), 302, 414, 420, 490

na.omit (*stats*), 332, 403, 409, 420, 427
names (*base*), 26, 45, 51, 85, 294, 326, 329, 334, 363, 397, 478, 480, 483
NBI (*gamlss.dist*), 357
ncol (*base*), 459
nrow (*base*), 60, 81, 142, 478
ns (*splines*), 225, 452
numeric (*base*), 61, 63, 142, 257, 314, 406, 490

onewayPlot (*DAAG*), 123
options (*base*), 35, 209, 211, 332, 366, 472, 484, 488
order (*base*), 105, 239, 339, 441
ordered (*base*), 279
outer (*base*), 82, 134
overimpute (*micemd*), 460, 461

p.adjust (*stats*), 124, 127, 432
pairs (*graphics*), 154, 157, 187
palette (*grDevices*), 494
panel.abline (*lattice*), 52
panel.dotplot (*lattice*), 13, 25, 492
par (*graphics*), 148, 262, 414, 421, 493, 494
paste (*base*), 15, 63, 84, 85, 127, 134, 152, 177, 184, 280, 302, 303, 339
paste0 (*base*), 27, 52, 54, 61, 116, 134, 153, 166, 181, 350, 386, 387, 408, 431, 460
pbinom (*stats*), 31, 95
plot (*base, generic*), 12, 15, ..., 471, 472, 485, 490, 491
plotCI (*gplots, plotrix*), 489
plotcp (*rpart*), 385
plotMDS (*limma*), 431, 437
plotMix2 (*inline code*), 418
plotQQunif (*DHARMa*), 353
plotResiduals (*DHARMa*), 353
plotSimDiags (*DAAG*), 181
plowerTransform (*car*), 163
pnorm (*stats*), 34
points (*graphics*), 15, 46, ..., 463, 490, 491
poisson (*stats*), 155, 357
poly (*stats*), 222, 225, 241, 242, 259, 288, 308
pool (*mice*), 459
posterior (*BayesFactor*), 62
power.t.test (*stats*), 54
powerTOlog (*inline code*), 272
powerTransform (*car*), 84, 113, 114, 140, 164, 165, 168, 169, 310
ppois (*stats*), 32, 95
prcomp (*stats*), 141, 403, 404, 406, 409
predict (aov()), 211
predict (gam()), 275
predict (glm()), 255, 262, 266
predict (lm()), 45, 109, 120, 121, 181, 188, 205, 272
predict (nls()), 201
predict (qgam()), 240, 272
predict (vglm()), 280
pretty (*base*), 17, 34, 334
printcp (*rpart*), 376, 385, 388, 398
prod (*base*), 440
profile (lmer()), 327, 328, 332
prop.table (*base*), 89
prune (*rpart*), 386, 388, 398
pt (*stats*), 50–52, 84, 85

qbinom (*stats*), 31
qdo (*qgam*), 240
qgam (*qgam*), 225, 238–240, 272
qnorm (*stats*), 34
qpois (*stats*), 32
qqmath (*lattice*), 84
qqnorm (*stats*), 236, 306

qreference (*DAAG*), 36, 46
qt (*stats*), 41, 63, 65, 87, 109, 134
qtukey (*stats*), 211
quasipoisson (*stats*), 357
quickplot (*ggplot2*), 406, 464, 465

rainbow (*grDevices*), 416
randomForest (*randomForest*), 390–399, 450, 455, 464
ranef (lmer()), 326, 334, 342, 344
range (*base*), 16, 17, 46, 227, 240, 266, 363, 479, 482, 484, 488
rbind (*base*), 23, 61, 65, 81, 96, 98, 101, 134, 327, 399, 413, 459
rbinom (*stats*), 31
refit (lmer()), 344
regsubsets (*leaps*), 185, 189
relevel (*stats*), 122, 209, 357
reorder (*stats*), 319
rep (*base*), 3, 35, 52, ..., 471, 475–477, 487
rePCA (lmer()), 365
residuals (gam()), 232, 235, 243, 305, 306, 309
residuals (gamlss()), 271
residuals (glm()), 262, 263, 276
residuals (lm()), 46, 105, 197
residuals (lmer()), 334, 343
rev (*base*), 484
rlm (*MASS*), 108, 140
rm (*base*), 472
rmvnorm (*mvtnorm*), 413
rnorm (*stats*), 34–36, 39, 52, 61, 82–84, 86, 184, 206, 314, 440, 484, 486
round (*base*), 11, 23, 27, 28, ..., 478
row (*base*), 303, 427, 441, 464
row.names (*base*), 175, 181, 401, 463, 465
rownames (*base*), 82, 97, 274, 332, 355, 357, 363, 425, 427, 464, 478
rowSums (*base*), 430
rpart (*rpart*), 376, 378, 380–383, 385–387, 389, 390, 393, 394, 396, 398
rpart.control (*rpart*), 384
rpart.plot (*rpart.plot*), 376, 378, 381, 386, 388
rpois (*stats*), 32, 83
rt (*stats*), 83

sammon (*MASS*), 407, 408, 465
sampdist (*DAAG*), 39
sample (*base*), 3, 82, 116, 142, 164, 257, 372, 374, 397–399, 406, 435
sapply (*base*), 16, 17, 25, 27, 28, 91, 126, 127, 177, 179, 216, 241, 263, 264, 326, 338, 363, 367, 397, 398, 403, 445, 459, 479, 492
scale (*base*), 11, 86, 344, 350, 351, 415
scam (*scam*), 225
scatter.smooth (*stats*), 106, 207, 380
scoreplot (*hddplot*), 436, 442
sd (*stats*), 27, 28, 50, 52, 84–86, 91, 121, 478, 479, 484, 488
search (*base*), 489, 490
seq (*base*), 3, 17, 62, 142, 339, 374, 484, 487
set.seed (*base*), 3, 32, 33, 35, 52, 67, 68, 70, 116, 119, 257
setNames (*stats*), 27, 29, 34, 49, 50, 63, 65, 85, 91, 96, 98, 127, 153, 178, 179, 239, 241, 266, 408, 460, 486
signif (*base*), 261
simulate (*stats*), 46, 344
simulateLinear (*DAAG*), 125
simulateResiduals (*DHARMa*), 352
sort (*base*), 85, 350, 362, 399, 410, 432, 484
split (*base*), 25, 27, 263, 326, 338, 344, 363, 367, 479, 492
splom (*lattice*), 401
spm (*car*), 149, 310, 398, 460
sqrt (*base*), 50, 52, 62, 63, 81, 84, 87, ..., 470, 472
str (*utils*), 80
strip.custom (*lattice*), 52, 307, 491
stripplot (*lattice*), 123
StructTS (*stats*), 314
subset (*base*), 13, 68, 85, 101, 110, 181, 207, 239, 264, 265, 268, 275, 366, 367, 445, 447, 454, 458, 487
substitute (*base*), 447, 485
substring (*base*), 357, 363, 431
sum (*base*), 24, ..., 427, 445, 465, 476, 488
summary (generic), 489
suppressMessages (*base*), 350, 376
suppressPackageStartupMessages (*base*), 135, 178, 303, 305, 314, 357, 390
Surv (*survival*), 283, 285–288
survfit (*survival*), 283, 285

t (*base*), 43, 86, 274, 399, 436, 484
t.test (*stats*), 50, 63, 83, 92, 93, 363, 483
table (*base*), 23, ..., 474, 476, 488
tapply (*base*), 334
teigen (*teigen*), 420, 422
termplot (aov()), 216
termplot (glm()), 256, 259
termplot (lm()), 163, 164, 201, 225
termplot (rlm()), 207
text (*graphics*), 82, 463, 465
time (*stats*), 293
title (*graphics*), 490
topTable (*limma*), 432, 443
ts (*stats*), 15, 294, 304
ttest.tstat (*BayesFactor*), 63–65, 85, 87, 133, 134
ttestBF (*BayesFactor*), 62–64, 87
tuneRF (*randomForest*), 390

unclass (*base*), 13, 334, 437, 465
unique (*base*), 25, 81, 262, 348, 350, 484
unit (*grid*), 454
unlist (*base*), 17, 425, 478, 479, 483
unname (*base*), 96, 174
update (*generic*), 16, 17, 36, 52, 176, 180, 304, 311, 319, 348, 351, 401, 491, 492

var (*stats*), 83, 124, 264, 315, 334
VarCorr (lmer()), 326, 330, 331, 334, 372
vif (*DAAG*), 189
voom (*limma*), 430, 431, 437
vooma (*limma*), 437, 442

WDI (*WDI*), 239
weighted.mean (*stats*), 96, 98
which (*base*), 484
which.max (*base*), 410, 484
which.min (*base*), 398, 484
white.test (*tseries*), 313
window (*stats*), 15, 293, 303, 316
with (*base*), 478, 479, 483, 484, 489, 491, 492
within (*base*), 149, 156, 165, 227, 251, 319, 350, 362, 363, 478

xtabs (*stats*), 23, 24
xyplot (*lattice*), 404, 408, 490, 491

yjPower (*car*), 168, 169, 236, 253, 272, 274

Index of Terms

abline (*graphics*), 15
Akaike information criterion (AIC and AICc), *see* model selection
allometric growth, 88, 114, 115
analysis of variance
  linear regression, 179
  multilevel experimental design, 335
analysis of variance, leave one out
  GAM model, 305
analysis of variance, sequential
  balanced incomplete block design, 214
  linear regression, 146
  multiple lines, 218, 241
  randomized block design, 213
argument, *see* function

Bayes Factor, 58, 61
  complement or replace p-value, 78
  null interval, 64
  prior odds, 63
  scale of evidence, 65
  Sellke et al. upper limit, 63, 132
  vs. BIC, 176
  vs. p-value
    sample size differences, 64
Bayesian estimation
  normal priors and likelihood, 132
Bayesian inference
  commentary, 131
  discrete prior probabilities, 48
  false discovery rate, 55
  Jeffreys Unit Information (JUI) family of priors, 65
  Jeffreys–Zellner–Siow (JZS) family of priors, 61
  Markov Chain Monte Carlo (MCMC), 134
  Monty Hall problem (prize behind one of three doors), 143
  positive predictive value (PPV), 55, 56, 139
  posterior, 49, 55, 61–63, 131, 132, 134, 136, 425, 427
  prior, 49, 51, 53–55, 57, 58, 61–63, 65, 78, 87, 132–134, 391, 392, 424, 426
Bayesian Information Criterion (BIC), *see* model selection
binomial models
  leverage, 277
binomial-like and count data
  deviance, 276
  dispersion (aka dispersion index) estimates, 276
bootstrap, *see* resampling methods
bootstrap estimate
  confidence interval, 69
  confidence interval for median, 69
  correlation coefficient, 69
  SE of median, 67
  when to use, 70

C_p statistic (Mallows), *see* model selection
case studies, 202
  birthweight paradox, 160
  Boeing 737 Max 8 2019 crashes, 73
  deaths from Atlantic hurricanes, 168
  dietary effects on health, 191
  Google flu trends, 74
  hurricane deaths data, 270
  IQ tests, 367
  left- vs. right-hander cricketer lifespans, 274, 288
  lifestyle effects on health, 159
  medical screening programs, 104
  moth habitats, 263
  spread of cholera, 257, 259
  UCB admissions data, 260
causal inference, 7, 202, 259
  balance and matching, 443
  Bradford Hill criteria, 158
  coarsened exact matching, 455
  confounders, 161
  directed acyclic graphs, 159
  graphical summary of differences from balance, 453
  interpretable regression coefficients, 158
  labor training data, complications, 448
  labor training data, regression comparisons, 449

causal inference (*cont.*)
propensity scores, 444
scores replace regression covariates, 450
use GAM fit to derive propensity scores, 452
use multiple evidence sources, 158
use randomForest proximities to compare groups, 450
censoring, *see* survival analysis
classification, *see* discriminant analysis
cluster analysis
k-means, 416
k-means vs. mixture model, 422
agglomerative clustering, dendrogram display, 413
hierarchical clustering, 412
mixture model-based clustering, 417
BIC is –BIC as used elsewhere, 420
EM algorithm, 419
single, average, and complete linkage, 413
comparisons, multiple
false discovery rate (FDR), 429
least significant difference (LSD) vs. Tukey's honest significant difference (HSD), 122
multiple range tests, 124
regression vs. qualitative comparisons, 124
comparisons, one-way
analysis of variance, 123
contingency table
chi-squared residuals, 101
chi-squared test for no association, 101
combining data across tables, 138
consistency of pattern, 103
Fisher exact test, 102
interpretation issues, 104
Mantel–Haenzel test, 138
mechanics of the chi-squared test, 101
correlation
alternative measures, 29
Fisher z-transformation, 94, 139
Kendall, 95
Pearson or product–moment, 94
spatial autocorrelation, 314
Spearman, 95
cross-validation, *see* resampling methods

data
acupuncture vs. sham, 137
comparison of inhaler instructions, 278
cuckoo eggs, 4, 12
drawings of dreams, 102
email spam (complete data), 396
guarding time vs. size of group (meerkats), 242
inhibition of current flow vs. protein concentration, 290
input and output from a file, 480
kidney stone surgery, 20
labor training data, available datasets, 444
machinist accident counts, 98
morphometric, 88, 114
painkiller experiment, 196
rare plant habitats, 103
weight gain, toxaphene in rat diet, 139
data analysis
advance planning, 9
challenges to results, 9
failures of human intuition, 75
organization and management of work, 70
risks of naive and misleading analyses, 75
the benefits of shared insights, 10
two-sample t-test, 91
data collection and analysis
planning, 6
data, *compositions*
Coxite, 187
data, *DAAG*
ACF1 (rat colon growths), 82, 261
ais (measures on athletes), 81
allbacks (book dimensions and weight), 144, 195, 204
anesthetic, 248
ant111b (corn yield measurements), 319
appletaste, 215
bomregions2021 (annual weather indices, Murray–Darling Basin, Australia), 304, 315
cities, 203
coralPval (coral gene expression comparison), 125
cricketer (left- vs. right-hander cricketer lifespans), 288, 291
cuckoohosts, 81
cuckoos, 84, 241, 479, 492
dewpoint, 234
frogs, 250
frostedflakes, 311, 315
fruitohms (resistance vs. juice content), 227, 244
geophones (seismic timing), 242
headInjury, 290, 396
hills2000, 172, 180, 204
houseprices, 119
humanpower1 (oxygen input vs. power output), 360
hurricNamed (deaths from Atlantic hurricanes), 168, 236, 270, 289
ironslag, 104
jobs, 17, 293, 479
kiwishade (kiwifruit vine yields), 25, 335
LakeHuron, 315
leafshape, 141, 464
leafshape17, 424
leaftemp, 218
litters (mouse brain vs. body weight), 47, 157
mdbAVtJtoD (monthly average temperatures, Murray–Darling Basin, Australia), 303
measles, 14
mifem, 290

mifem (female heart attack patient mortality), 384, 396
mignonette (crossed vs. self-fertilized plants), 92
moths, 264, 290, 356
nassCDS (road accident fatality data), 23
nihills, 148, 180, 197, 204
nswdemo (labor training evaluation data), 82, 100
nswpsid1 (labor training evaluation data), 22, 396, 465
oddbooks, 154, 204
orings (1986 space shuttle disaster), 80
ozone, 243
pair65 (stretch of elastic bands), 35, 140
possum, 12, 13, 80, 81, 139, 401, 427, 463
repPsych (psychology replication study), 207
rice, 128, 213
rockArt, 465
roller, 43
science (student attitudes to science), 7, 329
seedrates, 220, 242
socsupport, 7, 408
sorption, 372
spam7 (email spam), 374, 387, 390
sugar, 209
tinting, 344, 491
toycars, 241
two65 (elastic band stretch), 28, 91
wages1833, 242
worldRecords, 243

data, *DAAGbio*
plantStressCounts (mRNA gene expression counts), 430
primateDNA (bases at 232 mitochondrial locations, for 14 primates), 465

data, *datasets*
airquality, 309, 317, 460
cars (stopping distance vs. speed), 85
chickwts, 476
EuStockMarkets, 316
LakeHuron, 293
pressure (vapor pressure vs. temperature), 140
UCBAdmissions, 89, 138, 260, 479

data frame, 81, 477
as database, 478
vs. matrix, 478
vs. tibble, 481

data, *gamclass*
FARS (road accident fatality data), 24

data, *gclus*
wine (Italian wines, three cultivars), 464

data, *ggplot2*
diamonds (diamond prices), 86, 398

data, *hddplot*
Golub (cancer gene expression indices), 433

data, *HistData*
Cholera (deaths, London 1848–49), 259
GaltonFamilies, 110

data manipulation, 487
tidyverse packages, 481

data, *MASS*
Aids2, 282
Animals, 16, 81
biopsy (breast cancer biopsies), 397
cement (heat in setting), 204
cpus (performance, 209 CPUs), 204
galaxies (speeds of 82 galaxies), 82
painters (assessments of 54 classical painters), 463
Pima.tr (diabetes in Pima Indian women), 391, 398
whiteside (gas consumption vs. temperature), 231

data measurement issues, 7
Beck Depression Inventory (BDI), 8
DALYs and QALYs, 8

data, *MEMSS*
ergostool, 372
Gun, 372
MatchAchieve, 372
Orthodont, 362

data, *mice*
Boys (data on 748 Dutch boys), 458

data, *mlbench*
Vehicle, 464

data, *MPV*
radon (radon release in showers), 85
table.b1 (NFL team performance data), 207
table.b3 (gas mileage etc. for 32 cars), 205

data, *qra*
HawCon, 350
malesINfirst12, 96, 140

data, *rpart*
car.test.frame (mileage vs. weight), 381

data structures
matrices and arrays, 475

data, *tseries*
ice.river, 316

database, 490

datasets
in R packages, 489

dates
functions for use with, 474

dependence
Markov chain, 141
temporal or spatial, 6

deviance, 347, 357, 378–380
generalized additive model, 227–229, 232

deviance (*cont.*)
generalized linear model, 247–249, 253, 260, 262, 268, 276, 277
shape constrained additive model (SCAM), 231
vglm model, 280
discriminant analysis
linear discriminant analysis (LDA), 435
logistic discrimination vs. linear discriminant analysis (LDA), 422
misclassification costs, 424
distribution, 30
betabinomial, 96, 247
betabinomial vs. binomial, 96
binomial, 31
Cauchy, 61, 62, 65
changes in variability, 21
clustering, 21
dispersion index vs. dispersion parameter, 99, 247, 349
distributional asymmetry, 21
double binomial, 140
exponential, 34
extra-binomial and extra-Poisson, 95
extra-Poisson variation, 98
fitted vs. empirical centiles, 273
Jeffreys, 65
measures of variation, 27
negative binomial (NBI and NBII), 98, 247, 267
normal ('Gaussian'), 33, 34
normal approximation to binomial, 93
Poisson, 32, 262
quasibinomial adjustment, 247, 271
quasipoisson adjustment, 261, 264
t-, 40
technical notes on modeling extra-binomial or Poisson variation, 99
time trends, 22
uniform, 34

effect size, 29, 53
equation
Claudius–Clapeyron, 140
errors in x
classical vs. Berkson error model, 194
reliability ratio, 192
simulations, 192, 193
two explanatory variables, 193
experimental design, 6
multi-site, 344

factor
alternative choices of contrasts, 211
functions for working with, 475
missing values, 477
ordered factor, 476
false discovery rate (FDR), 125, 126
fitted values
calculation, 47
calculation from columns of model matrix, 210
frequentist inference
confidence intervals, 50
hypothesis testing and p-values, 50
p-value, 50, 56
p-value decision process, 51
p-value simulation, 51
power, 52
true and false positives, 53
function
anonymous, 486
argument, 404, 472, 473, 475, 477, 478, 481, 484, 486, 491, 492, 494
common useful built-in functions, 483
default argument, 485
generic (tune action to class of object), 485
in R packages, 489
operator, 486
return value, 485
user-written, 484

generalized additive mixed model (GAMM)
correlated errors, 308
generalized additive model (GAM), 225, 317
abilities in mgcv and related packages, 233
binomial errors, 275
check residuals for ARIMA errors, 305
choice of penalty, 226
diagnostic checks, 229
monotone curves, 230
multiple smoothing terms, 233
smooth for each factor level, 231
smooth surface, 235
generalized additive model, shape constrained (SCAM), 230
diagnostic plots, 231
generalized linear mixed model
betabinomial error, 349
diagnostic plots, 353
dispersion index, 352
intra-class correlation, 349, 352
lethal time confidence interval, Fieller's formula, 353
lethal time estimate, 353, 355
link function, 350
observation-level random effects, 356
scale correction, 351
generalized linear model
choice of link function and reference level, 265
common link functions, 246
complementary log-log link, 276
count data, 261
diagnostic checks, 269
fitted values, 255
linear predictor, 246
log(odds) scale with logit link, 247
logistic multiple regression, 250
logit link, 246

probit link, 276
square root link, 269
types of residuals, 276
variance inflation factor, 252
graphics
added variable plot, 197, 198
added variable plot, algebraic details, 199
boxplot, 5
boxplot, compared with density curve, histogram, and rug plot, 12
categorical data, 19
classification tree (email spam), 376
component+residual plot, 151, 163
component+residual plot or termplot, 163
density contours of fitted mixture model, 421
diagnostic checks for GAM model, 229
dotplot, 4
dotplot, with overlaid group means, 264
dynamic graphics, 174, 492
flawed graphs (variable selection bias), 435
influence plot, 176
interaction plot, 347
join separately created lattice objects, 492
lattice package, 491
leverage vs. fitted proportion, 278
linear discriminant analysis, scatterplot matrix for canonical variates, 428
logarithmic scale(s), 14, 15
logarithmic scale(s), labeling, 19
love plot (summarizes differences from balance), 454, 456
mean-variance relationship for gene expression counts, 431
mosaic plots, 20
normal quantile–quantile plot, 35, 36
plot characters, symbols, line types, and colors, 493
regression tree, 381
same vs. sliced logarithmic scale, 17, 18
scatterplot matrix, 149
scatterplot matrix, suggested power transformations, 169, 254
simulated diagnostic plots, 181
termplot, 151, 153, 164, 182, 197, 201, 225, 227, 255, 258, 305, 307
termplot equivalent for GAM model, 236
termplot equivalent for smooth terms in GAM model, 306
three-dimensional perspective plot, 402
time series autocorrelation and partial autocorrelation plots, 295
time series lag plots, 295
time series predictions, 301
time series seasonal effects, 303
time series trace plot, 294
univariate, breakdown by one or more factors, 13
worm plot, 98, 140
graphics packages
graphics, grid, lattice, latticeExtra, ggplot2, 490
graphics, generalized linear model, diagnostic plots, 269

imputation, *see* missing values

likelihood and log-likelihood, 42, 58
maximum likelihood estimation, 42
likelihood and maximum likelihood, 301
likelihood ratio test, 268
linear model, *see* regression
list, 482
as opposed to “atomic” vector, 482

machine learning
algorithmic motivations, 72
limits of current systems, 73
missing values, 243, 282, 309, 394, 487
alternative approaches, 74
counting and identifying, 488
in modeling functions, 488
missing at random (MAR), 457
missing completely at random (MCAR), 457
multiple imputation, 315, 457
model
allometric growth, 115
assumptions, 88
limitations, 90
outliers, 21
model matrix, 210
model object
extractor functions, 45
model predictions
fitted values vs. new observations, 109, 166
model selection
AIC, AICc, and BIC, 58, 176, 207, 300
BIC vs. Bayes Factor, 176, 178
drop1() and add1(), 178
Mallows C_p, 178, 207
over-fitting, 184–186
R-squared and adjusted R-squared, 176, 241
sampling properties of AIC differences, 60
multidimensional scaling (MDS), 406
binary data, 408
distance measures, 406
multilevel model
analysis of variance sums of squares, 339
balance, 318
best linear unbiased predictor (BLUP), 326
history, 369
instructive faulty analyses, 334
intra-class correlation, 324, 332
Kenward–Roger approximation, 325
key ideas, 318
levels of variation, 320
maximum likelihood (ML) vs. restricted maximum likelihood (REML) criterion, 346

multilevel model (*cont.*)
meta-analysis, 370
model selection, 346
nested factors, 322, 330
prediction levels, 322, 324
profile likelihood, 327, 332
random effects, 320
random vs. fixed effects, 322
simplistic error structure, 368
variance components vs. analysis of variance mean squares, 323, 338, 341
variance components, interpretation, 324
within and between block effects, 342
within and between class effects, 330
within and between site effects, 322, 344
within and between subject effects, 344
multiple imputation, *see also* missing values
overimputation graphs, 461
time series cross-sectional data, 460
multiple p-values
false discovery rate (FDR) estimates, 432, 442
multiway table
loglinear model, 281

observational data
inference, *see* causal inference
ordination, *see* multidimensional scaling (MDS)
outliers, *see* regression

p-value
adjusted, 127
threshold, 78
package
attach or load?, 489
permutation, 3, 66, 67
permutation tests, *see* resampling methods
pipe
using the |> operator, 485
positive predictive values, 54
posterior density or probability, *see* Bayesian inference
predictive accuracy, 116, 121, 148, 176, 256, 400, 422, 423, 425, 426, 429, 440, 462, 468
principal components
rotations ('loadings'), 404
stability relative to statistical variation, 405
prior density or probability, *see* Bayesian inference
publication
peer review of study plans, 78
reporting standards, 57
published experimental studies
independent replication, 57
power issues, 55

quantile regression, 238
smooths with 2SE bounds added, 238

R package task views, 469
R session
image file, 471
search list, 478, 490
working directory, 32, 70, 71
workspace, 33, 71, 471, 472, 477, 478, 484, 489, 490
random forest
boosting and bagging approaches, 396
bootstrap samples, 390
data values that are not independent, 392
importance measures, 391
out-of-bag (OOB) error, 390
prior probabilities, 391
proximity measure, 392
tree size, 390
tuning parameters, 390
random numbers, 35, 118
generation, 32
seed, 3, 32, 33
random sample, *see* sample, random
regression, *see also* generalized additive model (GAM), generalized additive mixed model (GAMM), generalized linear model,
analysis of variance, 106
confusion between explanatory and response variables, 195
contributions of basis terms to regression spline fit, 228
Cook's distance, 108, 148, 173
correlations between parameter estimates, 145
criteria for model choice, 162
cubic regression spline bases, 225
diagnostic checks, 171
diagnostic plots, 104, 147, 152, 170
diagnostic vs. simulated plots, 181
different parameterizations serve different purposes, 151
errors in x, 191, 206
factor contrasts, 209
fits to simulated data, 46
fitting multiple lines, 216
GLM vs. normal theory linear model, 248
hat matrix, 174
influence on coefficients (dfbetas), 175
influential point(s), 148
leverage, 173, 277
lm() vs. aov(), 209
locally weighted regression smooths, 237
low order polynomial, 114
many explanatory variables, 183
missing explanatory variables, 195
model fitting strategy, 161, 170
model formula and model objects, 44
model matrix, 47, 220
multicollinearity, 186
multicollinearity, remedies, 191
nonlinear methods, 200

omission of explanatory variables, 205
ordered categorical or categorical response, 278
orthogonal polynomials, 222
outliers and influence, 107, 173
polynomial, 220
polynomial bases, 220
polynomial fit vs. loglinear fit, 222
proportional odds logistic, 278
residuals and residual plots, 45, 46
resistant, 171–173, 202, 206, 237
ridge, 205
robust and resistant, 108, 140, 171–173, 202, 206, 207
roughness penalty methods, 220
SE of slope, 111
selection effects in observational data, 156
simulate variable selection procedures, 184
spline bases, 220, 223
structural equation models, 203
summary information, 144
test for main effect in presence of interaction, 212
thin plate regression bases, 224
variable selection penalty strategies, 186
variance inflation factor, 189, 252
y vs. x, or x vs. y, or functional relationship, 112
regression, model matrix
choice of factor contrasts, 211
repeated measures, 357
alternative approaches, 359
correlation structure, 359
random coefficients model, 361, 364
sequential correlation structure, 367
theory, 358
replicability
implying independent replication of a total study, 75
laboratory economics studies, 76
multiple replicates internationally of one study, 77
preclinical cancer research, 77
psychology, 76
studies where most published results fail, 76
replication ("reproducibility") studies, 56
reproducible reporting
gains from sharing data and code, 72
markup tools (mix code and text), 71
resampling methods, 66
assumptions, 121
bootstrap, 118
cross-validation, 116, 180
cross-validation, binary response, 256
one-sample permutation test, 66
permutation tests, 88
training/test, 116, 180
two-sample permutation test, 67
residuals, *see also* regression
randomized quantile (models with discrete error distributions), 95, 352
randomized quantile, simulation, 352, 353
robust and resistant methods, *see* regression

sample, cluster, 3
sample, nonresponse, 7
multiple vs. single imputation, 7
sample, random, 3
bootstrap, 4
with replacement, 3
without replacement, 3
sampling bias, 5
sampling distribution, 37
central limit theorem, 37, 38
of t statistic, 41
of mean (standard error of mean, or SEM), 38, 39
of median (SE of median), 39
of standard deviation, 39
search list, *see* R session
selection bias, 56, 146, 163, 182, 184–186, 191, 203
simulation
logistic regression model, 290
Poisson regression model, 291
standard deviation, 27
compared with inter-quartile range (IQR) and mean absolute deviation (MAD), 28
degrees of freedom, 27
pooled estimate, 28
summary measures
analysis using aggregated data, issues, 26
bias from omission of conditioning variable, 90
dengue status example, 26
R-squared and adjusted R-squared, 106, 176
tabulation, 23
uses and potential for distortions, 22
when to use aggregated data for analysis, 26
survival analysis
censoring, 282
Cox proportional hazards, 286
data collection process, 282
hazard rate, 283, 285
left- vs. right-hander cricketer lifespans, 288
reasons for right censoring, 284
survival analysis, Cox model
alternative tests for coefficient(s), 287
diagnostics, 287
time-dependent coefficients, 287

time sequence
test for sequential correlation, 232, 243, 305
time series
AR, ARMA, ARIMA, ETS, ARCH, GARCH, 292
AR(1) model, standard error of mean, 297
ARCH and GARCH models, 313

time series (*cont.*)
ARIMA (ARMA with differencing) model, 299
ARIMA errors, 304
ARIMA errors, drift, 299
autocorrelation and partial autocorrelation, 295
automatic model selection, 299, 307, 312
autoregressive (AR) models, 296
autoregressive model of order $p > 1$, 297
autoregressive moving average (ARMA) model, 299
calibration, 311
financial and economic, 313
innovations, 297
moving average (MA) processes, 298
residuals for ARIMA models, 308
seasonal effects, 303
simulation, 315, 317
stationarity, 296
univariate, 14
time series objects
functions, 293
time series predictions
ARMA, ARIMA, and ETS, 301
transformation
Box–Cox and Yeo–Johnson power, 112, 113, 164, 168, 252, 310
logarithmic, 112, 150
proportions and counts, 288
square or cube root, 304
to linearity, 21
tree
cost-complexity parameter, 383
event rate and survival data, 395
one-standard-deviation rule, 386
predictive accuracy, and the cost-complexity tradeoff, 382
predictive accuracy, cross-validation, 382
printed information on each split, 386
pruning, 383
splitting criteria, 378, 380
toy example, 378
tree, classification
relative vs. cross-validation error rate, 377
splitting criteria, 380
tree, regression
vs. loess regression smoothing, 380
tree-based methods
appropriate use, 374
as complement to other methods, 374, 395
history, 373
single-tree vs. random forests, 373, 393
vs. other approaches, 394
see also random forest

variance
Fligner–Killeen test for homogeneity, 263
heterogeneity, 105, 106, 166, 346, 348
variance inflation factor, 189

working directory, *see* R session
workspace, *see* R session